HAGUE LAW INTERPRETED

Given the centrality of Hague Law to the lawful prosecution of warfare, the relative paucity of dedicated works is surprising. The general formulation of Hague Law rules is largely uncontroversial, but this clarity stands in stark contrast to their interpretation and practical application. How precisely, for instance, the fundamental rules of distinction and proportionality in attack are to dictate and constrain the planning and practice of warfare continues to be highly uncertain. This important new publication fills the gap in the literature. Offering a comprehensive assessment of Hague Law, it explores questions of definitions and accountability and navigates the substantive rules and their application to different types of warfare.

Hague Law Interpreted

The Conduct of Hostilities under the Law of Armed Conflict

Stuart Casey-Maslen
with
Steven Haines

•HART•
OXFORD • LONDON • NEW YORK • NEW DELHI • SYDNEY

HART PUBLISHING

Bloomsbury Publishing Plc

Kemp House, Chawley Park, Cumnor Hill, Oxford, OX2 9PH, UK

HART PUBLISHING, the Hart/Stag logo, BLOOMSBURY and the Diana logo are trademarks of Bloomsbury Publishing Plc

First published in Great Britain 2018

A catalogue record for this book is available from the British Library.

Library of Congress Cataloging-in-Publication data

Names: Casey-Maslen, Stuart, author. | Haines, Steven, 1952- author.

Title: Hague law interpreted : the conduct of hostilities under the law of armed conflict / Stuart Casey-Maslen with Steven Haines.

Description: Oxford, UK ; Portland, Oregon : Hart Publishing, 2018.

Identifiers: LCCN 2018028910 (print) | LCCN 2018029825 (ebook) | ISBN 9781509921232 (Epub) | ISBN 9781509921225 (hardback : alk. paper)

Subjects: LCSH: War (International law)

Classification: LCC KZ6385 (ebook) | LCC KZ6385 .C369 2018 (print) | DDC 341.6—dc23

LC record available at https://lccn.loc.gov/2018028910

ISBN: HB: 978-1-50992-122-5
ePDF: 978-1-50992-124-9
ePub: 978-1-50992-123-2

Typeset by Compuscript Ltd, Shannon
Printed and bound in Great Britain by CPI Group (UK) Ltd, Croydon CR0 4YY

MIX
Paper from responsible sources
FSC® C013604

To find out more about our authors and books visit www.hartpublishing.co.uk. Here you will find extracts, author information, details of forthcoming events and the option to sign up for our newsletters.

THE AUTHORS

Stuart Casey-Maslen is an academic specialising in the use of force under international law. He is Honorary Professor at the Faculty of Law of the University of Pretoria and holds a doctorate in international humanitarian law, a master's degree in international human rights law and a master's degree in forensic ballistics. He previously worked for the Geneva Academy of International Humanitarian Law and Human Rights as head of research; for the International Committee of the Red Cross as a legal adviser; as a consultant to the United Nations Children's Fund (UNICEF) in New York and Geneva on the protection of civilians; as well as for the Office of the UN High Commissioner for Human Rights. In the 1990s, he was the main researcher for the UN Study on the Impact of Armed Conflict on Children headed by Ms Graça Machel.

Steven Haines is Professor of Public International Law at the University of Greenwich in London. He specialises in ocean governance, the law of the sea and international security law, as well as the roles of navies, from constabulary operations to conflict. As a Royal Navy Commander working within the Naval and Central Policy staffs in the Ministry of Defence, he was the lead author of British Maritime Doctrine (1999) and chaired the Editorial Board of the United Kingdom's *Manual of the Law of Armed Conflict* (2004), being also joint author of its chapter on 'Maritime Warfare'.

CONTENTS

TABLE OF CASES

International Criminal Court

International Criminal Tribunal for Rwanda

International Criminal Tribunal for Yugoslavia

International Military Tribunal

Permanent Court of International Justice

Special Court for Sierra Leone

TABLE OF LEGISLATION

International

Domestic

Pakistan

United States

Introduction

Hague Law is the branch of the law of armed conflict[1] that governs the conduct of hostilities: in the vernacular, who or what a party to an armed conflict may target during the fighting, and how. The general formulation of the rules is largely uncontroversial, but this clarity stands in stark contrast to their interpretation and practical application. How precisely, for instance, the fundamental rules of distinction and proportionality in attack are to dictate and constrain the planning and practice of warfare continues to be highly uncertain.

Successful prosecutions for war crimes allegedly committed during hostilities on land, at sea or during aerial operations are truly exceptional. One reason for this failure of accountability is doubt as to the circumscription of the rules. In 2012, for example, the contentious approach to the law by the Appeals Chamber of the erstwhile International Criminal Tribunal for the former Yugoslavia (ICTY) in the *Gotovina and Markac* case – acquitting the two defendants a Trial Chamber had earlier convicted and sentenced to prison terms of more than 20 years each – illustrates vividly how little is generally accepted in the law governing the conduct of hostilities. The case, which concerned use of artillery (in particular, field guns and rockets) against targets in populated areas during Operation Storm in Croatia in 1995, centred on the standard of accuracy that constitutes compliance with the rule of distinction in attack.

Accordingly, this work aims to fill a perceived and critical gap in the literature and understanding of Hague Law, going beyond an iteration of the rules to discuss how they must, should and may be interpreted. It is hoped that this book will provide greater clarity on all of Hague Law, not only identifying when and where it applies, but also detailing the constraints it imposes on acts of warfare on land, at sea, in the air, in space and in cyberspace. As such, it addresses Geneva law (which protects those in the power of a party to conflict, such as detainees or civilians in occupied territory) in only a cursory manner, and where it does so it focuses on areas where the delimitation of the boundary between Geneva Law and Hague Law is elusive. For while many instances of the use of force manifestly fall to be judged by one body of the law of armed conflict rather than the other, more controversial scenarios and situations do exist. Is it the presence, however few in number, of the enemy that is conclusive? The distance between the attacker and the defender? The type of weapons that are used?

[1] This descriptor for the branch of international law that regulates the acts of parties during and in connection with an armed conflict is generally preferred in this work to other common monikers such as international humanitarian law (the most widely used) and the (older) law of war. Gary Solis, for instance, notes 'the irony of how a body of law defining how non-combatants may lawfully be killed … is "humanitarian"': GD Solis, *The Law of Armed Conflict: International Humanitarian Law in War*, 2nd edn (New York, Cambridge University Press, 2016) 23. See also S Haines, 'War at sea: Nineteenth-century laws for twenty-first century wars?', *International Review of the Red Cross*, vol 98, no 2 (2016) 419–47, 420, fn 3.

The book is organised in 15 chapters. On a presumptive basis, which today is largely uncontroversial, that the same fundamental Hague Law rules generally apply in both international armed conflict (IAC) and non-international armed conflict (NIAC), no general differentiation is made between the two. Where a material distinction is deemed to exist, however, this is identified and explained. An obvious example of such a case is the issue of reprisals. In the chapter dedicated to promoting respect for Hague Law (chapter 15), the argument is discussed (and rejected) whereby any act ostensibly taken in reprisal is inherently unlawful in a NIAC.

Chapter 1 offers an overview of the relevant normative framework of *jus in bello*, the collective set of international legal rules that govern acts occurring simultaneously during, and in connection with, an armed conflict. It summarises the fundamental rules contained in Hague Law on the conduct of hostilities, particularly distinction and proportionality in attack, as well as weapon-specific rules such as the prohibition on the use of means and methods of warfare of a nature to cause superfluous injury or unnecessary suffering.

Chapter 2 describes how IAC and NIAC are defined in the law of armed conflict, and how these classifications have been refined and fleshed out by international criminal law since 1995. An armed conflict is an essential prerequisite for the application of Hague Law. In assessing the relevance and impact of other branches of international law, also discussed is *jus ad bellum* (the law on the inter-state use of force), but only insofar as is necessary to determine whether an IAC is in progress. Critical to this determination is whether valid consent has been given to the use of force by a foreign state. In contrast, cyberattacks are addressed both in the *ad bellum* discussions and, in subsequent chapters, as part of *in bello* rules.

Chapter 3 is devoted to identifying instances of hostilities within a situation of armed conflict. While a pitched battle between two parties to an armed conflict clearly amounts to acts of hostilities, how are other violent acts to be classified? Attacks on civilians may fall within Hague Law or Geneva Law, depending on the circumstances: what are the determinant factors? Moreover, even amid an armed conflict, acts governed by the law of law enforcement, the default position for state use of force, persist. What distinguishes an act of law enforcement from a hostile act *in bello*? If violent action occurs in a hitherto pacific area of the country or even abroad, what rules apply? And how do the rules differ if, according to the facts, violent action by the state falls to be judged by the international law of law enforcement?

Chapter 4 begins the treatment of the substantive rules of Hague Law, looking at distinction in attacks on objects. As in the following chapters, international criminal law is quoted and discussed where it benefits understanding of the scope and application of Hague Law rules, but also in order to identify the contours of what amount to serious violations of the rules attracting individual criminal responsibility. The *Gotovina* case as well as the earlier *Martić* case, both adjudged in the ICTY, are accorded particular attention.

Chapter 5 looks at the rule of distinction as it applies to attacks on persons. In so doing, the contentious 'interpretive guidance' proffered by the International Committee of the Red Cross (ICRC) in 2009 is discussed in detail. Also reviewed are ICTY cases in which it was controversially held that the use of an indiscriminate weapon may amount to a direct attack on civilians for the purpose of international criminal law. Relatively limited attention is accorded to international human rights law, which may impose additional restraint on the lawful conduct of hostilities, above and beyond those rules emanating from Hague Law. Readers are instead referred to the leading authorities engaged in the ongoing doctrinal debate about the interrelationship between the law of armed conflict and international human rights law.

Chapter 6 considers the rule of proportionality in attack. Arguably the most nebulous of all Hague Law rules in its application, too often its treatment in international fora and tribunals has lacked intellectual rigour and depth. Here it is discussed separately from other forms of indiscriminate attack, even though in the 1977 Additional Protocol I to the Geneva Conventions[2] it is explicitly considered under this rubric. Treaty and customary international criminal law standards for the accompanying war crime are also examined at length as they evidence a major obstacle to the successful prosecution of individuals for an alleged serious violation of the rule of proportionality in attack in all but the most flagrant cases.

Chapter 7 addresses the rule of precautions in attack. In which circumstances should a planned attack be cancelled? If the attack proceeds, what weapons may be used and which may not? Is there, for instance, a legal duty (likely *ferenda* – developing – rather than *lata*) to use precision-guided munitions rather than gravity ordnance in certain circumstances? When should a warning of an attack be given beforehand? What is the normative status of the rule governing precautions in attack, given that its observance is not, formally at least, an integral part of the prohibition of an indiscriminate attack?

Chapter 8 reflects on the superfluous injury rule. This is shorthand for the rule first enunciated in the Regulations annexed to 1899 Hague Convention II[3] and most recently incorporated in the 1998 Rome Statute of the International Criminal Court (ICC Statute)[4] potentially granting the Court, in the future, jurisdiction to try individuals who, in an IAC, '[employ] weapons, projectiles and material and methods of warfare which are of a nature to cause superfluous injury or unnecessary suffering'. Is this rule fast becoming obsolete, or does it retain normative merit and value? If so, what acts or weapons would be of such an inherently unlawful nature?

Chapter 9 applies the primary Hague Law rules to warfare on land. In addition to assessing the particularities of land warfare, the chapter considers the prohibition of perfidy, the use of human shields, the taking of hostages, sieges and humanitarian access, and starvation as a method of warfare. In assessing the legality of weapons typically employed during warfare on land, there is also specific discussion of ammunition whose use has been outlawed (notably expanding or exploding bullets), as well as of the trend among non-state armed groups to use improvised or locally produced explosive devices.

[2] Protocol Additional to the Geneva Conventions of 12 August 1949, and relating to the Protection of Victims of International Armed Conflicts (Protocol I); adopted at Geneva, 8 June 1977; entry into force, 7 December 1978.

[3] Regulations concerning the Laws and Customs of War on Land annexed to Convention (II) with Respect to the Laws and Customs of War on Land; adopted at The Hague, 29 July 1899; entry into force, 4 September 1900.

[4] Statute of the International Criminal Court; adopted at Rome, 17 July 1998; entry into force, 1 July 2002.

Chapter 10 applies the primary Hague Law rules to aerial warfare. The rules proposed by the contentious *Harvard Manual on International Law Applicable to Air and Missile Warfare*[5] receive particular attention. Also considered are an array of specific weapons and weapons platforms and munitions, including, notably, remotely piloted aircraft, incendiary weapons, barrel and other improvised bombs, and nuclear weapons.

In Chapter 11, Steven Haines describes how the primary rules of the law of armed conflict should be applied to warfare at sea. He argues that the 1994 *San Remo Manual*'s[6] focus on blockades is today anachronistic, and identifies where normative gaps, uncertainty or imprecision exist. It is, for instance, hard to imagine how a warship would exercise the right of visit and search of an 18,000-container-capacity vessel, especially when the vessel's master genuinely does not know the nature of his ship's cargo.

Chapter 12 assesses how Hague Law applies to armed conflict in space. A major issue during the Cold War, in recent years the threat of armed conflict in space has again moved up the international agenda, with several major military powers developing anti-satellite weapons. In 2015, responding to the growing fear that hostilities would occur in space, the ICRC cautioned the United Nations (UN) General Assembly that warfare in outer space would not occur in a legal vacuum (while noting that it in no way condoned the weaponisation that was occurring in that jurisdiction).

Chapter 13 looks at Hague Law regulation of cyberspace attacks. Since many modern military operations rely on the digital sphere, armed conflict increasingly involves the targeting of electronics through the Internet as well as software such as Universal Serial Bus (USB) sticks. The *Tallinn Manual on the International Law Applicable to Cyber Warfare*, published commercially in 2013,[7] is a key resource in this analysis.

Chapter 14 considers the relationship between counterterrorism and the law of armed conflict. While certain acts of terror are prohibited within the law of armed conflict and (rather more controversially) amount to a war crime within international criminal law, the ambit of the illegal conduct in Hague Law is often misunderstood. What is more, the relationship between international and domestic law prohibiting terrorism on the one hand, and Hague Law rules on the other, is perceived by some as a potentially fractious one.

Lastly, Chapter 15 is devoted to the measures required to promote respect for Hague Law. On the battlefield, reprisals are one brutal method that seeks to bring back into compliance a party to conflict that is violating the law governing the conduct of hostilities. But how are reprisals to be distinguished from acts of revenge in both law and practice? And, as mentioned above, are certain acts of reprisal potentially lawful not only in IAC but also, despite a widespread view to the contrary, in NIAC? The broader discussion of accountability in the aftermath of an alleged violation reviews the international law of state responsibility. Thereby, a state may be held responsible for a violation of Hague law where its action constitutes an internationally wrongful act.

[5] Program on Humanitarian Policy and Conflict Research at Harvard University, *HPCR Manual on International Law Applicable to Air and Missile Warfare*, 1st Edn, New York, Cambridge University Press, 2013.

[6] San Remo Manual on International Law Applicable to Armed Conflicts at Sea, 12 June 1994.

[7] M Schmitt (ed), *Tallinn Manual on the International Law Applicable to Cyber Warfare* (Cambridge, Cambridge University Press, 2013).

The final chapter also considers the international legal remedies foreseen by the law of armed conflict, most notably reparation, as well as the rules governing the transfer of arms to another state that is likely to misuse them. Individual criminal responsibility under international criminal law is then considered. At the last, the chapter assesses how far non-state armed groups that are party to an armed conflict, as well as international organisations and corporate actors, may be held accountable for violations of the rules governing the conduct of hostilities.

1

An Overview of the Normative Framework of *Jus in Bello*

I. Introduction

This chapter offers an overview of the normative framework of Hague Law. Section II summarises the fundamental rules on the conduct of hostilities, in particular the rules of distinction and proportionality in attack. Section III outlines the principles and rules that govern the use of weapons in the conduct of hostilities, defining and distinguishing means and methods of warfare and explaining the rules whereby the use of inherently indiscriminate weapons or of weapons that are of a nature to cause superfluous injury is unlawful.

Hague Law – together with Geneva Law, the other main branch of the law of armed conflict – is the mainstay of *jus in bello*, the collective set of international legal rules that governs acts occurring simultaneously during and in connection with an armed conflict. As noted in the Introduction to this book, Geneva Law governs the treatment of those 'in the power' of a party to a conflict, particularly aliens present in the territory of a party to an international armed conflict (IAC),[1] detainees (whether civilian or military, including prisoners of war) and any other persons *hors de combat*, notably the wounded, sick or shipwrecked.[2]

Hague Law derives its name from the city where most of its early rules were devised. In fact, though, the first modern treaty governing the conduct of hostilities was the 1868 Saint Petersburg Declaration, adopted, as its name suggests, not in The Hague but in that Baltic port city in northern Russia. The 1868 Declaration outlawed the use of exploding bullets against enemy personnel in warfare between states parties.[3] Six years later, states met in Brussels, once more at the initiative of the Russian Czar, Alexander II, and drafted an International Declaration concerning the Laws and Customs of War.[4] Although the 1874 Declaration never entered into force as binding international law, many of the provisions elaborated by the state representatives at the Brussels conference would formally become the letter of the law in a new treaty agreed at the end of the nineteenth century.

[1] See, eg, Convention (IV) relative to the Protection of Civilian Persons in Time of War; adopted at Geneva, 12 August 1949; entry into force, 21 October 1950 (hereinafter, 1949 Geneva Convention IV).

[2] See, eg, Arts 11, 17, 22, 41, 44, 45 and 72–79, Protocol Additional to the Geneva Conventions of 12 August 1949, and relating to the Protection of Victims of International Armed Conflicts (Protocol I); adopted at Geneva, 8 June 1977; entry into force, 7 December 1978 (hereinafter, 1977 Additional Protocol I).

[3] Declaration Renouncing the Use, in Time of War, of Explosive Projectiles Under 400 Grammes Weight; adopted at Saint Petersburg, 11 December 1868; entry into force on the same day.

[4] Project of an International Declaration concerning the Laws and Customs of War; draft elaborated at Brussels, 27 August 1874.

Indeed, as the International Committee of the Red Cross (ICRC) recalls, one of the purposes for which the First Hague Peace Conference of 1899 was convened was 'the revision of the declaration concerning the laws and customs of war elaborated in 1874 by the Conference of Brussels, and not yet ratified'.[5] Both the 1899 Hague Peace Conference and its 1907 sequel would adopt an array of international legal instruments governing the conduct of warfare between states, several of which remain in force and binding on the respective parties to this day. These include specific prohibitions on the use of 'asphyxiating or deleterious gases'[6] and expanding 'dum-dum' bullets,[7] both adopted in 1899, as well as binding rules ('regulations') for warfare on land, adopted in 1899 and revised minimally in 1907.[8] These regulations would be the central pillars of treaty-based Hague Law until the adoption, in 1977, of Additional Protocol I to the 1949 Geneva Conventions. Moreover, as the International Military Tribunal (IMT) held in 1946 with regard to 1907 Hague Convention IV, the rules laid down in the annexure had already attained customary law status by the outbreak of the Second World War:

> The rules of land warfare expressed in the Convention undoubtedly represented an advance over existing International Law at the time of their adoption ... but by 1939 these rules ... were recognized by all civilized nations and were regarded as being declaratory of the laws and customs of war.[9]

Section II of the Regulations annexed to both the 1899 Hague Convention II and 1907 Hague Convention IV is entitled 'Hostilities'. Chapter I of Section II, which addresses the 'means of injuring the enemy, sieges, and bombardments', reads in part as follows:

> **Article 22.**
>
> The right of belligerents to adopt means of injuring the enemy is not unlimited.
>
> **Article 23.**
>
> Besides the prohibitions provided by special Conventions, it is especially prohibited:
>
> (a) To employ poison or poisoned arms;
> (b) To kill or wound treacherously individuals belonging to the hostile nation or army;
> (c) To kill or wound an enemy who, having laid down arms, or having no longer means of defence, has surrendered at discretion;
> (d) To declare that no quarter will be given;
> (e) To employ arms, projectiles, or material of a nature to cause superfluous injury;

[5] Russian circular note of 30 December 1898; see introductory text to 1907 Hague Convention (IV) respecting the Laws and Customs of War on Land and its annex: Regulations concerning the Laws and Customs of War on Land, available at https://goo.gl/573cVB.

[6] Declaration (IV,2) concerning the Use of Asphyxiating Gases, adopted at The Hague, 29 July 1899; entry into force, 4 September 1900. The 1899 Declaration was effectively superseded by the 1925 Geneva Gas Protocol and later by the 1992 Chemical Weapons Convention.

[7] Declaration (IV,3) concerning the Use of Expanding Bullets, adopted at The Hague, 29 July 1899; entry into force, 4 September 1900. The Declaration prohibited use between states parties of bullets that 'expand or flatten easily in the human body, such as bullets with a hard envelope which does not entirely cover the core or is pierced with incisions'.

[8] The Conference of 1899 adopted Hague Convention II on land warfare to which the regulations are annexed. The Convention and the Regulations were revised slightly at the Second International Peace Conference in 1907, becoming 1907 Hague Convention IV, with its regulations again in annexure.

[9] IMT judgment reprinted in (1947) 41 *AJIL* 248–49.

(f) To make improper use of a flag of truce, the national flag or military ensigns and uniform of the enemy, as well as the distinctive badges of the Geneva Convention;
(g) To destroy or seize the enemy's property, unless such destruction or seizure be imperatively demanded by the necessities of war.[10]

These provisions were not entirely new – many were to be found in the spirit or the letter of the earlier 1874 Brussels Declaration[11] and even the 1863 Lieber Code, a set of instructions drafted during the American Civil War by Francis Lieber, a professor at Columbia College in New York, and approved by President Abraham Lincoln.[12] For instance, the language of the superfluous injury rule in Article 23(e) of the 1899 Hague Convention II Regulations was derived from Article 13(e) of the Brussels Declaration, but found its inspiration in the Lieber Code, which instructed the Union forces:

> Whoever intentionally inflicts additional wounds on an enemy already wholly disabled, or kills such an enemy, or who orders or encourages soldiers to do so, shall suffer death, if duly convicted …[13]

Notable by its absence from either set of Regulations (as had also been the case in the abortive 1874 Brussels Declaration and the subsequent 1880 Oxford Manual, a text drafted by non-governmental experts)[14] is an unequivocal and explicit prohibition on attacking civilians.[15] This is surprising given that already in the preamble to the 1868 St Petersburg Declaration it had been observed that 'the only legitimate object which States should endeavour to accomplish during war is to weaken the military forces of the enemy'.[16] The 1863 Lieber Code had even observed, while affirming that a 'citizen or native of a hostile country' is 'an enemy',[17] that

> as civilization has advanced during the last centuries, so has likewise steadily advanced, especially in war on land, the distinction between the private individual belonging to a hostile country and the hostile country itself, with its men in arms. The principle has been more and more acknowledged that the unarmed citizen is to be spared in person, property, and honor as much as the exigencies of war will admit.

[10] The text cited is from the Regulations annexed to the 1899 Hague Convention II for the reason that a slightly different wording is included in Art 23(e) of the 1907 version, replacing 'of a nature to cause' with 'calculated to cause'. That this more subjective formulation does not represent the state of the law is evidenced by the corresponding wording in Art 35(2) of the 1977 Additional Protocol I and Art 8(2)(b)(xx) of the 1998 Rome Statute of the International Criminal Court.

[11] Project of an International Declaration concerning the Laws and Customs of War; adopted at Brussels, 27 August 1874.

[12] G Oberleitner, *Human Rights in Armed Conflict: Law, Practice, Policy* (Cambridge, Cambridge University Press, 2015) 26–27; APV Rogers, *Law on the Battlefield*, 2nd edn (Manchester, Manchester University Press, 2004) 1; ICRC, 'Instructions for the Government of Armies of the United States in the Field (Lieber Code)' at https://goo.gl/WdyQii.

[13] Art 71, Instructions for the Government of Armies of the United States in the Field, General Order No 100 (hereinafter, '1863 Lieber Code'), promulgated by the War Department on 24 April 1863.

[14] The Laws of War on Land, a text drafted by Gustave Moynier and adopted by the non-governmental Institute of International Law at Oxford on 9 September 1880.

[15] Amanda Alexander argues that the genesis of the term 'civilian' can be traced back to the First World War: A Alexander, 'The Genesis of the Civilian' (2007) 20:2 *Leiden Journal of International Law* 2359. The notion of civilian protection – from aerial bombardment – was included in the 1923 Hague Draft Rules of Aerial Warfare.

[16] Declaration Renouncing the Use, in Time of War, of Explosive Projectiles Under 400 Grammes Weight, adopted at St Petersburg, 11 December 1868; entry into force the same day.

[17] Art 21, 1863 Lieber Code.

Nonetheless, as Solis points out, the Code did not consider it unlawful to starve civilians, 'so that it leads to the speedier subjection of the enemy'.[18]

The 1899 and 1907 Hague Regulations did explicitly prohibit 'attack or bombardment, by whatever means, of towns, villages, dwellings, or buildings which are undefended',[19] a prohibition corresponding in part to the immunity from attack of civilian objects, but this omits critical elements of the far broader rule of distinction that Hague Law has recognised for decades. This fundamental omission would not be formally rectified by treaty law until 1977.

In the intervening period, the most significant law of armed conflict treaties to be concluded were the four 1949 Geneva Conventions, which were drafted and adopted in the aftermath of the Second World War.[20] As their name indicates, the four Conventions are composed almost entirely of Geneva Law, offering protection in IAC to, respectively: wounded and sick members of the armed forces on land and in the air; wounded, sick and shipwrecked members of armed forces at sea; prisoners of war; and civilians, particularly those in occupied territories or 'aliens' on the territory of an enemy. The scarce provisions in the four Conventions that may relate to the conduct of hostilities concern primarily the immunity from attack of medical aircraft, ships, hospitals and other similar facilities. Thus, for example, the following extracts from the Geneva Conventions I, II, and IV stipulate:

> Fixed establishments and mobile medical units of the Medical Service may in no circumstances be attacked, but shall at all times be respected and protected by the Parties to the conflict.
>
> Hospital ships entitled to the protection of … Geneva Convention [II] … shall not be attacked from the land.
>
> …
>
> Medical aircraft … shall not be attacked, but shall be respected by the belligerents …[21]
>
> Military hospital ships … may in no circumstances be attacked or captured, but shall at all times be respected and protected …
>
> Establishments ashore entitled to the protection of … Geneva Convention [I] shall be protected from bombardment or attack from the sea.[22]
>
> Civilian hospitals organized to give care to the wounded and sick, the infirm and maternity cases, may in no circumstances be the object of attack, but shall at all times be respected and protected by the Parties to the conflict.[23]

[18] GD Solis (n 1) 47, citing Art 17, 1863 Lieber Code.

[19] Art 25, Regulations concerning the Laws and Customs of War on Land annexed to Convention (IV) respecting the Laws and Customs of War on Land; adopted at The Hague, 18 October 1907; entry into force, 26 January 1910 (hereinafter '1907 Hague Regulations'). The corresponding provision in the 1899 Convention II (also Art 25) had not included the phrase 'by whatever means'.

[20] The first instrument of Geneva law was adopted at Geneva on 22 August 1864: the Convention for the Amelioration of the Condition of the Wounded in Armies in the Field. It was subsequently revised and replaced by the Geneva Conventions of 1906 and 1929 prior to the adoption of the four 1949 Conventions.

[21] Arts 19, 20 and 36, 1949 Geneva Convention I.

[22] Arts 22 and 23, 1949 Geneva Convention II.

[23] Art 18, 1949 Geneva Convention IV.

In armed conflicts not of an international character, a legal notion introduced to the law of armed conflict for the first time by Article 3 common to the four 1949 Geneva Conventions ('Common Article 3'), it was specified inter alia that:

> Persons taking no active part in the hostilities, including members of armed forces who have laid down their arms and those placed *hors de combat* by sickness, wounds, detention, or any other cause, shall in all circumstances be treated humanely, without any adverse distinction founded on race, colour, religion or faith, sex, birth or wealth, or any other similar criteria.

It is generally (though not universally) agreed that Common Article 3 only concerns persons in the power of a party to a non-international armed conflict (NIAC) and does not regulate the conduct of hostilities.[24] Rogers, however, suggests a slight nuance of the accepted position, arguing that while indeed Common Article 3 does not deal *directly* with the conduct of hostilities, 'the principle of civilian immunity can be inferred' from the prohibition of 'violence to life and person' of anyone taking no active part in hostilities, a prohibition that, according to the language of Common Article 3, applies 'at any time and in any place whatsoever'.[25]

II. The Fundamental Rules on the Conduct of Hostilities

The two core Hague Law rules governing the conduct of hostilities are distinction in attack and proportionality in attack.[26] Although, as we have seen, the principles that underpin them are longstanding, the precise formulations were formally negotiated and adopted by states for the first time only in the 1977 Additional Protocol I, in a section entitled 'General Protection against Effects of Hostilities'. The notion of precautions in attack, discussed in chapter 4, does, as Théo Boutruche affirms,[27] certainly have an autonomous normative existence, but arguably its greater value is in buttressing the implementation of the rules of distinction and proportionality in attack.

An attack is defined in the 1997 Additional Protocol I as 'acts of violence against the adversary, whether in offence or in defence'.[28] As the 1987 ICRC commentary on the provision observes, 'It is quite clear that the meaning given here is not exactly the same

[24] See, eg, N Melzer, *Interpretive Guidance on the Notion of Direct Participation in Hostilities under International Humanitarian Law* (Geneva, ICRC, 2009) 28; ICRC commentary on 1949 Geneva Convention I, 2016, para 389. For a brief discussion of the position of various authors on the issue, see A Bellal, G Giacca and S Casey-Maslen, 'International law and armed non-state actors in Afghanistan', *International Review of the Red Cross*, vol 93, no 881 (March 2011) 53 at https://goo.gl/asNntR.

[25] Rogers (n 12) 221. See also L Moir, *The Law of Internal Armed Conflict* (Cambridge, Cambridge University Press, 2002) 58–61.

[26] They are also termed principles rather than rules by some. According to the International Court of Justice (ICJ), the two 'cardinal principles' of the law of armed conflict are the distinction between combatants and non-combatants, and the prohibition on causing unnecessary suffering to combatants. ICJ, *Legality of the Threat or Use of Nuclear Weapons*, Advisory Opinion, 8 July 1996 (hereinafter, '1996 Nuclear Weapons Advisory Opinion') para 78. Surprisingly – indeed regrettably – the ICJ did not discuss the application of the rule of proportionality in its 1996 Advisory Opinion.

[27] See T Boutruche, 'Expert Opinion on the Meaning and Scope of Feasible Precautions under International Humanitarian Law and Related Assessment of the Conduct of the Parties to the Gaza Conflict in the Context of the Operation "Protective Edge"' (Jerusalem, Diakonia, 2015) 10 at https://goo.gl/JRt194.

[28] Art 49(1), 1977 Additional Protocol I.

as the usual meaning of the word.' It notes that the closest ordinary meaning at the time was that found in the *Shorter Oxford Dictionary*: 'to set upon with hostile action'.[29] Thus, the ICRC suggests that the term 'attack' is effectively a synonym for 'combat action'.[30] Subsequently, the jurisprudence of the ICTY defined an attack as 'a course of conduct involving the commission of acts of violence'.[31] According to the *Tallinn Manual on the International Law Applicable to Cyber Warfare*, it is the 'use of violence against a target that distinguishes attacks from other military operations. Non-violent operations, such as psychological cyber operations or cyber espionage, do not qualify as attacks'.[32]

The core Hague Law rules of distinction and proportionality in attack are now discussed in turn.

A. The Rule of Distinction in Attack

This fundamental Hague Law rule holds that parties to any armed conflict must direct attacks only against lawful military objectives (military personnel or objects of concrete military value) and never against the civilian population, individual civilians or civilian objects. The rule of distinction in attack was first unequivocally expressed by law of armed conflict treaty in the 1977 Additional Protocol I[33] and, albeit in more limited terms, in the 1977 Additional Protocol II (which regulates certain high-intensity NIACs).[34] The basic rule, as set out in 1977 Additional Protocol I, is as follows:

> In order to ensure respect for and protection of the civilian population and civilian objects, the Parties to the conflict shall at all times distinguish between the civilian population and combatants

[29] Y Sandoz, C Swinarski, and B Zimmermann (eds), *Commentary on the Additional Protocols of 8 June 1977 to the Geneva Conventions of 12 August 1949* (Geneva, Martinus Nijhoff, 1987) (hereinafter, ICRC Commentary on the 1977 Additional Protocols), para 1879.

[30] ICRC Commentary on the 1977 Additional Protocols, para 1880.

[31] ICTY, *Prosecutor v Galić*, Judgment (Trial Chamber) (Case No IT-98-29-T), 5 December 2003, para 52, citing *Prosecutor v Krnojelac*, Judgment (Trial Chamber), 15 March 2002, para 54; and *Prosecutor v Kunarac*, Judgment (Trial Chamber), 22 February 2001, para 415. The ICTY further affirmed, albeit in the context of alleged crimes against humanity rather than war crimes, that 'the concept of "attack" is distinct and independent from the concept of "armed conflict"': *Prosecutor v Tadić*, Judgment (Appeals Chamber) (Case No IT-94-1-A), 15 July 1999, para 251.

[32] M Schmitt (ed), *Tallinn Manual on the International Law Applicable to Cyber Warfare* (Cambridge, Cambridge University Press, 2013) 106.

[33] See, in particular, Arts 48–57, 1977 Additional Protocol I. In its 1956 *Draft Rules for the Limitation of the Dangers incurred by the Civilian Population in Time of War*, however, the ICRC included a draft provision (Art 6), which stipulated that 'Attacks directed against the civilian population, as such, whether with the object of terrorizing it or for any other reason, are prohibited. This prohibition applies both to attacks on individuals and to those directed against groups. … In consequence, it is also forbidden to attack dwellings, installations or means of transport, which are for the exclusive use of, and occupied by, the civilian population.' In 1965, Resolution XXVIII of the 20th International Conference of the Red Cross Movement laid down a set of principles that were affirmed by UN General Assembly Resolution 2444 (XXIII) in December 1968, adopted by unanimous vote of 111 to nil. Two key principles were that 'it is prohibited to launch attacks against the civilian populations as such' and that 'distinction must be made at all times between persons taking part in the hostilities and members of the civilian population to the effect that the latter be spared as much as possible'.

[34] According to Art 13(2), Protocol Additional to the Geneva Conventions of 12 August 1949, and relating to the protection of victims of non-international armed conflicts (Protocol II); adopted at Geneva, 8 June 1977; entry into force, 7 December 1978 (hereinafter, 1977 Additional Protocol II): 'The civilian population as such, as well as individual civilians, shall not be the object of attack.' See also Art 14 ('Protection of Objects Indispensable to the Survival of the Civilian Population'); Art 15 ('Protection of Works and Installations Containing Dangerous Forces'); and Art 16 ('Protection of Cultural Objects and of Places of Worship').

> and between civilian objects and military objectives and accordingly shall direct their operations only against military objectives.[35]

According to an ICRC Study of Customary International Humanitarian Law (IHL) – the ICRC prefers this descriptor to that of the law of armed conflict – the core of the customary rule of distinction in attack is reformulated as two distinct norms:

> The parties to the conflict must at all times distinguish between civilians and combatants. Attacks may only be directed against combatants. Attacks must not be directed against civilians.
>
> …
>
> The parties to the conflict must at all times distinguish between civilian objects and military objectives. Attacks may only be directed against military objectives. Attacks must not be directed against civilian objects.[36]

Civilians are all persons who are not members of the armed forces (or organised armed groups akin to armed forces), while the civilian population comprises all persons who are civilians.[37]

Civilian objects are defined as any objects that are not military objectives, which in turn 'are limited to those objects which by their nature, location, purpose or use make an effective contribution to military action and whose partial or total destruction, capture or neutralization, in the circumstances ruling at the time, offers a definite military advantage'.[38] Thus, at any given point in time a specific object or piece of land is either a civilian object or a military objective: it cannot be both simultaneously. Where an object serves a 'dual-use' function, such as a road, bridge, power station or airport runway, whether it is a civilian object or a military objective under the law of armed conflict depends on the circumstances. As the definition delineates, notwithstanding simultaneous civilian use or occupation, when any specific object (or part of an object, such as a school classroom) makes an effective contribution to military action *and* its destruction or neutralisation, in the prevailing circumstances, offers a definite military advantage, Hague Law considers that object or part of the object to be a military objective.

In addition to prohibiting direct attacks on civilians and civilian objects, on the basis that attacks may only lawfully be directed against military objectives, the rule of distinction also prohibits indiscriminate attacks. Such attacks are those:

- which are not directed at a specific military objective;
- which employ a means or method of combat that cannot be directed at a specific military objective; or
- which employ a means or method of combat whose effects cannot be limited in accordance with law of armed conflict rules;

and consequently, in each such case, are of a nature to strike military objectives and civilians or civilian objects without distinction.[39]

[35] Art 48, 1977 Additional Protocol I.

[36] ICRC Study of Customary IHL, Rule 1 ('The Principle of Distinction between Civilians and Combatants') at https://goo.gl/1pxpDe; and ibid, Rule 7 ('The Principle of Distinction between Civilian Objects and Military Objectives') at https://goo.gl/hLX9Lq.

[37] ICRC Study of Customary IHL, Rule 5 ('Definition of Civilians') at https://goo.gl/Kn5CU3.

[38] ICRC Study of Customary IHL, Rule 8 ('Definition of Military Objectives') at https://goo.gl/8Ap8uH.

[39] ICRC Study of Customary IHL, Rule 11 ('Indiscriminate Attacks') at https://goo.gl/aNRtei; and Rule 12 ('Definition of Indiscriminate Attacks') at https://goo.gl/gxcHsw.

This means that if a weapon or tactic cannot be, or is not, directed with sufficient accuracy against a military objective (see chapters 2 and 3), or if the effects of the attack will inevitably extend or spread over such an area that they do not comply with the rule of distinction, the attack is indiscriminate and therefore unlawful.

Similarly considered an indiscriminate attack is a bombardment that 'treats as a single military objective a number of clearly separated and distinct military objectives located in a city, town, village or other area containing a similar concentration of civilians or civilian objects are prohibited'.[40] Area bombardment was a common tactic in the Second World War, and the phenomenon persisted among many local and regional armed conflicts that broke out after 1945, including, notoriously, during the Vietnam War. The rule of proportionality in attack, which is also deemed to be a form of indiscriminate attack by the 1977 Additional Protocol I,[41] is discussed in section I.B.

The war crime of attacking civilians is variously delineated in law of armed conflict and international criminal law treaties, and by the ICRC in its assessment of customary international law. It has arguably been broadened in scope by the jurisprudence of the ICTY, although as discussed below this may amount to an error of interpretation by the now moribund Tribunal. In the 1977 Additional Protocol I, it is stipulated that it is a 'grave breach' – one of a number of specific treaty-based war crimes occurring in an IAC[42] – to wilfully make the civilian population or individual civilians the object of attack, where the attacks causes 'death or serious injury to body or health'.[43] In the 1998 Rome Statute of the International Criminal Court (ICC Statute), the Court is potentially given jurisdiction over the war crime of 'Intentionally directing attacks against the civilian population as such or against individual civilians not taking direct part in hostilities';[44] there is, however, no specific requirement that death or serious injury result from the attack.

The ICRC affirms that under customary international law the war crime is '[m]aking the civilian population or individual civilians, not taking a direct part in hostilities, the object of attack'.[45] As the ICRC explains, to meet the requirement that the violation be of a serious nature, it is sufficient that the conduct *endangers* persons or objects that are protected by the law:

> The majority of war crimes involve death, injury, destruction or unlawful taking of property. However, not all acts necessarily have to result in actual damage to persons or objects in order to amount to war crimes. This became evident when the Elements of Crimes for the International Criminal Court were being drafted. It was decided, for example, that it was enough to launch an

[40] ICRC Study of Customary IHL, Rule 13 ('Area Bombardment') at https://goo.gl/Bo3fDH; see also Art 51(5)(a), Additional Protocol I.

[41] Art 51(5), 1977 Additional Protocol I.

[42] The term 'grave breach' is reserved by treaty for certain serious violations of the law of armed conflict that occur in an IAC. The corresponding term in a NIAC is 'serious violation', even though the ICC Statute also uses the term when referring to acts that are grave breaches of the 1977 Additional Protocol I. See, eg, Art 8(2)(b) and (c), ICC Statute.

[43] Art 85(3)(a), 1977 Additional Protocol I.

[44] Art 8(2)(b)(i), ICC Statute.

[45] ICRC Study of Customary IHL, Rule 156 ('Definition of War Crimes'), 'List of War Crimes', (ii)(i), at https://goo.gl/xIOyKz.

> attack on civilians or civilian objects, even if something unexpectedly prevented the attack from causing death or serious injury. This could be the case of an attack launched against the civilian population or individual civilians, even though, owing to the failure of the weapon system, the intended target was not hit.[46]

Arguably, though, the ICTY erred in its finding of law by holding, on a number of occasions, that indiscriminate attacks may qualify as direct attacks on civilians. Perhaps the best example of where the Tribunal went wrong is the *Galić* case. In his appeal against conviction by the Trial Chamber, General Galić's defence team presented its brief on 19 July 2004, arguing that neither disproportionate attacks nor indiscriminate attacks may qualify as direct attacks on civilians.[47] This is a correct statement of the law. The ICRC, for example, in its findings of customary law, distinguishes the war crime of making civilians the object of attack, set out above, from three other such crimes:

> Launching an indiscriminate attack resulting in loss of life or injury to civilians …;
>
> Using prohibited weapons;
>
> Launching an attack in the knowledge that such attack will cause incidental loss of civilian life, injury to civilians or damage to civilian objects which would be clearly excessive in relation to the concrete and direct military advantage anticipated.

Thus there is, despite its omission from the ICC Statute, the war crime, distinct from attacks on civilians, of an indiscriminate attack. There is a similarly distinct war crime of a disproportionate attack (discussed in section I.B). There is also the war crime of using an indiscriminate weapon (discussed further in section II.B). None of these should be conflated with the war crime of directly attacking civilians. In its brief for the Appeals Chamber in the *Galić* case, the Prosecution argued that the Trial Chamber properly relied on the principle of distinction, which obliges those directing attacks to do so only against military objectives, as distinguished from civilian targets. This is not contentious. It also claimed, though, that the Trial Chamber did not err in determining that indiscriminate and disproportionate attacks may qualify as making civilians the object of attack or direct attacks.[48]

How did the ICTY Appeals Chamber respond to this limb of the appeal? It noted that the Trial Chamber did not hold that such attacks *always* amount to direct attacks, but rather that they 'may qualify' as such. Despite the separate war crime of using prohibited weapons, it expressed its agreement with other Trial Chambers, which found that attacks using indiscriminate weapons are tantamount to direct targeting of civilians. This means that the Tribunal is holding that international criminal law deems that you are deliberately targeting someone with a weapon that, by definition, cannot be accurately targeted. This position should not be considered authoritative.

The Appeals Chamber referred to the judgment in the *Blaškić* case, wherein a Trial Chamber inferred from the weapons which had been used in an attack – inaccurate artisanal mortars known colloquially as 'baby bombs' – that the perpetrators wanted to target the

[46] Ibid, 'Serious nature of the violation', (i).

[47] Defence Appeal Brief, 19 July 2004, para 50; see ICTY, *Prosecutor v Galić*, Judgment (Appeals Chamber) (Case No IT-98-29-A), 30 November 2006, para 131.

[48] Prosecution Response Brief, paras 6.19, 6.17.

civilian population. This holding was, however, overturned on appeal. Indeed, on the basis of the trial and additional evidence, the Appeals Chamber in the *Blaškić* case declared that it was 'not satisfied beyond reasonable doubt either that the attack of 18 July 1993 resulted in heavy casualties among Muslim civilians, or that the attack was directed at the Muslim civilian population or civilian property in Stari Vitez'.[49] In addition, the Appeals Chamber noted that 'It need not be decided whether, in general terms, the use of "baby bombs" is illegal.'[50] Despite this fact, the Appeals Chamber in the *Galić* case found that the impugned finding 'does not conflate the two crimes but rather supports the view that a direct attack can be inferred from the indiscriminate character of the weapon used'.[51] This is a poor adjudication of the law.

In February 2017, the Commission of Inquiry on Syria released a report on respect for international law in the armed conflicts ongoing in that country. The report stated:

> Throughout the siege of eastern Aleppo, armed groups continuously shelled western Aleppo using mostly unguided and imprecise weaponry, such as improvised rockets and mortars. One of the most commonly used weapons were so-called 'hell canons [*sic*]'. The nature of the weapons used and the absence of a military presence in the majority of cases reviewed terrorized residents of western Aleppo in violation of the international humanitarian law principle of distinction. These attacks therefore amount to the war crime of indiscriminate attacks against a civilian population.[52]

The description of the Hague Law violation as one of an indiscriminate attack is here more appropriate, although the Commission appears to mix violations somewhat, as it then argues that the attack is 'against a civilian population'. Whether the nature of the weapons to which the Commission refers is such as to render them *inherently* indiscriminate is debatable, though in many specific instances their use may undoubtedly be so characterised.

B. The Rule of Proportionality in Attack

Even if an attack is targeted at a lawful military objective in accordance with the rule of distinction, the decision to launch the attack must also respect the rule of proportionality. According to this customary Hague Law rule, an attack against a lawful target will be unlawful where it 'may be expected' to cause incidental civilian harm that is 'excessive' compared with the projected 'concrete and direct military advantage'.[53] Civilian harm is explicitly defined as encompassing deaths or injuries to civilians, destruction of or damage to civilian objects, 'or a combination thereof'. Proportionality thus has 'nothing to do with injury to combatants or damage to military objectives' (except insofar as they amount to the expected

[49] ICTY, *Prosecutor v Thomir Blaškić*, Judgment (Appeals Chamber) (Case No IT-95-14-A), 29 July 2004, para 464.

[50] Ibid, para 465.

[51] *Galić* (n 47) para 132.

[52] Report of the Commission of Inquiry on Syria, UN Doc A/HRC/34/64, 2 February 2017, para 101.

[53] The ICRC has expressed the customary IHL rule as follows: 'Launching an attack which may be expected to cause incidental loss of civilian life, injury to civilians, damage to civilian objects, or a combination thereof, which would be excessive in relation to the concrete and direct military advantage anticipated, is prohibited.'

'concrete and direct military advantage'.[54] For, as the United States (US) Department of Defense's 2015 *Law of War Manual* observed:

> In conducting attacks, the proportionality rule only need be applied when civilians or civilian objects are at risk of harm from attacks on military objectives. It would not apply when civilians or civilian objects are not at risk.[55]

This excluded from the constraints of the proportionality rule situations where individuals with combatant status are *hors de combat* and may be affected by an attack against a lawful military objective.[56] In a more recent iteration of the Manual, however, the US Department of Defense has affirmed that:

> Although the prohibition on attacks expected to cause excessive harm to civilians and civilian objects generally does not require consideration of military personnel and objects, feasible precautions must be taken to reduce the risk of harm to military personnel and objects that are protected from being made the object of attack, such as military personnel placed *hors de combat*.[57]

It is important to recall that the assessment of likely civilian harm is made by the attacker in advance of the attack. It is not an *ex post facto* analysis based on the extent of any civilian casualties or damage to civilian objects actually inflicted (though such casualties or damage may oblige, and should certainly incite, the attacking party to review its information, assessment procedures and decision-making).[58]

The challenge in applying the proportionality rule is focused on the inherent imprecision of the term 'excessive'. Controversially, the ICRC has asserted that the rule 'does not provide any justification for attacks which cause extensive civilian losses and damages [*sic*]. Incidental losses and damages [*sic*] should never be extensive.' This is in all likelihood not the state of the law. As Yoram Dinstein has observed, the rule is a balancing act: the greater the anticipated military advantage, the greater the extent of foreseeable civilian harm that may not be unlawful.[59] In the view of the US Department of Defense in 2015:

> The weighing or comparison between the expected incidental harm and the expected military advantage does not necessarily lend itself to empirical analyses.[60] On the one hand, striking an ammunition depot or a terrorist training camp would not be prohibited because a farmer is plowing a field in the area.[61] On the other hand, a very significant military advantage would be

[54] Y Dinstein, *The Conduct of Hostilities under the Law of International Armed Conflict*, 2nd edn (Cambridge, Cambridge University Press, 2010) 129.

[55] US Department of Defense, *Law of War Manual*, June 2015 (hereinafter 'USDOD 2015 *Law of War Manual*'), para 5.12.1, at https://goo.gl/uZKhvk.

[56] On this basis, an attack could, for example, be lawfully conducted against three regular soldiers (ie not non-combatant army medics) who are evacuating a severely wounded colleague, even if it is highly likely that the soldier who is *hors de combat* will be killed by the attack, as long as he is not its target.

[57] US Department of Defense, *Law of War Manual*, June 2015, updated December 2016 (hereinafter 'USDOD December 2016 *Law of War Manual*') para 5.10.1, at https://goo.gl/QMkjqs.

[58] In the ICTY's final trial chamber judgment, of former Bosnian Serb army commander Ratko Mladić, Trial Chamber I cited testimony by Francis Thomas, a UN Military Observer in Sarajevo in 1993–94, whereby 'the indiscriminate nature of shelling by the Serbs was underscored by the fact that they never carried out target assessments, ie evaluated the damage done to a target and determining if further shelling was required': ICTY, *Prosecutor v Ratko Mladić*, Judgment (Trial Chamber I) (Case No IT-09-92-T), 22 November 2017, para 1876. See also The Minnesota Protocol on the Investigation of Potentially Unlawful Death (2016), Office of the UN High Commissioner for Human Rights, New York/Geneva, 2017, para 21, at https://goo.gl/Yu17ee.

[59] Dinstein (n 54) 131.

[60] ICTY, *Final Report to the Prosecutor by the Committee Established to Review the NATO Bombing Campaign Against the Federal Republic of Yugoslavia*, 13 June 2000, para 48.

[61] Ibid, citing also Rogers (n 12) 64–65.

> necessary to justify the collateral death or injury to thousands of civilians.[62] In less clear-cut cases, the question of whether the expected incidental harm is excessive may be a highly open-ended legal inquiry, and the answer may be subjective and imprecise ...[63]

The assertion that only 'very significant' military advantage could justify the incidental death of, or injury to, thousands of civilians was narrowed in the Department of Defense's revised *Law of War Manual* in December 2016. In coming closer to the state of Hague Law, it was now affirmed that 'an *extraordinary* military advantage would be necessary to justify an operation posing risks of collateral death or injury to thousands of civilians'.[64]

Nonetheless, the innate imprecision of the notion of 'excessive', combined with additional actus reus and mens rea requirements over and above the primary Hague Law rule, makes prosecution for the war crime of a disproportionate attack extremely challenging. A prosecutor at the ICC, for instance, would need to prove, inter alia, that the relevant commander 'intentionally' launched an attack 'in the knowledge' that it would cause 'clearly excessive' civilian harm in relation to the 'concrete and direct overall military advantage anticipated'.[65] There have been very few successful prosecutions for the war crime of a disproportionate attack, and none so far in the ICC.

According to the ICTY's Trial Chamber judgment in the *Galić* case, in determining whether an attack was proportionate it is necessary to examine 'whether a reasonably well-informed person in the circumstances of the actual perpetrator, ... making reasonable use of the information available to him or her, could have expected excessive civilian casualties to result from the attack'.[66] In so holding, the Tribunal cited, amongst others, the 1992 *Canadian Law of Armed Conflict at the Operational and Tactical Level*,[67] whereby 'consideration must be paid to the honest judgement of responsible commanders, based on the information reasonably available to them at the relevant time, taking fully into account the urgent and difficult circumstances under which such judgements are usually made'.[68] It 'indicates that the proportionality test must be examined on the basis of 'what a reasonable person would do' in such circumstances'.[69]

To establish the mens rea of the war crime of a disproportionate attack, the ICTY has held that the Prosecution must prove that the attack 'was launched wilfully and in knowledge of circumstances giving rise to the expectation of excessive civilian casualties'.[70]

III. Principles and Rules Governing Use of Weapons

Weapons are integral to any attack, but there is no accepted definition under international law of what constitutes a 'weapon'.[71] A weapon encompasses, but is not restricted to, devices

62 M Greenspan, *Modern Law of Land Warfare* (Berkeley, CA, University of California Press, 1959) 335.
63 USDOD 2015 *Law of War Manual*, para 5.12.4.
64 USDOD December 2016 *Law of War Manual*, para 5.12.3 (emphasis added).
65 See Art 8(2)(b)(iv), ICC Statute.
66 *Galić* (n 31) para 58.
67 At s 5, para 27.
68 *Galić* (n 31) para 58.
69 Ibid, fn 110.
70 Ibid, para 59.
71 A US Department of Defense Working Group reportedly suggested a definition of 'all arms, munitions, materiel, instruments, mechanisms or devices that have an intended effect of injuring, damaging, destroying or disabling personnel or property'. Cited in ICRC, *A Guide to the Legal Review of New Weapons, Means and Methods*

that cause harm by means of kinetic energy, such as a bullet fired from a gun. Damage to a human body can also be inflicted by weapons that operate through the transmission of heat, sound, electricity, bacteria, poison, radiation or electromagnetic energy.[72] Thus, a weapon includes a dual-use item, such as a knife, and adapted or locally produced explosive devices, as well as a radiological device ('dirty bomb'), wherein radioactive material is associated with conventional explosives. The term also applies to the use of the Internet in a cyberattack, wherein computer code is 'weaponised', for instance in viruses or worms.[73] The notion of a weapon is thus considerably broader than that of 'arms', which are generally defined as industrially produced weapons, especially when destined for the military market.[74]

A. Means and Methods of Warfare

According to the ICRC, the diplomatic conference that adopted the 1977 Additional Protocol I preferred the term 'methods and means of warfare' to 'methods and means of combat', which was used in the ICRC draft protocol, since combat 'might be construed more narrowly than "warfare"'.[75] The terms 'means of warfare' and 'method of warfare' are not, though, formally defined in international law. As Cameron noted in 1980, the 'term "methods and means of warfare" is of fairly recent vintage. One can sense vaguely, rather than know confidently, what it signifies.'[76] He suggests a collective definition: 'all strategies and tactics and every other measure which, by the use of manpower and weapons systems, an armed force may employ'.[77] Still as at the end of 2016, in the words of the US Department of Defense, they 'lack an established, specific meaning'.[78]

i. Means of Warfare

The ICRC commentary on use of the terms in Article 51, referring back to Article 35, states that 'The term "means of combat" or "means of warfare" … generally refers to the weapons being used, while the expression "methods of combat" generally refers to the way in which such weapons are used.'[79] Thus, in the ICRC commentary on the Protocol, poison is cited as a

of Warfare: Measures to Implement Article 36 of Additional Protocol I of 1977 (Geneva, ICRC, 2007) 8, fn 17. Within the context of the law of armed conflict, a weapon has been defined by one British military lawyer as connoting 'an offensive capability that can be applied to a military object or enemy combatant'. J McClelland, 'The Review of Weapons in Accordance with Article 36 of Additional Protocol I', *International Review of the Red Cross*, vol 85, no 850 (June 2003) 397, 404.

[72] See proposed definition in S Casey-Maslen (ed), *Weapons under International Human Rights Law* (Cambridge, Cambridge University Press, 2014) xx.

[73] See DP Fidler, 'Cyberattacks and international human rights law' in Casey-Maslen (ed) (n 72) ch 10, at 303.

[74] This is despite the fact that the equally authentic French version of the 1977 Additional Protocol I uses the term 'arme' and 'armes' to mean both weapon(s) and arms. A similar problem with translation occurs with respect to the Spanish version of the Protocol, as Spanish also does not distinguish between weapons and arms.

[75] ICRC Commentary on the 1977 Additional Protocols, para 1401.

[76] Col PJ Cameron, 'The Limitations on Methods and Means of Warfare' (1980) 9 *Australian Year Book of International Law* 247 at https://goo.gl/zjRpsF.

[77] Ibid, 255.

[78] USDOD December 2016 *Law of War Manual*, para 5.1.1.

[79] ICRC Commentary on the 1977 Additional Protocols, para 1957.

means of warfare,[80] while poisoning wells is a method of warfare.[81] It is sometimes suggested that the term 'means of warfare' is a synonym for a weapon, but the provision in Article 36 of 1977 Additional Protocol I, which refers to the duty to review any new 'weapon, means or method of warfare', implies that this is incorrect. Article 35 of the Protocol addresses 'weapons, projectiles and material and methods of warfare', a formulation that indicates that *means of warfare* include, in addition to weapons, 'projectiles and material' of warfare.[82]

The US Department of Defense considers that, in general, means of warfare 'has referred to weapons or devices used to conduct warfare'.[83] It also, though, cites Hays Parks, who, in 1997, opined that means of warfare 'traditionally has been understood to refer to the effect of weapons in their use against combatants'.[84] In its 2006 guide to implementation of Article 36 of 1977 Additional Protocol I, the ICRC affirmed simply that means of warfare designates 'the tools of war'.[85] Dinstein asserts that means of warfare 'consist chiefly of weapons and *matériel* (such as means of communications and signalling devices)'.[86] This is too wide, as means of communications and signalling devices are not means of warfare (though they may well be lawful military objectives). The most accurate definition of the Hague Law term is provided by the 2009 *Harvard Manual on International Law Applicable to Air and Missile Warfare*, which defines means of warfare as 'weapons, weapon systems or platforms employed for the purposes of attack'.[87]

ii. Methods of Warfare

In contrast, the *Harvard Manual*'s definition of methods of warfare as 'attacks and other activities designed to adversely affect the enemy's military operations or military capacity' is less accurate. It seemingly excludes attacks on enemy civilians, which may clearly fall within the definition of methods of warfare (even though such attacks are generally unlawful). The commentary on the *Manual* explains that methods of warfare 'are a subcategory of military operations', noting that military operations, 'such as resupply, transportation of troops and communications do not constitute methods of warfare unless they adversely affect the enemy's military operations or military capacity'.[88] It affirms that 'Bombing campaign [*sic*], missile attack, rocket attack, strafing, and conducting EW [electronic warfare] are specific methods of air warfare.'[89] In contrast, in seeking to explain the term *method of warfare*, Dinstein prefers to talk, in rather obscure terms, of 'operational modes'.[90]

[80] Ibid, para 1402.
[81] Ibid, para 1963.
[82] The 2009 *Harvard Manual on International Law Applicable to Air and Missile Warfare* refers to means of warfare used during military operations, 'such as weapons'. Available at https://goo.gl/tJX7bJ.
[83] USDOD 2015 *Law of War Manual*, para 5.1.1.
[84] W Hays Parks, Special Assistant to The Judge Advocate General of the Army for Law of War Matters, 'Memorandum of Law: Travaux Préparatoires and Legal Analysis of Blinding Laser Weapons Protocol', reprinted in *The Army Lawyer*, June 1997, 34–35.
[85] ICRC, *A Guide to the Legal Review of New Weapons, Means and Methods of Warfare: Measures to Implement Article 36 of Additional Protocol I of 1977* (Geneva, ICRC, 2006) 3.
[86] Y Dinstein, *The Conduct of Hostilities under the Law of International Armed Conflict*, 3rd edn (Cambridge, Cambridge University Press, 2001) 2.
[87] *Harvard Manual on International Law Applicable to Air and Missile Warfare*, s A, definition t.
[88] Ibid.
[89] Ibid.
[90] Dinstein (n 86) 2.

A better definition of the term is as follows: 'the form that military operations take during the conduct of hostilities and which involve the threat or use of force against the armed forces or other military objective of an adverse party to the conflict or civilians or civilian objects in that party's territory'. The *Harvard Manual* further usefully notes that 'In military terms, methods of warfare consist of the various general categories of operations, such as bombing, as well as the specific tactics used for attack, such as high altitude bombing.'[91] Other methods of warfare include starvation, perfidy, sieges and the denial of quarter.

The US Department of Defense has noted that, 'in some cases', the phrase

> may be a term of art in a legal instrument that has been specifically interpreted by the United States. For example, the Chemical Weapons Convention obligates Parties to undertake not to use riot control agents as a 'method of warfare', and the United States has interpreted that prohibition not to include certain uses of riot control agents.[92]

Such uses include where a riot breaks out in a prisoner-of-war camp or enemy combatant detainee facility managed by the US. In such a case, it argues therefore that any use of riot control agents, such as tear gas, would fall to be determined by the law of law enforcement, an issue considered further in chapter 3. This US understanding is a correct appreciation of the state of international law and does not affect the definition proposed above.

B. The Choice of Means or Methods of Warfare is not Unlimited

A fundamental Hague Law principle holds that the right of parties to an armed conflict 'to choose methods or means of warfare is not unlimited'.[93] This means that parties to an armed conflict are restricted by applicable treaty and customary rules in the weapons they may lawfully use, as well as in the way they may lawfully use them. Furthermore, according to the ICRC, '[m]ilitary necessity cannot justify any derogation from rules which are drafted in a peremptory manner'.[94]

The fundamental principle, which is also binding under customary law, applies to all armed conflict. According to the US Department of the Navy, for example, 'it is a fundamental tenet of the law of armed conflict that the right of nations engaged in an armed conflict to choose methods or means of warfare is not unlimited'.[95] In its 1996 Advisory Opinion on the *Legality of the Threat or Use of Nuclear Weapons*, the International Court of Justice (ICJ) reiterated that states 'do not have unlimited freedom of choice of means in the weapons they use'. In a strange holding, though, the Court then – incorrectly – limited the principle to the rule prohibiting use of weapons that cause unnecessary suffering to combatants.[96]

[91] *Harvard Manual on International Law Applicable to Air and Missile Warfare*, s A, definition v.

[92] USDOD 2015 *Law of War Manual*, para 5.1.1.

[93] Art 35(1), 1977 Additional Protocol I.

[94] ICRC Commentary on the 1977 Additional Protocols, para 1405.

[95] US Department of the Navy, *The Commander's Handbook on the Law of Naval Operations*, NWP 1-14M, 2007, para 9.1.

[96] 1996 Nuclear Weapons Advisory Opinion, para 78.

C. The Use of Inherently Indiscriminate Weapons is Unlawful

In addition to restricting the use of weapons in all military operations, whether offensive or defensive in nature,[97] the rule of distinction means that the use of any weapon that is 'incapable of distinguishing between civilian and military targets' is unlawful. The ICJ described this as a 'cardinal' principle in its 1996 Nuclear Weapons Advisory Opinion.[98] In 2005, the ICRC Study of Customary IHL concluded that 'The use of weapons which are by nature indiscriminate is prohibited.'[99] As the ICRC has correctly affirmed, the rule is a customary norm applicable in all armed conflicts.[100]

The UK's 2004 *Manual of the Law of Armed Conflict* describes the applicable rule as comprising two alternative tests: if a weapon cannot be targeted against a specific military objective (for instance, because it has a rudimentary guidance system), or if its effects cannot be limited to a military objective, it is an indiscriminate weapon.[101] While this understanding is not generally contentious, its application of the rule to specific weapons is. In its discussion of the customary rule, the ICRC cites numerous conventional weapons and weapons of mass destruction that have been alleged to be of an indiscriminate nature, but observes that 'insufficient consensus' [*sic*] exists 'to conclude that, under customary international law, they all violate the rule prohibiting the use of indiscriminate weapons'.[102]

Although the precise parameters for what is an inherently indiscriminate weapon are not clear, the strongest argument for a weapon in modern use that cannot be targeted sufficiently accurately is probably an early 'Scud' missile. This Soviet missile, the R-11, which was manufactured during the Cold War from 1959 to 1984, was intended to strike targets in Western Europe. Early Scuds, whose gyroscopes and electronics dated back to the technology of the 1950s, were notoriously inaccurate. In general, it was expected that half of the missiles fired at a single target would miss by more than one kilometre.[103]

Another weapon that has frequently been cited as 'indiscriminate' is the landmine. Here it is the fact that the weapon is activated by the victim that is at the heart of the argument. An anti-personnel mine can not 'distinguish' between the footfall of a soldier or that of a civilian: either will detonate the weapon. This would tend to suggest that its effects are indiscriminate. The flaw in the argument, though, is that the emplacement of anti-personnel mines in a marked and fenced area, especially one that is patrolled by military personnel,

[97] See Art 49(1), 1977 Additional Protocol I ('Definition of attacks and scope of application'): '"Attacks" means acts of violence against the adversary, whether in offence or in defence.'

[98] 1996 Nuclear Weapons Advisory Opinion, para 78. The Court's formulation is unfortunate, given that it implies there are civilian 'targets'. A better formulation would have been 'incapable of distinguishing between civilians and civilian objects and military objectives'.

[99] ICRC Study of Customary IHL, Rule 71 ('Weapons That Are by Nature Indiscriminate') at https://goo.gl/vrfRTg.

[100] Ibid. See also WH Boothby, *Weapons and the Law of Armed Conflict* (Oxford, Oxford University Press, 2009) 82.

[101] 'It is prohibited to employ weapons which cannot be directed at a specific military objective or the effects of which cannot be limited as required by Additional Protocol I and consequently are of a nature to strike military objectives and civilians or civilian objects without distinction.' UK Ministry of Defence, *The Manual of the Law of Armed Conflict* (Oxford, Oxford University Press, 2004) para 6.4.

[102] ICRC Study of Customary IHL, Rule 71 (n 99).

[103] See S Casey-Maslen, 'The use of nuclear weapons under rules governing the conduct of hostilities' in G Nystuen et al (eds), *Nuclear Weapons under International Law* (Cambridge, Cambridge University Press, 2014) 100.

can effectively ensure that the victims of any explosion are predominantly, if not exclusively, military and not civilian. That this is rarely the case in practice justifies their prohibition by treaty, but not the assertion that they are inherently indiscriminate weapons. Moreover, any state that believes instead that anti-personnel mines are inherently indiscriminate must surely accept that any use of an anti-vehicle mine is similarly unlawful, since such mines do not distinguish between, for instance, a tank and a school bus.

The US Air Force's *1976 Manual on International Law* cites biological weapons as a 'universally agreed illustration of … an indiscriminate weapon', observing that the uncontrollable effects from such weapons 'may include injury to the civilian population of other states as well as injury to an enemy's civilian population'.[104] These uncontrolled effects exist not only spatially but also over time.[105] The same applies to poison; as the ICRC has observed, 'poison is unlawful in itself, as would be any weapon which would, by its very nature, be so imprecise that it would inevitably cause indiscriminate damage'.[106]

D. The Use of Weapons Causing Superfluous Injury is Unlawful

One of the very few rules protecting combatants while they are fighting is the prohibition on means and methods of warfare that are of a nature to cause superfluous injury or unnecessary suffering. As noted in section I, the rule's origins can be traced back to the 1863 Lieber Code, which prohibited intentionally inflicting 'additional wounds on an enemy already wholly disabled'. While not constituting the rule as such, the notion of gratuitous infliction of pain and suffering beyond military necessity is already present. Five years later, the 1868 St Petersburg Declaration observed that since the only 'legitimate object' states should endeavour to accomplish through warfare is 'to weaken the military forces of the enemy', this objective 'would be exceeded by the employment of arms which uselessly aggravate the sufferings of disabled men, or render their death inevitable'.[107]

In 1899, the regulations on land warfare annexed to the Hague Convention II stipulated that 'it is especially prohibited … [t]o employ arms, projectiles, or material of a nature to cause superfluous injury'.[108] Today, the rule prohibiting the use of weapons causing superfluous injury is a customary norm applicable to all parties to any armed conflict.[109] In its Nuclear Weapons Advisory Opinion, the ICJ defined unnecessary suffering as 'harm greater than that unavoidable to achieve legitimate military objectives'.[110] Its application to specific

[104] US Department of the Navy, Annotated Supplement to the Commander's Handbook on the Law of Naval Operations 10–21, Naval Warfare Publication 9, 1987 (with Revision A (5 October 1989).

[105] In December 2017, states parties to the ICC amended the Statute to confer potential jurisdiction on the Court for the war crime of using biological weapons in both IAC and NIAC (as Art 8(2)(b)(xxvii) and Art 8(2)(e)(xvi), respectively).

[106] ICRC Commentary on the 1977 Additional Protocols, para 1402.

[107] Declaration Renouncing the Use, in Time of War, of Explosive Projectiles Under 400 Grammes Weight, adopted at St Petersburg, 11 December 1868; entry into force the same day.

[108] Art 23(e), Regulations concerning the Laws and Customs of War on Land annexed to Convention (II) with Respect to the Laws and Customs of War on Land; adopted at The Hague, 29 July 1899; entry into force, 4 September 1900.

[109] ICRC Study of Customary IHL, Rule 70 ('Weapons of a Nature to Cause Superfluous Injury or Unnecessary Suffering') at https://goo.gl/BdhGYj.

[110] 1996 Nuclear Weapons Advisory Opinion, para 78.

weapons is, though, frequently contested. For instance, it is not settled whether to kill or seriously injure combatants by deliberately burning them out in the open (using napalm or a flamethrower), to deliberately blind them (using a laser) or to kill them slowly through the irremediable effects of radiation (using a nuclear weapon) is a violation per se of the customary rule. The ICRC has asserted that the following are unlawful under the rule:

- Explosive bullets and projectiles filled with glass.
- Bullets which easily expand or flatten in the human body.
- Poison and poisoned weapons, as well as any substance intended to aggravate a wound.
- Asphyxiating or deleterious gases.
- Bayonets with a serrated edge and lances with barbed heads.[111]

It further claims that 'hunting shotguns are the object of some controversy, depending on the nature of the ammunition and its effect on a soft target'.[112]

The rule prohibiting means and methods of warfare of a nature to cause superfluous injury or unnecessary suffering is explained in chapter 8.

[111] ICRC Commentary on the 1977 Additional Protocols, para 1419.
[112] Ibid.

2

Defining an Armed Conflict

I. Introduction

A prerequisite for an attack to amount to the conduct of hostilities is that it must take place both during and in connection with an armed conflict. Both in theory and in practice, however, the type and level of violence that amount to an armed conflict may be vigorously contested, whether between the parties engaged in violent struggle or between the prosecution and the defence in a war crimes trial. What is certain is that any use of force by any individual that occurs either outside an armed conflict altogether, or in the course of an armed conflict but without sufficient nexus to it, cannot be a war crime. Accordingly, identifying when and where an armed conflict is in progress, the aim of this chapter, is critical both for the application of the correct international legal framework during all use of force and for the subsequent purpose of accountability.

The legality of any use of force by the state that occurs outside the bounds of an armed conflict must be adjudged not according to Hague Law rules but under the international legal rules governing law enforcement. In certain respects, these rules, which are described in the following chapter, differ markedly from those governing the conduct of hostilities, especially with regard to when recourse to potentially or intentionally lethal force is lawful. Furthermore, during an armed conflict each instance of state use of force may amount to an act either of law enforcement or of hostilities: it is not the case that all use of force must fall to be regulated by Hague Law rules purely on the basis that an armed conflict is ongoing on any given state's territory.

Despite occasional suggestions to the contrary, there are only two categories of armed conflict under the law of armed conflict and international criminal law: international armed conflict (IAC) and armed conflict not of an international character (non-international armed conflict (NIAC)).[1] A valuable and widely cited[2] general definition

[1] Some commentators have referred to 'transnational' or 'internationalised' armed conflict. Neither has any influence on the two law-of-armed-conflict categories of international and non-international armed conflict. The European Union (EU) also uses the term 'internal armed conflict'. This is employed to determine whether, for the purposes of protection under EU law, substantial grounds exist for believing that a third-country national who does not qualify as a refugee would, if returned to his or her country of origin, 'face a real risk of suffering serious harm … and is unable, or, owing to such risk, unwilling to avail himself or herself of the protection of that country': Art 2, EU Directive 2004/83. According to Article 15(c) of the Directive, serious harm consists of a 'serious and individual threat to a civilian's life or person by reason of indiscriminate violence in situations of international or internal armed conflict'. In a decision in January 2014, the Court of Justice of the EU determined that an internal armed conflict exists 'if a State's armed forces confront one or more armed groups or if two or more armed groups confront each other. It is not necessary for that conflict to be categorised as "armed conflict not of an international character" under international humanitarian law; nor is it necessary to carry out, in addition to an appraisal of the level of violence present in the territory concerned, a separate assessment of the intensity of the armed

of the two categories was proffered by the Appeals Chamber of the International Criminal Tribunal for the former Yugoslavia (ICTY) in a 1995 decision in the *Tadić* case:

> [A]n armed conflict exists whenever there is a resort to armed force between States or protracted armed violence between governmental authorities and organized armed groups or between such groups within a State.[3]

This definition is not beyond reproach, though, and accordingly this chapter discusses some of its flaws and proffers an alternative that, it is asserted, better reflects extant international law.

The types and constituent elements for each of the two categories of armed conflict are considered in turn. There are five types of IAC, as described in section II. The three types of NIAC are explained in section III, but the focus is on the most important of these: the one to which both Common Article 3 and customary Hague Law rules apply. Section IV endorses the widely held view that, as a matter of international law, a number of different armed conflicts (differing in type, extent, and parties) may co-exist over the same physical territory.

II. International Armed Conflict

A. The Five Types of International Armed Conflict

Article 2 common to the four 1949 Geneva Conventions ('Common Article 2') explicitly applies to 'all cases of declared war or of any other armed conflict which may arise between two or more of the High Contracting Parties, even if the state of war is not recognized by one of them'. Thus, *ab initio* two clear scenarios exist for an IAC: a declared war or another form of armed conflict between two or more states.

Common Article 2 goes on to clarify that the Conventions 'shall also apply to all cases of partial or total occupation of the territory of a High Contracting Party,[4] even if the said

confrontations, the level of organisation of the armed forces involved or the duration of the conflict.' *Aboubacar Diakité v Commissaire général aux réfugiés et aux apatrides*, Judgment (Fourth Chamber) (Case No C-285/12), 30 January 2014, para 35, at https://goo.gl/1PnH2D. This decision has no influence on the law of armed conflict/ international criminal law definition of armed conflict.

[2] See, eg, United States (US) Department of Defense, *Law of War Manual*, June 2015, Updated December 2016 (hereinafter, USDOD December 2016 *Law of War Manual*) para 3.4.2.2, fn 74, at https://goo.gl/QMkjqs; United Kingdom (UK) Ministry of Defence, *The Manual of the Law of Armed Conflict* (Oxford, Oxford University Press, 2005) para 3.3; French Ministry of Defence, *Manuel de Droit des Conflits Armés* (Paris, Ministère de la Défense, 2012) 33, 34, at https://goo.gl/xweVYn.

[3] ICTY, *Prosecutor v Tadić (aka 'Dule')*, Decision on the Defence Motion for Interlocutory Appeal on Jurisdiction (Appeals Chamber) (Case No IT-94-1), 2 October 1995, para 70, at https://goo.gl/4gHtjy. See generally also International Committee of the Red Cross (ICRC), 'How is the term "armed conflict" defined in international humanitarian law?', ICRC Opinion Paper, March 2008, at https://goo.gl/rtm694; and S Vité, 'Typology of armed conflicts in international humanitarian law: legal concepts and actual situations', *International Review of the Red Cross*, vol 91, no 873 (March 2009) 69–94, at https://goo.gl/TFnPhF.

[4] The term 'High Contracting Parties' is a synonym for states parties under the law of treaties, meaning a state that is party to, and thus bound by, an international convention or treaty.

occupation meets with no armed resistance'. This third scenario, a foreign military occupation, is also a form of IAC.[5] A further scenario is when one state attacks another by proxy, using an armed group rather than its own, regularly constituted armed forces. Lastly, in a highly contested provision, according to the 1977 Additional Protocol I, certain 'wars' of national liberation are deemed to be IACs rather than NIACs, which they would otherwise appear to be.

B. War

A war to which Common Article 2 applies is one that has to be declared.[6] Indeed, at the Second Peace Conference in The Hague of 1907, states adopted a treaty that obliged states parties not to initiate hostilities between themselves 'without previous and explicit warning, in the form either of a declaration of war, giving reasons, or of an ultimatum with a conditional declaration of war'.[7] A total of 36 states adhered to the 1907 Hague Convention III, including Austria, China, France, Germany, Japan, Russia, the United Kingdom (UK) and the United States (US). Its negotiation and adoption were prompted by the hostilities that broke out in 1904 between Japan and Russia without prior declaration of war by either side.[8]

Although the treaty is still nominally in force, the practice of declaring war has fallen into desuetude since the Second World War,[9] and is certainly not required by contemporary international law. Such declarations do occasionally occur today, though the practice is mainly the subject of political posturing rather than a prelude to active hostilities.

[5] The Elements of Crimes established under the International Criminal Court (ICC) provide that 'the term "international armed conflict" includes military occupation': ICC, 'Elements of crimes', UN Doc PCNICC/2000/1/Add.2 (2000), fn 34. See also, eg, A Cullen, 'The threshold of non-international armed conflict', SSRN (2008) 132 at https://goo.gl/xk3NYV.

[6] Dinstein offers the following definition of war in the latest edition of his masterpiece on *jus ad bellum: War, Aggression and Self-Defence*: 'War is a hostile interaction between two or more States, either in a material or in a purely technical sense. War in the purely technical sense is a formal status produced by a declaration of war. War in the material sense is generated by actual use of armed force, which is comprehensive on the part of at least one Belligerent Party.' Y Dinstein, *War, Aggression and Self-Defence*, 6th edn (Cambridge, Cambridge University Press, 2017) 17, para 43.

[7] Art 1, 1907 Hague Convention (III) Relative to the Opening of Hostilities, adopted at The Hague, 18 October 1907; entry into force, 26 January 1910.

[8] D Schindler and J Toman, *The Laws of Armed Conflicts* (Dordrecht, Martinus Nijhoff, 1988) 57–59.

[9] In December 1941, the US and Great Britain each declared war on Japan, and Japan in turn declared war on both the US and the British Empire, while the US declared war on Germany and Italy in response to those states' own declarations of belligerency, all in the space of a week. In accordance with its Constitution, which grants to Congress the power 'to declare War' in Art I(8), the US has declared war 11 times in its history, the first instance of which was against Great Britain in 1812 and the last against Bulgaria, Hungary and Romania, all on the same day: 4 June 1942. US Senate, 'Official Declarations of War by Congress' at https://goo.gl/ZkNhk2. Since the Second World War, the US Congress has authorised the use of military force rather than issuing a declaration of war. On 14 September 2001, for instance, in response to the 9/11 attacks, Congress passed Joint Resolution 23: 'Authorization for Use of Military Force', which authorised the use of 'all necessary and appropriate force against those nations, organizations, or persons [the President] … determines planned, authorized, committed, or aided the terrorist attacks that occurred on September 11, 2001, or harbored such organizations or persons, in order to prevent any future acts of international terrorism against the United States by such nations, organizations or persons'. Available at https://goo.gl/UDoPoV.

At the end of March 2013, for example, the Democratic People's Republic of Korea (DPRK) appeared to declare war formally on the Republic of Korea, its southern neighbour on the peninsula:

> From this moment, the north–south relations will be put at the state of war and all the issues arousing between the north and the south will be dealt with according to the wartime regulations.
>
> The state of neither peace nor war has ended on the Korean Peninsula.
>
> Now that the revolutionary armed forces of the DPRK have entered into an actual military action, the inter-Korean relations have naturally entered the state of war. Accordingly, the DPRK will immediately punish any slightest provocation hurting its dignity and sovereignty with resolute and merciless physical actions without any prior notice.[10]

After the November 2015 terror attacks in Paris, French President François Hollande said, 'This is an act of war. … An act committed by a terrorist army, Daesh [Islamic State], against France, our values, who we are, a free country that speaks to the entire planet.'[11] In July 2016, the then presumptive Republican presidential nominee, Donald Trump, said it was time to declare war on Islamic State. 'I would', Mr Trump said when he was asked on Fox News, shortly after the attack in Nice, if he would seek a declaration of war on Islamic State. 'This is war. If you look at it, this is war.'[12]

In the words of Yoram Dinstein, a declaration of war is 'a unilateral and formal announcement, issued by the constitutionally competent authority of a State, setting the exact point at which war begins with a designated enemy (or enemies)'.[13] In 2005, the Eritrea-Ethiopia Claims Commission stated that 'the essence of a declaration of war is an explicit affirmation of the existence of a state of war between belligerents'.[14]

In his 1952 commentary on Common Article 2, Jean Pictet affirmed that 'One may argue almost endlessly about the legal definition of "war". A State can always pretend, when it commits a hostile act against another State, that it is not making war, but merely engaging in a police action, or acting in legitimate self-defence.'[15] In fact, while a declaration of war may have far-reaching financial, legal and political consequences (on the neutrality of other states; for the economy of the belligerents and others; for insurance cover and premiums; and, under the 1949 Geneva Conventions, for the ability to detain aliens on a state's territory, amongst other things), until any hostile act occurs, Hague Law will not be relevant to action taken by a state.[16]

[10] See, eg, M Fisher, 'Here's North Korea's official declaration of "war"', *The Washington Post* (30 March 2013) at https://goo.gl/cezeZ1.

[11] See, eg, N Vinocur, '"An act of war"', *Politico* (13 November 2015) at https://goo.gl/xvUz69.

[12] M Thompson, 'How Donald Trump's Call to Declare War on ISIS Would Be Different', *Time* (15 July 2016) at https://goo.gl/qlLkTj.

[13] Dinstein (n 6) 32, para 84.

[14] Eritrea-Ethiopia Claims Commission, *Jus Ad Bellum, Ethiopia's Claims, Partial Award*, 2005, para 17.

[15] J Pictet (ed), *Geneva Convention for the Amelioration of the Condition of the Wounded and Sick in Armed Forces in the Field: A Commentary* (Geneva, ICRC, 1952) (hereinafter, 'Pictet Commentary on GC I'), Commentary on Art 2, 32, at https://goo.gl/YA4xU9.

[16] According to the ICRC's new commentary on 1949 Geneva Convention I, 'The Geneva Conventions become automatically applicable even when a declaration of war is not followed by armed confrontations between the declaring State and its designated opponent(s).' ICRC commentary on 1949 Geneva Convention I (2016) para 206, at https://goo.gl/48G3eS. This is a notable departure from the position held by Pictet in 1952, whereby he stated that 'The Convention becomes applicable as from the actual opening of hostilities.' Pictet Commentary on GC I (n 15) 32.

C. Other Types of International Armed Conflict

i. The Meaning of an Armed Conflict Between States

The term 'armed conflict' is more neutral, and less emotionally and politically charged, than the term 'war'.[17] It is also, potentially, far broader in scope, though in contrast to a declaration of war it may need to entail forcible action. According to Pictet's 1960 commentary on the 1949 Geneva Convention I:

> Any difference arising between two States and leading to the intervention of armed forces … is an armed conflict within the meaning of Article 2, even if one of the Parties denies the existence of a state of war. It makes no difference how long the conflict lasts, or how much slaughter takes place.[18]

In his later commentaries of 1958 and 1960 on the corresponding provisions in the 1949 Geneva Conventions II, III and IV, Pictet asserted that 'The occurrence of de facto hostilities is sufficient.'[19]

Similarly, in the view of the ICTY, as cited in section I, an international armed conflict exists 'whenever there is a resort to armed force between states'. The French and German Ministries of Defence adopt a similar position in their respective manuals on the law of armed conflict.[20] The US has interpreted the term 'armed conflict' in Common Article 2 to include 'any situation in which there is hostile action between the armed forces of two parties, regardless of the duration, intensity or scope of the fighting'.[21] These broad definitions are consonant with the amended 1998 Rome Statute of the International Criminal Court (ICC Statute), whereunder an act of aggression means the use of armed force by one state against the sovereignty, territorial integrity or political independence of another state, or in any other manner inconsistent with the 1945 Charter of the United Nations ('UN Charter').[22] Dinstein argues that the correct interpretation of the provision, which originates in Article 2(4) of the UN Charter, is that any inter-state use of force by (at least) UN member states 'for whatever reason' is unlawful, 'unless explicitly allowed by the Charter'.[23]

[17] Although neither the 1945 Charter of the United Nations (UN Charter) and the 1948 Universal Declaration of Human Rights (UDHR) refer to armed conflict, the UN Charter uses the term 'war' in a number of instances while the UDHR talks of 'rebellion'.

[18] Pictet Commentary on GC I (n 15) 32.

[19] See, respectively, J Pictet (ed), *Geneva Convention for the Amelioration of the Condition of the Wounded, Sick and Shipwrecked Members of Armed Forces at Sea: A Commentary* (Geneva, ICRC, 1960) 28 (hereinafter 'Pictet Commentary on GC II (1960)'); J Pictet (ed), *Geneva Convention Relative to the Protection of Prisoners of War: A Commentary* (Geneva, ICRC, 1960) 23 (hereinafter 'Pictet Commentary on GC III (1960)'); and J Pictet (ed), *Geneva Convention Relative to the Protection of Civilian Persons in Time of War: A Commentary* (Geneva, ICRC, 1958) 20 (hereinafter 'Pictet Commentary on GC IV (1958)').

[20] French Ministry of Defence (n 2) 33; German Ministry of Defence, *Law of Armed Conflict Manual*, Joint Service Regulation (ZDv) 15/2 (Berlin, 2013), paras 202, 203.

[21] US Department of State, Telegram 348126 to American Embassy at Damascus, 8 December 1983, in *Cumulative Digest of United States Practice in International Law*, vol III (1981–88) 3456, 3457, cited by USDOD December 2016 *Law of War Manual* (n 2), para 3.4.2.

[22] Art 8*bis*(2), ICC Statute. Surprisingly, some international lawyers dismiss any link with *jus ad bellum* qualification and would countenance the bombardment by one state of a non-state armed group on the territory of a foreign state without acknowledging that this amounts to an IAC between the two states in addition to, potentially, a NIAC between the extraterritorial state and the non-state armed group. This would mean that if the US were to attack a separatist armed group in Russia, for instance in the South Caucasus, no IAC would exist between the US and Russia, at least until a Russian military response. This is not credible.

[23] Dinstein (n 6) 94, para 258.

Moreover, while practice seems to indicate a need for some measure of armed violence, this is not the case in at least two scenarios. The first of these is a naval blockade. Thus, an act of aggression under the ICC Statute explicitly includes the blockade of the ports or coasts of a state by the armed forces of another state. This is an instance of use of force, but not necessarily an act of armed violence, for the blockade may be enacted and enforced without a gun being fired.[24]

A second possible instance of armed conflict without recourse to force of arms (which, traditionally understood, are industrially-produced weapons, especially when destined for the military)[25] is a cyber-attack. As Andrew Clapham observes, '[t]here seems to be little doubt that a cyber-attack by a state on another state, resulting in deaths or damage to property, would trigger the laws of IAC and the Geneva Conventions'.[26] In a similar vein, the International Committee of the Red Cross (ICRC), in its 2016 commentary on Common Article 2, affirms that it is 'generally accepted that cyber operations having similar effects to classic kinetic operations would amount to an international armed conflict'.[27] It tempers this conclusion somewhat by noting that

> cyber operations do not always and necessarily have such effects. Without physically destroying or damaging military or civilian infrastructure, cyber-attacks might also disrupt their operation. Could these still be considered as a resort to armed force under Article 2(1)? Would the low intensity approach still be appropriate for hostile actions carried out only through cyber operations? Would the threshold of harm tolerated by States affected by cyber operations be different depending on the military or civilian nature of the 'targeted' object? For the time being, these questions are left open and the law is uncertain on the subject. Therefore, it remains to be seen if and under what conditions States will treat such cyber operations as armed force amounting to armed conflict under humanitarian law in future operations.[28]

One of the best known cyber-attacks of recent years involved the Stuxnet worm, a form of malware apparently concocted by the US and Israel to damage centrifuges in Iranian uranium enrichment facilities, particularly at Natanz, in an operation codenamed 'Olympic Games'.[29] According to one media article, the Iranian centrifuges in question normally spin

[24] Art 8*bis*(2)(c), ICC Statute. In this, it can perhaps be considered analogous to a foreign military occupation, since Common Article 2 explicitly covers an occupation that meets with no armed resistance.

[25] Already in 1794, John Trusler distinguished arms and weapons in the following terms: 'By arms, we understand those instruments of offence generally made use of in war; such as firearms, swords, etc. By weapons, we more particularly mean instruments of other kinds (exclusive of fire-arms), made use of as offensive on special occasions.' Cyber-attacks are perhaps better characterised as weapons.

[26] A Clapham, 'The Concept of International Armed Conflict' in A Clapham, P Gaeta and M Sassòli (eds), *The 1949 Geneva Conventions: A Commentary* (Oxford, Oxford University Press, 2015) 3, 22.

[27] ICRC commentary on 1949 Geneva Convention I (n 16) para 255.

[28] Ibid, para 256, citing C Droege, 'Get off my cloud: cyber warfare, international humanitarian law, and the protection of civilians', *International Review of the Red Cross*, vol 94, no 886 (June 2012) 545–49.

[29] R Langner, 'Cracking Stuxnet, a 21st-century cyber weapon', *TED* (March 2011) at https://goo.gl/KhPrBM; and see DP Fidler, 'Cyberattacks and international human rights law' in S Casey-Maslen (ed), *Weapons under International Human Rights Law* (Cambridge, Cambridge University Press, 2014) 299, 303. Stuxnet 0.5, the oldest known version of the computer worm, was reportedly in development by November 2005, almost two years earlier than previously known, according to researchers from cyber-security firm Symantec. Stuxnet 0.5 is said to have disrupted Iran's nuclear program by surreptitiously closing valves in Natanz, whereas the later, better-known versions of the worm caused centrifuges to spin erratically. D Goodin, 'Revealed: Stuxnet "beta's" devious alternate attack on Iran nuke program' *Ars Technica* (26 February 2013) at https://goo.gl/1TA1w.

at 1,064Hz, but the resultant virus, which first infected the facility in June 2009, caused the frequency of its centrifuges to increase to 1,410Hz for 15 minutes and then return to their normal frequency. The virus took over control again 27 days later, this time slowing down the rotors in the centrifuge to a frequency of several hundred hertz for 50 minutes. The resulting excessive centrifugal force caused the aluminium tubes to expand, increasing the risk of parts coming into contact with one another and thereby destroying the centrifuges. Six cascades, each containing 164 centrifuges, were reportedly destroyed in this manner.[30] Thus, the Institute for Science and International Security, a Washington, DC-based think tank, claimed in December 2010 that Iran's centrifuges at Natanz suffered a series of failures in mid- to late 2009, which culminated in technicians taking 984 machines out of action. It identified Stuxnet as the likely cause of the failures.[31]

The *Tallinn Manual* asserts that Stuxnet amounted to a use of force.[32] If so, whether or not this use of force was lawful under *jus ad bellum*, this would seem to equate to an armed conflict (despite some doubt as to whether cyber-attacks or their underlying means of transmission amount to 'arms'[33]).[34] The fact that neither Iran nor the US characterised the incident as an armed conflict is relevant to that determination, but is not conclusive.

ii. The Level of Violence Necessary to Trigger an Armed Conflict Between States

Notwithstanding areas of uncertainty around certain acts in cyberspace, the jurisprudence and state practice previously cited posits that there is no floor of intensity for an armed conflict to exist between states once violence erupts. As we have seen, according to the ICTY, once one state uses violence on the territory of another (or, in the view of the US, at least when one armed force attacks another at any place), this is sufficient to trigger an armed conflict. Such an approach chimes with the rules of *jus ad bellum*, since an act of aggression includes both use of any weapons by one state against the territory of another and an attack by the armed forces of one state on the land, sea or air forces, or marine and air fleets of another state.[35]

[30] H Stark, 'Mossad's Miracle Weapon: Stuxnet Virus Opens New Era of Cyber War', *Der Spiegel* (8 August 2011) at https://goo.gl/bkwJxa.

[31] D Albright, P Brannan and C Walrond, 'Did Stuxnet Take Out 1,000 Centrifuges at the Natanz Enrichment Plant? Preliminary Assessment', *Institute for Science and International Security* (22 December 2010 at https://goo.gl/1AkQG.

[32] M Schmitt (ed), *Tallinn Manual on the International Law Applicable to Cyber Warfare* (Cambridge, Cambridge University Press, 2013) Commentary on Rule 10, para 9; see also MN Schmitt, 'The Use of Cyber Force and International Law' in M Weller (ed), *The Oxford Handbook of the Use of Force in International Law* (Oxford, Oxford University Press, 2015) 1127.

[33] See, eg, S Watts, 'Who is a Prisoner of War?' in Clapham, Gaeta and Sassòli (eds) (n 26) 889, 901.

[34] In fact, in early 2016 it was reported that the Stuxnet worm was only one element of a much larger US-prepared cyber-attack plan that would target Iran's air defences, communications systems and key parts of its power grid. The contingency plan, known internally as Nitro Zeus, was to be carried out in the event that diplomatic efforts to curb Iran's nuclear development programme failed and the US was pulled into a war between Iran and Israel. D Goodin, 'Massive US-planned cyberattack against Iran went well beyond Stuxnet', *Ars Technica* (17 February 2016) at https://goo.gl/rtQLbs, citing DE Sanger and M Mazzetti, 'US Had Cyberattack Plan if Iran Nuclear Dispute Led to Conflict', *New York Times* (16 February 2016) at https://goo.gl/JN2ZOD.

[35] See, eg, Art 8*bis*(2)(b) and (d), ICC Statute.

Many states and commentators subscribe to the so-called 'first shot' theory (also called the 'Pictet theory', after Jean Pictet's opinion in his 1960 commentary on 1949 Geneva Convention II),[36] whereby any act of armed violence by one state against or on the territory of another triggers an IAC.[37] The ICRC repeats this position in its 2016 commentary on Geneva Convention I: 'For international armed conflict, there is no requirement that the use of armed force between the Parties reach a certain level of intensity before it can be said that an armed conflict exists.'[38] This position is not universally held, though.[39] The International Law Association (ILA), for instance, has stated that 'The violence must be organized and intense – even between sovereign states – before the otherwise prevailing peacetime rules are suspended.'[40] Although, in its discussion of the use of force, the ILA appears at times to confuse IAC and NIAC (and its assertion that 'an armed attack that is not part of intense armed fighting is not part of an armed conflict'[41] is plainly wrong), at least insofar as a situation concerns use of force by one state against another, the 'first shot' theory is not without its problems.

In fact, at the bottom of the scale one could assess the detention by Iran of 15 UK Royal Navy personnel from *HMS Cornwall* in 2007: eight sailors and seven marines were held for 15 days beginning on 23 March. Even though it appears that not a single shot was fired, it was suggested in some quarters that their detention by Iranian armed forces triggered an armed conflict under Common Article 2 and thus that, according to the provisions of the 1949 Geneva Convention III,[42] they were prisoners of war.[43] Indeed, Mohammad Ali Hosseini, a spokesperson for the Iranian Ministry of Foreign Affairs, accused the UK of 'violating the sovereign boundaries', terming the action a 'blatant aggression'.[44] If it were an

[36] See, eg, 'Editorial: Delineating the Boundaries of Violence', *International Review of the Red Cross*, vol 96, no 893 (Spring 2014) 9; M Pedrazzi, 'The beginning of IAC and NIAC for the purpose of the applicability of IHL', XXXVIII Round Table on Current Issues of International Humanitarian Law: The Distinction between International and Non-International Armed Conflicts: Challenges for IHL?, San Remo, 3–5 September 2015, 2–3, at https://goo.gl/z69z59.

[37] In 2015, the ICRC seemed to soften its position on the issue slightly in its Challenges of Contemporary Armed Conflicts report to the 32nd International Conference of the Red Cross and Red Crescent. It wrote that 'The threshold for determining the existence of an IAC is therefore fairly low, and factors such as duration and intensity are generally not considered to enter the equation. For instance, the mere capture of a soldier or minor skirmishes between the armed forces of two or more States may spark off an international armed conflict and lead to the applicability of IHL, insofar as such acts may be taken as evidence of genuine belligerent intent': ICRC, *International humanitarian law and the challenges of contemporary armed conflicts*, Report for the 32nd International Conference of the Red Cross and Red Crescent, Geneva, October 2015 (hereinafter, 2015 ICRC Challenges Report) 8, at https://goo.gl/Bz8gnw.

[38] ICRC commentary on 1949 Geneva Convention I (n 16) para 236.

[39] See, eg, C Greenwood, 'Scope of Application of Humanitarian Law' in D Fleck (ed), *The Handbook of International Humanitarian Law*, 2nd edn (Oxford, Oxford University Press, 2008) 48; and A Paulus and M Vashakmadze, 'Asymmetrical War and the Notion of Armed Conflict – A Tentative Conceptualization', *International Review of the Red Cross*, vol 91, no 873 (March 2009) 101. Paulus and Vashakmadze suggest that 'mere incidents, in particular an isolated confrontation of little impact between members of different armed forces' may not amount to an IAC, whereas 'relatively low' violence, 'even short-lived cross-border armed clashes' may.

[40] ILA, 'Final Report on the Meaning of Armed Conflict in International Law', The Hague Conference (2010): Use of Force, 3, at https://goo.gl/JJxynT.

[41] Ibid, 8.

[42] Convention (III) relative to the Treatment of Prisoners of War; adopted at Geneva, 12 August 1949; entry into force, 21 October 1950.

[43] See, eg, J Grignon, 'The beginning of application of international humanitarian law: A discussion of a few challenges', *International Review of the Red Cross*, vol 96, no 893 (Spring 2014) 147–48. See also the discussion in Clapham (n 26) 14–16.

[44] Associated Press, 'Iran claims UK troops admit to illegal entry. Tehran blasts "blatant aggression"; Britain seeks return of 15 crew members', MSNBC (24 March 2007) at https://goo.gl/94n9t2.

armed conflict – an assertion that is unpersuasive – one of the key challenges would be to identify the cessation of active hostilities that would trigger the obligation to repatriate the prisoners under Geneva Convention III.[45] There were no 'hostilities' to begin with, so when would they cease? Immediately? An 'unjustifiable delay in the repatriation of prisoners of war or civilians' constitutes a grave breach of the 1977 Additional Protocol I,[46] and therefore a war crime entailing compulsory universal jurisdiction.[47]

Herein lies one of the problems with the 'first shot' theory. What if the first shot is the only shot? Or if one shot is followed only weeks or months later by another? When do active hostilities cease and when is the conflict over?[48] From time to time, one state's armed forces will shoot down an aircraft belonging to another's, for instance when it is alleged to have intruded into the former state's airspace. A notorious instance occurred on 24 November 2015, when Turkish Air Force F-16 Fighting Falcon combat aircraft shot down a Russian Su-24 all-weather attack aircraft over Turkey's border with Syria. This was said to be the first downing of a Russian Air Force combat aircraft by a North Atlantic Treaty Organization (NATO) member state since the Korean War in the 1950s.[49]

Whether or not the Russian aircraft was within Turkish territory (as Turkey claimed) or always within Syrian territory (as Russia claimed)[50] is relevant for *jus ad bellum* considerations, but not as to whether this was a short-lived IAC between Russia and Turkey.[51] In an interview with a French TV station two days after the incident, Turkish President Recep Tayyip Erdogan said, 'If we had known if it was a Russian plane maybe we would have warned it differently.'[52]

[45] Art 118, 1949 Geneva Convention III. The duty is also one of a customary nature. ICRC, Study of Customary IHL, Rule 128(a) ('Release and Return of Persons Deprived of Their Liberty') at https://goo.gl/rMik1j.

[46] Art 85(4)(b), 1977 Additional Protocol I. In this instance, however, the UK but not Iran was party to the Protocol.

[47] According to Art 85(5), 1977 Additional Protocol I, 'Without prejudice to the application of the Conventions and of this Protocol, grave breaches of these instruments shall be regarded as war crimes.' Russia is a state party to the 1977 Additional Protocol I, as is Syria, but Turkey is not. According to ICRC, however, under customary law, 'Making persons parachuting from an aircraft in distress the object of attack during their descent is prohibited.' ICRC Study of Customary IHL, Rule 48 ('Attacks against Persons Parachuting from an Aircraft in Distress') at https://goo.gl/zLCPux. The ICRC note that this is a longstanding rule, first enunciated by putative treaty in the abortive Hague Rules of Air Warfare (Art XX), drafted by a commission of lawyers in 1922–23.

[48] As the ICRC observes, 'Assessing the end of an armed conflict in the sense of [Common] Article 2(1) may be a very difficult enterprise. This is mainly due to the silence of the Geneva Conventions on this question but also to State practice, which indicates that States resort less and less to the conclusion of peace treaties.' ICRC commentary on 1949 Geneva Convention I (n 16) para 274. In its 'Challenges' report, issued the same year, the ICRC stated that the starting point was the 'general close of military operations'. In irregular cross-border incidents, however, this is not especially helpful, as the organisation itself acknowledges: 'The general close of military operations, however, is not always easily determined, especially in the absence of ongoing hostilities.' See 2015 ICRC Challenges Report (n 37) 8, 9.

[49] See, eg, T Gibbons-Neff, 'The last time a Russian jet was shot down by a NATO jet was in 1952', *The Washington Post* (24 November 2015) at https://goo.gl/ujvGQD.

[50] Two physicists poured scorn on the accounts of both governments, suggesting neither could be entirely accurate. C Mortimer, 'Turkey shoots down Russian plane: Physicists say both official accounts are scientifically impossible', *The Independent* (28 November 2015) at https://goo.gl/1F2MZ5.

[51] The plane crashed in the mountainous Jabal Turkmen area of the Syrian province of Latakia, which was being contested by Syrian government and rebel forces. Russia and Turkey disputed the exact location of the crash site, though both agreed that it was in Syrian territory. 'Turkey's downing of Russian warplane – what we know', *BBC* (1 December 2015) at https://goo.gl/zyvLQP.

[52] Agence France-Presse (AFP), 'Turkey would have acted differently if it had known jet was Russian: Erdogan' (26 November 2015) at https://goo.gl/KUFC4x.

The pilot and navigator ejected from the stricken aircraft as it was coming down. Both were fired upon during their descent in violation of Hague Law and the pilot was killed, instead of being given the opportunity to surrender on hitting the ground, as is required by Hague Law. According to the codification of the customary rule in 1977 Additional Protocol I, 'No person parachuting from an aircraft in distress shall be made the object of attack during his descent.'[53] However, to further complicate the scenario, the pilot was apparently killed by Turkmen rebel forces in Syria, not by Turkish forces, as he fell onto Syrian territory. The navigator was rescued, reportedly by Syrian government forces.[54]

One analysis of what transpired legally is that an IAC erupted at the instant Turkish forces fired on the Russian aircraft, and continued until they ceased firing, or even until the stricken aircraft hit the ground in neighbouring Syria. In between, the killing of the pilot amounted to a possible war crime, possibly committed by Syrian rebel forces. Since the pilot was *hors de combat* the instant he ejected in distress from his aircraft, this war crime would be a serious violation of Common Article 3 occurring within the NIAC between Syria (assisted by Russia) and the rebel group. It also violated a customary law rule, which in the view of the ICRC, also applies in NIAC. On 27 June 2016, however, President Erdogan wrote to Vladimir Putin expressing regret for what happened, and informing the Russian President that 'a judicial investigation is underway against the Turkish citizen said to be involved in the Russian pilot's death'.[55] It was not specified whether this concerned the air force pilot who shot down the jet, or potentially the individual who fired on the parachuting pilot in distress.

The better view is that this entire incident was a law enforcement action (albeit an ill-advised one). While tension had existed between Russia and Turkey for several weeks, given that Russia had been targeting Turkish-supported rebel groups in the Syrian conflict with air strikes, this was not the opening salvo in a war between two nations, only in a war of words between diplomats and between heads of state. If this analysis were correct, this would mean that the decision to fire on an aircraft that was in Turkish territory for no more than a matter of seconds – if indeed it ever were – would have to comply with the rules on the use of force under the law of law enforcement. These rules are discussed in more detail in chapter 3, but in brief, to be lawful it would have to be shown, at a minimum, that the incursive Russian aircraft presented either an imminent threat of death or serious injury, or a grave and temporally proximate threat to life in Turkey. There is no evidence that the Turkish action would pass this test.[56]

A further scenario to be considered in delineating the minimum threshold for an IAC is when regular or irregular border hostilities are occurring between the armed forces of two nations. In the *Nicaragua* case, the International Court of Justice (ICJ) discussed the point at which one state's support for rebel forces in another state would give rise to a situation where the latter state would be entitled to exercise its right of self-defence against the supportive foreign power. It referred to an operation that would, 'because of its scale and effects', have been 'classified as an armed attack rather than as a mere frontier incident

[53] Art 42(1), 1977 Additional Protocol I.

[54] See, eg, 'Turkey's downing of Russian warplane – what we know' (n 51).

[55] 'Vladimir Putin received a letter from President of Turkey Recep Tayyip Erdogan', Kremlin website (27 June 2016) at https://goo.gl/MmGPwi.

[56] Given the action taken, which was to fire an air-to-air missile at another aircraft, conceivably the standard might even be stricter: the decision to fire would only be lawful if it were strictly unavoidable to protect life.

had it been carried out by regular armed forces'.[57] This can, of course, be understood as implying that not every violation of Article 2(4) of the UN Charter gives rise to the right of self-defence. The reference to a 'mere frontier incident' could also, though, be read as suggesting that incidents involving use of force might not reach the threshold to trigger the existence of an IAC. The ILA cites a number of such incidents, including in 1981 and 1982, when the Swedish Navy used depth charges against Soviet submarines that were in Swedish waters.[58] These actions, the ILA notes, were classified by scholars as 'incidents' not an armed conflict.[59] Also in 1981, US combat aircraft engaged in a fire-fight with Libyan aircraft above the Gulf of Sidra, shooting them down.[60]

Another manifest example to consider in this regard is the continuing stand-off between India and Pakistan over the bitterly disputed territory of Kashmir. India and Pakistan first fought an IAC in October 1947, after Pakistan supported a Muslim insurgency in Kashmir.[61] Under UN supervision, the war ended on 1 January 1949, with the establishment of a ceasefire line that left one-third of the territory (comprising what Pakistan calls Azad Jammu and Kashmir as well as the Northern Areas) administered by Pakistan and the other two-thirds (Jammu, Ladakh and the Kashmir Valley) administered by India.[62] The status of the territory has, though, remained in dispute ever since.

In 1965, the two states again resorted to armed conflict after Pakistan launched a covert offensive across the ceasefire line into Indian-administered Jammu and Kashmir. India retaliated by crossing the international border at Lahore.[63] In 2001, tension rose along the ceasefire line, which had been formally renamed the Line of Control in 1972. A year later, the two states seemed to be on the verge of full-scale hostilities, potentially involving use of nuclear weapons. In November 2003, however, following an improvement in relations, India and Pakistan agreed to a formal ceasefire.

Ceasefire violations, including firing of mortars and small-arms fire across the Line of Control, continued every year for the next decade. In 2013, those violations increased significantly over previous years to potentially as many as 195,[64] causing 145 casualties. This, according to *The War Report* (edited at the time by the present author), went considerably beyond 'mere frontier incidents' and amounted to an IAC.[65] On 25 December, an agreement to reinstate the ceasefire agreed in 2003, which effectively ended the IAC,

[57] ICJ, *Case Concerning Military and Paramilitary Activities In and Against Nicaragua (Nicaragua v US)*, Judgment (Merits), 27 June 1986, para 195.

[58] ILA (n 40) 18.

[59] The ILA cites R Sadurska, 'Foreign Submarines in Swedish Waters: The Erosion of an International Norm' in WM Reisman and AR Willard (eds), *International Incidents: The Law that Counts in World Politics* (Princeton, NJ, Princeton University Press, 1988) 40, 41–44.

[60] SR Ratner, 'The Gulf of Sidra Incident of 1981: The Lawfulness of Peacetime Aerial Engagements' in Reisman and Willard (eds) (n 59) 181; AM Weisburd, *Use of Force: The Practice of States Since World War II* (University Park, PA, Pennsylvania State University Press, 1997) 289–90.

[61] 'Kashmir profile', *BBC* (31 January 2014) at https://goo.gl/ucZtvJ. Unless otherwise stated, the details of this case are taken from S Casey-Maslen (ed), *The War Report: Armed Conflict in 2013* (Oxford, Oxford University Press, 2014) 40–42.

[62] 'The Future of Kashmir', *BBC*, undated but accessed on 15 May 2018 at https://goo.gl/6Hg42U.

[63] '1965: Indian Army invades W Pakistan', *BBC* at https://goo.gl/a38daH.

[64] This amounted to more than all the ceasefire violations in the previous three years combined (93 occurred in 2012, 51 in 2011, and 44 in 2010).

[65] Casey-Maslen (ed) (n 61) 41.

was reached at the first meeting for 14 years of the Indian and Pakistani Director-Generals of Military Operations.[66]

The situation did not stay calm for long. Tensions along the Line of Control mounted, especially from the middle of 2014, and by October, the Indian Minister of Defence, Arun Jaitley, urged Pakistan to stop 'unprovoked' firing, warning that it would be made to pay an 'unaffordable' price if it persisted with 'adventurism'. In response, the Pakistan Minister of Defence, Khawaja Asif, stated that Pakistan would 'respond befittingly to Indian aggression'.[67] The head of the Pakistani forces patrolling the frontier, Major-General Khan Javed Khan, told Reuters news agency that India had fired 20,000 shells in the year to date, compared with 200 in 2012.[68] This latest IAC was ended by a high-level agreement between the two states in September 2015, in which they once again undertook to stop violating the ceasefire.[69]

Potentially more difficult to assess is the situation between Armenia and Azerbaijan. Longstanding enmity between ethnic Armenians and Azeris over the disputed region of Nagorno-Karabakh erupted into armed conflict in February 1992, which saw bitter fighting between the armed forces of Armenia and of Azerbaijan. The conflict resulted in the occupation of more than one-seventh of the territory of Azerbaijan, caused more than 20,000 casualties and provoked massive refugee flows from both sides. Ethnic Armenians were expelled from Azerbaijan and ethnic Azeris from Armenia.[70]

A ceasefire between the parties to the conflict was signed on 12 May 1994. Since February 1992, attempts to settle the conflict have been made under the framework of the Minsk Process led by the Presidents of the Organization for Security and Co-operation in Europe (OSCE) Minsk Group's co-chair states, namely France, Russia and the US. Despite the 20-year-long ceasefire, which is monitored by the OSCE, and continued negotiations for a peaceful settlement of the conflict, the Nagorno-Karabakh situation remains unresolved, with regular violations of the ceasefire involving armed incidents along the Line of Contact between Armenia and Azerbaijan.[71] (The Azerbaijan–Armenia border stretches for almost 1,000 km.) Ceasefire violations take place within an existing IAC by virtue of the military occupation by Armenian forces of Azerbaijan. Should that fact make the threshold of violence to trigger an active IAC lower than would otherwise be the case? There is no obvious reason to believe that it should, nor sufficient evidence to believe that it does.

In contrast, on 2–5 April 2016, heavy and sustained fighting erupted along the Nagorno-Karabakh frontline following the seizure of settlements and strategic heights along the front by Azerbaijani forces.[72] The fighting involved tanks, helicopters and artillery.[73]

[66] 'India, Pak agree to maintain LoC truce', *Deccan Herald* (25 December 2013) at https://goo.gl/MPtdrC.

[67] 'Kashmir: India and Pakistan warn each other over attacks', *BBC* (9 October 2014) at https://goo.gl/OVf4qb.

[68] Ibid.

[69] K Yousaf, 'Pakistan, India agree to stop ceasefire violations at working boundary', *Express Tribune* (Pakistan) (12 September 2015) at https://goo.gl/ZeKYqY.

[70] Unless otherwise stated, the details of this case are taken from Casey-Maslen (ed) (n 61) 45–46; and see 'Nagorno-Karabakh profile', *BBC* (6 April 2016) at https://goo.gl/evfyy3.

[71] In 2013, for instance, sporadic exchange of fire along the Line of Control continued, with fighting in August spreading to the highly sensitive Nakhichevan exclave. According to the OSCE, a total of 14 military personnel were killed and another 32 shot and injured during the year. In addition, five civilians were injured. OSCE, *Annual Report 2013* (2014) 21.

[72] 'Nagorno-Karabakh's war. A frozen conflict explodes', *The Economist* (9 April 2016) at https://goo.gl/7eJyTY.

[73] M Grigoryan and D Safarova, 'Azerbaijan-Armenia conflict: patriotism prevails on both sides', *Guardian* (7 April 2016) at https://goo.gl/dTQxXN.

According to one account, on the third day of fighting, dozens of Armenian and Azerbaijani tanks 'squared off against one another in open battle. By the fourth day, with at least one hundred and seventy two people killed and negligent territorial gains or losses, a temporary ceasefire was signed.'[74] The sustained and bitter fighting, the high number of casualties in such a short time, the range of arms employed and the agreement on a new ceasefire, all indicate that this amounted to an active, though short-lived, IAC.

In sum, not every firing of a gun by a member of an armed force against or on the territory of another state or its armed forces or citizens amounts to an IAC. Thus, as Solis affirms, a 'minor' armed incident between two states is not sufficient to constitute an armed conflict in the sense of Article 2 of the 1949 Geneva Conventions.[75] The determination is to be made on the basis of the facts and the evidence, which includes taking into account the views of the states involved. But, as discussed in section II.C.iv, even though 'in practice' the classification of a situation 'is often a subjective matter for the participants rather than an analysis of facts and law',[76] this is not the basis under international law on which a determination is to be made as to whether an armed conflict exists or not. Such subjectivity, which is often politically motivated, does not reflect a general principle of law.

In the *Tadić* judgment at trial, notwithstanding the Appeals Chamber's holding in its decision on jurisdiction, the Trial Chamber found that an active IAC existed on the territory of Bosnia and Herzegovina in 1991–92, and noted:

> It suffices for the moment to say that the level of intensity of the conflict, including the involvement of the JNA or the VJ in the conflict, was sufficient to meet the requirements for the existence of an international armed conflict for the purposes of the Statute.
>
> For evidence of this it is enough to refer generally to the evidence presented as to the bombardment of Sarajevo, the seat of government of the Republic of Bosnia and Herzegovina, in April 1992 by Serb forces, their attack on towns along Bosnia and Herzegovina's border with Serbia on the Drina River and their invasion of south-eastern Herzegovina from Serbia and Montenegro. That the hostilities involved in this armed conflict extended into opština Prijedor is also clear and is evidenced by the military occupation and armed seizure of power in the town of Prijedor itself on 30 April 1992 by JNA forces, aided by Bosnian Serb members of the police and administration and, following an unsuccessful revolt, their subsequent expulsion by force of arms of the majority of the non-Serb inhabitants from, and the bombardment and substantial destruction of, Stari Grad, the old, predominantly Muslim, section of Prijedor. These attacks were part of an armed conflict to which international humanitarian law applied up until the general cessation of hostilities.[77]

iii. Consent and the Need for Casus Belli*?*

It is uncontested that the prior consent of the territorial state to a foreign state's use of force on its territory precludes the possibility of an armed conflict between those two states, as

[74] P Liakhov, 'Behind the Four-Day War', *Jacobin* (13 April 2016) at https://goo.gl/MV5KLu.

[75] GD Solis, *The Law of Armed Conflict: International Humanitarian Law in War*, 2nd edn (New York, Cambridge University Press, 2016) 162; see also Y Dinstein, *War, Aggression and Self-Defence*, 5th edn (Cambridge, Cambridge University Press, 2012) 11.

[76] E Wilmshurst, 'Conclusions' in E Wilmshurst (ed), *International Law and the Classification of Conflicts* (Oxford, Oxford University Press, 2012) 499.

[77] ICTY, *Prosecutor v Tadić*, Judgment (Trial Chamber) (Case No IT-94-1-T), 7 May 1997, paras 569, 570.

long as the terms of the consent are respected by the intervening power. Thus, according to the Draft Articles on the Responsibility of States for Internationally Wrongful Acts presented by the International Law Commission in 2001, 'Valid consent by a State to the commission of a given act by another State precludes the wrongfulness of that act in relation to the former State to the extent that the act remains within the limits of that consent.'[78] But the requisite nature of the consent, and the individual or entity that is empowered or entitled under international law to give valid consent, are less settled.

a. The Nature of Consent

In the *Nicaragua* case, the ICJ noted, in a dictum in a single sentence, that foreign intervention[79] was 'already allowable at the request of the government of a State'.[80] A request is ordinarily defined as the 'act of asking [politely or] formally for something'; thus, consent must be expressly sought. Thus, Alexander Orakhelashvili affirms that 'Intervention by consent is lawful, provided that it rests on a *clearly expressed request*, authored by the government of the territorial state, to be interpreted strictly in terms of duration, space, and type of pertinent military activities.'[81]

The ICRC, however, considers that valid consent may also be given when it is established 'tacitly'.[82] This is not a correct assessment of the state of international law. A desire or a wish for something may be expressed tacitly, but a request to have foreign soldiers on your soil potentially killing your citizens may not: acquiescence to a state of affairs is not the same as consent. This is despite Kreß's factually accurate observation that, in the *Armed Activities in the Congo* case, which addressed the issue of consent by the territorial state, the ICJ did not expressly 'exclude the possibility that valid consent may be expressed *implicitly*'.[83]

b. Who Can Give Valid Consent?

'In general', as David Wippman states, 'any indigenous government in effective control of the state is deemed entitled to grant or withhold consent to intervention, whether or not the government at issue is democratically or popularly supported'.[84] This may not be the consensus view, but in the view of the present author, it is the correct one. Further, in assessing who has 'effective control of the state', the individual who commands and controls the

[78] Art 20, International Law Commission (ILC) Draft Articles on the Responsibility of States for Internationally Wrongful Acts, adopted on 10 August 2001, contained in annex to United Nations General Assembly Resolution 56/83 of 12 December 2001 (hereinafter, '2001 Articles on State Responsibility').

[79] As Kreß observes, although the dictum forms part of the judgment that deals with unlawful *intervention*, 'it is difficult not to extend it to the *use of force*': C Kreß, 'The ICJ and the 'Principle of Non-Use of Force' in Weller (ed) (n 32) 561, 577 (original emphasis). Indeed, if foreign intervention needs a request, *a fortiori* so would authority to a foreign state to use force.

[80] *Nicaragua v US* (n 57) para 246.

[81] A Orakhelashvili, 'Changing *Jus Cogens* through State Practice' in Weller (ed) (n 32) 167 (emphasis added).

[82] ICRC commentary on 1949 Geneva Convention I (n 16) para 263: 'Where a territorial State consents to the actions of an intervening State, thereby removing the existence of a parallel international armed conflict, the consent given must have been previously expressed or established (explicitly or tacitly).' It further asserts that the absence of protest by the territorial State 'is a strong indicator of the existence of – at least – tacit consent'. Ibid.

[83] Kreß (n 79) 577. See *Case concerning Armed Activities on the Territory of the Congo (DRC v Uganda)*, Judgment, 19 December 2005, paras 43–47.

[84] D Wippman, 'Pro-Democratic Intervention' in Weller (ed) (n 32) 797, 805.

armed forces (or the bulk of them when dissident forces exist) is a state representative capable of giving such consent to a foreign power.[85] To admit otherwise would be to allow legal fictions: '*L'Etat, c'est moi*' only works when the sovereign exercises effective control.[86]

As the ICRC acknowledges, the intervention of a third state 'may prompt contradictory statements by its authorities', a situation that 'remain[s] very complex and sensitive'.[87] This is evidenced in the case of Pakistan, as discussed in the subsection following.

c. Extraterritorial Use of Force Without Consent

As noted, some commentators argue that a state attacking a non-state armed group on the territory of a foreign state even without the consent of the territorial state does not automatically amount to an IAC.[88] One of the arguments advanced in support of the argument is that the use of force is not directed against the government of the territorial state and does not engage their armed forces, that is, there is no *casus belli*. This is not persuasive. Whether, without the express consent of the territorial state, extraterritorial use of force is lawful under *jus ad bellum* (for instance, on the basis of self-defence), there must be an IAC in play (if the low intensity criterion is met), since force is being used against both the territorial integrity and the political independence of the territorial state. In discussing these issues, Dapo Akande notes that a government is but one part of a state, and concludes, as does Dieter Fleck whom he cites, that a situation of IAC between the state using force and the territorial state 'automatically arises'.[89] This is a correct statement of the law in the present author's view.[90] Opponents of this approach[91] sometimes criticise the 'double classification' whereby a single strike might fall to be considered under both *in bello*

[85] Thus, the provisions in Art 7 of the 1969 Vienna Convention on the Law of Treaties should be distinguished, as they concern the capacity to adopt, authenticate and sign an international treaty. But *cp* GH Fox, 'Intervention by Invitation' in Weller (ed) (n 32) 816, 816ff.

[86] Indeed, the notional head of state may not only wield no effective power, he or she may 'coincidentally' be present on the territory of the state to which consent to use force is purported to be given. This could have legitimised under *jus ad bellum* the actions of Russia in the Crimean region of Ukraine and of Saudi Arabia in Yemen.

[87] ICRC commentary on 1949 Geneva Convention I (n 16) para 263.

[88] See, eg, the sources cited in D Akande, 'Classification of Armed Conflicts: Relevant Legal Concepts' in Wilmshurst (ed) (n 76) 32, 72, fnn 163 and 164.

[89] Ibid, 75, 74, citing D Fleck, 'The Law of Non-international Armed Conflict' in D Fleck (ed), *The Handbook of International Humanitarian Law*, 3rd edn (Oxford, Oxford University Press, 2013) 608.

[90] It is also the view of the ICRC, which cites both Fleck and Akande in affirming that 'Should the third State's intervention be carried out without the consent of the territorial State, it would amount to an international armed conflict between the intervening State and the territorial State.' ICRC commentary on 1949 Geneva Convention I (n 16) para 260. The ICRC further states that 'This position was implicitly confirmed by the International Court of Justice in *Armed Activities on the Territory of the Congo*, in which the Court applied the law governing international armed conflict to the military actions undertaken by Uganda in the Democratic Republic of the Congo (DRC) outside the parts of the DRC it occupied. According to the International Court of Justice, the conflict was international in nature even though Uganda claimed to have troops in the DRC primarily to fight non-State armed groups and not the DRC armed forces.' Ibid, para 261, citing ICJ, *Armed Activities on the Territory of the Congo case*, Judgment, 2005, paras 108, 146 and 208 et seq. The ICRC cites the UN Commission of Inquiry on Lebanon, *Report of the Commission of Enquiry on Lebanon pursuant to Human Rights Council resolution S-2/1*, UN Doc A/HRC/3/2, 23 November 2006, paras 50–62, recognising that an IAC took place in 2006 between Israel and Lebanon even if the hostilities only involved Hezbollah and Israeli armed forces. The difference between the DRC and Lebanon cases, however, is that in both cases part of the country was simultaneously being occupied by the foreign state. This is not the situation in Pakistan or Syria, both cases that are discussed below.

[91] See, eg, D Carron, *L'acte déclencheur d'un conflit armé international* (Zurich, Schulthess, 2016).

rules governing IAC and NIAC. In fact, however, this is little different from the use of force during an occupation. The occupation itself amounts to an IAC. Assessing the legality of any use of force will need to consider the target and whether this concerns the IAC or the NIAC (if such exists). Targeting the armed group clearly points to the latter, targeting national infrastructure indicates the former. This was the case with respect to Israel's action against Lebanon in 2006, where most Israeli attacks targeted Hezbollah, but they also targeted the Lebanese army.[92]

An obvious case to consider regarding consent to foreign power use of force is the US use of armed drones on the territory of Pakistan. According to available information, the US first used armed drones in Pakistan in 2004 in a Central Intelligence Agency (CIA) strike near Wana in South Waziristan that killed up to eight people, including a local Taliban commander (Nek Muhammad Wazir) and two children. The Pakistani army initially claimed responsibility for a 'rocket attack'.[93] According to a 2013 report in the *New York Times*, the target was

> not a top operative of al-Qaeda, but a Pakistan ally of the Taliban who led a tribal rebellion and was marked by Pakistan as an enemy of the state. In a secret deal, the CIA had agreed to kill him in exchange for access to airspace it had long sought so it could use drones to hunt down its own enemies.[94]

Thus, in April 2013 Pakistan's former president, Pervez Musharraf, admitted giving permission for the CIA to launch drone attacks inside Pakistan, directly contradicting repeated claims by the Pakistani Government that it had never authorised drone strikes.[95] The same month, a US media company, McClatchy, claimed that its review of US intelligence reports confirmed for the first time the existence of a long-term arrangement between the CIA and Pakistan's Inter-Services Intelligence Directorate (ISI), under which US drones were used against Pakistani Taliban militants at the ISI's request in exchange for helping the US to identify and hit al-Qaida targets. Reportedly, until mid-2008 the CIA had to obtain advance approval before each attack, but by 2010, an ISI veto on targets had been removed.[96]

In one strike, on 13 January 2006, and despite its secret deal with the US, the Pakistani Government publicly denounced a strike that was said to have killed up to 18 civilians. The main target at an alleged al-Qaeda and Taliban commanders' meeting was Ayman al-Zawahiri, then al-Qaeda's second in command, but he was not present when the strike was conducted. Despite initial claims that all the victims were al-Qaeda or Taliban figures, later reports by local officials suggested that most of the dead were civilians, including 14 from a single family, with up to six children killed. Pakistan's Ministry of Foreign Affairs

[92] 'The Commission found no indication that the Lebanese Armed Forces actively participated in the hostilities that ensued. For its part, IDF attacked the Lebanese Armed Forces and its [*sic*] assets (eg military airport at Qliat in northern Lebanon, all radar installations along the Lebanese coast, and the army barracks at Djamhour, 100 kilometres from the southern border with Israel).' *Report of the Commission of Inquiry on Lebanon pursuant to Human Rights Council resolution S-2/1*, UN Doc A/HRC/3/2, 23 November 2006, para 53 (footnotes omitted).

[93] M Mazzetti, 'A Secret Deal on Drones, Sealed in Blood', *New York Times* (6 April 2013) at https://goo.gl/98FFpL; and see The Bureau of Investigative Journalism, 'The Bush Years: Pakistan strikes 2004–2009' (10 August 2011) at https://goo.gl/zJUfn1.

[94] Mazzetti (n 93).

[95] J Boone in Islamabad and P Beaumont, 'Pervez Musharraf admits permitting "a few" US drone strikes in Pakistan', *Guardian* (12 April 2013) at https://goo.gl/MZzECh.

[96] Cited ibid.

summoned the US Ambassador, Ryan Crocker, to deliver an official protest.[97] Based on available information, it appears that this and similar protests were for public consumption and political expediency. Accordingly, no IAC existed between Pakistan and the US at that time.

It is possible, however, that the situation changed, at least for a limited period of time, upon or shortly after Nawaz Sharif assumed the position of Prime Minister in Pakistan in June 2013. In October of that year, during a meeting with US President Barack Obama, he 'brought up the issue of drones … emphasising the need for an end to such strikes'.[98] Responding to public disclosure by *The Washington Post* of Pakistani memoranda that indicated officials were routinely given classified briefings on drone strikes by the US, the Pakistani Ministry of Foreign Affairs stated that 'Whatever understandings there may or may not have been in the past, the present government has been very clear regarding its policy on the issue. … We regard such strikes as violation of our sovereignty as well as international law.'

From 25 December 2013 to 11 June 2014, the longest pause in the history of US drone strikes in Pakistan occurred. According to Zora Ahmed, the pause seems to have been in response to a request by the Pakistan Government to suspend strikes during its talks with the Pakistani Taliban (TTP), which had been, in part, frustrated by continued US bombing.[99] This might suggest that when Pakistani consent for drone strikes is genuinely withdrawn, the US stops.

When, on 12 June 2014, the US resumed the use of armed drones against targets in Pakistan, the Ministry of Foreign Affairs condemned the first and subsequent strikes.[100] Given past realities, however, healthy scepticism is needed: consent to foreign state use of force on a state's territory must be express, but it does not have to be public. According to the ICRC,

> if the territorial State has explicitly protested against the intervention and this protest has been made by authorities that are entitled to give or withdraw the consent, it should be presumed that the consent did not exist in the first place or has been withdrawn, triggering the application of humanitarian law to the relationship between the territorial State and the intervening State.[101]

This does not address the situation where one arm of the state has ostensibly given consent and another has not, or has sought to deny consent. Under Article 243 of the Constitution of Pakistan, the President is appointed civilian Commander-in-Chief of the armed forces. In March 2015, Pakistan President Manmoor Hussain told a Russian media agency that 'Pakistan has always maintained that drone strikes are a violation of its sovereignty, territorial integrity and international law.'[102] Clearly, though, this does not tell the whole truth and

[97] JS Landay, 'US secret: CIA collaborated with Pakistan spy agency in drone war', *McClatchy DC* (9 April 2013) at https://goo.gl/ht19Wt.

[98] 'Secret memos "show Pakistan endorsed US drone strikes"', *BBC* (24 October 2013) at https://goo.gl/9r6PgU.

[99] Z Ahmed, 'Strengthening Standards for Consent: The Case of US Drone Strikes in Pakistan' (2015) 23(2) *Michigan State International Law Review* 459, 504, citing K DeYoung and G Miller, 'US Curtails Drone Strikes in Pakistan as Officials There Seek Peace Talks with Taliban', *Washington Post* (4 February 2014) at https://goo.gl/TUs6iM.

[100] Ahmed (n 99) 504.

[101] ICRC commentary on 1949 Geneva Convention I (n 16) para 263.

[102] 'US Drone Strikes in Pakistan Breed Terrorism – President to Sputnik', *Sputnik* (16 March 2015) at https://goo.gl/zp9Ujt.

nothing but the truth, given earlier presidential agreements on drones. In June 2016, Chief of Army Staff General Raheel Sharif was reported as having stated that US drone strikes in Pakistani territory compromised the country's sovereignty.[103]

If an agency is said to have agreed that drone strikes (or any other form of force) can occur on the state's territory, and the executive does not agree with that decision, it is always open to the executive to remove the head of that agency from power and install someone who is more compliant. If the executive is unwilling or unable to do so, this would tend to suggest that consent has indeed been given, albeit with the benefits of plausible deniability.

Another possibility, as Akande suggests, is that despite the extraterritorial use of force by a state against a non-state armed group, 'the level of violence does not cross the threshold of an armed conflict'.[104] If one takes the position, as the present author does, that there is a minimum level of violence for an IAC, perhaps a targeted drone strike falls below this threshold? This possibility must be rejected. There is a material difference between members of one state's armed force taking occasional pot-shots at members of another's across a disputed boundary, and the deliberate killing, in planned attacks, of nationals belonging to, or living in, another state.

An example of this occurred in Syria on 21 August 2015. British-born Islamic State fighter Reyaad Khan was killed in a single strike by a UK Royal Air Force (RAF)-piloted drone in the Islamic State stronghold of Raqqah in Syria, in an action justified on the grounds of national self-defence.[105] This was the first British airstrike in Syria, and the first time the UK had launched a drone strike outside a situation of armed conflict in which it had been a party. The UK Prime Minister at the time, David Cameron, told Parliament on 7 September 2015:

> The strike was conducted according to specific military rules of engagement, which always comply with international law and the principles of proportionality and military necessity. The military assessed the target location and chose the optimum time to minimise the risk of civilian casualties. This was a very sensitive operation to prevent a very real threat to our country ...[106]

Whatever the merits of the action under *ad bellum* rules, and whether or not the action also amounted to an act in the conduct of hostilities in a NIAC with Islamic State (the better view is that it was a an act of law enforcement), the fact that the action occurred in Syria without that state's consent means that it amounted to an IAC between the UK and Syria.

At the beginning of October 2015, Walid Muallem, Syria's Minister of Foreign Affairs, affirmed that French and UK airstrikes against Islamic State on Syrian territory violated international law: 'What Britain and France are doing in the Syrian airspace flies in the face of international law and is a flagrant violation of the national sovereignty of the Syrian Republic.'[107] Six months later, Russia called the deployment of 150 US soldiers to Rumeilan in north-eastern Syria, without the consent of the Syrian Government, a 'violation of the

[103] 'Army chief says drone attacks threat to country's integrity', *Dawn* (2 June 2016) at https://goo.gl/pCzvTp.

[104] Akande (n 88) 71.

[105] M Wilkinson, P Dominiczak and S Swinford, 'David Cameron: Britain mounted fatal air strike in Syria', *Daily Telegraph* (7 September 2015) at https://goo.gl/uBhPfN.

[106] Ibid, col 27.

[107] 'Damascus Accuses US-Led Coalition of Breaking International Law, State Sovereignty', *Sputnik* (1 October 2015) at https://goo.gl/0fCjoP.

country's sovereignty'. Russia's Deputy Foreign Minister, Sergey Ryabkov, told the TASS news agency that 'such actions are being carried out by the US without the consent of the legitimate government of the Syrian Arab Republic'. He emphasised that Syria's Government had come to 'a similar political assessment'.[108] These statements reinforce the argument that France, the UK and the US are engaged in an IAC with Syria by virtue of their airstrikes on Syrian territory, which are manifestly conducted without the express consent of the Syrian Government.

iv. The Importance of the Views of the Parties

The views of affected parties as to whether the nature and extent of violence wrought by one state on another's territory is sufficient for an armed conflict to exist, without the requisite consent, are significant but not determinant. Indeed, although the threshold of armed violence to trigger an IAC may not be settled, that an IAC can exist is clear even when one of the involved states does not support the determination. This is made explicit in Common Article 2, though as the 1958 Pictet Commentary on the 1949 Geneva Convention IV notes:

> The Convention only provides for the case of one of the Parties denying the existence of a state of war. What would the position be, it may be wondered, if both the Parties to an armed conflict were to deny the existence of a state of war. Even in that event it would not appear that they could, by tacit agreement, prevent the Conventions from applying. It must not be forgotten that the Conventions have been drawn up first and foremost to protect individuals, and not to serve State interests.[109]

In its 2016 commentary on Common Article 2, the ICRC asserts that 'It follows from Article 2(1) that the factual existence of an armed conflict suffices for humanitarian law to apply.'[110] It further states:

> Even if none of the Parties recognize [*sic*] the existence of a state of war or of an armed conflict, humanitarian law would still apply provided that an armed conflict is in fact in existence. How States characterize the armed confrontation does not affect the application of the Geneva Conventions if the situation evidences that the State concerned is effectively involved in hostile armed actions against another State. The fact that a State does not, for political or other reasons, explicitly refer to the existence of an armed conflict within the meaning of Article 2(1) in a particular situation does not prevent it from being legally classified as such.[111]

In the case of the Stuxnet worm, for example, neither Iran nor the other presumed belligerents, Israel and the US (who did not even acknowledge publicly the action they had taken),[112] accepted that this amounted to an armed conflict. Of course, for the US and Israel

[108] RT, '"Violation of sovereignty": Moscow slams Obama decision to send 250 more US troops to Syria', *Infowars* (29 April 2016) at https://goo.gl/uUxf7W.
[109] Pictet Commentary on GC IV (1958) (n 19) 21.
[110] ICRC commentary on 1949 Geneva Convention I (n 16) para 210.
[111] Ibid.
[112] According to a 2011 report in *The New York Times*, 'Officially, neither American nor Israeli officials will even utter the name of the malicious computer program, much less describe any role in designing it.' WJ Broad, J Markoff and DE Sanger, 'Israeli Test on Worm Called Crucial in Iran Nuclear Delay', *New York Times* (15 January 2011) at https://goo.gl/jNkty.

it was not only politically sensitive, they would also have had some *ad bellum* issues to consider. For Iran, the political embarrassment at being hit by a cyber-attack meant it was keen to downplay the consequences.

D. Foreign Military Occupation

Common Article 2 stipulates that the Geneva Conventions 'shall also apply to all cases of partial or total occupation' of the territory of a state party, 'even if the … occupation meets with no armed resistance'. The Elements of Crimes established under the ICC provide that 'the term "international armed conflict" includes military occupation'.[113]

The issue of consent to foreign use of force, discussed in section II.C.iii, is equally relevant for the question of foreign military occupation. If valid consent to the presence of foreign troops has been given, there is no military occupation and the law of armed conflict does not apply (unless, for instance, the foreign forces are party to a NIAC in the territorial state).

During a belligerent occupation of foreign territory, the applicable law is set out in the 1907 Hague Regulations (Articles 42–56), the 1949 Geneva Convention IV, the 1977 Additional Protocol I and customary international law. The underpinning of the law of military occupation is that it is a temporary situation, which lasts until a political agreement is reached. During this period, the occupant does not enjoy sovereign rights over the territories it occupies and local law that was applicable prior to the occupation remains in force. At the same time, the occupying power is responsible for administering the local life of the population under its control – maintaining it as closely as possible as it was prior to the occupation – and for providing security.[114] In addition, international human rights law is binding on the occupying state extraterritorially with regard to the territories it occupies. Certain human rights treaty obligations may, though, be subject to derogation.[115]

In 2012 and 2013, at least nine situations of military occupation were recorded:

- Azerbaijan, partially occupied by Armenia
- Cyprus, partially occupied by Turkey
- Eritrea, partially occupied by Ethiopia
- Georgia, partially occupied by Russia
- Lebanon, partially occupied by Israel
- Moldova, partially occupied by Russia

[113] ICC, 'Elements of crimes', UN Doc PCNICC/2000/1/Add.2 (2000), fn 34.

[114] Art 43, Convention (IV) respecting the Laws and Customs of War on Land and its annex: Regulations concerning the Laws and Customs of War on Land; adopted at The Hague, 18 October 1907; entry into force, 26 January 1910 (hereinafter, 1907 Hague Regulations).

[115] Derogations from certain human rights in accordance with the 1966 International Covenant on Civil and Political Rights (ICCPR) may only occur in 'time of public emergency which threatens the life of the nation and the existence of which is officially proclaimed'. Any derogation must be only 'to the extent strictly required by the exigencies of the situation, provided that such measures are not inconsistent with their other obligations under international law and do not involve discrimination solely on the ground of race, colour, sex, language, religion or social origin'. Art 4(1), ICCPR. The right to life and the right to freedom from torture or other inhumane treatment are non-derogable.

- Palestine, partially occupied by Israel
- Syria, partially occupied by Israel
- Western Sahara, partially occupied by Morocco.[116]

As at the beginning of 2017, these occupations persisted, and a tenth had existed since 2014: Russia's occupation of Ukraine (Crimea). The consent to military intervention that Russia purported to have received from the President of Ukraine, Viktor Yanukovych, after his effective deposition from power – albeit one that was seemingly in violation of Ukrainian law[117] – was not valid for the purposes of *jus ad bellum*. President Yanukovych was no longer in effective control of the state, including the nation's armed forces.

There is some debate as to when a state of occupation actually starts: is it the invasion of/incursion into territory, or must a degree of control be exercised by the incursive forces? In its 2015 Challenges Report to the 32nd International Conference of the Red Cross and Red Crescent, the ICRC argued that a cumulative three-step test should determine whether a state of occupation has been established for the purposes of the law of armed conflict:

> 1) The armed forces of a State are physically present in a foreign territory without the consent of the effective local government in place at the time of the invasion.
> 2) The effective local government in place at the time of the invasion has been or can be rendered, substantially or completely, incapable of exerting its powers by virtue of the foreign forces' unconsented presence.
> 3) The foreign forces are in a position to exercise authority instead of the local government over the concerned territory (or parts thereof).[118]

In some ways this is a surprisingly high threshold. The third cumulative requirement implies that the initial invasion or incursion is an active IAC (even if no combat occurs), rather than an occupation. This in itself is not especially controversial. But the requirement that the foreign forces be 'in a position to exercise authority instead of the local government over the concerned territory' might, depending on the intent of the phrase, require a level of administration that would take some time to install. Orders can easily be issued, but the management of schools, hospitals, roads and the cleaning of streets, the collection of rubbish and the disposal of sewage are resource intensive. As Katja Schöberl has written, though, Common Article 2 has been interpreted to have a broader meaning than is the case under Article 42 of the 1907 Hague Regulations, which requires territory to be 'actually placed under the authority of the hostile army' and which considers occupation to extend 'only to the territory where such authority has been established and can be exercised'.[119]

[116] See S Casey-Maslen (ed), *The War Report: 2012* (Oxford, Oxford University Press, 2013); and Casey-Maslen (ed) (n 61), respectively.

[117] On 3 March 2014, in the UN Security Council, the Russian Ambassador, Vitaly Churkin, produced a letter from the ousted Ukrainian President asking Russia to send troops across the border 'to establish legitimacy, peace, law and order, stability and defending the people of Ukraine'. Thousands of Russian troops had already been pouring into the Crimea by then. See, eg, 'Ukraine's Yanukovych asked for troops, Russia tells UN', *BBC* (4 March 2014) at https://goo.gl/XxCkrC; 'Yanukovich sent letter to Putin asking for Russian military presence in Ukraine', RT (3 March 2014) at https://goo.gl/aWxNqp.

[118] 2015 ICRC Challenges Report (n 37) 11–12.

[119] K Schöberl, 'The Geographical Scope of Application of the Conventions' in Clapham, Gaeta, and Sassòli (eds) (n 26) 67, 74.

The ICRC test is also worded in a slightly unfortunate manner. The use of 'local' government might be taken to mean local or regional authority. In a breakaway republic (the Crimea or South Ossetia, for instance), the local or regional authorities may actively welcome the foreign troops. The language used should have been, in the view of the author, the national government in place at the time of the invasion. Gary Solis has suggested that Iraq in 2003 was only under US occupation from 1 May 2003, when US President George W Bush declared the effective end of the conflict that followed the coalition invasion of 20 March.[120] This is not a legally accurate assessment of the situation in Iraq.

The point at which an occupation ends is also difficult to establish. In this regard, Article 6 of the 1949 Geneva Convention IV states that the application of the Conventions generally continues until 'one year after the general close of military operations'.[121] In contrast, the 1977 Additional Protocol I provides that it applies until, 'in the case of occupied territories, … the termination of the occupation, except, in either circumstance, for those persons whose final release, repatriation or re-establishment takes place thereafter'.[122] The ICRC argues that its three-step 'effective-control test' also applies to the end of occupation, 'meaning that the criteria to be met should generally mirror those used to determine the beginning of occupation, only in reverse. Thus, if any of the three conditions listed above ceases to exist, an occupation should be considered to have ended.'[123]

The ICRC also, though, considers

> that in some specific and rather exceptional cases – in particular when foreign forces withdraw from occupied territory (or parts thereof) but retain key elements of authority or other important governmental functions usually performed by an occupying power – the law of occupation may continue to apply within the territorial and functional limits of such competences. Indeed, despite the lack of the physical presence of foreign forces in the territory concerned, the retained authority may amount to effective control for the purposes of the law of occupation and entail the continued application of the relevant provisions of this body of norms. This is referred to as the 'functional approach' to the application of occupation law. This test will apply to the extent that the foreign forces still exercise, within all or part of the territory, governmental functions acquired when the occupation was undoubtedly established and ongoing.[124]

Although not expressly stated, the ICRC's lawyers are likely to be thinking, in particular, of the situation in Gaza.[125]

E. A Proxy International Armed Conflict

One state can conduct warfare against another state by proxy, using the intermediary of an armed group. This also amounts to an IAC, although the requisite level of control over the

[120] Solis (n 75) 234.
[121] See, generally, J Grignon, 'The Geneva Conventions and the End of Occupation' in Clapham, Gaeta, and Sassòli (eds) (n 26) 1575.
[122] Art 3(b), 1977 Additional Protocol I.
[123] 2015 ICRC Challenges Report (n 37) 12.
[124] Ibid.
[125] This is clearer in the ICRC 2016 commentary on Geneva Convention I, when it refers, at a salient point, to Y Shany, 'Faraway, So Close: The Legal Status of Gaza after Israel's Disengagement', (2005) 8 *Yearbook of International Humanitarian Law* 369, 380–83.

group and the threshold of violence needed are both contentious. In the UN definition of aggression, reproduced in the ICC Statute, as amended, it is stipulated that an act of aggression includes

> The sending by or on behalf of a State of armed bands, groups, irregulars or mercenaries, which carry out acts of armed force against another State of such gravity as to amount to the acts listed above, or its substantial involvement therein.[126]

It is, though, not only the 'sending' but also a level of control over an armed group that will amount to an IAC by proxy. Mere support, whether political or financial, or in the form of the provision of resources, including armaments, is not sufficient. Two possible tests appear to have crystallised in the jurisprudence to date: 'effective control' and 'overall control'. In fact the situation is perhaps less uncertain, as the test of 'effective control' over the group, first mooted by the ICJ in *Nicaragua v US*, was destined for consideration of state responsibility for unlawful action, either because the armed group received and acted on specific instructions from the foreign power, or on the basis that the foreign power controlled the specific operation in which the violation of international law occurred.[127]

Following the approach taken by the ICJ in *Nicaragua v US*, Draft Article 8 of the ILC's 2001 Articles on State Responsibility provides:

> The conduct of a person or group of persons shall be considered an act of a State under international law if the person or group of persons is in fact acting on the instructions of, or under the direction or control of, that State in carrying out the conduct.[128]

The 'overall control' test proposed by the ICTY in the *Tadić* case in 1999 was as follows:

> In order to attribute the acts of a military or paramilitary group to a State, it must be proved that the State wields overall control over the group, not only by equipping and financing the group, but also by coordinating or helping in the general planning of its military activity. Only then can the State be held internationally accountable for any misconduct of the group. However, it is not necessary that, in addition, the State should also issue, either to the head or to members of the group, instructions for the commission of specific acts contrary to international law.

Thus, overall control involves coordinating or supporting the 'general planning' of the armed group's military operations but not necessarily specific operational instructions, including those that would involve violations of the law of armed conflict.

This 'overall control' test for an IAC by proxy has since received support in both the ICJ and the ICC. In the *Genocide* case between Bosnia and Herzegovina and Serbia and Montenegro, the ICJ stated that 'Insofar as the "overall control" test is employed to determine whether or not an armed conflict is international … it may well be that the test is

[126] Art 3(g), Definition of Aggression, annexed to UN General Assembly Resolution 3314 (XXIX), adopted without a vote on 14 December 1974; see also Art 8*bis*, ICC Statute.

[127] ICRC commentary on 1949 Geneva Convention I (n 16) para 269; see ICJ, *Nicaragua v US* (n 57) para 115.

[128] In its commentary on the draft provision, in distinguishing the 'overall control' test, the ILC stated that it is 'a matter for appreciation in each case whether particular conduct was or was not carried out under the control of a State, to such an extent that the conduct controlled should be attributed to it'. As Sassòli observes, 'This is true for the appreciation of the facts, while the applicable legal standard provided for by the secondary rule of attribution must be the same in all cases.' M Sassòli, 'State responsibility for violations of international humanitarian law', *International Review of the Red Cross*, vol 84, no 846 (June 2002) 407.

applicable and suitable.'[129] The Court did not, though, think it 'appropriate' to take a formal position on the point as there was no need to resolve it for the purpose of its judgment.[130]

In the *Bemba* case, an ICC Pre-Trial Chamber concluded that 'an international armed conflict exists in case of armed hostilities between States through their respective armed forces or other actors acting on behalf of the State'.[131] In the *Lubanga* case, ICC Trial Chamber I explicitly endorsed the ICTY's approach in *Tadić*, affirming that, '[a]s regards the necessary degree of control of another State over an armed group acting on its behalf', it had concluded 'that the "overall control" test is the correct approach'.[132] It further noted that a state 'may exercise the required degree of control when it "has a role in organising, coordinating or planning the military actions of the military group, in addition to financing, training and equipping or providing operational support to that group"'.[133]

The ICRC questions the wisdom of two different tests on the basis that the (stricter) effective control test might lead to an accountability gap:

> The notion of overall control might prevent the intervening Power from hiding behind the proxy's veil in order to avoid its obligations and international responsibilities under humanitarian law. It also makes it possible to challenge the third State's claim that the actions were in fact those of actors who could not be considered as officials or persons acting on its behalf and therefore that it could not itself be considered as a Party to the conflict.[134]

The ICRC's concern about a potential lack of accountability is well-founded (though it is also an accusation that could be directed against the law of armed conflict in general). It is particularly acute if the assertion is correct that once the overall control test has been met, an erstwhile NIAC is transformed into an IAC while the erstwhile NIAC is, under the law of armed conflict, effectively extinguished:

> In the view of the ICRC, the consequences of the notion of overall control will be decisive insofar as the non-State armed group then becomes subordinated to the intervening State. The members of the armed group become the equivalent of 'agents' of the intervening State under international law. This means that the intervening State becomes a Party to the existing conflict in lieu of the armed group and that the conflict has become entirely international in nature.[135]

However, this position is itself problematic. It assumes that there is a pre-existing NIAC in operation, which must of course have met the requisite criteria, as discussed in section III of this chapter. Why should the situation not be considered as two parallel armed conflicts – one international, the other non-international in character? The foreign state would still be responsible, as Andrew Clapham argues, for 'any failure to prevent violations of the Geneva Conventions which could reasonably have been prevented, as well as for ensuring respect for the Geneva Conventions through the exercise of its overall control over the organized

[129] ICJ, *Case Concerning Application of the Convention on the Prevention and Punishment of the Crime of Genocide (Bosnia and Herzegovina v Serbia and Montenegro)*, Judgment (Merits), 26 February 2007, para 404.

[130] Ibid.

[131] ICC, *Situation in the Central African Republic in the Case of the Prosecutor v Jean-Pierre Bemba Gombo*, Decision on the Charges (Pre-Trial Chamber II), Doc ICC-01/05-01/08-424, 15 June 2009, para 223.

[132] ICC, *Prosecutor v Thomas Lubanga Dyilo*, Judgment (Trial Chamber I) (*Lubanga*), 14 March 2012, para 541.

[133] Ibid.

[134] ICRC commentary on 1949 Geneva Convention I (n 16) para 273.

[135] Ibid.

armed group'.[136] The individuals participating would be responsible for any violations of international criminal law they commit, while the group *qua* entity could also be responsible under civil law for tortious acts.

Further, why is a prior NIAC a prerequisite? Why is the threshold not the same as the threshold for an IAC? What if, for example, one state were to 'send' a small armed group, perhaps comprising non-national mercenaries, to assassinate a foreign head of state on that state's territory. This could clearly amount to an act of aggression and would satisfy the effective control test, but would not seem to fall within the ICRC paradigm as no NIAC was ongoing at the time.

F. Wars of National Liberation

The final potential scenario for an IAC is what is sometimes termed a war of national liberation. According to Article 1(4) of the 1977 Additional Protocol I, situations covered by Common Article 2 include

> armed conflicts in which peoples are fighting against colonial domination and alien occupation and against racist régimes in the exercise of their right of self-determination, as enshrined in the Charter of the United Nations and the Declaration on Principles of International Law concerning Friendly Relations and Co-operation among States in accordance with the Charter of the United Nations.

The US and a number of other states opposed this provision vociferously when it was adopted. Until 2015, it had never been effectively applied in practice (which state would be content to accept that it is engaged in colonial domination or alien occupation, or is a racist regime?) and cannot be considered customary law, both for lack of state practice and especially *opinio juris*. On 21 June 2015, however, the Polisario Front made a unilateral declaration on behalf of the people of Western Sahara, undertaking to apply the 1949 Geneva Conventions and the 1977 Additional Protocol I to the conflict between it and Morocco. Morocco ratified the 1977 Additional Protocol I in 2011 without reservation.

According to Article 96(3) of the Protocol, the authority representing a people engaged against a state party in an armed conflict of the type referred to in Article 1(4), may undertake to apply the Geneva Conventions and the Protocol in relation to that conflict by means of a unilateral declaration addressed to the depositary. The depositary of the Protocol, the Swiss Federal Council, accepted Polisario's declaration and issued a corresponding notification to that effect to the other states parties. As has been observed, this is the first time the Council has accepted such a declaration by a national liberation movement and a non-state entity under international law.[137] The effects of the declaration are to bring into force the Conventions and this Protocol, while the Polisario Front assumes 'the same rights and obligations' as those assumed by Morocco, and the Conventions and the Protocol 'are equally binding' upon both parties to the conflict.

[136] Clapham (n 26) 18.

[137] K Fortin, 'Unilateral Declaration by Polisario under API accepted by Swiss Federal Council', Armed Groups and International Law blog (2 September 2015) at https://goo.gl/uvwyx9.

The threshold of armed violence for such a conflict to exist is not settled, but is probably the same as for an IAC – that is to say, much lower than it is for a NIAC. This is not the position of the UK, which argues that the threshold is the same as for a NIAC regulated by Common Article 3.[138] The example of the Polisario Front, though, might be taken to suggest that a low threshold is sufficient, as the extent of violence between Polisario and Morocco does not come close to being regular and intense, as is required for a NIAC.

G. The Geographical Scope of International Armed Conflict

Without prejudice to the rules of *jus ad bellum* and the law of neutrality, which continue to apply, an IAC can be fought anywhere: not only on the territory of the parties but on any territory, including the high seas.[139] This is despite the seemingly limiting decision in the *Tadić* case, whereby the law of armed conflict 'continues to apply in the whole territory of the warring States'.[140] The ICRC adds additional territory to the possible scope of application of IAC, affirming:

> As regards IAC, it is generally accepted that IHL applies to the entire territories of the States involved in such a conflict, as well as to the high seas and the exclusive economic zones (the 'area' or 'region' of war). A State's territory includes not only its land surface but also rivers and landlocked lakes, the territorial sea, and the national airspace above this territory.[141]

The UK Ministry of Defence seems to take a similar position,[142] as do a number of leading commentators.[143] Presumably, though, consonant with Common Article 2, 'the entire territories of the States involved' would encompass territory occupied by one of the parties, whether legally or illegally (otherwise this would be denying that much of the combat that took place during the Second World War was part of an IAC). Schöberl adds outer space to the list of possible geographical areas of an IAC: 'while other areas, such as the high seas and outer space, have been removed from claims of sovereignty and reserved for peaceful purposes, … they too would have to be considered being part of the Conventions' geographical scope in case of armed conflict'.[144]

Schmitt notes that the law of neutrality obliges neutral states to ensure that belligerents do not operate from their territory. Should a neutral state 'fail to comply with this duty, either because it will not or can not, the opposing belligerent may lawfully cross into neutral territory for the sole purpose of putting an end to its enemy's activities'. In contrast, the

[138] UK Ministry of Defence (n 2) para 3.4.2.

[139] The particular issue of outer space, generally defined as beginning at the Kármán line at an altitude of 100 kilometres (62 miles) above sea level, is addressed in ch 14.

[140] *Tadić* (n 3) para 70.

[141] 2015 ICRC Challenges Report (n 37) 13. For a discussion of the meaning of Art 88 of the UN Convention on the Law of the Sea, see Dinstein (n 6) 24, paras 64–65.

[142] In describing where naval warfare may be conducted, it refers to 'hostile actions … in, on, or over the territorial sea, internal waters, land territories, continental shelf, exclusive economic zone, and, where relevant, archipelagic waters of belligerent states (both enemy and allied)'; and also 'in, on, or over the high seas and those waters falling beyond the territorial limits of all states'. See UK Ministry of Defence (n 2) para 13.6.

[143] MN Schmitt, 'Charting the Legal Geography of Non-International Armed Conflict' (2014) 90 *International Law Studies* 5.

[144] Schöberl (n 119) 74.

ICRC argues that 'it is widely agreed that military operations cannot be carried out beyond the area or region of war as defined above, meaning that they may not be extended to the territory of neutral States'.[145]

In fact, despite the position of the ICRC on this issue, as Schöberl observes, while the law of neutrality, along with *ad bellum* rules, 'protects the inviolability of neutral territory, the Conventions will nevertheless apply if the law of neutrality is violated, for example in case of hostilities between belligerents on neutral territory'.[146] If that were not the case, these violent acts would not be regulated by the law of armed conflict. Presumably, the argument would be that either human rights law applied to the conduct of hostilities (a stance that is resolutely opposed by certain commentators), or, perhaps in the point of view of certain states, that no international law at all applied to the specific acts of violence. This is not credible. Indeed, as the US Department of Defense observes, in asserting that the law of armed conflict governs the conduct of hostilities in outer space, 'law of war treaties and the customary law of war are understood to regulate the conduct of hostilities, regardless of where they are conducted'.[147]

The better view is thus that there are no geographical limitations to an IAC. *Jus ad bellum* and the law of neutrality impose limitations on where war may lawfully be conducted according to those international legal corpora, but where it is conducted outside of the scope that they allow, Hague Law rules still apply. The corollary of this, of course, is that there are no geographical limitations on where war crimes can be committed.

H. The Temporal Scope of International Armed Conflict

The question as to when an active IAC and a military occupation ends has been addressed, in part, in section II.D. With respect to an active IAC, both the 1949 Geneva Convention IV and its 1977 Additional Protocol I stipulate that these treaties apply 'until the general close of military operations'.[148] As Gabriella Venturini observes, this has a wider meaning than 'cessation of active hostilities', which means, in her view, 'the mere termination of fighting'.[149] The general close of military operations entails, in the words of Derek Jinks, a 'complete cessation of all aggressive military maneuvers' by all belligerents.[150]

The ICTY, in its decision on jurisdiction in the *Tadić* case, held:

> International humanitarian law applies from the initiation of such armed conflicts and extends beyond the cessation of hostilities until a general conclusion of peace is reached; or, in the case of internal conflicts, a peaceful settlement is achieved.[151]

[145] 2015 ICRC Challenges Report (n 37) 13.

[146] Schöberl (n 119) 74.

[147] USDOD December 2016 *Law of War Manual* (n 2) para 14.10.2.2.

[148] Art 6, 1949 Geneva Convention IV; Art 3(b), 1977 Additional Protocol I.

[149] G Venturini, 'The Temporal Scope of Application of the Conventions' in Clapham, Gaeta, and Sassòli (eds) (n 26) 51, 58.

[150] D Jinks, 'The Temporal Scope of Application of International Humanitarian Law in Contemporary Conflicts', Background Paper prepared for the Informal High-Level Expert Meeting on the Reaffirmation and Development of International Humanitarian Law, Cambridge, 27–29 January 2003, HCPR, Harvard, MA, 3.

[151] *Tadić* (n 3), para 70.

But as the ICRC has observed:

> Assessing the end of an armed conflict in the sense of Article 2(1) may be a very difficult enterprise. This is mainly due to the silence of the Geneva Conventions on this question but also to State practice, which indicates that States resort less and less to the conclusion of peace treaties.[152]

It affirms that 'In any case, the determination that an international armed conflict has ended is based not on the existence of a peace agreement, but rather on an appreciation of the facts on the ground.'[153]

This is correct. Hague Law rules apply from the initiation of the conduct of hostilities during an armed conflict until those hostilities end. This is unrelated to the existence of any ceasefires or peace agreements, but depends on when the fighting actually stops (or, in Jinks' more poetic formulation, 'the silencing of the guns').[154] This is a factual determination of a legal status.

III. Non-International Armed Conflict

If issues around the existence of an IAC are complex, they pale into insignificance compared to those concerning armed conflicts not of an international character.[155] There is, for example, precious little general agreement, let alone consensus, as to precisely when, where, between whom and for how long a NIAC exists under the law of armed conflict and international criminal law. The only fact that is uncontested is probably that the term 'armed conflict not of an international character' was first included in a law of armed conflict treaty in Article 3 common to the four 1949 Geneva Conventions ('Common Article 3')[156] and that this provision governs all such conflicts.[157]

There are three types of NIAC: the general NIAC to which Common Article 3 and customary Hague Law rules apply; within that broader context, a smaller number of conflicts governed by the higher threshold of the 1977 Additional Protocol II; and, potentially, the 'protracted' armed conflicts in which the ICC has jurisdiction for certain war

[152] ICRC commentary on 1949 Geneva Convention I (n 16) para 274.

[153] Ibid, para 276.

[154] Jinks (n 150) 3.

[155] The term appears to have first been employed by the ICRC in text drawn up in preparation for the 17th International Conference of the Red Cross in Stockholm in 1948. ICRC commentary on 1949 Geneva Convention I (n 16) para 370.

[156] For the history leading to the adoption of Common Article 3, see, eg S Sivakumaran, *The Law of Non-International Armed Conflict* (Oxford, Oxford University Press, 2012) ch 2, *esp* 30–42; A Cullen, *The Concept of Non-International Armed Conflict in International Humanitarian Law* (Cambridge, Cambridge University Press, 2010) ch 2. Of course, domestic provisions already applied to what would later be termed NIACs. The 1863 Lieber Code, for example, was ostensibly governing a NIAC: the American Civil War. (Though see, eg, S Spillman, 'War, Civil War, or Revolution?', *New Republic* (30 August 2017) at https://goo.gl/o3YVVK, citing D Armitage, *Civil Wars: A History in Ideas* (New York, Alfred A Knopf, 2017.) The ICRC also notes that the 1928 Convention on Duties and Rights of States in the Event of Civil Strife stipulated rules for states parties in the event of civil strife in another state party. ICRC commentary on 1949 Geneva Convention I (n 16) para 359.

[157] ICRC commentary on 1949 Geneva Convention I (n 16) para 351. As the ICRC observes, 'The text of "common" Article 3 is identical in the four Geneva Conventions, except for in the Second Convention, which refers to the "wounded, sick and shipwrecked" as opposed to just the "wounded and sick" as referred to in the First, Third and Fourth Conventions.' Ibid, fn 3.

crimes by virtue of Article 8(2)(f) of the ICC Statute. By far the most important is the first of these scenarios.

A. The Importance of Common Article 3

As the ICRC observed in its 2016 commentary on the 1949 Geneva Convention I, Common Article 3 'remains the core provision of humanitarian treaty law for the regulation of non-international armed conflicts. As part of the universally ratified 1949 Geneva Conventions, it is the only provision that is binding worldwide and governs all non-international armed conflicts.'[158] It reflects customary international law, and thus the provision, which was already termed a 'Convention in miniature' during its negotiation,[159] is applicable to every NIAC. But Common Article 3 not only represents customary law governing all NIACs; in the words of the ICJ, '[t]here is no doubt that, in the event of international armed conflicts, these rules also constitute a minimum yardstick, in addition to the more elaborate rules which are also to apply to international conflicts'.[160]

It is widely accepted (though it is not a consensus position)[161] that Common Article 3 does not regulate the conduct of hostilities.[162] In fact, the provision is Geneva law in its purest form, requiring the humane treatment both of those *hors de combat* (albeit by other individuals who may themselves still be conducting hostilities) and of those in the power of a party to a NIAC, such as members of the civilian population or detainees.

B. The Constituent Elements of Non-International Armed Conflict

To amount to a NIAC, any given situation must involve regular and intense armed combat between state armed forces and a non-state armed group, or between two or more non-state armed groups. To be party to an armed conflict, the armed group or groups engaged in fighting must be sufficiently 'organised'. This means that such groups are military or paramilitary forces with a martial-style hierarchy, and that some of the members are equipped with, at the very least, firearms. They must be capable of mounting military operations, but they do not need to possess uniforms, nor do they need to actively or even passively control territory.

i. The Path to a Definition

Beyond referring to 'armed conflict not of an international character', and describing acts that are prohibited and certain acts that are obligatory during a NIAC, Common Article 3 proffers no guidance as to how such a conflict is to be objectively identified. Some further

[158] Ibid, para 354.
[159] Ibid, para 356.
[160] *Nicaragua v US* (n 57), para 218.
[161] See, eg, Sivakumaran (n 156) 336, for a discussion of sources that argue for, or oppose, the notion that Common Article 3 also regulates the conduct of hostilities.
[162] See, eg, ICRC commentary on 1949 Geneva Convention I (n 16) para 389. The commentary was published four years after Sivakumaran's excellent work.

guidance can be found in the 1977 Additional Protocol II, even though its scope of application is more limited than is Common Article 3.[163] Notably, the Protocol affirms that armed conflicts are not 'situations of internal disturbances and tensions, such as riots, isolated and sporadic acts of violence and other acts of a similar nature'.[164] While helpful, this exclusionary analysis does not greatly assist in the identification of the constituent elements of a NIAC.

Faced with this challenge, it was left to the subsidiary means of identifying international legal rules to seek to plug the gap. As the Statute of the ICJ indicates, these are 'judicial decisions and the teachings of the most highly qualified publicists of the various nations'.[165] Jean Pictet's commentaries on Common Article 3 are an extremely valuable example of the latter. Pictet enumerated a series of proposals made by states during the diplomatic conference that negotiated and adopted the four 1949 Geneva Conventions, suggesting that the 'criteria are useful as a means of distinguishing a genuine armed conflict from a mere act of banditry or an unorganized and short-lived insurrection or terrorist activities'.[166] The criteria were as follows:

> (1) That the Party in revolt against the de jure Government possesses an organized military force, an authority responsible for its acts, acting within a determinate territory and having the means of respecting and ensuring respect for the Convention.
> (2) That the legal Government is obliged to have recourse to the regular military forces against insurgents organized as military and in possession of a part of the national territory.
> (3) (a) That the de jure Government has recognized the insurgents as belligerents; or
> (b) that it has claimed for itself the rights of a belligerent; or
> (c) that it has accorded the insurgents recognition as belligerents for the purposes only of the present Convention; or
> (d) that the dispute has been admitted to the agenda of the Security Council or the General Assembly of the United Nations as being a threat to international peace, a breach of the peace, or an act of aggression.
> (4) (a) That the insurgents have an organisation purporting to have the characteristics of a State.
> (b) That the insurgent civil authority exercises de facto authority over persons within a determinate territory.

[163] According to Art 1(1), 1977 Additional Protocol II, the Protocol only applies to NIACs occurring in the territory of a state party 'between its armed forces and dissident armed forces or other organized armed groups which, under responsible command, exercise such control over a part of its territory as to enable them to carry out sustained and concerted military operations and to implement this Protocol.'

[164] Art 1(2), 1977 Additional Protocol II. That this exclusion applies also to Common Article 3 is implied by the ICC Statute, which in giving the ICC potential jurisdiction over serious violations of the acts prohibited in the article, stipulates that this 'applies to armed conflicts not of an international character and thus does not apply to situations of internal disturbances and tensions, such as riots, isolated and sporadic acts of violence or other acts of a similar nature'. The only textual difference is that the Statute uses 'or' rather than 'and' when referring to 'other acts of a similar nature'. The older formulation was employed a year later in the Second Hague Protocol on Protection of Cultural Property: Art 22(2), Protocol to the Hague Convention of 1954 for the Protection of Cultural Property in the Event of Armed Conflict; adopted at The Hague, 26 March 1999, entry into force, 9 March 2004. Art 22(1) refers simply to 'armed conflict not of an international character', without offering any definition. This was also the case in the Convention on Certain Conventional Weapons (CCW). At the Second CCW Review Conference, which took place in Geneva from 11 to 21 December 2001, states parties adopted an Amendment to Art 1 of the Convention, extending its scope of application to cover NIACs. See Art 1(3), CCW.

[165] Art 38(I)(d), 1945 Statute of the ICJ.

[166] Pictet Commentary on GC I (n 15) 50.

(c) That the armed forces act under the direction of the organized civil authority and are prepared to observe the ordinary laws of war.
(d) That the insurgent civil authority agrees to be bound by the provisions of the Convention.[167]

While indeed valuable, these criteria should only be considered as indicative and not probative, much less determinative. Pictet himself asserted that they were 'not obligatory and are only mentioned as an indication'.[168] It is, for example, possible that a situation may be on the agenda of the UN Security Council as being a threat to international peace, or actually claimed by the Council to be an armed conflict, without a NIAC factually being in existence.

A clear example of such a situation was the Central African Republic (CAR) during much of 2013. As Annyssa Bellal has written, 'The NIAC that took place in CAR from December 2012 to 24 March 2013 opposed governmental forces (the Forces armées centrafricaines (FACA) as well as the Presidential Guard) and a coalition of armed groups named "Séléka".'[169] After this date, however, Bellal strongly doubts whether an armed conflict in fact existed, as those engaged in violence were not sufficiently organised, a criterion discussed in section II.B.iv.[170] This is despite the adoption of UN Security Council Resolution 2127 on 5 December 2013, which strongly condemned 'the continued violations of international humanitarian law' (thereby making clear its view that an armed conflict was in progress). The Council called upon 'all parties to armed conflict in the CAR', to issue clear orders 'prohibiting all violations and abuses committed against children' and 'against sexual violence'.[171]

Bellal concluded that 'any determination of the existence of a NIAC by the UN Security Council (an intergovernmental body), as in the circumstances prevailing in CAR, needs to be considered with caution'.[172] In November 2014, the Commission of Inquiry whose establishment Security Council Resolution 2127 called for,[173] concluded that an armed conflict existed in the CAR in 2013 until 'late March' and then, by remarkable coincidence, from 4 December 2013 onwards.[174] No evidence is advanced in support of the assertion that, as a matter of international law, an armed conflict existed from that date.

In his 1952 commentary on the 1949 Geneva Convention I, Pictet distinguished a NIAC from 'a mere act of banditry or an unorganized and short-lived insurrection', which were not armed conflicts. This sets the bar quite high for a NIAC. At the same time, though, he called for Common Article 3 to be applied 'as widely as possible', arguing:

> There can be no reason against this. For, contrary to what may have been thought, the Article in its reduced form does not in any way limit the right of a State to put down rebellion. Nor does it increase in the slightest the authority of the rebel party. … What Government would dare to claim

[167] Ibid, 49–50.
[168] Ibid, 50.
[169] A Bellal, 'Central African Republic: from conflict to chaos and back again?' in Casey-Maslen (ed) (n 61) 412, 414.
[170] See also 'Armed Conflict in the Central African Republic in 2013' in Casey-Maslen (ed) (n 61), 104ff.
[171] See UN Security Council Resolution 2127, 5 December 2013, paras 17, 22–23.
[172] Bellal (n 169) 424.
[173] See UN Security Council Resolution 2127, para 24.
[174] Final report of International Commission of Inquiry on the Central African Republic, para 39, attached to Letter dated 19 December 2014 from the UN Secretary-General to the President of the UN Security Council, UN Doc S/2014/928, 22 December 2014.

> before the world, in a case of civil disturbances which could justly be described as mere acts of banditry, that, Article 3 not being applicable, it was entitled to leave the wounded uncared for, to inflict torture and mutilations and to take hostages?[175]

Pictet's plea for the broadest possible application of the humanitarian elements of Common Article 3 made sense, from a policy perspective, at the time. Indeed, few would argue for the right to be 'entitled to leave the wounded uncared for, to inflict torture and mutilations and to take hostages'. But suggesting that the provision applies as a matter of law is another thing entirely; one with broader and darker consequences, particularly for civilians as a result of the permissiveness of the law governing the conduct of hostilities during a NIAC. For given that Hague Law rules are, in general, far less restrictive as to when potentially and intentional lethal use of force may be employed, it is right that this extraordinary legal regime should only be applied when an armed conflict is truly in existence. Thus, in its 2016 commentary on Geneva Convention I, the ICRC noted:

> While common Article 3 contains rules that serve to limit or prohibit harm in non-international armed conflict, it does not in itself provide rules governing the conduct of hostilities. However, when common Article 3 is applicable, it is understood that other rules of humanitarian law of non-international armed conflict, including those regarding the conduct of hostilities, also apply. Thus, while there may be no apparent need to discern possible limits to the scope of application of common Article 3, it is important that the rules applicable in armed conflicts apply only in the situations for which they were created. …
>
> The existence of a situation that has crossed the threshold of an 'armed conflict not of an international character occurring in the territory of one of the High Contracting Parties' must therefore be neither lightly asserted nor denied. Humanitarian law standards must be applied only in the situation – armed conflict – for which they were intended and developed, carefully balancing considerations of military necessity and humanity.[176]

Perhaps inevitably given the reticence of many states on the issue, the criteria for a NIAC fell to be determined by judges in a trial under international criminal law. After all, the first line of defence for lawyers seeking to have their clients acquitted of war crimes charges is often that there was no armed conflict at the relevant place and time. If they sustain this position successfully, the charges against the defendant must fail. Duško Tadić was the first accused to stand trial before the ICTY, charged with a range of war crimes, including murder, torture and sexual violence, as well as crimes against humanity (which according to the ICTY Statute were limited to those committed during an armed conflict).[177]

[175] Pictet Commentary on GC I (n 15) 50. Over the course of the next eight years, Pictet's thinking evolved further. In his 1958 commentary on GC IV, he wrote that 'Speaking generally, it must be recognized that the conflicts referred to in Article 3 are armed conflicts, with armed forces on either side engaged in hostilities – conflicts, in short, which are in many respects similar to an international war, but take place within the confines of a single country. In many cases, each of the Parties is in possession of a portion of the national territory, and there is often some sort of front.' Pictet Commentary on GC IV (n 19) 36. The same language was included in his 1960 Commentary on Geneva Convention III on the Treatment of Prisoners of War (Pictet Commentary on GC III (1960) (n 19) 37), but not in his commentary, published the same year, on Convention II on the Wounded, Sick and Shipwrecked at Sea (Pictet Commentary on GC II (1960) (n 19)).

[176] ICRC commentary on 1949 Geneva Convention I (n 16) paras 389–90.

[177] Though, as the US Department of Defense has observed, he was 'a relatively low-level offender who – had he been caught only a few years later – would have been referred to Bosnia for domestic prosecution.' USDOD December 2016 *Law of War Manual* (n 2), para 1.9.1, fn 155.

Mr Tadić's lawyers argued, inter alia, that the Tribunal lacked jurisdiction *ratione materiae*, affirming that the Statute of the ICTY was limited to crimes committed in the context of an IAC, or, alternatively, that there was no armed conflict at all in the region where the crimes with which he was charged were allegedly committed.[178]

Before the ICTY's Appeals Chamber, Tadić's lawyers claimed that the concept of armed conflict covered only the precise time and place of actual hostilities. They further argued that the conflict in the Prijedor region (where the alleged crimes were said to have taken place) was limited to a political assumption of power by the Bosnian Serbs and did not involve armed combat (though movements of tanks were admitted).[179] The Appeals Chamber rejected the argument, holding that 'the temporal and geographical scope of both internal and international armed conflicts extends beyond the exact time and place of hostilities'.[180] It affirmed, correctly:

> Although the Geneva Conventions are silent as to the geographical scope of international 'armed conflicts,' the provisions suggest that at least some of the provisions of the Conventions apply to the entire territory of the Parties to the conflict, not just to the vicinity of actual hostilities. Certainly, some of the provisions are clearly bound up with the hostilities and the geographical scope of those provisions should be so limited. Others, particularly those relating to the protection of prisoners of war and civilians, are not so limited. With respect to prisoners of war, the Convention applies to combatants in the power of the enemy; it makes no difference whether they are kept in the vicinity of hostilities. In the same vein, Geneva Convention IV protects civilians anywhere in the territory of the Parties.

It applied the same logic to NIACs, which it termed, a little loosely, 'internal armed conflicts':

> The geographical and temporal frame of reference for internal armed conflicts is similarly broad. This conception is reflected in the fact that beneficiaries of common Article 3 of the Geneva Conventions are those taking no active part (or no longer taking active part) in the hostilities. This indicates that the rules contained in Article 3 also apply outside the narrow geographical context of the actual theatre of combat operations. Similarly, certain language in Protocol II to the Geneva Conventions … also suggests a broad scope. First, like common Article 3, it explicitly protects '[a]ll persons who do not take a direct part or who have ceased to take part in hostilities.'[181]

In concluding its analysis, the Tribunal famously found that a NIAC exists 'whenever there is … protracted armed violence between governmental authorities and organized armed groups or between such groups within a State'.[182] It further held that even if substantial clashes were not occurring in the Prijedor region at the time and place the crimes were alleged to have been committed, international humanitarian law still applied: 'It is sufficient that the alleged crimes were closely related to the hostilities occurring in other parts of the territories controlled by the parties to the conflict.'[183]

[178] *Tadić* (n 3) para 65.
[179] Ibid, para 66.
[180] Ibid, para 67.
[181] Ibid, para 68.
[182] Ibid, para 70.
[183] Ibid.

What is initially striking about the Appeals Chamber's definition of armed conflict is how little legal analysis it offers in support of its wide-reaching affirmations. It does offer textual and logical justification that once an armed conflict exists on the territory of a state, IHL applies throughout the territory, but its twin criteria of 'protracted armed violence' and the need for armed groups to be 'organised' are proffered without supporting evidence. It is true that Article 1(1) of the 1977 Additional Protocol II refers to 'organized armed groups', but the threshold for application of the Protocol is considerably higher than it is for Common Article 3. Organisation of the armed opposition was proposed during the negotiation of Common Article 3, but this was included among indicative criteria rather than prerequisites.

As for the criterion of protracted armed violence, perhaps the best that can be said in support of the formulation is that, *a priori*, it seems to correspond to Pictet's assertion that a 'short-lived' insurrection is not an armed conflict. This is on the basis that protracted tends to mean, in ordinary parlance, 'lasting for a long time or longer than expected or usual'.[184] The term does not seem to speak to intensity, even though this is clearly a relevant criterion. The ICTY was subsequently constrained to clarify that, despite its ordinary meaning, in fact 'protracted' actually meant 'intense' rather than prolonged. Indeed, by the time Mr Tadić came to trial, the Trial Chamber felt able to claim, without a hint of discomfiture:

> The test applied by the Appeals Chamber to the existence of an armed conflict for the purposes of the rules contained in Common Article 3 focuses on two aspects of a conflict; the intensity of the conflict and the organization of the parties to the conflict.[185]

Subsequent cases reaffirmed this understanding.[186]

The twin criteria have been supported, or at least cited as relevant, by states and in other judicial fora as relevant to determine the existence of a NIAC. Thus, although neither the ICC Statute nor the subsequent Elements of Crimes define 'armed conflict', the introduction to the Elements of Crimes stipulates that the elements for war crimes under Article 8(2) of the Statute 'shall be interpreted within the established framework of the international law of armed conflict'.[187] In its first-ever trial – of Thomas Lubanga – the ICC explicitly 'derived assistance from the jurisprudence of the ICTY' and cited the definition of armed conflict in *Tadić*.[188]

State practice tentatively supports the *Tadić* criteria. The US Department of Defense notes, citing *Tadić*, that the 'intensity of the conflict and the organization of the parties are criteria that have been assessed to distinguish between non-international armed conflict and "internal disturbances and tensions"'.[189] The French Ministry of Defence cites the *Tadić* criteria, noting that 'the jurisprudence of the former Yugoslav Criminal Tribunal has set out the definition of a non-international armed conflict, and specified what distinguishes

[184] *Collins English Dictionary*.

[185] *Prosecutor v Tadić* (n 77) para 562.

[186] ICTY, *Prosecutor v Ramush Haradinaj, Idriz Balaj, and Lahi Brahimaj*, Judgment (Trial Chamber) (Case No IT-04-84-T), 3 April 2008, paras 40 et seq.

[187] *Lubanga* (n 132) para 531.

[188] Ibid, para 533.

[189] USDOD December 2016 *Law of War Manual* (n 2), para 3.4.2.2.

it from situations of internal disturbances and tensions'.[190] The UK Ministry of Defence cites the *Tadić* definition as 'guidance' but claims, somewhat opaquely, that the criteria do not 'deal with the threshold of an armed conflict'.[191] In contrast, the German *Law of Armed Conflict Manual* does not cite *Tadić* but affirms:

> A non-international armed conflict is a sustained, intense, violent confrontation, normally carried out on national territory, between the existing governmental authority and an organised armed group as a non-governmental Party to the conflict, or among such armed, organised groups, even when a governmental authority no longer exists … Through mere internal disturbances and tensions, such as riots, isolated and sporadic acts of violence or other acts of a similar nature, the threshold into non-international armed conflict is not crossed; in these situations LOAC [the law of armed conflict] is thus not applicable.[192]

Thus Germany seems to include the protracted (in its ordinary meaning) nature of the violence ('sustained') as well as its intensity. As discussed in section III.B.ii, only one leading commentator appears to agree that the threshold is so high.

Leading commentators generally support the '*Tadić* definition' (at least as later clarified by the ICTY in its trial judgment in the *Tadić* case). Sivakumaran, for instance, thought that the 'core elements that featured in the various definitions that had been posited previously were thus encapsulated in a neat and concise definition'.[193] Rogers referred to it as 'useful guidance'.[194] Moir opined that the *Tadić* definition might have settled the issue, noting his view that the Appeals Chamber decision had set the threshold for a NIAC 'actually relatively low'.[195] Akande has asserted that the *Tadić* definition was 'determined by criteria which have been fleshed out by customary international law'.[196] Similarly, the International Group of Experts that drafted the *Tallinn Manual on Cyberwarfare* wrote that the 'holding' in *Tadić* 'is widely accepted as setting forth the two criteria for qualification as a non-international armed conflict – intensity of the hostilities and the involvement of an organized armed group'.[197]

ii. A Higher Threshold?

Yoram Dinstein does not accept the mainstream view of what amounts to a NIAC for the purposes of customary law and Common Article 3, claiming that the criteria of 'protracted' actually does not mean what the ICTY Trial Chamber said that it meant in 1997. He argues instead that there are two separate criteria in addition to organisation of the armed

[190] Author's translation from French original: 'C'est la jurisprudence du tribunal pénal pour l'ex-Yougoslavie qui a précisé la définition d'un conflit armé non international, et ce qui le distingue de situations de tensions internes et troubles intérieurs.'

[191] UK Ministry of Defence (n 2) para 3.3.

[192] German Ministry of Defence (n 20) para 210.

[193] Sivakumaran (n 156) 164.

[194] APV Rogers, *Law on the Battlefield*, 3rd edn (Manchester, Manchester University Press, 2012) 4.

[195] L Moir, *The Law of Internal Armed Conflict* (Cambridge, Cambridge University Press, 2002) 43.

[196] Akande (n 88) 51. He goes on to assert, though, that the test is adopted in Art 8(2)(f) of the ICC Statute. In fact, that provision talks of 'protracted armed conflict', not 'protracted armed violence', which is a different and higher threshold than the one relating to the war crimes resulting from serious violations of Common Article 3 (as covered by Art 8(2)(d) of the Statute). This issue is discussed further in section III.B.ii.

[197] Schmitt (ed) (n 32), Commentary on Rule 23, para 6.

group(s) – the intensity of the violence and its protracted nature – asserting that 'Violence that is protracted but not intense, or intense but not protracted, does not amount to a NIAC.'[198]

In so doing, he cites the decision of ICC Pre-Trial Chamber II in the *Gombo* case as evidence.[199] Indeed, the Chamber does refer to the duration of armed violence as a relevant criterion. But it does so not in relation to the definition *simpliciter* of a NIAC,[200] but in relation to the requirement set out in Article 8(2)(f) of the ICC Statute that the type of NIAC for which the Court will have jurisdiction over certain serious violations of Hague Law rules must itself be 'protracted'. No such requirement is set out with respect to serious violations of Common Article 3, potentially punishable under Article 8(2)(d) of the ICC Statute. Thus, the Chamber affirms:

> The Chamber is also mindful that the wording of article 8(2)(f) of the Statute differs from that of article 8(2)(d) of the Statute, which requires the existence of a 'protracted armed conflict' and thus may be seen to require a higher or additional threshold to be met – a necessity which is not set out in article 8(2)(d) of the Statute. The argument can be raised as to whether this requirement may nevertheless be applied also in the context of article 8(2)(d) of the Statute. However, irrespective of such a possible interpretative approach, the Chamber does not deem it necessary to address this argument, as the period in question covers approximately five months and is therefore to be regarded as 'protracted' in any event.[201]

Why should there be, in the ICC Statute, a higher threshold for individual criminal responsibility for war crimes committed in the conduct of hostilities than for the application of Geneva law? One explanation may be found in the widespread reluctance of states to see their military personnel or ordinary citizens liable to prosecution for offences committed 'in the heat of battle'. This was already evident in the high threshold set for the application of the 1977 Additional Protocol II, which is only legally binding in cases where a NIAC takes place in the territory of a state party

> between its armed forces and dissident armed forces or other organized armed groups which, under responsible command, exercise such control over a part of its territory as to enable them to carry out sustained and concerted military operations and to implement this Protocol.[202]

While not all of these cumulative criteria are picked up in the ICC Statute, the reference to 'protracted armed conflict' there should be taken to refer to its duration. In the trial judgment in the *Gombo* case, rendered in March 2016, the ICC considered that 'the intensity and "protracted armed conflict" criteria' do not require the violence 'to be continuous and uninterrupted'. Rather, 'as set out in the first sentence common' to Article 8(2)(d) and (f), the 'essential criterion is that it go beyond "isolated or sporadic acts of violence"'.[203] In adducing

[198] Y Dinstein, *Non-International Armed Conflict in International Law*, 1st edn (Cambridge, Cambridge University Press, 2014) 35.

[199] ICC, *Prosecutor v Jean-Pierre Bemba Gombo*, Decision on the Charges (Pre-Trial Chamber II) (Case No ICC-01/05-01/08), 15 June 2009. As already noted, of the state practice cited, only Germany seems to hold the same view.

[200] A phrase coined by Sivakumaran to mean a NIAC governed by the threshold for application of Common Article 3.

[201] *Gombo* (n 199) para 235.

[202] Art 1(1), 1977 Additional Protocol II.

[203] ICC, *Prosecutor v Jean-Pierre Bemba Gombo*, Judgment (Trial Chamber III) (Case No ICC-01/05-01/08), 21 March 2016, para 140.

support for its position, the Trial Chamber explicitly referred to the *travaux préparatoires* of Article 8(2)(f), noting that, at the 1998 Rome Diplomatic Conference,

> the Bureau's initial proposal for the content of Article 8(2)(f) was taken from Article 1(1) of Additional Protocol II, which referred to 'sustained and concerted military operations'. Several delegates were concerned that the use of this provision would set too high a threshold for armed conflicts not of an international character. In the amended text, in addition to other changes, 'sustained and concerted military operations' was replaced by the phrase that now constitutes part of Article 8(2)(f), 'protracted armed conflict'.[204]

Although the Trial Chamber's explanation of the criterion under Article 8(2)(f) of 'protracted armed conflict' cannot be considered a gem of flawless clarity, at least two main explanations for the use of the wording may exist. The first, ostensibly supported by a majority of commentators, is that it adds nothing substantive to the threshold set out in Article 8(2)(b) of the Statute. Akande, for instance, suggests that the protracted nature of the conflict (meaning its duration) is nothing more than 'a factor to be assessed in determining intensity'.[205] This is not persuasive. The better view, albeit one that is supported by a minority of publicists,[206] is that prosecutions for serious violations of Hague Law rules committed during a NIAC are only possible in the ICC if they take place within an armed conflict that is ongoing for a prolonged period of time. While this threshold is not expressly quantified, the Pre-Trial Chamber in the *Gombo* case had observed 'that the period in question covers approximately five months and is therefore to be regarded as "protracted" in any event'.[207] This implies, correctly, that the threshold is considerably shorter than this.

Dinstein's position that violence does not amount to a NIAC where it is protracted but not intense, or intense but not protracted, is thus not correct in toto as a matter of law. His first assertion that violence that is protracted but not intense is not a NIAC is true, since it is generally uncontested that isolated and sporadic acts of violence do not constitute an armed conflict. But violence that is intense but not protracted may still amount to a NIAC. Multiple instances of combat over the course of several days may thus be sufficient to ground the existence of such a conflict. Imagine a small, land-locked country ruled by a weak, oppressive government. A group of citizens band together in a military structure with ranks and uniforms, arm and equip themselves, and prepare an all-out assault on the main army and air force bases. There is bitter fighting for many hours on each occasion, with a high number of casualties on each side, but the 'freedom fighters' are successful, effectively destroying the state armed forces and taking the capital in a matter of only a few days. In Dinstein's view, it would appear, this would not be an armed conflict, even though it otherwise appears to fulfil all of the conditions and more under international law to be a NIAC.[208]

[204] Ibid, para 140, fn 318.

[205] Akande (n 88) 56. See similarly T Meron, 'The Humanization of Humanitarian Law' (2000) 94 *AJIL* 260; M Bothe, 'War Crimes' in A Cassese et al (eds), *The Rome Statute of the International Criminal Court: A Commentary* (Oxford, Oxford University Press, 2002) 423; A Cullen, 'The Definition of Non-international Armed Conflict in the Rome Statute of the International Criminal Court: An Analysis of the Threshold of Application Contained in Article 8(2)(f)' (2007) 12(3) *Journal of Conflict and Security Law* 445.

[206] See Vité (n 3) 82 (and the sources he cites).

[207] *Gombo* (n 199) para 235.

[208] But compare the *Abella* case, discussed in section III.B.iii, which fails to meet the threshold.

In sum, therefore, the two primary criteria to determine whether or not a NIAC exists are the intensity of the combat between state armed forces and a non-state armed group (or between two or more non-state armed groups) and the level of organisation of the armed group or groups engaged in the fighting. These criteria are now discussed in more detail.

iii. *Intense Armed Violence*

The intensity of the fighting is the first criterion to assess in any situation of armed violence. As we have seen, it is generally agreed that situations of internal disturbances and tensions, such as riots, isolated and sporadic acts of violence, and other acts of a similar nature, are not armed conflicts. In its commentary on this provision of the 1977 Additional Protocol II, the ICRC stated:

> The concept of internal disturbances and tensions may be illustrated by giving a list of examples of such situations without any attempt to be exhaustive: riots, such as demonstrations without a concerted plan from the outset; isolated and sporadic acts of violence, as opposed to military operations carried out by armed forces or armed groups; other acts of a similar nature, including, in particular, large scale arrests of people for their activities or opinions.[209]

Further, as a matter of law, it would appear that violence must be more intense than is the case with banditry or sporadic terrorist activities, and even an unorganised and short-lived insurrection, since these are also not armed conflicts. This phrasing, which, as noted above, originated in Pictet's 1952 commentary on 1949 Geneva Convention I, was picked up and endorsed by the ICTY in the *Tadić* trial judgment.[210] This sets quite a high threshold.

For there to be a NIAC, the violence does not need to be widespread across a country, nor does it need to continue for many weeks (much less months), though should these occur in any given scenario they may constitute evidence of both intensity and in all likelihood also organisation.[211] In cases before the ICTY, the Tribunal has tended to consider especially the number and severity of clashes in deciding whether armed violence is sufficiently intense for an armed conflict to exist. In its judgment at trial in the *Mrkšić* case, an ICTY Trial Chamber referred to 'the seriousness of attacks and potential increase in armed clashes, their spread over territory and over a period of time'.[212] In its judgment in the *Haradinaj* case, the ICTY stated that indicative factors for an armed conflict include 'the number, duration and intensity of individual confrontations'.[213] This notion of combat – direct conflict between two opposing armed groups – is particularly important, helping to distinguish a situation of armed conflict from terrorist and counterterrorism activities.[214]

[209] ICRC commentary on Art 1(2), 1977 Additional Protocol II, in Y Sandoz, C Swinarski and B Zimmermann (eds), *Commentary on the Additional Protocols of 8 June 1977 to the Geneva Conventions of 12 August 1949* (Geneva, Martinus Nijhoff, 1987) para 4474.

[210] *Tadić* (n 77) para 562.

[211] At the same time, of course, a late-night mass brawl at a pub or an afternoon fight at a football match between rival groups of supporters, however vicious it may be, is not even close to reaching the threshold for the existence of an armed conflict.

[212] See, eg, ICTY, *Prosecutor v Mile Mrkšić, Miroslav Radić, and Veselin Šljivančin*, Judgment (Trial Chamber II) (Case No IT-95-13/1-T), 27 September 2007, para 407, and sources cited in fn 1592.

[213] ICTY, *Prosecutor v Haradinaj*, Judgment (Trial Chamber) (Case No IT-04-84-T), 3 April 2008, para 49.

[214] *The War Report* argued that the requirement that there be actual combat was a third criterion for a NIAC to exist. Here it is subsumed into the criterion of intensity, as per the approach of the ICTY. See Casey-Maslen (ed) (n 61) 19.

In the *Limaj* case, the ICTY Trial Chamber, in finding that an armed conflict existed in Kosovo before the end of May 1998 between the Kosovo Liberation Army (KLA) and the Serb forces, observed that

> by the end of May 1998 KLA units were constantly engaged in armed clashes with substantial Serbian forces in areas from the Kosovo–Albanian border in the west, to near Prishtina/Pristina in the east, to Prizren and the Kosovo–Macedonian border in the south and the municipality of Mitrovice/Kosovka Mitrovica in the north.[215]

Other indicative factors of sufficient intensity include 'the type of weapons and other military equipment used; the number and calibre of munitions fired; the number of persons and type of forces partaking in the fighting; the number of casualties; the extent of material destruction; and the number of civilians fleeing combat zones. The involvement of the UN Security Council may also be a reflection of the intensity of a conflict.'[216] In its *Lubanga* trial judgment, the ICC endorsed the approach of the ICTY in determining intensity.[217]

In contrast, in the *Abella* case, the Inter-American Commission on Human Rights (in) famously held that an attack on 23 January 1989 by 42 armed persons on the barracks of an Argentinian infantry regiment at La Tablada in Buenos Aires province, which saw combat between the attackers and Argentine military personnel last for 30 hours, amounted to an armed conflict.[218] Its judgment, which intervened after both the *Tadić* decision on jurisdiction and subsequent trial judgment, but surprisingly did not quote from either, is flawed. It cited the fact that Common Article 3-type conflicts do not extend to 'unorganized and short-lived rebellions', but emphasised its view that since the attack was planned it must be organised and therefore this exclusion did not apply.[219] With all due respect to the Inter-American Commission, the two are not synonyms. Further, its characterisation of the situation as more than 'large-scale violent demonstrations, students throwing stones at the police, bandits holding persons hostage for ransom, or the assassination of government officials for political reasons' simply sets the threshold of intensity far too low. This was an isolated act of admittedly serious violence, but not one that forms part of an armed conflict.

iv. 'Organised' Armed Groups

Organised armed groups are those imbued with a military-style command-and-control structure, where their members typically possess and use effectively a variety of weapons, and which control a significant logistical capacity that gives them the capability to sustain military operations. When an organised armed group is engaged in intense armed confrontations with state armed forces or another organised armed group, such an armed group is

[215] ICTY, *Prosecutor v Limaj, Bala, and Musliu*, Judgment (Trial Chamber) 30 November 2005, para 172 (note omitted).

[216] *Haradinaj* (n 213) para 49. See also the long (and less helpful) listing of factors that were taken into account by an ICTY Trial Chamber in *Prosecutor v Boškoski and Tarčulovski*, Judgment (Trial Chamber II) (Case No IT-04-82-T), 10 July 2008, para 177.

[217] *Lubanga* (n 132) para 538.

[218] Inter-American Commission on Human Rights, *Juan Carlos Abella v Argentina*, Judgment (Case No 11.137), 18 November 1997, paras 1, 146–56.

[219] Ibid, paras 152, 155.

'party' to a NIAC. But, as the ICTY noted in the retrial of Ramush Haradinaj and others, although 'an armed group must have "some degree of organisation", the warring parties do not necessarily need to be as organised as the armed forces of a State'.[220]

In *Boškoski*, an ICTY Trial Chamber summarised in five categories the factors that the ICTY had assessed in its jurisprudence in determining whether or not any given armed group was sufficiently organised. These were: command structure; the ability to carry out operations in an organised manner; the level of logistics; the level of intra group discipline; and (more debatably) whether the armed group was able to 'speak with one voice'.[221] While the categories are somewhat overlapping, they are valuable headings under which to assess the level of organisation of a group. Of course, an armed group does not need to be successful in its overall aims in order to be party to an armed conflict.

a. Command Structure

A command structure is evidenced by, for example, the existence of a command headquarters and the establishment of a general staff or high command that appoints and gives directions to commanders and authorises (or blocks) military action. Also relevant is the issuing of internal regulations, which may, for example, establish ranks of soldiers and define duties of commanders and deputy commanders of a unit, company, platoon or squad, and/or create a chain of military hierarchy between the various levels of commanders.[222]

b. Organised Operations

The ICTY has held that relevant indicators are also an armed group's ability to determine a unified military strategy and/or to conduct large-scale military operations, its capacity to control territory, the capacity of operational units to coordinate their actions, and the effective dissemination of written and oral orders and decisions.[223] This combines elements of a devolved command structure at field level, as well as an ability to coordinate between different units of an armed group.

c. Logistics

The ability to put military plans and instructions into effect is dependent on a control of logistics. Logistics is 'a relatively new word used to describe a very old practice: the supply, movement, and maintenance of an armed force both in peacetime and under operational conditions'.[224] The importance of logistics should never be underestimated. In a contribution to the weblog of the S Rajaratnam School of International Studies in Singapore, it was

[220] ICTY, *Prosecutor v Ramush Haradinaj, Idriz Balaj, and Lahi Brahimaj*, Judgment (Trial Chamber II) (Case No IT-04-84*bis*-T), 29 November 2012, para 393.

[221] ICTY, *Boškoski and Tarčulovski* (n 216), paras 199–203.

[222] Ibid, para 199.

[223] Ibid, para 200.

[224] 'Military Logistics: A Brief History', *History of War*, at https://goo.gl/bVrV4r.

noted that in any military campaign or operation you need to 'get your logistics sorted out, or get ready to be defeated'.[225] Or, as Sun Tzu put it succinctly in his fifth-century BCE masterpiece, *Art of War*, 'The line between disorder and order lies in logistics'. Thus, the ICTY has appropriately noted the relevance of assessing the ability to recruit new members to the armed group, the provision of military training, the organised supply of military weapons, the supply and use of uniforms, and the existence of communications equipment for linking headquarters with units or between units.[226]

d. The Level of Discipline

With respect to discipline, factors to be considered are the ability to implement the basic obligations of Common Article 3 or the rule of distinction, including when a person is *hors de combat*, as well as the establishment of disciplinary rules and mechanisms, proper training and whether internal regulations are effectively disseminated to fighters.[227] In the 1977 Additional Protocol II, the conditions for the scope of application a little strangely talk of organised armed groups that exercise such control of territory 'as to enable them' to implement the Protocol.[228] This could be inferred as meaning that the ability to respect and ensure respect for the law of armed conflict is dependent on territory. This is not the case, either factually, or at law.

e. Unified Political Structure

A unity of structure as a relevant factor addresses itself less to the military wing of an armed group and more its political side (should one exist). Thus, the ICTY noted the relevance of the capacity of the group to act on behalf of its members in political negotiations with representatives of international organisations and foreign countries. More controversially, it refers also to the ability of the group to negotiate and conclude agreements such as a ceasefire or peace accord. In fact, while this category may have some relevance, the successful negotiation of ceasefires points more to the existence of an armed conflict on the basis of a sufficient level of intensity. Indeed, the sources that the Trial Chamber cites in support do not discuss ceasefires as constituent of the element of organisation. In the *Hadžihasanović* judgment, for example, it is noted that

> cease-fire orders issued by the general staffs of both armies and the political leaders representing the two parties to the conflict imply that there was an armed conflict between the two armies on the date of the agreements. … The fact that representatives from international organisations were there attempting to broker and enforce cease-fire agreements is additional evidence making it possible to infer that there was in fact an armed conflict in the municipalities and during the period referred to in the Indictment.[229]

[225] BFW Loo, 'The importance of logistics', weblog, S Rajaratnam School of International Studies, Singapore, 9 February 2012, at https://goo.gl/79wHFt.

[226] *Boškoski and Tarčulovski* (n 216) para 201.

[227] Ibid, para 202.

[228] Art 1(1), 1977 Additional Protocol II.

[229] ICTY, *Prosecutor v Enver Hadžihasanović and Amir Kubura*, Judgment (Trial Chamber) (Case No IT-01-47-T), 15 March 2006, para 23.

f. Designation of the Groups as Terrorist

Armed groups are sometimes termed rebels, insurgents, terrorists, criminal gangs or anti-government elements by states or other entities; such designations have no consequence for the determination of their status under international law with respect to an armed conflict. Thus, even though the KLA was condemned by Serbia and even members of the Clinton administration as 'terrorist',[230] this did not preclude it from being party to the armed conflict in Kosovo. The same applied to the (Macedonian) National Liberation Army operating in the former Yugoslav Republic of Macedonia.[231] Similarly, in 2006 the relevant UN Commission of Inquiry determined that there was an armed conflict between Hezbollah and Israel, regardless of Israel's characterisation of Hezbollah as a terrorist organisation.[232]

It is also not necessary that an armed group have a particular political or religious agenda for it to be party to a NIAC; in 2005 in the *Limaj* case, an ICTY Trial Chamber reiterated the *Tadić* criteria, recalling that the 'determination of the existence of an armed conflict is based solely on two criteria: the intensity of the conflict and organisation of the parties', and noting that 'the purpose of the armed forces to engage in acts of violence or also achieve some further objective is, therefore, irrelevant'.[233] In his thoughtful article in the *International Review of the Red Cross* on the qualification of armed conflict, Sylvain Vité, citing the *Limaj* judgment, wrote as follows:

> Some observers add a further condition to the notion of non-international armed conflict. They suggest that account needs to be taken of the motives of the non-governmental groups involved. This type of conflict would thus cover only groups endeavouring to achieve a political objective. 'Purely criminal' organizations such as mafia groups or territorial gangs would thus be eliminated from that category and could in no way then be considered as parties to a non-international armed conflict. … However, in the current state of humanitarian law, this additional condition has no legal basis.[234]

Accordingly, an organised armed group whose aim is purely or primarily lucrative, such as a drugs cartel or an organised crime network, can be a party to an armed conflict, as long as the combat with the authorities or another organised armed group is sufficiently intense. Thus, for example, in its analysis of armed conflicts existing in 2017, the Geneva Academy asserted that 'Mexico's security forces were arguably engaged in non-international armed conflicts with at least the Sinaloa Cartel and the Jalisco Cartel New Generation.'[235] It summarises the rationale for this classification as follows:

> [T]he violence related to organized crime in Mexico can be characterized as: violent battles between heavily armed and increasingly fragmented criminal groups fighting over control of

[230] See, eg, N Sebak, 'The KLA – terrorists or freedom fighters?', *BBC* (28 June 1998) at https://goo.gl/osB3z7; and G Sulyok, 'Terrorism or National Liberation: Remarks on the Activities of the Kosovo Liberation Army During the Kosovo Crisis' at https://goo.gl/Ro7urG.

[231] N Wood, 'Macedonia's "mujahideen" – immigrants or terrorists?', *BBC* (20 March 2002) at https://goo.gl/ycCb95.

[232] Report of the Commission of Inquiry on Lebanon, pursuant to Human Rights Council Resolution S-2/1, UN Doc A/HRC/3/2, 23 November 2006, para 62.

[233] See, eg, ICTY, *Prosecutor v Fatmir Limaj, Haradin Bala, and Isak Musliu*, Judgment (Trial Chamber II) (Case No IT-03-66-T), 30 November 2005, para 170.

[234] Vité (n 3) 78.

[235] J Lambin, 'Mexico: Armed Gang violence Sliding Into Armed Conflict?' in A Bellal (ed), *The War Report* (Geneva, Geneva Academy of International Humanitarian Law and Human Rights, 2018) 83, at https://goo.gl/3cpPkz.

> lucrative business opportunities from diverse criminal activities; violent confrontations between criminal groups and the state armed forces, involving heavy weaponry on both sides; a major impact on the civilian population as 'collateral damage' of both the clashes between criminal groups and the state's response to organized crime.[236]

It further states, though, that it 'is important to note that this classification is controversial'.[237]

v. Acts Excluded from Amounting to a Non-International Armed Conflict

While the labelling of an armed group or its activities as 'terrorist' has no legal effect in the determination of a NIAC, the extent to which acts of terrorism amount to, and fall within, an armed conflict may be debated. As noted, the Pictet Commentary[238] and the *Tadić* judgment[239] both excluded 'terrorist activities' from a NIAC. Further, NIACs to which Common Article 3 was to apply were 'conflicts which are in many respects similar to an international war, but take place within the confines of a single country', that is, where 'armed forces' on either side are engaged in 'hostilities'.[240] This implies, correctly, that even widespread placing of bombs, without any element of the combat between competing forces or groups that is integral to the notion of intensity, is insufficient to ground claims for the existence of a NIAC.

Thus, the rather careless dictum of the ICTY Appeals Chamber in the *Kordić* case, whereby the 'requirement of *protracted* fighting is significant in excluding mere cases of civil unrest or single acts of terrorism', should not be taken to lower the threshold for armed conflict.[241] In the *Boškoski* trial, judged four years later, an ICTY Trial Chamber affirmed that

> what matters is whether the acts are perpetrated in isolation or as part of a protracted campaign that entails the engagement of both parties in hostilities. It is immaterial whether the acts of violence perpetrated may or may not be characterised as terrorist in nature.[242]

It affirmed, somewhat implausibly, that its interpretation was 'consistent' with the Appeals Chamber's observation in *Kordić*.[243]

If by 'engagement of both parties in hostilities' the Chamber means combat against each other in addition to attacks against civilians or in indiscriminate attacks, it is correct. If it means only distinct acts of violence by both the state armed forces and an armed group, this is wrong. It is inherent in the notion of armed conflict that two parties conflict – with each other. That they also engage in other forms of unlawful violence not directed at a lawful military objective is of course relevant. But if all that transpires is the emplacement of improvised explosive devices (IEDs) by one element (ie the armed group) and the dropping

[236] Ibid, 86.
[237] Ibid, 83.
[238] Pictet Commentary on GC I (n 15) 50.
[239] *Tadić* (n 77) para 562.
[240] Pictet Commentary on GC II (n 19) 33, cited with approval in *Boškoski and Tarčulovski* (n 216) para 185.
[241] ICTY, *Prosecutor v Dario Kordić and Mario Čerkez*, Judgment (Appeals Chamber) (Case No IT-95-14/2-A), 17 December 2004, para 341.
[242] *Boškoski and Tarčulovski* (n 216) para 185.
[243] Ibid.

of aerial bombs by the other (ie the state), this is not an armed conflict. In such a scenario, the armed group will be violating domestic law, while the state is likely to be violating international human rights law. After all, as the Trial Chamber affirmed in *Haradinaj*, 'an armed conflict can exist only between parties that are sufficiently organized *to confront each other with military means*'.[244]

In a similar vein, upon its ratification of the 1977 Additional Protocol I, the UK entered a declaration whereby 'the term "armed conflict" of itself and in its context denotes a situation of a kind which is not constituted by the commission of ordinary crimes including acts of terrorism whether concerted or in isolation'.[245] In citing this declaration, the US Department of Defense, however, claims that 'States are not required to apply law of war rules when using domestic law enforcement tools to respond to ordinary crimes, including acts of terrorism'.[246]

This is poorly formulated. States are in fact prohibited from applying Hague Law rules on the conduct of hostilities when a situation is not an armed conflict. Stricter law of law enforcement rules (see chapter 3) govern the state's use of force in such a scenario.

In contrast, that acts of terror may be committed during the course of an armed conflict is not to be doubted. As the Trial Chamber noted in *Boškoski*, 'It would be nonsensical that international humanitarian law would prohibit such acts if these were not considered to fall within the rubric of armed conflict.'[247] Thus Article 4(2)(d) of the 1977 Additional Protocol II, for example, explicitly prohibits 'acts of terrorism'. Similarly, Article 13(2) of the same instrument prohibits '[a]cts or threats of violence the primary purpose of which is to spread terror among the civilian population'. Indeed, as Sandra Krähenmann has noted, the practice of both the ICTY[248] and the Special Court for Sierra Leone (SCSL) reveals that such acts of terror may be prosecuted as war crimes.[249] The inter-relationship between counterterrorism and the law of armed conflict is further explored in chapter 14.

C. The Geographical Scope of Non-International Armed Conflict

Also highly controversial is the geographical scope of NIAC. Whereas military operations in an IAC may be regulated by Hague Law wherever in the world they are conducted

[244] ICTY, *Prosecutor v Ramush Haradinaj, Idriz Balaj, and Lahi Brahimaj*, Judgment (Trial Chamber) (Case No IT-04-84-T), 3 April 2008, para 60 (emphasis added); cited with approval in *Boškoski and Tarčulovski* (n 216) para 198.

[245] Declaration of 28 January 1998, at https://goo.gl/kCB5L9; see Sivakumaran (n 156) 233. Sivakumaran refers to the 'understanding' of the UK as a 'reservation', but it is more accurately termed a 'declaration' because it does not seek to modify the terms of the Protocol with respect to the UK but rather to set out the UK's understanding of the term that is consonant with the state of the law. See also, eg, ICTY, *Prosecutor v Slobodan Milošević*, Decision on Motion for Judgment of Acquittal (Rule 98*bis* Decision) (Trial Chamber) (Case No IT-02-54-T), 16 June 2004, para 26. See also UK Ministry of Defence (n 2) para 5.21.1.

[246] USDOD December 2016 *Law of War Manual* (n 2), para 3.4.2.3.

[247] *Boškoski and Tarčulovski* (n 216) para 187. The Trial Chamber asserts that 'terrorist acts may be constitutive of protracted violence'; again, this must be against the backdrop of actual combat. Ibid, para 187; but see also paras 188–90 for a rather questionable assessment of national practice in this area.

[248] This includes the *Tadić* case itself (see, eg, para 575 of the Trial Judgment).

[249] S Krähenmann, 'Foreign Fighters under International Law', Academy Briefing No 7, Geneva Academy of International Humanitarian Law and Human Rights, October 2014, 24. Krähenmann further notes that the Statute of the International Criminal Tribunal for Rwanda (ICTR) also included acts of terrorism as a war crime, but that – perhaps surprisingly – no charges were brought under this heading.

(or, indeed, outside it, for instance in outer space), the geographical scope of a NIAC is far more limited. This is also reflected in the higher threshold imposed by states for its application, both in terms of intensity of armed violence and in relation to the organisational level of an armed group. That a state's armed forces are sufficiently organised is assumed, and, as described in section III.B.ii, the level of violence needed to trigger an IAC is far lower than it is for a NIAC.

The basic rule for application of Hague Law rules is simple and clear. In each state, a NIAC exists where there is intense armed combat between one or more states and an organised armed group, or between two organised armed groups. Thus, it is the fighting that leads to the existence of an armed conflict and the application of the law of armed conflict to that fighting: the conduct of hostilities.

The text of Common Article 3 refers to armed conflict not of an international character 'occurring in the territory of one of the High Contracting Parties'. This implies that such an armed conflict is territorially limited to a single state party to the 1949 Geneva Conventions, a fact supported by reference to the *travaux préparatoires*. In its proposals for the diplomatic conference, the ICRC had proposed a provision to the Twenty-Seventh International Red Cross Conference at Stockholm that included the phrase:

> In all cases of armed conflict which are not of an international character, especially cases of civil war, colonial conflicts, or wars of religion, which may occur in the territory of one *or more* of the High Contracting Parties ...[250]

The proposed words 'or more' were not incorporated in Common Article 3 by negotiating states at Geneva, which indicates a desire to limit the geographical scope of application of the provision.[251]

Common Article 3 stipulates that once a NIAC is occurring, 'the following acts are and shall remain prohibited at any time and in any place whatsoever'.[252] In the *Tadić* case, the ICTY Appeals Chamber declared that once a NIAC exists, 'international humanitarian law' applies to 'the whole territory under the control of a party, whether or not actual combat takes place there'.[253] As Schmitt notes, this (rather ham-fisted) formulation should in fact be taken to mean all sovereign territory belonging to the state on whose territory a NIAC exists.[254] In case of organised non-state armed groups fighting each other, the law of armed conflict similarly applies to the territory of each state in which intense combat is occurring. This is correct, insofar as the applicable law is *Geneva* Law. As discussed in chapter 3, though, Hague Law applies only to conduct in areas where hostilities are occurring. Indeed, Mr Tadić was accused of war crimes against detainees in a prison camp and of murder and other serious crimes against civilians amounting to serious violations of customary international law. These crimes comprised serious violations of Common Article 3 and

[250] Pictet Commentary on GC I (n 15) 42.

[251] In contrast, the ICRC affirms that, 'For unspecified reasons, the additional phrase "or more" was not adopted by the 1949 Diplomatic Conference' and determines, surprisingly, that 'no conclusion can be drawn from its absence for the interpretation of common Article 3'. ICRC commentary on 1949 Geneva Convention I (n 16) para 469.

[252] Ibid, para 457.

[253] *Tadić* (n 3) para 70.

[254] Schmitt (n 143) 10.

grave breaches of the 1949 Geneva Conventions (ie Geneva Law), as well as crimes against humanity which were similarly committed during armed conflict.

The situation with so-called 'cross-border' or 'spillover' conflicts is also debated. According to the ICRC, 'The object and purpose of common Article 3 supports its applicability in non-international armed conflict reaching beyond the territory of one State.'[255] This is not persuasive. Once armed violence occurs on the territory of any state, the fundamental conditions set for a NIAC apply: intense armed combat involving at least one organised armed group. As the ICRC acknowledges, if the NIAC does extend over the border, the issue of geographical applicability of the law of armed conflict within the foreign state again arises. Here, in seeming defiance of its own general stance, the ICRC asserts that 'As long as the State into whose territory the conflict has spilled does not become a Party to the conflict, there is reason to doubt that it applies throughout its whole territory.'[256]

Further, when coalitions of states support a state engaged in a NIAC on its own territory,

> questions have arisen in respect to whether international law [*sic*] also applies on the 'home' territory of States party to such conflicts. ... At the time of writing, there is insufficient identifiable State practice on its applicability in the territory of the home State.[257]

This is a rather surprising statement given that a senior ICRC legal advisor had previously argued publicly that law of armed conflict rules apply to all of the territory of every state that is party to a NIAC.[258] Schmitt similarly contends that the support of foreign states in one state's fight against an organised armed group potentially brings the conflict to their doorstep.[259] As he acknowledges, however, this 'fact' would have 'enormous implications in light of, for instance, international support of Afghanistan in its NIAC with the Taliban and associated armed groups'.[260] Although many states have pulled out of Afghanistan, at one stage members of some 50 states' armed forces were present in Afghanistan, including Canada, France, Denmark, Germany, Norway, the UK and the US.

This would equally well apply to the situation in Syria, where a series of armed conflicts were raging as of 2017. In Syria, the armed forces of Australia, Bahrain, Belgium, Canada, France, Germany, Iran, Jordan, the Netherlands, Qatar, Russia, Saudi Arabia, Turkey, the UK, the United Arab Emirates and the US (amongst others) have all been involved at some time and to some degree.[261] If the logic of applying law of armed conflict rules to the territory of any state party to an armed conflict in Syria were sound, this could mean that a single terrorist attack anywhere on the territory of such by a 'soldier' of Islamic State fell

[255] ICRC commentary on 1949 Geneva Convention I (n 16) para 467.

[256] Ibid, para 476.

[257] Ibid, para 473. Presumably, the ICRC meant to say 'international *humanitarian* law', as international law, including *jus ad bellum* and international human rights law, would, of course, be applicable.

[258] J Pejic, 'IHL's applicability to extra territorial drone strikes' in Panel Discussion – Scope of the law in armed conflict, Humanitarium, Geneva, 19 February 2015, at https://goo.gl/nV9pHp; see also J. Pejic, 'Extraterritorial targeting by means of armed drones: Some legal implications', *International Review of the Red Cross*, vol 96, no 893 (2014) 67, 102.

[259] Schmitt (n 143) 10. Indeed he claims, though without supporting evidence, that it is 'well-settled that IHL applies throughout the territory of parties to a NIAC irrespective of where the hostilities are underway (or likely to occur).' Ibid, 15.

[260] Ibid, 11.

[261] Iran and Russia are supporting the Government of Syria in their NIACs against a range of non-state armed groups, while Operation Inherent Resolve is the US operational name for the military intervention against Islamic State in both Iraq and Syria.

to be fought and governed by the rules governing hostilities. This is politically unpalatable but, more significantly, it is legally unsound.

Schmitt advocates that activities of organised armed groups operating across several countries should be 'combined to satisfy the intensity criterion' when such groups 'can reasonably be characterised as a single coherent organization operating collaboratively'.[262] This amounts to a globalised NIAC potentially without limit and without the need for combat given that these groups tend to engage in suicide or remotely controlled bombings. He rejects, though, the politically charged language on the Global War on Terror, a US construct that implied the ability to kill a 'terrorist' anywhere at any time but seemingly without any accompanying liability or criminal responsibility.[263] As the ICRC observes,

> the practice of States party to the Geneva Conventions in support of a global or transnational non-international armed conflicts remains isolated. … The ICRC has thus expressed the view that the existence of an armed conflict or the relationship of a particular military operation to an existing armed conflict has to be assessed on a case-by-case basis.[264]

D. The Temporal Scope of Non-International Armed Conflict

As the ICRC has stated,

> as with the initial existence of a non-international armed conflict, its end must be neither lightly asserted nor denied: just as humanitarian law is not to be applied to a situation of violence that has not crossed the threshold of a non-international armed conflict, it must also not be applied to situations that no longer constitute a non-international armed conflict.[265]

In the 1995 *Tadić* decision on jurisdiction, the ICTY Appeals Chamber had held that the law of armed conflict applies in a non-international armed conflict 'until a peaceful settlement is achieved'.[266] This is widely disregarded today. In the ICRC's view, which it proffers while paying lip service to support for the position of the Appeals Chamber,

> armed confrontations may also dissipate without any ceasefire, armistice or peace agreement ever being concluded, or before the conclusion of such an agreement. Thus, while the existence of such agreements may be taken into account when assessing all of the facts, they are neither necessary nor sufficient on their own to bring about the termination of the application of humanitarian law.[267]

The more widely held (and better) view is that Hague Law rules apply only when, and only for as long as, the twin criteria exist in relation to a situation and the concerned parties. 'What would matter', as Marko Milanovic contends, 'is whether the intensity of the hostilities or the organization of the non-State actor factually eroded to such an extent that the threshold is no longer met.'[268] Accordingly, once either of the two criteria is no longer

[262] Schmitt (n 143) 13.
[263] Ibid.
[264] ICRC commentary on 1949 Geneva Convention I (n 16) para 482; and see also paras 479–81.
[265] Ibid, para 485.
[266] *Tadić* (n 3) para 70.
[267] ICRC commentary on 1949 Geneva Convention I (n 16) para 490.
[268] M Milanovic, 'End of application of international humanitarian law', *International Review of the Red Cross*, vol 96, no 893 (March 2014) 163, 180.

met, whether because the violence is no longer intense (for a sustained period), or because the armed group can no longer be considered sufficiently organised,[269] a NIAC no longer exists. For the state, an end to a NIAC means its armed and other security forces must once more comply with the stricter rules of the law of law enforcement in their operations against the remnants of an armed group. For the armed group, this means domestic law continues to be applicable, but its actions may now be regulated by customary or at least peremptory international human rights law, without reference to law of armed conflict rules.

Of course, armed conflict ebbs and flows in its intensity. A temporary lull in hostilities is not an end to a NIAC. According to the ICRC:

> It is impossible to state in the abstract how much time without armed confrontations needs to pass to be able conclude with an acceptable degree of certainty that the situation has stabilized and equates to a peaceful settlement.[270]

Milanovic talks of 'a certain degree of permanence and stability so as to enable us to establish that the hostilities have, in fact, ended'.[271] This determination may also depend on factors such as the climate in a country. In Afghanistan, for example, the Quetta Shura Taliban have often significantly reduced combat during the winter, but only as a prelude to a spring offensive. Thus, in March 2016 an article in *Stars and Stripes* magazine affirmed:

> The fighting season traditionally begins in spring shortly after the start of the Persian New Year, or Nowruz. This past year, however, fighting barely abated during the normally quieter winter, leading some observers to forecast more intensive attacks by the insurgents in 2016. The capability of Afghan forces has already been severely challenged in some parts of the country where the Taliban have launched repeated, aggressive attacks.[272]

On 12 April 2016, the Taliban announced the start of its spring offensive in Afghanistan, affirming in an online statement that it would intensify its offensive on international forces and government officials in the country.[273]

In sum, whether a NIAC has ended is context specific and must be determined on a case-by-case basis, but in accordance with the twin criteria required for its establishment. When either criterion is no longer fulfilled, the conflict is over, at least as a matter of international law.

IV. Armed Conflicts Co-existing over the Same Territory

Different armed conflicts may co-exist over the same territory at the same time. This is generally, though not universally, accepted. In fact, the same hostile act may form part of an

[269] This may be, for example, because it has fragmented, has been defeated militarily, or has been victorious and becomes the, or part of the, government.

[270] ICRC commentary on 1949 Geneva Convention I (n 16) para 492.

[271] Milanovic (n 268) 180.

[272] PW Wellman, 'Afghanistan braces for season of Taliban attacks', *Stars and Stripes* (23 March 2016) at https://goo.gl/h1crxY. Similarly, it was asserted that 'Traditionally, fighting subsides in Afghanistan during winter because heavy snow blocks the movement of insurgents through mountain passes. But Afghan officials and military commanders said because of a mild winter there was no let-up in fighting in 2015.' 'Pashtun Taliban Insurgency – 2015', *Global Security*, at https://goo.gl/442Azf.

[273] 'Pashtun Taliban Insurgency – 2016', *Global Security*, at https://goo.gl/EgDWGh.

IAC and a separate NIAC. The logic of the IAC/NIAC distinction militates in favour of this understanding. Already in *Nicaragua v US*, the ICJ had accepted this possibility:

> The conflict between the contras' forces and those of the Government of Nicaragua is an armed conflict which is 'not of an international character'. The acts of the contras towards the Nicaraguan Government are therefore governed by the law applicable to conflicts of that character; whereas the actions of the United States in and against Nicaragua fall under the legal rules relating to international conflicts.[274]

The ICTY accepted the reality of parallel conflicts in its Appeal Chamber's decision on jurisdiction in the *Tadić* case, concluding that 'the conflicts in the former Yugoslavia have both internal and international aspects'.[275] This was confirmed in the judgment at trial, wherein the Trial Chamber held that both an IAC (between Bosnian government forces and Yugoslav armed forces) and a NIAC (between Bosnian government forces and Bosnian Serb armed groups) existed in Bosnia and Herzegovina.[276] Mr Tadić appealed against his conviction. In its judgment, the ICTY Appeals Chamber affirmed:

> It is indisputable that an armed conflict is international if it takes place between two or more States. In addition, in case of an internal armed conflict breaking out on the territory of a State, it may become international (or, depending upon the circumstances, be international in character alongside an internal armed conflict) if (i) another State intervenes in that conflict through its troops, or alternatively if (ii) some of the participants in the internal armed conflict act on behalf of that other State.[277]

In the *Lubanga* case, the ICC Trial Chamber endorsed the general view of the ICTY on mixed conflict, accepting 'that international and non-international conflicts may coexist'.[278] The ICRC similarly supports the existence of parallel armed conflicts under international humanitarian law.[279]

[274] *Nicaragua v US* (n 57) para 219.
[275] *Tadić* (n 3) para 77.
[276] *Tadić* (n 77) paras 568, 569.
[277] ICTY, *Prosecutor v Tadić*, Judgment (Appeals Chamber) (Case No IT-94-1-A), 15 July 1999, para 84.
[278] *Lubanga* (n 132) para 540.
[279] See, eg, ICRC commentary on 1949 Geneva Convention I (n 16) paras 261–62; ICRC, 'International Humanitarian Law and the challenges of contemporary armed conflicts', *Report for the 31st International Conference of the Red Cross and Red Crescent, 28 November–1 December 2011*, Geneva, October 2011, 9. See also S Vité, 'Co-existing international and non-international armed conflicts in one country', XXXVIII Round Table on Current Issues of International Humanitarian Law, San Remo, 3–5 September 2015, 2–3.

3

Identifying Situations of Hostilities

I. Introduction

As is the case with Geneva Law, Hague Law only applies during a situation of armed conflict and only regulates acts that are directly linked to an armed conflict. For, as the International Committee of the Red Cross (ICRC) has observed, the notion of hostilities

> is intrinsically linked to situations of international or non-international armed conflict. ... Therefore, the concept of direct participation in hostilities cannot refer to conduct occurring outside situations of armed conflict, such as during internal disturbances and tensions, including riots, isolated and sporadic acts of violence and other acts of a similar nature.[1]

But whereas Geneva Law seeks to ensure the humane treatment of those *hors de combat* or in the power of a party to an armed conflict (such as persons in detention or civilians in occupied territory), Hague Law attempts to minimise the suffering inflicted during or as a result of combat. The geographical scope of application of Hague Law is far narrower than is the case with Geneva Law.

A relevant act by a belligerent during an armed conflict falls to be judged by the rules of either Geneva Law or Hague Law. Indeed, in many instances it is perfectly clear which applies: Geneva Law to the conditions of detention and treatment of a prisoner; Hague Law to a pitched battle between the conflict parties, for example. But there are many circumstances in which it may be unclear which of the two legal regimes applies. In addition, the line between law enforcement and the conduct of hostilities during a situation of armed conflict is blurred to say the least, and the rules laid down by the two bodies of international law differ materially, especially with respect to how and when potentially or intentionally lethal force may be used. In general – though not in absolute terms – Hague Law rules are far less restrictive on a state that is party to an armed conflict than are the international legal rules laid down by the law of law enforcement.

Accordingly, this chapter describes what acts constitute hostilities for the purpose of Hague Law; where and for how long they may exist; and what distinguishes them from acts regulated by Geneva Law and the law of law enforcement. Section II defines hostilities, distinguishing them from attacks and from means and methods of warfare. Section III delineates the material scope of hostilities, identifying the elements that determine in any given scenario whether it is Geneva Law or Hague Law that applies, or whether it is Hague Law or the law of law enforcement. Section IV explains how the geographical

[1] ICRC, *Interpretive Guidance on Direct Participation in Hostilities under International Humanitarian Law* (Geneva, ICRC, 2009) (hereinafter 'ICRC DPH Guidance') 43.

scope of hostilities is generally unrestrained in international armed conflict (IAC) but very closely circumscribed in armed conflict not of an international character to areas of existing intense combat. Section V clarifies the temporal scope of hostilities, while section VI outlines in more detail the requisite nexus to hostilities for acts to be governed by Hague Law rules. Lastly, section VII summarises the law of law enforcement rules that apply when state use of force is governed by that corpus of international law.

II. Defining Hostilities

Nowhere in Hague Law (or elsewhere in the law of armed conflict) are 'hostilities' formally defined or explained. The ordinary meaning of the term is 'acts of warfare',[2] but while this simple definition is a useful starting point,[3] it is inadequate to delineate precisely which actions fall within the conduct of hostilities and which do not. Even dictionaries specific to international law are quite general in their definitions. Verri's 1992 *Dictionary of the International Law of Armed Conflict* defined 'hostilities' as 'acts of violence by a belligerent against an enemy in order to put an end to his resistance and impose obedience'.[4] The 2001 *Dictionnaire de droit international public* edited by Jean Salmon defined 'hostilities' as the 'set of offensive or defensive acts and military operations executed by a belligerent in the context of an armed conflict'.[5] More narrowly, the International Law Association (ILA) has defined the term 'hostilities' as referring to 'the actual fighting of an armed conflict',[6] mirroring the ordinary definition of the word.

Although no formal definition exists in the law of armed conflict, indications as to the scope of the notion of 'hostilities' can be gleaned from relevant headings and subjects relating to hostilities in relevant treaties. In the 1899 and 1907 Hague Regulations,[7] for example, Section II ('On Hostilities') governs means of injuring the enemy, sieges and bombardments; spies; flags of truce; capitulations; and amnesties. The 1977 Additional Protocol I[8] covers means and methods of warfare in one section, which covers the basic rules, perfidy, emblems, quarter, the safeguard of an enemy *hors de combat* and those parachuting from an

[2] *Oxford English Dictionary*.

[3] As the ICRC notes, law of armed conflict treaties do not establish uniform terminology for the conduct of hostilities but refer, in addition to 'hostilities', to 'warfare' (pt IV, s I and Art 35(1), 1977 Additional Protocol I), to 'military operations' (Art 53, 1949 Geneva Convention IV; Art 51(1), 1977 Additional Protocol I, and Art 13(1), 1977 Additional Protocol II), or simply to 'operations' (Art 48, 1977 Additional Protocol I). ICRC DPH Guidance (n 1) 43.

[4] P Verri, *Dictionary of the International Law of Armed Conflict* (Geneva, ICRC, 1992) 57.

[5] J Salmon (ed), *Dictionnaire de droit international public* (Brussels, Bruylant, 2001) 550 (author's translation). The original French reads 'Ensemble des actes offensifs ou défensifs et des opérations militaires accomplis par un belligérant dans le cadre d'un conflit armé'.

[6] ILA, *Final Report on the Meaning of Armed Conflict in International Law*, The Hague Conference (2010): Use of Force, 9, available at https://goo.gl/EDiCBJ.

[7] Convention (II) with Respect to the Laws and Customs of War on Land and its annex: Regulations concerning the Laws and Customs of War on Land; adopted at The Hague, 29 July 1899; entry into force, 4 September 1900; and Convention (IV) respecting the Laws and Customs of War on Land and its annex: Regulations concerning the Laws and Customs of War on Land; adopted at The Hague, 18 October 1907; entry into force, 26 January 1910.

[8] Protocol Additional to the Geneva Conventions of 12 August 1949, and relating to the Protection of Victims of International Armed Conflicts (Protocol I), adopted at Geneva, 8 June 1977; entry into force, 7 December 1978.

aircraft in distress. A separate section elsewhere in the Protocol headed 'General Protection against Effects of Hostilities' addresses the following:

- The basic rule
- The protection of the civilian population and individual civilians against dangers arising from military operations and the rules of distinction and proportionality in attack
- The protection of civilian objects
- The protection of cultural objects and places of worship
- The protection of objects indispensable to the survival of the civilian population
- The protection of the natural environment
- The protection of works and installations containing dangerous forces
- Precautions in attack
- Precautions against the effects of attacks
- The special protection afforded to non-defended localities and demilitarised zones
- The protection of civilian civil defence organisations and their personnel, and
- Military personnel assigned to civil defence organisations.

Dinstein defines 'hostilities' broadly as a 'portmanteau term embracing all forms of hostile acts undertaken against the enemy'.[9] He affirms that hostilities are conducted through means and methods of warfare, which extend beyond violent acts to encompass 'ancillary non-violent operations, such as gathering intelligence about the enemy; logistics (delivering to combatants armaments, equipment, transportation, food, fuel and other essentials); and running a network of communications (electronic or otherwise)'.[10]

In a similar vein, the ICRC variously refers to international law on the conduct of hostilities as regulating and limiting the methods and means of warfare used by parties to an armed conflict; 'the (collective) resort by the parties to the conflict to means and methods of injuring the enemy'; or 'the sum total of all hostile acts carried out by individuals directly participating in hostilities'.[11] With respect to civilians participating directly in hostilities, the ICRC also envisages the word 'hostilities' in broad terms as covering 'not only the time that the civilian actually makes use of a weapon, but also, for example, the time that he is carrying it, as well as situations in which he undertakes hostile acts without using a weapon'.[12]

These definitions and treaty elements give clues as to the scope of the term, but are too generic and broad to reflect those acts and situations in which Hague Law applies and over which it governs. It is certainly not correct to say, for example, that when a party to a conflict uses a weapon, this act is necessarily regulated by Hague Law. Weapons may be used during

[9] Y Dinstein, *The Conduct of Hostilities under the Law of International Armed Conflict*, 3rd edn (Cambridge, Cambridge University Press, 2016) 2.

[10] Ibid, para 4.

[11] ICRC, 'International law on the conduct of hostilities: overview' (29 October 2010) at https://goo.gl/4ow5Kx; ICRC DPH Guidance (n 1) 43, 44.

[12] Y Sandoz, C Swinarski and B Zimmermann (eds), *Commentary on the Additional Protocols of 8 June 1977 to the Geneva Conventions of 12 August 1949* (Geneva, Martinus Nijhoff, 1987) para 1943.

armed conflict in violation of Geneva Law or in violation of the law of law enforcement. To be governed by Hague Law, the act must either take place in the context of an IAC and have direct nexus to that conflict, or be similarly directly linked to an armed conflict not of an international character *and* occur in an area in which hostilities are ongoing (because the geographical scope of a non-international armed conflict (NIAC) is limited).

A. 'Hostilities' and 'Attacks'

In the experts' group discussions that led to the ICRC issuing its interpretive guidance on direct participation in hostilities in 2009, it was argued that the 'overall' use of the term in the Geneva Conventions suggested that the notion of 'hostilities' was narrower than that of 'armed conflict', but wider than the concept of 'attack'.[13] In the 1977 Additional Protocol I, 'attack' is formally defined as 'acts of violence against the adversary, whether in offence or in defence'.[14] This is ostensibly because '[n]on-violent acts tied to military operations – although subsumed under the overarching heading of 'hostilities' – do not come within the bounds of attacks'.[15]

B. 'Hostilities' and 'Means and Methods of Warfare'

As is the case with 'hostilities', the terms 'means of warfare' and 'method of warfare' are not formally defined in international law, and in the view of the United States (US) Department of Defense 'lack an established, specific meaning'.[16] As discussed in chapter 1, means of warfare are weapons and weapons platforms, including ammunition and munitions. Thus, an armed Reaper drone is a means of warfare, as is the Hellfire missile or Paveway bombs that it may carry. A method of warfare denotes the way force is used. In the case of the drone, that may be high-level or low-level bombing for example. Persistent flying above a locality so that the population hears the persistent 'drone' of the engine could also be a method of warfare, designed to intimidate and influence behaviour.

C. The Meaning of 'Hostilities'

In sum, hostilities are the use, during and in direct connection with an armed conflict, of means and methods of warfare by one party to the conflict against the armed forces or other military objective of an adverse party, or against civilians or civilian objects in that party's territory (insofar those acts are not governed by Geneva Law). The concept includes threats of unlawful acts, such as declarations that no quarter will be given and threats of

[13] N Melzer, 'Third Expert Meeting on the Notion of Direct Participation in Hostilities' (Geneva, ICRC, 23–25 October 2005) Summary Report, 17.

[14] Art 49(1), 1977 Additional Protocol I.

[15] Dinstein (n 9) 3.

[16] US Department of Defense, *Law of War Manual*, June 2015, updated December 2016, para 5.1.1 at https://goo.gl/jBfjt5.

violence, the primary purpose of which is to terrorise civilians. It also includes operational surveillance and intelligence gathering and communication.

III. Material Scope of Hostilities

A. Geneva Law or Hague Law?

Geneva Law covers those 'taking no active part in the hostilities, including members of armed forces who have laid down their arms and those placed *hors de combat* by sickness, wounds, detention, or any other cause'.[17] Thus, as the ICRC has noted, the law of armed conflict (or, as the ICRC prefers, international humanitarian law, IHL)

> makes a basic distinction between the conduct of hostilities and the exercise of power or authority over persons or territory. As a result, the infliction of death, injury, or destruction by civilians on persons or objects that have fallen into their 'hands' … or 'power' … within the meaning of IHL does not, without more, constitute part of the hostilities.[18]

The ICRC further cites the examples of use of armed force by civilian authorities to suppress riots and other forms of civil unrest, prevent looting, or otherwise maintain law and order in a conflict area as not 'generally' amounting to hostilities, despite the fact this may cause death, injury or destruction. Similarly, once military personnel have been captured, the suppression of riots and prevention of escapes are 'not designed to directly cause military harm to the opposing party to the conflict and, therefore, [lack] belligerent nexus'.[19] In fact, these acts of force would generally fall to be considered by the law of law enforcement, discussed in section VII of this chapter.[20]

Let us assume a situation we are considering is one in which an armed conflict is ongoing. For the purpose of this example, it does not matter whether that conflict is international or non-international. We are concerned with a region of the country where hostilities are ongoing between the two parties to the conflict. A group of soldiers belonging to one of the parties enters a village whose members are believed to be supporters of the enemy (in moral and political terms, but not materially). There is no evidence of the presence of enemy soldiers, no find of weapons, and no one within the village commits, or even threatens, a hostile act. The soldiers decide to rape and then murder the villagers and pillage from the houses. Some victims are shot at close range; others are stabbed; and some are bludgeoned

[17] Common Article 3.

[18] ICRC DPH Guidance (n 1) 61.

[19] Ibid, 62. At the same time, it is noted that 'to the extent practically possible, the guarding of captured military personnel as a means of preventing their liberation by the enemy should be distinguished from the exercise of administrative, judicial and disciplinary authority over them while in the power of a party to the conflict, including in case of riots or escapes, which are not part of a hostile military operation'. Ibid, 48, fn 99.

[20] Art 42 of the 1949 Geneva Convention III specifies that 'The use of weapons against prisoners of war, especially against those who are escaping or attempting to escape, shall constitute an extreme measure, which shall always be preceded by warnings appropriate to the circumstances.' Today, this may be deemed to be reflected in the law of law enforcement possibility to have recourse to firearms, where that is necessary to prevent the escape of a detainee who poses a grave threat to life. See 1990 Basic Principles on the Use of Force and Firearms by Law Enforcement Officials, Principle 9, as discussed in section VII.C below.

to death during interrogation. Are these acts serious violations of Geneva Law or of Hague Law? It seems fairly clear that they are the former, and the actions of the soldiers constitute murder and torture, amongst other war crimes. The civilians are in the power of the soldiers belonging to a party to the conflict who enter the village, and those soldiers are in effective control of the situation.

What if there had been unconfirmed reports of enemy soldiers in the village? Would this scenario change the legal situation? The soldiers entering the village may be on higher alert, but the villagers are still to be considered as being in their power for the purposes of the law.

But what if the soldiers had, based on the unconfirmed reports, chosen to fire mortar or artillery shells at the village from a distance rather than to enter it? At this point, arguably the scenario becomes one governed by Hague Law. What is different is the remoteness of the perpetrator from the victim (or, more neutrally, the actor from the target) and therefore the relative lack of control or power over the targets.[21]

The switch to Hague Law regulation is all the more likely if an enemy sniper fires at the incursive soldiers, because then we are in a combat situation between two adverse parties, the epitome of a situation of hostilities.

The 1998 Rome Statute of the International Criminal Court (ICC Statute)[22] does not lend much assistance to efforts to delineate the contours of hostilities. *A priori*, Article 8(2)(a) and (c) are pure Geneva Law, reflecting, respectively, grave breaches of the Geneva Conventions (in IAC) and serious violations of Common Article 3 (in NIAC). Subparagraphs (b) and (e) contain a mix of crimes, most committed during the conduct of hostilities, but some, such as 'Subjecting persons who are in the power of an adverse party to physical mutilation or to medical or scientific experiments',[23] which are clearly Geneva Law.

But certain crimes are clearly 'conduct of hostilities crimes'.[24] In the *Katanga* case, one of the charges against the defendant was of the war crime, during a NIAC, of '[i]ntentionally directing attacks against the civilian population as such or against individual civilians not taking direct part in hostilities'. A pre-trial chamber of the ICC noted that this war crime, which is set out in Article 8(2)(b)(i) of the ICC Statute, 'is the first in the series of war crimes for which one essential element is that the crime must be committed during the conduct of hostilities'.[25] The crime

> is applicable only to attacks (acts of violence) directed against individual civilians not taking direct part in the hostilities, or a civilian population, that has not yet fallen into the hands of the adverse or hostile party to the conflict to which the perpetrator belongs.[26]

In its decision to confirm this charge against an accused, Germain Katanga, the ICC Pre-Trial Chamber noted that the jurisprudence of the ICTY 'has emphasised that an

[21] The notion of remoteness leading to the application of Hague Law applies *a fortiori* to aerial bombing. It is not necessary that aircraft or the soldiers outside the village be coming under fire. Even though the victims are, in practice, equally helpless, they are not considered, for the purposes of the law of armed conflict, to be in the power of the party that is conducting the bombing.

[22] Statute of the International Criminal Court; adopted at Rome, 17 July 1998; entry into force, 1 July 2002.

[23] Art 8(2)(b)(x) and (e)(xi), ICC Statute.

[24] ICC, *Prosecutor v Germain Katanga and Mathieu Ngudjolo Chui*, Decision on the Charges (Pre-Trial Chamber I) (Case No ICC-01/04-01/07), 30 September 2008, para 267.

[25] Ibid.

[26] Ibid.

individual civilian, or a civilian population, falls into the hands of an adverse or hostile party to the conflict when it comes under the control of its members'. Once it does so, 'an act of violence against them does not fall under Article 8(2)(b)(i) … but under other provisions of the Statute'.[27] The ICTY jurisprudence cited by the ICC Pre-Trial Chamber was, notably, the *Martinovic* case. In this, the ICTY Trial Chamber accepted the Prosecution's argument 'that the expression "in the hands of" a party or occupying power, as it appears in Article 4 of [the 1949] Geneva Convention IV, refers to persons finding themselves on the territory controlled by that party or occupying power'.[28]

In the *Katanga* case, *Force de Résistance Patriotique en Ituri* (FRPI) soldiers under the command of Mr Katanga (along with other forces) attacked a village (Bogoro) in the Democratic Republic of the Congo (DRC) on 24 February 2003, having effectively encircled it. They were armed with heavy weapons and bladed weapons. The attack had a dual aim: to attack another party to the armed conflict whose forces were stationed in the village and to attack civilians, seemingly motivated by ethnic animus.[29] As many as 200 civilians were killed during and in the aftermath of the attack on the village, which included combat between the enemy forces pitted against each other. In the course of the action, the FRPI (and other) fighters destroyed many houses, shops, schools and/or public or private property belonging to the civilian population. They also pillaged civilian property, and raped and sexually enslaved civilian women and girls. Children under the age of 15 were used to participate actively in the hostilities conducted during the attack.[30]

The attack included the murder of 'women and small children, who were killed inside their houses with gunshots or machetes'.[31] This element of the war crimes committed during the attack is a serious violation of Geneva Law: 'unarmed civilians were attacked with firearms or machetes … or were burned alive inside their homes.'[32] As the Pre-Trial Chamber noted,

> as the attacking forces of a party to the conflict gradually gain control of a targeted village, individual civilians in these successive areas automatically become protected persons within the meaning of Article 4 of the [1949 Geneva Convention] IV, provided they do not claim allegiance to the party in question. Article 8(2)(a)(i) of the [ICC] Statute thus prohibits the wilful killing of those civilians in such a circumstance.[33]

At the same time, the Chamber found beyond reasonable doubt that *Ngiti* combatants directly targeted the predominantly *Hema* civilian population of Bogoro on 24 February 2003, which it deemed to be an intentional attack on civilians committed during the conduct of hostilities. It reached this finding on the basis of the

> timing of the attack and the means and method used – encirclement of the village whilst its inhabitants were still asleep; use of machetes to strike them directly and at close range; shooting

[27] *Katanga* (n 24) para 269.

[28] ICTY, *Prosecutor v Mladen Naletilic (aka 'Tuta') and Vinko Martinovic (aka 'Štela')*, Judgment (Trial Chamber) (Case No IT- 98-34-T), 31 March 2003, para 208. In its actual reference to the case, the ICC Pre-Trial Chamber seemingly mistook the date of the judgment and confused the submission of the prosecution for the holding, quoted here, of the ICTY Trial Chamber.

[29] *Katanga* (n 24) para 267.

[30] Ibid.

[31] ICC, *Prosecutor v Germain Katanga*, Judgment (Trial Chamber II) (Case No ICC-01/04-01/07), 7 March 2014, para 719.

[32] *Katanga* (n 24) para 300.

[33] Ibid, para 293.

> indiscriminately or directly at the villagers, whether during or after the fighting, in their homes, as they fled or when they had taken shelter in the Institute or in the bush; the civilian death toll, including 13 children, many women and elderly people …[34]

Some of these acts are governed by Hague Law (eg shooting indiscriminately) and some more readily fall within the scope of Geneva Law (eg the use of machetes). But is this all just semantics, whether acts fall within the conduct of hostilities or whether they are committed against someone in the power of a conflict party? It is not. In fact, as well as in law, the likelihood of a prosecution vastly diminishes when a situation is governed by Hague Law rather than Geneva Law, as, in particular, the mens rea element of the crime is far harder to establish. And once there is an exchange of fire with the enemy in a particular situation, the chances of prosecution are, in practice, extremely slim. Indeed, in the *Katanga* case, after the attack on Bogoro had been launched, some people fled the camp for the slopes of a nearby mountain. The Trial Chamber found that this group of people included both civilians and soldiers, who were also fleeing. The evidence admitted into the record in the case did not allow the Chamber

> to assess the exact proportion of civilians and soldiers within this group. … It is therefore difficult for the Chamber to find that one of the objectives, at that specific moment, was to attack the civilian population and that the civilian population was targeted as such. Therefore, the Chamber is unable to establish that these acts fall within Article 8(2)(e)(i) of the Statute, as this provision requires the Chamber to establish that the perpetrator meant the civilian population, as such, to be the object of the attack …[35]

Of course, though, if after the shelling or bombing of a village soldiers enter it and calmly perpetrate the acts of murder and torture described above while not under fire, these would again be governed by Geneva Law and the chance of a prosecution increases. Thus, Sergeant Alexander Blackman, a UK Royal Marine, who was given an eight-year prison sentence following a court-martial, was convicted of murder for the wilful killing of a seriously wounded Taliban fighter.[36] On 15 September 2011, while on patrol in Helmand Province, he shot an unknown Afghan insurgent in the chest and killed him. The Afghan fighter had been seriously wounded, 'having been engaged lawfully by an Apache Helicopter' (ie during the conduct of hostilities), but when Sgt Blackman found him 'he was no longer a threat'.[37] After his action, Sergeant Blackman explicitly acknowledged that he had just violated 'the Geneva Conventions'.[38] His conviction for murder was subsequently reduced to manslaughter on appeal on the basis of diminished responsibility at the time of the killing.[39] He was released in late April 2017 after serving three-and-a-half years in prison.[40]

[34] *Katanga* (n 31) paras 878–89.

[35] Ibid, para 875.

[36] Court Martial Appeal Court, *R v Alexander Wayne Blackman*, Judgment (Case No 2014/00049/B5), 22 May 2014, para 77, at https://goo.gl/voSSm4.

[37] Court Martial (Bulford), *R v Alexander Blackman*, Sentencing Remarks (Case No 2012CM00442) 1, at https://goo.gl/WgU7Dr.

[38] Ibid.

[39] Court Martial Appeal Court, *R v Alexander Wayne Blackman*, Judgment, [2017] EWCA Crim 190, 15 March 2017.

[40] See, eg, S Morris, 'Marine A, who killed wounded Taliban fighter, released from prison', *Guardian* (28 April 2017), at https://goo.gl/ZoWyJX.

B. Hague Law or Law of Law Enforcement?

Also difficult to distinguish are acts that fall within the conduct of hostilities from acts of law enforcement. As a 2013 publication by the ICRC noted, 'It is not entirely clear in international law which situations in the context of an armed conflict are governed by the conduct of hostilities paradigm and which are covered by the law enforcement paradigm.'[41] The default situation for use of force by the state, even in armed conflict, remains law enforcement; only in situations of combat do the rules governing the conduct of hostilities apply.

This subsection discusses which acts amount to hostilities and which to law enforcement within an area in which hostilities between parties to an armed conflict are already ongoing. The situation with respect to acts that occur during a situation of armed conflict but which are committed outside an area in which hostilities are being conducted between parties to an armed conflict is discussed in the following section (on the geographical scope of hostilities).

In November 2013, the ICRC published a report on its experts' group discussions on the use of force in armed conflicts. A number of scenarios the experts reviewed in assessing the 'interplay between the conduct of hostilities and law enforcement paradigms' deserve further analysis.

i. Use of Force at Checkpoints

The ICRC gives the following case scenario. In the context of a NIAC, a 'suspicious' car arrives at a checkpoint manned by the belligerent states' armed forces. Although the checkpoint is clearly indicated, the car arrives at high speed and does not stop when ordered to do so.[42] There is no evidence of firearms and the occupants of the car do not engage in hostile acts (at least in the information provided). Although the case study does not make it explicit, let us assume that this is in an area where hostilities are ongoing.

A checkpoint is generally a law enforcement tool, designed to facilitate the capture of fleeing suspects. It is not a military base or control post. A well-constructed checkpoint would have concrete blocks intelligently emplaced to force an incoming vehicle to slow, and spike strips ('stingers') ready for use to blow out the tyres of a fast incoming vehicle, while those manning the checkpoints might even be equipped with laser dazzlers.[43] These would likely ensure that the car is effectively brought to a standstill without any need to spray the vehicle (whose occupants may well be civilians) with small arms fire. Of course, not every checkpoint is so well constructed, and in not every instance is the time available

[41] G Gaggioli, *Expert Meeting: The Use of Force in Armed Conflicts. Interplay between the Conduct of Hostilities and Law Enforcement Paradigms, Report* (Geneva, ICRC, 2013) (hereinafter 'ICRC 2013 Use of Force Report') 1, at https://goo.gl/xtjyPH.

[42] Ibid, 39.

[43] The US military in Iraq announced in May 2006 that it was using a laser 'device' mounted on soldiers' M-4 rifles to 'dazzle' Iraqi drivers who failed to heed warnings to stop at checkpoints. Disingenuously (and incorrectly), the US asserted that the laser device should not be called a weapon because it was not intended to injure: 'They are a warning device. They are intended to minimize unnecessary casualties', particularly among Iraqi civilians. Associated Press, 'US military uses laser "dazzler" to stop Iraqis who ignore warnings to stop', Archive (18 May 2006), at https://goo.gl/Fgb338.

for the barrier to be carefully planned. There is, however, a significant difference in likely consequences between shooting at the tyres of a vehicle and shooting to kill the occupants. Depending on the circumstances, use of firearms (if feasible, against the car; but if not, against the driver) may be legitimate under the law of law enforcement.[44]

In the ICRC experts' discussion, there was 'a broad consensus' that an 'escalation of force procedure has to be used when dealing with the use of force against an unidentified person seemingly posing a threat at a checkpoint'. Several experts asserted that, if it was known that the person arriving at high speed in the car 'is a legitimate target' under the law of armed conflict (ie a fighter or a civilian directly participating in hostilities), this person could be targeted under a conduct of hostilities 'paradigm'.[45] In contrast, 'if it were known that the person arriving in the car travelling at high speed was a civilian (not directly participating in hostilities), the law enforcement paradigm would apply. No one questioned this position.' The likelihood of such advance knowledge is, however, fairly low.

ii. Riots During Armed Conflict

It is explicit in the law of armed conflict that riots do not amount to armed conflict situations. These are archetypical law enforcement scenarios. What if, though, as the ICRC postulates, during an existing NIAC, rebel fighters take advantage of a riot to attack government forces? The experts' discussion lent towards a parallel application of law of armed conflict and law of law enforcement rules; the former to the fighters, the latter to the rioting civilians. But, as was also pointed out, this would generate significant practical challenges:

> How could soldiers distinguish between fighters (who might not distinguish themselves), civilians directly participating in hostilities and rioters who are not directly participating in hostilities? How could soldiers be expected to apply two different paradigms at the same time and place? Moreover, in most situations of armed conflicts, belligerents may not have snipers able to target surgically fighters among the crowd and thus targeting them may cause excessive incidental civilian losses in violation of IHL.[46]

Indeed, in a situation where a party to a NIAC comes under fire in an area of ongoing hostilities, this entitles that party to have recourse to Hague Law rules, including intentional lethal use of firearms against lawful targets. The decision by enemy fighters to, in effect, use the rioters as human shields engages their own liability, but it does not void the duties of distinction and proportionality incumbent on the force returning fire. Moreover, one could envisage a scenario where the police were seeking legitimately to disperse the rioters using riot control agents, an option that would not be open to the military operating under Hague Law rules.

[44] In December 2015, a *gendarme* in Paris fired around 10 shots when a driver refused to stop and then forced his way through one of the main entrances of Les Invalides on Rue Grenelle in the French capital. The incident took place at the complex where a remembrance ceremony had recently been held for the 130 people killed in the 13 November Islamist attacks across Paris. Associated Press, 'Police open fire on car after driver tries to ram barrier at Paris's Invalides monument', *Daily Telegraph* (16 December 2015) at https://goo.gl/X5Nt6W.

[45] In fact, presumably the speed of the car would be irrelevant to those who assert that there is an unfettered right to kill a combatant/civilian directly participating in hostilities unless he or she was clearly surrendering or was otherwise *hors de combat*.

[46] ICRC 2013 Use of Force Report (n 41) 26.

Outside the geographical scope of a NIAC – that is, where hostilities are not already ongoing – the scenario would be regulated by law of law enforcement rules, not those governing the conduct of hostilities. This would potentially allow riot control agents, such as teargas, to be used, and where firearms could lawfully be used, they could fire expanding ammunition to reduce the risks of over-penetration and (allegedly also) ricochet, which could amount to a war crime if used as a method of warfare. That said, if the violence escalates in violent protests lasting days, and firearms are widely used, the situation might potentially transform the situation into one that over time might amount to hostilities.

iii. Armed Bank Robbery

Not discussed in the ICRC report is the fact that rebel groups may engage in armed bank robberies to fund their activities (and/or individuals' lifestyles). Although bank robberies by ordinary criminals are becoming rarer in many nations across Western Europe (in part, as cyber-crime is safer, easier and more lucrative), in many countries armed robberies are still relatively common. In general, combatting this phenomenon is to be considered a law enforcement task, even if hostages are taken and the robbers do not make a successful getaway. This is still the case even if it is known that the robbers belong to a party to a NIAC and the robbery is expected or intended to fund the group's future activities.

IV. Geographical Scope of Hostilities

As the ICRC has noted, the geographical scope of application of the law of armed conflict, 'and more specifically of the conduct of hostilities paradigm, is not crystal-clear'.[47] The 1995 *Tadić* Appeals Chamber decision on jurisdiction made it clear that, in the view of the ICTY, while the law of armed conflict applied throughout the territory of a state in which a conflict existed, areas where hostilities were being conducted were more geographically limited, and so was the applicable law:

> Although the Geneva Conventions are silent as to the geographical scope of international 'armed conflicts', the provisions suggest that at least some of the provisions of the Conventions apply to the entire territory of the Parties to the conflict, not just to the vicinity of actual hostilities. *Certainly, some of the provisions are clearly bound up with the hostilities and the geographical scope of those provisions should be so limited.* Others, particularly those relating to the protection of prisoners of war and civilians, are not so limited. …
>
> The geographical and temporal frame of reference for internal armed conflicts is similarly broad. This conception is reflected in the fact that beneficiaries of common Article 3 of the Geneva Conventions are those taking no active part (or no longer taking active part) in the hostilities. This indicates that the rules contained in Article 3 also apply outside the narrow geographical context of the actual theatre of combat operations.[48]

[47] Ibid, 17.

[48] ICTY, *Prosecutor v Tadić (aka 'Dule')*, Decision on the Defence Motion for Interlocutory Appeal on Jurisdiction (Appeals Chamber) (Case No IT-94-1), 2 October 1995, paras 68, 69 (emphasis added).

This holding is, though, open to diverse interpretation. The simple starting point is that whereas Geneva Law applies across the country during an armed conflict, Hague Law applies only to areas with ongoing hostilities. In deciding that Duško Tadić could stand trial for war crimes (serious violations of Geneva Law), the Chamber affirmed that it was 'sufficient that the alleged crimes were closely related to the hostilities occurring in other parts of the territories controlled by the parties to the conflict'. This is not, in and of itself, especially controversial.

What remains to be determined, however, is how an area may be one in which hostilities are conducted such as to be governed by Hague Law. Let us take a mythical country whose capital is in the north and whose government is engaged in armed violence with a rebel group based in and operating from the south. At some point the group becomes sufficiently organised and the combat between the two is sufficiently intense such that a NIAC exists. (Until that point, operations are governed by law of law enforcement rules, international human rights law and domestic criminal law). In the area in which the violence occurs between the two parties to the nascent armed conflict, hostilities are now regulated by Hague Law. In contrast, any Geneva Law violation by one of the parties anywhere in the country will be subject to law of armed conflict rules and the associated accountability, including under international criminal law. Thus, for example, a prison camp set up by the government in which captured rebel group fighters are held would be governed, inter alia, by the rules set out in Common Article 3.

Let us say that the rebel group decides to conduct a military operation in the capital. There has been no prior combat in the capital or indeed in the north of the country. A small contingent of fighters travels incognito to the capital and in a lightning operation captures the parliament while it is in session. No shots are fired during the operation. The rebel fighters hold the parliamentarians captive and declare that they will only release them once the government ceases military operations in the south and withdraws its troops. The government, predictably, refuses and launches an assault on the parliament, causing many casualties. Every rebel fighter is killed, with many reportedly shot to death when they were unable to defend themselves owing to wounds or were actively surrendering.

How is this scenario to be characterised? Some would argue that once they began their travel to the north, the rebels were already directly participating in hostilities. Thus, government soldiers would be entitled to use potentially lethal force, including explosive weapons, without warning and without mercy, unless and until any or all the fighters were *hors de combat*. An ambush or an aerial bombing that instantly annihilated the group would thus presumably be lawful; ostensibly there is no need under Hague Law to offer enemy fighters the opportunity to surrender. It is unlawful to kill (or mistreat) an enemy who is clearly surrendering and who abstains from any hostile act; to deny quarter (ie to proclaim in advance of an operation that there will be no survivors); or to kill and mistreat enemy fighters who are otherwise *hors de combat*.

The lawfulness of an annihilation of the group is not quite the position of the ICRC. The organisation would, it is assumed, advocate for its policy position in Chapter IX of its 2009 interpretive guidance on direct participation in hostilities, wherein:

> In addition to the restraints imposed by international humanitarian law on specific means and methods of warfare, and without prejudice to further restrictions that may arise under other applicable branches of international law, the kind and degree of force which is permissible against

> persons not entitled to protection against direct attack must not exceed what is actually necessary to accomplish a legitimate military purpose in the prevailing circumstances.[49]

In applying this 'rule', the ICRC argues that

> the fact that a particular category of persons is not protected against offensive or defensive acts of violence is not equivalent to a legal entitlement to kill such persons without further considerations. At the same time, the absence of an unfettered 'right' to kill does not necessarily imply a legal obligation to capture rather than kill regardless of the circumstances.[50]

As part of its rationale for the existence of the rule, it cites the principle of humanity, which 'forbids the infliction of suffering, injury or destruction not actually necessary for the accomplishment of legitimate military purposes'.[51] This is consonant with the preamble to the 1868 St Petersburg Declaration, whereby 'the only legitimate object which States should endeavour to accomplish during war is to weaken the military forces of the enemy' and 'for this purpose it is sufficient to disable the greatest possible number of men'.

But this is a stretch.[52] It is hard to see a considerable extent of state practice, much less *opinio juris*, that would sustain a Hague Law prohibition on, for example, deadly ambushes, simply on the basis that it was feasible to take the enemy alive. The decision to capture rather than kill may be a policy decision but very few states would consider it a legal obligation, at least under the law of armed conflict. The better view is that this rebel operation occurs outside the geographical scope of the conduct of hostilities, and therefore the government operation is to be regulated under, and judged by, law of law enforcement rules. As discussed in section VIII.A below, it must therefore seek to capture the rebels if possible. Recourse to firearms is lawful if necessary and where an imminent threat exists of death or serious injury (or a grave threat to life); intentional lethal use of force (ie shooting to kill or bombing) is only lawful if strictly unavoidable to protect life.

The same applies to the subsequent operation against the parliament. With respect to the detention of the parliamentarians, the rebel fighters are subject at all times to Geneva Law. The taking of hostages, which would encompass most if not all of the parliamentarians,[53] already constitutes a serious violation of Common Article 3 and a war crime. Any further mistreatment of the hostages/detainees is likely also amount to a war crime. But when the government forces storm the building, those soldiers' use of force is, initially at least, restrained by law enforcement rules. Once an individual or the group is in their power, however, Geneva Law will apply to their actions, so summary execution

[49] ICRC DPH Guidance (n 1) 77. Indeed, in its 2016 commentary on the 1949 Geneva Convention I (Common Article 3), the ICRC referred to the view (among three others) that Chapter IX would apply 'use of force against isolated individuals who would normally be considered lawful targets, under international humanitarian law but who are located in regions under the State's firm and stable control, where no hostilities are taking place and it is not reasonably foreseeable that the adversary could readily receive reinforcement': ICRC commentary on 1949 Geneva Convention I, 2016, para 462, 463.

[50] ICRC DPH Guidance (n 1) 78.

[51] Ibid, 79, citing UK Ministry of Defence, *Manual of the Law of Armed Conflict* (Oxford, Oxford University Press, 2005), para 2.4.

[52] As a number of experts noted during the ICRC experts' group discussions on the use of force in armed conflict, 'the principles of military necessity and humanity – although underlying principles of IHL – are not additional legal rules to be taken into account in the conduct of hostilities': ICRC 2013 Use of Force Report (n 41) 23.

[53] If, for example, the parliamentarians included the Minister of Defence, he or she would be a detainee not a hostage under the law of armed conflict.

or torture by government forces of rebel fighters who are *hors de combat* will amount to war crimes. Only if there is sustained fighting over days could that situation become one governed also by Hague Law.

The 1982 communication to the Human Rights Committee[54] from the husband of Ms Suarez de Guerrero[55] concerned a slightly different scenario. In the facts of the case, the Colombian police raided a house pursuant to judicial mandate, hoping to secure the release of a former Ambassador of Colombia to France, who had been kidnapped some days earlier by a guerrilla organisation. When seven innocent civilians later entered the house they were all summarily executed by the police. In seeking to evade responsibility, Colombia did not assert that these were acts of warfare during an armed conflict. This enabled the Human Rights Committee to determine a violation of the right to life purely on the basis of international law governing law enforcement.[56]

How, then, within a territory which is the subject of an armed conflict, does a previously peaceful area become one in which hostilities are being conducted and where Hague Law is the primary legal frame of reference? The answer is that it meets the criteria set down for the existence of a NIAC: intense armed violence over the course of at the very least, several days, in a locality arising from combat between a state armed force and an organised armed group (or between two organised armed groups). A static situation in which there is a stand-off is not sufficient. Nor is a terrorist attack (for instance, a vehicle-borne or body-borne suicide bombing). These are governed by the law of law enforcement and domestic law.

The attack on the Westgate Centre in Nairobi in 2013 by fighters belonging to or allied to al-Shabaab,[57] an armed group engaged in the NIAC in Somalia, is an instructive example. On 21 September 2013, at midday, four gunmen entered the Westgate shopping centre in the Kenyan capital, and started throwing grenades and shooting at fleeing shoppers.[58] The shopping centre employed some 40 private security guards, who manned entrances and searched vehicles before they were permitted into the shopping centre garages. Guards searched bags, used electronic wands to search for weapons, and checked vehicle interiors, boots and underneath for weapons and bombs.[59]

According to an investigation by the New York Police Department (NYPD), a review of video footage and ballistics evidence indicates the terrorists were carrying assault rifles as well as grenades, the latter of which were only used on their entrance to the mall, after which the terrorists fired single shots to target fleeing shoppers. Although carrying hundreds of rounds of ammunition in magazines strapped to their bodies, the attackers were believed not to be wearing any form of body armour or carrying handguns.[60]

[54] The Human Rights Committee oversees implementation by states parties of the 1966 International Covenant on Civil and Political Rights (ICCPR).

[55] Human Rights Committee, *Camargo & Suarez de Guerrero v Colombia*, Views (Comm No R.11/45), UN Doc CCPR/C/15/D/45/1979, 31 March 1982, at https://goo.gl/DHie3L.

[56] Ibid, esp paras 13.2–13.3.

[57] See Associated Press (Nairobi), 'FBI says all attackers probably died in Westgate mall siege in Nairobi', *Guardian* (11 January 2014) at https://goo.gl/UQspEJ.

[58] See S Casey-Maslen (ed), *War Report: Armed Conflict in 2013* (Oxford, Oxford University Press, 2014) 23–24.

[59] Kansas Intelligence Fusion Center, *Lessons Learned: Westgate Mall Attack*, No HSEC-03-00000-ST-KS-2010, 25 October 2013, 5, https://goo.gl/8mZtXw.

[60] 'NYPD investigation into Kenya's Westgate Mall terror attacks reveals the truth behind the massacre of more than 60 civilians', *news.com.au* (11 December 2013) at https://goo.gl/xhLutr.

Around one hour into the attack, security forces entered the building and gun battles ensued between police and the attackers.[61] Gunfire and explosions continued overnight, although it is claimed that the actual attack lasted only six hours, after which the NYPD's report asserted that the terrorists hid in a storeroom where they prayed and tended to one of their wounded. Further, despite claims to the contrary, the NYPD believes no heavy explosions were caused by the attackers. Instead, it claimed that all of the heavy damage to the shopping mall's structure had been caused by anti-tank missiles being fired into the building by Kenyan military.[62]

According to the BBC, security sources suggested that a breakdown in control of the counterterrorism operation occurred when the military took over the operation and soldiers launched an 'uncontrolled shooting spree'.[63] Several hours after the first shootings, the Kenyan Government had sent in the military, but rivalry between the army and the police started when a commander of the police's elite squad was killed by the military in friendly fire. The police left in protest at the change in effective responsibility. A military commander involved in the operation, who spoke to the BBC on condition of anonymity, said that is when things started to go wrong:

> We entered the mall blindly with no guide, with no concept of anything. Command and control was not there. … The police felt they were undermined. The military thought the police didn't want to give them enough information so everything went wrong.[64]

The attack resulted in confirmed deaths of 61 civilians and six security officers, with the Kenya Red Cross Society listing a further 23 people as missing.[65] More than 175 people were reported wounded.[66] Al-Shabaab claimed responsibility for the attack, which it characterised as 'retributive justice for crimes committed' by the Kenyan military in Somalia, against which it had been fighting since 2011.[67] It was even tweeting during the attack.[68]

If the incident at the Westgate centre were considered to fall within the conduct of hostilities of the armed conflict in Somalia, use by Kenyan soldiers or police officers of tear gas 'to smoke out the terrorists' would be a serious violation of Hague Law rules.[69] In contrast, use of rocket-propelled grenades inside the complex,[70] or mortar shells against the fighters, with the consequent risk to civilians, would not, per se, be unlawful. The better

[61] 'Nairobi siege: How the attack happened', *BBC* (18 October 2013) at https://goo.gl/ffypyj.

[62] 'NYPD investigation' (n 60).

[63] 'Nairobi siege: How the attack happened' (n 61).

[64] D Okari, 'Kenya's Westgate attack: Unanswered questions one year on', *BBC* (22 September 2014) at https://goo.gl/tUjyQj.

[65] Ibid. Officials initially claimed that 10 to 15 attackers were involved, but CCTV recordings show only four men: 'Westgate siege: Four charged over Nairobi attack', *BBC* (4 November 2013) at https://goo.gl/mYjV1g.

[66] See, eg, Dr FC Onuoha, 'Westgate Attack Al-Shabaab's Renewed Transnational Jihadism', *Aljazeera Center for Studies* (11 November 2013) at https://goo.gl/1sie8x.

[67] Kansas Intelligence Fusion Center (n 59) 9. In March 2015, Adan Garaar, the alleged 'mastermind' of the Westgate attacks, was fatally wounded in Somalia after the car he was travelling in was hit by Hellfire missiles fired from a US drone. C Bucktin, 'Westgate mall attack: Alleged mastermind of Kenyan shopping centre massacre "killed in US drone strike"', *Daily Mirror* (13 March 2015) at https://goo.gl/zF8JRr.

[68] H Alexander, 'Tweeting terrorism: How al Shabaab live blogged the Nairobi attacks', *Daily Telegraph* (22 September 2013) at https://goo.gl/2f7bs3.

[69] M Pflanz and H Alexander, 'Nairobi shopping mall attacks: Britons among those caught up in terrorist assault', *Daily Telegraph* (21 September 2013) at https://goo.gl/zHjLKM.

[70] S Tomlinson, 'The wreckage of Westgate: first pictures taken inside Kenyan massacre mall show wasteland of crumpled cars and twisted metal', *Daily Mail* (26 September 2013) at https://goo.gl/dm8w34.

view, though, is that this was a law enforcement operation (albeit one involving military forces),[71] the legality of which falls to be judged by the rules of the law of law enforcement.[72] Nairobi was not the prior scene of hostilities, which were ongoing hundreds of miles away abroad in Somalia.

As the African Commission on Human and Peoples' Rights has opined, '[o]rganised crime and terrorism can pose significant threats to the enjoyment of the right to life and require a robust State response, but one that at all times takes into account the requirements of international human rights law'.[73] This means use of minimum necessary force, with the possibility of intentional lethal use of force, including through use of missiles and rockets, only when strictly unavoidable to protect life. It is highly questionable whether use of force by the Kenyan military in this case complied with law of law enforcement rules. The African Commission has further noted that 'Derogation from the right to life is not permissible in a time of emergency, including a situation of armed conflict, or in response to threats such as terrorism.'[74]

V. Temporal Scope of Hostilities

Until an armed conflict exists, there can be no 'hostilities', *proprement dit*. Once an armed conflict exists, hostilities will continue in areas where intense armed violence persists, accepting that any conflict will ebb and flow. While a specific time limit cannot be imposed, a sustained reduction in violence for many months (other than a purely seasonal hiatus, for example because of snow or flooding) would amount to the effective end of hostilities in an area. If the requirement of 'protracted' armed conflict under Article 8(2)(f) of the ICC Statute is fulfilled by hostilities that occur over a period of no more than five months,[75] an absence of hostilities for this period of time should similarly be considered sufficient to end the existence of an armed conflict unless the interval is purely due to climatic factors.

VI. Nexus to Hostilities

The issue of nexus has been touched on in section IV in relation to the geographical scope of hostilities. As the ICTY Trial Chamber stated in 1999, for an offence to amount to a

[71] In accordance with the commentary to Art 1 of the 1979 Code of Conduct for Law Enforcement Officials, the term 'law enforcement officials' includes all officers of the law, whether appointed or elected, who exercise police powers, especially the powers of arrest or detention. In countries where police powers are exercised by military authorities, whether uniformed or not, or by state security forces, the definition of law enforcement officials shall be regarded as including officers of such services.

[72] Casey-Maslen (ed) (n 58) 24.

[73] ACHPR, 'General Comment No 3 on the African Charter on Human and Peoples' Rights: The Right to Life (Article 4)', para 2.

[74] Ibid, para 7.

[75] As noted in ch 2, the Pre-Trial Chamber in the *Gombo* case had observed 'that the period in question covers approximately five months and is therefore to be regarded as "protracted" in any event'. ICC, *Prosecutor v Jean-Pierre Bemba Gombo*, Decision on the Charges (Pre-Trial Chamber II) (Case No ICC-01/05-01/08), 15 June 2009, para 235.

violation of the law of armed conflict, it needed 'to be satisfied that each of the alleged acts was in fact closely related to the hostilities'. For this, the Trial Chamber felt that it

> would be sufficient to prove that the crime was committed in the course of or as part of the hostilities in, or occupation of, an area controlled by one of the parties. It is not, however, necessary to show that armed conflict was occurring at the exact time and place of the proscribed acts alleged to have occurred, as the Appeals Chamber has indicated, nor is it necessary that the crime alleged takes place during combat, that it be part of a policy or of a practice officially endorsed or tolerated by one of the parties to the conflict, or that the act be in actual furtherance of a policy associated with the conduct of war or in the actual interest of a party to the conflict; the obligations of individuals under international humanitarian law are independent and apply without prejudice to any questions of the responsibility of States under international law ...[76]

As the Trial Chamber concludes, the 'only question, to be determined in the circumstances of each individual case, is whether the offences were closely related to the armed conflict as a whole'.[77] This is an important statement of both law and policy.

VII. Law of Law Enforcement Rules

This section describes the international legal rules that apply to forcible acts by the state in enforcing its domestic law, in particular relating to crimes involving physical violence. Of course, members of rebel groups do not have the authority to arrest and detain as do many law enforcement officials, especially the police, so they are not empowered to use force. In their capacity as citizens, however, they do have the possibility to use force in lawful self-defence against unlawful attack, whether the attack emanates from a state official or another citizen.

A. Necessity and Proportionality

The two fundamental law of law enforcement principles governing any use of force are necessity and proportionality. First, any force used must be only the minimum necessary in the circumstances (the principle of necessity). Second, force used must be proportionate to the threat (the principle of proportionality). The two principles, whose normative content is explained below, are cumulative: violation of either principle will usually mean that the victim's human rights have been violated.

i. The Principle of Necessity

Article 3 of the 1979 Code of Conduct for Law Enforcement Officials, a soft-law instrument that reflects state practice across democratic nations, allows the police and other law enforcement officials to use force 'only when strictly necessary'. The accompanying official

[76] ICTY, *Prosecutor v Tadić*, Judgment (Trial Chamber), 7 May 1999, para 573.
[77] Ibid.

commentary stipulates that the provision 'emphasises' that any use of force by law enforcement officials 'should be exceptional'. Thus, in given circumstances no force may lawfully be used. This default position is confirmed in Basic Principle 4 of the 1990 Basic Principles on the Use of Force and Firearms by Law Enforcement Officials:[78]

> Law enforcement officials, in carrying out their duty, shall, as far as possible, apply non-violent means before resorting to the use of force and firearms. They may use force and firearms only if other means remain ineffective or without any promise of achieving the intended result.[79]

A second element of the principle of necessity is that each use of force, whatever its nature and extent, must be for a legitimate purpose. As Article 3 of the 1979 Code of Conduct stipulates, law enforcement officials may use force only 'to the extent required for the performance of their duty'. The accompanying commentary clarifies that law enforcement officials may use such force, and no more, 'as is reasonably necessary under the circumstances' to prevent crime or 'in effecting or assisting in the lawful arrest of offenders or suspected offenders'.

Use of force must therefore never be meted out vindictively or as a form of punishment, nor applied against an individual offering no resistance, and in any event must cease when a need for further force has passed (for example, when a suspect is safely and lawfully detained). Unlawful arrest or detention clearly do not amount to legitimate law enforcement purposes. Discriminatory practices, such as those executed, for example, against minorities, are clearly unlawful.

A third element of the principle of necessity is that when force is indeed necessary it must be only the minimum reasonably necessary in the circumstances and no more.[80] According to Basic Principle 5, 'Whenever the lawful use of force and firearms is unavoidable, law enforcement officials shall … [e]xercise restraint in such use and … [m]inimize damage and injury'[81] In interpreting this principle, the Inter-American Court of Human Rights has asserted:

> The level of force used must be in keeping with the level of resistance offered. … Thus, agents must apply the criteria of differentiated and progressive use of force, determining the degree of cooperation, resistance or violence of the subject against whom the intervention is intended and, on this basis, employ negotiating tactics, control or use of force, as required.[82]

[78] The Basic Principles were adopted by the Eighth UN Congress on the Prevention of Crime and the Treatment of Offenders, Havana, Cuba, 27 August to 7 September 1990. The UN General Assembly, in its Resolution 45/166, adopted without a vote on 18 December 1990, welcomed the Basic Principles and invited governments to respect them (para 4).

[79] Such non-violent means include the powers of persuasion, negotiation and mediation backed by the authority that comes from being a law enforcement official of the state with the authority to use force when strictly necessary.

[80] See Commentary (a) on Art 3, 1979 Code of Conduct; 'Report of the Special Rapporteur on extrajudicial, summary or arbitrary executions, Christof Heyns', UN Doc A/HRC/26/36, 1 April 2014, para 59; and NS Rodley, 'Integrity of the Person' in D Moeckli et al (eds), *International Human Rights Law* (Oxford, Oxford University Press, 2010) 223. Sir Nigel cites the 1982 Human Rights Committee case of *Guerrero v Colombia* noted in the text associated with n 55.

[81] 1990 Basic Principle 5(a) and (b).

[82] IAmCtHR, *Nadege Dorzema et al v Dominican Republic*, Judgment (Merits, Reparations and Costs), 24 October 2012, para 85(iii). See also NS Rodley with M Pollard, *The Treatment of Prisoners under International Law*, 3rd edn (Oxford, Oxford University Press, 2011) 499.

ii. The Principle of Proportionality

The principle of proportionality as it applies to use of force for law enforcement is much misunderstood. Proportionality does not mean that force must be used by a law enforcement official in strict accord with any use-of-force continuum, or as a 'tit-for-tat' response to violence. Instead, it sets a ceiling as to what is lawful use of force, in accordance with the threat posed by an individual or group of individuals and the offence that has been or is about to be committed.

Proportionality is only to be assessed when some use of force is already necessary and when the force used is no more than the minimum necessary to achieve a legitimate law enforcement objective (meaning that the principle of necessity is being respected). It may act to render such a minimum necessary level of force unlawful in the circumstances. Thus, for example, to break up a serious pub brawl or to stop an escaping thief may demand use of a firearm or other potentially lethal weapon as the minimum necessary force in the prevailing circumstances. But the principle of proportionality will intervene to prevent such use. As the European Court of Human Rights held in the *Nachova* case, an escaping suspect (at least when he or she does not pose a grave threat to life) may not be shot, 'even if a failure to use lethal force may result in the opportunity to arrest the fugitive being lost'.[83] An escaping military detainee may – but does not necessarily – pose a grave threat to life that could justify the use of a firearm if it is necessary to prevent the escape.

Thus, proportionality holds that the threat an individual poses, whether to a law enforcement official or to the general public, as well as the seriousness of the offence an individual is suspected of committing (or is about to commit), will determine the maximum level of force that may lawfully be used. This is particularly important when force that may have lethal consequences is used.[84] The implications for use of firearms are obvious: the specific rules to be applied where recourse to firearms is contemplated are discussed in sub section C below.

B. The Duty of Precaution

Law enforcement operations must be planned and organised so as to minimise recourse to use of a potentially lethal weapon by a law enforcement official, and to minimise the risk of death or serious injury to any member of the public or law enforcement official. This is not a duty inherent in the law of law enforcement but is added by international human rights law, especially the right to life. The precautionary principle was first enunciated by the European Court of Human Rights in its landmark 1995 judgment in the *McCann* case:

> [T]he Court must carefully scrutinise … not only whether the force used by the soldiers was strictly proportionate to the aim of protecting persons against unlawful violence but also whether

[83] European Court of Human Rights (ECtHR), *Nachova v Bulgaria*, Judgment (Grand Chamber), 6 July 2005, para 95.

[84] As the European Court of Human Rights has stated, 'the legitimate aim of effecting a lawful arrest can only justify putting human life at risk in circumstances of absolute necessity. The Court considers that in principle there can be no such necessity where it is known that the person to be arrested poses no threat to life or limb and is not suspected of having committed a violent offence'. *Nachova* (n 83) para 95.

> the anti-terrorist operation was planned and controlled by the authorities so as to minimise, to the greatest extent possible, recourse to lethal force.[85]

The Inter-American Court of Human Rights has similarly found that proportionality

> is also related to the planning of preventive measures, since it involves an assessment of the reasonableness of the use of force. Thus, it is useful to analyze the facts rigorously to determine: (a) whether the violations could have been avoided with the implementation of less harmful measures, and (b) whether there was proportionality between the use of force and the harm it sought to prevent.[86]

Further, with a view to preserving life, law enforcement officials must also ensure that 'assistance and medical aid are rendered to any injured or affected persons at the earliest possible moment'.[87] This applies even if the injured person is a suspected offender or fighter.

C. Use of Firearms

In addition to the general principles of necessity and proportionality, which apply to any use of force, specific provisions of both the 1979 Code of Conduct and the 1990 Basic Principles cover the use (including, but not limited to the discharge) of firearms. These are also widely misunderstood, or at least subject to varying interpretations. The commentary on Article 3 of the 1979 Code of Conduct provides, in part:

> Every effort should be made to exclude the use of firearms, especially against children. In general, firearms should not be used except when a suspected offender offers armed resistance or otherwise jeopardizes the lives of others and less extreme measures are not sufficient to restrain or apprehend the suspected offender.

These guiding principles are elaborated in the 1990 Basic Principles, with Principle 9 providing, in part:

> Law enforcement officials shall not use firearms against persons except in self-defence or defence of others against the imminent threat of death or serious injury, to prevent the perpetration of a particularly serious crime involving grave threat to life, to arrest a person presenting such a danger and resisting their authority, or to prevent his or her escape, and only when less extreme means are insufficient to achieve these objectives.[88]

This means that four scenarios may allow recourse to use of firearms, though in each such use is only lawful when less extreme means are insufficient:

1. Imminent threat of death or serious injury.
2. To prevent a particularly serious crime involving grave threat to life.
3. To enable a person resisting arrest to be arrested if he or she is about to commit a particularly serious crime that involves grave threat to life.

[85] ECtHR, *McCann and others v United Kingdom*, Judgment (Grand Chamber), 27 September 1995, para 194.
[86] *Dorzema* (n 82) para 87.
[87] 1990 Basic Principle 5(c).
[88] For Sir Nigel Rodley, Principle 9 'impose[s] a principle of proportionality'. Rodley with Pollard (n 82) 499.

4. To prevent a person resisting arrest from escaping where he or she is about to commit a particularly serious crime that involves grave threat to life.

These four scenarios each apply when firearms are not used with the intention of killing but only for stopping the suspect ('shooting to stop'). As discussed in sub section iii below, an additional, heightened standard applies to intentional lethal use of firearms.

i. In Case of Imminent Threat of Death or Serious Injury

The foremost, and by far the most common scenario permitting recourse to firearms is where such use is necessary owing to an imminent threat of death or serious injury, and in circumstances where other measures are not likely to be effective. This exists whether the threat posed is to a law enforcement official or to a member of the public. The threat posed by the suspect does not need to come from his wielding a firearm; a knife, iron bar, a car being driven at someone, a potentially lethal chokehold, or even a baseball bat could be sufficient, depending on the situation. Serious injury should, though, be construed narrowly to mean potentially fatal injuries.

According to the UN Special Rapporteur on extrajudicial, summary or arbitrary executions, 'an imminent or immediate threat' should be considered 'a matter of seconds, not hours'.[89] It may even be the case that imminence under the law of law enforcement should be construed as being limited to a second, or even a split second.[90]

ii. To Prevent a Serious Crime Involving Grave Threat to Life

Scenarios 2–4, as set out in Basic Principle 9, concern a grave threat to life (ie not also a threat of serious injury) and where use of firearms is necessary but where the threat is not necessarily imminent. Indeed, it is not the case that imminence is an element of every single scenario where a discharge of firearms may be lawful. An example could be a military detainee or a serial killer escaping from a high-security prison, or where an individual drives through a roadblock when a terrorist attack is feared. In the *Nachova* case cited in section VII.A.ii, which concerned use of firearms against army deserters, the European Court of Human Rights does not state that imminence is an integral element in assessing whether any use of firearms is lawful; rather it was a question of whether or not the suspects were themselves armed, and whether they were being arrested for a serious offence (the link potentially to the 'grave threat to life' criterion in Basic Principle 9).[91] The Inter-American Court of Human Rights similarly

> considers that, even when abstaining from the use of force would have allowed the individuals that were the subject of the State's action to escape, the agents should not have used lethal force against people who did not represent a threat or a real *or* imminent danger to the agents or third parties.[92]

[89] *Report of the Special Rapporteur on extrajudicial, summary or arbitrary executions, Christof Heyns*, UN Doc A/HRC/26/36, 1 April 2014, para 59, citing UN Docs A/68/382 (paras 33–37) and A/HRC/14/24.

[90] Thus, imminence under the law of law enforcement should be clearly distinguished from the notion of imminence under *jus ad bellum*: the law governing inter-state use of force.

[91] *Nachova* (n 83) para 95. See also *Putintseva v Russia*, Judgment (First Section), 10 May 2012 (as rendered final on 10 August 2012), paras 44–46.

[92] *Dorzema* (n 82) para 85(ii) (emphasis added).

The circumstances of a 'grave threat to life' where no imminent threat exists, but which potentially allow firearms to be discharged, are truly exceptional. The test is very tightly drawn: suspects may not be shot in the back, nor firearms used when the threat is actually to property alone. The then UN Special Rapporteur on extrajudicial, summary or arbitrary executions stated in a 2006 report on Nigeria that the risk of escape by an alleged violent criminal 'who presents no direct threat to the lives of others, cannot justify shooting to kill'.[93] The exception does not authorise shooting to kill, as discussed in sub section iii below. But there may be circumstances in which it is not unlawful to shoot to stop an individual even where the threat to life is not imminent. Thus, for example, in *MD v Turkey*, the erstwhile European Commission on Human Rights considered the shooting of an escaping terrorist bombing suspect to fall within the exception set out in Article 2(2)(b) of the European Convention on Human Rights (ECHR), namely, 'to prevent the escape of a person lawfully detained'.[94]

iii. Intentional Killing

A distinct and stricter standard applies when law enforcement officials 'shoot to kill'. An example would be to stop a suicide bomber or a hostage-taker from killing others.[95]

According to the final sentence of Basic Principle 9, 'In any event, intentional lethal use of firearms may only be made when strictly unavoidable in order to protect life.' In this heightened standard, imminence is an integral part of the test of lawful use of force. If a suspect is not about to pull the trigger of a firearm aimed at a hostage's head, or to detonate a bomb, intentional lethal use of force cannot be said to be strictly unavoidable to protect life.

The Special Rapporteur on extrajudicial, summary or arbitrary executions has affirmed:

> A common sense understanding of the scope of application of Principle 9 suggests that all weapons that are designed and are likely to be lethal should be covered, including heavy weapons such as bombs and (drone) missiles, the use of which constitutes an intentional lethal use of force.[96]

Landmines should also be considered as such weapons according to jurisprudence before the European Court of Human Rights.[97]

[93] *Report of the Special Rapporteur on extrajudicial, summary or arbitrary executions, Philip Alston: Mission to Nigeria*, UN Doc E/CN.4/2006/53/Add.4 (2006), para 47.

[94] European Commission on Human Rights, *MD v Turkey*, Decision, 30 June 1997.

[95] See, eg, B Frevel and P Kuschewski, 'Police Organization and Police Reform in Germany: The Case of North Rhine-Westphalia' (2009) 5(2) *German Policy Studies* 53, at https://goo.gl/Vk67R2.

[96] Ibid, para 71. See also, eg, *Esmukhambetov and others v Russia*, Judgment (First Section), 29 March 2011 (as rendered final on 15 September 2011).

[97] In *Alkin v Turkey*, the ECtHR affirmed that injury resulting from landmines is a violation of Art 2 of the 1950 ECHR because the very nature of the weapon makes its use unlawful: '[T]he Court considers that the laying of such indiscriminate and inhumane weapons as anti-personnel landmines, which affect the lives of a disproportionate number of civilians and children, amounts to intentional use of lethal force.' ECtHR, *Alkin v Turkey*, Judgment (Second Section), 13 October 2009, para 30.

4

The Rule of Distinction in Attack: Objects

I. Introduction

The rule of distinction (termed a principle by some)[1] is the primary canon of Hague Law and its most fundamental norm. In its most generic formulation as the 'basic rule' for the conduct of hostilities, Article 48 of the 1977 Additional Protocol I requires parties to an international armed conflict (IAC) to distinguish 'at all times' between civilians and combatants and between civilian objects and military objectives, and to direct their operations 'only against military objectives'.

This chapter looks at the rule of distinction in its application to attacks against objects, including areas of land. Section II describes and explains the primary rule, defining the key concepts. Section III outlines how the rule is to be applied, distinguishing direct attacks against civilian objects from indiscriminate attacks that may affect civilian objects. The requisite level of accuracy required by Hague Law is assessed along with the legality of mistakes in targeting. Certain objects that enjoy special protection from attack are then identified – particularly hospitals, cultural 'property' and installations containing dangerous forces – and the contours of that special protection are demarcated. Lastly, section IV sets out the international criminal law standards that govern direct attacks against civilian objects and indiscriminate attacks under both customary and conventional law, as well as in an instance of national law (the United States (US) attack on a Médecins sans Frontières (MSF) hospital in Yemen in 2015).

Chapter 5 addresses the rule of distinction insofar as attacks against persons are concerned.

[1] Some refer to the 'principles' of distinction and proportionality, while others prefer to talk of 'rules'. In its 1996 Advisory Opinion on the threat or use of nuclear weapons, the International Court of Justice (ICJ) affirmed that distinction was one of the 'cardinal principles' of the law of armed conflict and one of the 'intransgressible principles of international customary law': ICJ, *Legality of the Threat or Use of Nuclear Weapons*, Advisory Opinion, 8 July 1996 (hereinafter '1996 Nuclear Weapons Advisory Opinion'), paras 78, 79. The International Committee of the Red Cross (ICRC) refers to the 'principle of distinction between civilians and combatants' as one of the customary 'rules' of international humanitarian law: ICRC Study of Customary International Humanitarian Law (IHL), Rule 1 ('The Principle of Distinction between Civilians and Combatants') at https://goo.gl/1pxpDe. The preferred nomenclature does not affect normative status or content.

II. The Primary Rule

According to the International Committee of the Red Cross (ICRC), the customary law rule of distinction in attacks against objects is as follows:

> The parties to the conflict must at all times distinguish between civilian objects and military objectives. Attacks may only be directed against military objectives. Attacks must not be directed against civilian objects.[2]

The ICRC affirms that this customary rule applies in all armed conflicts.[3] This is true despite the fact that the 1998 Rome Statute of the International Criminal Court (ICC Statute) does not give the Court jurisdiction over the war crime of intentionally directing attacks against civilian objects in non-international armed conflict (NIAC), as it does in IAC.[4]

The rule demands that all attacks target only military objectives and not civilian objects. An attack is unlawful not only if it is targeted against a civilian object, but also if it is *not* targeted at a lawful military objective, in which case it amounts to an indiscriminate attack. A civilian object is, as discussed in sub section A.i below, any object or area that is not a lawful military objective.

A. Key Definitions

i. Civilian Object

A civilian object is defined simply under the law of armed conflict as any object that is not a military objective. The definition, not itself controversial, was first codified in Article 52(1) of the 1977 Additional Protocol I, and is part of customary international law.[5] According to the Protocol, objects that are 'normally dedicated to civilian purposes' include 'a place of worship, a house or other dwelling or a school'.[6] In the ICRC's analysis,

> State practice considers civilian areas, towns, cities, villages, residential areas, dwellings, buildings and houses and schools, civilian means of transportation, hospitals, medical establishments and medical units, historic monuments, places of worship and cultural property, and the natural environment as *prima facie* civilian objects, provided, in the final analysis, they have not become military objectives.[7]

The notion of an 'object' includes an area of land. Also encompassed are animals, particularly livestock.

According to the United Kingdom (UK) Ministry of Defence, civilian objects 'would normally include cities, towns, and villages as such but not military objectives within those places'. The concept also includes

> foodstuffs and food producing areas, springs, wells, water works and other water sources, buildings and facilities used by civilians (so long as they do not fall within the definition of military

[2] ICRC Study of Customary IHL, Rule 7 ('The Principle of Distinction between Civilian Objects and Military Objectives') at https://goo.gl/hLX9Lq.

[3] See ibid.

[4] Art 8(2)(b)(ii), ICC Statute.

[5] ICRC Study of Customary IHL, Rule 9 ('Definition of Civilian Objects') at https://goo.gl/Ns6LSr.

[6] Art 52(3), 1977 Additional Protocol I.

[7] ICRC Study of Customary IHL, Rule 9 ('Definition of Civilian Objects') [notes omitted].

> objectives) such as housing estates and houses; apartment blocks and flats; factories and workshops producing goods of no military significance; offices, shops, markets and warehouses; farms and stables; schools, museums, places of worship, and other similar buildings; and means of transport such as civil aircraft, cars, railway trains, trams, and buses. Special protection is also given to hospitals, internment and prisoner of war camps.[8]

The US Department of Defense offers the following indicative list of objects and locations that are protected from attack (always provided, of course, that they are not military objectives):

- military medical transport, facilities, and equipment
- cultural property
- historic monuments, museums, scientific, artistic, educational, and cultural institutions
- places of worship
- undefended villages, towns, or cities
- hospital and safety zones, and persons and objects within these zones, and
- neutralised zones, and persons and objects within neutralised zones.[9]

The Department of Defense also recognises that it is prohibited to destroy food or water supplies for the purpose of denying sustenance to the civilian population, as is set out in law of armed conflict treaties.[10] The Eritrea-Ethiopia Claims Commission (EECC) considered the legality of Ethiopia's bombing of a reservoir located in a village in a harsh desert region about 17 kilometres from the port of Assab. The air strikes were purportedly conducted because Ethiopia believed that the loss of drinking water would have restricted Eritrea's military capacity on the Eastern Front.[11] Eritrea submitted statements to the Commission indicating that the reservoir served only civilians and was the sole source of drinking water for the town of Assab, and that the Eritrean forces in that area had their own wells and underground storage tanks.[12]

Based on the available evidence, the EECC had 'no doubt' that Ethiopia knew that the reservoir was a vital source of water for Assab. Ethiopia's purpose in targeting the reservoir was, the Commission concluded, to 'deprive Eritrea of the sustenance value of its water', and not 'on an erroneous assumption that the reservoir provided water only to the Eritrean armed forces'.[13] In reaching its determination that the relevant treaty provision[14] had become customary law, the EECC found it 'highly significant' that none of the 160 states that were then party to the Protocol had made 'any reservation or statement of interpretation rejecting or limiting the binding nature of that prohibition'.[15] It also referred to the statement in the 1997 amendment to the US Naval Handbook that the rule prohibiting

[8] UK Ministry of Defence, *The Manual of the Law of Armed Conflict* (Oxford, Oxford University Press, 2004) para 5.24.2.

[9] US Department of Defense, *Law of War Manual*, June 2015, updated December 2016 (hereinafter 'USDOD December 2016 *Law of War Manual*') para 5.5.2, at https://goo.gl/QMkjqs.

[10] Ibid, para 5.20.1. See Art 54(2), 1977 Additional Protocol I; and Art 14, 1977 Additional Protocol II.

[11] EECC, *Partial Award: Western Front, Aerial Bombardment and Related Claims*, 19 December 2005, para 98, p 328, at http://legal.un.org/riaa/cases/vol_XXVI/291-349.pdf.

[12] Ibid, para 99.

[13] Ibid, para 100.

[14] Art 52(3), 1977 Additional Protocol I.

[15] EECC (n 11) para 104.

intentional destruction of objects indispensable to the survival of the civilian population for the specific purpose of denying the civilian population their use was a 'customary rule' accepted by the US.[16]

In sum, the following objects, amongst others, are generally to be considered civilian for the purpose of the rule of distinction:

- private dwellings (unless occupied by combatants)
- offices (without a military function)
- factories that manufacture non-military products
- a place of worship
- schools
- hospital and other medical facilities
- water sources
- agricultural land and farms
- livestock
- cultural property, and
- civilian means of transportation and infrastructure, especially minor roads and rail and tram networks[17] not used by the military.

The 1977 Additional Protocol I stipulates that, in case of doubt, objects are to be considered as civilian.[18] The US, though, does not accept that this provision is declaratory of customary law.[19] In contrast, the ICRC notes that at the Diplomatic Conference leading to the adoption of the Additional Protocols, Mexico stated that Article 52 was so essential that it 'cannot be the subject of any reservations whatsoever since these would be inconsistent with the aim and purpose of Protocol I and undermine its basis'.[20] Israel takes a more nuanced view than the US, arguing that the presumption of civilian status only applies when the field commander considers a 'significant' doubt exists as to status and not merely a slight possibility of being mistaken. As the ICRC explains, 'Accordingly, [in the practice of Israel] the decision whether or not to attack rests with the field commander who has to determine whether the possibility of mistake is significant enough to warrant not launching the attack.'[21]

[16] Ibid. The US was not (and is still not) a party to the 1977 Additional Protocol I.

[17] In the *Dragomir Milošević* case, a Trial Chamber of the International Criminal Tribunal for the former Yugoslavia (ICTY) held that, 'on the basis of the evidence, the Trial Chamber is satisfied that the trams targeted in the city of Sarajevo had civilian status. In this regard, the Trial Chamber notes that all evidence shows that a tram is not suitable for military use. Furthermore, it was a well-known fact among people living in Sarajevo that civilians used the trams. This was also made clear from media reports during the relevant time period. The fact that one or two soldiers were travelling on a tram which was targeted by sniper fire does not change its civilian status.' ICTY, *Prosecutor v Dragomir Milošević*, Judgment (Trial Chamber III) (Case No IT-98-29/1-T), 12 December 2007, para 224.

[18] Art 51(3), 1977 Additional Protocol I.

[19] See, e.g., USDOD December 2016 *Law of War Manual* (n 9) para 5.4.3.2; see also Y Dinstein, *The Conduct of Hostilities under the Law of International Armed Conflict*, 3rd edn (Cambridge, Cambridge University Press, 2016) paras 301, 379.

[20] Practice cited in ICRC Study of Customary IHL, Rule 10 ('Civilians Objects' Loss of Protection from Attack') at https://goo.gl/rVbk6K.

[21] Ibid.

ii. Military Objective

The logical definition of a civilian object as any object that is not a military objective nonetheless gives rise to the question of what constitutes a military objective. In the words of the International Criminal Tribunal for the former Yugoslavia (ICTY) Committee, established to review the 1999 North Atlantic Treaty Organization (NATO) bombing of the Federal Republic of Yugoslavia ('the ICTY Committee'), 'Everyone will agree that a munitions factory is a military objective and an unoccupied church is a civilian object.'[22] With respect to many objects, however, the legal determination is not so straightforward. Insofar as objects are concerned, 'the most widely accepted' definition of military objectives is given in Article 52(2) of the 1977 Additional Protocol I.[23] This definition, which represents customary law in all armed conflict in the view of the ICRC,[24] is as follows:

> [M]ilitary objectives are limited to those objects which by their nature, location, purpose or use make an effective contribution to military action and whose partial or total destruction, capture or neutralization, in the circumstances ruling at the time, offers a definite military advantage.

Thus, there are two cumulative elements to the definition. First, the nature, location, purpose or use of an object must make an effective contribution to military action. Second, the object's partial or total destruction, capture or neutralisation must, in the circumstances ruling at the time, offer a definite military advantage. These elements and their constituents are discussed in turn.

a. An Object's Military Nature

The 'nature' of an object refers to its 'type', according to the UK Ministry of Defence.[25] This implies that certain objects will, by their 'nature', be military objectives. In the view of the ICRC, this element comprises all objects directly used by the armed forces, such as weapons, equipment, transports, fortifications, depots, buildings occupied by armed forces,[26] staff headquarters, communications centres.[27] Similarly, as the UK states, the term includes military weapons, vehicles, equipment and installations of combatant members of enemy armed forces, as well as military transports, command and control centres, or communications stations.[28]

In the *Gotovina* case before the ICTY, which concerned Croatia's retaking of its Krajina region, evidence was presented that, 'on the tactical level, the targets for Operation Storm were command posts of brigades; firing positions of the artillery; communication centres

[22] *Final Report to the Prosecutor by the Committee Established to Review the NATO Bombing Campaign Against the Federal Republic of Yugoslavia*, 2000, para 37 (hereinafter 'ICTY Committee Final Report').

[23] Ibid, para 35.

[24] ICRC Study of Customary IHL, Rule 8 ('Definition of Military Objectives') at https://goo.gl/LSSuhX. The ICTY Committee also considered the definition in Art 52(2) to be 'generally accepted as part of customary law': ICTY Committee Final Report (n 22) para 42.

[25] UK Ministry of Defence (n 8) para 5.4.4.

[26] One should assume that the ICRC means 'permanently' occupied by the armed forces as, where the occupation of a building is merely temporary, this may fall under the heading of 'use' rather than 'nature'.

[27] Y Sandoz, C Swinarski and B Zimmermann (eds), *Commentary on the Additional Protocols of 8 June 1977 to the Geneva Conventions of 12 August 1949* (Geneva, ICRC/Martinus Nijhoff, 1987) para 2020 (hereinafter 'ICRC Commentary on the 1977 Additional Protocols').

[28] UK Ministry of Defence (n 8) para 5.4.4(c).

and relay nodes; depots for military equipment, combat reserves and troops; roads and bridges; fortified combat features and enemy defence trenches; and any targets that would emerge during combat'.[29] On the operational level, the targets were the Krajina Serb forces main staff and communications centre, the Ministry of Defence headquarters, bridges and the railway station, all in Knin; the police stations in Knin and Gračac (the police were deemed to be participating directly in hostilities on behalf of the Krajina Serbs); the military barracks facilities in Knin and other towns; and crossroads in the towns of Benkovac, Drvar, Gračac, and Knin.[30] Most of these targets, whose identification was aided by use of reconnaissance drone, were military objectives by their nature. The bridges, crossroads and railway station would become military objectives by virtue of their location or use, as discussed in section II.A.ii.b.

A valuable listing of objects whose nature would tend to make them military objectives has been proffered by Yoram Dinstein. His list is adapted and abridged as follows:

- Fixed military fortifications and military bases, barracks and installations (whether permanent or temporary).
- Means of warfare (armaments, weapon systems and related *matériel*).
- Military ports, shipyards and dry-docks.
- Military airfields.
- Military storage facilities.
- Raw materials for military use.
- Military repair facilities.
- Military research and development facilities.
- Intelligence-gathering facilities (even when not run by the military).
- Ministry of Defence.
- Power plants serving the military.
- Factories producing weapons and components for the military.[31]

b. An Object's Military Value by Reason of its Location

Dinstein also includes as military objectives 'by nature' transportation arteries of strategic importance, including railways, bridges, roads, navigable rivers and canals, and tunnels.[32] These are, though, better understood as having military value by reason of their location (or their use). For, as the ICRC commentary on the relevant provision in the 1977 Additional Protocol I notes, certain objects 'by their nature have no military function' but,

> by virtue of their location, make an effective contribution to military action. This may be, for example, a bridge or other construction, or it could also be … a site which is of special importance for military operations in view of its location, either because it is a site that must be seized or

[29] ICTY, *Prosecutor v Ante Gotovina and Mladen Markač*, Judgment (Trial Chamber I) (Case No IT-06-90-T), 15 April 2011, para 1189.
[30] Ibid.
[31] Adapted from Dinstein (n 19) para 296(a)–(p).
[32] Ibid, para 296(q).

> because it is important to prevent the enemy from seizing it, or otherwise because it is a matter of forcing the enemy to retreat from it.[33]

Dinstein rejects the comparison sometimes made between bridges and schools, intimating that in contradistinction to schools, there is a presumption that a bridge is a military objective. He argues that a bridge 'would fail to be a military objective only when it is neither actually nor potentially of any military benefit to the enemy (eg when located in a residential area away from the contact zone)'.[34] This is too broad. A bridge, unless fortified, is not by nature a military objective. It must, therefore, by its location, purpose,or use, make an effective contribution to military action.

As an example, during the 1999 Kosovo conflict between several NATO member states and the Federal Republic of Yugoslavia, a NATO aircraft launched two laser-guided bombs at the Leskovac railway bridge over the Grdelica gorge and Juzna Morava river in eastern Serbia. The case is notorious for other reasons, as discussed in chapter 6, but what concerns us here is whether or not the bridge was, *a priori*, a lawful military objective. According to General Wesley Clark, NATO's Supreme Allied Commander for Europe, the railroad bridge was 'part of the integrated communications supply network in Serbia', used to re-supply Serb forces in Kosovo.[35] Accordingly, the ICTY Committee was of 'the opinion' that the bridge was a 'legitimate' military objective.[36] This is an appropriate analysis of the status of the bridge under Hague Law.

An area of land, even one that has no object on or beneath it, can be a military objective by virtue of its location. For instance, in the view of the UK (citing as evidence the ICRC commentary on the 1977 Additional Protocol I), location 'includes areas which are militarily important because they must be captured or denied to the enemy or because the enemy must be made to retreat from them'.[37] When it ratified the Protocol, the UK entered a statement of understanding whereby 'a specific area of land may be a military objective if, because of its location or other reasons specified in Article 52, its total or partial destruction, capture or neutralisation in the circumstances ruling at the time offers definite military advantage'.[38] Understandings in a similar vein have been made before and since by, amongst others, Canada,[39] France,[40] Germany,[41] Italy[42] and New Zealand.[43]

To transform an area of land into a lawful military objective, Dinstein would require a 'distinctive feature', such as 'an important mountain pass or defile; a trail in the jungle or in a swamp area; a bridgehead or a spit of land controlling the entrance of a harbour'.[44] He accepts that in 'the turmoil of the battlefield, additional sites, such as a hill dominating the surrounding ground in the contact zone', may become a military objective by virtue

[33] ICRC Commentary on the 1977 Additional Protocols, para 2021.
[34] Dinstein (n 19) para 311.
[35] Cited in ICTY Committee Final Report (n 22) paras 59, 58.
[36] Ibid, para 62.
[37] UK Ministry of Defence (n 8) para 5.4.4(d); ICRC Commentary on the 1977 Additional Protocols, para 2022.
[38] UK Statement of Understanding, 28 January 1998, para j, at https://goo.gl/hX58ah.
[39] Canadian Statement of Understanding, 20 November 1990, at https://goo.gl/GiKfNR.
[40] French Statement of Understanding, 11 April 2001, para 12, at https://goo.gl/DDKWYK.
[41] German Statement of Understanding, 14 February 1991, para 7, at https://goo.gl/tQWY7L.
[42] Italian Statement of Understanding, 27 February 1986, at https://goo.gl/sAuekA.
[43] New Zealand Statement of Understanding, 8 February 1988, para 4, at https://goo.gl/ZbCRqR.
[44] Dinstein (n 19) para 308.

of their tactical value. But he cautions that 'the military necessity to take the high ground in such circumstances does not deprive civilian objects standing there of their protected status'.[45] This accurately describes the state of the law.

c. An Object's Military Purpose

The military purpose of an object refers to its 'future intended use' in the view of the ICRC and the UK.[46] The scope of this constituent has not been satisfactorily explained. For Dinstein, it means discerning the *intent* of the enemy to use a given object for a military purpose in the future. He gives as an example an enemy's announced intention during peacetime to commandeer a civilian cruise ship for use as a troop ship during armed conflict. Once such an announcement is made, he argues, upon the outbreak of hostilities the ship may lawfully be targeted as a military objective even before it has been used for any military purpose.[47]

This understanding is potentially extremely broad. Indeed, it appears somewhat incongruous at first glance, given that the accepted definition of 'military objective' refers to the object's making an effective contribution to military action and that its destruction must offer a definite military advantage *in the circumstances ruling at the time*. A possible future use of an object[48] could amount to a disturbing loophole for those intending to target civilian areas, especially where urban conflict is expected against a non-state armed group, on the basis that the enemy will be constrained to hide in civilian homes and schools.

Dinstein tempers his finding, though, by arguing that speculation is insufficient, and that field intelligence which claims, for example, that a given school will be used as a munitions depot 'does not justify an attack against that school as long as no practical steps have been taken to move the munitions in'.[49] The distinction he draws between the intended commandeering of the cruise ship and the intended use of the school is that the latter is based on intelligence that is partial and fragmented, which amounts to 'not more than estimates and evaluations'.[50] Thus, he cautions against targeting based on a 'worst case scenario'.[51] In light of the elaborate and detailed US and UK intelligence claims about the existence and location of weapons of mass destruction in Iraq, caution is well justified.

Dinstein notes that the EECC explicitly held a similar understanding of purpose to the UK as regards 'intended future use'.[52] The Commission considered the case of Ethiopia's bombing in May 2000 of an Eritrean power plant at Hirgigo, whose construction had been completed but which was still in the 'testing and commissioning phase'.[53] Eritrea had asserted that, as at May 2000, the Hirgigo plant was not yet producing power for use in Eritrea and that Eritrea's military forces had their own electric generating equipment

[45] Ibid.

[46] UK Ministry of Defence (n 8) para 5.4.4(e).

[47] Dinstein (n 19) para 304.

[48] Gary Solis, for instance, suggests possible use as an alternative to intended future use. See GD Solis, *The Law of Armed Conflict. International Humanitarian War in Law*, 2nd edn (New York, Cambridge University Press, 2016) 511.

[49] Dinstein (n 19) para 305.

[50] Ibid, paras 305, 306.

[51] Ibid, para 306.

[52] Ibid, para 303, citing EECC, *Partial Award: Western Front* (n 11) para 120, p 335.

[53] Dinstein (n 19) para 111.

and did not depend on general power grids in Eritrea. Eritrea also submitted evidence in support of its assertion that its Ministry of Defence used no more than 4 per cent of Eritrea's non-military power supply and that Eritrean manufacturing companies did not produce significant military equipment.[54]

The EECC agreed with Ethiopia's assertion in its pleadings that electricity generating stations 'are generally recognized to be of sufficient importance to a State's capacity to meet its wartime needs of communication, transport and industry so as usually to qualify as military objectives during armed conflicts'.[55] The Commission also agreed with Ethiopia's interpretation that a state at war should not be obligated to wait until an object is put into use, when its purpose is such that 'it will make an effective contribution to military action once it has been tested, commissioned and put to use'.[56] Thus the ICTY Trial Chamber in the *Gotovina* case appeared to accept that 'documentary evidence' that a civilian factory producing 'bolts, screws, and other metal products' would be used to produce ammunition at a future point in time would be sufficient to render the object a lawful military objective.[57]

d. An Object's Military Use

It is uncontested that what is, *a priori*, a civilian object may become a military objective as a result of its current use. The UK, for instance, affirms that military objectives 'may' also include other objects of military value, 'such as bridges, communications towers, and electricity and refined oil production facilities'.[58] This typically depends on their use. Positioning troops, weapons, military intelligence assets or military *matériel* in or on an object will all potentially transform it into a lawful military objective. Thus, for example, an ICTY Trial Chamber found that stationing police in a monastery in the Croatian town of Knin – in the conflict in the Krajina, ethnic Serb police were participating directly in hostilities – transformed a civilian object into a military objective.[59]

Among a number of controversial examples, during the 1999 Kosovo conflict, NATO forces bombed the Serbian TV and Radio Station (RTS) in Belgrade on the early morning of 23 April. Between 10 and 17 people are said to have been killed by the strike.[60] The bombing of the TV studio was part of a broader planned and coordinated attack that sought to disrupt and degrade the Yugoslav command, control and communications network. At a press conference on 27 April 1999, NATO officials justified the attack in terms of the dual military and civilian use to which the FRY communication system was routinely put, asserting that '[m]ost of the commercial system serves the military and the military system can be put to use for the commercial system'.[61] NATO further described civilian television as 'heavily dependent on the military command and control system and military traffic is also

[54] Ibid, para 117.

[55] Ibid. The Commission excluded from being military objectives power stations 'that are known, or should be known, to be segregated from a general power grid and are limited to supplying power for humanitarian purposes, such as medical facilities, or other uses that could have no effect on the State's ability to wage war'.

[56] Ibid, para 120.

[57] *Gotovina and Markač* (n 29) paras 1208, 1216.

[58] UK Ministry of Defence (n 8) para 5.4.1.

[59] *Gotovina and Markač* (n 29) para 1213.

[60] ICTY Committee Final Report (n 22) para 71.

[61] Ibid, para 72.

routed through the civilian system'.[62] It also claimed that the RTS facilities were being used 'as radio relay stations and transmitters to support the activities of the FRY military and special police forces, and therefore they represent legitimate military targets'.[63]

As the ICTY Committee observed, however, '[m]ore controversially', the strike 'was also justified on the basis of the propaganda purpose to which it was employed':[64]

> [We need to] directly strike at the very central nerve system of Milosevic's regime. This of course are [*sic*] those assets which are used to plan and direct and to create the political environment of tolerance in Yugoslavia in which these brutalities can not only be accepted but even condoned. … Strikes against TV transmitters and broadcast facilities are part of our campaign to dismantle the FRY propaganda machinery which is a vital part of President Milosevic's control mechanism.

The ICTY Committee concluded that the strike's legality as an attack against a propaganda machine was 'more debatable' but, '[i]nsofar as the attack actually was aimed at disrupting the communications network, it was legally acceptable'.[65] This assessment is too kind to NATO. Attacking a TV station because it supports the regime in power is unlawful. Indeed, NATO's assertion in a statement of 8 April 1999 that the TV studios would be targeted unless they broadcast six hours each day of Western media reports was fatuous from a political as well as a legal perspective:

> If President Milosevic would provide equal time for Western news broadcasts in its programmes without censorship 3 hours a day between noon and 1800 and 3 hours a day between 1800 and midnight, then his TV could be an acceptable instrument of public information.[66]

If the TV studio had been genuinely targeted on the basis that it was part of a military communications and/or command and control network, this could indeed comply with Hague Law. This judgment would not be affected even if an ancillary aim was to target the regime's propaganda apparatus.[67] But if the reality was that attacking the station for reasons of military command and control was only a rationale advanced *ex post facto* without adequate factual substance, the attack would have been unlawful. In that case, NATO would have been targeting a civilian object, one that potentially offered political rather than military advantage. According to the ICRC, indirect participation in hostilities – which does not lead to loss of civilian protection – encompasses war-sustaining actions, such as 'political propaganda'.[68] Human Rights Watch asserted that 'Even if one could justify legal attacks on civilian radio and television, there does not appear to be any justification for attacking urban studios, as opposed to transmitters.'[69]

[62] See ibid.

[63] Amnesty International, *NATO/Federal Republic of Yugoslavia: Violations of the Laws of War by NATO during Operation Allied Force*, Report, June 2000, 42.

[64] ICTY Committee Final Report (n 22) para 74.

[65] Ibid, paras 76, 75.

[66] Cited ibid, para 74.

[67] As Commander William Fenrick wrote, undermining civilian morale is not a legitimate military objective but securing it as a secondary benefit resulting from a lawful attack is not a law of armed conflict violation. W Fenrick, 'Targeting and Proportionality during the NATO Bombing Campaign against Yugoslavia' (2001) 12 *EJIL* 489, 497–98.

[68] ICRC, *Interpretive Guidance on Direct Participation in Hostilities under International Humanitarian Law* (Geneva, ICRC, 2009) 51.

[69] Human Rights Watch, 'Civilian Deaths in the NATO Air Campaign: The Crisis in Kosovo', 2000, at https://goo.gl/6vE5hW.

The UK Prime Minister, Tony Blair, in Washington, DC, for NATO's 50th anniversary summit at the time of the bombing, claimed that bombing television stations was 'entirely justified' since they were part of the 'apparatus of dictatorship and power of Milosevic'. At a 'heated' press briefing at the Ministry of Defence, Clare Short, the UK Secretary of State for International Development, said 'This is a war, this is a serious conflict, untold horrors are being done. The propaganda machine is prolonging the war and it's a legitimate target.' Admiral Sir Ian Garnett, chief of joint operations at the Ministry of Defence, said President Milosevic's 'propaganda machine consists of transmitters but also the studios from which the information is transmitted. That makes it part of the overall military structure. Both elements have to be attacked.'[70]

It is not certain what the truth of the reason for targeting RTS was. It is worth noting, however, that one of the attacks for which the commander of the Bosnian Serb forces above Sarajevo, Dragomir Milošević, was convicted of war crimes, was an attack on a TV building in Sarajevo. Commander Milošević had written in a letter:

> Our artillery forces are responding with precision to the Muslim artillery attacks. In one such response on 28 June they hit the BH Radio and Television Centre, the centre of media lies against the just struggle of the Serbian people.[71]

e. Destruction, Capture or Neutralisation Offering Definite Military Advantage

Any object whose nature, location, purpose or use makes an effective contribution to military action must also fulfil a second cumulative criterion: that, in the prevailing circumstances, its destruction, capture or neutralisation offers definite military advantage. According to the ICRC:

> In other words, it is not legitimate to launch an attack which only offers potential or indeterminate advantages. Those ordering or executing the attack must have sufficient information available to take this requirement into account; in case of doubt, the safety of the civilian population, which is the aim of the Protocol, must be taken into consideration.[72]

In acknowledging that the 1977 Additional Protocol I definition was the 'contemporary standard which must be used when attempting to determine the lawfulness of particular attacks', the ICTY Committee observed that it was 'not beyond criticism'.[73] As the ICTY notes, some argued that the definition was too restrictive. Hays Parks, for example, then Special Assistant for Law of War Matters to the US Army Judge Advocate General, argued that the focus on 'definite military advantage' might preclude attacks on economic targets that sustain a nation's ability to wage war.[74] Indeed, as Rogers notes, the definition of military objective 'excludes the general industrial and agricultural potential of the economy. Targets must offer a more specific military advantage.'[75]

[70] All cited in R Norton-Taylor, 'Serb TV station was legitimate target, says Blair', *Guardian* (24 April 1999) at https://goo.gl/6XssNB.
[71] *Dragomir Milošević* (n 17) para 836.
[72] ICRC Commentary on the 1977 Additional Protocols, para 2024.
[73] ICTY Committee Final Report (n 22) para 42.
[74] W Hays Parks, 'Air War and the Law of War' (1990) 32:1 *Air Force Law Review* 135.
[75] APV Rogers, *Law on the Battlefield*, 3rd edn (Manchester, Manchester University Press, 2012) 110.

In the case of the Hirgigo power plant, noted in section II.A.ii.c, the EECC held that the term 'military advantage' can 'only properly be understood in the context of the military operations between the Parties taken as a whole, not simply in the context of a specific attack'.[76] Thus, determining whether the attack on the power station offered a definite military advantage 'must be considered in the context of its relation to the armed conflict as a whole at the time of the attack'.[77] Controversially, the EECC affirmed that

> infliction of economic losses from attacks against military objectives is a lawful means of achieving a definite military advantage, and there can be few military advantages more evident than effective pressure to end an armed conflict that, each day, added to the number of both civilian and military casualties on both sides of the war.[78]

By a majority, the Commission found that in the prevailing circumstances, the Hirgigo power station was a lawful military objective.[79]

iii. Loss of Protection

Consonant with the definition of a military objective, a civilian object may lose its protection under Hague Law if it is used in hostile action, becoming for a time a military objective. Just as with a civilian participating directly in hostilities, the loss of protection is temporary: limited to the period during which it is used for hostile action, whether that be for firing at the enemy, storage of weapons, barracking of troops or military reconnaissance. As Dinstein records, 'Once military use of a civilian object has ceased, the object reverts to its initial status, which is not tainted by past military use.'[80]

During the period of its military use, an object (or, more accurately, the part of the object used for hostile purposes) effectively becomes a military objective in accordance with the customary law definition. As the ICRC observes:

> It follows that when a civilian object is used in such a way that it loses its civilian character and qualifies as a military objective, it is liable to attack. This reasoning can also be found in the Statute of the International Criminal Court, which makes it a war crime to intentionally direct attacks against civilian objects, provided they 'are not military objectives'.[81]

However, the fact that, for example, a school classroom or outbuilding is being used by a sniper, or contains military weapons or equipment does not make the entire school a lawful military objective. Each distinct object is treated on its own merits in the circumstances prevailing at the time. As previously noted, in the *Dragomir Milošević* case, an ICTY Trial Chamber held that, 'on the basis of the evidence', it was 'satisfied that the trams targeted in the city of Sarajevo had civilian status. … The fact that one or two soldiers were travelling on a tram which was targeted by sniper fire does not change its civilian status.'[82]

[76] EECC, *Partial Award: Western Front* (n 11) para 113, citing D Fleck, *The Handbook of Humanitarian Law in Armed Conflict* (Oxford, Oxford University Press, 1995) 162.
[77] EECC, *Partial Award: Western Front* (n 11) para 113.
[78] Ibid, para 121.
[79] Ibid.
[80] Dinstein (n 19) 112.
[81] ICRC Study of Customary IHL, Rule 10 ('Civilians Objects' Loss of Protection from Attack').
[82] *Dragomir Milošević* (n 17) para 224.

III. The Application of the Rule

As neither treaty nor customary law makes explicit how the rule of distinction is to be applied in practice, it is necessary to employ 'subsidiary means for the determination of rules of law'. These are, according to the 1945 Statute of the International Court of Justice ('the ICJ Statute'), 'judicial decisions and the teachings of the most highly qualified publicists of the various nations'.[83]

To date, the most valuable examples of judicial discussion of the targeting of objects under Hague Law rules have been in the *Galić*, *Dragomir Milošević*, *Mladić* and *Gotovina* cases before the ICTY. *Galić*, *Milošević* and *Mladić* all addressed the Bosnian Serb campaign of sniping and shelling in 'The Siege of Sarajevo' in the early 1990s, while *Gotovina* addressed the conflict to oust the ethnic Serb forces in the Krajina in Croatia in 1995.

Major-General Stanislav Galić was the commander of Bosnian Serb forces in and around Sarajevo from September 1992 to August 1994. The Prosecution alleged that over this period he conducted a protracted campaign of sniping and shelling against civilians in Sarajevo.[84] One of the charges against General Galić was that that he conducted 'a coordinated and protracted campaign of artillery and mortar shelling onto civilian areas of Sarajevo and upon its civilian population. The campaign of shelling resulted in thousands of civilians being killed or injured.'[85]

While the charge was formally one of attacking civilians, in fact and in law the reference to civilian areas is better framed as an attack on civilian objects. The Prosecution in the *Galić* case suggested that in accordance with the 'principle' of distinction, the following types of attack are unlawful:

(1) attacks deliberately directed against the civilian population as such, whether directed at particular civilian objects or at civilian areas generally;
(2) attacks aimed at military and civilian objectives without distinction; and
(3) attacks directed at legitimate military objectives, which cause civilian losses clearly disproportionate to the military advantage anticipated.[86]

These equate, respectively, to an attack on civilians or an attack on civilian objects; an indiscriminate attack; and a disproportionate attack. Although, under the 1977 Additional Protocol I, a disproportionate attack is to be considered an indiscriminate attack, these two forms of violation of Hague Law are better treated as distinct rules and tests.

A. Direct Attacks against Civilian Objects

A direct attack against a civilian object is one where an object is targeted with the knowledge that it is civilian in nature. According to the 1977 Additional Protocol I, civilian objects 'shall not be the object of attack'.[87] In its formulation of the corresponding customary law

[83] Art 38(1)(d), ICJ Statute.
[84] ICTY, *Prosecutor v Stanislav Galić*, Judgment (Trial Chamber I) (Case No IT-98-29-T), 5 December 2003, paras 2, 3.
[85] Ibid, para 15.
[86] Ibid, para 36, citing Prosecution Pre-Trial Brief, para 157 and Prosecution Final Trial Brief, para 17.
[87] Art 52(1), 1977 Additional Protocol I.

rule on the 'general principle of immunity of civilian objects',[88] the ICRC frames the prohibition as follows: 'Attacks must not be directed against civilian objects.'

The standard by which knowledge is to be judged with respect to individual responsibility under international criminal law is addressed in section V.C of this chapter. Here what is at issue is the knowledge required for state responsibility for violations of the primary rule. For this, it would be enough that either the commander launching the attack, or an individual engaged in the attack, was aware that a civilian object was more likely than not to be struck, taking into account the allowable margin of error under Hague Law (see section III.D). Evidence of a significant lack of care in selecting a military objective to attack should typically result in the finding of an indiscriminate attack rather than a direct attack on civilians or civilian objects, notwithstanding jurisprudence in the ICTY.[89]

B. Indiscriminate Attacks Affecting Civilian Objects

As with direct attacks against civilian objects, indiscriminate attacks are prohibited by both treaty and customary law.[90] An indiscriminate attack is one that is of a nature 'to strike military objectives and civilians or civilian objects without distinction'. This is because: the attack is not directed at a specific military objective; it uses a means or method of warfare that cannot be directed at a specific military objective; or it uses a means or method of warfare whose effects cannot be limited as required by Hague Law rules. As the UK Ministry of Defence has surmised, it 'seems that an attack can be indiscriminate even if no civilians are killed or injured by it'.[91]

The use of inherently indiscriminate means and methods of warfare is addressed in section III.C of this chapter. An attack that is not directed at a specific military objective encompasses not only situations where it is known that a military objective is not being targeted, but also instances where targeting is reckless. It likely does not comprehend situations where the targeting is only negligent.[92] As Dinstein explains, in contrast to a direct attack on a civilian object, in an indiscriminate attack any civilian harm is 'merely' a matter

[88] ICRC Commentary on the 1977 Additional Protocols, para 2011.

[89] In its final trial chamber judgment, of Bosnian Serb military leader Ratko Mladić, the ICTY reaffirmed its view that 'acts or threats of violence directed against civilians are not limited to direct acts or threats of violence against civilians, but may include indiscriminate or disproportionate acts or threats of violence'. ICTY, *Prosecutor v Ratko Mladić*, Judgment (Trial Chamber I) (Case No IT-09-92-T), 22 November 2017, para 3187.

[90] See Art 51, 1977 Additional Protocol I; ICRC Study of Customary IHL, Rule 12 ('Definition of Indiscriminate Attacks') at https://goo.gl/ZYReci. As Dinstein notes, the prohibition was first included in the abortive 1923 Hague Rules on Air Warfare, Art XXIV(3) of which stipulated that 'The bombardment of cities, towns, villages, dwellings, or buildings not in the immediate neighbourhood of the operations of land forces is prohibited. In cases where the objectives … are so situated, that they cannot be bombarded without the indiscriminate bombardment of the civilian population, the aircraft must abstain from bombardment.'

[91] UK Ministry of Defence (n 8), para 5.23.3.

[92] In the *Galić* case, the Appeals Chamber cited with approval the 1987 ICRC Commentary on Article 85 of the 1977 Additional Protocol I, which describes recklessness as 'the attitude of an agent who, without being certain of a particular result, accepts the possibility of its happening', distinguishing it from negligence, which describes a person who 'acts without having his mind on the act or its consequences'. See ICRC Commentary on the 1977 Additional Protocols, para 3474; see *Prosecutor v Galić*, Judgment (Appeals Chamber) (Case No IT-98-29-A), 30 November 2006, para 140.

'of no concern' to the attacking party.[93] He gives non-exhaustive examples of what would amount to an indiscriminate attack, which include:

- to fire 'carelessly' (without a clear idea of the nature of the target) into territory controlled by the enemy
- to jettison bombs at random over enemy territory
- to conduct bombing raids at night, in inclement weather or from extremely high altitudes (when visibility is impaired) without adequate means of target identification.[94]

In the *Gotovina* case, an ICTY Trial Chamber had found that, on 4 and 5 August 1995, Croatian army artillery units fired artillery shells and rockets at the so-called 'four towns' in the Krajina (Benkovac, Gračac, Knin and Obrovac). After carefully comparing the evidence on the locations of impacts in these towns with the locations of possible military targets, it concluded that they had targeted certain areas that did not contain military objectives. As such, the Chamber found that Croatian forces had treated the towns themselves as targets for artillery fire, holding that this shelling constituted an indiscriminate attack on the towns and an unlawful attack on civilians and civilian objects.

The controversial elements of the judgment concerned the focus on an (*ex-post-facto*) impact assessment as evidence of violations to be judged at the time of launch, and especially that the Trial Chamber determined that strikes more than 200 metres away from a possible military objective were unlawful. The logic by which it arrived at this conclusion is more than a little obscure. The Chamber judged the 'normal scattering dispersion of a 130-millimetre shell' as 'an area with a diameter of 35 metres'.[95] In ballistics, however, it is more common to refer to the circular error probable (CEP) of a weapon to measure its accuracy. This is the radius, not the diameter, of a circle within which half of the rounds are expected to land. A further figure, amounting to the radius of three times the CEP, is the area within which 95 per cent of the rounds are expected to land.[96] Thus, the 130 mm shell, fired from an accepted operational distance, would appear to have a CEP of 17.5 metres and 3 CEP of 52.5 metres. Very different figures were subsequently proffered by a US artillery expert, retired Lieutenant-General Wilson A Shoffner, who contributed a report to an *amicus curiae* brief submitted to the Tribunal in connection with General Gotovina's appeal against conviction. He calculated that a 'reasonable estimate' of CEP from a field gun firing at maximum range (27.5 kilometres, just beyond the firing of the guns against Knin) would be 165 metres, with 3 CEP extending to a radius of 495 metres.

The Trial Chamber cited evidence by Andrew Leslie, Chief of Staff of UNCRO Sector South in Knin from 1 March to 7 August 1995 and 'a military officer with extensive experience in artillery', who considered that when using 130 mm guns or multiple-barrel rocket

[93] Dinstein (n 19) para 393.
[94] Ibid, para 396.
[95] *Gotovina and Markač* (n 29) para 1898.
[96] See, eg, Comments by Lt-Gen (ret) Wilson A Shoffner on The Report by Major General Robert H Scales on Croatian Army ('HV') Use of Artillery and Rockets on Targets Based in Knin, Croatia, August 4–5, 1995, p 3 in ICTY, *Prosecutor v Gotovina* (Appeals Chamber) (Case No IT-06-90-A), Application and Proposed Amicus Curiae Brief Concerning the 15 April 2011 Trial Chamber Judgment and Requesting that the Appeals Chamber Reconsider the Findings of Unlawful Artillery Attacks during Operation Storm (hereinafter 'Proposed Amicus Curiae Brief to the Gotovina Appeals Chamber').

launchers (MBRLs), landing within a 400-metre radius of the target with the first shot would be 'acceptable'.[97] Despite his experience, they accorded less importance to his statement as he 'was not called as an artillery expert in this case and did not testify in detail about his basis for concluding that landing within a 400-metre radius of a target was acceptable for a first shot'.[98] Instead, the Trial Chamber, evaluating all of the evidence presented during the trial, 'consider[ed] it a reasonable interpretation of the evidence that those artillery projectiles which impacted within a distance of 200 metres of an identified artillery target were deliberately fired at that artillery target'.[99] This meant that, *a priori*, impacts that were more than 200 metres away from a lawful military objective were unlawful.

This conclusion by the Trial Chamber was of great concern to a number of leading law of armed conflict experts. In their *amicus curiae* to the Appeals Chamber (which was not formally considered as, inter alia, one of the experts, Professor Geoffrey Corn, had not formally disclosed in the brief that he had served as an expert for the defence in General Gotovina's trial),[100] the *Amici* argued that 200 metres was an 'unrealistic operational standard'. They encouraged the Appeals Chamber to 'carefully consider whether this 200-meter radius of acceptable error is: (1) sufficiently established by the Trial record, and if so (2) whether that radius is inherently inconsistent with the nature of artillery and indirect fire capabilities and employment'.[101] The *Amici* advocated for a 400-metre standard, as 'proposed by Brigadier General Leslie' and based on the realities of operational artillery employment.[102]

In its judgment, the ICTY Appeals Chamber noted – correctly – that the Trial Chamber 'did not explain the specific basis on which it arrived at a 200 metre margin of error as a reasonable interpretation of evidence on the record'.[103] It further observed that the trial judgment 'contains no indication that any evidence considered by the Trial Chamber suggested a 200 metre margin of error'.[104] The Appeals Chamber held, Judges Agius and Pocar dissenting, that absent 'an established range of error', it could not exclude

> the possibility that all of the impact sites considered in the Trial Judgement were the result of shelling aimed at targets that the Trial Chamber considered to be legitimate. The fact that a relatively large number of shells fell more than 200 metres from fixed artillery targets could be consistent with a much broader range of error. The spread of shelling across Knin is also plausibly explained by the scattered locations of fixed artillery targets, … along with the possibility of a higher margin of error. Although evidence on the record suggests that individual units of the HV aimed artillery in the general direction of the Four Towns rather than at specific targets, the Trial Chamber found that this evidence was not wholly conclusive when considered alone … and was indicative of an unlawful attack only in the context of the Trial Chamber's application of the 200 Metre Standard.[105]

[97] *Gotovina and Markač* (n 29) para 1898.
[98] Ibid.
[99] Ibid.
[100] ICTY, *Prosecutor v Gotovina and Markač*, Decision on Application and Proposed Amicus Curiae Brief (Appeals Chamber), 14 February 2012, para 12.
[101] Proposed Amicus Curiae Brief to the Gotovina Appeals Chamber (n 96) 20–21.
[102] Ibid, 21.
[103] ICTY, *Prosecutor v Gotovina and Markač*, Judgment (Appeals Chamber) (Case No IT-06-90-A), 16 November 2012, para 58.
[104] Ibid.
[105] Ibid, para 65.

The Appeals Chamber unanimously agreed that a 200-metre standard for artillery and rocket attacks in populated areas did not exist in Hague Law. But, as Judge Pocar pointed out in his excoriating dissent, where the Chamber found an error of law in the trial judgment 'arising from the application of an incorrect legal standard', it was duty bound to articulate what the correct standard was. The Chamber had manifestly failed to do so.[106] The putative *Amici* had expressed their belief that the *Gotovina* judgment had 'the potential to become the "Tadić of targeting law"'. Regrettably, their wish would be unfulfilled. As Judge Pocar observed:

> By not articulating the correct legal standard, the Majority falls short of correcting any legal errors in the Trial Judgement and clarifying the law the Trial Chamber should have applied when assessing the legality of an attack directed on civilians and civilian objects. It also fails to consider whether the artillery attacks on the Four Towns were lawful or not when the evidence is assessed in light of the principles of international humanitarian law ('IHL'). First, the Majority fails to give any indication as to what the correct legal standard was. Does the Majority consider that the correct legal standard was a 400-metre standard? A 100-metre standard? A 0-metre standard? The Appeal Judgement provides no answer to this question. Second, the Majority also fails to clarify on which basis the correct legal standard should have been established. Does the Majority consider that a legal standard can be established on a margin of error of artillery weapons? Does the Majority consider that a trial chamber is entitled in law to establish a presumption of legality to assess the evidence of the shelling attacks and the artillery impacts in order to establish the lawfulness of the attack? Is a trial chamber not limited in its analysis to the strict application of IHL principles? Here again, the Appeal Judgement is mute on these issues. Third, if the Majority considers that applying a presumption of legality to analyse the evidence of the shelling attacks and the artillery impacts in order to establish its lawfulness is incorrect, it further fails to articulate which legal principles the Trial Chamber should have applied. Does the Majority consider that the Trial Chamber should have applied the principles of customary IHL in its analysis? If so, which exact IHL principles should the Trial Chamber have applied in assessing whether the artillery attack was lawful? Does the Majority consider that the minimum applicable legal standard was to analyse whether the shelling was aimed at targeting military objectives offering a definite military advantage, whether it was done in respect of the principle of proportionality and after all precautionary measures had been taken? Silence.[107]

Attacks on 'undefended' populated areas have long been unlawful. Under the 1907 Hague Regulations, the 'attack or bombardment, by whatever means, of towns, villages, dwellings, or buildings which are undefended is prohibited'.[108] In the *Gotovina* case, one international observer, the UN Security Coordinator for Sector South in 1995, testified that attack on Knin by 120 mm and 81 mm mortars and tank fire continued in spite of its being clearly

[106] *Gotovina and Markač* (n 103), Dissenting Opinion of Judge Fausto Pocar, paras 8–9; see also Dissenting Opinion of Judge Carmel Agius, paras 7–10.

[107] ICTY, *Prosecutor v Gotovina and Markač*, Trial Judgment, 16 November 2012, Dissenting Opinion of Judge Fausto Pocar, para 13.

[108] See, eg, Art 25, Regulations concerning the Laws and Customs of War on Land, annexed to Convention (IV) respecting the Laws and Customs of War on Land; adopted at The Hague, 18 October 1907; entry into force, 26 January 1910 (hereinafter '1907 Hague Regulations'), adapting language in Art 15, Project of an International Declaration concerning the Laws and Customs of War; adopted at Brussels, 27 August 1874 (1874 Brussels Declaration); and then Art 25, Convention (II) with Respect to the Laws and Customs of War on Land and its annex: Regulations concerning the Laws and Customs of War on Land; adopted at The Hague, 29 July 1899; entry into force, 4 September 1900 ('1899 Hague Regulations').

visible at one point that the Krajina Serb forces had withdrawn from the town.[109] In his Dissenting Opinion in the Appeals Chamber, Judge Agius noted that 'in relation to Knin, at least 900 projectiles fell all over the town in just one and a half days, … and there are no findings of any resistance coming from the town.'[110]

It is also explicit in treaty and custom that an attack is indiscriminate where it involves a bombardment that treats clearly separated and distinct military objectives in an area containing civilian objects as a single military objective.[111] Syria has suffered countless instances of indiscriminate bombardment. In one report from 2012 by the Report of the Independent International Commission of Inquiry on the Syrian Arab Republic established by the United Nations (UN) Human Rights Council ('the Commission of Inquiry on Syria'), it was reported that the city of Al Qusayr was subjected to indiscriminate attacks between February and May 2012. One 'credible source' told the Commission of Inquiry on Syria, 'I witnessed what people call indiscriminate shelling – the Syrian army just spreads mortar fire across an entire neighbourhood.'[112] On the basis of its findings, the Commission of Inquiry on Syria

> determined that the legal threshold for an indiscriminate attack as a violation of customary international humanitarian law was reached. Government forces fired shells into areas inhabited by civilians while failing to direct them at a specific military objective.[113]

As everyone knows, the situation has deteriorated in the years that have followed. In 2015, the chair of the Commission of Inquiry on Syria, Paulo Sérgio Pinheiro, affirmed that since 2012, indiscriminate and disproportionate bombardments were the 'primary cause of civilian casualties and mass displacement' in Syria. Data from non-governmental organisations indicated that casualties from air strikes, shelling and explosions accounted for more than half of all documented deaths in 2014. Indiscriminate bombardments had also damaged homes, medical facilities, schools, water and electrical facilities, bakeries and crops.[114] The bombing of eastern Aleppo by Russian and Syrian forces in 2016 is an epitome of attacks that are indiscriminate under Hague Law.

C. Indiscriminate Weapons and Civilian Objects

In addition to restricting the use of weapons in all military operations, whether offensive or defensive in nature,[115] the rule of distinction means that any weapon that is 'incapable of

[109] *Gotovina and Markač* (n 29) para 1327.

[110] *Gotovina and Markač* (n 103), Dissenting Opinion of Judge Carmel Agius, para 18.

[111] See Art 51(5)(a), 1977 Additional Protocol I; ICRC Study of Customary IHL, Rule 13 ('Area Bombardment') at https://goo.gl/xrtxze.

[112] *Report of the independent international commission of inquiry on the Syrian Arab Republic*, UN Doc A/HRC/21/50, 16 August 2012, para 91.

[113] Ibid, para 94.

[114] 'The use of barrel bombs and indiscriminate bombardment in Syria: the need to strengthen compliance with international humanitarian law', Statement of Paulo Sérgio Pinheiro, Chair of the Syrian Commission of Inquiry, Presented at a side event hosted by the Permanent Mission of Austria and Article 36, Geneva, 12 March 2015, 1, at https://goo.gl/DXBB7u.

[115] See Art 49(1), 1977 Additional Protocol I ('Definition of attacks and scope of application'): '"Attacks" means acts of violence against the adversary, whether in offence or in defence.'

distinguishing between civilian and military targets' is unlawful.[116] The ICJ described this as a 'cardinal' principle in its 1996 Nuclear Weapons Advisory Opinion.[117] In 2005, the ICRC Study of Customary IHL concluded that 'The use of weapons which are by nature indiscriminate is prohibited.'[118] According to the ICRC, the rule is a customary norm applicable in all armed conflicts.[119]

Consonant with the 1977 Additional Protocol I, a means or method of warfare that either cannot be directed at a specific military objective, or whose effects cannot be limited as required by Hague Law rules is inherently indiscriminate and may not be employed. This encompasses a weapon that cannot be targeted with sufficient accuracy, or whose effects spread too far beyond the target in an uncontrolled manner. Similarly, the UK Ministry of Defence's 2004 *Manual of the Law of Armed Conflict* describes the applicable rule as comprising two alternative tests: if a weapon cannot be targeted against a specific military objective (for instance, because it has a rudimentary guidance system), or if its effects cannot be limited to a military objective, it is an indiscriminate weapon.[120] The first of these is discussed in the following subsection, while the second is addressed in chapter 5.

i. An Excessively Inaccurate Weapon

The use of a weapon that cannot be targeted with sufficient accuracy against a specific military objective is always unlawful. This is true irrespective of whether civilian harm is the result of its use – whether that be civilian death or injury, or destruction of or damage to civilian objects.

While the rule per se is not contentious, its application to specific weapons assuredly is. In its discussion of the customary law rule, the ICRC cites a number of conventional weapons and weapons of mass destruction that have been alleged to be of an indiscriminate nature, but observes that there is 'insufficient consensus … to conclude that, under customary international law, they all violate the rule prohibiting the use of indiscriminate weapons'.[121]

Although the precise parameters for what is an inherently indiscriminate weapon are not clear (see section III.D), the strongest argument for an armament in modern use that cannot be targeted with sufficient accuracy is probably an early 'Scud' missile.[122] This Soviet missile, the R-11, which was manufactured during the Cold War from 1959 to 1984, was intended to strike targets in Western Europe. Early Scuds, whose gyroscopes and electronics

[116] The unintended implication by the ICJ's wording that a civilian or civilian object is a 'target' was unfortunate. A better formulation would have been 'incapable of distinguishing between civilians and civilian *objects* and military objectives'.

[117] 1996 Nuclear Weapons Advisory Opinion (n 1) para 78.

[118] ICRC Study of Customary IHL, Rule 71 ('Weapons That Are by Nature Indiscriminate') at https://goo.gl/vrfRTg.

[119] Ibid. See also WH Boothby, *Weapons and the Law of Armed Conflict* (Oxford, Oxford University Press, 2009) 82.

[120] 'It is prohibited to employ weapons which cannot be directed at a specific military objective or the effects of which cannot be limited as required by Additional Protocol I and consequently are of a nature to strike military objectives and civilians or civilian objects without distinction.' UK Ministry of Defence (n 8) para 6.4.

[121] ICRC Study of Customary IHL, Rule 71.

[122] Gary Solis argues that the Second World War-era V-1 flying bomb and V-2 rockets and Scud missiles are 'by their nature indiscriminate': Solis (n 48) 525. The UK affirms that the V-1 flying bomb and the Scud rocket 'are examples of weapons likely to be caught by this provision': UK Ministry of Defence (n 8) para 6.4.1.

dated back to the 1950s, were notoriously inaccurate. In general, it was expected that half of the missiles fired at a single target would miss by more than one kilometre.[123]

In the *Blaškić* case, the Trial Chamber inferred from the weapons used (inaccurate artisanal mortars, nicknamed 'baby bombs' locally) that the perpetrators of the attacks wanted to target the civilian population. However, this holding was overturned on appeal. Indeed, on the basis of the trial and additional evidence, the Appeals Chamber declared that it was 'not satisfied beyond reasonable doubt either that the attack of 18 July 1993 resulted in heavy casualties among Muslim civilians, or that the attack was directed at the Muslim civilian population or civilian property in Stari Vitez'.[124] In addition, the Appeals Chamber noted that 'It need not be decided whether, in general terms, the use of "baby bombs" is illegal.'[125]

In the *Gotovina* case, the Trial Chamber, based primarily on the testimony of expert witness Professor Geoffrey Corn, considered that although multiple-barrel rocket launchers (MBRLs) 'are generally less accurate than Howitzers or mortars', their use by the Croatian army against Knin on 4 and 5 August 1995 'was not inherently indiscriminate'.[126] It did not offer a legal basis for this controversial finding. In the *amicus curiae* submitted for consideration in General Gotovina's appeal, retired Lieutenant-General Shoffner noted that the 122 mm 40-tube BM21 MBRL, with a firing range of up to 20 kilometres, was introduced into operational service with the Russian Army in 1963 and was 'widely used throughout the world'. Owing to its 'high volume of fire and large area coverage', he asserted that it is 'well suited for use against troops in the open or for use in artillery preparations'. He cautioned, however, that because the weapons have a large CEP, 'they are not suited for attacks against point targets'. He estimated the CEP at 300 metres, with a consequent figure for 3 CEP of 900 metres. This means that some 45 per cent of rockets would be expected to land between 300 and 900 metres from their target. On this basis, their use in a small built-up town such as Knin should have been considered generally indiscriminate.

Indeed, the Appeals Chamber decision in the *Gotovina* case contrasts unfavourably with one of the targets of the Croatian army's attacks against Knin, Milan Martić, the erstwhile President of the self-styled Republic of Serbian Krajina. In its judgment in the *Martić* case, which concerned the firing of cluster munitions against Zagreb in early May 1995, an ICTY Trial Chamber observed that the weapon, the M-87 Orkan, was a high-dispersion weapon fired 'from the extreme of its range'. The Trial Chamber held that the Orkan was 'an indiscriminate weapon, the use of which in densely populated civilian areas, such as Zagreb, will result in the infliction of severe casualties'.[127]

The Trial Chamber had based its decision on the fact that Orkan was a non-guided weapons system used to target soldiers and armoured vehicles that was 'incapable of hitting

[123] See also S Casey-Maslen, 'The use of nuclear weapons under rules governing the conduct of hostilities' in G Nystuen et al (eds), *Nuclear Weapons under International Law* (Cambridge, Cambridge University Press, 2014) 100.

[124] ICTY, *Prosecutor v Thomir Blaškić*, Judgment (Appeals Chamber) (Case No IT-95-14-A), 29 July 2004, para 464.

[125] Ibid, para 465.

[126] *Gotovina and Markač* (n 29) para 1897.

[127] ICTY, *Prosecutor v Milan Martić*, Judgment (Trial Chamber) (Case No IT-95-11), 12 June 2007, para 463. The Appeals Chamber subsequently clarified that the Trial Chamber had concluded that the Orkan '*was used* as an indiscriminate weapon': ICTY, *Prosecutor v Milan Martić*, Judgment (Appeals Chamber) (Case No IT-95-11-A), 8 October 2008, para 247 (emphasis added).

specific targets'. Each rocket holds a cluster warhead with 288 submunitions, each of which contains 420 pellets of 3 mm diameter. The bomblets are ejected from the rocket at a height of 800–1,000 metres above the targeted area and explode upon impact, blasting the pellets in all directions. The maximum firing range of the Orkan is 50 kilometres. The dispersion error when fired at its maximum range is about 1,000 metres in any direction. The area of dispersion of the submunitions on the ground is about 20,000 metres.[128] Just as with the BM21, the Orkan was suitable for use against troops in the open, but not for point targeting in civilian populated areas.

In the *Prlić, Praljak, and Ćorić* case, the Trial Chamber described the attack on the village of Duša on 18 January 1993 as indiscriminate, largely on the basis that the attackers had fired artillery shells 'the nature of which is such that it is impossible to distinguish military from civilian targets'.[129] As the Appeals Chamber observed, however, Trial Chamber III 'provided no references in support of the finding that "shells" are of such a nature that it is impossible to distinguish between civilian and military targets'.[130] The Appeals Chamber stated that it

> would have expected such a finding to be based on evidence that the weapon employed in the attack, when used in its normal or designed circumstances, will inevitably be indiscriminate, in the sense that it is incapable of being directed at a specific military objective or its effects are incapable of being limited as required by law.[131]

In the absence of such an assessment, the Appeals Chamber considered that 'no reasonable trier of fact could have found that "shells", without further specification, are inherently indiscriminate', and accordingly it reversed the finding of the Trial Chamber.[132] This reversal is clearly based on sound reasoning.

In February 2017, the Commission of Inquiry on Syria released its latest report on respect for international law in the armed conflicts in the country. The Commission reported that from September 2016 onwards,

> an alarming number of incidents involving cluster munitions were also reported. Although the Syrian Arab Republic is not a party to the Convention on Cluster Munitions, the use of cluster munitions in densely populated areas is inherently indiscriminate (given the typically wide dispersal pattern and high dud rate, which continues to endanger civilians years after a cessation of hostilities) and therefore prohibited by customary international humanitarian law. For this reason, their use in cities such as eastern Aleppo constitutes the war crime of indiscriminate attacks in a civilian populated area.[133]

This is not an accurate statement of the law. Cluster munitions can and have been used in an indiscriminate manner (see further section III.D), including in Syria, but their use

[128] Ibid, para 462.
[129] ICTY, *Prosecutor v Prlić and others*, Judgment (Trial Chamber III) (Case No IT-04-74-T), vol 3, 29 May 2013, para 663.
[130] ICTY, *Prosecutor v Prlić and others*, Judgment (Appeals Chamber) (Case No IT-04-74-A), 29 November 2017, para 434.
[131] Ibid.
[132] Ibid.
[133] Report of the Commission of Inquiry on Syria, UN Doc A/HRC/34/64, 2 February 2017, para 57. In an annex to the report on the applicable law the Commission again asserts that 'When used in densely-populated areas such weapons [cluster munitions] are inherently indiscriminate.' Ibid, Annex 1, para 44.

in even a densely populated area is not, per se, prohibited by customary international humanitarian law.

A better assessment of what amounts to an indiscriminate weapon is found in the judgments by the ICTY in the *Dragomir Milošević* case. Several of the charges against the accused involved the use of 'modified air-bombs'. These were air bombs to which Bosnian Serb forces attached rockets and then fired from launch pads on the ground. The FAB-100 had 100 kg of TNT as its explosive charge, whereas the typical explosive charge for a FAB-250 was a fuel-air mixture.[134] Lieutenant Commander Thomas Knustad, a Norwegian UN Military Observer in Sarajevo, estimated that a modified air bomb could deviate from its intended target by as much as one kilometre. Another witness testified that in addition to the inherent inaccuracy of air bombs, the 'unprofessional way' the rockets were mounted under the air bomb increased the risk of deviation of the bomb while in flight. Even a defence expert witness conceded that modified air bombs were 'completely inaccurate'.[135] Accordingly, the Trial Chamber found, based on the evidence, that the bombs were 'highly inaccurate' and 'indiscriminate' weapons, and that they 'could only be directed at a general area, making it impossible to predict where they would strike'.[136]

The issue of the modified air bombs was again considered by the ICTY in its final Trial Chamber case, against Bosnian Serb commander Ratko Mladić. This time, General Mladić's defence team had argued that the bombs were 'well-designed, accurate, and valid weapons' that had been 'extensively tested'.[137] Witness Stevan Veljović, however, who served as Assistant Chief of Staff for Operations and Training of the 1st Romanija Brigade from 19 May 1992 until December 1994, had testified that

> the engines of modified air bombs were very unreliable – sometimes one engine fired later than the other causing the bomb to drift either to the left or to the right; as a result, it was impossible to predict where the bomb would land. … For this reason they were not meant to be used in urban areas as this would risk hitting their own men or civilians. … [He further] testified that modified air bombs had not been tested, and there were no firing tables for the modified air bombs and there were no rules detailing how the modified air bombs and accompanying launchers were to be used. … [A]s a result, modified air bombs were also dangerous to the artillery crew firing it; some artillery crews dealing with modified air bombs were killed as the bombs exploded when they were activated.[138]

Based on all the evidence it heard from expert witnesses, the Trial Chamber concluded that as 'a result of their make-shift design, modified air bombs were highly inaccurate'.[139] The Trial Chamber further found that Mladić ordered the production of modified air bombs and that he 'personally oversaw' the programme of their development, which started in 1993.[140]

Another weapon that has frequently been cited as indiscriminate is the landmine. Here it is the fact that the weapon is activated by the victim that is at the heart of the argument.

[134] *Dragomir Milošević* (n 17) para para 92, 93.
[135] Ibid, para 97.
[136] Ibid, paras 912, 1001.
[137] *Ratko Mladić* (n 89) para 1892.
[138] Ibid, para 1895.
[139] Ibid, para 1913.
[140] Ibid, para 4792.

An anti-personnel mine cannot 'distinguish' between the footfall of a soldier or a civilian: either will detonate the weapon. This would tend to suggest that its effects are indiscriminate. The flaw in the argument, though, is that placing anti-personnel mines in a marked and fenced area, and especially one that is patrolled by military personnel, can effectively ensure that the victims of any explosion are predominantly military and not civilian. They can be used in a discriminate manner and are therefore not inherently indiscriminate. That this is rarely the case in practice justifies their prohibition by treaty, but not the assertion that they are indiscriminate by nature. Moreover, as noted in chapter 1 (section III.C), any state that accepts otherwise must surely accept that use of an anti-vehicle mine is similarly unlawful.

D. The Requisite Level of Accuracy

As the preceding discussion indicates, the level of accuracy required by the law is unclear. What is certain is that the targeting requirement applies when the attack is launched: it is not an *ex-post-facto* assessment of what is actually struck by the attack. But the circumstances of the attack, including the accuracy of the weapon(s) used and whether or not any lawful military objective was in the vicinity of the strike, will contribute to the determination of lawfulness at time of launch. It is also clear that Hague Law does not require an attacker or a defender to actually hit what they are intending to hit: the margin of error that is allowable remains unsettled, and is likely to be, to a certain extent, weapon-specific.

As noted in section III.B, in the *amicus curiae* submitted to the ICTY in advance of the Appeals Chamber hearings in the *Gotovina* case, several foremost law of armed conflict authorities argued that artillery fire into a populated area should not be deemed unlawful unless it fell at least 400 metres from a lawful military objective. The figure of 400 metres was derived from the remarks during the trial by a Canadian Brigadier General, who had referred to a reasonable figure for a 'first shot'. It also comprised less accurate rocket fire. But what is a reasonable achievement for the accuracy of artillery and rocket fire at distances of more than 20 kilometres is not necessarily lawful.

In the *Martić* case, the Trial and Appeal Chambers held the view that a weapon that would fall up to 1,000 metres from the target with an area of dispersion of about 20,000 metres could not lawfully be used to target specific sites in a heavily populated area. The cluster munition used in this case, and in the circumstances of its use, was designed for use against a concentration of troops in the open, and was being employed at the upper limits of its operational range, reducing its likely accuracy. The fact that it was the only weapon that the Krajina Serbs had at that time that could hit Zagreb was irrelevant. If a weapon's use is unlawful in the circumstances, it is unlawful notwithstanding the fact that the party using it has no alternative in its arsenal.

E. Targeting Mistakes

A targeting mistake that leads to a civilian object being unintentionally destroyed or damaged is not a serious violation of the law of armed conflict, unless the error is reckless. The standard for precautionary measures of feasibility (see chapter 7) suggests that simple negligence in targeting may not be sufficient to ground a finding of a violation of the rule of distinction, and will certainly not lead to a successful prosecution for a war crime.[141] The 'fog of war' is used to describe the fact that one's own troops or allies are sometimes killed by (the rather ironic term) 'friendly fire', while civilian objects are often hit by mistake even when a significant degree of care is taken to comply with Hague Law rules.

A well-known and oft-cited error of targeting occurred during the 1991 Gulf War, in which a bunker in the Amariyah suburb of south-western Baghdad was targeted and destroyed by US forces in the mistaken belief that it was purely a military command and control centre and therefore a lawful military objective. In fact, civilians were sheltering in the bunker and at least 204 people, most undoubtedly civilians, were killed by the strike. The US decision to target the bunker was based on an array of evidence: intelligence from a spy; signals intelligence that suggested command-and-control radio traffic was emanating from the bunker; the fact that the bunker was camouflaged, surrounded by barbed wire and guarded; and because military vehicles were regularly parked outside it.[142] As Solis notes, extensive reconnaissance had failed to discern that each night the wives and children of the Iraqi secret police sheltered from the US air raids in the basement of the bunker.[143] Had the US known this, it would have been obligated to target the bunker during the day (or at least have been constrained to conduct a proportionality assessment that took into account the significant civilian casualties likely to result from a night attack).

During the armed conflict in Gaza in the summer of 2014, four children were killed on 16 July while playing on a breakwater near the port in Gaza City; the area was hit by two missiles fired by the Israeli Air Force. According to information released by the Israeli Military Advocate General (MAG), a criminal investigation found that the incident took place in an area that was known to be a compound belonging to Hamas naval forces and which was 'utilized exclusively by militants'. An intelligence assessment had indicated that operatives would gather in the compound to prepare for military activity against the Israel Defence Forces (IDF). Aerial surveillance had identified figures running into the compound as militants. In contrast, journalists who attended the scene in the immediate aftermath of the attack 'saw a small and dilapidated fisherman's hut containing a few tools where the children had been playing hide-and-seek'.[144] One of the journalists, who worked for the *Guardian* newspaper, was surprised not to have been contacted during the investigation.[145]

On the basis of the investigation, the MAG concluded that 'the attack process … accorded with Israeli domestic law and international law requirements'.[146] A senior IDF figure affirmed on a blog entry that 'the tragic outcome of the incident does not affect the legality of the attack ex post facto'.[147] The UN Commission of Inquiry established by the Human Rights Council, however, found 'strong indications that the actions of the IDF were

[141] As the Trial Chamber in *Galić* held in relation to the offence of attack on civilians, 'the notion of "wilfully" incorporates the concept of recklessness, whilst excluding mere negligence. The perpetrator who recklessly attacks civilians acts "wilfully".' *Galić* (n 84) para 54.

[142] Solis (n 48) 275.

[143] Ibid.

[144] P Beaumont, 'Israel exonerates itself over Gaza beach killings of four children last year', *Guardian* (11 June 2015) at https://goo.gl/zig1bx.

[145] Ibid.

[146] 'Decisions of the IDF MAG Regarding Exceptional Incidents that Allegedly Occurred During Operation "Protective Edge"', Update No 4 of 11 June 2015, at http://mfa.gov.il/MFA/ForeignPolicy/IsraelGaza2014/Pages/Operation-Protective-Edge-Investigation-of-exceptional-incidents-Update-4.aspx.

[147] Lt-Col Peter Lerner, Facebook page entry, 11 June 2015, at https://goo.gl/VpYLqb.

not in conformity with international humanitarian law and that the investigation does not appear to have been carried out in a thorough manner'.[148] In this regard, the Commission found 'strong indications that the IDF had failed in its obligations to take all feasible measures to avoid or at least minimize incidental harm to civilians'.[149]

IV. Objects Enjoying Special Protection from Attack

A. Hospitals

The highest level of protection afforded to a civilian object by the law of armed conflict is for hospitals (or similar medical facilities). As noted in chapter 1, these are almost the only objects whose protection from attack during the conduct of hostilities is addressed in the 1949 Geneva Conventions. Geneva Convention I protects fixed establishments (which include hospitals) and mobile medical units (which include field hospitals) belonging to the armed forces' medical service,[150] while Geneva Convention IV accords protection to civilian hospitals. As Dinstein notes, however, that scope of protection from attack is extended to all types of medical units, whether military or civilian, by the 1977 Additional Protocol I.[151]

The ICRC has affirmed that it is a customary rule, applicable to all armed conflicts, that medical units 'exclusively assigned to medical purposes must be respected and protected in all circumstances'.[152] The ICRC concluded that the expansion of scope in the Additional Protocol I was widely supported in state practice, including those not party to the Protocol.[153] The ICC Statute prohibits in all armed conflicts intentionally 'directing attacks against hospitals and places where the sick and wounded are collected, provided they are not military objectives'.[154] Thus, medical units lose their protection 'if they are being used, outside their humanitarian function, to commit acts harmful to the enemy'.[155]

It is also required that, 'as far as possible', hospitals and medical units 'be situated in such a manner that attacks against military objectives cannot imperil their safety'.[156] The meaning of the phrase *as far as possible* is 'to the extent possible', and not 'as far away as possible'.[157]

[148] *Report of the detailed findings of the independent commission of inquiry established pursuant to Human Rights Council resolution S-21/1*, UN Doc A/HRC/29/CRP.4, 22 June 2015 (hereinafter 'UN Commission of Inquiry on the 2014 Gaza Conflict') para 663.

[149] Ibid, para 631.

[150] See, eg, E Mikos-Skuza, 'Hospitals' in A Clapham, P Gaeta and M Sassòli (eds), *The Geneva Conventions in Context: A Commentary* (Oxford, Oxford University Press, 2015) 207, 210.

[151] Dinstein (n 19) 220.

[152] ICRC Study of Customary IHL, Rule 28 ('Medical Units') at https://goo.gl/rg4LBE. Mikos-Skuza (n 150) inaccurately describes (at 213) the nature of the obligation in the Geneva Convention I as a 'recommendation', whereas the language employed is 'The responsible authorities shall ensure that …'. She is correct in relation to the Geneva Convention IV, given that the equivalent provision reads as follows: 'In view of the dangers to which hospitals may be exposed by being close to military objectives, it is recommended that such hospitals be situated as far as possible from such objectives.' Art 18(5), 1949 Geneva Convention IV.

[153] ICRC Study of Customary IHL, Rule 28 ('Medical Units').

[154] Art 2(b)(ix) and (e)(iv), ICC Statute.

[155] ICRC Study of Customary IHL, Rule 28 ('Medical Units').

[156] Art 19(2), 1949 Geneva Convention I.

[157] ICRC commentary on 1949 Geneva Convention I, 2016, para 1820, at https://goo.gl/PiMsS7.

According to the ICRC, though, the use (including presumably the placing) of medical units with a view to shielding military objectives from attack would amount to an 'act harmful to the enemy' entailing a loss of protection.[158]

The unlawful targeting of medical facilities, despite their special protection, is one of the many sad realities of armed conflict. In Syria, for example, hospitals and other medical care providers have been systematically targeted by many parties to the plethora of armed conflicts being fought out on Syrian territory. According to the Commission of Inquiry on Syria, reporting in September 2013:

> The deliberate targeting of hospitals, medical personnel and transports, the denial of access to medical care, and ill-treatment of the sick and wounded, has been one of the most alarming features of the Syrian conflict. According to multiple accounts collected by the Commission of Inquiry, Government forces and affiliated militias interfere with and instrumentalise medical care to further strategic and military aims. Evidence collected by the Commission leads to an overwhelming conclusion: Government forces deny medical care to those from opposition-controlled and affiliated areas as a matter of policy. The policy is implemented through attacks on medical units, by endangering hospitals, targeting medical personnel, and interfering with patients receiving treatment. Victims relay harrowing accounts of the wounded and sick languishing at checkpoints unable to reach medical treatment, coming under renewed attack in hospital and doctors providing impartial aid being arrested and targeted. There is also evidence that some anti-Government armed groups have attacked hospitals in certain areas.[159]

In the 2014 Gaza conflict, Palestinians alleged numerous violations of the immunity of medical facilities from attack. In one such case, witnesses reported that the only medical facility in Khuza'a, Dr Kamel Qdeih's Clinic, was struck by repeated Israeli air strikes on 23 and 24 July. One of the doctors running the clinic recounted:

> The clinic and its surroundings were hit by a number of rockets. About thirty people in total were killed, and several more injured in these attacks. They were mostly children and women. None of them were combatants. Among them was my brother who was killed before my own eyes. … They targeted the clinic with three rockets from drones. There were at least 25 or 30 explosions in the neighbourhood. The attacks on the clinic continued also on the 24th. Our clinic was deprived of the most basic provisions to treat patients … and in all this there was no communication or warnings. We were just attacked.[160]

As the Commission of Inquiry recalled, ambulances and medical personnel enjoy special protection under the law of armed conflict: they are to be protected from attack in all circumstances and only lose the protection 'if they are used outside of their humanitarian function to commit acts harmful to the enemy'. The Commission noted that some of the incidents in its report constituted a violation by the IDF of the prohibition of attacks on medical transports and medical personnel, 'and may amount to war crimes, in particular, if the vehicles or personnel attacked used the distinctive emblems of the Geneva Conventions'.[161]

The conflicts in the former Yugoslavia were also notorious for attacks on medical facilities. In the *Galić* case, the ICTY Trial Chamber noted that international observers and

[158] Ibid, para 1821, citing Art 12(4), 1977 Additional Protocol I; and Art 21, 1949 Geneva Convention I.

[159] Commission of Inquiry on Syria, 'Assault on Medical Care in Syria', UN Doc A/HRC/24/CRP.2, 13 September 2013, para 1.

[160] UN Commission of Inquiry on the 2014 Gaza Conflict (n 148) para 329.

[161] Ibid, para 464.

senior hospital staff testified that the state hospital in Sarajevo, located in Marin Dvor, was regularly fired upon from Bosnian Serb-controlled territory, including by shelling, 'resulting in injuries to patients and staff and significantly damaging the hospital infrastructure'.[162] As a result, by January 1993, 'shelling had reduced the bed capacity of the hospital to 200 from its pre-conflict level of 480 beds'.[163]

The Trial Record also contains 'extensive evidence from hospital staff and international observers indicating that Koševo hospital was regularly shelled throughout the Indictment Period, resulting in civilian casualties, as well as in damage to the hospital infrastructure'.[164] On 30 December 1992, the commander of the UN military observers conducted a battle damage assessment of the hospital in order to identify how the damage caused by shelling affected the hospital's operations. He found that the hospital had been hit by artillery, anti-aircraft artillery and possibly tank fire. The third floor had received several direct hits by 122 mm artillery and 40 mm anti-aircraft artillery. One room in the intensive care unit had also been directly hit and damaged beyond repair by 20 mm, 40 mm and 82 mm shells fired from a north-easterly direction. He established that the fire had originated from two areas within Bosnian Serb-held territory.[165]

The Trial Record disclosed that Bosnian Serb soldiers admitted targeting the hospital. Gun crews stationed in the south of Sarajevo claimed that the hospital was a legitimate military target 'because they had been told by an unspecified source that the ABiH [Bosnian army] used the Koševo buildings as army barracks'.[166] In the spring of 1992, Dragan Kalinić, the Minister of Health of Republika Srpska, said 'let me tell you this right now, if the Military Hospital is to end up in the hands of the enemy, I am for the destruction of the Koševo hospital so that the enemy has nowhere to go for medical help'.[167] Evidence also indicated, however, that on occasion ABiH soldiers had fired mortars from the hospital grounds or its vicinity, sometimes soliciting Bosnian Serb counter-fire. As the Trial Chamber noted, 'The Prosecution has conceded that ABiH mortar fire originated from hospital grounds.'[168]

The Trial Chamber declared itself 'satisfied beyond reasonable doubt that the Koševo hospital, a well-known civilian medical facility, was regularly targeted' by the Bosnian Serbs. The Chamber was also satisfied that Bosniak army mortar fire 'originated from the hospital grounds or from its vicinity and that these actions may have provoked' Bosnian Serb counter-fire. The Chamber was unable to establish what damage and which casualties resulted from exchange of fire, but 'the evidence does reveal that, on occasions, the Koševo hospital buildings themselves were directly targeted, resulting in civilian casualties, and that this fire was certainly not aimed at any possible military target'. The Trial Chamber held that the direct attacks on the hospital 'constitute examples of the campaign of attacks on civilians'.[169]

At the end of 2011, the ICRC and the broader Red Cross and Red Crescent movement launched a multi-year campaign entitled 'Health Care in Danger', to try to reduce

162 ICTY, *Prosecutor v Galić*, Judgment (Trial Chamber I), 5 December 2003, para 244.
163 Ibid, para 245.
164 Ibid, para 498.
165 Ibid, para 499.
166 Ibid, para 501.
167 Ibid, para 502.
168 Ibid, para 504.
169 Ibid, para 509.

the number of attacks against medical facilities and personnel during armed conflict.[170] It remains to be seen how effective this valiant effort will prove in practice.

B. Cultural 'Property'

In the *Jokić* case, which concerned naval[171] and land bombardment of the Old Town of Dubrovnik in 1991 during the conflicts raging in the former Yugoslavia, an ICTY Trial Chamber noted that 'the destruction and damage inflicted to the Old Town … were very serious crimes'. It found that 'since it is a serious violation of international humanitarian law to attack civilian buildings, it is a crime of even greater seriousness to direct an attack on an especially protected site, such as the Old Town'.[172] The Old Town of Dubrovnik had been inscribed on the United Nations Educational, Scientific and Cultural Organization (UNESCO)'s World Heritage List in 1975. Noting that damage 'was caused to more than 100 buildings, including various segments of the Old Town's walls, ranging from complete destruction to damage to non-structural parts', the Trial Chamber held that the unlawful attack on the Old Town 'must therefore be viewed as especially wrongful conduct'.[173]

In the *Prlić, Praljak, and Ćorić* case, one of the charges related to the destruction of the Old Bridge (Stari Most) over the Neretva river at Mostar in Bosnia and Herzegovina. The bridge was completed in 1566–67 and stood for 427 years. Throughout the day of 8 November 1993, a Bosnian Croat tank fired shells against it; the bridge collapsed following further shelling the following day.[174] The Trial Chamber found that the Old Bridge was used by both the Bosniak army and civilians living on either bank of the river between May and November 1993.[175] The Trial Chamber further found that the bridge was essential to the Bosniak army for front-line combat activities, evacuations and for the sending of troops, food and *matériel*, and that it was used for these purposes, rendering it a lawful military objective.[176] The Trial Chamber then engaged in a proportionality analysis (discussed further in chapter 6) before concluding that the destruction was wanton and not justified by military necessity.[177]

Judge Antonetti, in his Trial Chamber dissent, noted that the Indictment failed to characterise the Old Bridge as a 'cultural landmark' under Article 3(d) of the ICTY Statute.[178] At the time of its destruction, the bridge

> was not listed on the UNESCO World Heritage List. However, the Security Council, UNESCO and the Council of Europe were informed of the risk of destruction in a letter dated 9 July 1993,

[170] See healthcareindanger.org/hcid-project.

[171] Convention (IX) concerning Bombardment by Naval Forces in Time of War; adopted at The Hague, 18 October 1907; entry into force, 26 January 1910. Art 5 of the 1907 Convention requires that 'In bombardments by naval forces all the necessary measures must be taken by the commander to spare as far as possible sacred edifices, buildings used for artistic, scientific, or charitable purposes, historic monuments, hospitals, and places where the sick or wounded are collected, on the understanding that they are not used at the same time for military purposes.'

[172] ICTY, *Prosecutor v Jokić*, Sentencing Judgment (Trial Chamber I) (Case No IT-01-42/1-S), 18 March 2004, para 53.

[173] Ibid.

[174] *Prlić and others* (n 130) para 405.

[175] *Prlić and others* (n 129) para 1582.

[176] Ibid.

[177] Ibid, para 1587.

[178] *Prlić and others* (n 129), Dissenting Judgment of Judge Antonetti, 302.

> in which the Government of the Republic of Bosnia and Herzegovina requested that the destruction of the Stari Most be prevented and that a UNESCO committee of experts be sent to ensure its protection.[179]

Judge Antonetti concluded that the bridge was protected under the Convention for the Protection of Cultural Property in the Event of Armed Conflict ('the Hague Convention') of 1954 to which Bosnia and Herzegovina was a successor state party,[180] even though the bridge was not marked with any distinctive emblem conferring special protection upon it.[181]

He further observed that the protection of cultural objects remains subject to their military use.[182] Article 4(2) of the Hague Convention allows protection to be waived 'only in cases where military necessity imperatively requires such a waiver'. The Convention itself does not clarify the scope of the criterion of imperative military necessity, though the 1999 Protocol II to the Hague Convention explains that 'imperative necessity' may be invoked only when the property has been made into a military objective and no similar military advantage can be obtained without targeting the protected object.[183] He concluded that the requirements were met in this case: 'I fail to see how the principle of proportionality could be applicable in this case. If the Old Bridge was a military objective, it quite simply had to be destroyed. In any event, there is no such thing as proportionate destruction.'[184]

The Appeals Chamber recalled that the elements of wanton destruction included the destruction of property that is not justified by military necessity.[185] Since the Trial Chamber had found that the bridge was a military target at the time of the attack, and thus its destruction offered a definite military advantage, the Appeals Chamber, Judge Pocar dissenting, held that it could not be considered, 'in and of itself', as wanton destruction not justified by military necessity.[186] This is a correct application of Hague Law.

In his dissent, Judge Fausto Pocar asserted that the Majority of the Appeals Chamber had erred in 'conflating the well-established IHL notion of military target or military objective and the principle of military necessity'.[187] He 'strongly disagree[d]' with the Majority's reasoning that the fact that the bridge was a military objective was 'per se determinative of the issue of whether or not its destruction was justified by military necessity', since the 'notion of justified by military necessity is distinct from and more stringent than that of a military objective'.[188] He then referred to jurisprudence of the Appeals Chamber, whereby military necessity is defined as 'the necessity of those measures which are indispensable for securing the ends of the war, and which are *lawful* according to the modern law and

[179] Ibid, 306.
[180] Ibid, 307.
[181] Ibid, 308–09.
[182] Ibid, 316.
[183] Ibid, 317.
[184] Ibid, 325.
[185] *Prlić and others* (n 130) para 411, citing ICTY, *Prosecutor v Hadžihasanović and Kubura*, Decision on Joint Defence Interlocutory Appeal of Trial Chamber Decision on Rule 98bis Motions for Acquittal (Appeals Chamber) (Case No IT-01-47-AR73.3), 11 March 2005, fn 53; *Prosecutor v Kordić and Čerkez*, Judgment (Appeals Chamber) (Case No IT-95-14/2-A), 17 December 2004, para 74.
[186] *Prlić and others* (n 130) para 411.
[187] Ibid, Dissenting Opinion of Judge Fausto Pocar, para 8.
[188] Ibid.

usages of war'.[189] His argument was that because the attack on the bridge violated the rule of proportionality, it did not amount to a lawful attack.[190] He further noted, though,

> [*e*]*n passant*, … the missed opportunity of the Prosecutor in failing to specifically charge the destruction of the Old Bridge of Mostar as 'destruction or wilful damage done to institutions dedicated to religion, charity, education, the arts and sciences, historic monuments and works of art and science' under Article 3(d) of the [ICTY] Statute, which protects specifically cultural property …[191]

Judge Pocar continued: 'As exemplified in many recent armed conflicts, such as those in Mali, Syria, Libya, Yemen, and Iraq, the protection of cultural property is paramount.'[192]

Indeed, the protection of cultural property has received particular attention in recent years, in no small part owing to the actions of Islamic State in Iraq and Syria. Among the most notorious instances of violation of Hague Law rules protecting cultural property was the destruction at Palmyra, a UNESCO World Heritage site known as the 'Venice of the Sands' whose history dates back four millennia.[193] Islamic State took control of the central Syrian city in May 2015, and by June the group began destroying historical sites. The Syrian Government said that Islamic State had destroyed two Muslim holy sites: a 500-year-old shrine and a tomb where a descendant of the Prophet Mohammed's cousin was reportedly buried. Two months later, Islamic State destroyed more antiquities, including the 1,800-year-old Arch of Triumph that framed the approach to the city and the nearly 2,000-year-old Temple of Baalshamin. UNESCO called the temple's destruction a war crime.[194] This was also the position taken by the UN Commission of Inquiry on Syria: 'Deliberate attacks on properties of great cultural importance, such as those perpetrated by ISIS, stand as clear violations of international customary humanitarian law and are a war crime.'[195]

The protection of cultural property was not addressed in the 1949 Geneva Conventions, though buildings and works of art and science had been given a measure of protection in the 1863 Lieber Code and the 1899 and 1907 Hague Regulations.[196] Indeed, as Solis recalls, Alfred Rosenberg was sentenced to death by the International Military Tribunal at Nuremburg for widespread plunder of art during the Second World War.[197] Although the Hague Convention was only adopted in 1954, a draft of the treaty had been prepared before the 1949 Geneva Conventions.[198] Solis criticises, though, the vague definition of cultural

[189] Ibid, para 9, citing *Kordić and Čerkez* (n 185), para 686, quoting Art 14 of the Lieber Code (emphasis added by Judge Pocar).

[190] *Prlić and others* (n 130), Dissenting Opinion of Judge Fausto Pocar, para 11.

[191] Ibid, para 12.

[192] Ibid, para 16.

[193] S Jeffries, 'Isis's destruction of Palmyra: "The heart has been ripped out of the city"', *The Guardian* (2 September 2015) at https://goo.gl/tRmwT4.

[194] E McKirdy, 'Which ancient treasures did ISIS destroy in Palmyra?', *CNN* (29 March 2016) at https://goo.gl/A1Axmg. In fact, the devastation could have been even worse. In April 2016, it was reported that a plan to detonate 4,500 improvised mines linked to the telephone network was not carried out because the man responsible for triggering the explosions was killed by Syrian government regime loyalists working undercover. P Wintour, 'Isis destruction of Palmyra antiquities revealed in new pictures', *Guardian* (1 April 2016) at https://goo.gl/hAkK6L.

[195] 'Report of the Independent International Commission of Inquiry on the Syrian Arab Republic', UN Doc A/HRC/31/68, 11 February 2016, para 92.

[196] See, eg Solis (n 48), 711.

[197] Ibid, 712–13.

[198] Ibid, 713.

property in the 1954 Convention, in particular employment of terms such as 'importance' and 'artistic' interest.[199] He affirms that the Convention is not entirely reflective of custom, but endorses the ICRC's findings that 'the obligation of states both to protect cultural objects by not attacking them and not to endanger them by making military use of them clearly is customary law'.[200] That the duty to respect cultural property is applicable in both IAC and NIAC is evidenced by the ICC Statute, which is given jurisdiction over the war crime of 'Intentionally directing attacks against buildings dedicated to religion, education, art, science or charitable purposes, historic monuments … provided they are not military objectives.'[201]

In 2016, Ahmad Al Faqi Al Mahdi pleaded guilty before the ICC to the charge of intentionally directing attacks against historic monuments and buildings dedicated to religion as a war crime committed in a NIAC. He was sentenced to nine years' imprisonment for his involvement in the destruction of nine mausoleums and one mosque in Timbuktu, Mali, in June and July 2012. In the earlier confirmation of charges, the Pre-Trial Chamber I found:

> The Buildings/Structures were regarded and protected as a significant part of the cultural heritage of Timbuktu and of Mali. The community in Timbuktu was involved in their maintenance and used them for their religious practices. At the time of the destruction, all cemeteries in Timbuktu, including the Buildings/Structures within those cemeteries, were classified as world heritage and thus under the protection of UNESCO [UN Educational, Scientific and Cultural Organization], and as many as 16 mausoleums situated in Timbuktu were also themselves protected sites pursuant to the 1972 Convention concerning the protection of the world cultural and natural heritage. Furthermore, as of 28 June 2012, the conflict in Mali as a whole and Timbuktu in particular led UNESCO, upon request of the Malian authorities, to include the city in its entirety on the list of world heritage in danger. It is also apparent from the evidence that the Buildings/Structures did not constitute military objectives.[202]

C. Installations Containing Dangerous Forces

Special protection is also afforded by Hague Law to installations that contain 'dangerous forces' (dams, dykes and nuclear power stations).[203] As Article 56(1) of the 1977 Additional Protocol I provides:

> Works or installations containing dangerous forces, namely dams, dykes and nuclear electrical generating stations, shall not be made the object of attack, even where these objects are military objectives, if such attack may cause the release of dangerous forces and consequent severe losses among the civilian population. Other military objectives located at or in the vicinity of these works or installations shall not be made the object of attack if such attack may cause the release of

[199] Ibid.

[200] Ibid, 721, citing ICRC Study of Customary IHL, Rule 38 ('Attacks Against Cultural Property') at https://goo.gl/EikXpA. Also relevant is Rule 39 ('Use of Cultural Property for Military Purposes') at https://goo.gl/BCRFsi.

[201] Art 2(b)(ix) and (e)(iv), ICC Statute.

[202] ICC, *Prosecutor v Ahmad Al Faqi Al Mahdi*, Decision on the confirmation of charges (Pre-Trial Chamber I) (Case No ICC-01/12-01/15), 24 March 2016, para 36, at https://goo.gl/78s2x1.

[203] As Dinstein recalls, the list is exhaustive: a factory producing toxic chemicals is not accorded similar protection. Dinstein (n 19) 227, citing ICRC Commentary on the 1977 Additional Protocols, para 2148.

> dangerous forces from the works or installations and consequent severe losses among the civilian population.[204]

As the ICRC has recalled, when installations containing dangerous forces are civilian objects, they may not be attacked.[205] But practice, the organisation affirms, also shows that states 'are conscious of the high risk of severe incidental losses' that can result from attacks against installations even when they constitute military objectives. Consequently, states recognise that 'particular care must be taken in case of attack'.[206] The ICRC believes that the following is a customary rule in all armed conflict:

> Particular care must be taken if works and installations containing dangerous forces, namely dams, dykes and nuclear electrical generating stations, and other installations located at or in their vicinity are attacked, in order to avoid the release of dangerous forces and consequent severe losses among the civilian population.[207]

As Dinstein observes, the protection bestowed by the 1977 Additional Protocol I is 'unique'.[208] He rightly points out that the treaty provision is not merely an application of the proportionality principle (discussed in chapter 6), because 'severe' losses do not constitute a balancing against military advantage in the way that 'excessive' does. He argues, though, that Article 56(1) of the Protocol 'does not coincide' with customary international law.[209]

In any event, the special protection against attack provided by Article 56(1) ceases:

> a) for a dam or a dyke only if it is used for other than its normal function and in regular, significant and direct support of military operations and if such attack is the only feasible way to terminate such support;
> b) for a nuclear electrical generating station only if it provides electric power in regular, significant and direct support of military operations and if such attack is the only feasible way to terminate such support;
> c) for other military objectives located at or in the vicinity of these works or installations only if they are used in regular, significant and direct support of military operations and if such attack is the only feasible way to terminate such support.[210]

Dinstein believes that better protection would have been afforded to the civilian population if a duty of passive precautions had been imposed on parties to an armed conflict, such as to oblige a belligerent with nuclear reactors to shut them down during hostilities or switch off any hydroelectric facility linked to a dam, so as to 'extinguish any military rationale for attack by the enemy'.[211] How realistic this would be for states highly reliant on nuclear power or hydroelectric power is debatable. France, for example, derives about three-quarters of its electricity from nuclear energy.[212]

[204] The first sentence only is reproduced in Art 15, 1977 Additional Protocol II.
[205] ICRC Study of Customary IHL, Rule 42 ('Works and Installations Containing Dangerous Forces'), at https://goo.gl/6jCmvV.
[206] Ibid.
[207] Ibid.
[208] Dinstein (n 19) 227.
[209] Ibid, 228.
[210] Art 56(2), 1977 Additional Protocol I
[211] Dinstein (n 19) 229.
[212] World Nuclear Association, 'Nuclear Power in France', last updated March 2018, at https://goo.gl/e80sem.

V. Attacks against Civilian Objects under International Criminal Law

A. Under 1977 Additional Protocol I

The 1977 Additional Protocol provides for compulsory universal jurisdiction in case of grave breaches (which amount to war crimes),[213] where these are committed wilfully, in violation of the Protocol, and cause death or serious injury.[214] Although the term 'wilfully' is not defined in the Protocol, according to the relevant ICRC commentary it encompasses not only deliberate intent but also recklessness:

> [T]he accused must have acted consciously and with intent, ie, with his mind on the act and its consequences, and willing them ('criminal intent' or 'malice aforethought'); this encompasses the concepts of 'wrongful intent' or 'recklessness', viz, the attitude of an agent who, without being certain of a particular result, accepts the possibility of it happening; on the other hand, ordinary negligence or lack of foresight is not covered, ie, when a man acts without having his mind on the act or its consequences.[215]

This stance was quoted and explicitly approved by the ICTY in the *Galić* case: 'The Trial Chamber accepts this explanation, according to which the notion of "wilfully" incorporates the concept of recklessness, whilst excluding mere negligence. The perpetrator who recklessly attacks civilians acts "wilfully"'.[216]

The Protocol does not make attacks on civilian objects *simpliciter* a war crime, as it does 'making the civilian population or individual civilians the object of attack'.[217] Instead it criminalises the following:

- launching an indiscriminate attack affecting civilian objects in the knowledge that such attack will cause excessive damage to civilian objects (as defined in Article 57(2a)(iii) of the Protocol)[218]
- launching an attack against works or installations containing dangerous forces in the knowledge that such attack will cause excessive damage to civilian objects (as similarly defined)[219]

[213] Art 85(1), 1977 Additional Protocol I. This applies the rules laid down in the 1949 Geneva Conventions to the repression of grave breaches, which demands that each state party enact necessary criminal legislation to punish those who commit, or order the commission of, any grave breaches. The state parties are also obligated to search for those alleged to have committed, or ordered to be committed, grave breaches, and to prosecute them, regardless of their nationality, in their courts. A state party may also, 'if it prefers, and in accordance with the provisions of its own legislation', hand such persons over for trial to another state party concerned, where that state party has made out a prima facie case. See Art 146, 1949 Geneva Convention IV.

[214] Art 85(3), 1977 Additional Protocol I.

[215] ICRC Commentary on the 1977 Additional Protocols, para 3474.

[216] *Galić* (n 162) para 54. The Trial Chamber's finding was confirmed by the Appeals Chamber: *Galić* (n 92) para 140.

[217] Art 85(3)(a), 1977 Additional Protocol I.

[218] Art 85(3)(b), 1977 Additional Protocol I.

[219] Art 85(3)(c), 1977 Additional Protocol I.

- making non-defended localities and demilitarised zones the object of attack[220]
- attacking and causing extensive destruction to clearly-recognised historic monuments, works of art or places of worship, which constitute the cultural or spiritual heritage of peoples and to which special protection has been given by special arrangement (such as by UNESCO).[221]

By virtue of the requirement in the chapeau of Article 85(3), the indiscriminate (disproportionate) attacks that cause 'excessive' damage to civilian objects or dangerous installations must also cause death or serious injury. Thus destruction or damage alone is insufficient to ground a grave breach of the Protocol. Such 'disproportionate' attacks are discussed in more detail in chapter 6.

In the case of undefended localities, it is not required that civilian objects be damaged, merely that the attack has caused death or serious injury. In the case of attacks on cultural property, however, it is necessary that extensive destruction be caused, not that the attack caused death or serious injury.

B. Under Customary International Law

The ICRC Study of Customary IHL was more systematic in its approach to war crimes committed against civilian objects than were the states negotiating the Protocol. The Study found in particular that attacks on civilian objects *simpliciter* were a war crime under customary law. It identified the following specific war crimes as applicable in all armed conflict:[222]

- making civilian objects, that is, objects that are not military objectives, the object of attack[223]
- making objects involved in a humanitarian assistance or peacekeeping mission in accordance with the UN Charter the object of attack, as long as they are entitled to the protection given to civilian objects under the law of armed conflict
- making non-defended localities and demilitarised zones the object of attack
- making buildings dedicated to religion, education, art, science or charitable purposes or historic monuments the object of attack, provided they are not military objectives[224]
- launching an indiscriminate attack resulting in damage to civilian objects

[220] Art 85(3)(d), 1977 Additional Protocol I.

[221] Art 85(4)(d), 1977 Additional Protocol I. This is subject to there being no evidence of the enemy's having used the objects in support of the military effort and when they are not located in the immediate proximity of military objectives.

[222] See ICRC Study of Customary IHL, Rule 156 ('Definition of War Crimes') at https://goo.gl/YZLXn3.

[223] The ICRC's formulation in regard to NIAC is simpler than in IAC, just 'making civilian objects the object of attack', but this is not a substantive difference.

[224] The ICRC formulation in NIAC is materially different: 'making religious or cultural objects the object of attack, provided that they are not military objectives'. It is not clear why this should be the case. In the 1977 Additional Protocol II, Art 16 stipulates that 'it is prohibited to commit any acts of hostility directed against historic monuments, works of art or places of worship which constitute the cultural or spiritual heritage of peoples, and to use them in support of the military effort'.

- launching an attack against works or installations containing dangerous forces in the knowledge that such attack will cause excessive incidental loss of civilian life, injury to civilians or damage to civilian objects
- launching an attack in the knowledge that such attack will cause incidental damage to civilian objects, which would be clearly excessive in relation to the concrete and direct military advantage anticipated[225] and
- using inherently indiscriminate weapons.

In contrast to the 1977 Additional Protocol, and consonant with the approach taken in the ICC Statute, the ICRC found that

> not all acts necessarily have to result in actual damage to persons or objects in order to amount to war crimes. This became evident when the Elements of Crimes for the International Criminal Court were being drafted. It was decided, for example, that it was enough to launch an attack on civilians or civilian objects, even if something unexpectedly prevented the attack from causing death or serious injury.[226]

With respect to the mens rea needed, in accordance with its understanding of the term 'wilfully', the ICRC found that each of these war crimes demanded either deliberate intent (*dolus directus*) or recklessness (*dolus eventualis*).[227]

C. Under the ICC Statute

Although the ICC Statute does not require actual damage to a civilian object, much less death or serious injury, for a war crime committed by an attack against a civilian object,[228] its overall approach to the issue differs markedly between IAC and NIAC. The Statute does not provide for jurisdiction over the war crime of indiscriminate attacks affecting civilian objects in either category of conflict.

In IAC, the following war crimes may be subject to the Court's jurisdiction:

- intentionally directing attacks against civilian objects, that is, objects which are not military objectives[229]
- intentionally directing attacks against installations, material, units or vehicles involved in a humanitarian assistance or peacekeeping mission in accordance with the UN Charter, as long as they are entitled to the protection given to civilian objects under the law of armed conflict[230]

[225] These disproportionate attacks – and the ICRC's controversial formulation – are discussed in ch 6.

[226] ICRC Study of Customary IHL, Rule 156 ('Definition of War Crimes') at https://goo.gl/YZLXn3, 'Serious nature of the violation', point (ii).

[227] ICRC Study of Customary IHL, Rule 156.

[228] Thus, in the elements of crimes for Art 8(2)(b)(ii) of the ICC Statute (war crime of attacking civilian objects) the following elements are required: (i) The perpetrator directed an attack. (ii) The object of the attack was civilian objects, that is, objects which are not military objectives. (iii) The perpetrator intended such civilian objects to be the object of the attack. (iv) The conduct took place in the context of and was associated with an international armed conflict. (v) The perpetrator was aware of factual circumstances that established the existence of an armed conflict.

[229] Art 8(2)(b)(ii), ICC Statute.

[230] Art 8(2)(b)(iii), ICC Statute.

- intentionally launching an attack in the knowledge that such attack will cause incidental damage to civilian objects which would be clearly excessive in relation to the concrete and direct overall military advantage anticipated[231]
- attacking or bombarding, by whatever means, towns, villages, dwellings or buildings which are undefended and which are not military objectives[232]
- intentionally directing attacks against buildings dedicated to religion, education, art, science or charitable purposes, historic monuments, hospitals and places where the sick and wounded are collected, provided they are not military objectives[233]
- intentionally directing attacks against buildings, material, medical units and transport, and personnel using the distinctive emblems of the Geneva Conventions in conformity with international law.[234]

The list of crimes within the jurisdiction of the ICC when committed in NIAC, though, is markedly less developed, the most notable omission being the war crime of attacking civilian objects *simpliciter*:

- intentionally directing attacks against buildings, material, medical units and transport, and personnel using the distinctive emblems of the Geneva Conventions in conformity with international law[235]
- intentionally directing attacks against installations, material, units or vehicles involved in a humanitarian assistance or peacekeeping mission in accordance with the UN Charter, as long as they are entitled to the protection given to civilian objects under the law of armed conflict,[236] and
- intentionally directing attacks against buildings dedicated to religion, education, art, science or charitable purposes, historic monuments, hospitals and places where the sick and wounded are collected, provided they are not military objectives.[237]

In its 2016 judgment in the *Al Mahdi* case referred to in section IV.B, the Trial Chamber found that

> Mr Al Mahdi knew that he exercised joint control over the attack and was fully implicated in its execution. He was the head of the Hesbah, one of four primary institutions established by Ansar Dine and AQIM [al Qaeda in the Islamic Maghreb] upon occupying Timbuktu. He had overall responsibility for the execution phase of the attack, supervising the execution of the operations, using the Hesbah's members and determining the sequence in which the buildings would be destroyed, making the necessary logistical arrangements and justifying the attack to the broader world through media interviews. He also was present at all of the attack sites, giving instructions and moral support, and he personally participated in the attack that led to the destruction of at least five sites.[238]

[231] Art 8(2)(b)(iv), ICC Statute.
[232] Art 8(2)(b)(v), ICC Statute.
[233] Art 8(2)(b)(ix), ICC Statute.
[234] Art 8(2)(b)(xxiv), ICC Statute.
[235] Art 8(2)(e)(ii), ICC Statute.
[236] Art 8(2)(e)(iii), ICC Statute.
[237] Art 8(2)(e)(iv), ICC Statute.
[238] ICC, 'ICC Trial Chamber VIII declares Mr Al Mahdi guilty of the war crime of attacking historic and religious buildings in Timbuktu and sentences him to nine years' imprisonment', Press release ICC-CPI-20160927-PR1242, 27 September 2016, at https://goo.gl/Fca73r.

D. In the Jurisprudence of the Ad Hoc International Criminal Tribunals

The ICTY Statute seemed to privilege attacks against civilian objects. Article 3 of the Statute ('Violations of the laws or customs of war') gave the Tribunal the power to prosecute persons violating the laws or customs of war, which included:

- employment of poisonous weapons or other weapons calculated to cause unnecessary suffering
- wanton destruction of cities, towns or villages, or devastation not justified by military necessity
- attack, or bombardment, by whatever means, of undefended towns, villages, dwellings or buildings
- seizure of, destruction or wilful damage done to institutions dedicated to religion, charity and education, the arts and sciences, historic monuments and works of art and science, and
- plunder of public or private property.

In practice, though, the ICTY often treated attacks against civilian objects or indiscriminate attacks damaging civilian objects as either potential or actual direct attacks on civilians. In the *Galić* case, the Trial Chamber controversially held that indiscriminate or disproportionate attacks may amount to direct attacks against civilians.[239] General Galić appealed against his conviction for war crimes, arguing, inter alia, that the Trial Chamber had conflated a set of distinct war crimes. In response, the Appeals Chamber found that 'the impugned finding does not conflate the two crimes but rather supports the view that a direct attack can be inferred from the indiscriminate character of the weapon used'.[240] It further held that the Trial Chamber's finding 'that disproportionate attacks "may" give rise to the inference of direct attacks on civilians is … a justified pronouncement on the evidentiary effects of certain findings, not a conflation of different crimes'.[241] The Appeals Chamber then muddied the waters, averring:

> The Trial Chamber clearly stated that it limited itself to attacks on civilians pursuant to Article 51(2) of Additional Protocol I, which only contemplates direct attacks against the civilian population. The definition it adopted of the offence is equally clear. … No mention is made of indiscriminate or disproportionate attacks as the basis for conviction. Accordingly, this part of Galić's ground of appeal is dismissed.[242]

This might be taken to mean that the situations in which indiscriminate or disproportionate attacks may amount to direct attacks on civilians are indeed rare. The relevant parts of the judgments in the *Martić* case could therefore be viewed as an exception to a general rule that separates the different war crimes (and law of armed conflict violations). A direct attack on civilians differs from an indiscriminate attack affecting civilian objects, which in

[239] *Galić* (n 162) para 57.
[240] *Galić* (n 92) para 132.
[241] Ibid, para 133.
[242] Ibid, para 134.

turn is distinct from a disproportionate attack that is expected to cause excessive civilian damage.

In the case against Dragomir Milošević, who took over command of the Bosnian Serb forces above Sarajevo from General Galić, the Prosecution alleged that the accused perpetuated a 'campaign of shelling and sniping' of civilians, civilian areas and the civilian population of Sarajevo, and asserted that the attacks were deliberate, indiscriminate or disproportionate.[243] In testimony during the trial, the United Nations Protection Force (UNPROFOR) reported 'numerous incidents of shelling of Bosnian Muslim-held areas of Sarajevo', and witnesses described civilian areas being regularly targeted by shelling, such as parks, cemeteries, market places and places where people collected water. Evidence indicated that civilian buildings were regularly shelled and that shells regularly landed very near to peoples' houses. One witness said that there was 'nothing which could be done about the shelling except putting sandbags against the windows of the house and covering the windows with blankets'.[244] Based on the evidence, the Trial Chamber concluded that the behaviour of Bosnian Serb forces 'was characterised by indiscriminate shelling of civilian areas'.[245]

From October 1991, Vice Admiral Miodrag Jokić was commander of the Ninth Naval Sector of Boka in Montenegro. He was responsible, as a commander, for the naval shelling of Dubrovnik, although he had not ordered it.[246] As a result of naval and land shelling, two civilians were killed and three others wounded, and numerous buildings were destroyed, including those constituting cultural property. In 2004, Commander Jokić pleaded guilty to a range of war crimes, including murder, unlawful attack on civilians, devastation not justified by military necessity, unlawful attack on civilian objects, and destruction of or wilful damage done to institutions dedicated to religion, charity and education, the arts and sciences, historic monuments, and works of art and science. One of the treaties on which the ICTY Trial Chamber relied was the 1907 Hague Naval Bombardment Convention.[247] As a consequence of his failure to prevent or repress war crimes, Commander Jokić was sentenced to seven years' imprisonment by the ICTY,[248] a sentence confirmed on appeal.[249]

E. In National Law

A particularly grave incident involving an attack against a civilian object enjoying special protection (a hospital) occurred early on 3 October 2015 in the context of the NIACs in Afghanistan. At around 2am, a US Air Force AC-130 gunship attacked MSF's Kunduz Trauma Centre in the city of Kunduz in northern Afghanistan. It is estimated that, despite messages by MSF and others pleading for the attack to be halted, the airstrikes lasted

[243] *Dragomir Milošević* (n 17) para 6.
[244] Ibid, paras 422–24.
[245] Ibid, para 991.
[246] *Jokić* (n 172) para 26.
[247] Art 1 of the 1907 Convention prohibits the 'bombardment by naval forces of undefended ports, towns, villages, dwellings, or buildings'.
[248] *Jokić* (n 172) para 116.
[249] ICTY, *Prosecutor v Jokić*, Judgment on Sentencing Appeal (Appeals Chamber) (Case No IT-01-42/1-A), 30 August 2005, s IX ('Disposition').

approximately one hour, with some accounts saying the strikes continued for one hour and fifteen minutes, ending at approximately 3.15am.[250] Doctors and other medical staff were reportedly shot by the gunship's gunners while running to safety in a different part of the compound.[251] According to MSF's internal report on the air strike, the total number of dead was 'known to be at least 30, including: 10 known patients, 13 known staff, and 7 more bodies that were burnt beyond recognition'.[252] Subsequently, it was reported that 42 people had been killed and 37 wounded.[253]

On 7 October 2015, US President Barack Obama apologised for the airstrike and announced the US would be making condolence payments to the families of those killed. Subsequently, a US Department of Defense report, whose findings were made public on 29 April 2016, stated that condolence payments had been made to more than 170 individuals and families and US$5.7 million had been approved to reconstruct the MSF facility. General Joseph Votel, the commander of US Central Command, said in a news briefing to release the report that US$3,000 had been paid to the survivors, and US$6,000 to the relatives of those killed in the attack.[254]

The investigation found that a combination of factors had caused both the ground force commander and the air crew to believe mistakenly that the air crew was firing on the intended target, an insurgent-controlled site approximately 400 metres away from the MSF Trauma Centre. General Votel said that 'The investigation concluded that certain personnel failed to comply with the rules of engagement … [and][255] the law of armed conflict. However, the investigation did not conclude that these failures amounted to a war crime.'[256]

[250] Médecins sans Frontières (MSF), 'Initial MSF internal review: Attack on Kunduz Trauma Centre, Afghanistan', November 2015 (publicly released 5 November 2015) 7.

[251] Ibid, 10.

[252] Ibid, 12.

[253] I Ali, 'US strike on Afghan hospital in 2015 not a war crime: Pentagon', *Reuters Canada* (29 April 2016) at https://goo.gl/sWYZD6.

[254] Ibid.

[255] The CENTCOM press release issued the same day used the word 'and' rather than 'in', which was the word actually used by General Votel. 'April 29: CENTCOM releases investigation into airstrike on Doctors Without Borders trauma center', Press release 20160429-10, 29 April 2016, at http://www.centcom.mil/MEDIA/PRESS-RELEASES/Press-Release-View/Article/904574/april-29-centcom-releases-investigation-into-airstrike-on-doctors-without-borde/.

[256] News Transcript: Department of Defense Press Briefing by Army General Joseph Votel, Commander, US Central Command, 29 April 2016, at https://goo.gl/yhVT3z.

5

The Rule of Distinction in Attack: Persons

I. Introduction

Chapter 4 looked at the application of the rule of distinction to attacks against objects. This chapter addresses the rule of distinction as it applies to attacks against persons. This has grown in importance and controversy in tandem with the challenge in targeting only those participating directly in hostilities, especially in urban warfare occurring during non-international armed conflict (NIAC).

Section II describes the primary rule, including the key definitions of 'civilian', 'civilian population', 'combatant' and 'non-combatant'. It then details which acts amount to direct (civilian) participation in hostilities, one of the most controversial concepts in Hague Law. Section III articulates how the legal rule has been applied in practice, looking at case law regarding direct attacks against civilians or the civilian population and indiscriminate attacks affecting civilians, including by the use of indiscriminate weapons. Attacks against civilians as crimes against humanity are then identified and discussed. As was the case in chapter 4 with respect to civilian objects, the requisite level of accuracy demanded by Hague Law is given particular attention. The International Committee of the Red Cross's (ICRC's) 'Chapter IX' protection from use of lethal force is then assessed from the point of view of its normative status, the section concluding with analysis of which acts lead to loss of (legal) protection from attack.

Section IV describes which non-combatant individuals (other than protected civilians) enjoy special protection from attack under Hague Law, notably medical and religious personnel. Lastly, section V looks at how international criminal law addresses attacks against civilians under both conventional and customary international law. The section includes the analyses offered by the jurisprudence of the ad hoc international criminal tribunals. It concludes with an instance of prosecution under national military law: Staff Sergeant Robert Bales was emotively described by a magazine that interviewed him as 'America's most notorious war criminal'.

II. The Primary Rule

The prohibition on attacks against civilians and the civil population is included in both 1977 Additional Protocols. According to Article 48 of the 1977 Additional Protocol I,[1] 'Parties to

[1] Protocol Additional to the Geneva Conventions of 12 August 1949, and relating to the protection of victims of international armed conflicts (Protocol I); adopted at Geneva, 8 June 1977; entry into force, 7 December 1978.

the conflict shall at all times distinguish between the civilian population and combatants … and accordingly shall direct their operations only against military objectives.' According to Article 13(2) of the 1977 Additional Protocol II,[2] 'The civilian population as such, as well as individual civilians, shall not be the object of attack.'

Rule 1 of the 161 rules discerned by the ICRC in its Study of Customary International Humanitarian Law (IHL) provides that 'The parties to the conflict must at all times distinguish between civilians and combatants. Attacks may only be directed against combatants. Attacks must not be directed against civilians.'[3] The ICRC affirms that this fundamental customary rule applies in all armed conflicts.[4] The 1998 Rome Statute of the International Criminal Court (ICC Statute) gives the Court jurisdiction over the war crime of 'intentionally directing attacks against the civilian population as such or against individual civilians not taking direct part in hostilities' in both international armed conflict (IAC) and NIAC.[5]

The customary rule implies that a person has the status of either a civilian or a combatant. In fact, as the formulation in the ICC Statute suggests, the law is a little less straightforward. Civilians are not always protected from attack: they may be targeted if and for such time as they participate directly in hostilities. In addition, it is prohibited to attack non-combatant members of the armed forces (who are not civilians), or to attack combatants who are *hors de combat*, for example where, owing to wounds or sickness, they are unable or unwilling to continue participating directly in hostilities, or because they have clearly expressed their intention to surrender.

A. Key Definitions

i. Civilians and the Civilian Population

In an IAC, civilians are all persons who are not members of the armed forces. This definition of civilians is set out in Article 50 of the 1977 Additional Protocol I and has become part of customary law.[6] In turn, the civilian population comprises all persons who are civilians.[7] Civilians may become combatants without joining their nation's armed forces if, as an enemy approaches during an IAC, they spontaneously take up arms to resist the invading troops without having time to form themselves into an armed force. This longstanding

[2] Protocol Additional to the Geneva Conventions of 12 August 1949, and relating to the protection of victims of non-international armed conflicts (Protocol II); adopted at Geneva, 8 June 1977; entry into force, 7 December 1978.

[3] ICRC Study of Customary IHL, Rule 1 ('The Principle of Distinction between Civilians and Combatants') at https://goo.gl/qH7CwE.

[4] Ibid.

[5] Art 8(2)(b)(i) and (e)(i), Statute of the International Criminal Court; adopted at Rome, 17 July 1998; entry into force, 1 July 2002.

[6] ICRC Study of Customary IHL, Rule 1 ('The Principle of Distinction between Civilians and Combatants'). The International Criminal Tribunal for the former Yugoslavia (ICTY) has similarly defined civilians as those persons 'who are not, or no longer, members of the armed forces'. ICTY, *Prosecutor v Thomir Blaškić*, Judgment (Trial Chamber) (Case No IT-95-14-T), 3 March 2000, para 180.

[7] ICRC Study of Customary IHL, Rule 1.

rule, which is termed a *levée en masse* in the law of armed conflict, is codified in the 1899 and 1907 Hague Regulations and the 1949 Geneva Convention III.[8]

In the case of NIAC, a definition drafted for the 1977 Additional Protocol II clarified that 'a civilian is anyone who is not a member of the armed forces or of an organized armed group'. As the ICRC records,[9] even though it had been agreed by consensus during the Diplomatic Conference negotiations, the definition was deleted at the last moment as part of an agreement to adopt the Protocol, in particular in light of concerns voiced by Pakistan. The extent to which this reflects customary law, however, is questionable. According to the ICRC, 'practice is not clear' as to whether members of armed groups are civilians who lose protection from attack in case of direct participation, or whether 'members of such groups are liable to attack as such'.[10] Its position subsequently changed, as enunciated in its 2009 interpretive guidance on direct participation in hostilities.[11] This issue is discussed in section III.G.

The better view, as reflected in law of armed conflict treaty texts, is that civilians who do not join the state armed forces remain civilians but may be targeted when and for such time as they participate directly in hostilities. This reflects the call of the 20th International Conference of the Red Cross in 1965, which adopted a resolution stressing that a 'distinction must be made at all times between persons taking part in the hostilities and members of the civilian population, to the effect that the latter be spared as much as possible'.[12] The notion of 'membership' is often inappropriate to describe involvement in the activities of an armed group. An exception to the general rule would be where a section of the armed forces breaks away and engages in regular and intense combat with the rump of the armed forces. In this case, the members of the dissident armed forces are not to be considered civilians but may be targeted as if they were combatants.

ii. Combatant

All members of the armed forces of a party to an IAC are combatants, except dedicated medical and religious personnel.[13] A combatant has 'the right to participate directly in hostilities'.[14] Combatant status, which entitles a member of the armed forces to be treated as a prisoner of war upon capture, exists only in treaty law with respect to IACs. In the view of

[8] Art 2, Regulations concerning the Laws and Customs of War on Land annexed to Convention (II) with Respect to the Laws and Customs of War on Land; adopted at The Hague, 29 July 1899; entry into force, 4 September 1900; and Art II, Regulations concerning the Laws and Customs of War on Land, annexed to Convention (IV) respecting the Laws and Customs of War on Land; adopted at The Hague, 18 October 1907; entry into force, 26 January 1910 (1899 and 1907 Hague Regulations, respectively); and Art 4(A)(6), 1949 Geneva Convention III. For examples of *levées en masse* in recent history, see, eg, GD Solis, *The Law of Armed Conflict: International Humanitarian Law in War*, 2nd edn (New York, Cambridge University Press, 2016) 215–16.

[9] ICRC Study of Customary IHL, Rule 1.

[10] Ibid.

[11] ICRC, *Interpretive Guidance on Direct Participation in Hostilities under International Humanitarian Law* (Geneva, ICRC, 2009) (hereinafter 'ICRC DPH Guidance') at https://goo.gl/5CisPj.

[12] Resolution XXVIII ('Protection of civilian populations against the dangers of indiscriminate warfare'), 20th International Conference of the Red Cross, Vienna, 2–9 October 1965, at https://goo.gl/YXWf6j.

[13] ICRC Study of Customary IHL, Rule 3 ('The Definition of Combatants') at https://goo.gl/iD73pp.

[14] Art 43(2), 1977 Additional Protocol I.

the ICRC, for the purpose of the rule of distinction in attack, members of state armed forces may be considered combatants also in NIAC.[15]

Article 43(1) of the 1977 Additional Protocol I stipulates:

> The armed forces of a Party to a conflict consist of all organized armed forces, groups and units which are under a command responsible to that Party for the conduct of its subordinates, even if that Party is represented by a government or an authority not recognized by an adverse Party.

Paramilitary forces, such as the *gendarmerie* in France and many Francophone countries, may be encompassed within this definition as they are typically under the auspices of the Ministry of Defence. Thus, for instance, when adhering to the Protocol, France appended an understanding whereby its armed forces comprehend, on a permanent basis, the national *gendarmerie*.[16]

iii. Non-combatant

In addition to the status of combatant and civilian there is also the status of non-combatant. Dedicated medical and religious personnel who are members of the armed forces are considered non-combatants. This distinction within the armed forces was already reflected in both the 1899 and the 1907 Hague Regulations, which stipulated that 'the armed forces of the belligerent parties may consist of combatants and non-combatants'.[17] This status means that they shall not be attacked nor, unless they are willing to lose their protection, shall they engage in attacks. The customary rule is codified in Article 43(2) of the 1977 Additional Protocol I.

iv. Direct Participation in Hostilities

Both 1977 Additional Protocols make it explicit that civilians enjoy the protection afforded by Hague Law rules against attack, 'unless and for such time as they take a direct part in hostilities'.[18] The precise scope of the term 'direct participation in hostilities' (DPH), however, the action of which transforms a civilian who may not be attacked into one who no longer benefits from such protection, is one of the most contested norms in the law of armed conflict in its interpretation and application.

The fact that in 2009 the ICRC dedicated an 85-page report to offer its view ('interpretive guidance') of what amounts to direct participation in hostilities illustrates both the complexity of the topic and its importance.[19] For whether or not an individual is deemed to be directly participating in hostilities may determine whether he or she lives or dies. And when, for example, a combatant attacks an individual, if the target was not a direct participant in hostilities this may not only be a serious violation of the law of armed conflict, it may also require that the combatant is prosecuted for a war crime. So while the debate

[15] ICRC Study of Customary IHL, Rule 3 ('The Definition of Combatants').

[16] French Statement of Understanding, 11 April 2001, para 7, at https://goo.gl/eXsTTo.

[17] Art 3, 1899 and 1907 Hague Regulations.

[18] Art 51(3), 1977 Additional Protocol I; Art 13(3), 1977 Additional Protocol II.

[19] ICRC DPH Guidance (n 11). According to Solis, for instance, 'Although not perfect, the *Interpretive Guidance* provides a clarity previously absent.' Solis (n 8) 218.

surrounding participation in hostilities may seem to some to be rarefied or abstruse, the potential consequences of a determination of DPH are not.

The key elements that the ICRC's interpretive guidance identifies – threshold of harm, direct causation and belligerent nexus – mirror the key words 'participation', 'direct', and 'in hostilities'. This is both logical and reasonable and does not appear to be contested. The interpretation of the scope of the terms in the Guidance, however, certainly is, especially with regard to the first two elements.

As the issue of what amounts to hostilities was addressed in detail in chapter 3, the ins and outs of that debate are not repeated here. It suffices to recall that, in summary, hostilities in an IAC are not geographically limited, whereas in NIAC they are limited to areas where intense and regular combat is occurring. Of further note, the default scenario for the use of force in NIAC is law enforcement (on the part of the state) and potentially criminal violence under domestic law (on the part of individual citizens or members of armed groups). In any event, it is settled that violence must be directly linked to an armed conflict to even be considered as constituting direct participation in hostilities.[20] The focus of this section henceforth is therefore on what amounts to participation, and how one distinguishes direct from indirect participation.

a. 'Participation' in Hostilities

To participate in something means, in ordinary parlance, to be involved in it. It is clearly not enough, therefore, to be merely affected by combat or to support the struggle from a moral standpoint: one must contribute in some form to hostilities. The scope of this contribution is defined and limited by material, temporal and geographical issues.

1. Material Scope

In its judgment in the *Rutaganda* case, the International Criminal Tribunal for Rwanda (ICTR) explicitly applied the ICRC's commentary on the 1977 Additional Protocols as its basis for determining that direct participation in hostilities is constituted by 'acts of war which by their nature or purpose are likely to cause actual harm to the personnel and equipment of the enemy armed forces'.[21] Two decades after the publication of its commentary, though, the ICRC adopted a considerably broader stance in its interpretive guidance. While it still affirms that for a specific act to qualify as direct participation in hostilities the harm likely to result[22] must attain a certain threshold, it advocates that the requisite threshold

[20] One of the three elements discerned by the ICRC in its interpretive guidance is what it terms belligerent nexus: that the relevant act 'be specifically designed to directly cause the required threshold of harm in support of a party to the conflict and the detriment of another'. ICRC DPH Guidance (n 11) 58–64.

[21] ICTR, *Prosecutor v Georges Anderson Nderubumwe Rutaganda*, Judgement and Sentence (Trial Chamber I) (Case No ICTR-96-3-T), 6 December 1999, para 100; see Y Sandoz, C Swinarski, and B Zimmermann (eds), *Commentary on the Additional Protocols of 8 June 1977 to the Geneva Conventions of 12 August 1949* (Geneva, Martinus Nijhoff, 1987) para para 1944, 4788 (hereinafter 'ICRC Commentary on the 1977 Additional Protocols'). In para 1944 it is stated 'Thus "direct" participation means acts of war which by their nature or purpose are likely to cause actual harm to the personnel and equipment of the enemy armed forces.'

[22] 'The qualification of an act as direct participation does not require the *materialization* of harm reaching the threshold but merely the objective *likelihood* that the act will result in such harm. Therefore, the relevant threshold determination must be based on "likely" harm, that is to say, harm which may reasonably be expected to result from an act in the prevailing circumstances.' ICRC DPH Guidance (n 11) 47.

can be reached 'either by causing harm of a specifically military nature or by inflicting death, injury, or destruction on persons or objects protected against direct attack'.[23]

This position casts the net very broadly, with the ICRC thus arguing that participation in hostilities can be founded by an act which either does, or is likely to:

- adversely affect the military operations of a party to an armed conflict
- adversely affect the military capacity of a party to an armed conflict
- kill or injure civilians protected against direct attack, or
- destroy (or damage) civilian objects protected against direct attack.[24]

The ICRC terms this test the 'threshold of harm'.

Certain acts unequivocally constitute participation in hostilities: firing at an enemy from land, air or sea; capturing enemy personnel; the laying of landmines; clearing 'operational' minefields;[25] destroying, damaging or capturing military assets; damaging or blocking military communications, including through cyber-attacks; and transmitting tactical information directly to a party to the conflict with a view to an attack's being initiated.[26] For the purpose of ensuring compliance with Hague Law rules and subsequent accountability, it is logical that when and where an armed conflict exists, attacks harming civilians or civilian objects also form part of the hostilities.

That its proposed criterion of 'adversely affecting' military operations or military capacity was 'too wide and vague and could be misunderstood to authorise the killing of civilians without any military necessity' was raised by a number of experts engaged in the process leading to the elaboration by the ICRC of its interpretive guidance. The ICRC disregarded these concerns on the basis that its Chapter IX guidance, discussed in section III.F, would preclude use of deadly force where it was 'feasible' to use less violent means.[27] But this nonetheless implies that, *a priori*, it would not be unlawful under Hague Law for an unarmed civilian, standing in front of a tank and trying to impede its passage, to be machine-gunned or crushed under its tracks.[28] In the *Strugar* case, however, the ICTY's Appeals Chamber observed that a person is *hors de combat* if he 'is in the power of an adverse Party' and that 'the notion of active participation in hostilities encompasses armed participation in combat activities'.[29]

[23] Ibid.

[24] Ibid.

[25] That is, those being used operationally by a party to the conflict, even if that party had not originally laid the minefield.

[26] See ICRC DPH Guidance (n 11) 48.

[27] Ibid, 47, fn 97.

[28] Although the action did not take place during an armed conflict, the action of so-called 'Tank Man' during the Tiananmen Square repression in China on 4 June 1989 would presumably constitute direct participation in hostilities had it occurred in an armed conflict. See, eg, H Saul, 'Tiananmen Square: What happened to Tank Man?', *Independent* (4 June 2014) at https://goo.gl/CdaUUc. In Turkey, in July 2016, the short-lived *coup d'état*, the nature and extent of which seemingly amounted to a NIAC given the widespread nature and severity of the military action, also witnessed an instance of an unarmed man blocking the passage of a tank. This time, however, the tanks did not stop, and the man lay down on the road while two tanks passed over. He escaped unhurt. See, eg, N Morley, 'CCTV shows man get run over by two tanks and get up unharmed during Turkey coup', *Metro* (21 July 2016) at https://goo.gl/dkuLgW.

[29] ICTY, *Prosecutor v Pavle Strugar*, Judgment (Appeals Chamber) (Case No IT-01-42-A), 17 July 2008, paras 175, 176.

The ICRC asserts that the following acts do not constitute participation in hostilities: 'the building of fences or roadblocks, the interruption of electricity, water, or food supplies, the appropriation of cars and fuel, the manipulation of computer networks, and the arrest or deportation of persons'. While each of these acts 'may have a serious impact on public security, health, and commerce' (and may even be prohibited by the law of armed conflict), 'they would not, in the absence of adverse military effects, cause the kind and degree of harm required to qualify as direct participation in hostilities'.[30]

2. Temporal Scope

The ICRC also determined that in addition to acts that constitute DPH, preparatory acts and post-operational return by an individual 'may' also fall within the scope of the term.[31] In its general formulation in the interpretive guidance, though, this notion of doubt was forgotten: 'Measures preparatory to the execution of a specific act of direct participation in hostilities, as well as the deployment to and the return from the location of its execution, constitute an integral part of that act'.[32] This is despite the fact that, per se, such acts and movements adversely affect neither the military operations nor the military capacity of a party to an armed conflict, nor are they likely to. Thus, the ICRC's view of DPH, set out below, is too broad:

> A deployment amounting to direct participation in hostilities begins only once the deploying individual undertakes a physical displacement with a view to carrying out a specific operation. The return from the execution of a specific hostile act ends once the individual in question has physically separated from the operation, for example by laying down, storing or hiding the weapons or other equipment used and resuming activities distinct from that operation.[33]

The ICRC would perhaps have done better to remain consistent with its threshold of harm test. Once the act that adversely affects military operations or military capacity is over, so is the direct participation in hostilities, unless, for instance, the adverse party is in hot pursuit of the participants immediately following their act of hostilities.

Prior to the act, the planning of the act could also be considered preparatory. While the ICRC does not discuss in its interpretive guidance whether this is sufficient, during the earlier experts meetings one expert argued, correctly in the present author's view, that in terms of the beginning of DPH, threats, preparation and planning are to be excluded. The (unnamed) expert asserted that DPH starts with the actual carrying out of the act itself, and could be deemed to end when the individual no longer posed a direct threat to the enemy.[34] This is, I assert, the correct test.

It is not, though, supported by a majority of commentators. Dinstein, broadly citing the views of Kenneth Watkin, argues that 'it is necessary to go as far as is reasonably required

[30] ICRC DPH Guidance (n 11) 50.

[31] Ibid, 65.

[32] ICRC DPH Guidance (n 11), ch VI. See also ICRC Commentary on the 1977 Additional Protocols, para 4788, wherein the ICRC recalled that during the negotiation of the 1977 Additional Protocol I, 'several delegations considered that the term "hostilities" also covers preparations for combat and returning from combat'.

[33] ICRC DPH Guidance (n 11) 67.

[34] 'Direct Participation in Hostilities under International Humanitarian Law', Background Paper, Expert Meeting of 25–26 October 2004, 34.

both "upstream" and "downstream" from the actual engagement'.[35] The flaw in his argument is evidenced by the example he gives of cyber-warfare. He says that injecting a 'logic bomb' into an enemy computer

> is likely to be only the initial step: violent effects may be delayed until its activation after a lapse of time. As asserted in the Tallinn Manual, the duration of an individual's direct participation extends from the earliest point of planning the mission to the termination of his role in the operation (up to and including activation of the 'logic bomb').[36]

Let us apply this by direct analogy to the laying of mines. As already noted, the laying of mines is undoubtedly one act that can constitute direct participation in hostilities. If Dinstein were correct, this would imply that not only on his or her return from emplacement but potentially for years or even decades afterwards (if the conflict lasted that long) the mine-layer would be participating directly in hostilities and could be killed without warning at any time. This is so even if it were the only hostile act this individual ever performed in his or her life. Presumably only the detonation of the mine would end his or her participation and liability to attack. Such an approach is not credible.

Dinstein also appears to reject a general presumption of civilian status for an individual,[37] particularly once he or she has previously performed hostile acts.[38] He notes that the ICRC maintains that civilian immunity from attack is restored each time the person ends his or her engagement in a hostile act, and that no prediction as to future conduct is allowed.[39] He claims, however, that a 'soldier by night and peaceful citizen by day' should be considered 'an unlawful combatant at all times'. Citing Michael Schmitt, he approves the assertion that civilian protection from attack cannot be regained 'until he unambiguously opts out through extended nonparticipation or an affirmative act of withdrawal'.[40] How does one do this? And how does the enemy know that this is not the first and only time you have, for example, driven munitions to the front line? While the limited functional test has its critics, it better reflects the realities of *direct* participation in hostilities.

[35] Y Dinstein, *The Conduct of Hostilities under the Law of International Armed Conflict*, 3rd edn (Cambridge, Cambridge University Press, 2016) 177, para 476, citing K Watkin, 'Controlling the Use of Force: A Role for Human Rights Norms in Contemporary Armed Conflict' (2004) 98 *AJIL* 1, 17.

[36] Dinstein (n 35) 177, para 476.

[37] This is consonant with the United States (US) Department of Defense's view of customary international law. It states that 'Under customary international law, no legal presumption of civilian status exists for persons or objects, nor is there any rule inhibiting commanders or other military personnel from acting based on the information available to him or her in doubtful cases.' US Department of Defense, *Law of War Manual*, June 2015, Updated December 2016 (hereinafter 'USDOD December 2016 *Law of War Manual*') para 5.4.3.2, at https://goo.gl/QMkjqs. As the *Manual* notes, however, under Art 50(1) of the 1977 Additional Protocol I, 'In case of doubt whether a person is a civilian, that person shall be considered to be a civilian.' This presumption therefore applies to all states parties to the Protocol. France and the United Kingdom (UK), however, have declared that 'the rule … applies only in cases of substantial doubt still remaining after the [requisite] assessment … has been made, and not as overriding a commander's duty to protect the safety of troops under his command or to preserve his military situation, in conformity with other provisions of the Protocol'. See UK Declaration of 2 July 2002, at https://goo.gl/z8ENQ9; see also J Gaudreau, 'The reservations to the Protocols additional to the Geneva Conventions for the protection of war victims', *International Review of the Red Cross*, no 849 (March 2003) 143 ('Definition of civilians and civilian population – Article 50') at https://goo.gl/V5MXPT.

[38] Dinstein (n 35) 139, para 370; 180, para 485.

[39] Ibid., para 477, citing ICRC DPH Guidance (n 11), 70–71.

[40] Dinstein (n 35) 177, para 477, citing MN Schmitt, 'Targeted Killings and International Law: Law Enforcement, Self-defense and Armed Conflict' in R Arnold and N Quénivet (eds), *International Humanitarian Law and Human Rights Law: Towards a New Merger in International Law* (Leiden, Martinus Nijhoff, 2008) 525, 546.

3. Geographical Scope

As already noted, and discussed in detail in chapter 3, the geographical scope of participation in hostilities is limited to the areas where hostilities are taking place. In an IAC, this could be anywhere in the world (or indeed outside it, in outer space), whereas in a NIAC it is far more limited. Thus, acts that take place in the context of a NIAC outside the area of hostilities are not regulated by Hague Law but by applicable domestic law and international human rights law. They do not occur in a legal vacuum.

b. Direct Participation

The fact that to lose protection from attack one must participate *directly* in hostilities means that an individual participating *indirectly* in hostilities retains his or her civilian protection from attack. The distinction typically drawn is between fighting (direct) and war-sustaining or military capacity-building (indirect) acts of participation. First, though, the issue of language (active versus direct participation) needs to be discussed.

1. Active Versus Direct

The language of Article 3 Common to the four 1949 Geneva Conventions (Common Article 3) protects those 'taking no active part in the hostilities' while, as previously noted, the 1977 Additional Protocols protect those who 'who do not take a direct part or who have ceased to take part in hostilities'.[41] Despite the difference in language in the English version, it is generally accepted that no substantive difference exists between the notions of active and direct participation for the purpose of the rule of distinction.[42]

The issue was, though, indirectly addressed by the ICC in the *Lubanga* trial judgment and Mr Lubanga's subsequent appeal against conviction for using children under the age of 15 'to participate actively' in hostilities. The Trial Chamber had held that

> the expression 'to participate actively in hostilities', as opposed to the expression 'direct participation' (as found in Additional Protocol I to the Geneva Conventions) was clearly intended to import a wide interpretation to the activities and roles that are covered by the offence of using children under the age of 15 actively to participate in hostilities.[43]

In the judgment of his appeal, the ICC Appeals Chamber held:

> Mr Lubanga's argument is correct that, in the context of Common Article 3 of the Geneva Conventions, 'active' and 'direct' participation in hostilities are used interchangeably. This is supported not only by the French and English versions of this article, but also by the ICRC

[41] See Arts 51(3) and 77(2) and (3), 1977 Additional Protocol I; and Arts 4(1) and (3) and 13(3), 1977 Additional Protocol II.

[42] Dinstein (n 35) 174, para 470, citing with approval ICRC DPH Guidance (n 11) 33–34.

[43] ICC, *Prosecutor v Thomas Lubanga Dyilo*, Judgment (Trial Chamber) (Case No ICC-01/04-01/06), 14 March 2012, para 627. It noted that Art 4(3)(c) of the 1977 Additional Protocol II, which proscribes child participation, does not include the word 'direct'. The Trial Chamber also quoted from the *AFRC* case before the Special Court for Sierra Leone (SCSL), which included as use of children to participate actively in hostilities 'carrying loads for the fighting faction, finding and/or acquiring food, ammunition or equipment, acting as decoys, carrying messages, making trails or finding routes, manning checkpoints or acting as human shields [, which] are some examples of active participation as much as actual fighting and combat': SCSL, *Prosecutor v Alex Tamba Brima, Santigie Borbor Kanu, and Brima Bazzy Kamara*, Judgment (Trial Chamber I) (Case No SCSL-04-16-T), 20 June 2007, para 737.

> Interpretative Guidance on the notion of direct participation in hostilities under international humanitarian law, scholarly commentators and the ICTY/ICTR jurisprudence. Common Article 3 of the Geneva Convention is relevant to the distinction between persons who are afforded certain protection under the Geneva Conventions, including civilians, and those who are excluded from that protection. The purpose of Common Article 3 of the Geneva Conventions is to afford protection to those persons who are 'taking *no* active part in the hostilities' (emphasis added).[44]

The Court then proceeded to rather tie itself up in legal knots. The Appeals Chamber stated, sensibly enough, that the purpose of the prohibition on the active participation of children in hostilities was in the context of efforts to prevent children being involved in armed conflict; the prohibition of recruitment of children was further evidence of this. But the Court then relied on the 1987 ICRC commentary on the Additional Protocols, in which it was asserted that 'gathering and transmission of military information, transportation of arms and munitions, provision of supplies' were considered to be forms of indirect participation, but which nonetheless amount to services that children 'should' not be required to perform.[45]

The Court's approach is flawed in three respects. First, it transforms a high-minded 'should' into a 'shall' for the purpose of a war crimes conviction. Second, as evidenced above, the ICRC's thinking seems to have evolved materially since the commentaries on the Additional Protocols were published in 1987, and, depending on the nexus to hostilities, these indirect acts of participation could be considered as direct participation by the ICRC today. Third, it implies that a child may be deemed to be 'actively' participating in hostilities by acts that would still protect him or her from direct attack. Nonetheless, the ICC Appeals Chamber clearly held that law of armed conflict rules 'do not establish that the phrase "participate actively in armed hostilities" should be interpreted so as to only refer to forms of direct participation in armed hostilities, as understood in the context of the principle of distinction and Common Article 3 of the Geneva Conventions'.[46]

In mid-August 2016, the Saudi-led coalition forces attacking Houthis in Yemen were accused by Médecins sans Frontières (MSF) of an attack against a Koranic school in the Haydan district of Saada province, which killed 10 children.[47] The United Nations (UN) Secretary-General Ban Ki Moon condemned the attack and called for a swift investigation, noting 'with dismay that civilians, including children, continue to bear the brunt of increased fighting and military operations in Yemen'.[48] The coalition, however, denied targeting a school in Haydan, claiming that it had bombed a camp at which the Houthis were training child soldiers.[49] Coalition spokesman General Ahmed Assiri said that the site that was bombed was a 'major training camp for militia'. He affirmed that the deaths of the children 'confirm the Huthis' practice of recruiting and subjecting children to terror', and

[44] ICC, *Prosecutor v Lubanga*, Judgment (Appeals Chamber) (Case No ICC-01/04-01/06 A 5), 1 December 2014, para 323 (original note on emphasis; notes omitted).

[45] Ibid, para 326, citing ICRC Commentary on the 1977 Additional Protocols, para 3187.

[46] *Lubanga* (n 44) para 328.

[47] 'Yemen conflict: Air strike hits MSF hospital in Hajjah', *BBC* (15 August 2016) at https://goo.gl/w3G6GS.

[48] Statement from the Office of the UN Secretary-General, cited in G Balkiz, T Ap, A Moshtaghian, and H Almasmar (CNN), 'Saudi-led coalition denies targeting schools', *KRDO* (15 August 2016) at https://goo.gl/ntkg8v.

[49] *BBC*, 'Yemen conflict' (n 47).

claimed that the Houthis used children 'as scouts, guards, messengers and fighters', citing reports from Human Rights Watch on their use of underage recruits.[50]

According to the ICRC interpretive guidance, unless the children already had a 'continuous combat function' (see section III.G), the Saudis would need to know whether they were being trained for future service or for a specific military operation. The former would preserve their immunity from attack (though they could be lawful collateral victims in an attack targeting a lawful military objective); the latter would render them liable to being targeted and killed. If the intelligence were accurate, they were probably being used to participate actively in hostilities according to the ICC definition, demonstrating both the problem of identifying DPH for the purpose of the rule of distinction and also the dangers of the dual definition of 'active participation in hostilities' (APH) for the purpose of prosecuting use of children as soldiers.

2. Direct Versus Indirect

In the *Strugar* case, the ICTY Appeals Chamber rightly noted that DPH

> cannot be held to embrace all activities in support of one party's military operations or war effort. This is made clear by Article 15 of Geneva Convention IV, which draws a distinction between taking part in hostilities and performing 'work of a military character'. Moreover, to hold all activities in support of military operations as amounting to direct participation in hostilities would in practice render the principle of distinction meaningless.[51]

According to the ICRC report on its expert discussions on DPH, there was 'general agreement' among the experts that civilians working in a munitions factory are merely building up the capacity of a party to a conflict to harm its adversary, but do not directly cause harm themselves. Therefore, 'unlike civilians actually using the produced ammunition to cause harm to the adversary, such factory workers cannot be regarded as directly participating in hostilities'.[52] Attacking the factory would of course be lawful as it is a legitimate military objective, but the civilian workers would not be lawful objects of attack, so the risk to their lives and limbs would need to be factored in to the proportionality assessment before an attack was launched (see chapter 6).

More controversially, the ICRC asserts that it

> is neither necessary nor sufficient for a qualification as direct participation that a preparatory measure occur immediately before (temporal proximity) or in close geographical proximity to the execution of a specific hostile act or that it be indispensable for its execution.[53]

It cites as an example the loading of bombs onto an aircraft for a specific attack, which it argues does constitute a measure preparatory to a specific hostile act and, therefore, qualifies as direct participation in hostilities. Interestingly, it limits the example to situations where the attack is planned against military objectives in an area of hostilities.[54] The ICRC

[50] Agence France-Presse, 'Coalition denies targeting Yemen school as 10 children killed', *The Straits Times* (15 August 2016) at https://goo.gl/z9Jv16.

[51] *Strugar* (n 29) para 176.

[52] ICRC DPH Guidance (n 11), 53, fn 123.

[53] Ibid, 66.

[54] Presumably, though, this would also be the case if the attack was unlawful, such as if it was planned to target civilians or civilian objects.

further clarifies that this is the case even if the operation 'will not be carried out until the next day, if the target will be selected only during the operation, and if great distance separates the preparatory measure from the location of the subsequent attack'.[55] Conversely, it affirms, transporting bombs from a factory to storage at an airfield and then to an aircraft 'for shipment to another storehouse in the conflict zone for unspecified use in the future would constitute a general preparatory measure qualifying as mere indirect participation'.[56]

So somehow the enemy is supposed to know whether a particular munition is being transported for use in connection with a specific operation: if it is, those civilians engaged in the transport are directly participating in hostilities; if not, they are civilians whose lives and limbs must be incorporated into a proportionality analysis.[57] Dinstein seems to make a distinction between loading bombs onto a military aircraft prior to a sortie (whatever the distance from the destination) and transporting munitions in a truck (which does depend on the proximity to the conflict zone).[58] So the driver who delivers the bomb to the airport thousands of miles away from the area of hostilities cannot be directly targeted but the person who loads it onto the plane can? This is lacking in intellectual rigour.

Likewise, if Dinstein is correct in asserting that 'ancillary acts' such as the gathering of information suffice for DPH, this means for instance that a seven-year-old boy or girl standing by a tree as a look-out can be targeted and killed without warning. But how does one know whether the child is merely standing by a tree? Or watching soldiers pass by? As discussed in chapter 7, according to Hague Law rules parties to a conflict only need to take 'feasible' measures to ensure that they target only lawful military objectives.

In the *Strugar* case, the Appeals Chamber offered examples, based on analysis of 'military manuals, soft law, decisions of international bodies, and the commentaries to the Geneva Conventions and the Additional Protocols', of what constitutes indirect participation in hostilities:

- participating in activities in support of the war or military effort of one of the parties to the conflict
- selling goods to one of the parties to the conflict
- expressing sympathy for the cause of one of the parties to the conflict
- failing to act to prevent an incursion by one of the parties to the conflict
- accompanying and supplying food to one of the parties to the conflict
- gathering and transmitting military information
- transporting arms and munitions and providing supplies, and
- providing specialist advice regarding the selection of military personnel, their training or the correct maintenance of the weapons.[59]

[55] ICRC DPH Guidance (n 11) 66.
[56] Ibid.
[57] Moreover, the concrete and direct military advantage anticipated from destroying weapons that may only be used at some unspecified juncture in the future is going to be pretty low at best (indeed, how is it deemed direct rather than indirect?).
[58] Dinstein (n 35) 179, para 482; 180, para 483.
[59] *Strugar* (n 29) para 177.

Examples of general preparation not entailing loss of protection against direct attack, according to the ICRC, include purchase, production, smuggling and hiding of weapons; general recruitment and training of personnel; and financial, administrative or political support to armed actors.[60] But again, how is the enemy supposed to know whether individuals are being trained for the cause or for a specific operation? Or whether weapons are being bought, produced, smuggled or hidden to sustain capacity or to equip a unit for a particular attack? The application of the rules, discussed in section III, indicates how difficult that may be in practice.

III. The Application of the Rule

As neither law of armed conflict treaty nor custom makes explicit how the rule of distinction is to be applied in practice, it is necessary to employ 'subsidiary means for the determination of rules of law'. These are, according to the 1945 Statute of the International Court of Justice (ICJ Statute), 'judicial decisions and the teachings of the most highly qualified publicists of the various nations'.[61] The most valuable examples of judicial discussion of the targeting of objects under Hague Law rules are to be found in the *Jokić*, *Strugar*, *Galić* and *Dragomir Milošević* cases before the ICTY. The *Jokić* and *Strugar* cases addressed the Yugoslav army and navy attacks on the Croatian town of Dubrovnik in 1991, while *Galić* and *Milošević* both concerned the Bosnian Serb campaign of sniping and shelling in 'The Siege of Sarajevo' in 1992–95.

A. Direct Attacks against Civilians or the Civilian Population

Under the 1977 Additional Protocols I and II, it is stipulated that the civilian population as such, as well as individual civilians, shall not be the object of attack.[62] It is implicit in this treaty prohibition (made explicit in other provisions)[63] that civilians only receive this protection when they are not participating directly in hostilities. Attacks can of course be launched from land, the air or the seas. Case law in different fora has addressed these scenarios to varying degrees.

To firmly ground an allegation of an attack directed against civilians, it is necessary both to establish where the firing originated (at least the area and under whose control the area fell at the relevant time) and to confirm that no military objective nearby could have been lawfully targeted. In general, an individual who is hit by a ricochet or is caught in crossfire during combat between two parties to an armed conflict (if a lawful military objective is being targeted) cannot be said either to have been under attack as a civilian or to have been the victim of an indiscriminate attack. This is also the case where an individual is accidentally hit by a shell or by shrapnel (shell fragmentation), unless the targeting was reckless or involved the use of an indiscriminate weapon.

[60] ICRC DPH Guidance (n 11) 66–67.
[61] Art 38(1)(d), ICJ Statute.
[62] Art 51(2), 1977 Additional Protocol I; Art 13(2), 1977 Additional Protocol II.
[63] Art 51(3), 1977 Additional Protocol I; Art 13(3), 1977 Additional Protocol II.

i. *The* Galić *Case*

This case demonstrates some of the challenges in finding serious violations of Hague Law rules. General Galić, who commanded Bosnian Serb forces in and around Sarajevo for much of the war in Bosnia and Herzegovina, was accused of conducting a protracted campaign of sniping and shelling against civilians in Sarajevo.[64] Inter alia, the Indictment referred to

> Violations of the Laws or Customs of War (attacks on civilians as set forth in Article 51 of Additional Protocol I and Article 13 of Additional Protocol II to the Geneva Conventions of 1949) punishable under Article 3 of the Statute of the Tribunal.[65]

The paragraph introducing that count of the indictment alleged that General Galić, as commander of Bosnian Serb forces, 'conducted a coordinated and protracted campaign of sniper attacks upon the civilian population of Sarajevo, killing and wounding a large number of civilians of all ages and both sexes, such attacks by their nature involving the deliberate targeting of civilians with direct fire weapons'.[66] A further count of the indictment was similar, except that it concerned 'a coordinated and protracted campaign of artillery and mortar shelling onto civilian areas of Sarajevo and upon its civilian population. The campaign of shelling resulted in thousands of civilians being killed or injured.'[67]

The Trial Record contained evidence that civilians were deliberately targeted while engaged in civilian activities or while in civilian locations.[68] One witness, a Bosnian Serb soldier, testified that the brigade commander gave orders to his mortar battery to target ambulances, a marketplace, funeral processions and cemeteries.[69] The main avenue in Sarajevo, which runs parallel to the Miljacka River from Stari Grad into the western part of town, became known as 'Sniper Alley'.[70] David Fraser, an UNPROFOR (UN Protection Force) representative in Sarajevo from April 1994, stated that 'in the area of Sniper Alley, there were no military positions … just civilians walking along the street'. They were the main targets of the shooting.[71]

On 3 September 1993, in one incident in Hrasno, a neighbourhood in Sarajevo, Nafa Tarić went out to get school books at approximately 5pm with her eight-year-old daughter, Elma. It was a 'sunny and peaceful day'. They crossed a street behind a line of containers that had been installed to provide protection against Bosnian Serb snipers. As the two emerged from the cover of the containers, they were shot. A single bullet hit Nafa Tarić's left thigh, then grazed her daughter's hand and penetrated her stomach. They fell to the ground. Nafa Tarić said that another bullet 'whizzed past our bodies as we lay there'. They managed to crawl away from the exposed position and were taken to hospital.[72]

The Trial Chamber noted Nafa Tarić's testimony that no military activity was ongoing at the time of the incident and that neither soldiers nor any items of military equipment

[64] ICTY, *Prosecutor v Galić*, Judgment (Trial Chamber I) (Case No IT-98-29-T), 5 December 2003, para 3.
[65] Ibid, para 13. The Trial Chamber held, citing other Tribunal jurisprudence, that the prohibition of attack on civilians embodied in those treaty provisions 'reflects customary international law'. Ibid, para 19.
[66] Ibid, para 14.
[67] Ibid, para 15.
[68] Ibid, para 217.
[69] Ibid, para 219.
[70] Ibid, para 229.
[71] Ibid, para 230.
[72] Ibid, para 267.

were in the immediate vicinity. According to the witness, the closest Bosniak army military command post was located between 500 and 800 metres from Hrasno neighbourhood. Moreover, the Chamber observed that the fact that the two were shot at as they emerged from behind the containers, and that a second shot was fired at them as they lay wounded, reveals that they were deliberately targeted and not wounded by accident.[73] The Chamber was satisfied beyond reasonable doubt that Nafa and Elma Tarić, both civilians, were deliberately targeted from a Bosnian Serb-controlled position.[74]

While this instance was uncontroversial from a legal perspective, Judge Nieto-Navia, in his Dissenting Opinion in the trial judgment, identified a number of other sniping and shelling incidents in which he believed reasonable doubt existed as to the guilt of forces under General Galić's command. Of course, the standard for culpability under international criminal law (beyond reasonable doubt) is considerably higher than the proof needed to find a party to an armed conflict responsible for a violation of a primary rule (generally, this would be judged on the balance of probabilities), but in some instances, the civil law standard of proof might not even have been reached.

In one such incident, Almasa Konjhodzic, a civilian, was found by the Majority to have been deliberately targeted and killed by a shot fired from Bosnian Serb-controlled territory on 27 June 1993. (The incident is discussed in further detail in chapter 9.) Judge Nieto-Navia noted that the location where Ms Konjhodzic was shot lay directly across from the Marshal Tito barracks, which had been occupied for a time by the Bosniak army and was in an area where fighting took place, including on the day of the incident. The evidence established that two shots were fired during the incident. The first was claimed by one witness not to have been aimed at the victim because it 'was flying much too high', while the second was said to have hit the victim only after having 'ricocheted from the asphalt'. Judge Nieto-Navia found that the evidence did not 'conclusively exclude the possibility that the victim was hit by a stray bullet, perhaps originating from the fighting taking place in the area during the day of the incident'.[75]

Judge Nieto-Navia's Dissenting Opinion also identified a number of shelling incidents in which reasonable doubt existed as to the guilt of forces under General Galić's command. One such case concerned the finding by the Majority of the Trial Chamber that a group of civilians queueing for water in the Dobrinja 'C5' area was deliberately targeted on 12 July 1993 by an 82 mm mortar shell fired from Bosnian Serb-held territory.[76] Since the mortar shell responsible for the deaths of the civilians exploded in flight when striking a person, it left no crater, only radial imprints on the pavement surface. These imprints enabled a local police investigator and UN representative to conclude that the direction of fire was 'most probably' from the west-north-west, towards where Bosnian Serb forces were located. But the lack of a crater prevented the determination of the distance of fire of the shell, which would have established conclusively that it had been fired from beyond a confrontation line some 250 to 300 metres away, in Bosnian Serb-controlled territory.[77]

[73] Ibid, para 269.
[74] Ibid, para 271.
[75] *Galić* (n 64) Dissenting Opinion of Judge Nieto-Navia, paras 30–33.
[76] Ibid, para 66.
[77] Ibid, para 67.

But even if the provenance of the shell had been established, Judge Nieto-Navia was of the view that the evidence would not establish that the projectile had been aimed deliberately at civilians given the significant Bosniak army presence in the vicinity of the water pump. A local commander had testified that when the shelling occurred, the army was digging a tunnel from Dobrinja to Butmir, which was completed less than three weeks later. Sources in evidence offered varying estimates of the distance from the entrance of the tunnel to the site of the incident, ranging from 30 metres to 200 metres. The Trial Record established that the Bosnian Serb forces knew about the Butmir end of the tunnel, which it shelled intensively, but it was not clear whether it was also aware of the Dobrinja entrance. The Bosniak army had also set up a command post about 100 metres from the water pump. This and other evidence meant that lawful military objectives were in the vicinity of the strike, and on that basis Judge Nieto-Navia concluded that the Prosecution had not established beyond a reasonable doubt that the 82 mm mortar shell which exploded at the water pump was fired deliberately at civilians by the Bosnian Serbs.[78] His reasoning is sound, illustrating once more the difficulty of prosecuting serious violations of Hague Law, particularly when hostilities are being conducted in cities or towns.

ii. The Strugar *Case*

The *Strugar* case confirmed that it is not only essential to assess evidence of the civilian status of a victim of an attack, but a tribunal should also make explicit how it reached its findings based on that evidence. Pavle Strugar was a Lieutenant-General of the erstwhile Yugoslav Peoples' Army (JNA), charged by the ICTY with a range of war crimes, including attacks against civilians and civilian objects and murder in connection with the attacks on Dubrovnik, particularly the Old Town. He denied the charges. Two people were killed by the shelling, one a shop worker, the other a photographer. In both cases, the Trial Chamber was satisfied that at the time of their deaths they were civilians 'taking no active part in the hostilities'.[79] This finding of fact and law, which was based on witness statements and their civilian clothing, was subsequently confirmed by the Appeals Chamber.[80]

General Strugar was also convicted of 'cruel treatment' for shelling that resulted in serious wounds to Mato Valjalo. After being hit by shrapnel, Mr Valjalo was taken to a nearby hospital where he was found to have shrapnel lodged in his leg, head and lungs. As a result of his injuries, Mr Valjalo was assessed to be 30 per cent disabled and suffering from psychoneurosis.[81] With regard to his civilian status, the Trial Chamber found that as a driver for the Dubrovnik Municipal Crisis Staff who was injured on his way to work, 'there is nothing in the evidence to suggest that, as a driver, in this capacity, he was taking an active part in the hostilities'.[82]

General Strugar appealed against his conviction, arguing, inter alia, that Mato Valjalo was in fact taking active part in hostilities when he was injured. Mr Valjalo had testified that during the attacks in December 1991, he was driving the President of the Executive

[78] Ibid, para 70.
[79] ICTY, *Prosecutor v Pavle Strugar*, Judgment (Trial Chamber II) (Case No IT-01-42-T), 31 January 2005, paras 244, 252.
[80] *Strugar* (n 29) para 183.
[81] *Strugar* (n 79) paras 271, 272.
[82] Ibid, para 274.

Council of Dubrovnik, who also served as the President of the Dubrovnik Municipal Crisis Staff. Valjalo specified that the President did not wear a military uniform. Mr Valjalo also asserted that he was himself a civilian, that he wore civilian clothes and that he was unarmed. Although he was a reserve in the Croatian army, he was not mobilised during the war.[83] General Strugar, however, observed that Mr Valjalo was subsequently granted the status of a 'disabled veteran of the Croatian war of defence', indicating a military status. During his testimony, however, Mr Valjalo had explained that although members of the Dubrovnik Municipal Crisis Staff were civilians and 'didn't fight', they were nonetheless granted the status of a 'military war invalid'.[84] The Appeals Chamber stated that 'while it would have been preferable for the Trial Chamber to make more explicit findings on this issue', it was satisfied that it had been 'established beyond a reasonable doubt that, in substance' Mato Valjalo was a civilian.[85]

B. Indiscriminate Attacks Affecting Civilians

As with direct attacks against civilian objects, indiscriminate attacks are prohibited by both treaty and customary law.[86] An indiscriminate attack is one that is of a nature 'to strike military objectives and civilians or civilian objects without distinction'. This is because the attack is not directed at a specific military objective; uses a means or method of warfare that cannot be directed at a specific military objective; or because it uses a means or method of warfare whose effects cannot be limited as required by law of armed conflict rules. As the UK Ministry of Defence has observed, it 'seems that an attack can be indiscriminate even if no civilians are killed or injured by it'.[87]

The use of inherently indiscriminate means and methods of warfare is addressed in section III.C. The present section illustrates through case law the first of the three scenarios: where an attack is not directed at a specific military objective. In contrast to a direct attack on a civilian object, in an indiscriminate attack the attacker does not care whether any civilian harm results.[88] This encompasses not only situations where it is known that a military objective is not being targeted, but also where targeting is reckless.

i. Benzer v Turkey

In the *Benzer* case, the European Court of Human Rights applied Hague Law rules to the bombing by aircraft belonging to the Turkish military of two Kurdish villages in

[83] See *Strugar* (n 29) para 182.

[84] Ibid, para 183.

[85] Ibid, para 188.

[86] See Art 51, 1977 Additional Protocol I; ICRC Study of Customary IHL, Rule 12 ('Definition of Indiscriminate Attacks') at https://goo.gl/T8JMMe. The prohibition was first included in the abortive 1923 Hague Rules on Air Warfare, Art XXIV(3) of which stipulated that 'The bombardment of cities, towns, villages, dwellings, or buildings not in the immediate neighbourhood of the operations of land forces is prohibited. In cases where the objectives … are so situated, that they cannot be bombarded without the indiscriminate bombardment of the civilian population, the aircraft must abstain from bombardment.'

[87] UK Ministry of Defence, *The Manual of the Law of Armed Conflict* (Oxford, Oxford University Press, 2005) para 5.23.3.

[88] Dinstein (n 35) para 393.

south-eastern Turkey in March 1994. As a result, 13 people in Koçağili village and 25 people in Kuşkonar village lost their lives. Most of those who were killed were children, women or elderly.[89] The Court considered 'that an indiscriminate aerial bombardment of civilians and their villages … cannot be reconcilable with … the customary rules of international humanitarian law'.[90] The Court held that the attacks violated the right to life of those killed by the bombing, as well as those severely injured but who survived.[91]

ii. The Dragomir Milošević *Case*

In this case, the ICTY Trial Chamber heard evidence that civilians in Sarajevo were often caught in the fighting, but that they were also direct targets of shelling and sniping or casualties of indiscriminate firing.[92] According to one witness (a Civil Affairs Officer with UNPROFOR), 'in 1993 and 1994, but probably more in the latter half of 1994, the shelling was not concentrated against military targets. Instead, shells were dropped apparently randomly across densely-populated civilian areas in a way that would cause a small number of casualties in a large number of places'. According to another witness, one of the consequences of using mortars as 'harassing fire', as it was used in Sarajevo, was the infliction of 'a lot of harm, especially against civilians'.[93]

In Dragomir Milošević's appeal, the Appeals Chamber considered that Article 51(5)(a) of the 1977 Additional Protocol I, 'although mainly concerned with cases of carpet bombing and similar military activities' rather than 'with a protracted campaign of sniping and shelling during a siege-like situation', was 'undoubtedly instructive of the approach belligerents are required to take in establishing and pursuing military targets'.[94] The Appeals Chamber considered that Mr Milošević had not substantiated his assertion that the attacks carried out by the Bosnian Serbs under his command were 'combat activities within military installations'.[95]

iii. The Commission of Inquiry on Syria

In Syria, already in 2012 the Independent International Commission of Inquiry reported that 'Accounts indicated that Government forces on occasion directed shelling to target small opposition strongholds. In many attacks, however, those firing projectiles did not distinguish between civilian and military targets.'[96] On the basis of its findings, the Commission determined 'that the legal threshold for an indiscriminate attack as a violation

[89] European Court of Human Rights, *Benzer v Turkey*, Judgment (Former Second Section), 12 November 2013, para 11.

[90] Ibid, para 184.

[91] Ibid, para 185.

[92] ICTY, *Prosecutor v Dragomir Milošević*, Judgment (Trial Chamber III) (Case No IT-98-29/1-T), 12 December 2007, para 148.

[93] Ibid, para 420.

[94] ICTY, *Prosecutor v Dragomir Milošević*, Judgment (Appeals Chamber) (Case No IT-98-29/1-A), 12 November 2009, para 53, fn 149.

[95] Ibid, para 101.

[96] *Report of the Independent International Commission of Inquiry on the Syrian Arab Republic*, UN Doc A/HRC/21/50, 16 August 2012, para 90.

of customary international humanitarian law was reached. Government forces fired shells into areas inhabited by civilians while failing to direct them at a specific military objective.'[97]

In 2015, the Commission noted that none of the armed actors had made 'any apparent effort to review its targeting practices in order to reduce or prevent civilian casualties. The parties continue to conduct hostilities in an indiscriminate, often disproportionate and unlawful manner.'[98] In addition to direct targeting of civilians, indiscriminate and disproportionate attacks by government forces also contributed significantly to civilian casualties.[99]

C. Indiscriminate Weapons and Civilians

i. Inaccurate Weapons

Weapons that cannot be targeted with sufficient accuracy are inherently indiscriminate. The degree of inaccuracy required to amount to an unlawful weapon is uncertain, although a certain level of clarity has been afforded by jurisprudence.

a. The *Galić* Case

One of the shelling incidents for which General Galić was held criminally responsible concerned the firing into the Alipašino Polje area of Sarajevo of at least three mortar shells, two of 82 mm calibre and one of 120 mm calibre.[100] The shells struck open civilian areas (two streets and a neighbouring park), killing six children and injuring several other civilians. A possible military objective was a Bosniak detachment (Kulin Ban), reportedly located between 150 metres and 500 metres away from the impact of the shells, but the Prosecution cited evidence that Bosnian Serb mortar units could expect their first shot to be accurate to within 50 metres.[101] Galić's defence counsel denied a law of armed conflict violation had occurred, arguing variously: that the site of origin of the shells had not been established; that even if the shells in question originated in Bosnian Serb-controlled territory, a military unit had its headquarters a few dozen metres away from the site of the impact, so the resulting civilian casualties must be understood as collateral; that the possibility of a mistake could not be completely excluded; that the possibility of a staged attack by the Bosniak army (for propaganda purposes, presumably) against territory under its control could not be completely excluded; and that one witness (a former Bosnian Serb fighter) testified that he had never received an order to fire at children or playgrounds, from which the Defence claimed it might be inferred that no other Bosnian Serb side soldiers had received such orders.[102]

[97] Ibid, para 94.

[98] *Report of the Independent International Commission of Inquiry on the Syrian Arab Republic*, UN Doc A/HRC/28/69, 5 February 2015, para 92.

[99] Ibid, para 47.

[100] 'Scheduled Shelling Incident 3' in *Galić* (n 64) paras 331 et seq.

[101] Ibid, para 338.

[102] Ibid, para 337.

In its decision, the Trial Chamber rejected the Defence's assertions. With respect to the suggestion that the attack could have been staged by the Bosniak army, the Trial Chamber stated 'that a mere hypothesis is not a basis for reasonable doubt. Some fact or allegation must be relied on to turn a mere possibility into a reasonable one.'[103] Concerning the targeting of a military objective, the Chamber rejected the claim that a military unit had its headquarters a few dozen metres away from the site of the impact, and observed that the first shell impacted closest to the location of a detachment of Bosniak forces with the second and third landing further away:

> Considering the sequence of the explosions, together with the fact that the shelling ceased after just three volleys were fired, all of which landed wide of Kulin Ban (two at a distance of at least 150 metres), the Trial Chamber concludes that Kulin Ban was not the intended target of this attack.[104]

It therefore found that the shelling constituted 'an attack that was, at the very least, indiscriminate as to its target (which … was primarily if not entirely a residential neighbourhood), and was carried out recklessly, resulting in civilian casualties'.[105]

Thus, in this instance criminal responsibility was founded on a mortar shelling where the shells landed between 100 and 150 metres away from a target in a crowded city centre that could have represented a lawful military objective. What distinguishes the different findings in the cases cited so far? It does not appear that all instances of the conduct of hostilities have been treated equally, even within the same international criminal tribunal. Is it remoteness from the target? Or the overall context? Milan Martić had said that 'we will continue to attack Zagreb and destroy their cities'.[106] The siege of Sarajevo was infamous for the deliberate sniping of civilians by Bosnian Serb forces. Yet General Gotovina's order of 2 August 1995 was 'to put Drvar, Knin, Benkovac, Obrovac, and Gračac under artillery fire', without providing 'clear guidelines for artillery units regarding the specification and details of military targets, or the effects to be achieved'.[107]

b. The Commission of Inquiry on the 2014 Gaza Conflict

The UN Commission of Inquiry on the 2014 Gaza conflict reported that most of the projectiles fired by Palestinian armed groups were rockets 'that at best were equipped with only rudimentary guidance systems and in the vast majority of cases had none at all'.[108] The rockets available to armed groups in Gaza at the time 'were unguided and inaccurate'. Estimates, confirmed by the Commission, indicated that the Fajr-5[109] and similar J-80 and M-75 rockets can land as far as 3 kilometres from any intended target. The longer-range

[103] Ibid, para 342.
[104] Ibid, para 344.
[105] Ibid, para 345.
[106] ICTY, *Prosecutor v Milan Martić*, Judgment (Trial Chamber) (Case No IT-95-11), 12 June 2007, para 319.
[107] ICTY, *Prosecutor v Ante Gotovina and Mladen Markač*, Judgment (Trial Chamber I) (Case No IT-06-90-T), 15 April 2011, para 1172.
[108] *Report of the detailed findings of the independent commission of inquiry established pursuant to Human Rights Council resolution S-21/1*, UN Doc A/HRC/29/CRP.4, 22 June 2015 (hereinafter 'UN Commission of Inquiry on the 2014 Gaza Conflict') para 97.
[109] Army Recognition, *Fadjr-5 333 mm Multiple rocket launcher system*, indicating that the Fajr-5 has a circular error of probability of '4 per cent'.

rockets, such as the R-160, can land as far as 6 kilometres away from the target because their accuracy decreases with range.[110]

The Commission concluded that the rockets could not be directed at a specific military objective and therefore were indiscriminate attacks in violation of the customary rule codified in Article 51(4) of the 1977 Additional Protocol I. The fact that Palestinian armed groups did not possess more accurate weapons was rejected as a justification for their failure to attack precisely military targets. As the Commission noted, the 'military capacity of the parties to a conflict is irrelevant to their obligation to respect the prohibition against indiscriminate attacks'.[111] It stated that the launching of rockets by Palestinian armed groups may therefore amount to war crimes.[112]

c. The Commission of Inquiry on Syria

In the case of Syria, the Commission of Inquiry argued that the Syrian regime's use of indiscriminate shelling and aerial bombardment

> has been informed by its use of a variety of weaponry. The Government began hostilities by employing artillery shells, mortars and rockets against restive and sometimes besieged areas. By mid-2012, the use of cluster munitions, thermobaric bombs and missiles was documented, often used against civilian objectives, such as schools and hospitals. The Government has also used incendiary weapons.
>
> … The first reported use of barrel bombs was in August 2012 in Homs city. It was not, however, until mid-2013 that government forces began an intense campaign of barrel bombing of Aleppo city and governorate. … Throughout 2013, 2014 and into 2015, the Government has made liberal use of barrel bombs. These makeshift explosive containers have caused thousands of civilian casualties. Barrel bombs are regularly dropped on crowded areas, such as bakery lines, transportation hubs, apartment buildings and markets. Aid distributions have also been targeted.[113]

The Commission reported that civilian deaths continued to be

> recorded as a result of the Government's aerial bombardment campaign of anti-Government armed-group-controlled areas of Aleppo city as well in towns in Rif Damascus and Dara'a governorates. In the eastern neighbourhoods of Aleppo city, notably Al-Sukkari, civilians were killed when barrel bombs were dropped indiscriminately by Government helicopters flying at high altitudes. Government barrel-bombing also killed civilians in Qadi Askar neighbourhood in January, June and October 2014.[114]

In this, the Commission nuanced its description of barrel bombs as inherently indiscriminate weapons. It seemingly believes that the weapons are indiscriminate because they are 'unguided or poorly guided'.[115] Still, in the 2015 Report, the Commission recommended

110 Amnesty International, *Unlawful and deadly. Rocket and Mortar Attacks by Palestinian Armed Groups during the 2014 Gaza/Israel Conflict*, March 2015, 10.

111 UN Commission of Inquiry on the 2014 Gaza Conflict (n 108) para 97.

112 Ibid, para 98, citing Art 8, ICC Statute.

113 *Report of the Independent International Commission of Inquiry on the Syrian Arab Republic*, UN Doc A/HRC/28/69, 5 February 2015, paras 13, 14.

114 Ibid, para 49.

115 *Report of the Independent International Commission of Inquiry on the Syrian Arab Republic*, UN Doc A/HRC/25/65, 12 February 2014, para 158.

that the Syrian regime '[h]alt immediately the use of illegal and indiscriminate weapons, including barrel bombs'.[116] As the Geneva Academy of International Humanitarian Law and Human Rights has observed:

> There is no authoritative definition of a barrel bomb under international law. In common parlance the term refers to an improvised container (eg an oil drum or gas cylinder) dropped from an aircraft and filled with explosive, incendiary or other substances and often additional materials to increase fragment projection.[117]

When barrel bombs contain chemical agents,[118] they are unequivocally unlawful; in other instances (especially in Syria), their use has almost invariably been indiscriminate, but it is not correct to say that they are inherently unlawful (see further chapter 10).

ii. A Weapon with Uncontrolled Effects

The US Air Force's *1976 Manual on International Law* cites biological weapons as a 'universally agreed illustration of ... an indiscriminate weapon', observing that the uncontrollable effects from such weapons 'may include injury to the civilian population of other states as well as injury to an enemy's civilian population'.[119] These uncontrolled effects exist not only spatially but also over time. The same applies to poison; as the ICRC has observed, 'poison is unlawful in itself, as would be any weapon which would, by its very nature, be so imprecise that it would inevitably cause indiscriminate damage'.[120] The huge emission of poisonous radiation by the detonation of a high-yield nuclear weapon, and especially a 'salted' bomb in which the device is surrounded by cobalt-60[121] or gold-98, would likely also violate this prohibition.

D. Attacks against Civilians as Crimes against Humanity

Attacks against civilians, particularly when they involve acts intended to terrorise the civilian population (see chapter 14), may also amount to crimes against humanity. According to the ICC Statute, these crimes, which may occur within or outside an armed conflict, encompass a range of acts of violence or cruelty, 'when committed as part of a widespread or systematic attack directed against any civilian population, with knowledge of the attack'.[122]

[116] *Report of the Independent International Commission of Inquiry on the Syrian Arab Republic*, UN Doc A/HRC/28/69, 5 February 2015, para 144(a).

[117] Glossary: 'Barrel Bombs', *Weapons Law Encyclopedia*, Geneva Academy of International Humanitarian Law and Human Rights, at https://goo.gl/ZbRHRY.

[118] *Report of the Independent International Commission of Inquiry on the Syrian Arab Republic*, UN Doc A/HRC/28/69, 5 February 2015, para 15.

[119] US Department of the Navy, Annotated Supplement to the Commander's Handbook on the Law of Naval Operations 10–21, Naval Warfare Publication 9, 1987 (with Revision A) (5 October 1989).

[120] ICRC Commentary on the 1977 Additional Protocols, para 1402.

[121] In February 1950, Leó Szilárd, the physicist and, subsequently, anti-nuclear weapon campaigner, famously publicised a cobalt-salted hydrogen bomb as the ultimate doomsday machine. A thick cobalt metal blanket is used to capture the fusion neutrons to maximise fallout. Instead of generating additional explosive force from fast fission ^{238}U, the cobalt is transmuted into ^{60}Co, which produces energetic and penetrating gamma rays. *The Physics Hypertextbook* at https://goo.gl/c46E2Z.

[122] Art 7, ICC Statute.

i. The Katanga *Case*

In the *Katanga* case,[123] an ICC Trial Chamber explained that the crime entails three stages of reasoning:

- The existence of an attack (an operation or course of conduct involving the multiple commission of proscribed acts that is directed against a civilian population, and which took place pursuant to or in furtherance of a state or organisational policy).[124]
- The characterisation of the attack as widespread (large-scale in nature) or systematic (of an organised nature).[125]
- Proximate nexus between the attack and the proscribed act and knowledge of that nexus by the perpetrator.[126]

The civilian population, which comprises all but members of the armed forces 'and other legitimate combatants', must be the primary target of the attack and not the incidental victim.[127] There must also be a policy to attack the civilian population, defined broadly as the intent of a state or organisation, 'whether through action or deliberate failure to take action'.[128] In distinguishing a policy from a systematic attack, the Chamber stated that the systematic nature of the attack goes 'beyond the existence of any policy seeking to eliminate, persecute or undermine a community', to represent 'a series of repeated actions seeking to produce always the same effects on a civilian population'. These were undertaken 'with consideration – identical acts or similarities in criminal practices, continual repetition of a same modus operandi, similar treatment meted out to victims or consistency in such treatment across a wide geographic area'.[129]

In its submission to the Trial Chamber, Mr Katanga's defence counsel contended that the attack on Bogoro was directed not against the civilian population but against a military camp in the village.[130] The Chamber, however, considered that the camp 'was not the attackers' sole and prime target'. It recalled that the camp, which was 'at the heart of the village', was 'geographically circumscribed' and that the attackers 'did not solely take the camp to secure control of the village'.[131] Moreover, even when the camp had been captured and fighting had ceased, 'the attackers relentlessly pursued, wounded or killed by machete and firearm the villagers who were in their homes, had taken flight, or were seeking refuge … or in the bush and who had no part in combat'.[132]

[123] ICC, *Prosecutor v Germain Katanga*, Judgment (Trial Chamber II) (Case No ICC-01/04-01/07), 7 March 2014.
[124] Ibid, para 1097.
[125] Ibid, para 1098.
[126] Ibid, para 1099.
[127] Ibid, paras 1102, 1104.
[128] Ibid, para 1108. As it is relatively rare that a state or organisation adopts and disseminates a pre-established design or plan to that effect, in most cases, the existence of the policy can be inferred by 'repeated actions occurring according to a same sequence, or the existence of preparations or collective mobilisation orchestrated and coordinated by that State or organisation'. Ibid, para 1109.
[129] Ibid, para 1113.
[130] Ibid, para 1129.
[131] Ibid, para 1136.
[132] Ibid.

ii. The Dragomir Milošević *Case*

In this case, the commander of the Bosnian Serbs in and around Sarajevo was accused of murder as a crime against humanity. The ICTY Statute limited jurisdiction for crimes against humanity to those 'committed in armed conflict'. According to the Tribunal's case law, this notion required only 'the existence of an armed conflict at the relevant time and place'. Thus, the Trial Chamber concluded:

> The underlying crimes need not be closely related to the armed conflict; it suffices that they be linked geographically and temporally with it. … This requirement is purely jurisdictional and does not constitute a substantive element of a crime against humanity.[133]

As to the widespread nature of the attack, the Chamber found adequate evidence of 'a very large number of attacks by way of mortars, modified air bombs and sniping, spread out over the entire city of Sarajevo over a prolonged period of time'.[134] In addition, the circumstances were such, the Chamber held, 'that it must have been obvious' to the Bosnian Serb troops 'that they were targeting a civilian population'.[135] The requisite acts amounted to both murder and 'other inhumane acts' (where civilians were seriously injured but survived) as crimes against humanity.[136]

iii. The Commission of Inquiry on Syria

The frequent link between acts carried out with a view to punishing and terrorising civilians and crimes against humanity has been all too clearly illustrated in Syria. In 2014, the UN Commission of Inquiry of Syria found that the Government had employed

> a strategy of controlling the population, combining long-lasting sieges with continuous air and ground bombardment. In neighbourhoods around Damascus, including Yarmouk, Darayya, Babbila and Barzah, civilians were targeted on the basis of their perceived opposition to the Government. Merely living in or originating from those neighbourhoods led to targeting.[137]

It concluded that the Syrian regime 'has carried out a widespread and systematic attack against the civilian population of Aleppo to punish and terrorize civilians for supporting or hosting armed groups, in an apparent strategy to erode popular support for those groups'.[138]

E. The Requisite Level of Accuracy

It is clear that while attackers should do 'everything feasible' to 'verify' that an individual who is targeted by or during an attack is a military objective,[139] an attack does not have to

[133] *Dragomir Milošević* (n 92) para 915.
[134] Ibid, para 927.
[135] Ibid, para 930.
[136] Ibid, paras 932, 934.
[137] *Report of the independent international commission of inquiry on the Syrian Arab Republic*, UN Doc A/HRC/27/60, 13 August 2014, para 104.
[138] Ibid.
[139] Art 57(2)(a)(i), 1977 Additional Protocol I.

strike what it is aiming at in order to comply with Hague Law. Attacks may miss their target, bullets may ricochet or over-penetrate, intelligence may be faulty, and accidents or mistakes may and do occur, especially in the heat of battle when combatants or others directly participating in hostilities are often tired, angry and fearful.

With respect to snipers, there is no requirement under Hague Law that they use telescopic sights rather than iron sights. But if they do, the margin of permissible error may be lessened. A sniper who shoots and kills an elderly woman in broad daylight instead of a combatant 50 metres to her left will struggle to justify why that is not to be considered an unlawful attack against a civilian. It is implicit, at least in ICTY case law, that attacks that occur outside the context of a pitched battle may be held to a higher standard.

The precise standard of accuracy for artillery[140] is unclear, but it is safe to say that medium- or long-range artillery shells or projectiles delivered by artillery that cannot regularly be directed to within one kilometre of their target are inherently indiscriminate. A first shot's lack of accuracy may be accorded a greater degree of margin, but if firing is not adjusted on available intelligence, an inference may be drawn that an attack was indiscriminate or even directed against civilians. It is not necessary under Hague Law rules that direct-fire weapons be used, that is those with a direct line of sight between the artillery piece and the target, or that they fire precision-guided shells.

i. The Gotovina *Case*

In the *Gotovina* case, the Trial Chamber concluded that multiple-barrel rocket launchers (MBRLs) were not 'inherently indiscriminate' in an urban setting,[141] even though some 45 per cent of rockets would be expected to land between 300 and 900 metres from their target. On this basis, I believe their use in a small built-up town such as Knin should generally have been considered an indiscriminate attack, but this was not the judgment of the Tribunal.

ii. The Martić *Case*

In the *Martić* case, the firing of submunitions dispersed from rockets against Zagreb in early May 1995 was found to involve 'an indiscriminate weapon, the use of which in densely populated civilian areas, such as Zagreb, will result in the infliction of severe casualties'.[142] The dispersion error of the rockets when fired at maximum range is said to be about 1,000 metres in any direction. The area of dispersion of the submunitions on the ground was about 20,000 metres.[143] Just as with the BM21 MBRLs used by Gotovina's forces, the Orkan rocket system was suitable for use against troops in the open, but not for point targeting in densely populated areas.

[140] Artillery as a category encompasses 'cannon' artillery, such as howitzers, mortars and field guns, and 'rocket' artillery.

[141] *Gotovina* (n 107) para 1897.

[142] *Milan Martić* (n 106) para 463. The Appeals Chamber subsequently clarified that the Trial Chamber had concluded that the Orkan '*was used* as an indiscriminate weapon': ICTY, *Prosecutor v Milan Martić*, Judgment (Appeals Chamber) (Case No IT-95-11-A), 8 October 2008, para 247 (emphasis added).

[143] Ibid, para 462.

iii. The Dragomir Milošević *case*

In the *Dragomir Milošević* case, the 'modified air-bombs' were said to deviate from the intended target by as much as one kilometre.[144] Even a defence expert witness conceded that modified air bombs were 'completely inaccurate'.[145] Accordingly, the Trial Chamber found, based on the evidence, that the bombs were 'highly inaccurate' and 'indiscriminate' weapons, and that they 'could only be directed at a general area, making it impossible to predict where they would strike'.[146]

In the *Mladić* case, as discussed in section III.C.i of chapter 4, the legality of the bombs was again considered by the ICTY in its final Trial Chamber case, against Ratko Mladić. This time, General Mladić's defence team had argued that the bombs were 'well-designed, accurate, and valid weapons' that had been 'extensively tested'.[147] Based on all the evidence it heard from expert witnesses, however, the Trial Chamber concluded that as 'a result of their make-shift design, modified air bombs were highly inaccurate'.[148]

The Commission of Inquiry on the 2014 conflict in Gaza correctly found that the Palestinian Fajr-5 and similar rockets, which could land as far as three kilometres away from an intended target, were inherently indiscriminate.[149] This applies *a fortiori* to longer-range rockets, such as the R-160, which could land as far as six kilometres away from the target.

Short-range mortars will be held to a much stricter standard. In testimony during the *Dragomir Milošević* case, it was asserted that 'a proficient detachment with training can easily hit targets, throughout its ranges, to an accuracy of less than 40 metres'.[150] The defence counsel, though, suggested that the first shells fired at a target could deviate as far as '128 metres in direction and up to 312 metres in distance'.[151] Factors that could reduce the effectiveness of mortars include inexperience of a mortar crew, inexperience and poor skills of the observer, an unstable base plate, movement of the mortar, firing at targets of opportunity and changes in the weather.[152]

iv. The Galić *Case*

In the *Galić* case, a defence expert witness testified during the trial that an experienced mortar crew could reach to within 200 metres or 300 metres of their target on the very first shot.[153] However, the Prosecution cited evidence that Bosnian Serb mortar units could expect their first shot to be accurate to within 50 metres. As noted in section III.C.i.a, one of the shelling incidents for which General Galić was held criminally responsible

[144] *Dragomir Milošević* (n 92) paras 92, 93, 97.
[145] Ibid, para 97.
[146] Ibid, paras 912, 1001.
[147] ICTY, *Prosecutor v Ratko Mladić*, Judgment (Trial Chamber I) (Case No IT-09-92-T), 22 November 2017, para 1892.
[148] Ibid, para 1913.
[149] *Report of the detailed findings of the independent commission of inquiry established pursuant to Human Rights Council resolution S-21/1*, UN Doc A/HRC/29/CRP.4, 22 June 2015, para 97.
[150] *Dragomir Milošević* (n 92), para 91.
[151] Ibid, para 91.
[152] Ibid.
[153] See ICTY, *Prosecutor v Galić*, Judgment (Appeals Chamber) (Case No IT-98-29-A), 30 November 2006, para 335.

concerned the firing into the Alipašino Polje area of Sarajevo of at least three mortar shells, two of 82 mm calibre and one of 120 mm calibre.[154] The shells struck open civilian areas (two streets and a neighbouring park), killing six children and injuring several other civilians. A possible military objective was a Bosniak detachment (Kulin Ban) reportedly located between 150 metres and 500 metres away from the impact of the shells.[155] The Trial Chamber observed that the first shell impacted closest to the location of a detachment of Bosniak forces, with the second and third landing further away:

> Considering the sequence of the explosions, together with the fact that the shelling ceased after just three volleys were fired, all of which landed wide of Kulin Ban (two at a distance of at least 150 metres), the Trial Chamber concludes that Kulin Ban was not the intended target of this attack.[156]

It therefore found that the shelling constituted 'an attack that was, at the very least, indiscriminate as to its target (which nevertheless was primarily if not entirely a residential neighbourhood), and was carried out recklessly, resulting in civilian casualties'.[157] So here criminal responsibility was founded on a mortar shelling, where the shells landed between 100 and 150 metres away from a target in a crowded city centre that could have represented a lawful military objective.

v. The Commission of Inquiry on the 2014 Gaza Conflict

In contrast, the UN Commission of Inquiry on the 2014 Gaza conflict held:

> On the basis of the information available, it appears that the weapons the IDF [Israel Defence Forces] used in this incident were high explosive 120 mm mortars, which have a circular error probability of 136 meters, and are therefore imprecise.[158]

The Commission does not disclose the evidence for its assertion of a CEP of 136 metres,[159] but is suggesting that mortars should not be used in civilian-populated areas with the population density of Gaza. It went on to affirm:

> Mortars are considered a wide-area weapon which, if used in a built-up, densely populated area, are likely to strike military objectives and civilians without distinction – particularly given a scenario in which over 50 per cent of the 120 mm mortar shells fired are likely to fall between 136 and 300 metres from the intended target.[160]

Lastly, it appears that a more proficient mortar team may effectively be held to a higher standard than one that is not so proficient. In attacks that struck Koševo hospital and the

[154] 'Scheduled Shelling Incident 3' in *Galić* (n 64) paras 331 et seq.
[155] Ibid, para 338.
[156] Ibid, para 344.
[157] Ibid, para 345.
[158] UN Commission of Inquiry on the 2014 Gaza Conflict (n 108) para 380.
[159] In 2005, a US army expert asserted that 120 mm mortar shells generally had a CEP of 160 metres with 3 CEP of 480 metres, with the consequence that rounds could land as far as 1 kilometre from each other. R Trohanowsky, '120 mm Mortar System Accuracy Analysis', US Army RDECOM-ARDEC, Picatinny, NJ, 17 May 2005, at https://goo.gl/vZ28SW.
[160] Ibid, para 388.

state hospital, the Trial Chamber in the *Dragomir Milošević* case stated that, in light of all the available evidence, 'including that of the skill of the mortar crews', it was satisfied that both hospitals were intentionally targeted by the Bosnian Serb forces.[161]

F. ICRC's 'Chapter IX' Protection from Use of Lethal Force?

In Chapter IX of its 2009 interpretive guidance, the ICRC elaborated a curious theory to restrain use of lethal force against those it had deemed were participating directly in hostilities. It articulated the theory as follows:

> In addition to the restraints imposed by international humanitarian law on specific means and methods of warfare, and without prejudice to further restrictions that may arise under other applicable branches of international law, the kind and degree of force which is permissible against persons not entitled to protection against direct attack must not exceed what is actually necessary to accomplish a legitimate military purpose in the prevailing circumstances.[162]

The Guidance further suggested:

> Clearly, the fact that a particular category of persons is not protected against offensive or defensive acts of violence is not equivalent to a legal entitlement to kill such persons without further considerations. At the same time, the absence of an unfettered 'right' to kill does not necessarily imply a legal obligation to capture rather than kill regardless of the circumstances.[163]

'Clearly' is not a legal argument, and the institution did not enunciate protection based on the tenets of international human rights law;[164] instead, the juridical basis was said to be 'the fundamental principles of military necessity and humanity, which underlie and inform the entire normative framework of IHL and, therefore, shape the context in which its rules must be interpreted'.[165] In conjunction, the ICRC argued, these two principles act to 'reduce the sum total of permissible military action from that which IHL does not expressly prohibit to that which is actually necessary for the accomplishment of a legitimate military purpose in the prevailing circumstances'.[166]

The problem here is that there is no evidence to suggest that the ICRC has done anything other than to invent a new legal rule out of (justified) concern that its guidance on DPH was otherwise too permissive. Moreover, military necessity as a principle tends to be permissive

[161] *Dragomir Milošević* (n 92), paras 427, 428.
[162] ICRC DPH Guidance (n 11) 77.
[163] Ibid, 78.
[164] In 2013, the President of the ICRC spoke to the UN Human Rights Council in the following terms: 'Is it not wise to stress from the outset that IHL is based on a realistic behavioural approach that, to be applied, must propose a fair balance between protection and security, whereas human right [*sic*] stem from a broader, even philosophical, aspiration, to protect and defend what characterizes human beings as such? From a more technical perspective, IHL and human rights also differ in certain respects, particularly in the case of the indisputable extraterritorial application of IHL, its direct application to non-State armed groups and even their respective control and supervision mechanisms.' 'ICRC and Human Rights Council: complementary activities, respect for differences', Statement by Peter Maurer, President of the ICRC, Twenty-second session of the Human Rights Council, High-level Segment, Geneva, 26 February 2013, at https://goo.gl/FZbKVe.
[165] ICRC DPH Guidance (n 11) 78.
[166] Ibid, 79.

not restrictive,[167] whereas humanity – to the extent it is a core Hague Law principle[168] – already informs the rules of distinction and proportionality in attack and the underpinning of these rules provided by the duty to take all feasible precautions. It cannot, therefore, be lucidly reintroduced as an extra brake on what amounts to lawful force.[169]

What is more illuminating is that the guidance suggests that situations in which its Chapter IX rule was most applicable were akin to 'peacetime policing'.[170] This would suggest a law of law enforcement approach, which would mean a duty to seek to capture rather than kill; and use of firearms only in self-defence or for the protection of others faced with an imminent threat of death or serious injury, or in case of a proximate grave threat to life.

The ICRC offered a number of examples of how its Chapter IX protection would apply. In one,

> an unarmed civilian sitting in a restaurant using a radio or mobile phone to transmit tactical targeting intelligence to an attacking air force would probably have to be regarded as directly participating in hostilities. Should the restaurant in question be situated within an area firmly controlled by the opposing party, however, it may be possible to neutralize the military threat posed by that civilian through capture or other non-lethal means without additional risk to the operating forces or the surrounding civilian population.[171]

Presumably the requisite tactical targeting intelligence would include the location of a platoon marching past the restaurant. What if someone were to tweet that same intelligence to his or her followers, which included the enemy air force? Or if he or she were to post it on Facebook? How about those who retweeted the information to a broader audience? Would almost everyone with a smartphone potentially become a direct participant in hostilities? In this respect, the interpretive guidance looks suspiciously like an analogue solution to a digital problem.

Another oft-cited example is the member of an armed opposition group who visits his or her family (or goes shopping) in a town or an area under the effective control of the government. His or her asserted 'continuous combat function' is discussed in the following subsection. Those who would allow the government to kill that person without warning would extend the area of hostilities to all areas of the country (and presumably even beyond if necessary) even though no hostilities were ongoing at the time. The better view is simply that, outside the area of hostilities, law of law enforcement rules apply.

The third example proffered in the interpretive guidance was where 'large numbers of unarmed civilians … deliberately gather on a bridge in order to prevent the passage of governmental ground forces in pursuit of an insurgent group'. The ICRC asserts that they 'would probably have to be regarded as directly participating in hostilities'. But Chapter IX rules would intervene to restrain use of force (firing shells, machine-gunning or crushing them under the tracks of tanks, for instance) since, in most cases, 'it would be reasonably possible for the armed forces to remove the physical obstacle posed by these civilians

167 See, eg, N Hayashi, 'Requirements of Military Necessity in International Humanitarian Law and International Criminal Law' (2010) 28 *Boston University International Law Journal* 39.

168 See, eg, Solis (n 8) 305–09.

169 See, eg, JK Kleffner, 'Section IX of the ICRC Interpretive Guidance on Direct Participation in Hostilities: The End of *Jus In Bello* Proportionality As We Know It?' (2012) 45 *Israel Law Review* 35.

170 ICRC DPH Guidance (n 11) 80.

171 Ibid, 81.

through means less harmful than a direct military attack on them'.[172] The ICRC does not indicate what those less harmful means might be.

G. Loss of Protection from Attack

What is relatively uncontested is that the loss of protection only extends for the period of time in which the civilian is participating directly in hostilities. The 1977 Additional Protocol I is unequivocal, stating that civilians enjoy the protection afforded by the Hague Law rules it stipulates, 'unless and for such time as they take a direct part in hostilities'.[173] This sets clear material and temporal boundaries. Civilians are defined under of the Protocol as all those individuals other than members of organised armed forces, groups and units that are under a command responsible to a Party to armed conflict for the conduct of its subordinates.[174]

In its interpretive guidance, the ICRC elaborated a new concept of 'continuous combat function' to designate members of organised armed groups belonging to a non-state party to the conflict who cease to be civilians for as long as they remain members.[175] This status

> distinguishes members of the organised fighting forces of a non-state party from civilians who directly participate in hostilities on a merely spontaneous, sporadic, or unorganised basis, or who assume exclusively political, administrative or other non-combat functions.[176]

Dinstein complains that this status does not go far enough, omitting valuable support staff who enable the fighters to engage in warfare ('technicians, drivers, secretaries, cooks, and the like').[177] In fact, the ICRC's position goes too far. The treaty texts are clear as to who is or is not a civilian. As Jann Kleffner notes, 'the better view on the temporal scope of the loss of protection is to distinguish between those who are not and those who are members of the armed forces of a party to a NIAC'.[178]

IV. Individuals Enjoying Special Protection from Attack

It is settled that certain members of the armed forces, specifically dedicated medical and religious personnel, are non-combatants.[179] They may not be the object of attack; indeed, they must be both respected and protected, unless and for such time as they engage in acts harmful to the enemy.[180] The core provision of the 1949 Geneva Conventions with respect

[172] Ibid.
[173] Art 51(3), 1977 Additional Protocol I.
[174] Arts 43(1) and 50(1), 1977 Additional Protocol I.
[175] ICRC DPH Guidance (n 11) 71.
[176] Ibid, 34.
[177] Dinstein (n 35) 178, para 479.
[178] J Kleffner, 'The Beneficiaries of the Rights Stemming from Common Article 3' in A Clapham, P Gaeta and M Sassòli (eds), *The 1949 Geneva Conventions: A Commentary* (Oxford, Oxford University Press, 2015) 433, 439.
[179] See, generally, S Casey-Maslen, 'The Status, Rights, and Obligations of Medical and Religious Personnel' in Clapham et al (eds) (n 178) 807.
[180] According to the ICRC, this encompasses situations when they 'are used, outside their function, to interfere, directly or indirectly, in military operations and thereby cause harm to the enemy'. ICRC commentary on 1949

to medical and religious personnel is set out in the 1949 Geneva Convention I. The relevant provision stipulates:

> Medical personnel exclusively engaged in the search for, or the collection, transport or treatment of the wounded or sick, or in the prevention of disease, staff exclusively engaged in the administration of medical units and establishments, as well as chaplains attached to the armed forces, shall be respected and protected in all circumstances.[181]

The protection afforded by the Geneva Convention I is limited to army medical personnel and army chaplains in IAC, though in the view of the ICRC Study of Customary IHL, state practice has resulted in the broader rule that 'medical personnel exclusively assigned to medical duties must be respected and protected in all circumstances', attaining the status of a customary norm applicable in all armed conflict.[182] State practice and *opinio juris* for the rule are stronger with respect to IAC than NIAC, though the rule can also be seen as deriving from the customary obligation in Common Article 3, under which the wounded and sick 'shall be collected and cared for'.

A. Medical Personnel

Under the 1949 Geneva Convention I, the term 'medical personnel' is broad in scope, encompassing 'doctors, surgeons, dentists, chemists, orderlies, nurses, stretcher-bearers, etc, who give direct care to the wounded and sick',[183] as long as they are members of the armed forces. Such personnel shall be 'respected and protected in all circumstances'. The only qualifying condition is that they be 'exclusively engaged' in searching for, transporting, treating, or caring for the wounded or sick, or in preventing disease (or a combination of such tasks).[184] The words 'exclusively engaged' require that the assignment be permanent,[185] which is not the case in the provision addressing auxiliary medical personnel.[186]

A combatant on the battlefield who evacuates his or her wounded colleague for the purpose of medical care may, though, still be fired upon. The wounded soldier is *hors de combat*, and therefore immune from attack, but the soldier evacuating him or her is not,

Geneva Convention I, 2016, para 1841. It is therefore much broader than the concept of DPH. Military medical or religious personnel may, however, be armed with light weapons, which they may use for their own defence or for the defence of the wounded and sick in their care without losing protection. Thus, under Art. 22(1) of the 1949 Geneva Convention I, the fact that personnel of a medical unit or establishment are armed, and even that they use the arms in their own defence or in defence of wounded and sick in their charge, does not deprive a medical unit or establishment of the protection guaranteed by Art. 19.

[181] Art 24, 1949 Geneva Convention I

[182] ICRC Study of Customary IHL, Rule 25 ('Medical Personnel') at https://goo.gl/v2bcuY.

[183] J Pictet (ed), *Geneva Convention for the Amelioration of the Condition of the Wounded and Sick in Armed Forces in the Field: A Commentary* (Geneva, ICRC, 1952) 218.

[184] According to the ICRC's 2016 commentary on Geneva Convention I, 'a veterinarian who, as a member of the armed forces, takes care of animals that are deployed to assist combat activities would, for example, be deemed a combatant. Historically, this has been the dominant paradigm. However, when a veterinarian engages exclusively in the protected activity of "prevention of disease" vis-à-vis human beings, for example when inspecting the hygiene of food supplies for able-bodied combatants, as more and more veterinarians who are members of the armed forces do, this person qualifies to be "respected and protected" in the sense of Article 24.' ICRC commentary on 1949 Geneva Convention I, 2016, para 1959.

[185] Ibid, 219.

[186] Under the 1949 Geneva Convention I, similar protection is afforded to 'auxiliary medical personnel', namely members of the armed forces 'specially trained' for use as hospital orderlies, nurses or auxiliary stretcher-bearers, who look for, transport, treat, or care for the wounded or sick. Art 25, 1949 Geneva Convention I.

and may be attacked. This is regrettable, but it is the law. It appears clear that the soldier *hors de combat* is not to be considered a civilian for the purpose of a proportionality assessment. In contrast, if civilians respond to an appeal from a party to the conflict to help care for the wounded or sick (they may not be compelled to assist), they must be granted 'the necessary protection and facilities'.[187]

B. Religious Personnel

According to the 1949 Geneva Convention I, 'chaplains attached to the armed forces ... shall be respected and protected in all circumstances'.[188] The position of chaplain was not defined in the 1949 Geneva Conventions but was ordinarily understood as meaning a member of the clergy of a Christian church. This denominational limitation is clearly anachronistic,[189] and accordingly the 1977 Additional Protocol I included a more general definition of 'religious personnel' as meaning 'military or civilian persons, such as chaplains, who are exclusively engaged in the work of their ministry' and who are attached to the armed forces, medical units, medical transports or civil defence organisations of a party to an IAC.[190]

According to the 1977 Additional Protocol I, the attachment of religious personnel may be either permanent or temporary, 'unless otherwise specified',[191] but only religious personnel exclusively assigned by the state to religious duties are protected. The ICRC Study of Customary IHL concluded that state practice has established that the rule protecting religious personnel is a customary norm applicable in all armed conflict. It is formulated as follows:

> Religious personnel exclusively assigned to religious duties must be respected and protected in all circumstances. They lose their protection if they commit, outside their humanitarian function, acts harmful to the enemy.[192]

V. Attacks against Civilians under International Criminal Law

A. Under 1977 Additional Protocol I

According to the 1977 Additional Protocol I, making the civilian population or individual civilians the object of attack is a grave breach of the Protocol, when committed wilfully, in violation of the Protocol, and if it causes death or serious injury to body or health.[193] This grave breach amounts to a war crime.[194] There is no corresponding provision on individual criminal responsibility in the 1977 Additional Protocol II.

[187] Art 18, 1949 Geneva Convention I.
[188] Art 24, 1949 Geneva Convention I.
[189] ICRC commentary on 1949 Geneva Convention I, 2016, para 1967.
[190] Art 8(d)(i), (ii), and (iv), 1977 Additional Protocol I. Indeed, to accept otherwise would be to discriminate between religions: a violation of a fundamental principle underlying the Geneva Conventions.
[191] Art 8(k), 1977 Additional Protocol I.
[192] ICRC Study of Customary IHL, Rule 27 ('Religious Personnel') at https://goo.gl/RRf83c.
[193] Art 85(3)(a), 1977 Additional Protocol I.
[194] Art 85(5), 1977 Additional Protocol I.

B. Under Customary International Law

The ICRC Study of Customary IHL identified a number of war crimes under customary law that concern the targeting of persons:[195]

- making the civilian population or individual civilians, not taking a direct part in hostilities, the object of attack
- making persons involved in a humanitarian assistance or peacekeeping mission in accordance with the UN Charter the object of attack, as long as they are entitled to the protection given to civilians under the law of armed conflict,[196] and
- launching an indiscriminate attack resulting in loss of life or injury to civilians.

These war crimes are applicable in all armed conflict.

C. Under the ICC Statute

The ICC Statute gives the Court jurisdiction over the war crime of 'intentionally directing attacks against the civilian population as such or against individual civilians not taking direct part in hostilities' in both IAC and NIAC.[197] It also has similar jurisdiction over the war crime in all armed conflict of intentionally directing attacks against personnel involved in a humanitarian assistance or peacekeeping mission in accordance with the UN Charter, as long as they are entitled to the protection given to civilians or civilian objects under the international law of armed conflict.[198]

D. In the Jurisprudence of the Ad Hoc International Criminal Tribunals

i. The Mandate to Prosecute Attacks against Civilians

Surprisingly, the ICTY did not have an explicit mandate to prosecute attacks against civilians. Article 3 of the ICTY Statute ('Violations of the laws or customs of war') gives the Tribunal the power

> to prosecute persons violating the laws or customs of war. Such violations shall include, but not be limited to:
>
> (a) employment of poisonous weapons or other weapons calculated to cause unnecessary suffering;
> (b) wanton destruction of cities, towns or villages, or devastation not justified by military necessity;

[195] ICRC Study of Customary IHL, Rule 156 ('Definition of War Crimes') at https://goo.gl/YZLXn3.
[196] The ICRC notes that in the case of 'attack on troops, the act would only be criminal if, at the time, the troops had not become involved in hostilities and had not thereby lost the protection afforded to civilians under international humanitarian law'.
[197] Art 8(2)(b)(i) and (e)(i), ICC Statute.
[198] Art 8(2)(b)(iii) and (e)(iii), ICC Statute.

(c) attack, or bombardment, by whatever means, of undefended towns, villages, dwellings, or buildings;
(d) seizure of, destruction or wilful damage done to institutions dedicated to religion, charity and education, the arts and sciences, historic monuments and works of art and science;
(e) plunder of public or private property.

Nonetheless, the Trial Chamber in the *Galić* case found that an unlawful attack on civilians giving rise to deaths or injuries is an extremely serious violation, 'transgressing a core principle of international humanitarian law'.[199]

Beginning in October 1991, Vice Admiral Miodrag Jokić was commander of the Ninth Naval Sector of Boka in Montenegro. He was responsible, as a commander, for the naval shelling of Dubrovnik, although he had not ordered it.[200] As a result of naval and land shelling, two civilians were killed and three others wounded, and numerous buildings were destroyed, including those constituting cultural property. In 2004, Commander Jokić pleaded guilty to several war crimes, including murder, unlawful attack on civilians, devastation not justified by military necessity, unlawful attack on civilian objects, and destruction or wilful damage done to institutions dedicated to religion, charity and education, the arts and sciences, historic monuments and works of art and science. One of the treaties on which the ICTY Trial Chamber relied was the 1907 Hague Naval Bombardment Convention.[201] As a consequence of his failure to prevent or repress war crimes, Commander Jokić was sentenced to seven years' imprisonment by the ICTY,[202] a sentence confirmed on appeal.[203]

ii. Attacking Civilians as Murder

In a number of cases, the ICTY considered sniping or shelling of civilians as 'murder' rather than an attack on civilians. This seems, at first view, to conflate a serious violation of Geneva Law (eg Common Article 3) with a serious violation of Hague Law.[204] But consonant with the fine line between Geneva Law and Hague Law, the Tribunal's approach is defensible, as it is often challenging to appreciate the distinction between murdering someone you are detaining with a firearm and doing it at a distance (close by in the case of sidearms and considerably further away in the case of a sniper).

The line is harder to hold when it concerns indiscriminate shelling. However, many national jurisdictions consider different forms of recklessness or indifference to outcome as sufficient to ground a charge of murder under domestic law. In the US, for example, under domestic law 'depraved indifference' murder is where a defendant's conduct is 'so wanton, so deficient in a moral sense of concern, so lacking in regard for the life or lives of others,

[199] *Galić* (n 64), para 27.
[200] ICTY, *Prosecutor v Jokić*, Sentencing Judgment (Trial Chamber I) (Case No IT-01-42/1-S), 18 March 2004, para 26.
[201] Convention (IX) concerning Bombardment by Naval Forces in Time of War; adopted at The Hague, 18 October 1907; entry into force, 26 January 1910. Art 1 of the 1907 Convention prohibits the 'bombardment by naval forces of undefended ports, towns, villages, dwellings, or buildings'.
[202] *Jokić* (n 200) para 116.
[203] ICTY, *Prosecutor v Jokić*, Judgment on Sentencing Appeal (Appeals Chamber) (Case No IT-01-42/1-A), 30 August 2005, s IX ('Disposition').
[204] See, eg, S Knuckey, 'Murder in Common Article 3' in Clapham et al (eds) (n 178) 449, 455–56.

and so blameworthy as to warrant the same criminal liability as that which the law imposes upon a person who intentionally causes a crime'. Depraved indifference focuses on the risk created by the defendant's conduct, not on the injuries actually resulting.[205] In one case decided by the Court of Appeals of the State of New York, *People v Register*, the Court ruled that to amount to murder,

> the People were required to establish also that defendant's act was imminently dangerous and presented a very high risk of death to others and that it was committed under circumstances which evidenced a wanton indifference to human life or a depravity of mind. … The crime differs from intentional murder in that it results not from a specific, conscious intent to cause death, but from an indifference to or disregard of the risks attending defendant's conduct.[206]

The case concerned a defendant who fired the gun three times in a 'packed' bar room, 'conduct which presented a grave risk of death and did in fact result in the death' of one man.[207]

Similarly, in South Africa in early December 2015, the Supreme Court famously installed a conviction for murder on Oscar Pistorius based on *dolus eventualis*: a form of mens rea where a perpetrator foresees the possibility of his or her conduct causing death and nonetheless persists recklessly in carrying out the act. As Justice Eric Leach stated, 'in firing the fatal shots the accused must have foreseen that whoever was behind the toilet door might die, but reconciled with that event occurring, and gambled with that person's life'.[208]

E. In National Law

In 2015, a world-famous international monthly men's magazine based in New York City described Staff Sergeant Robert Bales as 'America's most notorious war criminal'.[209] *GQ* ('Gentleman's Quarterly') included the first public interview with former Sergeant Bales after his conviction; he was sentenced to a full-life prison term without parole for the murder of 16 Afghan villagers in 2012. Shortly after midnight on 11 March, Bales left his base at Village Stability Platform Belambai in Kandahar province and walked to a nearby village, where he killed four Afghans, including a three-year-old girl, and wounded six others. He returned to his base to reload, told another soldier what he had done (who apparently did not believe him) and then left again to murder 12 more people in another village just down the road. Of the 16 people he killed, four were men, four were women and eight were children. The youngest was two years old. This was said to be the deadliest atrocity committed by an American soldier since the My Lai massacre in 1968 during the Vietnam War.[210]

[205] 'Depraved Indifference Law and Legal Definition', *USLegal*, at https://goo.gl/Bj3Yzm.

[206] *People v Register*, 60 NY2d 274 (1995).

[207] Ibid, 275.

[208] See, eg, S Allison, 'Oscar Pistorius guilty of murder as court overturns previous conviction', *Guardian* (3 December 2015) at https://goo.gl/NDX7EF.

[209] B Vaughan, 'Robert Bales Speaks: Confessions of America's Most Notorious War Criminal', *GQ* (21 October 2015) at https://goo.gl/W4mRHJ.

[210] Ibid.

Bales' defence counsel proposed a deal to the army to take the death penalty off the table in exchange for which Bales would plead guilty,

> sparing the government a trial at which sensitive or even damaging details about the Army might emerge. After months of legal wrangling – including a pre-trial hearing in November of 2012 that included graphic testimony offered by survivors via live video feed from Afghanistan – the two sides agreed on terms.[211]

In June 2013, Bales pleaded guilty to charges that included 16 counts of murder and six of attempted murder. The six-member military jury sentenced him to life in prison with no possibility of parole.

In May 2016, it was reported that an 'unusual coalition of largely older and conservative former military men and younger, left-leaning law students' were campaigning for clemency for troops convicted of killing civilians in Iraq and Afghanistan, including Robert Bales.[212] The campaigners argued that the army had determined that Sergeant Bales had post-traumatic stress disorder and a traumatic brain injury after his third combat deployment in 2010, but still deployed him to Afghanistan. One of the campaigners was asking President Barack Obama to reduce Mr Bales's sentence to 100 years, which would make him eligible for parole in 2023.[213]

In September 2017, the US Army Court of Criminal Appeals, at Fort Belvoir, Virginia, rejected Bales' appeal against his conviction and life sentence. In his appeal, he had argued that the Army had withheld information about a witness in the case and presented evidence he may have been prescribed a psychosis-inducing malaria drug. The three-judge panel rejected those arguments as unfounded.[214]

[211] Ibid.

[212] D Philipps, 'Shared Mission to Pardon US Soldiers Who Killed Civilians', *New York Times* (19 May 2016) at https://goo.gl/amLsUh.

[213] Ibid.

[214] Associated Press, 'Court upholds ex-soldier's life sentence in slayings of Afghan civilians', *Army Times* (28 September 2017) at https://goo.gl/HKvzCV.

6

The Rule of Proportionality in Attack

I. Introduction

In armed conflict, civilians 'almost always suffer when hostilities are raging'.[1] Indeed, incidental harm to civilians and damage to civilian objects is, as the United States (US) Department of Defense has observed, 'unfortunate and tragic' but 'inevitable'.[2] The issue is thus how much foreseeable suffering the law of armed conflict allows. Accordingly, this chapter addresses the rule of proportionality in attack, undoubtedly among the most nebulous of all Hague Law rules.[3] For, as Hays Parks has asserted, 'by American domestic law standards, the concept of proportionality … would be constitutionally void for vagueness'.[4]

Section II of the chapter sets out the primary rule, which holds that an attack targeting a lawful military objective will nonetheless be unlawful if there is a substantial risk that it will cause *excessive* civilian harm when compared to the expected military advantage.[5] It is thus a forward-looking assessment of what might happen, not an *ex-post-facto* quantification of how civilians suffered, to be equated to the military benefit actually accrued. Although treated under the 1977 Additional Protocol I as a form of indiscriminate attack, proportionality is best considered distinctly, as state practice and commentators tend to do.

There are six elements in judging proportionality, which are addressed in turn in section II. The first is the existence of an 'attack' (which therefore demands to be defined). The second is that the attack must be directed at a lawful military objective. The third is that the standard of foreseeability of harm – 'which may be expected' – is low. The fourth is that the expected harm must be civilian in nature. The fifth is the nature of the anticipated military advantage with which the foreseen harm is compared. The sixth, and most challenging, is to determine what, in practice, amounts to 'excessive' civilian harm.

Section III addresses the application of the rule, considering both indiscriminate attacks affecting civilians or civilian objects and 'disproportionate' weapons. Section IV looks at

[1] Y Dinstein, *The Conduct of Hostilities under the Law of International Armed Conflict*, 3rd edn (Cambridge, Cambridge University Press, 2016) 149, para 397.

[2] US Department of Defense, *Law of War Manual*, June 2015, Updated December 2016 (hereinafter 'USDOD December 2016 *Law of War Manual*'), para 2.4.1.2, at https://goo.gl/QMkjqs.

[3] Geoffrey Best described the word proportionality as 'lumbering, unattractive and inexpressive'. G Best, *War and Law since 1945* (Oxford, Oxford University Press, 1994) 324.

[4] W Hays Parks, 'Air War and the Law of War' (1990) 32:1 *Air Force Law Review* 1, 173. See GD Solis, *The Law of Armed Conflict: International Humanitarian Law in War*, 2nd edn (New York, Cambridge University Press, 2016) 292–93.

[5] As the US Department of Defense has also noted, 'Under the law of war, judgments of *proportionality* often involve difficult and subjective comparisons.' USDOD December 2016 *Law of War Manual*, para 2.4.1.2 (original emphasis).

disproportionate attacks under both conventional and customary international criminal law. The jurisprudence of the International Criminal Tribunal for the former Yugoslavia (ICTY), in particular in the *Galić* and *Prlić* cases, is considered. The chapter concludes with a case under national law in Poland, which concerns an attack by Polish soldiers operating in Afghanistan in 2007.

II. The Primary Rule

According to Article 51(5)(b) of the 1977 Additional Protocol I, one form of indiscriminate attack is

> an attack which may be expected to cause incidental loss of civilian life, injury to civilians, damage to civilian objects, or a combination thereof, which would be excessive in relation to the concrete and direct military advantage anticipated.[6]

There are six key elements to this rule:

- there must be a (planned) attack
- the attack must be directed at a lawful military objective
- the standard of foreseeability of harm is low
- the expected harm must be to civilians (death or physical injury) or concern damage to civilian objects
- the civilian harm foreseen by the attacker must be compared to the anticipated concrete and direct military advantage
- the attack is unlawful where the foreseen civilian harm is excessive in comparison to that expected military advantage.[7]

These elements are discussed in turn.

A. The Six Elements in Judging Proportionality

i. The Existence of an Attack

There must be an attack. Attacks (in the plural) are defined in the 1977 Additional Protocol I as 'acts of violence against the adversary, whether in offence or in defence'.[8] Such acts of violence involve the use of weapons or weapon systems,[9] and therefore exclude non-violent

[6] Art 51(5)(b), Protocol Additional to the Geneva Conventions of 12 August 1949, and relating to the Protection of Victims of International Armed Conflicts (Protocol I); adopted at Geneva, 8 June 1977; entry into force, 7 December 1978.

[7] As discussed in the following chapter, where this is the case, the duty to take precautions in attack requires that the attack be cancelled or postponed, or that the plans be amended in order to respect the rule of proportionality in attack.

[8] Art 49(1), 1977 Additional Protocol I.

[9] See APV Rogers, *Law on the Battlefield*, 3rd edn (Manchester, Manchester University Press, 2012) 31.

military operations such as reconnaissance. It is implicit, but not explicit, in the nature of the rule that the attack must have been at least in some sense planned in advance, and not an instant response to an involuntary situation of combat.

ii. The Attack Must be Directed at a Lawful Military Objective

It inheres in the use of the term 'incidental' that the attack must have been directed against a lawful military objective. If it is not, it directly violates the rule of distinction. At the least, such an attack will already be indiscriminate, but it even may be deemed, depending on the circumstances, to amount to a direct attack on civilians or civilian objects (see the previous two chapters for details).

iii. A Low Standard of Foreseeability

The required amount of risk for the incidental harm to be taken into account in the assessment of proportionality is remarkably low: the formulation 'which may be expected to cause' is substantially less exacting than possible alternatives such as 'which is expected to cause', 'which is likely to cause' or 'which would cause'.

The US Department of Defense, though, frames the 'proportionality rule' in slightly different terms:

> Combatants must refrain from attacks in which the expected loss of civilian life, injury to civilians, and damage to civilian objects incidental to the attack would be excessive in relation to the concrete and direct military advantage expected to be gained.[10]

Thus, the US sets a higher threshold for what will amount to a disproportionate attack, requiring that the 'expected' incidental harm *would* be excessive: seemingly a well-founded fear or lesser level of risk is, in its view, not sufficient. This potentially narrows the protective element of the rule. It is nonetheless an objective test, not a subjective one that is dependent on the whims of an individual commander.

Neither the Protocol nor customary law (see section II.B) identifies who is responsible for the proportionality assessment. It is assumed to be the relevant 'commander', but the effective commander for any given attack may be holding one among a range of military posts, from platoon lieutenant (or even a sergeant) all the way up to a full general.

It is not made explicit in the Protocol that commanders or individual soldiers are required to assess the likelihood of each individual attack causing incidental civilian harm, but this duty is subsumed in both the rule of proportionality in attack and the rule of precautions in attack. Under this latter rule (the subject of the following chapter), parties to an armed conflict must do everything feasible to verify that an attack is targeting one or more military objectives.[11] This is a prerequisite for the rule of proportionality, as it is predicated on the fact that a lawful military objective is being attacked.

Parties are also required to take all feasible precautions in their choice of means and methods of warfare in an attack, 'with a view to avoiding, and in any event to minimizing,

[10] USDOD December 2016 *Law of War Manual*, para 5.12.
[11] Art 57(2)(a)(i), 1977 Additional Protocol I.

incidental loss of civilian life, injury to civilians and damage to civilian objects'.[12] Here too it is understood that an assessment of the likelihood of civilian harm has been performed, at least where it is feasible in the prevailing circumstances to do so. Where a disproportionate attack may be expected to occur, the planned attack must be either cancelled or suspended, or the operational plans duly amended so that the attack conforms to the requirements of Hague Law.[13]

For sure, the assessor must act in good faith. He or she has concomitant obligations on information gathering to inform his or her assessment. According to the ICTY Committee established to review the 1999 North Atlantic Treaty Organization (NATO) bombing of the Federal Republic of Yugoslavia ('the ICTY Committee'), for example, 'A military commander must set up an effective intelligence gathering system to collect and evaluate information concerning potential targets.'[14] At the same time, a commander can only make decisions based on the information he or she has at the time the decision is made to launch the attack, a point that has been made by many states.[15]

But the ICTY Committee has also asserted that

> in combat military commanders are required … when directing their operations against military objectives, to ensure that the losses to the civilian population and the damage to civilian property are not disproportionate to the concrete and direct military advantage anticipated.[16]

This misstates the standard under both the Additional Protocol I and customary law. To ensure something is to guarantee an outcome, a standard that no commander, however diligent, can always meet.

iv. The Expected Harm Must be Civilian in Nature

Expected deaths of and injuries to enemy combatants and civilians taking a direct part in hostilities or damage to military *matériel* are not part of the assessment.[17] As Yoram Dinstein recalls, the rule 'does not protect fighters'.[18] This is generally the case even with respect to combatants who have laid down their arms, or who have been placed *hors de combat* by sickness, wounds, detention or any other cause. As the US Department of Defense affirms, however:

> Although the prohibition on attacks expected to cause excessive harm to civilians and civilian objects generally does not require consideration of military personnel and objects, feasible

[12] Art 57(2)(a)(ii), 1977 Additional Protocol I.
[13] Art 57(2)(a)(iii) and (b), 1977 Additional Protocol I.
[14] ICTY Committee Final Report, para 29.
[15] For instance, the International Committee of the Red Cross (ICRC) Study of Customary International Humanitarian Law (IHL) cites the practice of Algeria, Australia, Austria, Belgium, Canada, Ecuador, Egypt, Germany, Ireland, Italy, the Netherlands, New Zealand, Spain, the United Kingdom (UK) and the US. ICRC Study of Customary IHL, Rule 14 ('Proportionality in Attack') at https://goo.gl/rnDetJ.
[16] *Final Report to the Prosecutor by the ICTY Committee* (2000) para 28 (hereinafter 'ICTY Committee Final Report').
[17] See, eg, US Department of Defense, *Law of War Manual*, June 2015 (hereinafter 'USDOD 2015 *Law of War Manual*'), para 5.12.3.1, at https://goo.gl/uZKhvk; see, for the revised text on this issue, USDOD December 2016 *Law of War Manual*, para 5.10.1.
[18] Y Dinstein, *Non-International Armed Conflict in International Law*, 1st edn (Cambridge, Cambridge University Press, 2014) 217, para 693. Indirectly, however, as discussed below, it may protect the soldiers of the attacking party.

> precautions must be taken to reduce the risk of harm to military personnel and objects that are protected from being made the object of attack, such as military personnel placed *hors de combat*.[19]

Moreover, the risk of harm to civilians who were, in the past, participating directly in hostilities, but are no longer doing so, will form part of the proportionality equation.

The type of civilian harm likely to be assessed is broad: either deaths or injuries to civilians, or damage to civilian objects, or a combination thereof.[20] Accordingly, expected civilian harm that amounts to a small number of deaths, a few injuries and some damage to civilian objects may cumulatively render the attack unlawful. But, as the US Department of Defense has observed, the rule 'would not apply when civilians or civilian objects are not at risk'.[21]

More controversially, the Department asserts that the presence of 'civilian workers who place themselves in or on a military objective, knowing that it is susceptible to attack, such as workers in munitions factories', would 'be understood not to prohibit attacks under the proportionality rule'.[22] Dinstein rejects the proposed category of 'quasi-combatant', but observes that in 'certain sets of circumstances' civilians 'run continuous risks'.[23] Rogers believes that civilians working in a munitions factory must be part of the proportionality assessment, even though he believes that such a factory 'is such an important military objective that the death of a large proportion of the civilians working there cannot be said to be disproportionate to the military gain achieved by destroying the factory'.[24]

An ICTY Trial Chamber reaffirmed that parties to a conflict are 'under an obligation to remove civilians, to the maximum extent feasible from the vicinity of military objectives and to avoid locating military objectives within or near densely populated areas'. As also observed, however, 'the failure of a party to abide by this obligation does not relieve the attacking side of its duty to abide by the principles of distinction and proportionality when launching an attack'.[25] The ICTY Committee similarly observed that civilians present within or near military objectives must be taken into account in the proportionality equation, 'even if a party to the conflict has failed to exercise its obligation to remove them'.[26]

In its *Law of War Manual*, the US Department of Defense has argued that 'the party that employs human shields in an attempt to shield military objectives from attack assumes responsibility for their injury', though it tempers this conclusion by making it subject to the attacker's taking 'feasible precautions in conducting its attack'.[27] The UK Ministry of Defence affirms that even where human shields are being used, 'the proportionality rule must be considered'. It further notes, though, that 'if defenders put civilians or civilian

[19] USDOD December 2016 *Law of War Manual*, para 5.10.1.

[20] As the US Department of Defense has noted, 'Lesser forms of harm, such as mere inconveniences or temporary losses, need not be considered in applying the proportionality rule.' USDOD December 2016 *Law of War Manual*, para 5.12.1.2. It also gives examples of remote forms of harm, such as the economic harm caused by the death of an enemy combatant to his or her family, or the loss of jobs caused by the destruction of a tank factory. Ibid, para 5.12.1.3.

[21] USDOD December 2016 *Law of War Manual*, para 5.12.1.

[22] Ibid, para 5.12.3.2.

[23] Dinstein (n 1) 151, para 403; p. 150, paras 401, 402.

[24] Rogers (n 9) 22.

[25] ICTY, *Prosecutor v Galić*, Judgment (Trial Chamber I) (Case No IT-98-29-T), 5 December 2003, para 61.

[26] ICTY Committee Final Report, para 51.

[27] USDOD 2015 *Law of War Manual*, para 5.12.3.3; see USDOD December 2016 *Law of War Manual*, para 5.12.1.4.

objects at risk by placing military objectives in their midst or by placing civilians in or near military objectives, this is a factor to be taken into account in favour of the attackers in considering the legality of attacks on those objectives'.[28] Thus, even if so-called 'human shields' are placed, or position themselves, in or near a military objective, the risk to their lives and limbs must be assessed. This would seem to reward the unscrupulous party or the reckless individual, but to do otherwise would be tantamount to inviting indiscriminate attacks. And as the UK asserts, the actions of the defenders would be taken into account in assessing proportionality, effectively giving the attacker a greater margin of discretion than would otherwise be the case.

The proportionality rule does not ostensibly privilege lives and limbs over property. In 1991, however, the US had asserted:

> While collateral damage to civilian objects should be minimized, … collateral damage to civilian objects should not be given the same level of concern as incidental injury to civilians. Measures to minimize collateral damage to civilian objects should not include steps that will place US and allied lives at greater or unnecessary risk.[29]

In its latest iteration of the *Law of War Manual*, the US Department of Defense asserts that 'In light of the humanitarian objectives of the law of war, the expected loss of civilian life and injury to civilians should be given greater consideration than the expected damage to civilian objects.'[30] It does, though, qualify that stance by clarifying that 'expected damage to civilian objects (such as schools, hospitals, and religious facilities) should be given greater consideration when such damage is expected to involve the risk of harming civilians present inside such objects'. It also asserts that expected damage to cultural property 'should be afforded greater consideration than expected damage to ordinary property'.[31]

It has also been suggested, paraphrasing George Orwell, that while all civilians are equal, some are more equal than others. According to Dinstein, those who benefit from special protection from attack, such as the wounded and sick, or, 'even more so', medical personnel,

> do not seem to be counted on a par with ordinary civilians. Differently put, a dozen civilians dining in a restaurant do not weigh as much as a dozen patients and doctors in an infirmary. Otherwise, what is the real meaning of the special protection accorded to the latter?[32]

Dinstein further suggests that 'intuitively', adult men 'in their prime'

> are not seen in the same light as women, children and the elderly who are more vulnerable. When an air strike or an artillery barrage leaves a trail of civilian deaths behind, nobody would equate a score of adult men in a pub with a score of toddlers in a kindergarten.[33]

As already noted, there is no specific exemption in the way in which the proportionality rule is phrased for civilians who participate directly in hostilities. In principle, therefore,

[28] UK Ministry of Defence, *The Manual of the Law of Armed Conflict* (Oxford, Oxford University Press, 2004) para 2.7.2.

[29] Comments on the International Committee of the Red Cross's Memorandum on the Applicability of International Humanitarian Law in the Gulf Region, 11 January 1991, *Digest of United States Practice in International Law 1991–1999*, 2063.

[30] USDOD December 2016 *Law of War Manual*, para 5.12.1.1.

[31] Ibid.

[32] Dinstein (n 1) 159–60, para 428(a).

[33] Ibid, 160, para 428(b).

they fall within the balancing. Indeed, common sense dictates that those who are engaged in fighting, even on a short-term basis, have lost their immunity from attack, and therefore not only should be excluded from being considered as civilians for the purpose of the rule but their death or serious injury as a result of the attack may also be included as part of the anticipated direct and concrete military advantage.

The extent to which civilian harm should be assessed beyond that which is likely to be instantly wrought by the attack is unsettled.[34] The *Commentary on the Harvard Manual on International Law Applicable to Air and Missile Warfare* (which sought to describe the law applicable to international armed conflict (IAC)) states that

> harm to civilians and civilian objects that the attacker did not expect is not collateral damage included in proportionality calculations, so long as the lack of expectation of harm was reasonable in the circumstances … The key question with regard to such harm is whether there is compliance with the requirement to take feasible precautions in attack.[35]

Attacks may, for instance, provoke displacement and accompanying misery, such as separation of families. They are likely to lead to hazardous unexploded ordnance (UXO) that may be detonated later by unsuspecting civilians, particularly children. The US Department of Defense has observed that the rule 'would not be required to consider in the proportionality analysis the possibility that a munition might not detonate as intended and might injure civilians *much later* after the attack because the risk of such harm is too remote'.[36] The short-term threat from UXO is, though, capable of assessment, and this may be required. The Department of Defense cited Christopher Greenwood's 2002 presentation to the Group of Governmental Experts set up under the Convention on Certain Conventional Weapons:

> If, for example, cluster weapons are used against military targets in an area where there are known to be civilians, then the proportionality test may require that account be taken both of the risk to the civilians from sub-munitions exploding during the attack and of the risk from unexploded sub-munitions in the hours immediately after the attack. It is an entirely different matter, however, to require that account be taken of the longer-term risk posed by [Explosive Remnants of War (ERW)], particularly of the risk which ERW can pose after a conflict has ended or after civilians have returned to an area from which they had fled. The degree of that risk turns on too many factors which are incapable of assessment at the time of the attack, such as when and whether civilians will be permitted to return to an area, what steps the party controlling that area will have taken to clear unexploded ordnance, what priority that party gives to the protection of civilians and so forth. The proportionality test has to be applied on the basis of information reasonably available at the time of the attack. The risks posed by ERW once the immediate aftermath of an attack has passed are too remote to be capable of assessment at that time.[37]

[34] Thus, Sandesh Sivakumaran likely overstates *lex lata* (and the views of leading commentators) when he asserts that 'it is now accepted that longer-term effects have to be taken into account, such as deaths resulting from the impact of the destruction of the civilian infrastructure'. S Sivakumaran, *The Law of Non-International Armed Conflict* (Oxford, Oxford University Press, 2012) 350 and fn 30. See, eg, Dinstein (n 1) 159, para 425(d).

[35] *Commentary on the Harvard Manual on International Law Applicable to Air and Missile Warfare* (Cambridge, Cambridge University Press, 2013) 33, para 4.

[36] USDOD 2015 *Law of War Manual*, para 5.12.2.1 (emphasis added).

[37] C Greenwood, 'Legal Issues Regarding Explosive Remnants of War, Group of Government Experts of States Parties to the Convention on Prohibitions or Restrictions on the Use of Certain Conventional Weapons', UN Doc CCW/GGE/I/WP.10, 2002, 8.

It has also been questioned whether the likely cumulative effect on the civilian population of attacks against infrastructure should also be taken into account when judging the legality of attacks.[38] This proportionality assessment seems particularly apposite when attacks against electricity generating stations are being entertained.[39]

In the *Prlić* case, both the Trial and Appeals Chambers looked at the application of the proportionality rule in assessing the consequences of destroying the Old Bridge at Mostar. The Trial Chamber found that, at the time of the attack by Bosnian Croat forces, the Old Bridge was a military objective.[40] The Chamber, however, also noted

> that the destruction of the Old Bridge put the residents of Donja Mahala, the Muslim enclave on the right bank of the Neretva, in virtually total isolation, making it impossible for them to get food and medical supplies resulting in a serious deterioration of the humanitarian situation for the population living there. ... The Chamber determined that there were very few supply routes available to the inhabitants, other than the Old Bridge; that between May and November 1993, in addition to the Old Bridge, they could only use the *Kamenica* bridge, a makeshift bridge constructed by the ABiH [Bosniak army] in March 1993 and used until November 1993, or a path over the mountain from the neighbourhood of Donja Mahala to Jablanica, which was considered very dangerous; ... and that, as such, the destruction of the *Kamenica* bridge by the armed forces of the HVO [Bosnian Croat army] on 10, 11 or 17 November 1993, that is, only a few days after the destruction of the Old Bridge, cut off all access across the Neretva River in Mostar definitively. ... The Chamber also determined that the destruction of the Old Bridge had a very significant psychological impact on the Muslim population of Mostar.[41]

Based on its analysis, the Trial Chamber held that although the destruction of the Old Bridge by the Bosnian Croat army 'may have been justified by military necessity', the damage caused to civilians 'was indisputable and substantial'. It held, by a Majority, with Judge Antonetti dissenting, 'that the impact on the Muslim civilian population of Mostar was disproportionate to the concrete and direct military advantage expected by the destruction of the Old Bridge'.[42]

The problem with the Trial Chamber's analysis is that the rule of proportionality in attack does not require 'psychological impact', or even a 'serious deterioration of the humanitarian situation for the population' to be taken into account. It is, of course, prohibited to starve the civilian population as a method of warfare (see chapter 9), but it is not suggested that this is what was sought (or expected) by the attack, much less what was achieved. The vectors of civilian harm are, as described at the start of section II, 'incidental loss of civilian life, injury to civilians, damage to civilian objects, or a combination thereof'. In his Dissenting Opinion, Judge Antonetti similarly concluded that the bridge was a legitimate military objective,

[38] F Hampson, 'Means and Methods of Warfare in the Conflict in the Gulf' in P Rowe (ed), *The Gulf War 1990–91 in International and English Law* (London, Routledge, 1983) 100.

[39] The *Harvard Manual* has an unusual formulation of the proportionality rule, referring to 'collateral damage', which 'means incidental loss of civilian life, injury to civilians and damage to civilian objects or other protected objects or a combination thereof, caused by an attack on a lawful target'. *Harvard Manual on International Law Applicable to Air and Missile Warfare* (Cambridge, Cambridge University Press, 2013) para 1(l), 3. The *Commentary to the Manual* does not explain what it understood to constitute 'other protected objects'.

[40] ICTY, *Prosecutor v Prlić and others*, Judgment (Trial Chamber III) (Case No IT-04-74-T), vol 3, 29 May 2013, para 1582.

[41] Ibid, para 1583.

[42] Ibid, para 1584.

'whose destruction gave the HVO a definite military advantage by cutting off communications and the supply of food'. Without explaining further he stated that he 'fail[ed] to see how the principle of proportionality could be applicable in this case. If the Old Bridge was a military objective, it quite simply had to be destroyed. In any event, there is no such thing as proportionate destruction.'[43]

In their appeal, lawyers for Prlić and others questioned the Trial Chamber's application of the rule on proportionality in attack. In response, the Prosecution submitted that the Trial Chamber had

> appropriately considered the psychological harm as well as the physical impact caused by isolation as these effects were not mere incidental by-products of an attack on a military objective, but were the primary aim of the HVO as part of its campaign of terror against the civilian population.[44]

The Appeals Chamber dodged the issue of proportionality, finding that there had been adequate military necessity for the destruction of the bridge, which was a military objective, and that no other (civilian) object was incidentally destroyed.[45]

In his Dissenting Opinion, Judge Fausto Pocar endorsed the findings of the Trial Chamber with respect to proportionality. He affirmed that the Appeals Chamber had left untouched Trial Chamber III's 'overall conclusion that the attack was disproportionate in nature'.[46] He did not, though, address the nature of the proportionality rule and how issues other than incidental loss of civilian life, injury to civilians and damage to civilian objects are part of the rule.

v. *The Military Advantage*

The civilian harm that is foreseen must be compared to the 'concrete and direct military advantage' that is 'anticipated' to result from the attack. This is quite a high standard. Indirect military advantage is insufficient, as is intangible military benefit. Military advantage may, in the view of the US Department of Defense, include:

> (1) denying the enemy the ability to benefit from the object's effective contribution to its military action (eg using this object in its military operations);
> (2) improving the security of the attacking force; and
> (3) diverting the enemy's resources and attention.[47]

As Dinstein notes, the military value of given military objectives will vary significantly depending on the circumstances:

> A functioning command and control centre is inherently worth more than empty military barracks … When industrial plants are attacked, there is a considerable difference between a factory producing F-16 fighter aircraft and one manufacturing M-16 rifles.[48]

[43] Ibid, Dissenting Judgment of Judge Antonetti, 325.
[44] ICTY, *Prosecutor v Prlić and others*, Judgment (Appeals Chamber) (Case No IT-04-74-A), 29 November 2017, para 409.
[45] Ibid, para 411.
[46] Ibid, Dissenting Opinion of Judge Fausto Pocar, paras 10–11.
[47] USDOD 2015 *Law of War Manual*, para 5.12.5.
[48] Dinstein (n 1) 161, para 433.

He affirms that the difference 'projects on the extent of lawful collateral damage that may ensue for any civilians/civilian objects affected by the attack'.[49]

According to the ICRC Commentary on the 1977 Additional Protocols, the expression 'concrete and direct' military advantage was used to indicate that the advantage must be 'substantial and relatively close, and that advantages which are hardly perceptible and those which would only appear in the long term should be disregarded'.[50] Dinstein challenges the assertion that the advantage need be '*substantial*', though he accepts that it must be 'particular, perceptible and real as opposed to general, vague and speculative'.[51] The US Department of Defense has affirmed that it is not required that the military advantage be 'immediate', nor is it is 'restricted to immediate tactical gains', though it too concedes that the advantage 'may not be merely hypothetical or speculative'.[52]

The *Commentary on the Harvard Manual on International Law Applicable to Air and Missile Warfare* suggests an example whereby

> an attack on a bridge to deny the enemy the capability to cross a river may seemingly be of low military advantage if the enemy is actually not using that bridge. However, if the purpose of the attack on the bridge is to block avenues of retreat which the commander knows will be taken once he launches his planned offensive, the military advantage of destroying the bridge will be high.[53]

In adhering to the 1977 Additional Protocol I, several major military states, such as, for example, the UK, have asserted that 'the military advantage anticipated from an attack is intended to refer to the advantage anticipated from the attack considered as a whole and not only from isolated or particular parts of the attack'.[54] This, though, poses some difficult challenges, as the attack 'as a whole' may engage different forces and different commanders (and thus the problem of legal interoperability). How the proportionality assessment is to be effectively conducted in such circumstances is unclear.

The *Commentary on the Harvard Manual on International Law Applicable to Air and Missile Warfare* notes that 'Aerial attacks are often conducted by multiple military aircraft, in which case it would be improper to consider the impact of each single sortie in isolation. It is rather necessary to assess the overall mission.' The *Commentary* offers a specific example of a

> contemplated series of attacks against a number of bridges across the same river when they are in proximity to each other. Although the first attack on one of these bridges might appear to yield only a limited military advantage, considering that the enemy can still use the remaining bridges, the military advantage will become apparent once subsequent attacks against the other bridges take place.[55]

[49] Ibid.

[50] Y Sandoz, C Swinarski and B Zimmermann (eds), *Commentary on the Additional Protocols of 8 June 1977 to the Geneva Conventions of 12 August 1949* (Geneva, ICRC, 1987) para 2209 (hereinafter 'ICRC Commentary on the 1977 Additional Protocols').

[51] Dinstein (n 1) 161, para 430 (original emphasis]).

[52] USDOD December 2016 *Law of War Manual*, para 5.6.7.3.

[53] *Commentary on the Harvard Manual on International Law Applicable to Air and Missile Warfare* (n 35) 92, para 10.

[54] Declaration of the United Kingdom, (i), at https://goo.gl/9qnra4.

[55] *Commentary on the Harvard Manual on International Law Applicable to Air and Missile Warfare* (n 35) 93, para 11.

It is not unreasonable for the attacking party to consider privileging the application of lawful means and methods of warfare in an attack that may result in fewer of its own troops being lost, as long as the expected civilian harm is not excessive. According to New Zealand, for instance, 'the term "military advantage" involves a variety of considerations, including the security of attacking forces'.[56] The UK has observed:

> The application of the proportionality principle is not always straightforward. Sometimes a method of attack that would minimize the risk to civilians may involve increased risk to the attacking forces. The law is not clear as to the degree of risk that the attacker must accept. The proportionality principle does not itself require the attacker to accept increased risk. Rather, it requires him to refrain from attacks that may be expected to cause excessive collateral damage. It will be a question of fact whether alternative, practically possible methods of attack would reduce the collateral risks. If they would, the attacker may have to accept the increased risk as being the only way of pursuing an attack in a proportionate way.[57]

For, as Solis observes, force protection 'does not supersede the requirements of proportionality. Nor is a proportionality exception granted because an attacker's casualties are heavier than anticipated, or because a defender disregards'[58] the duty to take precautions against the effects of attacks 'to the maximum extent feasible'.[59] Moreover, according to the rule of precautions in attack, when an attack that is likely to produce similar military advantage may target different military objectives in so doing, it should target the objective that may be expected to cause the least danger to civilian lives and civilian objects.[60]

vi. What is 'Excessive'?

At the heart of the rule on proportionality in attack, and at the centre of its lack of clarity (and therefore controversy), is the identification and prevention of civilian harm that may be expected to be 'excessive' in comparison to the anticipated military benefits of the attack. As Judith Gardam has stated:

> The key to the dilemma is the subjective nature of assessing proportionality. It requires balancing between two opposing goals: the swift achievement of the military goal with the minimum losses of one's own combatants and the protection of the other party's civilian population.[61]

Nonetheless, the test is that where the assessed civilian harm 'may be expected' to be 'excessive'[62] compared to the anticipated military advantage, the attack will be indiscriminate and therefore unlawful.

[56] Declaration of New Zealand upon ratification of the 1977 Additional Protocol I, 8 February 1988, No 3, at https://goo.gl/6EBM77.

[57] UK Ministry of Defence (n 28) para 2.7.1.

[58] Solis (n 4) 305.

[59] Art 58, 1977 Additional Protocol I.

[60] Art 57(3), 1977 Additional Protocol I. The US has expressed the view that this rule is not a requirement of customary international law. See USDOD 2015 *Law of War Manual*, para 5.11.5 and fn 303.

[61] J Gardam, 'Proportionality and Force in International Law' (1993) 87(3) *AJIL* 391, 409.

[62] This standard is less stringent than the one enunciated in the 1863 Lieber Code, which described military necessity as admitting of 'all direct destruction of life or limb of *armed* enemies, and of other persons whose destruction is incidentally *unavoidable* in the armed contests of the war'. Art 15, 1863 Lieber Code (original emphasis).

The notion of comparison is inherent in the rule, as very significant anticipated military advantage may allow foreseeable civilian harm also to be substantial. The ICRC is therefore incorrect in its assertion that 'The Protocol does not provide any justification for attacks which cause extensive civilian losses and damages. Incidental losses and damages should never be extensive.'[63] As Rogers notes, such an interpretation would make 'nonsense of the rule of proportionality, the whole idea of which is to achieve a balance between the military advantage and the incidental loss'.[64] But at the same time, the US Department of Defense's assertion in 2015 that 'a very significant military advantage would be necessary to justify the collateral death or injury to *thousands* of civilians'[65] is a dangerous understatement of the restrictions imposed by Hague Law. As noted in chapter 1, however, the claim that 'a very significant' military advantage could justify the incidental death of, or injury to, thousands of civilians was narrowed in the Department's revised *Law of War Manual* in December 2016. In coming closer to the state of Hague Law, it was now affirmed that 'an *extraordinary* military advantage would be necessary to justify an operation posing risks of collateral death or injury to thousands of civilians'.[66]

A further issue is that the standard of assessment is not made explicit. As the US Department of Defense noted in 2015, 'The weighing or comparison between the expected incidental harm and the expected military advantage does not necessarily lend itself to empirical analyses.'[67] The sentiment was maintained in the revised *Law of War Manual* of December 2016, although the language differed: 'Determining whether the expected incidental harm is excessive does not necessarily lend itself to quantitative analysis because the comparison is often between unlike quantities and values.'[68] The ICTY Committee suggested 'that the determination of relative values must be that of the "reasonable military commander"'.[69] These issues are explored further in section III of this chapter.

As the facts change, so does the application of the proportionality rule. Thus, as the *Commentary on the Harvard Manual on International Law Applicable to Air and Missile Warfare* stipulates, the principle of proportionality

> applies throughout all stages of an attack, from planning to execution. Anyone with the ability and authority to suspend, abort or cancel an attack, must do so once he reaches the conclusion that the expected collateral damage would be excessive in relation to the anticipated military advantage. For instance, a pilot who has the target in view and unexpectedly observes civilians in the target area – who were not supposed to be there, based on the information provided to him during the briefing preceding the attack – must assess the collateral damage expected to befall them and cancel the attack if he concludes that the principle of proportionality will be violated.[70]

[63] ICRC Commentary on the 1977 Additional Protocols, para 1980.
[64] Rogers (n 9) 25.
[65] USDOD 2015 *Law of War Manual*, para 5.12.4 (emphasis added).
[66] USDOD December 2016 *Law of War Manual*, para 5.12.3 (emphasis added).
[67] USDOD 2015 *Law of War Manual*, para 5.12.4.
[68] USDOD December 2016 Law of War Manual, para 5.12.3 (emphasis added).
[69] ICTY Committee Final Report, para 50.
[70] *Commentary on the Harvard Manual on International Law Applicable to Air and Missile Warfare* (n 35) 94, para 15.

B. The Customary Rule

The rule of proportionality in attack is also of a customary law nature, applicable in all armed conflict according to the ICRC.[71] As Sivakumaran recalls, commenting on the non-international armed conflict (NIAC) in Sri Lanka as it drew to a brutal close in 2009, the US stated that the customary laws of war 'require all parties to a conflict to comply with the principles of distinction and proportionality in the conduct of hostilities'.[72] Dinstein maintains that the application of the rule in NIAC 'cannot be rebutted', despite its 'perplexing absence' from the 1977 Additional Protocol II.[73] Its customary formulation in both IAC and NIAC is, in the view of the ICRC, very similar to its codification in the 1977 Additional Protocol I:

> Launching an attack which may be expected to cause incidental loss of civilian life, injury to civilians, damage to civilian objects, or a combination thereof, which would be excessive in relation to the concrete and direct military advantage anticipated, is prohibited.

There is no evidence that, despite great uncertainty as to its application generally, the rule on proportionality in attack is to be applied differently in NIAC compared to IAC. In contrast, it is clear that the notion of proportionality in Hague Law differs materially from the concept as it is understood in other branches of international law, notably international human rights law or *jus ad bellum*.

III. The Application of the Rule

As the ICTY Committee noted:

> The main problem with the principle of proportionality is not whether or not it exists but what it means and how it is to be applied. It is relatively simple to state that there must be an acceptable relation between the legitimate destructive effect and undesirable collateral effects.[74]

This much is true. Unfortunately, the Committee went on to make a fatuous (and legally incorrect) claim about proportionality in attack, writing in its Final Report that 'bombing a refugee camp is obviously prohibited if its only military significance is that people in the camp are knitting socks for soldiers'.[75] Refugees knitting socks for soldiers are not by any stretch of the imagination directly participating in hostilities. They are therefore civilians protected from attack, pure and simple. This is not, therefore, by definition, a proportionality assessment, as the attack would be directly targeting civilians. One of the prerequisites

[71] ICRC Customary IHL Study, Rule 14 ('Proportionality in Attack').

[72] Sivakumaran (n 34) 349, citing US Department of State, *Report to Congress on Incidents during the Recent Conflict in Sri Lanka* (2009) 7.

[73] Dinstein (n 18) 217, para 693. One might add that its absence from the war crimes punishable by the International Criminal Court in NIAC is similarly perplexing.

[74] ICTY Committee Final Report, para 48.

[75] Ibid.

for the application of the rule of proportionality in attack, as discussed, is that the attack must have targeted a lawful military objective.

As Dinstein observes, while the difficulties of applying the proportionality rule are 'disquieting', it 'would be wrong to believe that weighing the expected collateral damage as against the anticipated military advantage is not doable'.[76] Famously, in the *Galić* case, an ICTY Trial Chamber stated:

> In determining whether an attack was proportionate it is necessary to examine whether a reasonably well-informed person in the circumstances of the actual perpetrator, … making reasonable use of the information available to him or her, could have expected excessive civilian casualties to result from the attack.[77]

The Chamber cited military manuals as providing guidance as to the practical application of this test; in particular the 1992 Canadian Manual indicates, for example, that 'consideration must be paid to the honest judgement of responsible commanders, based on the information reasonably available to them at the relevant time, taking fully into account the urgent and difficult circumstances under which such judgements are usually made', and that the proportionality test must be examined on the basis of 'what a reasonable person would do' in such circumstances.[78]

A. Potentially Disproportionate Attacks

The ICTY Committee affirmed that 'an air strike on an ammunition dump should not be prohibited merely because a farmer is plowing a field in the area'.[79] That is correct, but it hardly tells the whole story. A strike could be timed when no civilians, including a farmer, are present. It is also to be expected that a strike on an ammunition dump will lead to throw-outs from the storage area, which, depending on the size of the facility, may render vast swathes of agricultural land unsafe for use.[80] The ammunition storage area may be far from hostilities, and contain unsafe or unusable munitions. Beguiling simple statements may actually be overly simplistic when the rule on proportionality in attack is concerned.

Rogers constructs a scenario of a counterattack on an enemy stronghold in a village: 'If the commander directs his attack at the stronghold, the risk of excessive incidental loss is minimal. If he destroys the whole village, there is a much greater risk of infringing the proportionality rule.'[81] As he observes, the commander's decision may be 'questioned later' by a war crimes tribunal, for example on the basis that any 'civilian object damaged was clearly separate, or that the military advantage was either nil or negligible'.[82]

[76] Dinstein (n 1) para 426.
[77] *Galić* (n 25) para 58.
[78] *Canadian Law of Armed Conflict at the Operational and Tactical Level* (1992) s 5, para 27.
[79] ICTY Committee Final Report, para 48.
[80] Though this eventuality may be considered too remote by some to require its incorporation in the rule's practical application.
[81] Rogers (n 9) 26.
[82] Ibid.

He affirms that the following factors are to be taken into account in assessing the legality of a planned attack:

- the military importance of the target
- the density of the civilian population in the target area
- the likely incidental effects of the attack, including the possible release of hazardous substances
- the types of weapon available to attack the target and their accuracy
- whether the defenders are deliberately exposing civilians or civilian objects to risk
- the mode of attack, and
- the timing of the attack, especially in the case of a mixed target.[83]

In applying the proportionality rule to theoretical situations, Solis distinguishes two scenarios. In one, an enemy sniper in a remote and isolated desert could lawfully be targeted and killed with a 2,000lb bomb. In another, where the sniper is in a crowded orphanage, killing him or her 'with a mere hand grenade' could 'easily' violate the rule of proportionality in attack owing to the close presence of so many civilians.[84] Dinstein adds the scenario where a village is destroyed in order to kill a single enemy sniper. This, as he observes, is an 'obvious manifestation of "excessive" collateral damage'.[85] More controversially, though, he suggests that if an entire artillery battery operates from the village, the total destruction of the village 'may be warranted'.[86]

A more difficult scenario, he argues, is where a pilot of a fighter aircraft is attacking a railway bridge and as he begins his bombing run he sees a passenger train just starting across the bridge. 'Should he break off his attack or carry out the mission? There is no matrix, no order, no formula that resolves that dilemma.'[87] This scenario recalls a real-life incident that occurred during the 1999 conflict over Kosovo. On 12 April 1999, a NATO aircraft launched two laser-guided bombs at the Leskovac railway bridge in eastern Serbia. A five-carriage passenger train, travelling from Belgrade to Ristovac on the Macedonian border, was crossing the bridge at the time, and was struck by both missiles. At least 10 people were killed in this incident and at least 15 individuals were injured.[88]

The designated target was the railway bridge, which was claimed to be part of a re-supply route being used for Serb forces in Kosovo. After launching the first bomb, the person controlling the weapon, at the last instant before impact, sighted movement on the bridge. The controller was unable to dump the bomb at that stage and it hit the train, the impact of the bomb cutting the second of the passenger coaches in half. Realising the bridge was still intact, the controller picked a second aim point on the bridge at the opposite end from where the train had come and launched the second bomb. In the meantime the train had slid forward as a result of the original impact and parts of the train were also hit by the second bomb.[89]

[83] Ibid, 27.
[84] Solis (n 4) 296–97.
[85] Dinstein (n 1) 156, para 418.
[86] Ibid.
[87] Solis (n 4) 297.
[88] ICTY Committee Final Report, para 58.
[89] Ibid.

The ICTY Committee did not believe that the train was targeted deliberately. US Deputy Secretary of State for Defense John Hamre stated that 'one of our electro-optically guided bombs homed in on a railroad bridge just when a passenger train raced to the aim point. We never wanted to destroy that train or kill its occupants. We did want to destroy the bridge and we regret this accident.'[90] According to General Wesley Clark, NATO's Supreme Allied Commander for Europe,

> all of a sudden at the very last instant with less than a second to go he caught a flash of movement that came into the screen and it was the train coming in. Unfortunately he couldn't dump the bomb at that point, it was locked, it was going into the target and it was an unfortunate incident which he, and the crew, and all of us very much regret. We certainly don't want to do collateral damage.[91]

These statements could be taken to imply either that the incidental damage caused to the train would have been unlawful if the pilot had had time to postpone the attack, or that it was a policy position to minimise incidental damage beyond what is required by Hague Law.

Solis asks rhetorically, in the context of the US invasion of Iraq in 2003, how many civilian lives

> would be [an] acceptable forfeit for the targeting and killing of Sadaam Hussein and his two sons, the three of whom were legitimate military targets? Would the anticipated military advantage gained by their deaths, while the international armed conflict was still in progress, mitigate the deaths of ten civilians? Twenty? A hundred?[92]

As he recalls, following the receipt of information that the three men were in Baghdad near a restaurant, the US launched four precision-guided munitions. The bombs killed at least a dozen people (presumably civilians) but not the Husseins. Solis asked: 'Did that alter the proportionality equation?'[93]

An analogous scenario was in the US pursuit of the Pakistani Taliban leader, Baitullah Mehsud. On 23 June 2009, the US Central Intelligence Agency (CIA) killed Khwaz Wali Mehsud, a mid-ranking Pakistan Taliban commander. They planned to use his body as 'bait' to target Baitullah Mehsud, who was expected to attend his namesake's funeral. In fact, as many as 5,000 people attended, including not only Taliban fighters but many civilians. US drones struck the funeral gathering, killing up to 83, of whom as many as 45 were reportedly civilians, including 10 children and four tribal leaders. Baitullah Mehsud himself escaped unharmed, reportedly dying six weeks later along with his wife in a fresh CIA drone strike while on a drip being treated for a kidney problem.[94] According to a journalist writing for *The New Yorker* magazine, the CIA conducted 16 missile strikes, killing a total of up to 321 people before they managed to kill Mr Mehsud.[95]

[90] Ibid, para 59.
[91] Ibid.
[92] Solis (n 4) 298.
[93] Ibid.
[94] See, eg, P Finn and J Warrick, 'Under Panetta, a more aggressive CIA', *The Washington Post* (21 March 2010); see also C Woods and C Lamb, 'Obama terror drones: CIA tactics in Pakistan include targeting rescuers and funerals', *Bureau of Investigative Journalism* (4 February 2012).
[95] J Meyer, 'The Predator war', *New Yorker* (26 October 2009).

In the *Galić* case, one of the shelling incidents for which General Galić was prosecuted for war crimes before the ICTY, involved the shelling of a football match. On 1 June 1993, some residents of Dobrinja decided to organise a football tournament. The residents looked for a safe place to hold the matches. The football pitch was in the corner of a car park, bounded by six-storey apartment blocks on three sides and by a hill on the fourth side; it was not visible from any point on the Bosnian Serb side of the confrontation line. Some 200 spectators, among whom women and children, gathered to watch the games.[96]

About 10 to 20 minutes into the second game, a shell landed among the players in the centre of the pitch. The referee was hit by shrapnel, sustaining serious injuries in both legs as well as in other parts of his body. He saw that 11 young men were on the ground, eight of whom had died on the spot. Three players were 'totally dismembered'; only their tracksuits 'held them together' and many people around the pitch were on the ground.[97] A second shell, which landed at almost the same spot within seconds of the first shell, fell in front of a young man and tore his leg off.[98]

General Galić's defence counsel submitted that the intended target of this attack was a legitimate military objective, arguing, inter alia, that the Bosnian government army had headquarters located close to the car park and that a system of trenches ran only a dozen metres away from that site.[99] In addition, a number of army soldiers were at the football match. The commander of a local brigade acknowledged that off-duty soldiers amounted to around half of the casualties.[100] The Majority of the Trial Chamber nonetheless held:

> Although the number of soldiers present at the game was significant, an attack on a crowd of approximately 200 people, including numerous children, would clearly be expected to cause incidental loss of life and injuries to civilians excessive in relation to the direct and concrete military advantage anticipated.[101]

Judge Nieto-Navia dissented from the holding of the Majority in respect of its conclusion of an indiscriminate (disproportionate) attack, both on the basis that it had not been proven beyond a reasonable doubt that the shell was fired by Bosnian Serb forces and that the foreseeable incidental civilian harm was not excessive compared to the anticipated military advantage.[102] This included the possible targeting of objects as well as personnel that constituted lawful military objectives.

In the *Gotovina* case, a charge of disproportionate attack was levelled against the accused for the attack on the residence of Milan Martić in Knin.[103] A prosecution expert witness with expertise in the use of artillery in military operations, Lieutenant-Colonel Harry Konings of the Royal Netherlands army, affirmed that although the presence of the commander-in-chief of the Krajina Serb forces could make his residence a lawful military objective, 'the likelihood of killing the commander by artillery was very low, considering the degree

[96] *Galić* (n 25) para 372.
[97] Ibid, para 373.
[98] Ibid, para 374.
[99] Ibid, para 382.
[100] Ibid, para 386.
[101] Ibid, para 387.
[102] ICTY Galić (n 25), Dissenting Opinion of Judge Nieto-Navia, paras 63–65.
[103] ICTY, *Prosecutor v Ante Gotovina and Mladen Markač*, Judgment (Trial Chamber I) (Case No IT-06-90-T), 15 April 2011, para 1166.

of protection in a strong building and that the commander was unlikely to be on the top floor'.[104] Nonetheless, the Trial Chamber concluded that, given Mr Martić's position within the Krajina Serb forces, it was satisfied that 'firing at his residence could disrupt his ability to move, communicate, and command and so offered a definite military advantage, such that his residence constituted a military target'.[105]

The Chamber recalled that the Croatian army reported firing a total of 12 130 mm shells at Milan Martić's apartment on two occasions between 7.30am and 8am on 4 August 1995. Since the apartment was located in an otherwise civilian building in an otherwise predominantly civilian residential area, and given the fact that civilians could have reasonably been expected to be present on the streets of Knin near Mr Martić's apartment, firing the shells from a distance of approximately 25 kilometres created a significant risk of a high number of civilian casualties and injuries, as well as of damage to civilian objects. The Trial Chamber considered that this risk was excessive in relation to the anticipated military advantage and therefore amounted to a disproportionate attack.[106]

In connection with General Gotovina's appeal, an *amicus curiae* brief was submitted by a number of law of armed conflict experts. The *Amici* noted that, in their collective experience,

> few targets are designated as higher in value than enemy strategic leadership. Disrupting the ability of such leaders to influence ongoing operations is traditionally anticipated to produce critically important operational effects favouring friendly forces. Indeed, it is an axiom of military operations that enemy command, control, and communications capability is always a high value target. Any assessment of compliance with the proportionality rule vis-à-vis enemy strategic leadership must account for this value attribution. Furthermore, Amici endorse the views of the two experts relied on by the Trial Chamber to reach its conclusion that artillery is often used to produce a harassing or disrupting effect on enemy command, control, and communication, and that the inability to achieve a destructive effect does not render artillery ineffective as a weapon to use against strategic leadership. We also note that because the Trial Chamber chose not to articulate the values it concluded must have been properly attributed to each side of the proportionality balance by the defendant, it is impossible to determine whether those values comport with traditional operational practice. Accordingly, Amici encourage the Appeals Chamber to consider whether the conclusion of illegality was in fact consistent with the anticipated extremely high value any reasonable commander would attribute to disrupting a supreme commander's (Milan Martić's) ability to influence the battle, with the limited number of projectiles fired at his residence, and with the apparent absence of civilian casualties produced by those attacks.[107]

The *Amici* had a 'strong consensus' that the attacks against Martić's home 'fully complied with the proportionality obligation'. It believed that the evidence at trial indicated that General Gotovina 'would have reasonably believed' that most of the civilians had left the residential area in the vicinity of the Martić's apartment at the time; that Gotovina and his

[104] ICC, *Prosecutor v Germain Katanga*, Judgment (Trial Chamber II) (Case No ICC-01/04-01/07), 7 March 2014, para 1174.

[105] Ibid, para 1899.

[106] Ibid, para 1910.

[107] ICTY, *Prosecutor v Gotovina* (Appeals Chamber) (Case No IT-06-90-A), Application and Proposed Amicus Curiae Brief Concerning the 15 April 2011 Trial Chamber Judgment and Requesting that the Appeals Chamber Reconsider the Findings of Unlawful Artillery Attacks during Operation Storm, para 26.

subordinates took great care to target only military targets and to avoid civilian casualties; that they used a limited number of projectiles against the building; and that the attacks resulted in no civilian casualties.[108]

The Appeals Chamber did not formally consider the *amicus* brief but seemed to have taken note of it. It criticised the Trial Chamber's analysis of the attacks for a lack of a concrete assessment of comparative military advantage, and for not making any findings on resulting damages or casualties: 'Especially when considered in the context of the Trial Chamber's errors with respect to the Impact Analysis, … this finding of a disproportionate attack was thus of limited value in demonstrating a broader indiscriminate attack on civilians in Knin.'[109] In his Dissenting Opinion, Judge Agius affirmed:

> At no time did the Trial Chamber doubt the legitimacy of targeting Martić's residence, however it came to the conclusion that the attack was disproportionate because of the number of shells fired, the kind of artillery used, the distance from where the shells were fired, the location of both residences within a residential area, and the times when the shells were fired. … In my view, given these findings, the Trial Chamber did not necessarily need to tie its finding that the shelling was disproportionate to any findings on resulting damages or casualties. The Majority may only reach a decision to overturn the Trial Chamber's finding of disproportionality if it is clear that no reasonable trial chamber could reach that decision. In my opinion, this is certainly not the case. I therefore cannot agree with the Majority. I also disagree with the Majority that the decision reached by the Trial Chamber was of 'limited value' in establishing that there was a broader indiscriminate attack. In my view, this evidence is indeed revealing and a reasonable trier of fact could attach importance to it.[110]

In the *Katanga* case, an ICC Trial Chamber held that despite the fact that civilians and soldiers were fleeing together and that the fleeing soldiers 'may have constituted a military target for the attackers', the Chamber considered that the loss of human life resulting from the shots fired at the group of fleeing persons 'was excessive in relation to the military advantage which the attackers could have anticipated, specifically given that the … soldiers were already fleeing'.[111]

B. 'Disproportionate' Weapons

There is no such thing as an inherently 'disproportionate' weapon. The contextualisation that is part and parcel of the rule of proportionality in attack prohibits this classification in the same way that it applies to indiscriminate weapons. There is a slight caveat to the unequivocal nature of this assertion: those weapons whose effects cannot be limited as required by Hague Law rules might be said to be 'inherently disproportionate' on the basis that while they can be directed at a specific military objective, their effects may go far and beyond to strike civilians. As noted in chapters 1 and 5, biological weapons are a generally accepted example of such a weapon.

[108] Ibid, para 27.
[109] ICC, *Prosecutor* v *Gotovina*, Judgment (Appeals Chamber) (Case No IT-06-90-A), 16 November 2012, para 82.
[110] Ibid, Dissenting Opinion of Judge Carmel Agius, para 44.
[111] *Katanga* (n 104) para 865.

As Solis observes, 'weapons such as cluster bombs in populated areas, even aerial bombardment by "dumb" bombs, raise proportionality issues'.[112] The *Martić* case before the ICTY, discussed in chapter 4, involved the firing of submunitions from ground-launched rockets against the city of Zagreb in early May 1995.[113] The Trial Chamber noted that the weapon was fired 'from the extreme of its range' and that it was 'a non-guided high dispersion weapon'. It therefore concluded that the weapon, 'by virtue of its characteristics and the firing range in this specific instance, was incapable of hitting specific targets' and its use in densely populated civilian areas, such as Zagreb, would result in the infliction of severe casualties. Further, the decision to once again use the weapon on a second day meant that 'the full impact of using such an indiscriminate weapon was known beyond doubt as a result of the extensive media coverage on 2 May 1995 of the effects of the attack on Zagreb'. In contrast, the ICTY Committee's cursory examination of NATO's use of cluster bombs in the conflict with the Federal Republic of Yugoslavia, dealt with in a single paragraph and omitting all discussion of the mistaken attack on the city of Niš that killed 14 and seriously injured 27 others,[114] was woefully inadequate.[115]

In the *Gotovina* case, Geoffrey Corn testified that any commander considering the use of rocket artillery in a civilian area is obliged to assess the anticipated collateral damage and incidental injury. As the Trial Chamber summarised, he asserted that rocket artillery 'is not necessarily the most indiscriminate option of attack when compared to cannon artillery: the comparison depends on the location of the civilian population (indoors or outdoors), the timing of the attack, the protection afforded to civilians by hardened structures, and the potential comparative impact of cannon and rocket rounds'.[116] Depending on these factors, Corn 'considered it conceivable that a commander could make a good faith determination that rocket artillery is better suited to achieve the desired effect'.[117]

In practice, the less accurate the weapon, the more likely it is that civilian harm should be 'expected' to occur in the proportionality assessment. Thus, for example, a reasonable commander cannot assume that no incidental harm may occur if there is only a 25 per cent chance that the weapon will hit the intended target (which has no civilians or civilian objects within a 50 metre radius) but a 75 per cent chance that it will strike 100 to 300 metres away. This is one instance where precautionary measures in the choice of means of warfare help to ensure compliance with the rule of proportionality in attack.

IV. Disproportionate Attacks under International Criminal Law

The intentional launching of an attack against one or more military objectives that is expected to cause disproportionate harm to civilians or damage to civilian objects compared

[112] Solis (n 4) 294. Solis describes the weapons as indiscriminate, tending to suggest that this is their nature, but he likely means to say 'indiscriminate use'.

[113] ICTY, *Prosecutor v Milan Martić*, Judgment (Trial Chamber) (Case No IT-95-11), 12 June 2007, para 463.

[114] See, eg, Norwegian People's Aid, *Yellow Killers: The Impact of Cluster Munitions in Serbia and Montenegro* (Belgrade, 2007) esp 21–26, at https://goo.gl/YT5ckE.

[115] ICTY Committee Final Report, para 27.

[116] *Gotovina and Markač* (n 103), para 1166.

[117] Ibid.

to the military advantage reasonably likely to accrue from the attack is a war crime. That is so, whether or not such disproportionate harm to civilians or damage to civilian objects in fact transpires.

The standard required for a successful prosecution, though, differs materially between treaties and between certain treaties and customary international law, as now discussed.

A. Under 1977 Additional Protocol I

i. Disproportionate Attacks Affecting Civilians

The default standard is set out in Article 85(3) of the 1977 Additional Protocol I. When the act is committed wilfully, *and when it results in death or serious physical or mental injury*, it is a war crime to:

> Launch … an indiscriminate attack affecting the civilian population or civilian objects in the knowledge that such attack will cause excessive loss of life, injury to civilians or damage to civilian objects, as defined in Article 57(2)(a)(iii).[118]

In turn, the relevant provision in Article 57 stipulates that parties to conflict should refrain from launching any attack

> which may be expected to cause incidental loss of civilian life, injury to civilians, damage to civilian objects, or a combination thereof, which would be excessive in relation to the concrete and direct military advantage anticipated.

The formulation of the war crime of disproportionate attacks is thus rather clumsy, but the following elements of actus reus and mens rea constitute the offence.

a. Actus Reus

The actus reus of a disproportionate attack is that:

- there must have been an indiscriminate attack affecting the civilian population or civilian objects, and
- the attack must have resulted in death or serious physical or mental injury or damage to civilian objects.

Thus, under the Protocol the attack must have impacted on civilians or civilian objects; but even if it impacted on civilian objects, it must have resulted in death or serious injury. An attack that merely caused excessive damage to civilian objects without concomitant loss of life or serious physical or mental injury would not be encompassed. This sets a far higher standard than the primary rule of proportionality in attack. It also runs somewhat counter to the logic of the rule, which is, as we have seen, forward-looking (to what is expected), while the essence of the actus reus of the war crime is looking back to what actually transpired as a result of the attack.

[118] Art 85(3)(b), 1977 Additional Protocol I.

Interestingly, though, it is not made explicit that the actual loss of life or serious physical or mental injury must occur to civilians, as is generally required by the rule of proportionality in attack. Thus, it would appear that, exceptionally, the death of, or injury to, combatants might meet this requirement, at the very least when they are *hors de combat*.

b. Mens Rea

The mens rea of a disproportionate attack is that it must have been committed:

- wilfully (ie deliberately and either with intent that the harm would result, or recklessly as to the risk of the harm occurring),[119] and
- (in the knowledge that) the attack would cause excessive loss of life, injury to civilians, or damage to civilian objects, or a combination thereof, compared to the concrete and direct military advantage anticipated.

The term 'knowledge' is not elaborated on in the Protocol, though it is defined in the ICC Statute as 'awareness that a circumstance exists or a consequence will occur in the ordinary course of events'.[120]

Thus, in sum, the commander who launches the attack must have been aware that the attack would, in the ordinary course of events, cause excessive loss of life or injury to civilians, or damage to civilian objects (or a combination thereof) compared to the concrete and direct military advantage anticipated, and have intended that to occur or have been reckless as to the risk of it occurring. And the attack must have resulted in death or serious injury.

ii. Disproportionate Attacks against Dangerous Installations

Similar requirements are set out in the Protocol for the war crime of attacking dangerous installations where it has a disproportionate impact on civilians, that is,

> launching an attack against works or installations containing dangerous forces in the knowledge that such attack will cause excessive loss of life, injury to civilians or damage to civilian objects, as defined in Article 57(2)(a)(iii).[121]

a. Actus Reus

The actus reus of a disproportionate attack against dangerous installations is that:

- there must have been an indiscriminate attack affecting the civilian population or civilian objects, and
- the attack must have resulted in death or serious injury.

[119] According to the ICRC commentary on the term, 'the accused must have acted consciously and with intent, ie, with his mind on the act and its consequences, and willing them ("criminal intent" or "malice aforethought"); this encompasses the concepts of "wrongful intent" or "recklessness", viz, the attitude of an agent who, without being certain of a particular result, accepts the possibility of it happening; on the other hand, ordinary negligence or lack of foresight is not covered, ie, when a man acts without having his mind on the act or its consequences … (although failing to take the necessary precautions, particularly failing to seek precise information, constitutes culpable negligence punishable at least by disciplinary sanctions)'. ICRC Commentary on the 1977 Additional Protocols, para 3474.

[120] Art 30(3), ICC Statute.

[121] Art 85(3)(c), 1977 Additional Protocol I.

b. Mens Rea

The mens rea of a disproportionate attack is that it must have been committed:

- wilfully (ie deliberately and either with intent that the harm would result, or recklessly as to the risk of the harm occurring), and
- (in the knowledge that) the attack would cause excessive loss of life, injury to civilians or damage to civilian objects, or a combination thereof, compared to the concrete and direct military advantage anticipated.

B. Under Customary International Law

The ICRC has identified the intentional launching of a disproportionate attack as a war crime under customary law. Its proposed formulation in an IAC is, though, at best controversial and at worst incorrect. According to the organisation, it is a war crime in an IAC to:

> Launch … an attack in the knowledge that such attack will cause incidental loss of civilian life, injury to civilians or damage to civilian objects which would be clearly excessive in relation to the concrete and direct military advantage anticipated.[122]

This standard differs materially from that set out in the 1977 Additional Protocol I in two respects. First, to be punishable the civilian harm must be 'clearly excessive'. Second, a cumulative harm of civilian death, injury and/or damage to civilian objects does not suffice. Taken together, the requirements set the bar extremely high for any prosecution, effectively making it extremely unlikely that any prosecution would be successful. Potentially only in a scenario of the type articulated by Solis – where a party destroys an entire village to kill one sniper – would the standard be met in practice. The ICRC does not justify the inclusion of the modifier 'clearly' other than to say that it 'follows more closely the wording' found in the ICC Statute. However, as Article 10 of the Statute iterates, nothing in the articulation of the crimes falling under the jurisdiction of the Court 'shall be interpreted as limiting or prejudicing in any way existing or developing rules of international law for purposes other than this Statute'. I would not seek to imply that identifying custom is purely a numbers game, but it is noteworthy that as at 1 April 2018, a total of 174 states were party to the 1977 Additional Protocol I compared to 123 states parties to the ICC Statute.

In contrast (and without explanation, much less justification), in the context of a NIAC, the ICRC sticks more closely to the Protocol formula, that is,

> launching an indiscriminate attack resulting in death or injury to civilians, or an attack in the knowledge that it will cause excessive incidental civilian loss, injury or damage.[123]

Here, the word 'clearly' is simply omitted, indicating (almost certainly incorrectly) that the standard for the customary law war crime is lower in a NIAC than it is in an IAC.

[122] ICRC Study of Customary IHL, Rule 156 ('Definition of War Crimes'), '(ii) Other serious violations of international humanitarian law committed during an international armed conflict', point (ii), at https://goo.gl/iSY6Z6.

[123] Ibid, '(iv) Other serious violations of international humanitarian law committed during a non-international armed conflict', point (ii).

Similarly, in the context of indiscriminate attacks affecting dangerous installations (in both classifications of armed conflict), the ICRC follows the wording of the 1977 Protocol, that is,

> launching an attack against works or installations containing dangerous forces in the knowledge that such attack will cause excessive incidental loss of civilian life, injury to civilians or damage to civilian objects.

C. Under the ICC Statute

The ICC Statute only gives the Court potential jurisdiction to prosecute disproportionate attacks that occur in an IAC. The formulation is as follows:

> Intentionally launching an attack in the knowledge that such attack will cause incidental loss of life or injury to civilians or damage to civilian objects ... which would be clearly excessive in relation to the concrete and direct overall military advantage anticipated.

The ICRC suggests that the word 'overall', which is not contained in Articles 51 and 85 of the 1977 Additional Protocol I or in the substantive rule of customary international law, is included in the ICC Statute

> to indicate that a particular target can have an important military advantage that can be felt over a lengthy period of time and affect military action in areas other than the vicinity of the target itself. As this meaning is included in the existing wording of Additional Protocol I and the substantive rule of customary international law, the inclusion of the word 'overall' does not add an extra element.[124]

The elements of crime are as follows (the footnotes are as in the original):

> 1. The perpetrator launched an attack.
> 2. The attack was such that it would cause incidental death or injury to civilians or damage to civilian objects ... and that such death, injury or damage would be of such an extent as to be clearly excessive in relation to the concrete and direct overall military advantage anticipated.[125]
> 3. The perpetrator knew that the attack would cause incidental death or injury to civilians or damage to civilian objects ... and that such death, injury or damage would be of such an extent as to be clearly excessive in relation to the concrete and direct overall military advantage anticipated.[126]

[124] ICRC Study of Customary IHL, Rule 156, '(ii) Other serious violations of international humanitarian law committed during an international armed conflict', point (ii). See also K Dörmann, *Elements of War Crimes under the Rome Statute of the International Criminal Court: Sources and Commentary* (Cambridge, Cambridge University Press, 2003) 169, esp 169–70.

[125] 'The expression "concrete and direct overall military advantage" refers to a military advantage that is foreseeable by the perpetrator at the relevant time. Such advantage may or may not be temporally or geographically related to the object of the attack. The fact that this crime admits the possibility of lawful incidental injury and collateral damage does not in any way justify any violation of the law applicable in armed conflict. It does not address justifications for war or other rules related to *jus ad bellum*. It reflects the proportionality requirement inherent in determining the legality of any military activity undertaken in the context of an armed conflict.'

[126] '[T]his knowledge element requires that the perpetrator make the value judgement as described therein. An evaluation of that value judgement must be based on the requisite information available to the perpetrator at the time.'

4. The conduct took place in the context of and was associated with an international armed conflict.
5. The perpetrator was aware of factual circumstances that established the existence of an armed conflict.

In contradistinction to its formulation in the 1977 Additional Protocol I, damage to civilian objects without accompanying death or injury would be sufficient for the ICC potentially to have jurisdiction to prosecute the war crime.

In the *Katanga* case, the ICC Trial Chamber held that the civilians who fled the safety of a building in the village were killed intentionally. This is despite the fact that civilians and soldiers were fleeing together and that the soldiers 'at that moment may have constituted a military target for the attackers'. The Chamber's conclusion was that 'the loss of human life ensuing from the shots fired at the group of fleeing persons was excessive in relation to the military advantage which the attackers could have anticipated, specifically given that the … soldiers were already fleeing'. By 'shooting indiscriminately at fleeing persons', the attackers 'showed scant regard for the fate of the civilians among the … soldiers in the mêlée and knew that their death would occur in the ordinary course of events. The Chamber finds that they thus intended to cause their death.'[127]

D. In the Jurisprudence of the Ad Hoc International Criminal Tribunals

In the *Galić* case, an ICTY Trial Chamber recalled that the actus reus of a disproportionate attack was one that involved an attack against a target whose 'military character' has been ascertained. Commanders must consider whether striking this target is 'expected to cause incidental loss of life, injury to civilians, damage to civilian objectives or a combination thereof, which would be excessive in relation to the concrete and direct military advantage anticipated.' If such casualties are expected to result, and the attack is pursued, an offence may have been committed.[128]

In determining culpability, the Chamber noted that the basic obligation to spare civilians and civilian objects as much as possible 'must guide the attacking party when considering the proportionality of an attack'. Further, in determining whether an attack was proportionate it is necessary to examine 'whether a reasonably well-informed person in the circumstances of the actual perpetrator, making reasonable use of the information available to him or her, could have expected excessive civilian casualties to result from the attack'.[129]

The Chamber held that to establish the mens rea of a disproportionate attack the Prosecution must prove the attack 'was launched wilfully and in knowledge of circumstances giving rise to the expectation of excessive civilian casualties'.[130] The Chamber further held that certain apparently disproportionate attacks may give rise to the inference that civilians

[127] *Katanga* (n 104) para 865. Of note, the Chamber did not make it explicit that the civilian harm was 'clearly' excessive, as the Statute requires.
[128] *Galić* (n 25), para 58.
[129] Ibid.
[130] Ibid, para 59.

were actually the object of attack. This is to be determined 'on a case-by-case basis in light of the available evidence'.[131]

In judging General Galić's appeal against conviction, the Appeals Chamber was satisfied that the Trial Chamber had correctly assessed the legality of disproportionate attacks.[132] It rejected his claim that 'overabundant evidence according to which many [military targets] were spread all over Sarajevo' was 'never fairly considered' by the Trial Chamber.[133] With regard to Galić's arguments that the weapons his forces had used had increased the likelihood of collateral damage because they were 'error-prone', the Prosecution averred this did not 'explain how such errors could be acceptable in the context of international humanitarian law when these problems are known in advance'.[134]

E. Under National Law

A potentially relevant case under national law concerns the action of Polish soldiers operating in Afghanistan. On 16 August 2007, Polish soldiers opened fire with 24 mortar shells (and possibly automatic weapons)[135] against the Afghan village of Nangar Khel, killing at least six civilians, including women and children, who were at a wedding taking place in the village. The attack may have been in response to injuries suffered by two other Polish soldiers earlier that day when their vehicle hit a Taliban mine/improvised explosive device located near the village. According to a number of witnesses, the Polish captain and commander of the relevant unit told his men to 'fuck over a couple of villages'. It is possible that Polish officers who ordered the attack believed that the Taliban forces involved in the prior attack on Polish soldiers earlier on the same day were present at Nangar Khel, which would give rise to a possible issue of proportionality.[136]

In 2011, the Warsaw district court acquitted seven soldiers of war crimes charges for lack of evidence. The defendants had blamed the attack on faulty weaponry and had sought to portray the attack as a response to enemy fire.[137] Following an appeal by the prosecutor, the court ordered a retrial for four of them. This is said to have been the first time Polish soldiers had been accused of violating the Hague and Geneva Conventions protecting civilians.[138] A Polish Supreme Court judge said the men had given conflicting accounts of why the village was attacked: at times they said they were responding to Taliban fire, at others they said they were following orders or that their mortar equipment was faulty.[139] On 19 March 2015, at the end of the retrial of four of the soldiers, the Military District Court in Warsaw cleared them of war crimes, declaring 'a lack of convincing proof that the war crime was committed'. A Court spokesman, Tomasz Krajewski, reportedly stated, 'The court did not

[131] Ibid, para 60.

[132] ICTY, *Prosecutor v Galić*, Judgment (Appeals Chamber) (Case No IT-98-29-A), 30 November 2006, para 192.

[133] Ibid, paras 233, 235.

[134] Ibid, para 234.

[135] See, eg, 'Lukasz Bywalec', Trial International, Updated 15 June 2016, at https://goo.gl/RgsLk8.

[136] M Sterio, 'Polish Soldiers Acquitted of War Crimes for Nangar Khel Incident', *Jurist* (20 April 2015) at https://goo.gl/vqw3Tu.

[137] Ibid.

[138] W Rylukowski, 'Court: Nangar Khel massacre is not war crime', *WBJ* (19 March 2015) at https://goo.gl/zstTKr.

[139] 'New trial for Polish soldiers over Afghanistan killings', *BBC* (9 January 2013) at https://goo.gl/gTZoWW.

establish that the soldiers' actions were deliberate. The shooting of the village was not on purpose; neither was the killing of the civilians.'[140]

Three troops were also charged with the lesser violation of improper execution of an order (failing to perform proper reconnaissance before opening fire) and use of an incorrect type of weaponry, inconsistent with the rules implemented by the Polish military contingent in Afghanistan. The soldiers were found guilty of failing to carry out a military order;[141] three were given suspended jail sentences, while the fourth was conditionally discharged. The convictions were upheld by the Supreme Court in February 2016, while the Prosecution's appeal against the acquittal on war crimes charges was rejected.[142]

[140] D Niemitz, 'Military court clears four Polish soldiers of war crimes in Afghanistan', *World Socialist Web Site* (25 March 2015) at https://goo.gl/JjZj14.

[141] Sterio (n 136).

[142] PAP, 'Killing of Afghan civilians was not war crime, Polish court rules', *Radio Poland* (17 February 2016) at https://goo.gl/kzqy5T.

7

The Rule of Precautions in Attack

I. Introduction

It is only exceptionally made explicit in law of armed conflict treaties, but the rules of distinction and proportionality in attack are directly underpinned by the duty on the attacker to take certain 'precautions'. The overriding aim of all precautions in attack is to minimise civilian harm, either by seeking to ensure that civilians are not present when an attack strikes, or by limiting, as far as reasonably possible, the ambient effects of an attack to a military objective.

In addressing the issue, section II of this chapter sets out the primary rules, which are codified in Article 57 of the 1977 Additional Protocol I.[1] As the International Committee of the Red Cross (ICRC) recalls, this provision was the subject of lengthy and difficult negotiations in the diplomatic conference, and the text that emerged was 'the fruit of laborious compromise'.[2] Section III details the measures that, in practice, constitute precautions in attack. These involve, amongst others: verifying that an attack is targeting military objectives; timing an attack to minimise the risk of civilian harm; issuing an effective warning of an impending or future attack to the civilian population; and selecting weapons that are likely to minimise the risks to civilians and civilian objects, and then using them in a manner that does so.

Section IV describes the strict nature of the duties to both refrain from deciding to launch a disproportionate attack and to cancel or suspend an attack that will violate the rules of distinction or of proportionality in attack. Section V summarises the duties of the defender to minimise the risk to civilians as set out in Article 58 of the 1977 Additional Protocol I. Lastly, section VI outlines the potential consequences of a violation of the duty to take precautions in attack.

II. The Primary Rules

The primary treaty rules governing the duty to take precautions in attack are set out in Article 57 of the 1977 Additional Protocol I. These treaty rules, which apply to international armed conflict (IAC), can be summarised as follows:

- In the conduct of military operations, constant care must be taken to spare the civilian population, civilians and civilian objects.[3]

[1] Protocol Additional to the Geneva Conventions of 12 August 1949, and relating to the Protection of Victims of International Armed Conflicts (Protocol I); adopted at Geneva, 8 June 1977; entry into force, 7 December 1978.

[2] Y Sandoz, C Swinarski, and B Zimmermann (eds), *Commentary on the Additional Protocols of 8 June 1977 to the Geneva Conventions of 12 August 1949* (Geneva, Martinus Nijhoff, 1987) (hereinafter 'ICRC Commentary on the 1977 Additional Protocols') para 2184.

[3] Art 57(1), 1977 Additional Protocol I.

- Those who plan or decide on an attack must do everything feasible to verify that the objectives to be attacked are military objectives that may lawfully be attacked.[4]
- Those who plan or decide on an attack must take all feasible precautions in the choice of means and methods of attack so as to avoid, or at least minimise, incidental civilian harm.[5]
- Those who plan or decide on an attack must refrain from deciding to launch any attack which may be expected to cause excessive incidental civilian harm compared to the concrete and direct military advantage anticipated.[6]
- An attack must be cancelled or suspended if it becomes apparent that the target is not a military objective or is subject to special protection, or that the attack may be expected to cause excessive incidental civilian harm.[7]
- Effective advance warning must be given of attacks that may affect the civilian population, unless circumstances do not permit.[8]
- When an attack that is likely to produce similar military advantage may target different military objectives in so doing, it should target the objective that may be expected to cause the least danger to civilian lives and civilian objects.[9]
- In the conduct of naval or aerial military operations, all reasonable precautions must be taken to avoid civilian deaths and damage to civilian objects.[10]

It is overt that Article 57 may not be construed as authorising any attacks against the civilian population, civilians or civilian objects.[11] According to the ICRC, the prescribed precautions 'will be of greatest importance in urban areas because such areas are most densely populated'.[12]

No corresponding obligations on precautions in attack are included in the 1977 Additional Protocol II, although they had been incorporated in the draft Protocol discussed at the 1977 diplomatic conference that would ultimately adopt the two Protocols. In the view of the ICRC, however, the duty to take precautions in attack is of a customary nature, which it articulates in the following manner:

> In the conduct of military operations, constant care must be taken to spare the civilian population, civilians and civilian objects. All feasible precautions must be taken to avoid, and in any event to minimize, incidental loss of civilian life, injury to civilians and damage to civilian objects.[13]

[4] Art 57(2)(a)(i), 1977 Additional Protocol I.
[5] Art 57(2)(a)(ii), 1977 Additional Protocol I.
[6] Art 57(2)(a)(iii), 1977 Additional Protocol I.
[7] Art 57(2)(b), 1977 Additional Protocol I.
[8] Art 57(2)(c), 1977 Additional Protocol I.
[9] Art 57(3), 1977 Additional Protocol I. The United States (US) has expressed the view that this rule is not a requirement of customary international law. See US Department of Defense, *Law of War Manual*, June 2015 (hereinafter 'USDOD 2015 *Law of War Manual*') para 5.11.5 and fn 303, at https://goo.gl/uZKhvk.
[10] Art 57(4), 1977 Additional Protocol I.
[11] Art 57(5), 1977 Additional Protocol I.
[12] ICRC Commentary on the 1977 Additional Protocols, para 2190.
[13] ICRC Study of Customary International Humanitarian Law (IHL), Rule 15 ('Precautions in Attack') at https://goo.gl/KjqGtr. The Eritrea-Ethiopia Claims Commission (EECC) similarly asserted that the rule set out in Art 57 is of a customary nature, although surprisingly it asserted that the rule articulated the 'basic requirement of proportionality'. EECC, *Partial Award: Western Front, Aerial Bombardment and Related Claims*, 19 December 2005, 348, para 9, at https://goo.gl/1UxzJS.

The ICRC further affirms that the customary duty applies in all armed conflict.[14] In 2012, in its judgment in the *Santo Domingo massacre* case, discussed further in section VI, the Inter-American Court of Human Rights (IACtHR) found a violation of human rights by applying the duty to take precautions to the non-international armed conflict (NIAC) between Colombia and the non-state armed group, the Colombian Revolutionary Armed Forces (FARC).[15] It cited the position of the ICRC on the status of the norm as authoritative.[16]

III. Feasible Precautions

This section details the precautionary measures that variously can, should and must be taken when a party to an armed conflict is planning an attack. As the ICRC has identified in its enunciation of the customary law rule, the underlying principle is the duty upon the attacker (which by virtue of the definition of attack, though, includes also the defender)[17] to take 'constant care' to spare the civilian population, civilians and civilian objects. The nature of this binding duty is articulated first in a series of measures subject to a standard of feasibility, and then in a set of obligations with which compliance is strictly required.

A. Efforts to Verify Attack is Targeting Military Objectives

Those who plan or decide upon an attack shall do 'everything feasible' to verify that the objectives to be attacked are neither civilians nor civilian objects; are not subject to special protection; and that it is not prohibited to attack them. This is both a factual and a legal demand, requiring that, in the case of an object, its nature and use be first established as well as any contribution to military action; while in the case of a person, his or her status, function and participation (if any) in the hostilities must similarly be determined.

The standard of 'feasibility' of action required of a party to an armed conflict is a relatively low one, considerably lower than 'all necessary measures', and one that is even substantively lower than 'all possible measures'. In declarations relating to Article 57 of the 1977 Additional Protocol I, several states followed Italy's lead in interpreting 'feasible' as meaning that which is 'practicable or practically possible, taking into account all circumstances ruling at the time, including humanitarian and military considerations'.[18] The US has expressed the view that feasible precautions are 'reasonable precautions, consistent with mission accomplishment and allowable risk to attacking forces'.[19] As the ICRC explains, 'What is required of the person launching an offensive is to take the necessary identification measures in good time in order to spare the population as far as possible.'[20]

[14] See ICRC Study of Customary IHL, Rule 15 ('Precautions in Attack').

[15] IACtHR, *Santo Domingo massacre v Colombia*, Judgment (Preliminary Objections, Merits and Reparations), 30 November 2012, esp paras 229–30.

[16] Ibid, para 216.

[17] These obligations thus complement those set out in Art 58 of 1977 Additional Protocol I.

[18] Statements of Understanding of Italy, 27 February 1986. The other states include Australia, Belgium, Canada, Egypt, Germany, The Netherlands and Spain.

[19] US Comments on the ICRC's Memorandum on the Applicability of International Humanitarian Law in the Gulf Region, 11 January 1991, in *Digest of United States Practice in International Law 1991–1999*, 2063.

[20] ICRC Commentary on the 1977 Additional Protocols, para 2198.

The task of decision-making falls especially to the 'commander', who must use the best information available to him or her at the time the decision to attack is made. But the ICRC's assertion that 'in case of doubt, even if there is only slight doubt', commanders 'must call for additional information and if need be give orders for further reconnaissance to those of their subordinates and those responsible for supportive weapons (particularly artillery and air force) whose business this is, and who are answerable to them'[21] overstates the requirements of the law. Naturally, as Rogers observes, no commander 'could ever be absolutely sure that an objective to be attacked was a military objective unless he inspected it himself which, of course, is quite impracticable'.[22] In the past, human spotters were sometimes used to direct fire accurately onto a military target. Today, this human intelligence can be supplemented by the use of remotely piloted aircraft to provide real-time surveillance.[23] At the same time, Dinstein cautions against the dangers of information overload, which, he asserts, 'is as grave as "seeing too little"'.[24]

While '[m]istakes based on faulty intelligence can be made',[25] there is an obligation of due diligence and a duty to act in good faith.[26] The well-known incident during the 1991 Gulf War, discussed already in chapter 4, in which a bunker in south-west Baghdad housing hundreds of civilians during the night was bombed by the US in the mistaken belief that it was a purely military objective, is instructive. As Solis notes, extensive reconnaissance had failed to discern that each night the wives and children of the Iraqi secret police sheltered from the US air raids in the basement of the bunker.[27] This was a clear failure of intelligence, but while tragic and avoidable – and possibly even negligent – it did not amount to a violation of Hague Law rules.

B. Avoiding Excessive Incidental Civilian Harm

Once it has been established, as far as practically possible in the prevailing circumstances, that the target is a lawful military objective, the rule of proportionality in attack must then be complied with. If there is a risk of civilian harm, measures that can reduce that risk include the appropriate timing of an attack, warning the civilian population of an impending attack, and careful selection of the means and methods of warfare to be used.

i. Timing of an Attack

The timing of an attack may be crucial in determining the extent of civilian harm that results, although it is not specifically cited as a precautionary measure in Article 57 of the 1977 Additional Protocol I. For instance, had it been known that the bunker in Al Amariyah

[21] Ibid, para 2195.

[22] APV Rogers, *Law on the Battlefield*, 2nd edn (Manchester, Manchester University Press, 2004) 97.

[23] Y Dinstein, *The Conduct of Hostilities under the Law of International Armed Conflict*, 3rd edn (Cambridge, Cambridge University Press, 2016) 166, para 445.

[24] Ibid, 166, para 444.

[25] Rogers (n 22) 97.

[26] Dinstein (n 23) 165, para 442.

[27] GD Solis, *The Law of Armed Conflict: International Humanitarian Law in War*, 2nd edn (New York, Cambridge University Press, 2016) 275.

was being used as an air-raid shelter at night, a day-time attack could have been considered. In contrast, targeting a school building that is firmly believed to contain weapons would logically be safer for the civilian population, especially the children, if conducted at night.[28]

Whether or not the same is true for a munitions factory could depend on whether the factory is working 24 hours a day, seven days a week – a distinct possibility during an armed conflict. Nonetheless, as the ICRC recalls, Allied bombardments during the Second World War against factories located in territories occupied by German forces were carried out 'on days or at times when the factories were empty; the desired effect was to destroy the factories without killing the workers'.[29]

With respect to the 2014 Gaza conflict, the United Nations (UN) Commission of Inquiry stated that

> many of the attacks took place in the evening as families gathered for *iftar*, the Ramadan meal to break the fast, during the night when people were asleep; or in the early morning during *suhhur*, the last meal before dawn, which increased the likelihood that many persons, often entire families, were at home. If the target was an individual, it can be questioned whether the individual could not have been targeted at another time or location.[30]

There may of course be increased danger to the attacker arising, for example, from a daylight bombing raid. If the rule of proportionality is not breached, it is not a Hague Law requirement that significant additional risk be accepted by the attacker's forces. The notion of 'constant care' does not impose an additional duty of care over and above the requirement to do 'everything feasible' and to take 'all feasible precautions', where so doing would further endanger the attacking forces.

Waiting for the right moment to attack may also be a longer-term endeavour than a simple 'day or night' calculation. For instance, the US Department of Defense observes that 'it may be appropriate to wait until enemy forces have departed from populated areas before attacking such forces in order to reduce the risk of civilian casualties'.[31] It cites the example from the 1991 Gulf War wherein the decision was taken not to attack Iraqi forces in Kuwait City even though the concentration of military personnel and vehicles, including tanks, 'invited attack'. The reasons were that such attacks 'could lead to substantial collateral damage to Kuwaiti civilian property and could cause surviving Iraqi units to decide to mount a defense from Kuwait City rather than depart'.[32] There was also the fear that Iraqi units remaining in Kuwait City

> would cause the Coalition to engage in military operations in urban terrain, a form of fighting that is costly to attacker, defender, innocent civilians, and civilian objects. The decision was made to permit Iraqi forces to leave Kuwait City and engage them in the unpopulated area to the north.[33]

[28] The US Department of Defense recalls that during Operation Desert Storm, attacks on known dual-use facilities were normally scheduled at night, 'because fewer people would be inside or on the streets outside'. US Department of Defense, *Law of War Manual*, June 2015, Updated December 2016 (hereinafter 'USDOD December 2016 *Law of War Manual*') para 5.11.3, fn 352, at https://goo.gl/QMkjqs.

[29] ICRC Commentary on the 1977 Additional Protocols, para 2200.

[30] *Report of the detailed findings of the independent commission of inquiry established pursuant to Human Rights Council resolution S-21/1*, UN Doc A/HRC/29/CRP.4, 22 June 2015 (hereinafter 'UN Commission of Inquiry on the 2014 Gaza Conflict') para 232.

[31] USDOD December 2016 *Law of War Manual*, para 5.11.3.

[32] Ibid, fn 353.

[33] Ibid.

ii. Warnings

Effective advance warning must be given of attacks which may affect the civilian population, *unless circumstances do not permit*. The notion of warnings has a long pedigree: already in the 1907 Hague Regulations it was stipulated that 'The officer in command of an attacking force must, before commencing a bombardment, except in cases of assault, do all in his power to warn the authorities.'[34]

Warnings may, though, allow an enemy to escape or to better prepare his defences, bringing with them a measure of danger for the attacker. Rogers cites an instructive example from the First World War, described by Michael Walzer in *Just and Unjust Wars*.[35] In a village that soldiers were in the process of taking, it was known that civilians were using some of the cellars in buildings as sanctuary from the firefights above. In one case, two soldiers shouted down towards the cellar and, receiving no response, were about to pull the pins out of their hand grenades when a young civilian woman came up the stairs. She had initially been too fearful to respond to the warnings shouts. Walzer points to the risk the soldiers had knowingly run, as had enemy soldiers been lurking in the cellar they could have rushed up the stairs, firing as they came.

In the 2014 Gaza conflict, on numerous occasions the Israel Defence Forces (IDF) used a controversial warning technique known as 'roof knocking'. This typically involved use of a low-yield or even non-explosive munition, which was dropped on the roof of a building with a view to warning the inhabitants that a major strike against the building was imminent. In some instances, this was accompanied by text or phone warnings to the inhabitants.

Israel believes that the procedure used by the IDF was 'highly effective, preventing many civilian injuries and deaths during the 2014 Gaza Conflict'.[36] The UN Commission of Inquiry on the conflict, while noting in its report that four buildings were totally destroyed in the latter days of hostilities using this procedure without consequent loss of life,[37] expressed considerable concern in relation to a number of other attacks. The Commission stated that sometimes the warnings were not understood; that the direction of safety for escaping civilians was often unclear; or the time given for evacuation between the warning and the actual strike was insufficient.[38]

Based on its findings, the Commission concluded that the 'roof-knocking' technique was not 'effective' – as the law requires – 'in particular if not combined with other specific warnings'.[39] The judgment of the Commission may, though, have been too harsh in this regard. Lives and limbs were undoubtedly spared by this technique, and while it was not universally effective, it is rare for a party to an armed conflict to provide such warnings. Moreover, there may also be a process of learning for the civilian population during

[34] Art 26, Regulations concerning the Laws and Customs of War on Land annexed to Convention (IV) respecting the Laws and Customs of War on Land; adopted at The Hague, 18 October 1907; entry into force, 26 January 1910 (hereinafter '1907 Hague Regulations').

[35] Rogers (n 22) 101, citing M Walzer, *Just and Unjust Wars*, 2nd edn (New York, Basic Books, 1992) 152.

[36] Israeli Ministry of Foreign Affairs, *IDF Conduct of Operations during the 2014 Gaza Conflict*, 37, at https://goo.gl/wZ3TXy.

[37] UN Commission of Inquiry on the 2014 Gaza Conflict, paras 210–11.

[38] Ibid, paras 235–38.

[39] Ibid, para 239.

an armed conflict. The fact that the four buildings were totally destroyed towards the end of the conflict without civilian loss of life might be adduced as evidence to support this assertion.

In April 2016, it was reported by the Reuters news agency that the US had used an adapted version of the technique in a bombing operation in the Iraqi city of Mosul earlier in the month.[40] Air Force Major-General Peter Gersten, Deputy Commander for Operations and Intelligence for the US-led coalition, said the airstrike targeted a building that housed a member of Islamic State in charge of distributing money to fighters, as well as being a cash storage site. Intelligence and reconnaissance aircraft tracking the site had made the US forces aware that a woman and children also frequented the house. Major-General Gersten stated that the US had fired a Hellfire missile 'so it wouldn't destroy the building, simply knocked on the roof to ensure that she and the children were out of the building'. Unfortunately, the woman ran back into the building after the weapon had been fired. General Gersten said this was 'very difficult for us to watch and it was within the final seconds of the actual impact'.[41] The extent to which the tactic has since been used in the course of air strikes in Iraq and Syria is not known.

iii. Selection of Means and Methods of Warfare

Those who plan or decide upon an attack must take all feasible precautions in the choice of means and methods of attack to seek to avoid, but at least to minimise, incidental civilian harm. With respect to the means of warfare, there are two broad issues to consider: the accuracy of a munition and its explosive yield (or other hazardous effects). Corresponding methods of warfare that can reduce the risk to civilians include planning the angle of attack[42] to direct much of the consequent blast and fragmentation away from civilians and civilian objects. Arguably, the timing of an attack, addressed in section II.B.i, may also be considered a relevant method of warfare.

a. A Duty to Use Precision-Guided Munitions?

Hague Law does not generally require a party to armed conflict to use any precision-guided munitions (PGM) it may possess in the conduct of hostilities.[43] However, if an attack might otherwise be expected to cause excessive civilian harm, for example if it does not successfully hit the intended target, using such munitions may be the only lawful means to achieve the military mission without violating the law.[44] The advantage for the attacker of using PGM is that fewer assets are likely to be required to be in play to destroy or significantly damage a military objective. This means fewer pilots are put at direct risk, or at least fewer aircraft need to be used (if the attack is to be conducted through a remotely piloted aircraft).

[40] Y Torbati and I Ali, 'US military used "roof knock" tactic in Iraq to try to warn civilians before bombing', *Reuters*, Washington, DC (26 April 2016) at https://goo.gl/IaWlav.

[41] Ibid.

[42] Dinstein (n 23) 164, para 441.

[43] USDOD December 2016 *Law of War Manual*, para 5.2.3.2, citing also the military manuals of Australia, Canada and Germany; see also Dinstein (n 23) 170, para 454; Solis (n 27) 294.

[44] Dinstein (n 23) 167, para 447; and 169, para 453.

In its 2015 *Law of War Manual*, the US Department of Defense agreed that, 'under certain circumstances, it may be advantageous to use … precision-guided munitions to minimize the risk of incidental harm'.[45] Controversially, however, it also argues that use of cluster munitions may similarly minimise the risk to civilians. In justifying this statement it refers to work by Hays Parks about the aerial bombing of North Vietnam during the Vietnam War. Hays Parks cites a specific attack in which anti-personnel cluster munitions were used, among other weapons, to hit 'AAA [Anti-aircraft Artillery] gun positions, ground-controlled intercept … radar, and surface-to-air missile (SAM) sites atop or adjacent to dikes'.[46] In fact, instances are likely to be very few in number in which cluster munitions reduce, rather than significantly enhance, the risk of civilian harm.

b. A Duty to Use Low-Explosive-Yield Munitions?

There is, correspondingly, no general *legal* duty on a party to armed conflict to use low-explosive-yield munitions.[47] As Solis describes, using a B-52 bomber's load of 2,000lb bombs to kill a solitary sniper in a remote and isolated desert hiding spot would be a gross waste of munitions, but it would not, per se, violate Hague Law rules.[48] The situation changes markedly, though, when civilians may be expected to be exposed to the effects of an attack. Again, the advantages of employing PGM can be readily appreciated. In addition to achieving greater accuracy of strike, such munitions often contain a smaller explosive charge than do 'their unguided counterparts',[49] reducing the risk of incidental civilian harm.

Dinstein remarks that the choice of means of warfare should lead an attacker to 'shun "overkill" effects that may be lethal to civilians'.[50] An example of good practice he proffers is of the use of a cyber-attack to neutralise enemy air force defence systems in heavily populated areas.[51] Similarly, a cyber-attack that renders an electrical generating station inoperable is likely to result in significantly less civilian harm than a 'comparable kinetic attack from an aerial bomber'.[52]

IV. Refraining from Deciding to Launch an Indiscriminate Attack

As Green notes, the duty to abandon or suspend a planned attack if it becomes apparent that the attack is not targeting a military objective or that excessive civilian harm may be

[45] USDOD 2015 *Law of War Manual*, para 5.11.3.

[46] Ibid and fn 297.

[47] Thus, the ICRC is correct when it affirms that 'When a well-placed 500 kg projectile is sufficient to render a military objective useless, there is no reason to use a 10 ton bomb or a series of projectiles aimed without sufficient precision.' ICRC Commentary on the 1977 Additional Protocols, para 2200. But this does not mean that using a 10-ton bomb is a *violation* of the duty to take precautions.

[48] Solis (n 27) 296.

[49] MN Schmitt, 'Asymmetrical Warfare and International Humanitarian Law' in W Heintschel von Heinegg and V Epping (eds), *International Humanitarian Law Facing New Challenges: Symposium in Honour of Knut Ipsen* (Berlin, Springer, 2007) 42.

[50] Dinstein (n 23) 164, para 441.

[51] Ibid.

[52] Ibid, citing M Gervais, 'Cyber Attacks and the Laws of War' (2012) 30 *Berkeley Journal of International Law* 570.

expected to result means that the commander 'must always ensure that his intelligence is up to date'.[53] This duty underpins, respectively, the rule of distinction set out in Article 48 of the 1977 Additional Protocol I (requiring each party to an IAC to direct its operations only against military objectives) and the rule of proportionality codified in Article 51(5)(b), which determines that an indiscriminate attack includes one which may be expected to cause excessive incidental civilian harm compared to the concrete and direct military advantage anticipated. Of course, it is always open to the party to identify another target that does constitute a lawful military objective, and to take additional precautions that will ensure the attack is no longer expected to inflict disproportionate civilian harm.

The ICRC claims that it is

> principally by visual means – in particular, by means of aerial observation – that an attacker will find out that an intended objective is not a military objective, or that it is an object entitled to special protection. Thus, to take a simple example, an airman who has received the order to machine-gun troops travelling along a road, and who finds only children going to school, must abstain from attack. However, with the increased range of weapons, particularly in military operations on land, it may happen that the attacker has no direct view of the objective, either because it is very far away, or because the attack takes place at night. In this case, even greater caution is required.[54]

V. The Duties of the Defender

By virtue of Article 58 of the 1977 Additional Protocol I, parties to an armed conflict are required, though only 'to the maximum extent feasible', to 'endeavour to remove the civilian population, individual civilians and civilian objects under their control from the vicinity of military objectives and to avoid locating military objectives within or near densely populated areas'.[55] According to the ICRC:

> As regards civilian objects, it seems clear that moveable objects should be removed whenever possible away from military objectives; thus a food depot intended for the civilian population should not be placed next to a fortified position or other defensive installations. However, the circumstances of war can change very rapidly and a building or installation which does not seem to be of any military interest can quickly become a major military objective.[56]

More vaguely, the parties are further required by Article 58 to 'take the other necessary precautions to protect the civilian population, individual civilians and civilian objects under their control against the dangers resulting from military operations'.[57] The ICRC explains that as regards persons, a party to armed conflict can make available shelters that provide adequate protection to the civilian population against the effects of weapons:

> In some countries real efforts are made to supply the population with such shelters, both collectively and individually, the latter when every dwelling includes a shelter for the occupants.

[53] LC Green, *The Contemporary Law of Armed Conflict*, 3rd edn (Manchester, Manchester University Press, 2008) 182, fn 228.
[54] ICRC Commentary on the 1977 Additional Protocols, para 2221.
[55] Art 58(a) and (b), 1977 Additional Protocol I.
[56] ICRC Commentary on the 1977 Additional Protocols, para 2249.
[57] Art 58(c), 1977 Additional Protocol I.

> The organization of well-trained civil defence services, adequately equipped, can also alleviate the fate of the civilian population.[58]

With respect to civilian objects, 'the presence of well-trained civil defence services will serve to limit damage, for example, through effective fire-fighting'.[59]

In his appeal against conviction for war crimes in the attack on Zagreb in May 1995, Milan Martić alleged that the failure of Croatia to take precautions against the effects of attacks according to Article 58 of Additional Protocol I led directly to the loss of civilian life. The Appeals Chamber however, 'squarely reject[ed] this argument'.[60] Without entering into an assessment of whether Croatia had failed to take the necessary precautions, it stated simply that one party to an armed conflict cannot 'claim that its obligations are diminished or non-existent just because the other side does not respect all its obligations'.[61]

VI. Consequences of a Violation

While a failure to comply strictly with the duty to take precautions in attack does not formally render the attack an indiscriminate one, the definition of the corresponding war crime of a disproportionate attack indicates the relevance of the provision. Thus, as discussed in chapter 6, Article 85(3)(b) of the 1977 Additional Protocol I stipulates that launching an indiscriminate attack inflicting civilian harm in the knowledge that such attack will cause excessive loss of life, injury to civilians or damage to civilian objects, as defined in Article 57(2)(a)(iii), is a grave breach of the Protocol entailing compulsory universal jurisdiction.

The ancillary nature of the duty to take precautions is reflected in (albeit limited) international criminal law jurisprudence. In the *Galić* case, the Prosecution urged the Trial Chamber of the International Criminal Tribunal for the former Yugoslavia (ICTY), in seeking to establish whether the rule of proportionality in attack had been violated, 'to consider whether the precautionary provisions contained in Article 57 of Additional Protocol I were complied with'.[62] In response, the Defence referred to the obligations of the parties to an armed conflict to undertake the precautionary measures against the effects of attacks in order to protect civilians in their own territory.[63]

The Trial Chamber held that the 'practical application of the principle of distinction requires that those who plan or launch an attack take all feasible precautions to verify that the objectives attacked are neither civilians nor civilian objects, so as to spare civilians as much as possible'.[64] Thus, in relation to an attack that killed and injured players and supporters at a football match in Sarajevo, discussed in chapter 6, the Trial Chamber stated that, 'Had the SRK [Bosnian Serb] forces launched two shells into a residential neighbourhood

[58] ICRC Commentary on the 1977 Additional Protocols, para 2257.
[59] Ibid, para 2258.
[60] ICTY, *Prosecutor v Milan Martić*, Judgment (Trial Chamber) (Case No IT-95-11), 12 June 2007, para 170.
[61] Ibid.
[62] ICTY, *Prosecutor v Galić*, Judgment (Trial Chamber I), 5 December 2003, para 37.
[63] Ibid, para 40.
[64] Ibid, para 58.

at random, without taking feasible precautions to verify the target of the attack, they would have unlawfully shelled a civilian area.'[65] Here the Court was equating the hypothetical failure to take feasible precautions with an indiscriminate attack.

A failure to take all feasible precautions in attack may also ground a claim of a human rights violation. The *Santo Domingo massacre* case concerned the dropping by the Colombian Air Force of a Second World War-era cluster bomb containing six explosive submunitions on the hamlet of Santo Domingo on 13 December 1998. The attack killed 17 civilians, including four boys and two girls, and injured 27 others (including five girls and four boys). To its great discredit, Colombia sought to attribute the deaths to a bomb placed by FARC guerrillas. The IACtHR said that given the lethal capacity and limited precision of the device used, its launch over the hamlet was contrary to the duty of precautions in attack.[66] Based in particular on this finding, the Court found a violation of the right to life of those who were killed and a violation of the prohibition on inhumane treatment of the injured.[67]

[65] Ibid, para 387.

[66] IACtHR, *Santo Domingo massacre v Colombia*, Judgment (Preliminary Objections, Merits and Reparations), 30 November 2012, para 229.

[67] Ibid, para 230.

8

The Superfluous Injury Rule

I. Introduction

The 'superfluous injury' rule (to give it a convenient shorthand name) was first enunciated in a binding law of armed conflict treaty in the Regulations annexed to 1899 Hague Convention II.[1] There it is stipulated that 'it is especially prohibited … [t]o employ arms, projectiles, or material of a nature to cause superfluous injury'.[2] The language of the rule was derived from Article 13(e) of the abortive 1874 Brussels Declaration,[3] but found its inspiration in the earlier Lieber Code of 1863, which instructed the Union forces that '[w]hoever intentionally inflicts additional wounds on an enemy already wholly disabled, or kills such an enemy, or who orders or encourages soldiers to do so, shall suffer death, if duly convicted'.[4] The underpinnings of the superfluous injury rule can also be seen clearly reflected in the following preambular paragraphs of the 1868 St Petersburg Declaration:

> That the only legitimate object which States should endeavour to accomplish during war is to weaken the military forces of the enemy;
>
> That for this purpose it is sufficient to disable the greatest possible number of men;
>
> That this object would be exceeded by the employment of arms which uselessly aggravate the sufferings of disabled men, or render their death inevitable;
>
> That the employment of such arms would, therefore, be contrary to the laws of humanity.[5]

It is thus important to bear in mind, despite occasional suggestion to the contrary, that the superfluous injury rule seeks to protect *combatants*, not civilians (unless they are participating directly in hostilities). Civilians are protected by the rules of distinction and proportionality in attack, amongst others. The superfluous injury rule is seeking to restrict the pain and suffering that may lawfully be inflicted on those who are fighting, while they are fighting. In so doing, the rule is exceptional in the law of armed conflict.

As is the case with the rules of distinction and proportionality in attack, while no one doubts the existence or normative import of the superfluous injury rule, there all

[1] Regulations concerning the Laws and Customs of War on Land annexed to Convention (II) with Respect to the Laws and Customs of War on Land; adopted at The Hague, 29 July 1899; entry into force, 4 September 1900 (hereinafter '1899 Hague Regulations').

[2] Art 23(e), 1899 Hague Regulations.

[3] Project of an International Declaration concerning the Laws and Customs of War; adopted at Brussels, 27 August 1874.

[4] Art 71, Instructions for the Government of Armies of the United States in the Field, General Order No 100 (hereinafter '1863 Lieber Code'), promulgated by the War Department on 24 April 1863.

[5] Declaration Renouncing the Use, in Time of War, of Explosive Projectiles Under 400 Grammes Weight, adopted at St Petersburg, 11 December 1868; entry into force the same day. We should note, though, that this

agreement largely ceases. Precisely which means and methods of warfare are of a nature to cause superfluous injury or unnecessary suffering finds no consensus among states in their practice or doctrine, nor between commentators. It is a core principle of Hague Law, but one that operates without a clear and accepted understanding of how it should be interpreted and applied.

Section II of this chapter sets out the primary rule and assesses its normative status. Section III discusses how the rule is, or should be, applied in practice, looking especially at the types of weapons that are said to have fallen foul of the prohibition. Section IV looks at the extent to which a serious violation of the superfluous injury rule during the conduct of hostilities is criminalised as a war crime.

II. The Primary Rule

Although the classic expression of the rule is perhaps best articulated in Article 35(2) of the 1977 Additional Protocol I,[6] according to the International Committee of the Red Cross (ICRC), the superfluous injury rule is expressed simply in customary law as follows: 'The use of means and methods of warfare which are of a nature to cause superfluous injury or unnecessary suffering is prohibited.'[7]

States accept that the superfluous injury rule – a core law of armed conflict concept in the words of Gary Solis[8] – is binding on them. The United Kingdom (UK) *Manual of the Law of Armed Conflict*, for example, states that it is a *guiding principle* of the regulation of weapons during the conduct of hostilities that 'It is prohibited to employ weapons, projectiles and material and methods of warfare of a nature to cause superfluous injury or unnecessary suffering.'[9] France similarly endorses the prohibition on use of means and methods of warfare with such effects in its national military manual.[10] According to Germany's Ministry of Defence, the St Petersburg Declaration 'codified the customary principle that the use of weapons that cause unnecessary suffering is prohibited, which is still valid today'.[11]

was unacceptable to some at the time. As Lawrence Freedman recalls, Von Moltke, for instance, wrote that in 'no way' could he agree with the St Petersburg Declaration whereby the only justifiable measure was the 'weakening of the enemy's military power'. He believed rather that 'all the sources of support for the hostile government must be considered, its finances, railroads, foodstuffs, even its prestige'. H Moltke, Letter to Johann Kasper Bluntschi 'On the Nature of War', 11 December 1880; see L Freedman, *The Future of War: A History* (London, Allen Lane, 2017) 39.

[6] 'It is prohibited to employ weapons, projectiles and material and methods of warfare of a nature to cause superfluous injury or unnecessary suffering.'

[7] ICRC Study of Customary IHL, Rule 70 ('Weapons of a Nature to Cause Superfluous Injury or Unnecessary Suffering') at https://goo.gl/BdhGYj.

[8] GD Solis, *The Law of Armed Conflict: International Humanitarian Law in War*, 2nd edn (New York, Cambridge University Press, 2016) 289.

[9] UK Ministry of Defence, *The Manual of the Law of Armed Conflict* (Oxford, Oxford University Press, 2005) para 6.1.

[10] French Ministry of Defence, *Manuel de Droit des Conflits Armés* (2012) 44 and 65.

[11] German Ministry of Defence, *Law of Armed Conflict Manual*, Joint Service Regulation (ZDv) 15/2 (2013) para 119 and see also para 401.

The customary rule, the ICRC asserts, applies to all parties in any armed conflict. It was most recently incorporated in the body of the 1998 Statute of the International Criminal Court (the ICC Statute), wherein an individual is liable to prosecution for the war crime of 'employing weapons, projectiles and material and methods of warfare which are of a nature to cause superfluous injury or unnecessary suffering'.[12] This only applies, though, in an international armed conflict (IAC), and in any event is dependent on a specific means or method of warfare being included in an annex to the Statute (which had yet to occur as of the time of writing).[13]

Earlier in the 1990s, in their submissions to the International Court of Justice (ICJ) in the context of the Nuclear Weapons Advisory Opinion, several states referred to the superfluous injury rule. In its Advisory Opinion, the Court affirmed that the prohibition of means and methods of warfare of a nature to cause superfluous injury or unnecessary suffering was one of the 'cardinal principles' of international humanitarian law (ie Hague Law).[14] The Advisory Opinion did not, though, address the tenets of Hague Law during a situation of non-international armed conflict (NIAC).

The generalised application of the rule in all armed conflict seems, though, to be uncontroversial. For instance, at the end of April 2012, in his speech to the Woodrow Wilson Center on 'The Ethics and Efficacy of the President's Counterterrorism Strategy', John O Brennan, then Assistant to the United States (US) President for Homeland Security and Counterterrorism, stated that 'targeted strikes conform to the principle of humanity which requires us to use weapons that will not inflict unnecessary suffering'.[15] As most of the (drone) strikes that have occurred in the conduct of hostilities have been in the context of a NIAC, one can safely assume that the US accepts that the superfluous injury rule applies as a matter of custom in all armed conflict.

There is some residual controversy as to the proper formulation of the rule. The US Department of Defense confines the prohibition to 'weapons that are *calculated* to cause superfluous injury'.[16] In so doing, it mistranslates the authentic French text ('*propres à causer*'), as translators did in the 1907 Hague Regulations, by encompassing a notion of intent that is not in the original text. Such intent, which might belong to the realm of international criminal law (see section IV), is out of place in the construction of the primary rule.

[12] Art 8(2)(b)(xx), ICC Statute.

[13] According to Art 8(2)(b)(xx), the jurisdiction of the Court is limited to 'such weapons, projectiles and material and methods of warfare [that] are the subject of a comprehensive prohibition and are included in an annex to th[e] Statute, by an amendment in accordance with the relevant provisions set forth in articles 121 and 123'.

[14] ICJ, *Legality of the Threat or Use of Nuclear Weapons*, Advisory Opinion, 8 July 1996 ('ICJ Nuclear Weapons Advisory Opinion') para 78. In a strange limitation of Hague Law rules, in its 1996 Nuclear Weapons Advisory Opinion, the ICJ reiterated justly that states 'do not have unlimited freedom of choice of means in the weapons they use', but – incorrectly – limited the principle to the superfluous injury rule. See ibid. In fact, the principle would equally apply to inherently indiscriminate weapons.

[15] Speech by John O Brennan, Assistant to the President for Homeland Security and Counterterrorism, 'The Ethics and Efficacy of the President's Counterterrorism Strategy', Woodrow Wilson Center, Washington, DC (30 April 2012) at https://goo.gl/XhYgjJ.

[16] US Department of Defense, *Law of War Manual*, June 2015, Updated December 2016 (hereinafter 'USDOD December 2016 *Law of War Manual*') para 2.3.2.2, at https://goo.gl/QMkjqs. As noted in section IV of this chapter, the Statute of the International Criminal Tribunal for the former Yugoslavia (ICTY) similarly used the formulation 'calculated', although that choice is perhaps more forgivable owing to the international criminal law context, where intent is an integral element of a successful prosecution.

The French phrase sets an objective standard, best translated as 'having the characteristic of [inflicting]' or 'of a nature to [inflict]', rather than as importing a subjective notion of an 'evil genius' weapons designer.[17]

III. The Application of the Rule

The rule is cast in English as 'superfluous injury or unnecessary suffering', with a view to accurately reflecting the broad scope of the authentic French original term, '*maux superflus*'. 'Injury' describes identifiable wounds or other physical harm to limbs, organs, senses or other parts of the body, including through burns. Injuries may thus inflict temporary incapacitation on a person, or may comport permanent disability, such as blindness or loss of hearing, or a soldier may become a single, double, triple or even quadruple amputee. In contrast, 'suffering' denotes primarily pain,[18] but also extends to comprehend severe psychological distress.[19] Amputees who suffered traumatic amputation during combat routinely describe the loss of a limb as especially devastating from a psychological point of view.[20]

In its Nuclear Weapons Advisory Opinion, the ICJ defined unnecessary suffering as 'harm greater than that unavoidable to achieve legitimate military objectives'.[21] The US Department of Defense believes the test is 'whether the suffering caused by the weapon provides no military advantage or is otherwise clearly disproportionate to the advantage reasonably expected from the use of the weapon'.[22] The UK Ministry of Defence provides that 'The correct criterion is whether the use of a weapon is of a nature to cause injury or suffering greater than that required for its military purpose.'[23] For Germany, means and methods of warfare cause superfluous injury or unnecessary suffering 'if the expected impairment does not serve any military purpose or if injuries or suffering are caused by the effects of weapons or projectiles that are not necessary to neutralise the adversary forces'.[24] While there are differences in the expression of the test, what is clear is that, as with proportionality, there is a balancing between the military advantage sought through

[17] Hays Parks' argument is thus flawed that 'calculated to cause unnecessary suffering' is 'a clearer expression of the intent of governments to focus on design and intended purpose rather than every remote possibility of weapon injury', first and foremost because of the French language issue; and second, since 'of a nature to' simply does not imply that every remote possibility of weapon injury falls within the scope of the rule. If it were so, the formulation would more logically be 'could be used to cause unnecessary suffering'. See Hays Parks, 'Conventional Weapons and Weapons Reviews' (2005) 8 *Yearbook of International Humanitarian Law* 87.

[18] Second-degree burns, for example, can be excruciating, and further pain is caused when the wounds are cleansed and the dressings changed.

[19] See, eg, Y Dinstein, *The Conduct of Hostilities under the Law of International Armed Conflict*, 3rd edn (Cambridge, Cambridge University Press, 2016) 74.

[20] See, eg, V Bhatnagar, E Richard, T Melcer, J Walker and M Galarneau, 'Lower-limb amputation and effect of posttraumatic stress disorder on Department of Veterans Affairs outpatient cost trends' (2015) 52:7 *Journal of Rehabilitation Research and Development* 827, at https://goo.gl/Mg4Ut4; N Breslau, 'The epidemiology of posttraumatic stress disorder: what is the extent of the problem?' (2001) 62 *Journal of Clinical Psychiatry* 16.

[21] 1996 Nuclear Weapons Advisory Opinion (n 14) para 78.

[22] USDOD December 2016 *Law of War Manual*, para 6.6.3.

[23] UK Ministry of Defence (n 9) para 6.2.

[24] German Ministry of Defence (n 11) para 402.

the use of a weapon or tactic and the typical humanitarian effects. As Bill Boothby has observed, 'both adjectives, "unnecessary" and "superfluous", are comparative, not absolute, concepts'.[25]

The UK thus argues that, in applying the rule to a set of facts with a view to determining the legality of use of a specific weapon, it is necessary to assess the weapon's effects in battle and the military task it is required to perform, and to then compare these two elements.[26] For as the US has recalled, weapons 'that may cause great injury or suffering or inevitable death are not prohibited, if the weapon's effects that cause such injury are necessary to enable users to accomplish their military missions'.[27]

The corollary of this is that once a combatant is effectively rendered *hors de combat*, there is no military need to uselessly aggravate the wounds, or for the wounds inflicted to be of such a nature as to render death inevitable. During the Vietnam War, for example, punji sticks were employed by the Vietcong using a sharpened piece of bamboo. After hardening by fire, bamboo will maintain an extremely sharp point for a considerable period of time. When placed in lightly covered holes or pits they can inflict very serious injuries on their victims who fall onto the bamboo points. To increase their wounding potential, however, the points were often smeared with poison or excreta, making infection and even death far more likely. This is a clear instance of additional injury that was superfluous to the military need.

This understanding chimes with the position of the US Department of Defense, which states in the December 2016 version of its *Law of War Manual* that 'Weapons that have been modified for the purpose of aggravating the harm inflicted upon incapacitated persons are weapons that are prohibited by the superfluous injury rule.' It cites the preamble to the St Petersburg Declaration as evidence for this assertion. The *Manual* goes on:

> For example, adding poison to bullets or other substances to weapons for the purpose of increasing the pain caused by the wound, to make wounds more difficult to treat, or to make death inevitable, would be prohibited. Such a substance would not increase the military utility of the weapon to incapacitate the enemy (ie, it would have no corresponding military advantage); thus, the additional injury would be superfluous when compared to the injury caused by the weapon without such a substance.[28]

A. The US Department of Defense Approach

In its 2015 *Law of War Manual*, the US Department of Defense set out in considerably more detail than many other states its approach to determining whether a weapon or method of warfare is captured – and thus its use rendered unlawful – by the superfluous injury rule. Its approach is valuable and bears repeating. First of all, it is necessary to note that in determining a weapon's legality, 'the weapon's planned uses and the normal circumstances

[25] W Boothby, *Weapons and the Law of Armed Conflict*, 1st edn (Oxford, Oxford University Press, 2009) 62.
[26] UK Ministry of Defence (n 9) para 6.2.1.
[27] USDOD December 2016 *Law of War Manual*, para 6.6.3.
[28] Ibid, para 6.6.4.

in which it would be used should be considered'. This conforms to the notion of the inherent capabilities of the weapon being paramount in the assessment. As the US notes, it is 'not necessary to assess all possible uses or all possible circumstances'.[29]

The legitimate military necessity that may be considered in assessing the legality of a weapon includes its capability to disable or incapacitate enemy combatants, including, for example:

- the probability of striking a person against whom the weapon is aimed or directed
- the probability that a person who is struck by the weapon will be incapacitated
- the speed at which a person who is struck by the weapon will be incapacitated, and
- the number of persons the weapon could strike.[30]

However, as the US observes, a weapon's military utility is often broader than its capacity to disable enemy combatants. This may extend to other factors, such as the:

- destruction or neutralisation of military *matériel*
- restriction of military movement
- interdiction of military lines of communication
- effects on the morale, command and control, stamina and cohesion of opposing forces
- weakening of the enemy's war-making resources and capabilities
- enhancement of the security of forces employing the weapon or other friendly forces
- effectiveness of the weapon against particular types of targets
- availability of alternative weapons and their effects
- logistics of providing the weapon and its ammunition where and when it is needed
- amount of ammunition required
- the cost of using the weapon in terms of time, money and other resources
- efficacy of the weapon compared to the adversary's defences
- efficacy of the weapon in light of the weapons and tactics of the adversary, and the
- risk to the civilian population when the weapon is used for its intended purposes.[31]

These other factors, the US posits, can justify weapons that inflict injuries on enemy combatants that are much greater than the minimum needed to render them *hors de combat*:

> For example, an artillery shell designed to destroy field fortifications or heavy material causes injuries to enemy personnel that are much greater than those necessary to make enemy combatants *hors de combat*. However, the artillery shell is not prohibited because these military advantages are not clearly disproportionate to the injuries it inflicts.[32]

The humanitarian effects of the weapon must also be carefully studied. The types of harm addressed by the superfluous injury rule include, in the view of the US Department

[29] US Department of Defense, *Law of War Manual*, June 2015 (hereinafter 'USDOD 2015 Law of War Manual'), para 6.6.3.4, at https://goo.gl/uZKhvk.

[30] Ibid, para 6.6.3.1.

[31] Ibid.

[32] Ibid.

of Defense, 'mortality rates, the painfulness of wounds, the severity of wounds, and the ease with which they may be treated (including the incidence of permanent damage or disfigurement)'.[33] However, the US believes that only where these harms are 'clearly or manifestly disproportionate' to the military necessity is a weapon's use outlawed by the superfluous injury rule.[34] This is a narrow understanding of the rule, more akin to a formulation of the actus reus of the corresponding war crime.

B. The ICRC's SIrUS Project

In the 1990s, the ICRC embarked on an ambitious and ultimately ill-fated project[35] entitled SIrUS (an acronym for Superfluous Injury or Unnecessary Suffering). The aim was to elucidate criteria that could be applied to any weapon to make a clear, evidence-based determination whether or not it was lawful under the superfluous injury rule. The ICRC, and a panel of experts it convened to support the initiative, identified four criteria by which a weapon's legality could be determined. The criteria, which were to be applied to the design-dependent, foreseeable effects of weapons when used against human beings, were as follows:

- Specific disease, specific abnormal physiological state, specific abnormal psychological state, specific and permanent disability or specific disfigurement (Criterion 1), or
- Field mortality of more than 25 per cent or a hospital mortality of more than 5 per cent (Criterion 2), or
- Grade 3 wounds as measured by the Red Cross wound classification (Criterion 3), or
- Effects for which there is no well recognised and proven treatment (Criterion 4).[36]

Criterion 1 would apply to a weapon designed to disorientate, confuse, induce calm, or precipitate seizures or psychosis causing a known neuroendocrine response to an agent or energy form, but without the infliction of physical injury (which would represent a specific normal physiological response). It would also encompass weapons whose method of wounding would predictably demand a blood transfusion. The implications of the need for blood transfusion are particularly important given that, without a reliable and safe blood bank (which is difficult to establish in a war zone), there is a risk of transfusing blood that has not been cross-matched or tested for communicable diseases such as syphilis, hepatitis B and HIV.[37]

[33] Ibid, para 6.6.3.2.

[34] Ibid.

[35] As the US Library of Congress notes, 'Criticism of this well-intentioned, but flawed methodology – which ignored consideration, for example, of military necessity – was raised at the ICRC Meeting of Experts on the SIrUS Project in Geneva, May 10–11, 1999. Growing opposition at the XXVIIth International Conference of the Red Cross and Red Crescent Movement – held from October 31 to November 6, 1999 – led to the ICRC announcing the withdrawal of the project at the Expert Meeting on Legal Reviews of Weapons and the SIrUS Project, Jongny-sur-Vevey, January 29–30, 2001.' US Library of Congress, 'The SIrUS Project: Towards a determination of which weapons cause "superfluous injury or unnecessary suffering"', 16 July 2010, at https://goo.gl/jy4Z2C.

[36] *The SIrUS Project: Towards a determination of which weapons cause 'superfluous injury or unnecessary suffering'* (Geneva, ICRC, 1997) 23, at https://goo.gl/VQ9Eoo.

[37] Ibid, 23–24.

With respect to Criterion 2, the ICRC argued that the use of weapons whose design renders death inevitable is already prohibited as part of the same legal concept that prohibits those causing superfluous injury or unnecessary suffering. According to the ICRC, the figures of 25 per cent and 5 per cent for field and hospital mortality, respectively, were proposed 'as limits which are on the conservative side of the established baseline'.[38]

Criterion 3 applies to weapons which, without targeting a particular part of the body, simply inflict large wounds, such as is the case for exploding and expanding bullets.[39] Grade 3 wounds under the Red Cross classification denote skin wounds of 10 cm or more with a cavity.[40]

Criterion 4 (effects for which no well recognised and proven treatment exists) is closely linked to Criterion 1. This would apply, for instance, to blindness for, as the ICRC specifically observed, 'for laser-damaged retina there is no known successful treatment even in the best facilities'.[41]

Falling foul of any criterion, the ICRC argued, would mean that the weapon in question was indeed of a nature to cause superfluous injury or unnecessary suffering. Therein lay the critical flaw, since the ICRC approach neglected the military necessity element of the equation, a fact the US and others were not slow to point out. For instance, in an article subtly entitled 'Just Say No! The SIrUS Project: Well-Intentioned, But Unnecessary and Superfluous', Major Donna Marie Verchio of the US Air Force attacked the ICRC for the mere fact of having initiated the project.[42] While a little poorly expressed and reasoned in parts (for instance, the author states that it is the responsibility 'of sovereign nations, *not non-governmental organizations (NGOs), such as the United Nations (UN)*, to determine whether a weapon causes unnecessary suffering or superfluous injury'),[43] the article did draw attention to the absence of the balancing element. It is regrettable that in its haste to apply the hatchet to the ICRC's work, the US failed to appreciate the benefits to states of such a set of systematic and carefully-reasoned criteria. The project could have been usefully recalibrated rather than binned.

C. Application of the Rule to Specific Means and Methods of Warfare

The application of the superfluous injury rule to specific weapons is, as one would expect, highly contested. For instance, as discussed in this section, it is not settled whether to kill or seriously injure combatants by deliberately burning them in the open (using napalm or a flamethrower), to deliberately blind them (using a laser) or to kill them slowly through the irremediable effects of radiation (using a nuclear weapon) is a violation *per se* of the customary rule. The ICRC has asserted that use of the following is unlawful under the rule:

- explosive bullets and projectiles filled with glass
- bullets which easily expand or flatten in the human body

[38] Ibid, 24.

[39] Ibid.

[40] Ibid, 15. Grade 1 denotes skin wounds of less than 10 cm without a cavity, while Grade 2 denotes skin wounds of less than 10 cm but with a cavity.

[41] Ibid, 25.

[42] Major DM Verchio, 'Just Say No! The SIrUS Project: Well-Intentioned, But Unnecessary and Superfluous' (2001) 51 *Air Force Law Review* 183.

[43] Ibid, 183 (emphasis added).

- poison and poisoned weapons, as well as any substance intended to aggravate a wound[44]
- asphyxiating or deleterious gases, and
- bayonets with a serrated edge and lances with barbed heads.[45]

i. Expanding Ammunition

Of this list, perhaps the most controversial is bullets that easily expand or flatten in the human body. According to the ICRC, 'there is general agreement that … [expanding] bullets would cause unnecessary suffering'.[46] Expanding bullets typically deposit greater kinetic energy when entering the body, inflicting graver wounds than is the case with their full-metal-jacketed counterparts.

Expanding ammunition is defined under the law of armed conflict as 'bullets which expand or flatten easily in the human body, such as bullets with a hard envelope which does not entirely cover the core or is pierced with incisions'.[47] Such bullets, use of which was prohibited as a means of warfare in IAC by the 1899 Hague Declaration IV,3,[48] are generally agreed to include hollow-point and soft-point rounds. More controversial are open-tip-match rounds, which have a small aperture in the nose. This is the result of the manufacturing process, which sees the core poured in through the aperture, and is ostensibly with a view to improving the bullet's accuracy as they were originally developed for match competition. Nonetheless, these bullets, which have been used by US Marines in Afghanistan, clearly fit the international legal definition. The US Department of Defense has noted that 'The US armed forces have used expanding bullets in various counterterrorism and hostage rescue operations, some of which have been conducted in the context of armed conflict'.[49]

The strength of the Hague Law prohibition is, though, evidenced by the fact that the use of expanding bullets as a means of warfare is individually criminalised under international criminal law, as well as in numerous domestic criminal law jurisdictions. Reflecting the text of the 1899 Declaration, the ICC Statute gave the Court possible jurisdiction over the war

[44] This applies to the punji sticks referred to at the beginning of section III.

[45] Y Sandoz, C Swinarski and B Zimmermann (eds), *Commentary on the Additional Protocols of 8 June 1977 to the Geneva Conventions of 12 August 1949* (Geneva, Martinus Nijhoff, 1987) (hereinafter 'ICRC Commentary on the 1977 Additional Protocols') para 1419.

[46] ICRC Study of Customary International Humanitarian Law (IHL), Rule 77 ('Expanding Bullets'), at https://goo.gl/aKsvJ2.

[47] In the French original and authentic version of the Declaration, the text reads as follows: 'Les Puissances contractantes s'interdisent l'emploi de balles qui s'épanouissent ou s'aplatissent facilement dans le corps humain, telles que les balles à enveloppe dure dont l'enveloppe ne couvrirait pas entièrement le noyau ou serait pourvue d'incisions.'

[48] Declaration (IV,3) concerning Expanding Bullets; adopted at The Hague, 29 July 1899; entry into force, 4 September 1900. Thirty-three states were party to the Declaration as at 1 April 2018, including the UK, with the most recent adherent being Ukraine. The states parties are the following: Austria, Belarus, Belgium, Bulgaria, China, Denmark, Ethiopia, Fiji, France, Germany, Greece, Hungary, Iran, Italy, Japan, Luxembourg, Mexico, Montenegro, the Netherlands, Nicaragua, Norway, Portugal, Romania, the Russian Federation, Serbia, South Africa, Spain, Sweden, Switzerland, Thailand, Turkey, Ukraine and the UK. Previously, the most recent ratification had been by South Africa, in 1978. See https://goo.gl/JdSKJo. Significantly, however, the US is not a state party and it does not accept that the prohibition in the Declaration is binding upon it through custom. USDOD December 2016 *Law of War Manual*, para 6.5.4.4.

[49] USDOD December 2016 *Law of War Manual*, para 6.5.4.4.

crime, in IAC, of '[e]mploying bullets which expand or flatten easily in the human body, such as bullets with a hard envelope which does not entirely cover the core or is pierced with incisions'.[50] An amendment to the ICC Statute adopted by states parties in 2010 extends the court's jurisdiction to cover use of expanding bullets in NIACs for those states that ratify the amendment.[51] The amendment had been ratified by 36 states as at 1 April 2018.[52]

The challenge to the rule is that, increasingly, law enforcement agencies around the world are using expanding bullets, especially with a view to reducing the risk of over-penetration through the body of the intended target, because the bullet might then strike and potentially kill an unintended bystander.[53] Within Western Europe, for instance, expanding bullets are used more or less routinely by police forces in many states, including Austria, Belgium, Denmark, Finland, France, Germany, the Netherlands, Spain, Sweden, Switzerland and the UK.[54] In June 2014, Norway announced plans to equip its police forces with expanding ammunition.[55]

Thus, it is lawful for a state's police force to use expanding ammunition against its own citizens under strict law of law enforcement rules, but a war crime to do so when firing on an enemy in the conduct of hostilities. This is the case even where the realities of urban warfare mean that over-penetration may result in the unnecessary death or serious injury of civilians. Controversially, Vincent Di Maio, an expert in wound ballistics, argued in his capacity as forensic pathologist that he had not seen someone killed by hollow-point rounds who would have survived had the bullet been fully metal jacketed.[56]

In its study of customary international humanitarian law published in 2005, the ICRC wrongly asserted that in general only handguns – using expanding ammunition – are used for law enforcement tasks:

> [E]xpanding bullets commonly used by police in situations other than armed conflict are fired from a pistol and therefore deposit much less energy than a normal rifle bullet or a rifle bullet which expands or flattens easily. Police forces therefore do not normally use the type of expanding bullet that is prohibited for military rifles.[57]

[50] Art 8(2)(b)(xix), ICC Statute.

[51] Art 8(2)(e)(xv), ICC Statute.

[52] Andorra, Austria, Belgium, Botswana, Chile, Costa Rica, Croatia, Cyprus, the Czech Republic, El Salvador, Estonia, Finland, Germany, Georgia, Latvia, Liechtenstein, Lithuania, Luxembourg, the former Yugoslav Republic of Macedonia, Malta, Mauritius, the Netherlands, Norway, Palestine, Panama, Poland, Portugal, Samoa, San Marino, Slovakia, Slovenia, Spain, Switzerland, Trinidad and Tobago, and Uruguay. Updated list available at the United Nations (UN) Treaty Section website.

[53] It is also argued that expanding ammunition reduces the risk of ricochet, but only limited evidence is publicly available to support this assertion.

[54] In South Africa, it is not permitted for law enforcement officials to use expanding bullets, but private citizens may purchase them for self-defence. Oscar Pistorius killed Reeva Steenkamp using Ranger T series expanding bullets manufactured by Winchester, which had produced the controversial Black Talon rounds on which they were based. S Wiley, 'Black Talon and Today's Best Self-Defense Ammo', *Ammunition* (website) (12 October 2014) at https://goo.gl/J6EoxM; P Ross, 'What Are Expanding Bullets? "Dum-Dums" Used by Oscar Pistorius to Shoot Reeva Steenkamp Cause More Damage than Regular Bullets', *International Business Times* (11 March 2014) at https://goo.gl/LzXj4n.

[55] 'Police seek to use expanding bullets', *NewsinEnglish.no* (5 June 2014) at https://goo.gl/r7Exuh. This followed the terror attacks of 22 July 2011 for which Anders Behring Breivik himself reportedly used expanding ammunition during the shootings on Utøya island in which he murdered 68 people.

[56] VJM Di Maio, *Gunshot Wounds: Practical Aspects of Firearms, Ballistics, and Forensic Techniques* (Boca Raton, FL, CRC Press, 1985) 309–11, 'Appendix A: Hollow-Point Pistol Ammunition, Myths and Facts'.

[57] ICRC Study of Customary IHL, Rule 77 ('Expanding Bullets').

This is clearly factually incorrect.[58] It is also a dangerous assertion to make from the standpoint of Hague Law, as it could be taken to suggest that the prohibition on expanding bullets does not somehow extend to handgun ammunition.

For some time, I have argued that the prohibition on expanding ammunition, as it stands, is no longer fit for purpose. The original motivation for the prohibition was humanitarian and is applauded as such. But the situation today is very different to the end of the nineteenth century in terms of rifle ammunition, and many bullets that routinely fragment within the body causing terrible wounds are not remotely captured by the specific prohibition, whereas ammunition that is used by law enforcement to protect the public is criminalised during warfare. The status of the prohibition, and of rifle ammunition more broadly, is ripe for review.

ii. Shotguns

The ICRC has claimed that the use of hunting shotguns is 'the object of some controversy, depending on the nature of the ammunition and its effect on a soft target.'[59] In 1979, the US army regulation, *Review of Legality of Weapons under International Law*, addressed the use of the combat shotgun, noting that it raised two issues with regard to legality:

> First, does a weapon capable of inflicting multiple wounds upon a single enemy combatant cause superfluous injury … Second, does the No 00 buckshot projectile … expand or flatten easily, in violation of the Hague Declaration Concerning Expanding Bullets of 29 July 1899?[60]

Solis notes that the *Review* concluded that neither the shotgun nor the double-nought ammunition violated the superfluous injury rule (or the prohibition on use of expanding ammunition).[61]

iii. Mines

The issue of landmines has been discussed in chapter 1, but rather under the notion of discrimination and the rule of distinction in attack. In 1997, a leading ICRC surgeon argued that buried blast anti-personnel mines would have been outlawed under the superfluous injury rule (had the ICRC's four criteria been generally accepted):

> Buried or 'point-detonating' anti-personnel mines are the only weapons in widespread use which cause specific and severe injury resulting in specific and permanent disability. The treatment of the injury requires, on average, twice as many operations and four times as many blood transfusions as an injury from other weapons. This is a surgeon's view.[62]

The ICRC did not pursue the issue of whether the use of buried blast anti-personnel mines did indeed violate the superfluous injury rule. In its study of customary international

[58] Authorised firearms officers in the Metropolitan Police Service, for example are often equipped with Heckler & Koch G36 or SiG Sauer SG516 or MCX carbines, which fire soft-point 5.56 mm rounds. Similar situations exist in other European law enforcement jurisdictions.

[59] ICRC Commentary on the 1977 Additional Protocols, para 1419.

[60] *Review of Legality of Weapons under International Law*, US Army Regulation 27-53, 1 January 1979; see Solis (n 8) 291.

[61] Solis (n 8) 291.

[62] R Coupland and P Herby, 'Review of the Legality of Weapons: a New Approach, The SIrUS Project', *International Review of the Red Cross*, vol 81, no 835 (1999) 583.

humanitarian law, the organisation duly noted that negotiating states that adopted the 1997 Anti-Personnel Mine Ban Convention included a preambular provision in which they stated that they were basing themselves, in part, on the superfluous injury rule. This is, of course, scarcely robust evidence that the point is generally accepted among states.

iv. Blinding Laser Weapons

According to Article 1 of the 1995 Protocol IV to the Convention on Certain Conventional Weapons (CCW),

> It is prohibited to employ laser weapons specifically designed, as their sole combat function or as one of their combat functions, to cause permanent blindness to unenhanced vision, that is to the naked eye or to the eye with corrective eyesight devices.

The ICRC suggests that this prohibition is derived from the superfluous injury rule.[63]

Donna Verchio, though, expressed the view in her 2001 article that deliberate blinding of a combatant may be lawful. Solis appears to agree with this stance, without making it explicit,[64] while the US Department of Defense asserts that 'it would not be prohibited for a soldier to use a non-prohibited laser system to blind an enemy combatant to save the user's life'.[65] It is clear that laser target designator systems are not captured by the Protocol IV prohibition – indeed Article 3 makes it explicit that blinding 'as an incidental or collateral effect of the legitimate military employment of laser systems, including laser systems used against optical equipment, is not covered by the prohibition'. Dinstein, however, argues that since the temporary flash blinding of enemy personnel would be sufficient for military purposes (the US has employed so-called 'dazzling' lasers at checkpoints in certain theatres of combat), the intentional permanent deprivation of vision amounts to unnecessary suffering.[66]

v. Flamethrowers

During the negotiation of the CCW, several states called for a total prohibition on the use of incendiary weapons, particularly napalm, following the horrific injuries suffered by many civilians during indiscriminate US attacks in the Vietnam War. These calls were ultimately rejected in favour of an agreement to prohibit direct attacks on civilians or attacks that would be expected to have incidental effects that would be disproportionate compared to the expected military advantage.[67] But as the ICRC observed in the late 1980s:

> It is worth noting that none of the rules explicitly protects combatants from incendiary weapons such as flame-throwers or napalm. However, it is generally admitted that these weapons should

[63] ICRC Study of Customary IHL, Rule 70 ('Weapons of a Nature to Cause Superfluous Injury or Unnecessary Suffering') at https://goo.gl/KncHLB, citing statement of Sweden and military manual of France; see also Rule 86: 'Blinding Laser Weapons' at https://goo.gl/8A8XQn.

[64] See Solis (n 8) 744–45.

[65] USDOD 2015 *Law of War Manual*, para 6.15.2.1. In December 2017, states parties to the ICC Statute added the war crime in both IAC and NIAC of 'Employing laser weapons specifically designed, as their sole combat function or as one of their combat functions, to cause permanent blindness to unenhanced vision, that is to the naked eye or to the eye with corrective eyesight devices'.

[66] Dinstein (n 19) 90.

[67] Art 2, Protocol III on Incendiary Weapons to the CCW.

> not be used in such a way that they will cause unnecessary suffering … which means that in particular they should not be used against individuals without cover.[68]

In its study of customary international humanitarian law published in 2005, the ICRC discerned a rule whereby the 'anti-personnel use of incendiary weapons is prohibited, unless it is not feasible to use a less harmful weapon to render a person hors de combat'. The ICRC explained that 'very few reports of use of napalm and similar incendiary weapons against combatants' have occurred since the adoption of the CCW: 'What reports there are, have been in the form of accusations condemning their use and are unconfirmed.'[69] It concluded from this practice that incendiary weapons 'may not be used against combatants if such use would cause unnecessary suffering, ie, if it is feasible to use a less harmful weapon to render a combatant hors de combat'. It further asserted that it was 'reasonable to conclude that the rule is applicable in non-international armed conflicts'.[70]

Solis gently rubbishes the position of the ICRC, arguing that 'Individual napalm or flame-thrower targets will be killed, cover or no cover, but that does not constitute unnecessary suffering.'[71] Dinstein observes that some weapons, such as napalm, 'play an essential role in attacks against solid (inanimate) military targets, yet have frightful consequences for flesh-and-blood combatants caught in them'.[72] He further notes that four of the five peace treaties that ended the First World War enunciated a prohibition on the use of flame-throwers, but that state practice in the Second World War showed their value against pillboxes and similar structures.[73]

vi. Nuclear Weapons

Nuclear weapons are the most powerful explosive devices yet invented by mankind. Temperatures of a nuclear explosion reach those in the interior of the sun and produce a brilliant fireball.[74] In addition to the tremendous heat that results from nuclear fusion or fission, huge doses of radioactive material are typically diffused by a nuclear weapon detonation:

> The release of radiation is a phenomenon unique to nuclear explosions. There are several kinds of radiation emitted; these types include gamma, neutron, and ionizing radiation, and are emitted not only at the time of detonation (initial radiation) but also for long periods of time afterward (residual radiation).[75]

The effects of radiation on the body are prodromal, hematologic, gastrointestinal, pulmonary, cutaneous and neurovascular in nature.[76] According to the Mayor of Nagasaki, 'All people exposed to large doses of radiation generated during the one-minute period

[68] ICRC Commentary on the 1977 Additional Protocols, para 1424.

[69] ICRC Study of Customary IHL, Rule 85 ('The Use of Incendiary Weapons against Combatants') at https://goo.gl/mvrSHR.

[70] Ibid.

[71] Solis (n 8) 291.

[72] Dinstein (n 19) 90.

[73] Ibid, 88.

[74] 'Thermal Radiation' at https://goo.gl/KPqQeq.

[75] 'Nuclear Radiation', at: https://goo.gl/8FjGHr.

[76] Fun Fong MD et al, 'In-Depth Medical Management for Nuclear/Radiological/Conventional Terrorism Agents', PowerPoint Presentation, undated but accessed on 11 December 2017, at https://goo.gl/qcDWKG.

after the Nagasaki atomic bomb explosion died within two weeks.'[77] It has been reported that leukaemia appears two or three years after an atomic bombing and that the incidence declines after reaching a peak six or seven years after the bombing. Cancer is said to appear after a latency of more than 10 years and then to increase in frequency over time.[78]

In reporting on its SIrUS project, the ICRC noted *en passant* that three of its four criteria (1, 2 and 4) would apply to nuclear weapons, notably the extent and severity of burns and the prevalence of radiation sickness.[79] O'Connor further argues that when the superfluous injury rule is applied to nuclear weapons, 'the obligation to consider, and choose, alternative means of warfare if the foreseen suffering is disproportionate to its military effectiveness, arguably renders the actual option to use nuclear weapons very slim'.[80]

Michael Matheson, in reviewing the ICJ's 1996 Nuclear Weapons Advisory Opinion, referred to the argument by some that 'any uses' of nuclear weapons would violate the superfluous injury rule, 'because of the extreme thermal and radiation effects of nuclear weapons'.[81] He noted that while the Court did not find all use of nuclear weapons illegal under the law of armed conflict, 'it did indicate that it had serious concerns because of the severe effects of nuclear weapons'.[82] Solis, after citing from Matheson, concludes that the 'moral questions attending the use, or threat of use, of nuclear weapons may be beyond the scope of the law of armed conflict, or any law'.[83]

IV. Violation of the Rule under International Criminal Law

A serious violation of the superfluous injury rule may amount to a war crime when the actus reus of the crime is committed with the requisite mens rea. Arguably, it will be necessary to prove that the accused was aware both of the factual elements concerning the cruelty of the means or methods of warfare he or she employed and of the likelihood that these would cause injury or suffering substantially beyond what was militarily necessary in the prevailing circumstances. There is scant relevant jurisprudence to assess in this regard.

A. Under the Hague Conventions

The 1899 and 1907 Hague Regulations did not provide for the criminalisation of their provisions. This includes the prohibition on 'employ[ing] arms, projectiles, or material of a nature to cause unnecessary suffering', included in the 1899 Hague Regulations

[77] Statement of the Mayor of Nagasaki to the International Court of Justice, 7 November 1995, 36.

[78] Fun Fong et al (n 76).

[79] R Coupland (ed), *The SIrUS Project: Towards a Determination of which Weapons Cause 'Superfluous Injury or Unnecessary Suffering'* (Geneva, ICRC, 1997), 26.

[80] S O'Connor, 'Nuclear weapons and the unnecessary suffering rule' in G Nystuen et al (eds), *Nuclear Weapons under International Law* (Cambridge, Cambridge University Press, 2014) 128, at 144.

[81] MJ Matheson, 'The Opinion of the International Court of Justice on the Threat or Use of Nuclear Weapons' (1997) 91:3 *AJIL* 417, 428–29.

[82] Ibid, 429.

[83] Solis (n 8) 317.

and then in amended form eight years later. Nonetheless, these treaties served as the basis for the prosecution of German war criminals in the Nuremburg and other trials that followed the end of the First World War, and the provision may be considered to be reflective of at least the actus reus of international crimes.

B. Under 1977 Additional Protocol I

Article 35(2) of the 1977 Additional Protocol I provides that 'It is prohibited to employ weapons, projectiles and material and methods of warfare of a nature to cause superfluous injury or unnecessary suffering.' This, together with the prohibition in the Hague Regulations, served as the basis for the potential inclusion of the crime in the ICC Statute (see section IV.D). Violation of the provision in the Additional Protocol is not, though, made a grave breach of the Protocol.

C. Under Customary International Law

The ICRC gives relatively scant consideration to the war crime of using means or methods of warfare that are of a nature to cause superfluous injury or unnecessary suffering. Under the rubric of 'Using prohibited weapons', it affirms that the crime certainly exists the case in an IAC. With respect to NIACs, it merely provides:

> As most States define a 'war crime' as being a 'violation' or a 'serious violation' of international humanitarian law, it is reasonable to conclude that they would consider the use of prohibited weapons in non-international armed conflicts to fall within this category.[84]

The position of the International Criminal Tribunal for the former Yugoslavia (ICTY) is perhaps less equivocal in its assertion that a serious violation of prohibitions on certain means and methods of warfare (without enumerating them) applied equally to NIACs.[85]

D. Under the 1998 Statute of the International Criminal Court

The ICC Statute accords the Court potential jurisdiction over individuals belonging to a party to an IAC who 'employ weapons, projectiles and material and methods of warfare which are of a nature to cause superfluous injury or unnecessary suffering'.[86] The Court's jurisdiction is, however, limited to 'such weapons, projectiles and material and methods of

[84] ICRC, Customary IHL Study, Rule 156 ('Definitions of War Crimes') at https://goo.gl/gTGYSQ.

[85] ICTY, *Prosecutor v Tadić*, Decision on the defence motion for interlocutory appeal on jurisdiction (Appeals Chamber) (Case No IT-94-1), 2 October 1995, para 127. Certain states criminalise the rule as a war crime in their domestic legislation. Such is the case with the Philippines, for example, in its 'Philippine Act on Crimes Against International Humanitarian Law, Genocide, and Other Crimes Against Humanity', ch III, s 4(c)(25)(iv): 'Weapons, projectiles and material and methods of warfare which are of the nature to cause superfluous injury or unnecessary suffering or which are inherently indiscriminate in violation of the international law of armed conflict.'

[86] Art 8(2)(b)(xx), ICC Statute.

warfare [that] are the subject of a comprehensive prohibition and are included in an annex to th[e] Statute, by an amendment in accordance with the relevant provisions set forth in articles 121 and 123'. To date, no such weapons, projectiles, material or methods of warfare have been so included.[87]

E. In the Jurisprudence of the Ad Hoc International Criminal Tribunals

Article 3 of the Statute of the ICTY included as one of the violations of the laws and customs of war within its jurisdiction the employment of weapons 'calculated to cause unnecessary suffering'. This is, as has been argued, an incorrect formulation of the primary rule, though as Dinstein points out, '[t]he reversion to the term "calculated" – concentrating on intention – makes more sense … when penal proceedings are instigated'.[88] No prosecution of this crime took place before the ICTY.[89]

[87] Accordingly, in the Elements of Crimes it is stipulated that for the requisite war crime, the 'Elements will have to be drafted once weapons, projectiles or material or methods of warfare have been included in an annex to the Statute.' ICC, 'Elements of crimes', UN Doc PCNICC/2000/1/Add.2 (2000), 27.

[88] Dinstein (n 19) 76.

[89] O'Connor (n 80) 135.

9

Warfare on Land

I. Introduction

Warfare on land dates back to the dawn of human civilisation. We do not know exactly when the first 'war'[1] erupted between rival groups of humans, nor what motivated the hostilities, though it may have been scarcity of food or arable land. The first war in recorded history is said to have taken place in Mesopotamia in 2700 BCE between Sumer and Elam; the Sumerians defeated the Elamites and, it is recorded, 'carried away as spoils the weapons of Elam'.[2] But this is certainly not the first true war. Archaeologists believe that a fortified city stood on the site of Jericho, perhaps the world's oldest city, before 7000 BCE, where

> [s]urviving arrowheads indicate that as well as being experienced and skilled in engineering and fortification, these people had developed the bow and arrow. To have made such large-scale military preparations they must have had powerful enemies to fear.[3]

The first clash whose details have come down to us with some measure of reliability is the Battle of Megiddo in the fifteenth century BCE. Combat between Egyptian forces under the command of Pharaoh Thutmose III and a coalition of Canaanite vassal states led by the king of Kadesh resulted in the Canaanites fleeing the battlefield and taking refuge in the city walls of Megiddo. This prompted a seven-month siege by the victorious Egyptian forces, at the issue of which the remaining forces surrendered. Remarkably, it is recorded that the city and the lives of its citizens were spared.[4] It is somewhat ironic, therefore, that the city's name bequeaths to us the word *Armageddon*. Some historians believe that Egypt's victory in this conflict was the foundation of its empire.

A. The Particularities of Land Warfare

While warfare for most of human history has persisted firmly on land (and occasionally at sea), increasingly hostilities occur from the air. It is likely that cyberspace and possibly even outer space will be key battlegrounds in the future. Nonetheless, the continuing importance

[1] According to Joshua Mark, the word *war* came into English from the old High German word 'Werran' (meaning to confuse or to cause confusion). JJ Mark, 'War: Definition', *Ancient History Encyclopedia* (2 September 2009) at https://goo.gl/YXd8A8.

[2] Ibid.

[3] Field-Marshal Viscount Montgomery of Alamein, *A History of Warfare* (London, Book Club Associates, 1982) 29.

[4] EH Cline, *The Battles of Armageddon: Megiddo and the Jezreel Valley from the Bronze Age to the Nuclear Age* (Ann Arbor, MI, University of Michigan Press, 2002).

of land or 'ground' warfare may not be overstated, for this is still where men and women live and die for the most part, and this is likely to remain the case for generations to come. As Colin Gray reminds us, 'For 3,000 years, organised society has been defined by values derived from territorial consciousness, making land the principal geographical medium on which conflict occurs.'[5]

Land warfare typically involves destroying or defeating enemy forces or taking objectives on land that reduce the enemy's effectiveness or will to fight. Four characteristics are said to distinguish combat on land: scope, terrain, duration and permanence.[6]

- *Scope.* Land combat involves contact with an enemy throughout an operational area, with forces conducting simultaneous and sequential operations in contiguous and non-contiguous terrain. Commanders manoeuvre their forces to seize and retain key and decisive territory and to defeat enemy forces. Land combat normally entails close and continuous contact with civilians.
- *Duration.* Land combat is repetitive and continuous. It is conducted with a view to rendering an enemy incapable or unwilling to conduct further action.
- *Terrain.* Land combat takes place among a complex variety of natural and man-made features. The complexity of the ground environment contrasts starkly with the relative transparency of air, sea and space. Plans for land combat must account for the visibility and clutter of the terrain and the effects of weather and climate.
- *Permanence.* Land combat frequently requires seizing or securing ground. With control of the territory comes control of populations and productive capacity. Thus, land combat makes permanent the temporary effects of other operations.

As Gray notes, modern battlespace is often more complex and more decentralised than in the past. This imposes greater responsibility on ever more junior commanders to make tactical decisions that may have strategic repercussions: 'The phenomenon of the "strategic corporal" is likely to become highly significant in future land operations.'[7] Such commanders will be legally responsible for their own decisions, as well as for the unlawful actions of their subordinates (unless they could not reasonably have foreseen and prevented them).

B. The Content of the Chapter

The remainder of this chapter is divided into two main sections, one addressing the means of warfare on land, the other concerning certain methods of land warfare. Means of warfare given particular consideration are the assault rifle and associated ammunition; artillery; tanks; mines; improvised explosive devices; and (ground-launched) cluster munitions. Methods of warfare addressed include the denial of quarter, perfidy and sieges (including the starvation of the civilian population).

The rules of distinction and proportionality in attack and the prohibition of using means and methods of warfare of a nature to cause superfluous injury or unnecessary suffering

[5] CS Gray, 'The Nature of Land Warfare' at https://goo.gl/Z1XiRj, 1.
[6] 'Land Power', *Global Security*, at https://goo.gl/ry9ayd.
[7] Gray (n 5) 5.

apply to all defensive and offensive land warfare operations, as supplemented and underpinned by the duties on attacker and defender to take all feasible precautions to protect the civilian population.

II. Means of Warfare

Land warfare is typically prosecuted by means of a wide array of weapons, especially artillery, and often with naval or air support. As the United States (US) military strategist Rear Admiral JC Wylie noted in 1967, however, 'the ultimate determinant in war is the man on the scene with the gun'.[8] This is especially the case in urban warfare, where greater firepower may be as dangerous to the attacker as it is to the defender.

A. Assault Rifles

Assault rifles – that is, selective-fire rifles with an effective range typically of the order of 300–600 metres and whose ammunition is fed from a detachable magazine – were developed by the Germans in the Second World War. They swiftly became the soldier's primary weapon in land warfare. In addition to killing or injuring the enemy, they also provide covering fire for one's own troop movements.

There is no North Atlantic Treaty Organization (NATO) standard for assault rifles as there is for the ammunition they fire. The US service rifle is the FN Herstal M4A1, a fully automatic carbine upgraded from the M4.[9] Russia's service rifle is still the AK-74M, developed in the early 1970s by Russian designer Mikhail Kalashnikov, which fires 5.45 x 39 mm rounds (though more inaccurately than equivalent NATO rifles).[10] China uses a range of assault rifles, including the QBZ-95, which uses 5.8 x 42 mm ammunition developed by China. It is claimed to have greater penetration than the standard NATO 5.56 x 45 mm round.[11] Its rate of fire is 650 rounds per minute, with 800 rounds per minute for the carbine version. France still uses the FAMAS, designed and manufactured by MAS in St Etienne, which has a rate of fire of some 1,000 rounds per minute,[12] although it is replacing the

[8] Rear Admiral JC Wylie, *Military Strategy: A General Theory of Power Control* (Annapolis, MD, Naval Institute Press, 1967) 72; see Gray (n 5) 1.

[9] FN America, 'M4A1' at https://goo.gl/bTm2t3. The M4A1 will need to improve on its predecessor's reputation for needing constant maintenance and being highly susceptible to jamming when sand or dirt gets into the firing mechanism.

[10] The AK-74M retains the advantages of the earlier Kalashnikov rifles, including reliability of fire, ruggedness, simplicity of operation and ease of maintenance. Its drawbacks are said to be poor balance and ergonomics, as well as inferior accuracy in comparison to most Western assault rifles. See 'AK-74: Assault rifle' at https://goo.gl/TrzxbN. In 2015, it was reported that improvised upgrades were expected to improve significantly the accuracy of the weapon. 'Russian Improvised AK-74M To Be 50 Per Cent More Accurate' (7 May 2015) at https://goo.gl/xA6Dtw.

[11] 'PLA Type 95 Rifle: Breaking with Convention', *Small Arms Defense Journal* (21 October 2013) at https://goo.gl/jErfGH.

[12] See, eg, H Hutchison, 'French Firepower: The FAMAS Rifle', *The Daily Caller* (29 December 2015) at https://goo.gl/jv4SBy.

weapon with the more powerful Heckler & Koch HK416 assault rifle.[13] The United Kingdom (UK) military uses the SA-80 (despite continuing grumbles about its reliability).[14] Typical rates of fire are about 1,300 rounds per minute.

There is, of course, no general prohibition on the use of fully automatic fire in the conduct of hostilities as there is during law enforcement operations. In a crowded urban area, however, fully automatic fire may be indiscriminate.

i. Jurisprudence

In the International Criminal Tribunal for the former Yugoslavia (ICTY), General Galić was charged, inter alia, with responsibility for attacks on civilians as a violation of the laws or customs of war as a result of his command of Bosnian Serb forces from September 1992 to August 1994 during the siege of Sarajevo.[15] Evidence for the charges included the 'sniping' of civilians resulting in their death or injury. The Prosecution defined the term 'sniping' as 'fire from a small calibre weapon, such as a rifle or machine-gun, from a concealed, or partially concealed, position'.[16] The Defence's objection that this definition was too broad and that 'sniping' should be limited to fire from 'a special rifle with optical sight'[17] was rejected by the ICTY Trial Chamber, which noted that the common understanding of sniping concerned the direct targeting of an individual or object, 'a special rifle not being a necessary part of the definition'.[18] It applied a definition of sniping that encompassed direct targeting of individuals at a distance using any type of small calibre weapon.[19]

The Prosecution alleged that

> for forty-four months, the [Bosnian Serb] Sarajevo Romanija Corps [SRK] implemented a military strategy which used shelling and sniping to kill, maim, wound and terrorise the civilian inhabitants of Sarajevo. The shelling and sniping killed and wounded thousands of civilians of both sexes and all ages, including children and the elderly.[20]

Two streets in Sarajevo – Zmaja od Bosne Street and especially Meša Selimović Boulevard – were nicknamed 'Sniper Alley' during the conflict.[21] In its evaluation of the evidence, the Trial Chamber assessed whether a 'scheduled' incident was 'beyond reasonable doubt representative of the alleged campaign of sniping and shelling or whether it is reasonable to believe that the victim was hit by ABiH [Bosniak] forces, by a stray bullet, or taken for a combatant'.[22] Such alternative circumstances would not have constituted unlawful action by the Bosnian Serb forces and thus would have obviated legal responsibility.

[13] N de Larrinaga, 'French Army selects HK416 to replace FAMAS', *IHS Jane's Defence Weekly* (30 September 2016) at https://goo.gl/zp7RF4.

[14] For one commentator's history of the problems, see 'SA80 (Small Arms for the 1980s): The Sorry Saga of the British Bulldog's Bullpup', *Historyofwar.org* at https://goo.gl/EPjGe.

[15] ICTY, *Prosecutor v Galić*, Judgment (Trial Chamber) (Case No IT-98-29-T), 5 December 2003.

[16] Prosecution Pre-Trial Brief, fn 3.

[17] Defence Final Trial Brief, para 11; and Acquittal Motion, para 11.

[18] *Galić* (n 15) para 183.

[19] Ibid, para 184.

[20] Indictment, para 4(a).

[21] *Galić* (n 15) para 229; and see Martin Bell's report for BBC News: 'Sarajevo: Inside "sniper alley"', *BBC* (5 April 2012) at https://goo.gl/PjkKbz.

[22] *Galić* (n 15) para 188.

One of the scheduled sniping incidents considered by the Trial Chamber concerned the shooting to death of Almasa Konjhodzić, the mother of Milada Halili with whom she was walking on the morning of 27 June 1993 at around noon along with Milada's husband, Sabri Halili. In a sad irony, they were commemorating the death by sniper fire of a relative. As they approached the traffic lights at the intersection of a street close to the Marshal Tito Barracks, they heard the sound of gunfire. Almasa Konjhodzić was subsequently struck by another bullet. She was taken to hospital, where she died from the wound.[23]

The Trial Chamber accepted the description of the incident as recounted by the witnesses and was satisfied that the victim was a civilian wearing civilian clothes. It noted that although Sabri Halili was a member of the Bosniak army, 'he was off-duty that day and was not dressed in uniform or carrying weapons'.[24] The Defence submitted that the victim was hit by a stray bullet, which ricocheted during an exchange of fire, and that she was not deliberately targeted; or, alternatively, that the bullet was fired from Bosniak army positions and then ricocheted, striking the victim.[25]

The testimony of the witnesses indicated that no soldiers or other military targets were in the vicinity of the incident. A United Nations Protection Force (UNPROFOR) document from 13 June 1993 confirmed that a cease-fire was in place, but reported the situation as being 'relatively tense due to SA [small-arms] fire and RT [artillery] shelling in the vicinity of Tito Barracks'. The Majority of the Trial Chamber found that the UNPROFOR report did not contradict the testimonies of the witnesses, as it did not provide sufficient information on the situation at the intersection at the time of the incident. Since the exact trajectory of the bullet which struck the victim was unclear from the evidence, the Majority could not exclude the possibility that the victim was hit by a bullet that ricocheted:

> Nevertheless, the Majority understands the evidence to show beyond reasonable doubt that no military activity which could have accounted for the shooting was underway at the time of the incident in the vicinity of Marshal Tito Barracks and that the victim and her family were being targeted deliberately.[26]

Two witnesses claimed that a tall white building in Grbavica, on the Bosnian Serb side of the confrontation line, was the source of fire. While the Trial Chamber accepted that the evidence was insufficient to conclude beyond reasonable doubt that the two shots were fired from that building,

> the visual evidence shows that there was an unobstructed line of sight from Grbavica to the intersection where the victim was shot. The fact that containers had been placed at the intersection to give protection from gunfire coming from Grbavica proves that that intersection was a dangerous one and had been targeted before. Based on these considerations, and on the testimony of the two witnesses as a whole, the only reasonable conclusion to be drawn from the evidence is, in the Majority's opinion, that the bullet which killed Almasa Konjhodzić was fired from Grbavica. The evidence demonstrates Grbavica was under SRK control at the time of the incident.[27]

[23] Ibid, para 247.
[24] Ibid, para 248.
[25] Ibid, para 249.
[26] Ibid, para 251.
[27] Ibid, para 252.

The Majority found that Almasa Konjhodzić, a civilian, was deliberately targeted and killed by a shot fired from SRK-controlled territory in Grbavica.[28]

Judge Rafael Nieto-Navia, however, dissented from the Majority's finding because he was not satisfied that the Prosecution had shown beyond a reasonable doubt that she was targeted deliberately.[29] The location where Ms Konjhodzić was shot lay directly across from the Marshal Tito barracks, which had been occupied for a time by the Bosniak army and was in an area where fighting took place. Indeed, as UNPROFOR had reported, there was small-arms fire in the vicinity of the barracks on the day of the shooting.[30] The evidence also established that two shots were fired during the incident. Sabri Halili believed that the first bullet had not been aimed at the victim because it 'was flying much too high'. He also believed that the second shot had hit the victim only after having 'ricocheted from the asphalt'. His wife, though, thought that the second bullet hit the victim directly. Thus, as Judge Nieto-Navia observed,

> the first shot fired during the incident was not aimed at the victim and the second bullet, which hit Konjhodzic, may have ricocheted first. … In my view, this evidence does not conclusively exclude the possibility that the victim was hit by a stray bullet, perhaps originating from the fighting taking place in the area during the day of the incident.[31]

Judge Nieto-Navia's logic is sound. The substance of the rule of distinction is that fire must be directed at a legitimate military objective. But how accurate that fire must be is, as we saw in chapters 4 and 5, unclear. In the case of the shooting of Ms Konjhodzić, a legitimate military objective was nearby; there appear to have been exchanges of small-arms fire during the day; and it may have been that the bullet that killed Ms Konjhodzić ricocheted before hitting her. Judge Nieto-Navia might also have noted that the bullet could have legitimately been aimed at Sabri Halili, for in the views of many he remained a lawful military target as a member of the Bosniak army even though he was off-duty and unarmed at the time. (The fact that the Bosnian Serb forces would in all likelihood not have known that he was a soldier does not preclude a finding of legality.) One sees again how hard it is to identify a violation of the rule of distinction during urban warfare.

A scheduled sniping incident accepted by all of the Trial Chamber as one that involved the targeting of a civilian concerned the wounding of 'Witness G'. On 25 June 1993, he was picking lettuces in the vegetable plot of his farm when, around 1.20pm, he heard sounds of shooting. He lay down for a couple of minutes but when he got up, he was shot in the back. 'Witness K' went to get help from a neighbour to take Witness G to safety. While they were carrying him, they heard intense shooting directed towards them and they dropped on the ground. The shooting stopped. They then ran several metres until the shooting restarted. Four or five times, they ran short distances, then fell to the ground to avoid being shot. Witness K counted 10 to 15 shooting periods in total, and it took them 15 to 20 minutes to carry Witness G to the house. He was then transported to hospital, where he was treated for his injuries over the period of a month.[32]

[28] Ibid, para 253.
[29] *Galić* (n 15), Dissenting Opinion of Judge Nieto-Navia, para 30.
[30] Ibid, para 31.
[31] Ibid, para 31.
[32] *Galić* (n 15) para 547.

The Trial Chamber was in no doubt that Witness G had civilian status on the day of the incident: what he was doing at the time of the shooting and the manner in which he was dressed (wearing only a pair of shorts) 'were without any doubt the activity and dress of a civilian'.[33] Witness G testified that his property was about 500 metres from the frontline. Both witnesses said there was no other military presence or military equipment in the close vicinity of his property. Witness G further recounted that before being shot in the back, he heard sounds of shooting from an area where a group of houses was on the frontline on the hills overlooking his property. According to Witness G, the complex of houses was held by Bosnian Serb snipers. He further testified that was 'the only location where there was a line of visibility' to his vegetable plot and from which a shooter could have seen him in the vegetable plot. Witness K testified similarly that the source of fire was from that area.[34] The Trial Chamber firmly rejected the defence suggestion that the victim of the shooting could have been hit by a stray bullet.[35]

As this incident shows, it is generally necessary for a very clear set of facts, outside active combat and any exchange of fire, for a war crimes charge to be successfully founded. An accused who can show he or she was returning fire or aiming towards a lawful military objective, even if he or she misses the target by many metres and kills or wounds civilians, is highly unlikely to be held criminally responsible for the war crime of attacking civilians.

ii. Ammunition

It is generally unlawful to use expanding or exploding bullets against individuals during the conduct of hostilities. Rifle bullets, at least for anti-personnel use, should thus be fully metal jacketed and not contain explosive material (although, of course, the primer in the cartridge housing the bullet is explosive, designed to propel the round out of the gun). Beyond those stipulations, it is only required that a bullet not be of a nature to cause superfluous injury or unnecessary suffering.

Around 1980, the Belgian (FN-designed) 62gr[36] SS109 round, which contains a closed-nose, copper-jacketed lead core, became the generally accepted standard for NATO member states.[37] The SS109-type bullet remains NATO standard ammunition for assault rifles. The heavier 62gr SS109 design was selected for standardisation rather than the US-produced 55gr M193, whose wounding potential and greater tendency to fragment[38] were considered unacceptable, based partly on humanitarian concerns.[39] As noted above, a particular tendency of any given bullet to fragment does not render it unlawful on the basis of the prohibition on the use of expanding ammunition, as it is not of a nature to 'expand or flatten easily in the human body', but the wound ballistics effects are sometimes graver than

[33] Ibid, para 548.
[34] Ibid, para 549.
[35] Ibid, para 551.
[36] Bullets are classified by mass in 'grains', whereby 1lb is equal to 7,000 grains.
[37] Muzzle velocity is 945 m/s according to Barnes. FC Barnes, *Cartridges of the World*, 14th Edn (Iola WI, Gun Digest Books, 2014) 489.
[38] For some detail on this fragmentation, see, eg, 'Q. So which ammo is better, M193 or M855? And what is all this discussion about fragmentation? Are these dumdum bullets?' at https://goo.gl/dMHBVg; see also D Zimmerman, 'ShootingTheBull410 on 5.56 Ball Ammo: Federal 55gr M193', *The Truth About Guns* (6 July 2014) at https://goo.gl/iRzm68.
[39] '5.56x45 mm NATO', undated but accessed at https://goo.gl/DndpK5.

expanding ammunition. Thus, this may mean they are of a nature to cause superfluous injury or unnecessary suffering. In the earthy language of one online commentator on guns:

> The irony is that fragmenting rounds are much worse than expansive rounds for the purposes of medical treatment as finding a bunch of little pieces of lead is harder than plugging one hole. … It's almost as if the folks coming up with conventions weren't scholars of modern military ballistics and pulled these ideas out of their own hole.[40]

B. Artillery

Artillery as a category encompasses 'cannon' artillery that fire shells, such as howitzers, mortars and field guns, and 'rocket' artillery. It is used to target hard structures and other ground targets, including military personnel, although anti-aircraft guns are also to be considered a form of artillery. The general role of artillery is 'the application of fire, coordinated with the manoeuvre of forces to destroy, neutralise, or suppress the enemy'.[41] Shelling during the conduct of hostilities can be both intense and prolonged, with a powerful shock value on both combatants and civilians alike during combat. In 1944, Stalin famously declared that artillery was the 'God of war'.[42]

In the first eight days of the Battle of the Somme during the First World War, British guns are reported to have fired more than 1.7 million shells. In the course of the four-year-long siege of Sarajevo, one UN expert estimated that 500,000 shells were fired at Sarajevo:

> Sometimes we were able to determine very exactly where they came from and sometimes [we] weren't. In nearly a hundred per cent of the cases, that is, with the exception of two or three, when we could confirm, we confirmed that they came from the Serb side.

In 1993–95, some 1,000 shells landed each day on the city, aside from a lull in 1994 due to a cease-fire.[43]

As discussed in chapters 4 and 5, the precise standard of accuracy Hague Law rules require for artillery is unclear, but it is safe to say that medium- or long-range artillery shells or projectiles delivered by artillery that cannot regularly be directed to within one kilometre of their target are inherently indiscriminate. As discussed in chapter 4, in the *Dragomir Milošević* case, 'modified air-bombs' were said to deviate from the intended target by as much as one kilometre.[44] The ICTY Trial Chamber found that the bombs were 'highly inaccurate' and 'indiscriminate' weapons, and that they 'could only be directed at a general area, making it impossible to predict where they would strike'.[45] The Commission of Inquiry on the 2014 conflict in Gaza found that the Palestinian Fajr-5 and similar rockets, which could land as far as 3 kilometres away from an intended target, were inherently indiscriminate.[46]

[40] Comment by 'Hannibal' at https://goo.gl/iRzm68.
[41] *NATO Glossary of Terms and Definitions*, Doc AAP-6, 2006.
[42] C Bellamy, 'Artillery' in R Holmes (ed), *Oxford Companion to Military History* (Oxford, Oxford University Press, 2001).
[43] ICTY, *Prosecutor v Dragomir Milošević*, Judgment (Trial Chamber III) (Case No IT-98-29/1-T), 12 December 2007, para 415.
[44] Ibid, paras 92, 93, 97.
[45] Ibid., paras 912, 1001.
[46] Report of the detailed findings of the independent commission of inquiry established pursuant to Human Rights Council resolution S-21/1, UN Doc A/HRC/29/CRP.4, 22 June 2015, para 97.

This applies *a fortiori* to longer-range rockets, such as the R-160, which could land as far as 6 kilometres away from the target.

Short-range mortars will be held to a much stricter standard than howitzers, field guns and unguided rockets. In testimony during the *Dragomir Milošević* case, it was asserted that 'a proficient detachment with training can easily hit targets, throughout its ranges, to an accuracy of less than 40 metres'.[47] The defence counsel, though, suggested that the first shells fired at a target could deviate as far as '128 metres in direction and up to 312 metres in distance'.[48] Factors that could reduce the effectiveness of mortars include inexperience of a mortar crew, inexperience and poor skills of the observer, an unstable base plate, movement of the mortar, firing at targets of opportunity and changes in the weather.[49]

Indeed, a first shot's lack of accuracy may be accorded a greater degree of margin, but if firing is not adjusted on available intelligence an inference may be drawn that an attack was indiscriminate or even directed against civilians. It is not necessary under Hague Law rules that direct-fire weapons be used, that is, those with a direct line of sight between the artillery piece and the target, or that they fire precision-guided shells. As recorded in the trial judgment in the *Dragomir Milošević* case, Major Veljović, who testified for the Defence, claimed that

> 'there was no mistake-free firing'; a projectile might miss a target by 50 to 100 metres and fall 'into a built-up inhabited area of town' if, for example, the sufficient charge was not used, the gunpowder was damp or a soldier who was 'upset, psychologically' forgot to measure the right angle.[50]

Ballistics evidence, correctly assessed, is critical to establishing the origin of an artillery shell (and therefore determining responsibility for a strike). On 8 November 1994 (the Trial record incorrectly states 1995 at one point), three mortar shells impacted on Livanjska Street in Centar municipality between, it appears, 3.25pm and 5.30pm. Witnesses testified that this was a purely residential area, with houses, a school and a police station at the end of the street, without military establishments in the vicinity. However, there was a military kitchen on a nearby street, which was used to prepare meals for the Bosniak soldiers deployed on the confrontation lines around Sarajevo. It remained closed through the day, shutting down at 5am and opening again only at 5pm in order to enable delivery of food to the soldiers in the evening or through the night until 5am. Everyone working at the kitchen wore civilian clothes and nobody in uniform was allowed near the kitchen, not even soldiers returning from the front. The confrontation line was an estimated one kilometre away from this area. A cease-fire was in force on 8 November 1994 and there had been no shelling for some time.[51]

The impact of the first shell on Livanjska Street was investigated both by the French Battalion of UNPROFOR and the Bosnian police. Local police arrived within 45 minutes of the explosion; they secured the scene and asked that children be kept inside the school building for fear of another shell's being fired. The police investigative team found the tail-fin embedded in the crater in the asphalt, as occurs most commonly in softer grounds.

[47] *Dragomir Milošević* (n 43) para 91.
[48] Ibid, para 92.
[49] Ibid.
[50] Ibid, para 419.
[51] Ibid, paras 444–45.

While the criminal investigation was ongoing at the scene, two more shells struck Livanjska Street.[52] UNPROFOR investigators arrived, but left after the police prevented them from removing the tail-fin of the first shell from the ground.[53]

The police investigation concluded that the first shell had come 'from the north, five degrees west'. The subsequent and more detailed investigation report by Bosnia's Counter Sabotage Protection Department (KDZ) determined that the shell was fired from the north-west, 'in the direction of Poljine', and the angle of descent was determined to be 62 degrees. The KDZ, which subsequently conducted a more detailed investigation into the shelling, reported that the mortar shell was an 82 mm type M74, which had formerly been used by the Yugoslav National Army. The UNPROFOR report corresponded with the police findings but identified the most 'suspected area' of firing as between Brijeg and Izlaze 'on the Serbian side', slightly north-west of Livanjska Street.[54] Quartermaster sergeant (QMS) Higgs, the Prosecution's expert on mortars, testified that, on the basis of the angle of descent and the position of the tail-fin found embedded at the site, the shell might have originated in Poljine, about 500 to 600 metres north of the confrontation line.[55]

Livanjska Street was shelled twice more on 8 November 1994, first at 5.25pm and then again five minutes later. The second shell exploded on the asphalt surface about 40 metres behind where people were assembled, near the entrance of the school building. The third shell landed in the yard of a house about 10 metres away from the impact of the second. A woman, Razija Šteta, who was found injured in the street, was driven to hospital where she succumbed to her wounds.[56] In total, the Trial Chamber found that at least four civilians were killed and six others seriously injured as a result of the three shells that impacted on Livanjska Street on 8 November 1994.[57]

Investigations by the KDZ and UNPROFOR into these shelling incidents were conducted simultaneously, but independently of one another, on 9 November 1994. While coinciding in several aspects, the investigative teams reached differing conclusions regarding the possible direction of fire. The KDZ report ascertained the angle of descent of the shells, both 82 mm M68 mortar shells, also formally used by the Yugoslav National Army (JNA), was 67 degrees. The report concluded the shells had been fired '20 degrees from the east, probably from the wider area of Špicasta Stijena occupied by the aggressors', although later in the report it stated the direction of fire was north-east. Prosecution expert QMS Higgs testified that this inconsistency was an error of presentation, not of the ballistics calculations. Another expert witness attributed the error to the fact that the inspector who compiled the report was a homicide investigator. Both witnesses interpreted '20 degrees from the east' as 'from the north to the east', that is, north-east, and concurred in this finding.[58]

The UNPROFOR investigation was convinced that the same mortar had fired the two shells, and concluded that the angle of descent of the two shells was between 70 to 75 degrees. It believed that to fire the 82 mm shells from Bosnian Serb-controlled territory,

[52] Ibid, para 449.
[53] Ibid, para 450.
[54] Ibid, para 451.
[55] Ibid, para 452.
[56] Ibid, para 455.
[57] Ibid, para 465.
[58] Ibid, para 456.

the angle had to be below 60 degrees. As a result, UNPROFOR found that 'it is possible to conclude that the most suspected areas are under the control of BiH'.[59] The inconsistency between the assessed directions of fire was attributed to the fact that the UNPROFOR team employed Finnish mortar tables for an 82 mm shell, which differed from the tables for JNA-produced mortars used by the police investigative team.[60]

Prosecution expert QMS Higgs testified that the spray pattern indicated that the angle of descent was closer to 60 to 65 degrees, which made it possible for the shells to have been 'fired from a distance in excess of four kilometres away' that was 'well beyond the confrontation line'. He noted that no one had heard the second and third shells being fired, even though the shells passed along very built-up residential areas. He also considered the lack of witnesses to the 'tremendous muzzle flash' that the mortar gives off upon being fired, which would have been visible at 5.25pm in winter from miles away. He testified that the shells could have been fired from the other side of the confrontation line, over and behind a steep escarpment, which would have muffled the sound. He concluded that the 'most logical position' from which the second and third shells were fired was in territory held by the SRK, though he could not rule out the possibility that the shell came from Bosniak-controlled territory.[61]

On the possible purpose of such mortar attacks, QMS Higgs said that 'a single round fired into the centre of a populated area' does not present the prospect of obtaining any military objective. The only possible purpose would have been 'to cause civilian casualties and to put basically terror into the minds of the people in that area'. In his opinion, the delay of several minutes between the second and third shell at Livanjska Street was not intended to achieve any military objective. Given that 82 mm mortars are capable of firing 20 rounds a minute, the delay was aimed to allow time for people from the area to gather around and treat casualties, thereby 'catch[ing] more people in the area than [were] there in the first place' – 'a tactic used by terrorist organisations with bombs'.[62]

Dragomir Milošević appealed against his conviction, including in relation to the Trial Chamber's holding that Bosnian Serb forces had fired the three shells at Livanjska Street on 8 November 1994. The Appeals Chamber rejected his appeal on this ground.[63] The tranquillity of the conflict on the day in question and the lack of any real military objective that could have been destroyed or damaged by the attack demonstrated that the civilian population was actually the target of the attack.

C. Tanks

Tanks are, in effect, a mobile form of artillery. They were first deployed by the British Army at Cambrai in November 1917 during the latter stages of the First World War. They are especially effective at swift incursions, as the Germans proved during the early part of the

[59] Ibid, para 457.
[60] Ibid, para 458.
[61] Ibid, para 459.
[62] Ibid, para 461.
[63] ICTY, *Prosecutor v Dragomir Milošević*, Judgment (Appeals Chamber) (Case No IT-98-29/1-A), 12 November 2009, paras 210–18.

Second World War. Guderian's movement of his tank divisions through The Ardennes, an adaptation of Erich von Manstein's plan to capture France, remains one of the most skilful examples of how tanks can spearhead attacks that win conflicts, particularly when underpinned by air superiority.[64] Although the vulnerability of tanks to aerial attack remains a weak point, armoured warfare continues to have an important role to play in land warfare, at least in certain theatres and for most armies. As one commentator argued in 2016, 'The future of the tank is secure.'[65]

> Men build machines that are faster, but more importantly to protect them from weapons on the field, and enable them to carry more devastating firepower than they could on foot. We must not forget that the tank was not developed to defeat the tank. It was developed in World War I to defeat the machine-gun and to penetrate layered defenses in torn terrain.

Two years earlier, however, in January 2014, a *Washington Post* headline ran 'The end of the tank? The Army says it doesn't need it, but industry wants to keep on building it'. The US Army, the article explained, wanted submarines, long-range bombers and drones – weapons that can project power over great distances. But with 6,000 main battle tanks (MBTs) in its arsenal, it could be argued that this number was sufficient. Looking to Asia, one commentator observed in 2015 that countries had gone on a 'tank-buying spree'.[66] Given ongoing sabre-rattling in the South China Sea, this trend is unlikely to end soon.

As with other modern weaponry, a generally higher standard of accuracy will be expected from MBTs under Hague Law rules than was the case during the Second World War or the Korean War. During Operation 'Protective Edge', the Israeli operation against Gaza in the summer of 2014, 14,500 tank shells and approximately 35,000 artillery shells were fired.[67] Israel's primary MBT is the 65-tonne Merkava Mk4, which fires 120 mm ordnance (including both high-penetration projectiles and anti-tank guided missiles reaching 8 kilometres away with a claimed accuracy of 70 centimetres CEP).[68] The Merkava also fires 60 mm mortar shells to a range of 2.7 kilometres. It appears that the Merkava was used in the incident that damaged Gaza's only power plant, located at Nusseirat.

i. *The Nusseirat Power Plant Incident*

The UN Commission of Inquiry established to assess compliance by the parties to the armed conflict discussed the use of tanks in relation to specific attacks by Israeli forces. One such attack concerned the damage to Gaza's only power plant, located at Nusseirat. This plant normally supplies about 30 per cent of the electricity in the Gaza Strip, with the rest provided from Israel and Egypt. Under normal circumstances, the three sources cater to half of Gaza's

[64] Of course, this is not to downplay the importance of heavy German bombing of the tank crossing points, nor to underestimate the significance of the ground troops that followed the tanks.

[65] P Donahoe, 'Heavy Armor; The Tank's Role in the Future of War', *National Interest* (24 May 2016) at https://goo.gl/TSDP2w.

[66] F-S Gady, 'The Main Battle Tanks of Asia: Junk or Still Useful', *The Diplomat* (10 January 2015) at https://goo.gl/D3s3YA.

[67] '16 Facts on Operation Cast Lead', *Bayabasha* (IDF Ground Forces magazine), Issue 29 (October 2014) 47, at https://goo.gl/Vebrvf.

[68] 'LAHAT Laser Guided Missile: IAI MBT Space & Missile Division', Defense Update (4 March 2006) at https://goo.gl/no9rQd.

overall electricity needs.[69] As the result of shelling on 29 July 2014, one of the plant's fuel tanks exploded, causing the plant to be shut down.[70] In May 2015, Israel stated that on 29 July,

> IDF [Israel Defence Forces] tank shells unfortunately missed their intended target and hit fuel tanks serving Gaza's power plant (but not the power plant itself). In this incident, IDF tank forces had legitimately directed an attack against several individuals who were believed to be carrying anti-tank rockets intended for immediate use.[71]

Owing to the limited evidence available to the Commission, it was unable to determine whether the power plant suffered incidental damage from an attack directed elsewhere, or whether it was the object of a deliberate attack. The Commission noted that the electricity infrastructure servicing the civilian population constitutes a civilian object, which is protected from attack unless it makes an effective contribution to military action and its destruction offers a definite military advantage.[72] This is a correct statement of the law.[73] More controversially, however, the Commission also argued that electricity plants are

> also protected by the customary law rule prohibiting parties to a conflict from attacking, destroying, or rendering useless objects indispensable to the survival of the civilian population. Deliberate targeting of such objects would be in violation of this prohibition.[74]

Here, the Commission appears to go beyond extant Hague Law rules. Destroying critical water supplies or crops or foodstuffs would constitute objects indispensable to the survival of the civilian population. An attack on an electricity power plant would, in general, not.[75]

This does not mean, though, that the attack was lawful. Indeed, Human Rights Watch declared that 'Deliberately attacking the power plant would be a war crime.' The organisation stated:

> The shutdown of the Gaza Power Plant has had an impact on the population far beyond power outages. It has drastically curtailed the pumping of water to households and the treatment of sewage, both of which require electric power. It also caused hospitals, already straining to handle the surge of war casualties, to increase their reliance on precarious generators. And it has affected the food supply because the lack of power has shut off refrigerators and forced bakeries to reduce their bread production.
>
> 'If there were one attack that could be predicted to endanger the health and well-being of the greatest number of people in Gaza, hitting the territory's sole electricity plant would be it,' said Eric Goldstein, deputy Middle East and North Africa director [of Human Rights Watch].[76]

[69] *Report of the detailed findings of the independent commission of inquiry established pursuant to Human Rights Council resolution S-21/1*, UN Doc A/HRC/29/CRP.4, 22 June 2015 (hereinafter, UN Commission of Inquiry on the 2014 Gaza Conflict) para 450.

[70] Ibid, paras 452, 451.

[71] Israeli Ministry of Foreign Affairs, *IDF Conduct During the 2014 Gaza Conflict*, 28, at https://goo.gl/Y0WgKa.

[72] UN Commission of Inquiry on the 2014 Gaza Conflict, para 454.

[73] For a discussion of this issue in relation to a power plant in Eritrea, see Eritrea-Ethiopia Claims Commission (EECC), *Partial Award: Western Front, Aerial Bombardment and Related Claims*, 19 December 2005, paras 211–21, at https://goo.gl/C19YIe.

[74] UN Commission of Inquiry on the 2014 Gaza Conflict, para 454.

[75] Though in relation to power plants that support the purification and pumping of drinking water, see Y Dinstein, *The Conduct of Hostilities under the Law of International Armed Conflict*, 3rd edn (Cambridge, Cambridge University Press, 2016) 252, para 683, citing H Shue and D Wippman, 'Limiting Attacks on Dual-Use Facilities Performing Indispensable Civilian Functions' (2002) 35 *Cornell International Law Journal* 573.

[76] Human Rights Watch, 'Gaza: Widespread Impact of Power Plant Attack' (10 August 2014) at https://goo.gl/TiuJVk.

The Commission of Inquiry reported that the Military Advocate General (MAG) had referred the power plant incident of 29 July 2014 to the IDF's Fact-Finding Assessment Mission, and its findings were provided to the MAG. As at May 2015, the MAG's decision 'whether to order the opening of a criminal investigation into this incident' was still pending.[77] The Commission argued that if the strike against the power plant were accidental, as Israel claimed,

> there remain nonetheless questions as to whether all appropriate precautions were taken by the IDF to avoid damage to a civilian object. The IDF's latest version of events concerning the 29 July incident says that it targeted several individuals alleged to be transporting weapons in the vicinity of the plant. If that is the case, the choice of means needs to be examined, namely whether tank shells were the most appropriate ammunition, and whether other types of ordnance, presenting fewer risks of incidental damage, could have been used instead. In addition, the fact that the power plant had been struck several times in the preceding days should have led the IDF to issue stringent orders to units operating near the power plant to exercise restraint, given the importance of the plant for the civilian population in Gaza. The IDF therefore appears not to have complied with its obligation to take all feasible precautions to avoid or at least to minimize incidental damage to civilian objects in the attack of 29 July that struck the power plant.[78]

In August 2016, the results of the MAG inquiry were reported publicly.[79] This report noted that MAG had referred the incident to the General Staff Mechanism for Fact-Finding Assessments (the FFA Mechanism), for examination. The FFA Mechanism had found that the power plant in Nusseirat was designated as a 'sensitive site' on the relevant operational systems of the IDF. This means that any military operation to be conducted in the vicinity of such sites requires the adoption of special precautions. On the day of the incident, an IDF armoured force operating in the area was found to have identified

> a squad of terror operatives, bearing anti-tank weaponry ('anti-tank squad'). The anti-tank squad was identified while it was close to what would later turn out to be the fuel tanks of the power plant. In light of the imminent threat posed by the squad to the armored force, the force fired, in a measured and direct manner, at the anti-tank squad, using the most precise munition the force had at its disposal. It appears, that as a result of this fire, one of the power plant's fuel tanks was damaged (the power plant itself was not hit). It was further found, that the IDF force which carried out the fire, did not make the connection between the facilities, in proximity to which it identified the anti-tank squad, and the power plant, and was not aware that the structures in question contained flammable material.
>
> After reviewing the factual findings and the material collated by the FFA Mechanism in regard to this incident, the MAG found that the targeting process carried out with regard to the anti-tank squad accorded with Israeli domestic law and international law requirements.
>
> The fire which was carried out by the IDF force over the course of the incident was aimed at a military object – an anti-tank squad of the terror organizations, which posed an immediate threat to the force. The attack on the squad complied with the principle of proportionality, as at the time the decision to attack was taken, it was considered that the collateral damage expected to arise as a result of the attack would not be excessive in relation to the military advantage anticipated from

[77] Israeli Ministry of Foreign Affairs (n 71) 29.

[78] UN Commission of Inquiry on the 2014 Gaza Conflict, para 455.

[79] 'Decisions of the IDF MAG regarding Exceptional Incidents that Allegedly Occurred During Operation "Protective Edge" – Update No 5', IDF, 24 August 2016, at https://goo.gl/bp4Rbz.

> it. This estimation was not unreasonable under the circumstances, when taking into consideration the immediacy of the threat posed to the force by the anti-tank squad, and in light of the fact that the force was not aware of the nature of the facilities in proximity to which they identified the squad.
>
> Moreover, the attack was carried out in conjunction with various precautionary measures, including the selection of the munition used (taking into account the distance between the force and the anti-tank squad, and the weaponry that was at the force's disposal), and the way in which the fire was carried out. These measures were carried out in order to minimize, to the extent possible under the circumstances, the collateral damage expected to result to structures and facilities in the vicinity of the target. In light of the immediacy of the threat, and the danger which was posed to the IDF force, the force did not have any latency in which to enquire into the nature of the facilities in proximity to which it had identified the squad, and the potential consequences, immediate, or long term, of collateral damage thereto.
>
> In light of the above, the MAG did not find that the actions of IDF forces raised grounds for a reasonable suspicion of criminal misconduct. As a result, the MAG ordered the case to be closed, without opening a criminal investigation.
>
> At the same time, the MAG made a recommendation to the relevant operational authorities that they review the processes for the integration of the operational instructions concerning operations carried out in proximity to 'sensitive sites', as well as the ways in which IDF forces' ability to locate and identify such sites might be improved.[80]

D. Mines

The use of anti-personnel mines in the conduct of hostilities is unequivocally unlawful for the 164 states parties to the 1997 Anti-Personnel Mine Ban Convention.[81] Although the treaty prohibition on use has not yet attained customary status, with several major military powers still outside its purview, it can be seen as *de lege ferenda*.[82] But, as discussed in chapter 1, the argument that anti-personnel mines are inherently indiscriminate is flawed on the basis that their emplacement in marked and fenced areas, especially one that is patrolled by military personnel (such as the Demilitarized Zone separating the two Koreas), can effectively ensure that the victims of any explosion are predominantly military and not civilian. This is not to deny the widespread indiscriminate use of anti-personnel mines witnessed in practice, which fully justified their prohibition by disarmament treaty.

Although many major military states are still outside the Anti-Personnel Mine Ban Convention, several (China, India, the Republic of Korea, Pakistan, Russia and the US, amongst others) are nonetheless party to Amended Protocol II to the Convention on Certain Conventional Weapons (CCW). The Protocol prohibits the use of 'non-detectable'

[80] Ibid.

[81] Convention on the Prohibition of the Use, Stockpiling, Production and Transfer of Anti-Personnel Mines and on Their Destruction; adopted at Oslo, 18 September 1997; entry into force 1 March 1999.

[82] Cryer et al suggest that among other weapons frequently mentioned as a candidate for a comprehensive prohibition, '[p]erhaps the closest to achieving the status as a war crime is the use of anti-personnel mines'. R Cryer, H Friman, D Robinson and E Wilmshurst, *An Introduction to International Criminal Law and Procedure* (Cambridge, Cambridge University Press, 2010) 305.

anti-personnel mines,[83] and generally outlaws the use of long-lived anti-personnel mines outside perimeter-marked areas that are monitored by military personnel and protected by fencing or other means.[84] Anti-personnel mines that are manually emplaced outside such marked and protected areas must comply with the requirements for self-destruction and self-deactivation set out in the Technical Annex to the Protocol. This means that 90 per cent of 'activated' mines must self-destruct within 30 days after emplacement, while the back-up self-deactivation feature (typically the exhaustion of a battery) must ensure that, in combination with the self-destruction mechanism, a total of 99.9 per cent (one in one thousand) of the activated mines can no longer be detonated 120 days after emplacement.[85] All remotely delivered anti-personnel mines (where they are ground-launched by artillery, for example) must meet these standards for self-destruction and self-deactivation.[86]

Anti-vehicle mines, whose use is not prohibited by treaty, are also not rendered illegal under customary law. According to CCW Amended Protocol II, it is prohibited to use remotely-delivered anti-vehicle mines, unless,

> to the extent feasible, they are equipped with an effective self-destruction or self-neutralization mechanism and have a back-up self-deactivation feature, which is designed so that the mine will no longer function as a mine when the mine no longer serves the military purpose for which it was placed in position.[87]

The lack of any standards or defined time period renders this obligation largely impotent in practice.

There remains a need to strengthen significantly the Hague Law restrictions on the use of anti-vehicle mines, primarily because of their effects on civilians and civilian transport. A 2014 study by the Geneva International Centre for Humanitarian Demining (GICHD) and the Stockholm International Peace Research Institute (SIPRI) concluded:

> Anti-vehicle mines (AVMs) have always had a humanitarian impact, but their significance has often been overshadowed by the higher-profile topic of anti-personnel mines (APMs), and thus the need to address AVMs has been neglected. In some countries, AVMs now present a greater threat to civilian populations than APMs, yet they are often viewed as a marginal issue in international fora.[88]

[83] Art 4, Protocol on Prohibitions or Restrictions on the Use of Mines, Booby Traps and Other Devices as amended on 3 May 1996, annexed to the CCW (hereinafter '1996 Amended Protocol II'). According to para 2(a) of the Technical Annex, 'With respect to anti-personnel mines produced after 1 January 1997, such mines shall incorporate in their construction a material or device that enables the mine to be detected by commonly-available technical mine detection equipment and provides a response signal equivalent to a signal from 8 grammes or more of iron in a single coherent mass.'

[84] Art 5(1), 1996 Amended Protocol II. According to para 3(a) of the Technical Annex, 'All remotely-delivered anti-personnel mines shall be designed and constructed so that no more than 10% of activated mines will fail to self-destruct within 30 days after emplacement, and each mine shall have a back-up self-deactivation feature designed and constructed so that, in combination with the self-destruction mechanism, no more than one in one thousand activated mines will function as a mine 120 days after emplacement.'

[85] Art 5(1), 1996 Amended Protocol II, and para 3(b) of the Technical Annex.

[86] Art 6(2), 1996 Amended Protocol II, and para 3(a) of the Technical Annex.

[87] Art 6(3), 1996 Amended Protocol II.

[88] See, eg, *The Humanitarian and Developmental Impact of Anti-Vehicle Mines* (Geneva, GICHD and SIPRI, 2014) 10, at https://goo.gl/BiwmMF.

E. Improvised Explosive Devices

Improvised explosive devices (IEDs), a term which is typically used to denote improvised mines[89] or command-detonated explosives, have come to the fore as a major challenge to armed forces in the past two decades.[90] An IED has not been defined under international law, although the US Department of Defense describes it as 'A weapon that is fabricated or emplaced in an unconventional manner incorporating destructive, lethal, noxious, pyrotechnic, or incendiary chemicals designed to kill, destroy, incapacitate, harass, deny mobility, or distract.'[91] Within CCW Amended Protocol II, it is provided that '"Other devices" means manually emplaced munitions and devices including improvised explosive devices designed to kill, injure or damage and which are actuated manually, by remote control or automatically after a lapse of time.'[92]

The injuries caused by certain IEDs, notably those buried devices containing explosives created from ammonium nitrate fertiliser and laid by insurgents in Afghanistan, Iraq and elsewhere, are often horrific. In some cases, the traumatic amputations that result from the explosion occur so close to soldiers' hips that it is difficult to fit prosthetic legs. It could be argued that the amount of explosive is far higher than that required to put a soldier *hors de combat*. A rebuttal to the assertion is that these weapons are often intended to penetrate soft-skinned or even armour-plated vehicles and therefore the high explosive content is militarily necessary.

F. Cluster Munitions

The use of all cluster munitions is outlawed for states parties under the 2008 Convention on Cluster Munitions.[93] As of 1 April 2018, 103 states were party to it. The evidence for customary law status of the general treaty prohibition on use is weaker in the case of cluster munitions than it is for anti-personnel mines. Many major military states not party to the Convention continue to use, or expressly reserve the right to use, cluster munitions in the conduct of hostilities. These states may be considered as specially affected for the purpose of determining customary law. In September 2016, the non-governmental Cluster Munition Monitor reported that since 1 July 2015, new use of cluster munitions was identified

[89] An IED that fulfils the definition of anti-personnel mine in the Anti-Personnel Mine Ban Convention (or 1996 Amended Protocol II) is indeed an anti-personnel mine and is therefore prohibited. Islamic State produced huge numbers of anti-personnel mines in local factories in areas under its control in Syria and Iraq in 2015–17. In April 2015, the research organisation Conflict Armament Research stated that Islamic State forces were producing and deploying 'IEDs' on 'an industrial scale'. Reported in Forum on the Arms Trade and Stimson, 'Tracking arms in conflict: Lessons from Syria and Iraq', 7 April 2015, at https://goo.gl/j6THwb.

[90] See, eg, UN Office for Disarmament Affairs, 'Improvised Explosive Devices (IEDs)' at https://goo.gl/1juo9v.

[91] US Department of Defense, *Department of Defense Dictionary of Military and Associated Terms*, Joint Publication 1-02, 8 November 2010 (as amended through 15 February 2016) 108. The notion of construction in an unconventional manner may be taken to exclude locally produced mines in workshops and small factories, which Islamic State and other non-state armed groups do increasingly commonly. This is presumably not the intent of the description.

[92] Art 2(5), Amended Protocol II.

[93] Convention on Cluster Munitions, adopted at Dublin, 30 May 2008; entry into force 1 August 2010.

in the armed conflicts in Syria (by Syrian government forces and likely Russia)[94] and in Yemen by at least Saudi Arabia.[95,96] In addition, the Monitor believed there was strong, but unconfirmed evidence that cluster munitions were used in Nagorno-Karabakh in April 2016. Azerbaijan and Armenia both denied using cluster munitions in the brief conflict.[97] Subsequently, Cluster Munition Monitor noted 'reports that cluster munitions may have been used in Iraq and Libya, but the Monitor could not independently verify the evidence of possible use'.[98]

In its judgment in the *Martić* case before the ICTY, which concerned the firing from rockets on land of cluster munitions against Zagreb in May 1995, the ICTY's Trial Chamber noted

> that the weapon was fired from the extreme of its range. Moreover, the Trial Chamber notes the characteristics of the weapon, it being a non-guided high dispersion weapon. The Trial Chamber therefore concludes that the M-87 Orkan, by virtue of its characteristics and the firing range in this specific instance, was incapable of hitting specific targets. For these reasons, the Trial Chamber also finds that the M-87 Orkan is an indiscriminate weapon, the use of which in densely populated civilian areas, such as Zagreb, will result in the infliction of severe casualties.[99]

The statement of the Trial Chamber might be understood to affirm that the Orkan is an inherently indiscriminate weapon. This would be a mistake. It was 'the firing range in this specific instance' and its claimed use against point targets within an urban environment that made it an indiscriminate weapon.[100] The distance from which the rockets were fired was close to the maximum range (50 kilometres) of the M-87 Orkan, at which the dispersion error is about 1,000 metres in every direction, with the area of the dispersion of the sub-munitions on the ground being about 20,000 square metres.[101] Thus, a different (ie shorter) firing range and a dissimilar environment for its use would potentially have led to a different outcome.

III. Prohibited Methods of Warfare

A range of methods of warfare are specifically outlawed under Hague Law rules, some of which are discussed in this section. Certain can be traced back to the notion of chivalry

[94] According to the Monitor, Syrian government forces used at least 13 types of air-dropped and ground-launched cluster munitions from July 2012 until July 2016. During that period there were at least 360 cluster munition attacks in 10 of Syria's 14 governorates, but the actual number is likely far higher as many attacks are not recorded. The Monitor also reported that Russia had denied using cluster munitions in Syria, 'but there is compelling evidence that it is using them'.

[95] Saudi Arabia, as well as, possibly, other members of the coalition that it has led in Yemen since 25 March 2015 against Houthi forces, has used air-dropped and ground-launched cluster munitions. Between April 2015 and February 2016, at least 19 cluster munition attacks were documented involving the use of seven types of cluster munitions. The United Arab Emirates has denied using cluster munitions, while Saudi Arabia has admitted to just one attack, in April 2015.

[96] *Cluster Munition Monitor Report 2016* at https://goo.gl/ufPTCe.

[97] Ibid.

[98] *Cluster Munition Monitor Report 2017* at https://goo.gl/7EuP5e.

[99] ICTY, *Prosecutor v Milan Martić*, Judgment (Trial Chamber) (Case No IT-95–11), 12 June 2007, para 463.

[100] This understanding is confirmed by the Appeal Chamber's judgment, in which it stated that 'The Trial Chamber concluded that the M-87 Orkan *was used as* an indiscriminate weapon.' ICTY, *Prosecutor v Milan Martić*, Judgment (Appeals Chamber) (Case No IT-95–11-A), 8 October 2008, para 247 (authors' emphasis).

[101] *Martić* (n 98) para 462.

that underpinned some of the laws of war in bygone centuries. Others are more recent rules intended to offer protection to the civilian population in addition to the rules of distinction and proportionality in attack.

A. Denial of Quarter

The denial of quarter – the statement that no one surrendering will be allowed to live – was already outlawed under the Hague Regulations.[102] As is the case with any fighter who is *hors de combat*, he or she must be respected and protected. This rule reflects military utility, as if fighters believe they are not going to be killed or tortured they are more likely to surrender than to fight on.

To violate the rule it is not necessary that any survivors actually be summarily executed while seeking to surrender, it is enough that the statement be made. This conduct is criminalised. Thus, the customary nature of the prohibition was reflected in the jurisdiction given to the International Criminal Court (ICC) under the 1998 Statute for the war crime in both international armed conflict (IAC) and non-international armed conflict (NIAC) of 'declaring that no quarter shall be given'.[103]

B. Perfidy

Also specifically illegal in the Hague Regulations is perfidy, which includes acts such as 'To make improper use of a flag of truce'[104] with a view to attacking the enemy. Article 37(1) of the 1977 Additional Protocol I sets out the modern prohibition on perfidy as follows:

> It is prohibited to kill, injure or capture an adversary by resort to perfidy. Acts inviting the confidence of an adversary to lead him to believe that he is entitled to, or is obliged to accord, protection under the rules of international law applicable in armed conflict, with intent to betray that confidence, shall constitute perfidy. The following acts are examples of perfidy:
>
> a) the feigning of an intent to negotiate under a flag of truce or of a surrender;
> b) the feigning of an incapacitation by wounds or sickness;
> c) the feigning of civilian, non-combatant status; and
> d) the feigning of protected status by the use of signs, emblems or uniforms of the United Nations or of neutral or other States not Parties to the conflict.

As Dinstein explains, there are thus three main elements to perfidy: first, a Hague Law norm must exist that requires a party to an armed conflict to grant protection to the enemy in a relevant scenario; second, the enemy commits an act that invites the granting of that protection; and third, the beneficiary deliberately betrays that trust.[105] In the ICC Statute, the

[102] See Art 23(d), Regulations concerning the Laws and Customs of War on Land annexed to Convention (IV) respecting the Laws and Customs of War on Land; adopted at The Hague, 18 October 1907; entry into force, 26 January 1910 (hereinafter '1907 Hague Regulations').

[103] Arts 8(2)(b)(xii) and 2(e)(x), Statute of the International Criminal Court; adopted at Rome, 17 July 1998; entry into force, 1 July 2002 (ICC Statute).

[104] See Art 23(e), 1907 Hague Regulations.

[105] Dinstein (n 75) 266, para 725.

prohibition on perfidy is captured in IAC by the provision on 'Killing or wounding treacherously individuals belonging to the hostile nation or army';[106] while in NIAC the formulation is slightly different: 'Killing or wounding treacherously a combatant adversary'.[107]

C. Human Shields

The deliberate placing of civilians in or around military objectives by a party to armed conflict with a view to preventing attacks is, in the words of Yoram Dinstein, a 'flagrant breach'[108] of Hague Law rules. The 1949 Geneva Convention IV stipulates that 'The presence of a protected person may not be used to render certain points or areas immune from military operations.'[109] This is reinforced in the 1977 Additional Protocol I, which provided:

> The presence or movements of the civilian population or individual civilians shall not be used to render certain points or areas immune from military operations, in particular in attempts to shield military objectives from attacks or to shield, favour or impede military operations. The Parties to the conflict shall not direct the movement of the civilian population or individual civilians in order to attempt to shield military objectives from attacks or to shield military operations.[110]

Dinstein asserts that 'Irrefutably, this norm mirrors customary international law.'[111] This is certainly the case in IAC wherein it is criminalised. Thus, it is reflected in the ICC Statute, which encompasses the war crime in IAC only of 'Utilizing the presence of a civilian or other protected person to render certain points, areas or military forces immune from military operations'.[112] No corresponding war crime is included in the provisions relating to NIAC.

So-called human shields may be forced, or they may be acting in an entirely voluntary manner. Where they are forced (or tricked) into being used to try to shield a military objective from attack, they remain civilians who are protected from attack[113] and their expected harm must be taken into account in the implementation of the rule of proportionality in attack. (Of course, it may not be clear to an attacking force whether individuals are acting as a result of coercion or of their own volition.) In contrast, Schmitt argues that voluntary human shields ought to be excluded from consideration in the proportionality equation by

[106] Art 8(2)(b)(xi), ICC Statute. Dinstein argues that the formulation in the ICC Statute, which derives from Art 23(b) of the Hague Regulations, is broader than Art 37(1) of the 1977 Additional Protocol I as, for example, it would also encompass the bribing of an enemy soldier to assassinate his commander. Dinstein (n 75) 267, para 727, citing WA Solf, 'Article 37' in M Bothe, KJ Partsch and WA Solf, *New Rules for Victims of Armed Conflicts: Commentary on the two 1977 Protocols additional to the Geneva Conventions of 1949* (The Hague, Martinus Nijhoff, 1982) 232 at 235.

[107] Art 8(2)(e)(ix), ICC Statute.

[108] Dinstein (n 75) 181, para 486.

[109] Art 28, 1949 Geneva Convention IV.

[110] Art 51(7), 1977 Additional Protocol I.

[111] Dinstein (n 75) 181, para 486.

[112] Art. 8(2)(b)(xxiii), ICC Statute.

[113] Indeed, as Solis observes, where a civilian is forcibly placed in or around a military objective, he or she is a hostage, which is a grave breach of the 1949 Geneva Convention IV. GD Solis, *The Law of Armed Conflict: International Humanitarian Law in War*, 2nd edn (New York, Cambridge University Press, 2016) 350.

the attacker,[114] a stance approved by Dinstein.[115] Whether or not this is correct may hang on whether, by their own actions, they are directly participating in hostilities.

In this regard, the ICRC asserts:

> Where civilians voluntarily and deliberately position themselves to create a physical obstacle to military operations of a party to the conflict, they could directly cause the threshold of harm required for a qualification as direct participation in hostilities.[116]

If this is indeed the case, clearly they have lost their protection from attack. This scenario, the ICRC goes on to argue, 'may become particularly relevant in ground operations, such as in urban environments, where civilians may attempt to give physical cover to fighting personnel supported by them or to inhibit the movement of opposing infantry troops'.[117]

Again, we may question how, in many practical instances, the attackers will know whether or not a civilian obstructing their view of a combatant or other military objective is acting in a purely voluntary manner. In these circumstances, it should be presumed that the individual is not so acting, and therefore he or she retains civilian status. As Article 50(1) of the 1977 Additional Protocol I provides, 'In case of doubt whether a person is a civilian, that person shall be considered to be a civilian.'[118]

D. Sieges and Starvation as a Method of Warfare

It is not prohibited to starve combatants into submission. Indeed, as the US Department of Defense observes, it is 'a legitimate method of warfare'.[119] Starvation may often be the intent of a siege, as taking a heavily fortified city or other area may prove very costly for the attacker. The starvation of the civilian population as a method of warfare is, however, unlawful, which, in practice, renders sieges of towns and cities that contain civilians generally prohibited once food and water supplies are insufficient.[120] It is further prohibited

> to attack, destroy, remove or render useless objects indispensable to the survival of the civilian population, such as foodstuffs, agricultural areas for the production of foodstuffs, crops, livestock, drinking water installations and supplies and irrigation works, for the specific purpose of denying them for their sustenance value to the civilian population.[121]

[114] MN Schmitt, 'War, Technology and the Law of Armed Conflict' (2006) 82 *International Legal Studies* 137, 177.

[115] Dinstein (n 75) 183, para 491.

[116] ICRC, *Interpretive Guidance on Direct Participation in Hostilities under International Humanitarian Law* (Geneva, ICRC, 2009) (hereinafter 'ICRC DPH Guidance') 56.

[117] Ibid, 57.

[118] As discussed in ch 5, the US does not regard this rule as reflective of customary law.

[119] US Department of Defense, *Law of War Manual*, June 2015 (hereinafter 'USDOD 2015 *Law of War Manual*') para 5.20, at https://goo.gl/uZKhvk.

[120] Dinstein objects quite forcefully to the notion that it is no longer lawful to starve the enemy into submission where to do so would also amount to intent to starve the civilian population. He suggests that allowing civilians safe passage out of the besieged area might allow the siege to be continued even if the civilian population decline to take advantage of the offer. Dinstein (n 75) 253–57, paras 688–99.

[121] Art 54(2), 1977 Additional Protocol I. Slightly different language is employed in the corresponding provision in the 1977 Additional Protocol II (Art 14): 'It is … prohibited to attack, destroy, remove or render useless, for that purpose [starvation of the civilian population], objects indispensable to the survival of the civilian population, such as food stuffs, agricultural areas for the production of foodstuffs, crops, livestock, drinking water installations and supplies and irrigation works.'

The siege of Aleppo in 2016 is an instance of siege warfare with apparent intent to starve both (rebel) fighters and civilians. It was claimed in late November that residents were 10 days from starvation; this included both combatants and civilians.[122] The UN declared that Russia and Syria were preventing essential humanitarian aid from reaching starving, sick civilians in east Aleppo.[123] On 9 December 2016, with the UN Security Council unable to pass a resolution addressing the issue in the face of Russia's opposition, the General Assembly adopted a resolution demanding an immediate and complete end to all attacks on civilians, as well as an end to all sieges in war-ravaged country.[124] A week later, the Security Council adopted a fairly anodyne resolution that expressed alarm at the 'continued deterioration of the devastating humanitarian situation in Aleppo', stressing that 'protection must be provided to all civilians who choose or who have been forced to be evacuated and those who opt to remain in their homes'.[125]

As noted above, the prohibition on starvation as a method of warfare, as such, was first decreed in the 1977 Additional Protocol I. It is also a war crime in IAC, as set out in the ICC Statute:

> Intentionally using starvation of civilians as a method of warfare by depriving them of objects indispensable to their survival, including wilfully impeding relief supplies as provided for under the Geneva Conventions.[126]

The Elements of Crime adopted for the Court do not help to elucidate the content of the prohibition, although they do imply that starvation need only be the intent, not the result, of an individual's actions:

1. The perpetrator deprived civilians of objects indispensable to their survival.
2. The perpetrator intended to starve civilians as a method of warfare.
3. The conduct took place in the context of and was associated with an international armed conflict.
4. The perpetrator was aware of factual circumstances that established the existence of an armed conflict.[127]

No equivalent war crime is included in the Statute with respect to NIACs, even though the prohibition on intentionally starving civilians is also a violation of the 1977 Additional Protocol II. The ICRC asserts that the prohibition is both a customary rule and a war crime in all armed conflicts under customary international law;[128] indeed, this seems generally uncontested.[129]

[122] See, eg, 'Syria's war: Aleppo residents "10 days from starvation"', *Aljazeera* (25 November 2016) at https://goo.gl/7Ry6Hn.

[123] 'Humanitarian aid blocked as Aleppo civilians starve', *Sky News* (1 December 2016) at https://goo.gl/JBk8yC.

[124] UN General Assembly Resolution 71/130, adopted on 9 December 2016 by 122 votes to 13 with 36 abstentions. The resolution 'recall[ed]' that 'all Syrian parties to the conflict shall enable the immediate and unhindered delivery of humanitarian assistance, and stress[ed] that the arbitrary denial of humanitarian access, depriving civilians of objects and assistance indispensable to their survival, including wilfully impeding relief supplies such as food aid and lifesaving medical supplies, and the use of starvation as a method of warfare may constitute a war crime'. Preambular para 18.

[125] UN Security Council Resolution 2328, adopted on 19 December 2016, Preambular para 3 and Operative para 2.

[126] Art 8(2)(b)(xxv), ICC Statute.

[127] ICC, 'Elements of crimes', UN Doc PCNICC/2000/1/Add.2 (2000) 31.

[128] ICRC Study of Customary International Humanitarian Law (IHL), Rule 156 ('Definition of War Crimes'), at https://goo.gl/HVEnCt.

[129] See, eg, USDOD 2015 *Law of War Manual*, para 17.9.2. UK Ministry of Defence, *The Manual of the Law of Armed Conflict* (Oxford, Oxford University Press, 2005) para 5.27.

The ICRC observes that the prohibition of starvation of civilians as a method of warfare was considered a new rule at the time of the adoption of the 1977 Additional Protocol I. However, practice since then has not only made this a customary rule, but its inclusion in the ICC Statute as a war crime was not controversial:

> Destroying objects indispensable to the survival of the civilian population also reflects a customary prohibition. There had, in fact, been a prosecution relating to a case of destruction of crops in a scorched earth operation during World War II, although the basis of the prosecution was the destruction of property not required by military necessity.[130]

According to the UK, as a result of the prohibition of starvation of civilians as a method of warfare, the customary law rule that permitted measures to dry up springs and to divert rivers and aqueducts must now be considered as applying only to water sources used exclusively by military personnel or for military purposes.[131]

In contrast, as the US Department of Defense argues, the rule in the Protocol that prohibits attacking, destroying, removing or rendering useless objects indispensable to the survival of the civilian population would not apply to attacks carried out for specific purposes other than to deny sustenance. It cites as an example of permitted conduct destroying a field of crops to prevent it from being used as concealment by the enemy, or destroying a supply route that is used to move military supplies but which is also used to supply the civilian population with food.[132] This is subject to the prohibition whereby 'in no event shall actions against these objects be taken which may be expected to leave the civilian population with such inadequate food or water as to cause its starvation or force its movement'.[133] An exception is also foreseen in the Protocol that allows a state to engage in a 'scorched earth' defence of a party's own territory.[134]

[130] ICRC Study of Customary IHL, Rule 156 ('Definition of War Crimes').
[131] UK Ministry of Defence (n 128) para 5.27.2.
[132] USDOD 2015 *Law of War Manual*, para 5.20.4.
[133] Art 54(3), 1977 Additional Protocol I.
[134] Ibid, citing Art 54(5), which allows such action 'by a Party to the conflict within such territory under its own control where required by imperative military necessity'.

10

Aerial Warfare

I. Introduction

Aerial warfare[1] has a long history,[2] but it came to the fore of international legal concern first in the Second World War, where it has remained ever since. Early attempts at aerial warfare, using kites (in China) and then balloons, involved reconnaissance or signalling more often than combat, with such devices being deployed primarily to identify or report enemy troop concentrations and movements.[3] The first – and only – general treaty prohibition on aerial warfare was incorporated in the 1899 Hague Declaration (IV,1), prohibiting the launching of projectiles or explosives from balloons 'or by other new methods of a similar nature'.[4] The declaration, which was ratified by the major powers of the time save for the United Kingdom (UK) and the United States (US), was only in force for five years, and was replaced by the 1907 Hague Declaration (XIV) Prohibiting the Discharge of Projectiles and Explosives from Balloons.[5] This agreement applies only to armed conflicts between states parties, as was the case with its 1899 antecedent. But as the 1907 treaty applies until the convening of the Third Hague Peace Conference (which has never occurred), it technically remains in force today.[6]

[1] The *Harvard Manual on International Law Applicable to Air and Missile Warfare*, the work of a number of law of armed conflict experts that was finalised in June 2009, stipulates that '"Air" or "airspace" means the air up to the highest altitude at which an aircraft can fly and below the lowest possible perigee of an earth satellite in orbit. Under international law, airspace is classified as either national airspace (that over the land, internal waters, archipelagic waters, and territorial seas of any State) or international airspace (that over contiguous zones, exclusive economic zones, the high seas, and territory not subject to the sovereignty of any State).' *Harvard Manual on International Law Applicable to Air and Missile Warfare* (2009) s A(1), p 1, at https://goo.gl/Ihkc4o. The highest recorded flight by a conventional aircraft is by American test pilot Robert White, who, on 17 July 1962, took the X-15 to an altitude of 96 km. Officially, however, Alexandr Fedotov holds the world altitude record, set on 31 August 1977, when his MiG E-266M reached a height of 37.6 km. This is explained by the fact that Mr Fedotov took off from the ground, whereas the X-15 was launched in the air. R Maksel, 'Who holds the altitude record for an airplane?', *Air Space Magazine* (28 May 2009) at https://goo.gl/stXmF9.

[2] In his work originally published in 1921, General Giulio Douhet sought to demonstrate how air warfare would render irrelevant fighting on the ground by taking the battle straight to the heartland of the enemy. G Douhet, *The Command of the Air*, at https://goo.gl/djMvAd; see L Freedman, *The Future of War: A History* (London, Allen Lane, 2017) 56.

[3] See, eg, G de Syon, 'Kites' in WJ Boyne (ed), *Air Warfare: an International Encyclopedia*, vol 1 (Santa Barbara, CA, ABC-CLIO, 2002) 352; and Ojibwa, 'Ancient China: Kites', *Daily Kos* (25 November 2012) at https://goo.gl/XjhgEc.

[4] Russia's proposed programme for the First Hague Peace Conference of 1899 had suggested 'the prohibition of the discharge of any kind of projectile or explosive from balloons or by similar means'. Balloons had been used on a small scale in previous wars, and there was much speculation about the future use of aircraft in war. D Schindler and J Toman, *The Laws of Armed Conflicts* (Dordrecht, Martinus Nijhoff, 1988) 202–04.

[5] Adopted at The Hague, 18 October 1907; entry in force, 27 November 1909.

[6] Since the UK and the US are still party to the Declaration, should the two nations decide to go to war against each other, technically they would be legally prevented from engaging in aerial warfare!

Following the invention of propeller-powered aircraft by the Wright brothers in the US in 1903, it quickly became clear that therein lay the future of warfare. The first use of airplanes in warfare occurred eight years later, in the war between Italy and Turkey, when Italian Air Corps planes bombed a Turkish camp near Tobruk in Libya.[7] In the First World War, balloons and airplanes were still largely used for information gathering or to direct artillery fire onto targets. To counter this reconnaissance capability, airplane pilots took to shooting down these aircraft, initially using side-arms they carried in the cockpit. All in all, though, as Field-Marshal Montgomery describes in *A History of Warfare*, air power was 'never of more than minor importance' during the First World War:[8]

> Aeroplanes ... were most useful for reconnaissance and attacking supply lines, but until the last year of the war they played only a minor part in the tactics of land warfare. The exploits of some of the air aces ... became celebrated, but really they hardly mattered. Nor did bombing make any real material impact, although the raids by Zeppelin airships over British cities caused a flurry of alarm.[9]

In contrast, as John Buckley observes, in the years following the end of the First World War the development of air power would fundamentally and irrevocably alter the way in which wars were wrought. For, as Montgomery outlines, between the two globalised conflicts of the first half of the twentieth century, aircraft developed 'enormously'.[10] It was both a cause and a crucial accelerating factor contributing to the theory and practice of 'total war'.[11] In 1923, states elaborated the Hague Draft Rules of Aerial Warfare, but did not go on to adopt them.[12] They sought to outlaw aerial bombardment 'for the purpose of terrorizing the civilian population, of destroying or damaging private property not of a military character, or of injuring non-combatants' and even 'the indiscriminate bombardment of the civilian population'.[13]

During the Second World War,

> air power became a mighty weapon which transformed the conception of war at sea, as well as ground tactics, enabling land battles to be won in less time and with fewer casualties than would otherwise have been the case. Strategic bombing played a large part in warfare and Allied air power was a decisive factor in the war in Europe.[14]

Germany developed the first short-range ballistic missiles during the war, but after the US dropped nuclear bombs on Hiroshima and Nagasaki, the Cold War that ensued between the US and the Soviet Union after 1945 saw tens of thousands of nuclear warheads fitted onto intercontinental ballistic missiles deployed on land, at sea and in the air. The strategy of mutually assured destruction persists to this day.

[7] J Buckley, *Air Power in the Age of Total War* (London, Routledge, 1998) 38.

[8] Field-Marshal Viscount Montgomery of Alamein, *A History of Warfare* (London, Book Club Associates, 1982) 482.

[9] Ibid. On 31 May 1915, Zeppelins bombed London for the first time, killing seven and injuring 35, while a Zeppelin raid on 8 September caused more than £500,000 of damage.

[10] Montgomery (n 8) 503.

[11] See, generally, Buckley (n 7).

[12] See, eg, R Bierzanek, 'Commentary to the 1923 Hague Rules for Aerial Warfare' in N Ronzitti (ed), *The Law of Naval Warfare. A Collection of Agreements and Documents with Commentaries* (Dordrecht, Martinus Nijhoff, 1988); see at https://goo.gl/tnpGdz.

[13] Arts XXII and XXIV(3), 1923 Hague Draft Rules of Aerial Warfare, at https://goo.gl/o2YsLm.

[14] Montgomery (n 8) 503–04.

Today, the doctrine of 'air power' predominates in military theory. As a major in the US Air Force wrote in 1997:

> Through emphasis on the unique capabilities of air power, Air Force doctrine stresses the strategic pre-eminence of the air power mission. As a result of air power's outstanding success in the [1991] Gulf War, many air power advocates believe that air power has finally matured and assumed a dominant role in warfare.[15]

In Australia, air power has become 'an essential component' of its national military power. As *The Air Power Manual* explains, for the Australian armed forces the four core air power roles and their associated missions are:

> a. **control of the air** [offensive counter air/defensive counter air],
> b. **strike** [strategic attack/close air support/air interdiction/anti-surface warfare/anti-submarine warfare/electronic warfare/information operations],
> c. **air mobility** [air logistic support/airborne operations/air-to-air refuelling/aeromedical evacuation], **and**
> d. **intelligence, surveillance and reconnaissance** ...[16]

The current (sixth) edition of the *Manual* (of 2013) notes that the law of armed conflict

> should not be seen as an impediment to a combatant in the execution of operations. The military mission should be balanced by judgement at the strategic level regarding the extent of permissible collateral damage or incidental injury to non-combatant persons or protected infrastructure. Air power can create devastating effects and failure to employ this power with discrimination and proportionality can have serious adverse consequences for the individual, Air Force and the Government.[17]

Any history of the opening decades of the twenty-first century must also, though, mention the use of remotely piloted aircraft, colloquially known as drones. Already in 1981, Edward Teller, the 'father of the hydrogen bomb', had claimed that '[t]he unmanned vehicle today is a technology akin to the importance of radars and computers in 1935'.[18] In a reconnaissance role, remotely piloted aircraft are fast becoming a mainstay of armed forces. But when weaponised, the technology offers states the capability to use lethal force within armed conflict, largely shorn of direct and immediate risk to a state's own pilots. Indeed, in 2015, on the basis of their ability to surveil for long periods without interruption and to kill at less than a minute's notice by remote control thousands of miles away, the American political

[15] Maj DH Fehrmann, 'Air Power Doctrine and the Strategic Label', Naval War College, Newport, RI, 13 June 1997, ii.

[16] *The Air Power Manual*, 6th edn (Canberra, Air Force Headquarters, 2013) ch 3, at https://goo.gl/m8PRQm. The UK defines the four roles of air power as follows: '[(i)] Control of the air secures our freedom of action within the air environment. [(ii)] Intelligence, surveillance and reconnaissance informs [*sic*] the development of understanding across all environments. [(iii)] Attack can coerce and influence actors into changing or maintaining behaviour. [(iv)] Air mobility enables movement, manoeuvre and sustainment.' UK Ministry of Defence, *UK Air and Space Power*, 2nd edn (Swindon, DCDC, 2017) para 1.5, at https://goo.gl/pQQUT7.

[17] *The Air Power Manual* (n 16) para 2.46.

[18] 'DOD's use of remotely piloted vehicle technology offers opportunities for saving lives and dollars: report to the Congress: summary, by the Comptroller General of the United States', US General Accounting Office, Washington, DC, 1981; see L Hancock with S Wexler, *Shadow Warfare: The History of America's Undeclared Wars* (Berkeley, CA, Counterpoint, 2014) 455; and S Shane, *Objective Troy* (New York, Tim Duggan Books, 2015) 70–71.

scientist Peter Warren Singer affirmed that such unmanned systems are a 'game-changer'.[19] They are also the future of air warfare, with ever greater autonomy of action and reaction the focus of research and development programmes worldwide. The days of manned combat aircraft appear to be numbered.

Air warfare may of course target other aircraft as well as targets at sea, but the focus of legal concern is, predictably, on bombardment of personnel and objects on the ground. The remainder of this chapter is divided into two sections. Section II looks at selected means of warfare such as weapons platforms, notably combat aircraft (including remotely piloted aircraft) and attack helicopters, as well as the munitions they ordinarily fire. A subsection looks first at the broad legal issues surrounding gravity ordnance and precision-guided munitions, picking up on a theme addressed in chapter 7 on precautions in attack. Consideration then turns to specific ordnance and the associated Hague Law rules: air-to-ground missiles, air-dropped mines, cluster munitions, incendiary weapons, 'barrel' bombs, chemical weapons, nuclear weapons and directed energy weapons. Section III looks at particular methods of warfare, especially high-level and (indiscriminate) 'carpet' bombing, and attacks against, or severely affecting, the natural environment.

II. Means of Warfare

A. Combat Aircraft

Combat aircraft are the mainstay of aerial warfare, used to attack other military aircraft, ships, submarines and ground-based military objectives. The category of combat aircraft is not formally defined under international law, though a valuable definition is offered by states within the auspices of the United Nations Register of Conventional Arms (UNROCA), a voluntary mechanism designed to increase transparency in arms transfers. The definition was given added status by its indirect incorporation into the 2013 UN Arms Trade Treaty (ATT). As at 24 December 2014, the date of the ATT's entry into force,[20] the definition of 'combat aircraft' was as follows:

> Includes fixed-wing or variable-geometry wing aerial vehicles as defined below:
>
> (a) Manned fixed-wing or variable-geometry wing aircraft, designed, equipped or modified to engage targets by employing guided missiles, unguided rockets, bombs, guns, cannons or other weapons of destruction, including versions of these aircraft which perform specialized electronic warfare, suppression of air defence or reconnaissance missions.
>
> (b) Unmanned fixed-wing or variable-geometry wing aircraft, designed, equipped or modified to engage targets by employing guided missiles, unguided rockets, bombs, guns, cannons or other weapons of destruction.
>
> The terms 'combat aircraft' and 'unmanned combat aerial vehicles (UCAV)' do not include primary trainer aircraft, unless designed, equipped or modified as described above.[21]

[19] P Singer, 'The Five Deadly Flaws of Talking About Emerging Military Technologies and the Need for New Approaches to Law, Ethics, and War' in PL Bergen and D Rothenberg (eds), *Drone Wars* (Cambridge, Cambridge University Press, 2015) 215, 216.

[20] This event was set as the date on which the relevant definitions within the UNROCA would apply to the conventional arms whose transfers were covered by the ATT. See Art 5(3), ATT.

[21] UNROCA, 'Categories of major conventional arms' at https://goo.gl/oDATTE.

The term is thus generic, covering fighter jets and strategic bombers as well as military reconnaissance aircraft, but not ordinary trainer aircraft used as such. With respect to fighter jets, it is common to talk of 'generations' of aircraft, a classification that began with the first jet-powered fighter aircraft in 1945 in the closing stages of the Second World War. These reflect greater speed and a higher level of technology, but also, generally speaking, greater accuracy of targeting. According to the Russian system of classification of fighter aircraft (others dispute how many generations exist), technological developments fall into the following chronological order:

- First Generation (1945–55) comprising Second World War-era fighters such as the Me 262 and 'mature' first-generation fighters such as the F-86 used in the Korean War.
- Second Generation (1955–60) with aircraft possessing more advanced avionics and engines, and using the first guided air-to-air missiles.
- Third Generation (1960–70) covering fighter aircraft such as the MiG-21 and MiG-23, and fighter-bombers and tactical bombers including the Su-24 and the F-4s and A-7s built by the US. As one authority explains, the major change brought about by this generation of aircraft was that it was no longer necessary to visually acquire opponents to neutralise them and gain control of the air.[22]
- Fourth Generation (1970–90) which continued the trend towards multi-role fighters and emphasising manoeuvrability rather than speed to succeed in air-to-air combat. Fourth-generation fighters include the US-designed F-14, F-15, F-16, and F/A-18; the Soviet-built SU-27 and MIG-29; and the European Mirage 2000.
- Fifth Generation (1990–2010) fighters use integrated avionics systems that provide the pilot with complete battlespace awareness combined with stealth technology. The F-22 and F-35 were the first fifth-generation fighters, with Russia following with the Mikoyan Gurevich MFI prototype and the Sukhoi PAK-FA, and China with the J-20.[23] In February 2018, the Sukhoi Su-57 fighter aircraft were spotted in Syria.[24]

In 2009, *Air Force Magazine* proposed a sixth generation (to come) that would be characterised by extreme stealth, morphing capability, smart skins and extremely sensitive sensors; the aircraft would be only optionally manned, would be equipped with directed energy weapons and would be 'highly networked'.[25] In fact, the next generation of fighter aircraft will probably be unmanned. In April 2015, then Secretary of the US Navy Ray Mabus famously said the Lockheed Martin F-35 Joint Strike Fighter, which will ultimately cost an estimated $1.5 trillion to develop and procure,[26] 'almost certainly will be the last manned

[22] 'Five Generations of Jets', *Fighterworld* at https://goo.gl/m6pTLS.

[23] 'Fighter Aircraft Generations', Global Security, undated but accessed on 1 March 2017, at https://goo.gl/q3b75K. Fifth generation fighter capabilities are largely defined by their software, and it will be the ongoing development of their software that will ensure they maintain their edge against evolving threats. The F-35 has more software than any other air combat aircraft, with seven million lines of code in the aircraft, and a further seven million lines of code in the supporting ground systems. An example of the complexity and sophistication of the F-35 software is that it uses about 100 times the number of parameters than a fourth generation fighter does to define a potential threat: 'Five Generations of Jets' (n 22). Necessary upgrades to software were expected to cost at least $1 billion annually over the next seven years: O Pawlyk, 'Upgrades, Development to F-35 Jet Will Cost $1 Billion Per Year', *Military.com* (8 March 2018) at https://goo.gl/m4Y3gU.

[24] A Roth, 'New Russian stealth fighter spotted in Syria', *Guardian* (22 February 2018) at https://goo.gl/A3eQs2.

[25] JA Tirpak, 'The Sixth Generation Fighter', *Air Force Magazine* (October 2009) at https://goo.gl/a1auGx.

[26] See, eg, D Francis, 'How DOD's $1.5 Trillion F-35 Broke the Air Force', *CNBC* (31 July 2014) (updated 14 December 2016), at https://goo.gl/p3Z5y7.

strike fighter aircraft the Department of the Navy will ever buy or fly'. He further asserted that 'Unmanned systems, particularly autonomous ones, have to be the new normal in ever-increasing areas.'[27]

The advance of technology should enable much greater precision and far fewer targeting mistakes, heightening the ability of combat aircraft to '[avoid], and in any event to [minimise], incidental loss of civilian life, injury to civilians and damage to civilian objects' in the words of the 1977 Additional Protocol I.[28] In some respects, this has occurred. With the general exception of the armed conflicts in Syria, and especially the aerial bombardment of Aleppo, as well as incidents in many other armed conflicts, a desire to reduce civilian harm resulting from aerial warfare can be evinced from the conduct of hostilities in many cases. Whether this trend persists, and even generalises further beyond many NATO members, remains to be seen.

i. Remotely Piloted Combat Aircraft

The UNROCA definition of combat aircraft explicitly covers both manned and remotely piloted aircraft. A number of commentators both prior to and following the adoption of the ATT had asserted – incorrectly – that the treaty would not and did not encompass remotely piloted aircraft (see further chapter 15).[29] Given their importance to existing and especially future warfare, this subsection describes their development and identifies the nations that use or are likely to use these aerial robots.

Armed aerial drones have a relatively long history, existing, at least in research and development circles, since the end of the First World War. In 1918, based on technological innovations by the American entrepreneur and inventor Elmer Sperry, the US Army began experiments with an aircraft nicknamed the Kettering Bug, 'a pilotless biplane with gyroscopic guidance that could carry 180 pounds of explosives for about forty miles before dive-bombing into a target'.[30] In 1919, Sperry successfully sunk a captured German battleship using the pilotless aircraft.[31] But the unmanned system remained rudimentary, with the in-flight guidance system offering stability rather than directional control.[32]

[27] S LaGrone, 'Mabus: F-35 Will Be "Last Manned Strike Fighter" the Navy, Marines "Will Ever Buy or Fly"', US Naval Institute (15 April 2015) at https://goo.gl/ajw6jZ. The US Air Force seemingly disagreed with the Navy's assessment. According to Lieutenant-General Stephen Hoog, Assistant Vice Chief of Staff of the Air Force, 'The essence is not whether a human being is in the cockpit, the essence is where your decision-making is going to be made. … The way to achieve "Sixth Generation Air Dominance" may not be an airplane. Instead of looking at the platform, we have to look at the mission set and figure out the best way to attack it.' R Whittle, 'Air Force Begs To Differ With Mabus: F-35 Not Last Manned Fighter', *Breaking Defense* (29 April 2015) at https://goo.gl/MUwe2F.

[28] Art 57(2)(a)(ii), 1977 Additional Protocol I.

[29] See, eg, T Brück and P Holtom, 'Will the arms trade treaty be stuck in the past?', Stockholm International Peace Research Institute (SIPRI) (26 March 2013) at https://goo.gl/xNtBvH; and R Alley, 'Firing Blanks? The Arms Trade Treaty', Discussion Paper No 16/14, Centre for Strategic Studies, University of Wellington, New Zealand (2014) 2, at https://goo.gl/SMXZms.

[30] Shane (n 18) 69.

[31] US Army UAS Center of Excellence, *'Eyes of the Army', US Army Unmanned Aircraft Systems Roadmap 2010–2035*, ARMY.MIL, No 4 (2010); see RP Barnidge, Jr, 'A Qualified Defense of American Drone Attacks in Northwest Pakistan under International Humanitarian Law' (2012) 30 *Boston University International Law Journal* 409, 413.

[32] 'A Brief History of Precision Guided Weapons', Twenty-First Century Books, at https://goo.gl/TUyrhH.

In subsequent decades, US efforts at developing the technology to increase control of armed drones during flight often disappointed. Greater success was achieved in the use of unarmed drones for information gathering; the Vietnam War was the setting for the first widespread deployment of surveillance and reconnaissance drones.[33] But after Vietnam it was not until the 1990s and the armed conflicts in Bosnia and Herzegovina,[34] and later with Yugoslavia over Kosovo,[35] that US remotely piloted aircraft would again see extensive deployment. Of particular note, Bosnia would be the theatre for the first use during armed conflict of General Atomics' (then unarmed) Predator drone.[36]

a. Predator and Reaper Drones

Although its operational lifetime is now drawing to a close,[37] the Predator is, in many ways, the iconic combat drone. While it is irrevocably linked to extraterritorial use of force by the US, the design of the Predator was actually the brainchild of an Iraqi-born Israeli citizen, Abraham Karem.[38] The first Predator strike in anger is said to have hit a Taliban camp in Kandahar on 7 October 2001. The attack, which was targeting Mullah Omar, missed its intended target but killed two of the Taliban leader's bodyguards.[39] Nonetheless, as a journalist from *The New York Times*, Scott Shane, observes, 'A new era in warfare had begun, with unpredictable consequences. … The Predator would be the first drone to become famous – and infamous – generating newspaper editorials, protest marches, secret legal opinions, and outlandish artworks.'[40]

The Predator, which can fire two laser-guided air-to-ground Hellfire ('helicopter-launched fire-and-forget') AGM-114 missiles against armour and personnel (see section II.D), can be seen as a first-generation armed drone. Its obsolescence was foretold in early 2017 with the announcement that the US Air Force would be phasing out the aircraft in favour of its faster and more heavily armed successor, the Reaper.[41] That said, as one commentator noted

[33] D Cenciotti, 'The dawn of the robot age: US Air Force testing air-launched UCAVs capable to fire Maverick and Shrike missiles in 1972', *The Aviationist* (weblog) (14 March 2012) at https://goo.gl/6xyMw3.

[34] RQ-1 Predator drones have been operational in Bosnia and Herzegovina since 1995 in support of NATO, UN and US operations. 'Predator RQ-1/MQ-1/MQ-9 Reaper UAV, United States of America', *Airforce-Technology.com*, at https://goo.gl/QSoAYB.

[35] D Abel, 'Downing the Drones', *Boston Globe* (10 June 1999) at https://goo.gl/Cfhsrd.

[36] HA Crumpton, *The Art of Intelligence: Lessons from Life in the CIA's Clandestine Service* (New York, Penguin Press, 2012) 150–51.

[37] In February 2018, the US Air Force announced that it was officially 'retiring' the MQ-1 Predator from operational service on 9 March of the same year as it completed the transition to MQ-9 Reapers. Senior Airman James Thompson, 'Sun setting the MQ-1 Predator: A history of innovation', Creech Air Force Base, United States, 14 February 2018, at https://goo.gl/mKG6sr.

[38] R Whittle, 'The Man Who Invented the Predator', *Air & Space* (April 2013) at https://goo.gl/rQZpM4; see also A Cockburn, *Kill Chain* (London, Verso, 2016) 50. In 2012, *The Economist* described Karem as the 'dronefather', although he denied any responsibility for the decision to weaponise the Predator. 'The dronefather', *The Economist* (1 December 2012) at https://goo.gl/c2ngr.

[39] AH Michel, 'How Rogue Techies Armed the Predator, Almost Stopped 9/11, and Accidentally Invented Remote War', *Wired* (17 December 2015) at https://goo.gl/m3oU2R.

[40] Shane (n 18) 69.

[41] Senior Airman Christian Clausen, 'AF to retire MQ-1, transition to MQ-9', 432nd Wing/432nd Air Expeditionary Wing Public Affairs, 24 February 2017, at https://goo.gl/VYvxHy.

in 2014, the Reaper's standard version 'suffers the same inadequacies' that plague the original Predator:

> It can't fly in bad weather and its satellite-relayed control signal tends to lag, which can cause crashes when operators sitting in trailers in the US can't respond fast enough to problems. ... It's also possible to hack the Reaper's video stream ... and jam its GPS.[42]

As at September 2015, the US Air Force had 93 Reapers in its inventory.[43]

Since the first drone strike more than a decade and a half ago, US use of remotely piloted aircraft in Afghanistan has expanded and increased, to the extent that in 2015 there were more drone strikes over the course of the year than there were strikes by combat aircraft with a pilot in the cockpit.[44] One media outlet specialising in reporting on the use of armed drones assessed total strikes for 2016 in Afghanistan at 1,071, killing between 1,389 and 1,597 people, of whom up to 105 were probably civilians.[45] In May, a US drone strike killed the Afghan Taliban leader, Mullah Akhtar Mansoor, in neighbouring Pakistan.[46] On 23 October, a senior al-Qaeda leader, Faruq al Qatani, was killed in a drone strike in Kunar province, in an operation confirmed by the Pentagon. A second strike the same day is believed to have killed Bilal al Utabi, another senior al-Qaeda leader.[47]

But strikes were also responsible for significant civilian casualties in 2016. The Bureau of Investigative Journalism identified 15 civilians killed by a single US drone strike in Nangarhar province on 28 September, the biggest loss of civilian life in one strike since the (piloted) attack on the Médecins Sans Frontières hospital in Kunduz in October 2015.[48] The US claimed to have conducted a counterterrorism strike against Islamic State fighters in Nangarhar. But the next day the UN Assistance Mission in Afghanistan (UNAMA) issued a statement saying the strike had killed 15 civilians and injured 13 others who had gathered at a house to celebrate a tribal elder's return from the *Hajj* (pilgrimage to Mecca).[49] In its statement, UNAMA reiterated the need for 'all parties to the conflict to adhere to their obligations under international humanitarian law', and called on the Afghan Government and international military forces 'to launch a prompt, independent, impartial, transparent, and effective investigation into this incident'.[50]

[42] D Axe, 'The US Air Force Was Not Fond of the Next-Gen Predator Drone: Flying branch blew off General Atomics' Predator C as too modest, too flimsy', *War is Boring* (website) (13 November 2014) at https://goo.gl/CCvBft.

[43] US Air Force (USAF), 'MQ-9 Reaper', Fact Sheet, 23 September 2015, at:https://goo.gl/1qmia8. In the summer of 2016, it was announced that the US Air Force was procuring 30 more MQ-9 Reapers under a $370 million contract, with the aircraft due to be delivered by May 2019. F-S Gady, 'US Air Force to Receive 30 New Reaper Killer Drones', *The Diplomat* (18 August 2016) at https://goo.gl/XiWAEu.

[44] Reuters, 'Exclusive: Afghan drone war – data show unmanned flights dominate air campaign' (20 April 2016) at https://goo.gl/My5hcR.

[45] J Serle, P Sargand and J Purkiss, 'US strikes in Afghanistan: Get the data: A list of US air and drone strikes, Afghanistan 2016', Bureau of Investigative Journalism, accessed on 16 January 2017 at https://goo.gl/jjfmSR.

[46] A Gul and C Babb, 'Afghan Intel: Afghan Taliban Leader Killed in US Drone Strike', *Voice of America* (22 May 2016) at https://goo.gl/PNT6dB; see also J Boone and SE Rasmussen, 'US drone strike in Pakistan kills Taliban leader Mullah Mansoor', *Guardian* (22 May 2016) at https://goo.gl/iAvmTJ.

[47] J Purkiss and J Serle, 'US strikes in Afghanistan: Al Qaeda leader killed in US strike in Afghanistan', Bureau of Investigative Journalism (11 November 2016) at https://goo.gl/ep4WfR.

[48] J Purkiss and R Khapalwak, 'US strikes in Afghanistan: The Bureau identifies 15 civilians killed in a single US airstrike', Bureau of Investigative Journalism (4 November 2016) at https://goo.gl/wOxWS1.

[49] UNAMA, 'UNAMA condemns killing of at least 15 civilians in airstrike' (29 September 2016) at https://goo.gl/jC5ENv.

[50] Ibid.

The Iraq conflict in 2003 saw considerable, and initially under-reported, use of armed drones. Indeed, based on the Iraqi experience, a Predator ground controller, Major Mark Lilly of the Air Force 46th Expeditionary Reconnaissance Squadron, predicted, with great foresight, that 'It won't be too many more years before pilots are flying this thing and probably nothing more.'[51]

Lieutenant-Colonel T Mark McCurley, a drone operator during the conflict (and later a drone squadron commander), notes that by 2005 unmanned aircraft were 'integrated into the operational scheme'.[52] Reflecting on their inability to prevail in dogfights, though, McCurley relates the shooting down of a Predator by an Iraqi Air Force MiG during the invasion. Unusually, the drone was equipped with AIM-92 Stinger air-to-air missiles.[53] It is claimed that during the initial period of the invasion, some older Predators were stripped down and used as decoys to entice Iraqi air defences to reveal their positions by opening fire.[54]

United States drone strikes in Libya and Syria began much later, after armed violence followed peaceful protests across the Arab world. In Libya, drone use epitomised Obama's decision to 'lead from behind', though a US drone strike on Gaddafi's convoy out of Sirte was instrumental in the former leader's demise.[55] There were reports that in June 2016 a drone strike had killed Islamic State leader Abu Bakr al-Baghdadi in Syria.[56] At the end of 2016, though, the US Department of Defense acknowledged that he was still alive and 'in charge'.[57] In autumn 2014, at the beginning of the air campaign in Syria, President Obama relaxed[58] the 'near certainty of no civilian casualties' requirement that he had established a year earlier for drone strikes against Islamic State.[59]

b. Development and Use by Israel

Israel was quicker than the US to appreciate the potential military applications of drones; indeed, Air Force 200 squadron was established in 1971 specifically to operate unmanned reconnaissance vehicles.[60] After losing many of their piloted planes to surface-to-air missiles, the nation used Vietnam-era reconnaissance drones procured from the US to locate anti-aircraft sites during the Yom Kippur War with Egypt and Syria.[61] The aerial drones proved

[51] B Cosgrove-Mather (Associated Press), 'Pilotless Warriors Soar to Success', *CBS News* (25 April 2003) at https://goo.gl/tNhp7c.

[52] Lt-Col TM McCurley with K Maurer, *Hunter Killer* (London, Allen & Unwin, 2016) 94.

[53] Ibid, 43.

[54] Cosgrove-Mather (n 51).

[55] 'US Drone Involved in Final Qaddafi Strike, as Obama Heralds Regime's "End"', *Fox News* (20 October 2011) at https://goo.gl/QT7cKf.

[56] 'US military officials "sceptical" of reports ISIS leader al-Baghdadi killed', *Fox News* (14 June 2016) at https://goo.gl/tFycDt.

[57] 'Isis leader Abu Bakr al-Baghdadi is still alive and in charge, says Pentagon', *Independent* (30 December 2016) at https://goo.gl/UV9nel.

[58] J Acosta and K Liptak, 'White House exempts ISIS strikes from civilian casualty guidelines', *CNN* (2 October 2014) at https://goo.gl/Q9kI4f.

[59] Associated Press, 'No drone strikes without "near certainty" of no civilian casualties: Obama', *Dawn* (23 May 2013) at https://goo.gl/TDDqw7.

[60] See, eg, https://goo.gl/av2r.

[61] See JF Kreis, 'Unmanned Aircraft in Israeli Air Operations', *Air Power History*, vol 37, no 4 (Winter 1990) 46.

to be vital assets during combat, and the Israelis began to develop their own unmanned aircraft.[62]

Israel used drones to effect in Lebanon, beginning in the 1980s. Unmanned aircraft played a substantial part in the destruction of the Syrian integrated air defence system in Lebanon.[63] One authority claims that armed Israeli drones may have attacked ground targets by dive-bombing into them[64] in a precursor to the Harpy, an autonomous weapons platform whose integrated sensors identify and target radar sites by detecting electromagnetic emissions from radar equipment. In 1996, during Operation Grapes of Wrath in Lebanon, drones equipped with video cameras relayed pictures and coordinates back to command posts in northern Israel, where the information was computerised and used to direct artillery and aircraft attacks.[65]

Israel is secretive about its drone programme, but it is believed that armed variants exist of both the Heron and the subsequent larger and more powerful Heron TP, whose wingspan is the length of a Boeing 737,[66] known as Eitan. Both unmanned systems are produced by Israel Aerospace Industries (IAI). The IAI Heron is capable of operating at a maximum altitude of 10.5 kilometres for up to 52 hours. The Eitan, which is supposedly able to carry a one-ton bomb,[67] can fly at 230 mph for more than 35 hours (some sources claim 70 hours).[68] In a November 2014 interview on Eitan use in Gaza, an Israeli drone commander by the assumed name of 'Major Yair' admitted to making some 'wrong calls'.[69]

Miniaturisation is also a feature of drone technological development. In November 2015, it was reported that Israel was marketing a 7lb drone, the Hero 30, a low-speed loitering aircraft that could crash-bomb into an identified target with its 1lb explosive warhead.[70] Launched by air pressure from a canister, the Hero can then fly on its electrical engine for up to 30 minutes. According to its manufacturer, Israeli defence company UVision, the Hero 30 is capable of speeds of up to 100 knots and 'is ideal for anti-personnel missions'.[71] In June 2016, it was announced that UVision had teamed up with US defence corporation Raytheon to adapt the Hero 30 to US military requirements.[72]

[62] D Tepper, V Mentasti and J Raab, 'Discover How Drones Are Made', *Time* (23 October 2015) at https://goo.gl/BGF28b; D Rodman, 'Unmanned Aerial Vehicles in the Service of the Israel Air Force', Rubin Center, 7 September 2010, at https://goo.gl/CPQs8J/.

[63] Rodman (n 62).

[64] RA Gabriel, *Operation Peace for Galilee: Israeli/Palestine Liberation Organization War in Lebanon* (New York, Hill & Wang, 1985) 99; see D Rodman, *Sword and Shield of Zion: The Israel Air Force in the Arab–Israeli Conflict, 1948–2012* (Eastbourne, Sussex Academic Press, 2014) ch 4, esp 85–86.

[65] J Cusack, '"Operation Grapes of Wrath" is a virtual war Israel is waging on computer screens', *Irish Times* (26 April 1996) at https://goo.gl/hZZebF.

[66] Rodman (n 62).

[67] Ibid.

[68] IAI, 'Heron TP MALE UAV System', at https://goo.gl/Xzqvey; and 'Heron/Machatz 1 Unmanned Aerial Vehicle (UAV), Israel', *Airforce Technology* (2017) at https://goo.gl/BsMQTp.

[69] D Blair, 'Israeli drone commander: "The life and death decisions I took in Gaza"', *Daily Telegraph* (19 November 2014) at https://goo.gl/tn5qHR.

[70] D Hambling, 'Israel Is Already Selling Kamikaze Micro-Drones That Will Change Modern Warfare', *Popular Mechanics* (3 November 2015) at https://goo.gl/3f0vbq.

[71] UVision, 'Hero 30' (2015) at https://goo.gl/nQY1YZ.

[72] Y Lappin, 'US army may soon use Israeli-designed "suicide drones"', *The Jerusalem Post* (1 June 2016) at https://goo.gl/AWM5WK.

c. Development by China

China's unmanned systems production is entrusted to the China Aerospace Science and Technology Consortium (CASC). The Cai Hong ('Rainbow') series to date comprises the CH-1[73] and CH-2, both of which are unarmed, and the CH-3, CH-4 and CH-5, each of which can be used for surveillance and/or offensive operations. The CH-3, a small drone with a width of seven metres and a length of eight metres, was initiated in 2008, though its capabilities have since been upgraded. The CH-3A can carry at least 130lbs of missiles and bombs under its wings, and possibly a heavier weapons payload. Its ability to loiter in the air is, though, limited to around six hours, roughly half of the original model.[74]

The CH-4 is similar in size and aspect to the Predator. It has an operational ceiling of 8 kilometres, a maximum range of 3,500 kilometres, and can fly continuously for up to 14 hours when operating to maximum payload and fully fuelled. It can carry up to six AR-1 semi-active laser-guided missiles, or FT-9 satellite-guided bombs or conventional gravity ordnance (or, alternatively, a mix of bombs and missiles).[75] Singer and Lin argue that until a technological advance in the remote operation of the CH-4, 'Chinese-made armed drones could not truly conduct what is known as a "remote split operation". … Up to this point, Chinese-made drones relied on direct line-of-sight communications with their ground control station, which dramatically limits their range to within a few hundred kilometres of their base.'[76]

The CH-5 is twice as big as its predecessors, can stay in the air for up to 60 hours, with a maximum operating ceiling of 10 kilometres. The CH-5 can carry up to one tonne of equipment and weapons. Its largest capacity is said to be 24 missiles in a single flight. Designers are reportedly planning to develop a variant capable of staying in the air for up to 120 hours, with a 20,000 kilometres range.[77]

ii. Hague Law Rules Applicable to Combat Aircraft

Hague Law rules apply equally and without qualification to both manned and remotely piloted aircraft during the conduct of hostilities. No allowance is made for the thousands of miles of distance between the aircraft and its pilot, nor is an additional burden imposed on the user by virtue of that fact by the law of armed conflict.

The general rules of distinction and proportionality in attack apply to all military aircraft engaged in the conduct of hostilities, as underpinned by the rule of precautions in attack. Although not limited to ordnance dropped or fired from the air, the prohibition codified in Article 51(5)(a) of the 1977 Additional Protocol I on 'attack by bombardment …

[73] The CH-1 dates back to the 1980s. E Kania and KW Allen, 'Inside the Secret World of Chinese Drones', *The National Interest* (26 May 2016) at https://goo.gl/4fxEn8.

[74] 'CASC CH-3 Rainbow Unmanned Aerial Vehicle (UAV) (2012)', *Military Factory* (13 April 2016) at https://goo.gl/kmpob1; and A Rawnsley, 'Meet China's Killer Drones', *Foreign Policy* (14 January 2016) at https://goo.gl/ttcKaF.

[75] 'CASC CH-4 Unmanned Combat Aerial Vehicle', *SinoDefence* (13 December 2015) at https://goo.gl/mvZ8rk.

[76] J Lin and PW Singer, 'Chinese Drones Make Key Breakthrough, Firing On Command By Satellite. Dial one to a CH-4 for missile delivery', *Popular Science* (8 June 2016) at https://goo.gl/o3VpJ6.

[77] Z Lei, 'Unmanned combat drone to be exported', *China Daily*, updated 11 January 2016, at https://goo.gl/4YgVgG.

which treats as a single military objective a number of clearly separated and distinct military objectives located in a city, town, village or other area containing a similar concentration of civilians or civilian objects' is of particular relevance to combat aircraft. High-level bombing and carpet bombing as methods of warfare are discussed further in section III.

The *Harvard Manual on International Law Applicable to Air and Missile Warfare* suggests that 'The destruction of the natural environment carried out wantonly is prohibited.'[78] In the accompanying commentary on the rule, it is stated that 'Despite the lack of a generally recognized definition of the term "natural environment", there is evidence in State practice of the customary character of the prohibition laid down in this Rule.'[79] This issue is also considered further in section III.

B. Attack Helicopters

An attack helicopter is an armed helicopter that has the capability to attack targets on the ground, such as tanks or enemy infantry. It is sometimes termed a helicopter gunship. Attack helicopters do not have the speed of combat aircraft but possess remarkable manoeuvrability, including the ability to hover over and land on very small areas of ground. As is the case with combat aircraft, no treaty definition of attack helicopters exists, but a valuable description is provided by the UNROCA, as follows:

> Rotary-wing aircraft designed, equipped or modified to engage targets by employing guided or unguided anti-armour, air-to-surface, air-to-subsurface, or air-to-air weapons and equipped with an integrated fire control and aiming system for these weapons, including versions of these aircraft which perform specialized reconnaissance or electronic warfare missions.[80]

The classification into 'generations' of attack helicopters has not been performed in the systematic way that has been the case with combat aircraft. Nonetheless, it is possible to piece together a set of criteria that could amount to such a classification:

- First Generation (1944–65) attack helicopters begin with US and German helicopters armed with bazookas or Panzerfaust anti-tank grenade launchers in the last stages of the Second World War. Early first-generation attack helicopters include the Sikorsky H-34s, in service with the US Air Force, and armed Mil Mi-4s, in service with the Soviet Air Force. 'Mature' first-generation attack helicopters encompass the armed Bell UH-1s and Mil Mi-8s used during the Vietnam War.
- Second Generation (1965–85) describes the first modern attack helicopters, beginning with the AH-1 'Huey' Cobra, which pioneered the format of pilot and weapons officer seated in tandem in a narrow fuselage with rockets and missiles mounted on stub wings. The Soviet Air Force has operated the Mil Mi-24 attack helicopter since 1972.

[78] *Harvard Manual* (n 1) Rule 88.

[79] *Commentary on the Harvard Manual on International Law Applicable to Air and Missile Warfare* (2010) 206, para 1.

[80] UNROCA (n 21).

- Third Generation (1986–2000) covers all-weather and night-capable helicopters that are faster, better protected and more heavily armed, such as the Boeing AH-64 Apache with nose-mounted sensors for target acquisition and night vision systems. The four hard-points mounted on stub-wing pylons typically carry a mixture of Hellfire missiles and Hydra 70 rocket pods.
- Fourth Generation (2000–15) attack helicopters, such as the AH-64D Apache Longbow, are equipped with advanced sensors that are capable of target detection even when the helicopter is behind obstacles such as hills, trees or buildings. The Longbow's target acquisition system can simultaneously track up to 128 targets and engage up to 16 at once.
- Fifth Generation (2015–) refers to attack helicopters with a low radar signature, extended flying range, advanced weapons control system, the capability to combat fighter jets, and possessing a speed of up to 600 kilometres per hour. Examples include the US Air Force's AH-64E Guardian and, probably, the Russian Mi-28NM, whose operational deployment was imminent.[81] As with fighter jets, unmanned systems are expected to be remotely piloted in future years, and incorporate ever-increasing autonomy of action and reaction.

Helicopters are currently the mainstay of the Afghan Air Force. As of 30 November 2016, it operated at least 48 aircraft capable of conducting offensive aerial operations, including 13 Mi-17 helicopters with fixed forward-firing guns (seven of which are capable of deploying rockets) and 27 MD-530 light helicopters.[82] During 2016, according to the United Nations Assistance Mission to Afghanistan (UNAMA), helicopter strikes caused 90 per cent of aerial operation civilian casualties attributed to the Afghan Air Force, amounting to 70 killed and 154 injured.[83] This included an incident on 22 September, when an Mi-35 helicopter conducted an airstrike targeting Taliban in the Such Bala area of Jurm district, Badakhshan province, which killed an eight-year-old boy and injured six members of the same family, including one woman and four children.[84] The MI-35 is a fourth-generation attack helicopter with advanced navigation and avionics, and a target sights system that includes a thermal imager, laser range finder and location finder.[85] In its annual report on the protection of civilians in 2016, UNAMA called for an 'immediate halt to the use of airstrikes in civilian-populated areas and … greater restraint in the use of airstrikes where civilians are likely to be present'.[86]

[81] 'Innovations Make Russia's Mi-28NM Copter an "Almost Perfect Combat Vehicle"', *Sputnik International* (4 January 2017) at https://goo.gl/pmpOvJ. In December 2017, the Russian Ministry of Defence ordered two improved variants of the Mi-28NM. According to Russian Deputy Defense Minister Yuri Borisov, the Mi-28NM will be the main attack helicopter of the Russian Armed forces for the coming decade. D Malyasov, 'Russia orders improved Mi-28NM attack helicopters', *Defense Blog* (21 December 2017) at https://goo.gl/e7wXnL.

[82] See US Department of Defense, *Report on Enhancing Security and Stability in Afghanistan* (December 2016) 54–59.

[83] UNAMA, *Protection of Civilians in Armed Conflict, Annual Report 2016*, Kabul (February 2017) 84–85.

[84] Ibid, 85.

[85] 'MI-35M: Attack Helicopters' (2017) at https://goo.gl/z6pfkZ.

[86] UNAMA (n 83) 85.

Helicopters were widely used by Israel in the 2014 Gaza conflict, deploying significant numbers of Hellfire missiles. Months after the end of the fighting, Ofer Shelah, a member of the Knesset Foreign Affairs and Defense Committee, declared:

> In the first three weeks of the conquest of Iraq, in 2003, the US armed forces captured cities and destroyed 1,600 armoured vehicles of the Iraqi army, half of them tanks. In Gaza, the IDF fought against an enemy that had no armoured vehicles, and Israeli soldiers probably saw no more than a few hundred armed Hamas militants. On average, an Israeli tank fired seven times as many shells a day as an American tank in Iraq. We fired more anti-tank missiles from the ground than the Americans, and twice as many Hellfire rockets from helicopters – Israel requested more of them during the war, but the Americans delayed their supply.[87]

C. Gravity Ordnance and Precision-guided Munitions

The first air-dropped bombs were 'unguided', meaning that once dropped from an aircraft, gravitational forces determined when they would land while the ballistic trajectory of the weapons upon release would determine where they would land. This was the case with all aircraft bombs in general service until the latter part of the Second World War,[88] and included the vast majority of all air-dropped ordnance until the Gulf War in the early 1990s.[89] Such gravity ordnance is contrasted with precision-guided weapons, defined by the *Harvard Manual on International Law Applicable to Air and Missile Warfare* as 'weapons that can be directed against a target using either external guidance or a guidance system of their own'.[90]

The formal *Commentary on the Harvard Manual* definition notes that it generally applies to any weapon 'that employs a guidance system to strike a target accurately'.[91] The *Commentary* cautions, though, that the notion of precision is

> sometimes wrongly characterized as a weapon's capacity to strike the precise point at which it is aimed (known as the 'aimpoint'). In fact, this ability is correctly labelled 'accuracy'. It is measured

[87] Quoted in 'This lawmaker won't let the Gaza War be pushed under the rug', *Haaretz* (24 April 2015) at https://goo.gl/Ba9r9b.

[88] The German Air Force in 1943 is said to be the first armed force to have introduce precision-guided munitions (PGMs) in combat, using the manual command to line of sight (MCLOS) Fritz X gliding munition to attack and sink the Italian battleship *Roma*. The PGM gave the German aircraft the possibility to remain out of range of the ship's anti-aircraft guns yet be able to strike accurately. See, eg, B McNally, 'The Sinking of the Battleship Roma and the Dawn of the Age of Precision Guided Munitions', *Defense Media Network* (1 June 2014) at https://goo.gl/ck1oTg.

[89] In 1991, it was claimed in the media that laser-guided bombs greatly enhanced the effectiveness of the US attacks during the War. 'Even small, armored targets like tanks and personnel carriers, previously almost impossible to destroy with bombs, have now fallen victim to the new bombs' accuracy. The same accuracy has substantially reduced the accidental damage that would otherwise have befallen civilian buildings.' An allied military spokesman claimed in February 1991 that of the many thousands of precision-guided bombs and missiles launched at Iraqi military targets, fewer than 0.1% had gone astray and fallen in civilian areas. MW Browne, 'Invention That Shaped the Gulf War: the Laser-Guided Bomb', *New York Times* (26 February 1991) at https://goo.gl/gCKktt. In fact, the truth was not as rosy. In 1997, the US Congress's General Accounting Office (GAO) produced a report on Operation Desert Storm in which it affirmed that many of the Department of Defense's and manufacturers' post-war claims about weapon system performance – particularly the F-117, cruise missiles and laser-guided bombs – were 'overstated, misleading, inconsistent with the best available data, or unverifiable'. GAO, *Operation Desert Storm: Evaluation of the Air Campaign*, US Doc NSIAD-97-134, 12 June 1997 (publicly released on 30 June 1997) 19, at https://goo.gl/2QsoFP. The report also concluded that air power was inhibited by the limited ability of aircraft sensors to identify and acquire targets in a timely manner; and that there was no apparent link between the cost of aircraft and munitions and their performance in Operation Desert Storm.

[90] *Harvard Manual* (n 1) para 1(bb).

[91] *Commentary on the Harvard Manual* (n 79) 51, para 1 (bb).

> in terms of circular error probable, the radius of a circle within which one-half of weapons launched will fall. Precision is a broader concept. It encompasses the ability to locate and identify a target, strike it accurately in a timely fashion, and determine whether desired effects have been achieved or restrike is needed.[92]

As the *Commentary* goes on to explain, such weapons have different degrees of autonomy. Some rely on a radar or laser signal from an aircraft, GPS or alternative source operated by a person to home in on the target. Some weapons have inbuilt capabilities to guide them to a target in the air or on the ground without external input. When an air-delivered guided weapon is independent of any signal from the launching aircraft, it has a 'fire-and-forget' capability;[93] this is the case with the Hellfire discussed in section II.D following.

As discussed in chapter 7 on the rule of precautions in attack, Hague Law does not generally require a party to armed conflict to use any PGMs it may possess in the conduct of hostilities.[94] However, if an attack might otherwise be expected to cause excessive civilian harm, for example if it is unlikely successfully to hit the intended target, such guided munitions may be the only lawful means to achieve the military mission without violating the law.[95] This reality is reflected in Rule 8 of the *Harvard Manual*.[96] In contrast, if a PGM hits a civilian or civilian object rather than a military objective, in many instances it may well be harder than would be the case with gravity ordnance to dismiss out of hand an alleged violation of the rule of distinction (unless of course the intelligence on which the attack was based was faulty). In any event, if the only form of munition in a conflict party's arsenal is an unguided weapon that is inherently indiscriminate, it is prohibited to use that weapon. To do so may amount to a war crime.

D. Air-to-ground Missiles

There are many types and models of air-to-ground missiles, though perhaps the best known publicly is the Hellfire, by virtue of its use from remotely piloted combat aircraft. The development of the Hellfire missile system began in 1974, with the US Army's requirement for an air-to-ground missile launched from helicopters against armoured fighting vehicles. This explains the name given to the missile, which is a shortened form of 'helicopter-launched fire and forget'. Production of the base model AGM-114A began in 1982.[97]

[92] Ibid, 51–52, para 2.

[93] Ibid, 52, para 4.

[94] US Department of Defense, *Law of War Manual*, June 2015 (hereinafter 'USDOD 2015 *Law of War Manual*') para 5.11.3, at https://goo.gl/uZKhvk, citing also the military manuals of Australia, Canada and Germany; see also Y Dinstein, *The Conduct of Hostilities under the Law of International Armed Conflict*, 3rd edn (Cambridge, Cambridge University Press, 2016) 170, para 454; GD Solis, *The Law of Armed Conflict: International Humanitarian Law in War*, 2nd edn (New York, Cambridge University Press, 2016) 294.

[95] Dinstein (n 94) 167, para 447; 169, para 453.

[96] 'There is no specific obligation on Belligerent Parties to use precision guided weapons. There may however be situations in which the prohibition of indiscriminate attacks, or the obligation to avoid – or, in any event, minimize – collateral damage, cannot be fulfilled without using precision guided weapons.'

[97] 'AGM-114 Hellfire II Missile, United States of America', *Army Technology*, undated but accessed on 17 January 2017 at https://goo.gl/CuJKn1.

The standard explosive charge in a Hellfire missile is typically 8 kg or 9 kg, with a reported 'kill radius' of 15 metres and a 'wounding radius' of 20 metres.[98] Scott Shane claims that after a 2010 strike killed several civilian women and children in Pakistan, President Barack Obama asked the Central Intelligence Agency (CIA) to reduce the size of the explosive they were incorporating in the Hellfire missiles being fired from drones.[99] The change is reported to have been implemented.[100]

E. Air-dropped Mines

Remotely delivered mines are dispersed from combat aircraft and attack helicopters. States parties to the 1997 Anti-Personnel Mine Ban Convention may not use any anti-personnel mines in the conduct of hostilities, including when they are remotely delivered. For other states that are party to the 1996 Amended Protocol II to the Convention on Certain Conventional Weapons (CCW), all remotely delivered anti-personnel mines must meet the standards for self-destruction and self-deactivation set out in the Technical Annex to the 1996 Protocol.[101] This requires that 90 per cent of 'activated' mines self-destruct within 30 days after emplacement, while the back-up self-deactivation feature (typically the exhaustion of a battery) must ensure that, in combination with the self-destruction mechanism, a total of 99.9 per cent (one in 1,000) of the activated mines can no longer be detonated 120 days after emplacement. These specific requirements may not yet form part of customary law.

Under Amended Protocol II, it is prohibited to use remotely-delivered anti-vehicle mines, unless,

> to the extent feasible, they are equipped with an effective self-destruction or self-neutralization mechanism and have a back-up self-deactivation feature, which is designed so that the mine will no longer function as a mine when the mine no longer serves the military purpose for which it was placed in position.[102]

The lack of any standards or defined time period renders this obligation largely impotent in practice.

F. Cluster Munitions

Any state party to the 2008 Convention on Cluster Munitions is prohibited from using cluster munitions as defined therein in the conduct of hostilities. The definition is generally broad, although specifically excluded from the scope of the treaty prohibition are all mines delivered as sub-munitions (both anti-personnel and anti-vehicle)[103] as well as a

[98] See, eg, G Chamayou, *La théorie du drone* (Editions de la Fabrique, 2013).
[99] Shane (n 18) 212.
[100] J Becker and S Shane, 'Secret "Kill List" Proves a Test of Obama's Principles and Will', *New York Times* (29 May 2012) at https://goo.gl/ojTiha.
[101] Art 6(2), 1996 Amended Protocol II, and para 3(a) of the Technical Annex.
[102] Art 6(3), 1996 Amended Protocol II.
[103] Art 1(3), 2008 Convention on Cluster Munitions.

specific form of fully autonomous weapon. This munition dispenses sensor-fuzed explosive sub-munitions 'designed to detect and engage a single target object'.[104] The conditions for exclusion are that the munition has *all* of the following characteristics:

(i) Each munition contains fewer than ten explosive submunitions
(ii) Each explosive submunition weighs more than four kilograms
(iii) Each explosive submunition is designed to detect and engage a single target object
(iv) Each explosive submunition is equipped with an electronic self-destruction mechanism
(v) Each explosive submunition is equipped with an electronic self-deactivating feature.[105]

Although it was not made explicit during the negotiations, much less within the text of the Convention itself, particularly envisaged by this exception were the Textron Systems (US)-produced CBU-105 cluster munitions. These munitions dispense 10 BLU-108 sub-munitions, each of which contains four small sensor-fuzed projectiles called skeets, which the sub-munition releases during high-speed rotation. The centrifugal force carries the skeets away from the empty canister. An infrared seeker on each skeet scans for targets on the ground by detecting heat signatures, such as those emitted by the engine of a vehicle, while a laser-ranging device calculates the range for release timing. Once it locks onto a target, the skeet fires explosively formed penetrators that hit the top of the target. A shrapnel ring causes damage around the target.[106]

Human Rights Watch has criticised the use of these munitions in Yemen, seemingly by Saudi Arabia. In 2015, the organisation stated that the weapons had been used in or near civilian areas, in apparent violation of US export law:

> A woman and two children were injured in their homes by CBU-105 Sensor Fuzed Weapons used on December 12, 2015, on the port town of Hodaida, while at least two civilians were wounded in an attack that used CBU-105 Sensor Fuzed Weapons near al-Amar village in Saada governorate on April 27, 2015.[107]

The organisation has also criticised the reliability of the self-destruct mechanism, which is supposed to ensure that 99 per cent of all cluster munitions dispersed either detonate as intended, or subsequently self-detonate.

G. Incendiary Weapons

As the Geneva Academy's *Weapons Law Encyclopedia* recalls, napalm and white phosphorous are probably the best-known incendiary substances used in incendiary weapons.[108] Protocol III to the CCW defines incendiary weapons as

> any weapon or munition which is primarily designed to set fire to objects or to cause burn injury to persons through the action of flame, heat, or combination thereof, produced by a chemical reaction of a substance delivered on the target.[109]

[104] Art 2(2)(c), 2008 Convention on Cluster Munitions.
[105] Ibid.
[106] See, eg, 'CBU-105 Sensor Fuzed Weapon: USAF's Ultimate Tank-buster', *Defencyclopedia* (12 June 2015) at https://goo.gl/3GYrv8.
[107] Human Rights Watch, 'Yemen: Saudis Using US Cluster Munitions' (6 May 2016) at https://goo.gl/8AbNNh.
[108] 'Incendiary weapons', *Weapons Law Encyclopedia*, Geneva Academy of International Humanitarian Law and Human Rights, at https://goo.gl/ijWvMG.
[109] Art 1(1), Protocol III to the CCW.

The Protocol prohibits only certain uses of incendiary weapons (despite a widespread, but mistaken public perception that the use of napalm is unlawful). Thus, efforts by some states in the 1970s to ban outright the use of incendiary weapons, particularly napalm, following their extensive use by the US in the war in Indochina, proved unsuccessful. The Protocol prohibits direct attacks on civilians or attacks that would be expected to have disproportionate effects[110] (consonant with the general rule on proportionality in attack).

Aerial delivery, in the conduct of hostilities, of incendiary weapons within a concentration of civilians is prohibited.[111] Upon its ratification of the Protocol in 2009, the US included a reservation whereby it retained 'the right to use incendiary weapons against military objectives located in concentrations of civilians where it is judged that such use would cause fewer casualties and/or less collateral damage than alternative weapons'. It pledged that, in so doing, it would take 'all feasible precautions with a view to limiting the incendiary effects to the military objective and to avoiding, and in any event to minimizing, incidental loss of civilian life, injury to civilians and damage to civilian objects'.[112]

Certain uses of white phosphorus (WP),[113] which bursts into flame when mixing with oxygen, also fall to be regulated by the 1980 Protocol III on Incendiary Weapons. Excluded from the definition of an incendiary weapon under Protocol III, and, hence, from the Protocol's scope, are munitions with 'incidental incendiary effects' and combined effects munitions 'in which the incendiary effect is not specifically designed to cause burn injury to persons'. Use of munitions containing WP that are primarily designed to illuminate or obscure rather than to harm through fire or heat are not regulated by the Protocol on the ground that their incendiary effects are considered incidental.[114] It is acknowledged, for instance, that US-led Coalition forces employed WP smokescreens in order to support the evacuation of Mosul in June 2017. According to New Zealand Brigadier-General Hugh McAslan, forces used WP 'to screen areas within west Mosul to get civilians out safely'.[115]

In a decision of 9 July 2013, Israel's Supreme Court sitting as the High Court of Justice dismissed a petition for order nisi in *Yoav Hess and others v Chief of Staff*[116] concerning use, by the Israeli Defence Forces, of WP in populated areas in Gaza during Operation Cast Lead (27 December 2008 to 18 January 2009). The petitioners had asked the Court to instruct the Israel Defence Forces (IDF) to refrain from using WP in populated areas, and to prohibit the use of any weapon containing WP whenever an alternative exists that would pose less risk to civilians while providing a similar military advantage.

In May 2009, four months after Operation Cast Lead ended, the military had published the results of its inquiry into the use of WP during the operation, concluding that although its use had been lawful, it would stop using shells containing WP. However, the military

[110] Art 2, Protocol III to the CCW.

[111] Art 1(2) of the Protocol defines a concentration of civilians as 'any concentration of civilians, be it permanent or temporary, such as in inhabited parts of cities, or inhabited towns or villages, or as in camps or columns of refugees or evacuees, or groups of nomads'.

[112] The text of the reservation is available at https://goo.gl/5FkT6q.

[113] White phosphorus is an allotrope of phosphorus that can be produced in a variety of ways. It is known informally as 'Willie Pete', the Second World War phonetic words for WP.

[114] 'White Phosphorus', *Weapons Law Encyclopedia*, Geneva Academy of International Humanitarian Law and Human Rights, last updated 4 August 2017, at https://goo.gl/hNxSPL.

[115] A Meuse, 'US-Led Coalition Has Used White Phosphorus In Fight For Mosul, General Says', *NPR* (June 2017) at https://goo.gl/h9sLHd.

[116] Israel Supreme Court, *Yoav Hess and others v Chief of Staff*, Case No HCJ 4146/11, 9 July 2013.

decided it would continue its practice of using such shells for the purpose of smokescreens. In the Court's ruling, Justice Edna Arbel rejected the state's argument that the Court did not have jurisdiction to review the use of munitions: 'Clearly, when there are allegations that military measures have been used in a manner that contravenes the laws of war, the court must go "to the battleground" and examine the arguments presented to it'.[117] Despite dismissing Hess's petition, the Court did recommend that the IDF conduct a detailed examination of its use of WP, including consideration of alternatives.[118]

The International Committee of the Red Cross (ICRC) acknowledged in its commentary on 1977 Additional Protocol I that none of the rules in CCW Protocol III explicitly protects combatants against incendiary weapons such as flame-throwers or napalm. It observed, however, that 'it is generally admitted that these weapons should not be used in such a way that they will cause unnecessary suffering ... which means that in particular they should not be used against individuals without cover'.[119] In its study of customary law of armed conflict rules, the ICRC affirmed that a rule existed whereby the 'anti-personnel use of incendiary weapons is prohibited, unless it is not feasible to use a less harmful weapon to render a person hors de combat'.[120] It further claimed that it was 'reasonable to conclude that the rule is applicable in non-international armed conflicts'.[121] Whether the proposed rule is indeed black-letter law is not settled. As noted in the previous chapter, Gary Solis's view is that 'Individual napalm or flame-thrower targets will be killed, cover or no cover, but that does not constitute unnecessary suffering.'[122]

H. 'Barrel' Bombs

Although no definition exists under international law,[123] barrel bombs are improvised devices – oil barrels, fuel tanks or gas cylinders packed with explosives, fuel and metal fragments (or containing chemical agents, especially chlorine).[124] They have been dropped from

[117] B'Tselem, 'HCJ dismisses petition demanding the military cease use of white phosphorous' (14 July 2013) at https://goo.gl/sxCm9R.

[118] 'White phosphorus petition (Israeli High Court of Justice)', *Weapons Law Encyclopedia*, Geneva Academy of International Humanitarian Law and Human Rights, last updated 8 August 2017, at https://goo.gl/F1q15d.

[119] ICRC Commentary on the 1977 Additional Protocols, para 1424.

[120] ICRC, Study of Customary IHL, Rule 85 ('The Use of Incendiary Weapons against Combatants') at https://goo.gl/8EuxGS.

[121] Ibid.

[122] Solis (n 94) 291.

[123] 'Barrel Bombs', *Weapons Law Encyclopedia*, Geneva Academy of International Humanitarian Law and Human Rights, at https://goo.gl/4WxCZb.

[124] See, eg, Report of the Independent International Commission of Inquiry on the Syrian Arab Republic (hereinafter 'Report of the Commission of Inquiry on Syria'), UN Doc A/HRC/34/64, 2 February 2017, paras 14, 17. As the *Weapons Law Encyclopedia* also recalls, in its eighth report (published on 13 August 2014), the Commission of Inquiry on Syria found strong evidence that chemical agents, likely chlorine, were used on Kafr Zeita, Al-Tamana'a and Tal Minnis in eight incidents, and that those agents were likely dropped in barrel bombs from government helicopters. The Commission recalled that chlorine gas is a chemical weapon as defined in the 1992 Chemical Weapons Convention, whose use is prohibited in all circumstances under customary law of armed conflict and is a war crime under the ICC Statute. Eighth Report of the Commission of Inquiry on Syria, UN Doc A/HRC/27/60, 13 August 2014, paras 177–78. Convention on the Prohibition of the Development, Production, Stockpiling and Use of Chemical Weapons and on Their Destruction, adopted at Geneva, 3 September 1992; entry into force 29 April 1997.

helicopters or other aircraft by Syrian government forces in the non-international armed conflicts (NIACs) across its territory since 2012.

Despite occasional claims to the contrary, especially in the media,[125] these weapons are not unlawful per se, either by virtue of their improvised nature or on the basis that they often have a high explosive yield. Thus, the Commission of Inquiry on Syria does not identify barrel bombs as weapons whose use is always prohibited.[126] It is certainly true, however, that in Syria they have been very widely used in an indiscriminate manner. In May 2015, Amnesty International issued a report entitled *'Death everywhere': War crimes and human rights abuses in Aleppo*, which concluded that some of the Government's actions in Aleppo amounted to crimes against humanity. The report describes the carnage caused by barrel bombs dropped by government forces on schools, hospitals, mosques and crowded markets. According to Amnesty, attacks using barrel bombs killed more than 3,000 civilians in Aleppo governorate in 2014, and more than 11,000 in Syria since 2012.[127]

A Syrian human rights organisation claimed in early 2017 that Syrian regime helicopters had dropped 12,958 barrel bombs in 2016 in total, killing 653 civilians, including 166 children and 86 women. Most were dropped on rebel-held suburbs of Damascus, followed by Aleppo, Hama, Idlib, Daraa and Homs. The highest number of barrel bombs was dropped during the month of November 2016, at the height of government efforts to retake Aleppo.[128]

I. Chemical Weapons

The use in warfare of asphyxiating and poisonous gases, such as chlorine or sulphur mustard, was first prohibited by an 1899 Hague Declaration.[129] In 1925, however, following their widespread use against combatants during the First World War, a new protocol was negotiated at a conference held in Geneva under the auspices of the League of Nations.[130] The preamble to the 1925 Geneva Gas Protocol noted the intention of states parties to ensure that the prohibition of the use of 'asphyxiating, poisonous or other gases, and of all analogous liquids materials or devices' would become 'universally accepted as a part of International Law, binding alike the conscience and the practice of nations'. However, subsequent reservations by more than 20 states parties effectively reduced the Protocol in many cases to only a ban on first use.

It took a further 67 years to transform the law of armed conflict prohibition on use into a comprehensive disarmament treaty prohibiting unequivocally all use of chemical weapons in the conduct of hostilities. Thus, the development, production, stockpiling, transfer

[125] B McKernan, 'Assad "dropped 13,000 barrel bombs on Syria in 2016", watchdog claims', *Independent* (11 January 2017) at https://goo.gl/55zHFX.

[126] Report of the Commission of Inquiry on Syria (n 124) 32–33.

[127] Amnesty International, *'Death everywhere': War crimes and human rights abuses in Aleppo* (May 2015) at https://goo.gl/PYXm4r.

[128] McKernan (n 125).

[129] Declaration (IV,2) concerning the Use of Asphyxiating Gases, adopted at The Hague, 29 July 1899; entry into force, 4 September 1900.

[130] Protocol for the Prohibition of the Use of Asphyxiating, Poisonous or Other Gases, and of Bacteriological Methods of Warfare, adopted at Geneva, 17 June 1925; entry into force, 8 February 1928.

and use of chemical weapons are generally prohibited under the 1992 Chemical Weapons Convention, and their use as a method of warfare in armed conflict is prohibited under customary international law. Use of chemical weapons is also a war crime for which potential jurisdiction is given to the International Criminal Court through the prohibition in international armed conflict (IAC) and NIAC of '[e]mploying asphyxiating, poisonous or other gases, and all analogous liquids, materials or devices'.[131] While the use of riot control agents such as tear gas is specifically prohibited as a method of warfare, the Chemical Weapons Convention admits an exception for their use for law enforcement, 'including domestic riot control'.[132]

Oversight of the implementation of the Convention was tasked to the Organisation for the Prohibition of Chemical Weapons (OPCW), specially created by the Chemical Weapons Convention for the purpose. Despite the OPCW's involvement in Syria, though, following that state's accession to the Chemical Weapons Convention in October 2013, chemical weapons have been used on many occasions during the many armed conflicts that were ongoing in that country as of writing. In March 2016, it was claimed that some 1,500 people had been killed by chemical attacks during the previous five years of armed conflict. The report by the Syrian-American Medical Society documented 161 chemical attacks in Syria on the basis of testimony from doctors operating in the areas that had borne the brunt of chemical attacks, leading to the deaths of 1,491 people and injuries to 14,581 others. More than a third of the attacks used chlorine gas.[133]

J. Nuclear Weapons

The Treaty on the Prohibition of Nuclear Weapons was adopted by states participating in a UN diplomatic conference in July 2017.[134] In accordance with its Article 13, the Treaty was opened for signature by all states at the UN headquarters in New York on 20 September 2017. As at 1 April 2018, there were 57 signatories of which seven had also deposited their instrument of ratification, the latest being Venezuela. In accordance with its Article 15(1), the Treaty will enter into force 90 days after the 50th instrument of ratification, acceptance, approval or accession has been deposited.

In its 1996 Nuclear Weapons Advisory Opinion, the International Court of Justice (ICJ) had determined, by seven votes to seven, by the President's casting vote,

> that the threat or use of nuclear weapons would generally be contrary to the rules of international law applicable in armed conflict, and in particular the principles and rules of humanitarian law;
>
> However, in view of the current state of international law, and of the elements of fact at its disposal, the Court cannot conclude definitively whether the threat or use of nuclear weapons would be

[131] Art 8(2)(b)(xviii) and 8(2)(e)(xiv), ICC Statute.

[132] Arts I(5) and II(9), 1992 Chemical Weapons Convention.

[133] See, eg, K Shaheen, '"Almost 1,500 killed in chemical weapons attacks" in Syria', *Guardian* (14 March 2016) at https://goo.gl/SfJ2Zw.

[134] The Treaty was adopted on 7 July 2017 by the UN conference to negotiate a legally binding instrument to prohibit nuclear weapons, leading towards their total elimination, held in New York from 27 to 31 March and 15 June to 7 July 2017.

> lawful or unlawful in an extreme circumstance of self-defence, in which the very survival of a State would be at stake.[135]

The Court unanimously held that there exists 'an obligation to pursue in good faith and bring to a conclusion negotiations leading to nuclear disarmament in all its aspects under strict and effective international control'.[136]

The Treaty will not directly affect the determination of the nuclear-armed states to maintain a nuclear arsenal. It will, though, dent a little further the notion that these weapons could ever be used lawfully when the risk is perhaps higher than at any time since the Cuban missile crisis. In 2015, an article by the managing editor of *The National Interest*, a US foreign policy website, entitled 'The Most Dangerous Nuclear Weapon in America's Arsenal', argued that the US' upgraded 50kT B61-12 nuclear weapon was so dangerous because of 'its usability'.[137] This usability, the article argues, is derived from a combination of accuracy and low yield: 'A lower-yield and more accurate bomb can … be used without having to fear the mass, indiscriminate killing of civilians through explosive force or radioactive fallout.'[138]

This stance was given support in 2016 by US General James E Cartwright, a retired vice-chair of the Joint Chiefs of Staff, who told *The New York Times* that he backed the upgraded, precision-guided nuclear weapons because precise targeting allowed the US to hold fewer weapons. But he acknowledged that 'what going smaller does is to make the weapon more thinkable'.[139] James N Miller, the former Under Secretary of Defense for Policy who helped develop the modernisation plan, said the smaller, more precise weapons would maintain the nation's nuclear deterrent while reducing risks for civilians near foreign military targets: 'Minimising civilian casualties if deterrence fails is both a more credible and a more ethical approach.' The B61-12 has a 'dial-a-yield' feature whose lowest setting is only 2 per cent as powerful as the bomb dropped on Hiroshima in 1945.[140] In July 2015, following testing of the B61-12 bomb (without, of course, a nuclear detonation), Russia's Deputy Minister of Defence Anatoly Antonov called the test 'irresponsible' and 'openly provocative'.[141]

As of the time of writing, the US was locked in discussions with the Democratic People's Republic of Korea (DPR Korea), which had developed a nuclear deterrent. On 9 October 2006, DPR Korea had announced it had successfully conducted its first nuclear test; its latest, as of writing, was of a hydrogen (thermonuclear) device on 3 September 2017. A month earlier, Patricia Lewis had warned that 'History is littered with near misses, but the latest tensions between the US and North Korea offer their own special risks of Armageddon.'[142] In December 2017, according to a statement by DPR Korea,

[135] ICJ, *Legality of the Threat or Use of Nuclear Weapons*, Advisory Opinion, 8 July 1996 ('Nuclear Weapons Advisory Opinion') para 105, dispositive E.

[136] Ibid, dispositive F.

[137] Z Keck, 'The Most Dangerous Nuclear Weapon in America's Arsenal', *The National Interest* (28 July 2015) at http://nationalinterest.org/blog/the-buzz/the-most-dangerous-nuclear-weapon-americas-arsenal-13433.

[138] Ibid.

[139] WJ Broad and DE Sangerjan, 'As US Modernizes Nuclear Weapons, "Smaller" Leaves Some Uneasy', *New York Times* (11 January 2016) at https://goo.gl/1RcGGX.

[140] Ibid.

[141] 'Russia slams US test of B61-12 atomic bomb as "provocative"', *Press TV* (13 July 2015).

[142] P Lewis, 'How Worried Should We Be About a Nuclear War With North Korea?', Chatham House (9 August 2017) at https://goo.gl/FuKwV8.

'The remaining question now is: when will the war break out? We do not wish for a war but shall not hide from it.'[143] A meeting and signed agreement between Chairman Kim and President Trump in June 2018 had not yet resulted in concrete progress towards disarmament.

K. Directed Energy Weapons

Directed energy weapons may soon be fielded by major military powers. What is true is that many military research and development programmes have been seeking to produce a viable laser weapon for offensive and defensive purposes. Some of the most promising research has focused on solid-state lasers for use on warships; earlier hopes that air and space-based directed energy weapons would soon be ready for trials have receded, although at the end of 2016, Lieutenant-General Robert Walsh, the head of the Marine Corps Combat Development Command, said that he could 'absolutely' see putting a laser on the F-35B combat aircraft in the future: 'Because of the size and weight requirements for a laser, we'd probably start off with a KC-130. As soon as we could miniaturise it, we'd put them on F-35s, Cobras, any of those attack aircraft.'[144]

Therein lies one of the challenges, as discussed at the second annual Directed Energy Summit in June 2016, hosted by defence contractor Booz Allen Hamilton and the Center for Strategic and Budgetary Assessment, a Washington think tank. A directed energy weapon needs great heat to excite the crystal at the heart of the solid-state laser (and considerable power to cool the equipment as well.)[145] As the *Air Force Times* reported, when the US Air Force first developed a directed energy weapon early in the new millennium, it was so large it took up an entire modified Boeing 747 aircraft. The Navy's test version, installed aboard the amphibious transport dock Ponce, is estimated to weigh more than could be lifted by the average aircraft.[146]

Also of concern to the US military is the legal and policy framework for the new weapons. Lieutenant-General William Etter, interviewed by the *Air Force Times*, expressed his desire for a laser weapon that could knock down an incoming missile, even ones travelling at hypersonic speed (Mach 5). But, as he noted, using a laser to hit a missile means making sure the laser does not cause collateral damage. 'We've got an additional consideration, though, and this is pretty important to us: We've got to make sure that we don't hit the other folks', Etter said. 'Because in the homeland we have civilian airliners, we have small aircraft, you can range even up to a satellite. … We have to be exactly precise.' He observed that 'The policy's actually more difficult than the actual technology. I need rules of engagement. Are we shooting down a [small drone], are we shooting down an aircraft?'[147]

[143] S Kim and H Yang, 'North Korea says U.S. threats make war unavoidable, China urges calm', *Reuters* (6 December 2017) at https://goo.gl/65ofrz.

[144] J Klimas, 'Marine general wants lasers on the F-35', *Washington Examiner* (30 December 2016) at https://goo.gl/EQiMqn.

[145] See, eg, A Robinson, 'Directed Energy Weapons: Will They Ever Be Ready?', *National Defense* (July 2015) at https://goo.gl/fuCmwu.

[146] P Swarts, 'Air Force has directed energy weapons; now comes the hard part', *Air Force Times* (25 June 2016) at https://goo.gl/GhQUc9.

[147] Ibid.

III. Methods of Warfare

A. High-level Bombing

High-level bombing is not generally unlawful, even when it is carried out using gravity ordnance. If conducted in densely populated areas, however, the likelihood that the attack will be indiscriminate increases significantly. This is not to say that all guided munitions delivered from high altitude successfully hit their targets. The 1997 report by the US Congress's General Accounting Office (GAO) on the conduct of the 1991 Gulf War found that while higher-altitude bombing

> clearly reduced aircraft casualties, [it] also caused target location and identification problems for guided munitions and exposed unguided bombs to uncontrollable factors such as wind. Medium- and high-altitude tactics also increased the exposure of aircraft to clouds, haze, smoke, and high humidity, thereby impeding IR [infrared] and electro-optical … sensors and laser designators for LGBs [laser-guided bombs]. These higher altitude tactics also reduced target sensor resolution and the ability of pilots to discern the precise nature of some of the targets they were attacking.[148]

The report further notes that while 'pilots and planners reported that unguided bombs were substantially less accurate and target discrimination problems were sometimes severe, these unguided bombs were employed with radar against area targets in poor weather'.[149]

B. Carpet Bombing

Carpet bombing of cities, also sometimes known as area bombardment or saturation bombing, was widely conducted during the Second World War, especially by the US Air Force against Japanese cities and by the British Royal Air Force against German cities.[150] While their actions were not unequivocally unlawful at the time, they certainly would be now. As noted in section II.A.ii, an indiscriminate attack includes one that 'treats as a single military objective a number of clearly separated and distinct military objectives located in a city, town, village or other area containing a similar concentration of civilians or civilian objects are prohibited'.[151]

According to the ICRC commentary on this provision, as included in the 1977 Additional Protocol I, 'it is understandable that the drafters of the Protocol wished to mention it specifically, even though such attacks already fall under the general prohibition [on indiscriminate attacks]'.[152] But the provision was only adopted 'with some difficulty; the

[148] GAO, *Operation Desert Storm: Evaluation of the Air Campaign* (n 88) 21.

[149] Ibid.

[150] Reflecting on his decision to call for the bombing of Hamburg in 1945, which was subsequently performed by a fleet of 1,000 bombers, Montgomery mused later that it would have been 'less horrible, and produced the same strategic results, to have put the entire population out of action for forty-eight hours with the use of suitable "bugs" or even gas. … There are great possibilities in the use of nerve gases to produce short-term disablement, without killing – and political leaders might well examine this question.' Montgomery (n 8) 546–47.

[151] ICRC Study of Customary IHL, Rule 13 ('Area Bombardment') at https://goo.gl/zgsYX1; see also Art 51(5)(a), 1977 Additional Protocol I.

[152] ICRC Commentary on the 1977 Additional Protocols, para 1968.

expression "clearly separated and distinct" in particular led to lengthy discussions'.[153] The ICRC acknowledged that the 'interpretation of the words "clearly separated and distinct" leaves some degree of latitude to those mounting an attack'. It recommends that in case of doubt, parties to an armed conflict can refer to the rule of proportionality in attack 'and assess whether the attack is of a nature to cause losses and damage which would be excessive in relation to the military advantage anticipated'.[154]

C. Attacks on the Environment

The protection of the environment from the effects of armed conflict has risen in importance in recent decades, and is an element of the proportionality equation insofar as the natural environment is a civilian object. It is, though, highly premature to talk of a 'principle of ambituity' as one suffusing Hague Law.[155] Indeed, the US has not 'accepted' the provisions on environmental protection set out the 1977 Additional Protocol I, and has 'repeatedly expressed the view that these provisions are "overly broad and ambiguous" and "not a part of customary law"'.[156] Similarly, Gary Solis asserts that despite 'noble intentions', the provisions on the environment included in the Protocol are not customary law.[157] Nonetheless, the inclusion in the ICC Statute of the war crime of '[i]ntentionally launching an attack in the knowledge that such attack will cause … widespread, long-term and severe damage to the natural environment which would be clearly excessive in relation to the concrete and direct overall military advantage anticipated' is significant, even though the Court's jurisdiction is limited to IAC. This war crime has developed from the corresponding prohibition in Article 35(3) of the 1977 Additional Protocol I.[158]

As noted above, no accepted definition of the 'natural environment' exists in the law of armed conflict, although the ICRC explains that the term refers to the 'system of inextricable interrelations between living organisms and their inanimate environment'.[159] In a work published the year the Additional Protocol was adopted, William Rodgers Jr, an international environmental lawyer, distinguished the 'natural' environment, which encompasses the physical condition of the land, air and water, from the 'human' environment, which includes health, social and other man-made conditions.[160] In 1997, Gretchen Daily referred

[153] Ibid, para 1969.

[154] Ibid, para 1972.

[155] See EV Koppe, 'The principle of ambituity and the prohibition against excessive collateral damage to the environment during armed conflict' (2013) 83 *Nordic Journal of International Law* 53.

[156] USDOD 2015 *Law of War Manual*, para 6.10.3.1, citing US Response to the ICRC Customary IHL Study: 'France and the United States repeatedly have declared that Articles 35(3) and 55 of AP I, from which the Study derives the first sentence of rule 45, do not reflect customary international law.' John B Bellinger, III, Legal Adviser, Department of State, and William J Haynes II, General Counsel, Department of Defense, Letter to Dr Jacob Kellenberger, President, ICRC, Regarding Customary International Humanitarian Law Study, 3 November 2006, reprinted in (2007) 46 *International Legal Materials*, 514, 521.

[157] Solis (n 94) 513. Dinstein agrees with this assertion: Dinstein (n 94) 238, para 644.

[158] 'It is prohibited to employ methods or means of warfare which are intended, or may be expected, to cause widespread, long-term and severe damage to the natural environment.' See also the duty of care installed by Art 55 of the Protocol, which focuses on the potential dangers for the civilian population of environmental damage. ICRC Commentary on the 1977 Additional Protocols, para 1449.

[159] Ibid, para 1451.

[160] WH Rodgers, *Handbook on Environmental Law* (Boulder, West Publishing Co., 1977).

to natural resources, plant and animal species, the atmosphere, oceans, rivers, lakes, terrestrial habitats and other elements of the natural world that provide ecosystem services.[161]

As Dinstein observes, although the natural environment is not formally designated as a civilian object, unless it or its constituent elements are a military objective, it is protected from attack.[162] Moreover, if such is the case, it must also be part of the proportionality equation in any event, notwithstanding the provision in Article 35(3). The UK *Manual of the Law of Armed Conflict* stipulates:

> These provisions do not automatically prevent certain types of military objectives such as nuclear submarines or super tankers from being legitimate targets nor do they automatically prevent the use of certain means of warfare such as herbicides or chemical agents. The effects of attacking these targets or using these means must be considered.[163]

The formulation in the 1977 Protocol is of environmental damage that is widespread, long-term *and* severe, that is to say, the elements of the prohibition are cumulative. The polluting effects of hostilities in the short or medium term (ie days, months, or years) will clearly not meet the definition. During the negotiations, the Rapporteur from the Working Group that discussed the provision stated:

> The time or duration required (ie, long-term) was considered by some to be measured in decades. References to twenty or thirty years were made by some representatives as being a minimum. Others referred to battlefield destruction in France in the First World War as being outside the scope of the prohibition. The Biotope report states that 'Acts of warfare which cause short-term damage to the natural environment, such as artillery bombardment, are not intended to be prohibited by the article', and continues by stating that the period might be perhaps for ten years or more. However, it is impossible to say with certainty what period of time might be involved. It appeared to be a widely shared assumption that battlefield damage incidental to conventional warfare would not normally be proscribed by this provision.[164]

The ICRC commentary on the provision in Article 35(3) of the 1977 Protocol states:

> Ecological warfare refers to the serious disruption of the natural equilibrium permitting life and the development of man and all living organisms, a disruption of which the effects may be felt for one or more decades. The paragraph under consideration here prohibits this, whether it is committed intentionally or not, for example, by the deliberate use of the tools of chemical warfare, or whether it is simply the result of the use of weapons which inevitably have the same effect on vast stretches of land, whether these are populated or not. Because of the transnational aspect of this problem in particular, the prohibition is absolute; it even continues to apply in the absence of any direct threat to the population or to the flora and fauna of the enemy State.[165]

Iraq's releasing of oil into the Persian Gulf and its subsequent setting fire to the oil wells in Kuwait is often cited as an instance where the rule in Article 35(3) of the 1977 Additional

[161] GC Daily (ed), *Nature's Services: Societal Dependence on Natural Ecosystems* (Washington, DC, Island Press, 1997); see International Environmental Agreements Database Project, University of Oregon, 2016, at https://goo.gl/ZYBJLM.
[162] Dinstein (n 94) 237, para 641.
[163] UK Ministry of Defence, *The Manual of the Law of Armed Conflict* (Oxford, Oxford University Press, 2005) para 5.29.3 (notes omitted).
[164] Cited in ICRC Commentary on the 1977 Additional Protocols, para 1454.
[165] Ibid, para 1462.

Protocol I was violated. In fact, as Dinstein records, while the environmental effects were undoubtedly severe (and the action itself probably wanton), the action fails this particular test by virtue of the relatively short duration of the impact.[166] The most obvious armaments whose use could meet the test are evidently high-yield nuclear weapons, particularly those whose explosive yield is greater than half a megaton.[167]

The ICRC commentary on Article 35(3) concludes, somewhat poetically, by averring that 'It is the natural environment itself that is protected. It is common property, and should be retained for everyone's use and be preserved.'[168]

[166] Dinstein (n 94) 245–47, paras 666–71.

[167] In its official response to the ICRC Customary IHL Study, and particularly Rule 45, the US offers the example of country A, which has hidden its chemical and biological weapons arsenal in a large rainforest, and plans imminently to launch the arsenal at country B. Under the ICRC customary rule, country B could not launch a strike against that arsenal if it expects that such a strike may cause widespread, long-term and severe damage to the rainforest, even if it has evidence of country A's imminent launch, and knows that such a launch itself would cause environmental devastation. US Response to the ICRC Customary IHL Study, 528, endnote 30.

[168] ICRC Commentary on the 1977 Additional Protocols, para 1462.

11

Naval Warfare

I. Introduction

The law of armed conflict generally has become one of the most reviewed and examined areas of public international law over the course of the last three decades. That element of it governing the conduct of hostilities at sea, however, has received relatively little attention. The reason for this is usefully revealed via a brief analysis of the recognised sources of law over that time.[1]

A. Treaties

There has been no conventional law negotiated dealing with the conduct of hostilities in naval war since before the Second World War. The most recent treaty negotiated was the 1936 London Procès-Verbal (or Protocol) Relating to the Rules of Submarine Warfare.[2] It is perhaps telling that the International Committee of the Red Cross (ICRC) stated towards the end of the Cold War that 'the conditions of sea warfare were radically transformed during the Second World War and in subsequent conflicts [and] it is difficult to determine which are the rules that still apply'. In terms of general treaty law, it went on to say that 'there are hardly any specific rules relating to sea .... warfare, and insofar as they do exist, they are controversial and have fallen into disuse'.[3] This view is not entirely supported here, but it does, nevertheless, serve to warn of notable shortcomings in the conventional law regulating the conduct of hostilities at sea.

B. State Practice

There have been relatively few wars involving naval forces since 1945. When naval hostilities have occurred, they have been markedly limited in scope. Significantly, there has been

[1] Sources listed in Art 38 of the 1945 Statute of the International Court of Justice.

[2] 1936 London Procès-Verbal Relating to the Rules of Submarine Warfare Set Forth in Part IV of the Treaty of London of 22 April 1930. The 1949 Geneva Convention II for the Amelioration of the Condition of Wounded, Sick and Shipwrecked Members of the Armed Forces at Sea (hereinafter '1949 Geneva Convention II') is clearly an important part of the body of law relating to naval war, but it deals with the treatment of the victims of war at sea and not with the conduct of hostilities. The 1977 Protocol Additional to the Geneva Conventions of 12 August 1949, and Relating to the Protection of Victims of International Armed Conflicts (hereinafter '1977 Additional Protocol I') does affect the conduct of hostilities in general, but it avoids addressing the particulars of war at sea.

[3] Y Sandoz, C Swinarski and B Zimmermann (eds), *Commentary on the Additional Protocols of 8 June 1977 to the Geneva Conventions of 12 August 1949* (Geneva: Martinus Nijhoff, 1987) paras 1896–97.

no general naval war between major maritime powers for more than 70 years. The majority of post-1945 conflicts involving naval hostilities – around a dozen – were fought before the end of the Cold War in 1990, since when there have been only two: the invasion of Iraq in 2003, and the non-international armed conflict (NIAC) in Sri Lanka (which actually commenced in 1983 but continued until 2009).[4] These conflicts have not resulted in substantial evidence of actual state practice sufficient to prompt the significant development of customary law. There have been several official legal manuals compiled by significant naval powers in recent years, however, all having chapters or sections focused on the law applicable to naval war.[5] As these posit their state's positions on legal rights and obligations during naval war, they can be described as 'verbal practice' and represent useful evidence of *opinio juris*. Importantly, all deal with other relevant bodies of law insofar as they affect the conduct of naval war. In particular, the law of the sea provides for zones of coastal state jurisdiction, which influence the sea areas within which naval hostilities can be conducted,[6] and human rights law has become an important consideration since the end of the Cold War.

C. Jurisprudence

There have been three notable international cases with a naval dimension (*Corfu Channel*, *Nicaragua* and *Oil Platforms*) dealt with by the International Court of Justice (ICJ),[7] but these have generally not been especially significant in relation to the conduct of hostilities at sea, despite their focus on sea-mining (in *Corfu Channel* and *Nicaragua*); rights of passage (in *Corfu Channel*); and on attacks on offshore installations (*Oil Platforms*). None of the cases dealt with by the *ad hoc* international tribunals has addressed naval issues.

[4] The Cold War era conflicts included: the Arab-Israeli Wars from 1948; the Korean War (1950–53); the 1956 Anglo-French assault on Suez; the Vietnam War (1955–75); the Indo-Pakistan War (1971); the 'Troubles' in Northern Ireland (which arguably became a NIAC in 1971–74); the Battle of the Paracels (1974); the Iran–Iraq War (1980–88); the Falklands/Malvinas War (1982); the Sri Lankan Civil War (1983–2009); and the Gulf of Sidra action (1986). These are the most obvious naval conflicts. There are difficulties in classifying naval interactions of lower intensity and duration, as very usefully pointed out in W Heintschel von Heinegg, 'The difficulties of Conflict Classification: Distinguishing Incidents at Sea from Hostilities', *International Review of the Red Cross*, vol 98, no 902 (August 2017) 449. Quite why there has been a noticeably lower frequency of naval conflicts since the end of the Cold War would be worth speculating about, but this is not the place to do so.

[5] Examples are: Australian Defence Force, *Law of Armed Conflict*, Doctrine Publication 06.4, 2006; United Kingdom (UK) Ministry of Defence, *The Manual of the Law of Armed Conflict* (Oxford, Oxford University Press, 2005); Canadian Department of National Defence, *Law of Armed Conflict at the Operational and Tactical Levels*, Joint Doctrine Manual B-GJ-005-104/FP-021, 2001; German Federal Ministry of Defence, *Law of Armed Conflict Manual*, Joint Service Regulation (ZDv) 15/2, 2013 (a previous German manual was published commercially as D Fleck (ed), *The Handbook of Humanitarian Law in Armed Conflicts* (Oxford, Oxford University Press, 1995); while this title was essentially the official German manual with added academic commentary, subsequent editions – the 2nd from 2008 and the 3rd from 2013 – have not been based on the official manual); US Department of the Navy and Department of Homeland Security, *Commander's Handbook on the Law of Naval Operations*, NWP 1-14M, 2007; and US Department of Defense *Law of War Manual* (2015).

[6] See discussion in section V on 'Regions of Operations'.

[7] ICJ, *Corfu Channel (United Kingdom v Albania)*, Judgment, 9 April 1949, [1949] ICJ Rep 4; *Military and Paramilitary Activities in and against Nicaragua (Nicaragua v United States of America)*, Judgment (Merits), [1986] ICJ Rep 14; and *Oil Platforms (Iran v United States of America)*, Judgment [2003] ICJ Rep 161.

D. Specialist Opinion

The body of academic literature dealing with the law applicable during armed conflict at sea is substantially smaller than that dealing with land and air operations in war. The United States (US) Naval War College's International Law Studies series contains the greatest number of papers on the subject, and the staff in its Stockton Center deserve praise for maintaining a steady flow of commentary.[8] There are several texts on the law of armed conflict, most of which have separate chapters or sections devoted to naval war.[9] Undoubtedly, however, the single most significant and influential publication has been the *San Remo Manual*, published in 1995. It was the product of an eight-year process that brought together a significant number of operational lawyers, academics and naval operators to discuss their perspectives on armed conflict at sea and the then state of the law regulating it.[10] Those involved in its production sought to develop the law where they deemed it appropriate and necessary, but were generally conservative in doing so. The *Manual* is certainly regarded as authoritative.[11] It was not prepared for formal state endorsement, however, and in itself is neither conventional nor customary law.[12] A recent 'practitioners' guide' has addressed the issue of human rights law in armed conflict.[13]

With no new treaties and precious little practice to develop custom, the law governing the conduct of naval hostilities has remained remarkably similar to that which applied until the end of the Second World War. Much has happened since then, however, with the seas and oceans subject to greater change than at any time in history.

All of the various dimensions of the maritime environment – political, economic, physical, technological, social, normative and military – have been transformed, with the changes in each dimension having an impact on all others. This wide-ranging transformation has had inevitable strategic, operational and tactical level consequences, with the purposes and roles of navies affected, as well as the characteristics of the wars in which they may have to engage.

[8] See the extensive series of 'Blue Books' – International Law Studies – dating back to 1895, the more recent of which are available online at https://stockton.usnwc.edu/ils/. This series, assiduously produced by the staff of the Stockton Center at the United States Naval War College in Newport, Rhode Island, has become the main global forum for debate on the subject.

[9] Three currently available examples of texts including naval war are: Y Dinstein, *The Conduct of Hostilities under the Law of International Armed Conflict* (Cambridge, Cambridge University Press, 2004); R Kolb and R Hyde, *An Introduction to the International Law of Armed Conflicts* (Oxford, Hart Publishing, 2008); and L Green, *The Contemporary Law of Armed Conflict*, 2nd edn (Manchester, Manchester University Press, 2000). In contrast, Rogers deliberately excluded any discussion of naval war: A Rogers, *Law on the Battlefield*, 2nd edn (Manchester, Manchester University Press, 2004).

[10] L Doswald-Beck (ed), *San Remo Manual on International Law Applicable to Armed Conflicts at Sea* (Cambridge, Cambridge University Press, 1995 (hereinafter 'SRM').

[11] Its authority is derived from the quality of the expert group that provided input and the reputation and status of the principal institutions under whose auspices it was developed (the ICRC and the International Institute for Humanitarian Law).

[12] The 'Maritime Warfare' chapter of the UK's Manual was based on the SRM but did not adopt it in its entirety, departing from, modifying or excluding some of the rules contained therein. For an account of the differences between the two, see S Haines, 'The United Kingdom's Manual of the Law of Armed Conflict and the San Remo Manual: Maritime Rules Compared' in Y Dinstein (ed) (2006) 36 *Israel Yearbook on Human Rights* 89.

[13] D Murray, *Practitioners' Guide to Human Rights Law in Armed Conflict* (Oxford, Oxford University Press, 2016).

The law governing the conduct of hostilities applies, of course, at the tactical level, not the strategic. But strategic considerations determine what navies are used for, and strategic decisions will be influenced by the environment within which military force is to be applied. The normative dimension of the maritime strategic environment will have an influence on strategy, and that will in turn influence what navies, as instruments of political purpose, do at the tactical level.[14] In this chapter in particular, in which the focus is on rarely used naval force, considerations at the strategic level will be of some importance in determining what is tactically feasible; and what the law has to regulate.

E. The Content of the Chapter

The law governing the conduct of naval hostilities is not divorced from that governing hostilities in general. Indeed, navies are subject to the general rules applicable to targeting, precautions in attack and in relation to the law on weapons, for example. A significant maritime force today will almost certainly deploy with its own aircraft, but it is not necessary to repeat here the rules for aerial warfare already discussed in chapter 10. Similarly, when navies project power ashore, the kinetic results of their actions come under the influence of the laws of land warfare. This chapter does not stand on its own, therefore, but needs to be read in conjunction with the rules discussed elsewhere in the volume.

It starts by describing in section II the different categories of operation that navies might engage in during armed conflict at sea; it approaches the subject from a naval doctrinal perspective. This is followed in section III by a brief résumé of the law as it stands, focusing on the extant naval specific conventional law and the rules established in the *San Remo Manual*. These two sections inform and provide necessary context for the sections that follow. Section IV deals with the means of naval warfare: essentially the platforms and the weapons deployed on or by them. Section V describes the regions within which naval hostilities can legitimately be conducted and discusses the constraints imposed on navies when they are operating in sea areas under the jurisdiction of neutral states. Section VI turns to the methods of naval warfare. It is deliberately structured by reference to the categories of operations outlined above, but also includes mention of hybrid warfare, naval zones, deception and permitted ruses of war. Lastly, although the focus of this chapter is on naval warfare during international armed conflicts (IACs), it is necessary briefly to address the conduct of naval hostilities in NIACs. The chapter then draws some general conclusions.

II. Naval Doctrine for War at Sea

Traditionally, naval operations in war have had the ultimate aim of influencing developments ashore, as the naval strategic theorist Sir Julian Corbett noted more than a

[14] See S Haines, 'The Influence of Law on Maritime Strategy' in D Moran and J Russell (eds), *Maritime Strategy and Global Order: Markets, Resources, Security* (Washington, DC, Georgetown University Press, 2016) 239.

century ago.[15] Maritime strategy in war has to be related to the overall strategy of the state, and naval action taken at the tactical level needs to be consistent with strategic objectives. The three traditional categories of operations reflecting this have been as follows.

A. Sea-control/Sea-denial Operations

These operations involve navies in conflict with enemy naval forces, each belligerent force having the object of securing control of the sea for itself while denying its use to the enemy. A navy secures control of the sea not simply for its own sake and to 'hold' an area of ocean (as an army would hold territory ashore) but in order that it will be free itself to manoeuvre and conduct one or other, or both, of the other categories of operation. Although it was argued by Mahan that a naval power ought to seek 'command of the sea',[16] this has always been largely impractical, and became especially so following the emergence of effective sea denial capabilities. The mine and the submarine armed with torpedoes were, and remain, capable of rendering the most powerful surface combatants vulnerable.

Since the early twentieth century, air power has become an important factor as well. It revealed its potential during the Second World War, in the context of both the Battle of the Atlantic, during which the Royal Air Force's Coastal Command played a substantial role in combating the threat from German U-boats, and the Pacific campaign, during which the aircraft carrier came of age as the principal capital warship. Subsequently, missiles – both sea and land-based – have become significant sea-denial systems. Sea-denial capabilities have consigned any ambitions for sea command to the pages of traditional theory, the achieving of the lesser condition of sea control becoming the accepted – and sufficient – precursor for the mounting of the operations described in the following subsections.

B. Power Projection Operations

These operations are about navies applying force directly to influence matters ashore, directing fire against shore targets, mounting amphibious landings, including into enemy-held territory, and supporting friendly ground forces. While historically, navies have always had a capacity for power projection (Nelson himself lost both his right arm and the use of one eye during amphibious operations[17]), it tended to be limited in the extent of its

[15] In Corbett's words, 'Since men live upon the land and not upon the sea, great issues between nations at war have always been decided – except in the rarest of cases – either by what your army can do against your enemy's territory and national life, or else by the fear of what the fleet makes it possible for your army to do'. See J Corbett, *Some Principles of Maritime Strategy* (Annapolis, MD, Naval Institute Press, 1988) (first published by Longmans, Green and Co, London, 1911) 16.

[16] Something which Mahan believed Britain had achieved during its period of naval dominance, including during the 19th-century *Pax Britannica*. See A Mahan, *The Influence of Sea Power Upon History, 1660–1783* (London, Sampson Low, Marston & Co, 1889). Set-piece sea battles, especially those fought during the Revolutionary and Napoleonic Wars, certainly gave the Royal Navy a pre-eminent position. See B Gough, *Pax Britannica: Ruling the Waves and Keeping the Peace before Armageddon* (Basingstoke, Palgrave Macmillan, 2014).

[17] A fact noted by the House of Commons Select Committee on Defence in its report, *Sunset for the Royal Marines? The Royal Marines and UK Amphibious Capability*, Third Report of Session 2017–19 (HC622), 4 February 2018, at para 16.

immediate effect. Today, with sea-based air-power and ship- and submarine-launched cruise missiles available to the more advanced navies, power can be projected hundreds of miles inland, and at short notice.

C. Economic Warfare Operations

These operations have involved navies interfering with an enemy's trading activities at sea, the aim being to apply pressure on its economic activity at the tactical and operational levels in order to influence its strategic decision-making, by undermining its ability to sustain war effort over time. Offensive economic warfare has been achieved historically through a combination of high-seas commerce raiding (or *guerre de course*) and the blockading of the enemy's ports and coast. Defensive economic warfare involves navies protecting their own state's trade from interdiction by the enemy; it has typically involved warships protecting convoys of merchant vessels during passage.

While these three long-accepted categories of naval action have all featured in more recent wars, they were last experienced together and in full during the naval conflicts between major maritime powers in the Second World War. Although they certainly remain relevant today, they must now be joined by another category of potential operations.

D. Coastal Jurisdiction Integrity Operations

Profound extensions and enhancements of coastal state jurisdiction, negotiated during the United Nations (UN) conferences on the Law of the Sea, have confounded one of the defining assumptions of nineteenth-century naval strategic thinking. When Corbett wrote on naval strategy at the beginning of the twentieth century, he was at pains to point out that the command (or control) of the sea 'is not identical in its strategic conditions with the conquest of territory … You cannot conquer sea because it is not susceptible of ownership, at least outside territorial waters.' He went on to state that 'the only right that we or our enemy can have on the sea is the right of passage'.[18]

He was correct at the time he was writing, when the oceans were principally regarded as a medium for navigation. His conclusion is no longer valid, however, because the resources of the oceans have become an important factor to take into consideration. Through technological innovations relating to both exploration and exploitation, previously unknown ocean resources (principally minerals) have been revealed, and traditionally harvested living resources have been over-exploited, leading to scarcity and, in some cases, near exhaustion. Both developments have generated a desire for some measure of control through ownership. The extension of coastal state jurisdiction, from the mere three nautical miles of territorial sea (with which Corbett was familiar), has included not only the extension of territorial waters to 12 nautical miles, but also the generation of archipelagic waters, the contiguous zone, the exclusive economic zone and the continental shelf. The last of these has the potential to extend coastal state jurisdiction to more than 100 times the width of the traditional territorial sea.

[18] Corbett (n 15) 93.

Since the outcomes of both the First and Third UN Conferences on the Law of the Sea, states do now have the ability to claim substantial areas of the seas adjacent to their coasts. This has increased the potential for international disputes over the ownership of areas of sea and of the vitally important economic resources both in and below them.[19] The 1982 UN Convention on the Law of the Sea (UNCLOS) not only created new sources of international dispute, it also provided an agreed framework for their peaceful resolution. Early, and somewhat pessimistic, predictions of a significant risk of conflict between states have not come to pass. Nevertheless, there remain a great many excessive and overlapping claims, some of which have taken states to the brink of conflict; they will probably continue to do so.[20] Currently, the most intense areas of dispute are in the East and South China Seas. There is certainly clear potential for states in that region to become involved in combat operations at sea, with the risk that major maritime powers (including China, Japan and the US) will be drawn into conflict with each other for the first time in more than 70 years.

This is the reason why it is necessary to add the fourth category of naval operations during war to the traditional three already mentioned.

These operations involve navies in asserting and challenging the control of substantial sea areas adjacent to their own and enemy coasts. These operations are notable in having relevance in both peace and war. In peacetime, naval (including coastguard) operations are essentially about law enforcement (constabulary operations), during which the law of the coastal state is enforced against those engaged in illicit activity that threatens the peace and good order of the relevant zone, including illicit resource exploitation. In disputed waters there is a risk of escalation from constabulary to conflict, as rival claims are asserted by the states concerned. Defending a sea area today is, therefore, a potential feature of naval war that simply did not figure in naval strategic thinking prior to the middle of the twentieth century.[21]

E. The Relative Importance of the Categories of Operations

Naval hostilities today and into the foreseeable future will be conducted within the framework of the categories of operations outlined in the preceding subsections. First and foremost, the establishment of *sea control* will always be a necessary precursor to the successful conduct of the others. Navies need to ensure their own security to be in a position to operate, and they need also to deny their opponents the security to do likewise. While the need for *sea control* is a given, a major influence on the characteristics of future naval war will be the relative importance assumed by each of the other three categories of operation; this deserves some discussion.

[19] A consequence well recognised halfway through the Third UN Conference on the Law of the Sea (UNCLOS III); see B Buzan, *A Sea of Troubles? Sources of Dispute in the New Ocean Regime* (London, International Institute for Strategic Studies, 1978).

[20] J Roach and R Smith, *Excessive Maritime Claims*, 3rd edn (Leiden, Brill, 2012). This work is closely associated with the US response to excessive claims, with the US Navy used as an instrument to challenge such claims at sea.

[21] It is interesting to quote Corbett once again as a way of emphasising this development. Referring to the rights of belligerents, he remarked that 'we exclude fishery rights, which are irrelevant to the present matter' (Corbett (n 15) 93). Today, they are anything but irrelevant; conflicting claims over resources are a significant (perhaps even the principal) reason why navies are likely to confront each other.

During the era of major imperial naval wars (from roughly the beginning of the seventeenth to the middle of the twentieth century), the principal means by which a maritime power used its navy to apply pressure on an enemy was through *economic warfare*; with *power projection* being generally the less influential role – and *coastal jurisdiction integrity* operations playing no part at all. While capital warships were crucial for securing *sea control*, they were also employed to interdict trade. During the two World Wars of the twentieth century, significant major warships (cruisers in particular) were procured with *guerre de course* as a principal role.

To comply with the laws regulating economic warfare, which latterly have had an important humanitarian dimension,[22] warships needed sufficient space on board to accommodate the crews of merchant vessels seized as prize or sunk on the high seas. They also had to carry additional suitably qualified personnel to provide prize crews for the manning and steaming of captured merchant vessels. Twentieth-century cruisers were heavily armed and armoured, and capable of defending themselves against enemy attempts to prevent them conducting their interdiction of shipping. A very good example of a major surface vessel intended and used for this purpose was the German pocket-battleship *Graf Spee*. She was employed on *guerre de course* operations against British merchant shipping in the south Atlantic and southern Indian Ocean between September and December 1939. She stopped and boarded British flagged ships, removed their crews to safety and accommodated them on board (subsequently transferring them to her tender, the *Altmark*) before sinking the vessels on the high seas. Her need to be capable of defending herself was well demonstrated by the manner of her eventual demise in the Battle of the River Plate, when she was confronted by three cruisers of the Royal Navy's South America Cruiser Squadron (*HMS Ajax*, *HMS Exeter* and *HMNZS Achilles*). She put up a credible defence, entered the neutral port of Montevideo for repairs and might even have prevailed subsequently if her commanding officer had not been fooled into thinking he was facing a much enhanced force, prompting him to scuttle his ship in the River Plate Estuary (both to avoid her being taken as booty and to spare his ship's company from becoming casualties or being taken as prisoners of war).[23]

The *Graf Spee's* commerce raiding activities commenced on 26 September 1939, less than a month after war was declared but prior to Germany's resort to unrestricted submarine attacks on merchant shipping. Despite the prominent role of U-boats in economic warfare throughout the war, capital warships continued to play a role. In May 1941, the battleship *Bismarck* and the heavy cruiser *Prinz Eugen* were tasked with raiding Allied shipping in the Atlantic. They each had prize crews embarked when intercepted by the Royal Navy. The *Bismarck* was sunk on 27 May 1941 (after she and *Prinz Eugen* had together sunk the British battlecruiser *HMS Hood*).[24] The *Prinz Eugen* escaped to occupied France and then

[22] As now reflected in the 1949 Geneva Convention II, for the latest interpretation of which see ICRC, *Commentary on the Second Geneva Convention* (Cambridge, Cambridge University Press, 2017).

[23] D O'Connell, *The Influence of Law on Sea Power* (Manchester, Manchester University Press, 1975) 27–39. For a more recent treatment of this engagement, see E Grove, *The Price of Disobedience: The Battle of the River Plate Reconsidered* (Stroud, Sutton Publishing, 2000).

[24] C Barnett, *Engage the Enemy More Closely: The Royal Navy in the Second World War* (London, Hodder and Stoughton, 1991) 287–88. She was torpedoed by Fairey Swordfish aircraft launched from the aircraft carrier *HMS Ark Royal*.

back to Germany.[25] The actions of these 'surface raiders' were entirely consistent with the recognised laws regulating *guerre de course* operations. Their disappointing performance in that role was one factor that led to the German High Command's reliance on submarines to attack Allied shipping. Capital warships had a significant role to play in lawful economic warfare operations. Very much smaller submarines were wholly unsuited for conducting such operations in accordance with the law, hence their resort to unlawful unrestricted attacks on shipping.

Economic warfare has been a feature of post-1945 conflicts at sea, but only through the use of blockade.[26] There has been no general, high seas *guerre de course* campaign waged since the end of the Second World War.[27] A clear reason for this has been the absence of conflict between great powers, involving economic pressure applied through naval action as a significant strategic lever. Although some have argued that great power war is probably not likely to recur, it may be foolish to rule it out altogether.[28] If it were to recur, an *economic warfare* campaign might well become a feature. There can be little doubt, however, that any future such campaign would take on different characteristics from those experienced in the past.

The international shipping industry today is profoundly different in both structure and practices from that which existed during the most recent general naval war. The emergence of open shipping registries, their domination of substantially increased global maritime trade, the containerisation of general cargoes and the substantial increase in the size of merchant vessels of all types, combine to render previous practices in *guerre de course* operations almost impossible to repeat. There is no possibility, for example, of conducting a search of a container ship at sea to establish whether or not it is carrying contraband. If these changes are not enough to justify new thinking on the conduct of economic warfare operations, the currently topical potential development is the introduction of unmanned and semi-autonomous ships.[29] The existing law governing the conduct of *economic warfare* evolved in a different era. It is arguably unsuited in large part to the regulation of future such operations.[30]

It is far from obvious that *economic warfare* will be a major feature of any future armed conflict at sea; it has certainly declined in importance in recent decades. *Power projection*, in contrast, has become the principal means by which major navies are used as instruments of strategic influence. It seems likely that this will continue to be the case.

[25] The *Prinz Eugen* survived the war, was taken as booty and commissioned in the US Navy, subsequently being used as a target/test bed during the Bikini Atoll nuclear tests in 1946. Having survived those, she was towed to Kwajalein Atoll, where she capsized and sank.

[26] Naval blockades since 1945 have included the Indian blockade of Bangladesh in 1971, the blockading of Haiphong in 1972 and, more recently, the Israeli blockade of Gaza.

[27] The so-called 'Tanker War' in the Gulf is the closest to such. It is significant that there was no attempt by Britain to interdict maritime trade during the Falklands War in 1982.

[28] For contributions to the debate about the likelihood of major war, see R Väyrynen (ed), *The Waning of Major War: Theories and Debates* (London/New York, Routledge, 2006). For a robust rejection of the dismissal of such, see C Gray, *Another Bloody Century: Future Warfare* (London, Weidenfeld and Nicolson, 2005).

[29] Rolls-Royce is a leader with technological development; see the company's briefing document at https://goo.gl/2b8roC. A recent UK Government report suggests that fully autonomous shipping 'could be in operation as early as 2035'. See Chief Scientific Adviser, *Foresight: Future of the Sea* (London, Government Office for Science, 2018) 47.

[30] An issue raised in S Haines, 'War at Sea: 19th Century Laws for 21st Century Wars?' *International Review of the Red Cross*, vol 98, no 902 (September 2017) 419.

From 1945 until the end of the Cold War, the naval operational focus of the major maritime powers reflected what had gone before. The rivalry between the Soviet Union and its Warsaw Pact allies, on the one hand, and the US and its North Atlantic Treaty Organization (NATO) allies, in particular, on the other, created the impression that a war at sea would be about sea control/denial (including denying Soviet submarines free rein in the North Atlantic) and economic warfare, with a likely campaign to protect sea lines of communication between North America and Europe. The NATO Alliance navies certainly exercised with this in mind, even to the point of chartering merchant ships to simulate convoys during NATO exercises.[31] Since 1990, however, economic warfare has ceased to be regarded as a major driver for NATO's maritime posture. It is also no longer an influence on force development. Capital ships are no longer designed with *guerre de course* in mind. The term 'escort' once implied vessels suitable for convoy escort missions in defensive economic warfare operations, with anti-submarine capabilities considered an essential feature given the threat posed by submarines during the most recent general naval war. Today, the term is used principally to describe both air-defence and anti-submarine frigates and destroyers used as defensive screening escorts for aircraft carriers and amphibious forces (the principal purpose of both being power projection).

This brings us to the fourth category of operations, to do with *coastal jurisdiction integrity*, which prompts two comments. First, while it was previously possible to argue that combat operations involving naval forces directly against other naval forces were essentially about sea control/denial, today they may also be about the assault on, and defence of, maritime space. Navies do now have a role in relation to the defence of substantial maritime areas in a way they did not when Corbett was thinking about maritime strategy. These areas are not, of course, restricted to the defence and integrity of territorial waters but also encompass that of the other jurisdictional zones, within which economically important resource rights are at risk.

Second, such defensive operations may well pose a particular challenge because they are likely to involve naval forces engaging in a fluid set of circumstances, with potential shifts across the spectrum from constabulary to conflict and back again. It is this type of situation in particular that has helped to give rise to the label 'hybrid warfare',[32] in which there is considerably less clarity than previously as to the commencement and termination of armed conflict (and the parallel applicability or non-applicability of the law regulating naval hostilities).

The extant law on the conduct of naval hostilities was not developed with either the defence of maritime jurisdiction or an essential fluidity between constabulary and combat operations in mind. So far, there has been little practice to assist in shaping the law to take account of either of these developments, but this situation may change. Informed opinion seems to suggest that maritime hybrid warfare is becoming a significant phenomenon, especially in relation to coastal jurisdiction. Legal issues are bound to be a major factor

[31] The author experienced such exercises himself when serving in a frigate tasked with convoy escort, and spent some time steaming slowly around the North Sea during Exercise Northern Merger in 1974 – not his most exciting NATO exercise!

[32] For an informed naval view of this, see Adm J Stavridis, 'Maritime Hybrid War is Coming', *US Naval Institute Proceedings*, vol 142 (December 2016), pt 12, 1,366, at https://goo.gl/bLDEfm.

to consider. It is not necessarily assumed here that the law will prove inadequate, but this cannot in all honesty be ruled out. It is as well that this is appreciated.

One certainly needs to be aware of the mismatch between the law as it stands (and developed in the past in very different circumstances) and the contemporary challenges to be faced in the event of a resurgence in naval hostilities. It is not enough simply to state the law as it is when considering the conduct of future hostilities in naval war. If that law is unsuited for prevailing circumstances, this needs to be pointed out and an attempt made to assess how operations might be conducted in a legally acceptable manner. In the (perhaps unlikely) event of major naval war, the law would need to evolve rapidly through practice to take account of the challenges of *economic warfare* against a backdrop of the contemporary shipping industry. If, as seems more likely, hostilities occur in response to hybrid forms of threat, those conducting naval operations in a fluid situation on the spectrum from law enforcement to combat will need a sophisticated understanding of the circumstances they are facing and the risk of escalation. Judging what law applies will not be easy. With that caveat declared, what about the law governing combat at sea?

III. The Extant Law of Naval Warfare

It is entirely possible to make significant claims about the longevity of a body of law dealing with naval war. One could, for example, trace it back to antiquity and suggest that the law applying today has developed over centuries – millennia even. There were rules that seem to have been applied in pre-modern times, and the conduct of economic warfare at sea was certainly influenced by generally acknowledged norms during the era of maritime imperial rivalry between the seventeenth and nineteenth centuries.[33] Indeed, there is also significant evidence that sailors frequently cared for their defeated enemies by rescuing them from the sea once the fighting stopped.[34] In reality, however, there is little to be gained from dwelling on this history when describing the current law governing the conduct of hostilities at sea. For all practical purposes we need go back no further than the middle of the nineteenth century. Indeed, we can be very specific and use 1856 as our basic date. In that year agreement was reached over the Paris Declaration Respecting Maritime Law.[35]

[33] Marsden contains a number of documents on Prize Law dating back to the 13th century in England (R Marsden, *Documents Relating to the Law and Custom of the Sea* (London, Navy Records Society, 1915). The law on economic warfare at sea developed significantly during the period of maritime imperial and naval rivalry from the 17th to the 19th centuries. Even Napoleon, not renowned for consulting legal advisers about his own use and deployment of military force on land, had something to say about the legitimacy of the Royal Navy's seizure of French goods at sea. He was not favourably disposed: 'The law of nations governing maritime war has remained in its state of utter barbarism'. See B Colson (ed), *Napoleon On War* (Oxford, Oxford University Press, 2015) 36. Writing in exile on St Helena, Napoleon was being critical of Britain's decision to seize private goods.

[34] Humanity has not been entirely absent in the context of sea warfare, and certainly preceded the advent of Geneva Law (which followed the Battle of Solferino and the founding of the Red Cross Movement in the middle of the 19th century), as evidenced, for example, by accounts of acts of humanity after the fighting at Trafalgar. See A Nicolson, *Men of Honour: Trafalgar and the Making of the English Hero* (London, Harper Collins, 2005).

[35] For a comprehensive discussion of the *Paris Declaration* and its consequences, see J Lemnitzer, *Power, Law and the End of Privateering* (Basingstoke, Palgrave Macmillan, 2014). All relevant and extant treaties on the Laws of Naval Warfare referred to below are available in A Roberts and R Guelff (eds), *Documents on the Laws of War*, 3rd edn (Oxford, Oxford University Press, 2000) and in N Ronzitti (ed), *The Law of Naval Warfare: A Collection of Agreements and Documents with Commentaries* (Dordrecht/Boston/London, Martinus Nijhoff, 1988).

The history of the development of conventional law regulating the conduct of naval hostilities is focused on the 80 years between 1856 and 1936. There were no treaties dealing with it prior to that period but none has been agreed since. Indeed, the period of development is in reality much more concentrated than even this suggests. After 1856, there was a gap of almost half a century before further negotiations concentrated on aspects of naval war. At the 1910 Hague Peace Conference, a convention (1910 Hague Convention III) was agreed to adapt the provisions of the 1864 Geneva Convention for the protection of the victims of naval war. This was followed by a 1904 convention dealing with the treatment of hospital ships. It was not until the 1907 Hague Peace Conference, however, that conventional law relating to the conduct of hostilities was negotiated. Eight of the total of 14 conventions negotiated in 1907 were maritime-related, although only five of those remain extant, as follows:[36]

- Convention VII Relating to the Conversion of Merchant Ships into Warships
- Convention VIII Relative to the Laying of Automatic Submarine Contact Mines
- Convention IX Concerning Bombardment by Naval Forces in Time of War
- Convention XI Relative to Certain Restrictions with Regard to the Exercise of Capture in Naval War
- Convention XIII Concerning the Rights and Duties of Neutral Powers in Naval War.

Two years after the Hague Conference, a further meeting was convened to negotiate what became the 1909 London Declaration Concerning the Laws of Naval War. The purpose of this was to provide detailed rules on the conduct of economic warfare operations to support the anticipated future proceedings of the International Prize Court to be established in accordance with the 1907 Hague Convention XII. Ultimately, however, neither Hague Convention XII nor the associated London Protocol entered into force.[37] Formally, at least, the law relating to economic warfare remained essentially that which had been promulgated in the 1856 Paris Declaration.

The Institute of International Law, meeting in Oxford in 1913, did attempt to clarify the legal situation for war at sea and adopted a *Manual of the Laws of Naval War*, intended as a comprehensive rule book. While undoubtedly an important document, it has been suggested that its significance today is, first, as a key to naval and legal thinking at that time and, second, as a hint, through its silences, at the degree of disagreement that prevented unanimous acceptance of particular aspects of the law.[38] On the eve of the First World War there was by no means unanimous international agreement about what the laws of naval warfare were.

During the First World War, the two most contentious legal issues relating to naval war were to do with the conduct of economic warfare. The first was the British naval blockade of Germany and the second was about German submarine operations, especially unrestricted

[36] The Convention VI Relative to the Legal Status of Enemy Merchant Ships at the Outbreak of Hostilities has fallen into desuetude; the substance of the Convention X is now covered by the 1949 Geneva Convention II, and the Convention XII Relative to the Establishment of an International Prize Court did not enter into force. See Roberts and Guelff (eds) (n 35), 67.

[37] For the text of the Declaration, see Ronzitti (ed) (n 35) 223–56 and also, in the same volume, F Kalshoven, 'Commentary' (on the Declaration), 257–75.

[38] See Ronzitti (ed) (n 35) 277–328 and, in the same volume, P Verri 'Commentary', 329–41.

attacks on shipping, which occurred in two phases: from the spring of 1915; and from early 1917 onwards.[39] No attempts were made to develop the law on belligerent blockade in the years from 1918 to 1939, but there was a serious attempt to regulate submarine operations – an attempt which initially failed but then appeared to have succeeded.

In 1922, a treaty was agreed that attempted to regulate the use of submarines (alongside banning the use of poison gases). Unfortunately, the 1922 Washington Treaty never entered into force because France broke the consensus. The submarine aspects of it were revisited, however, through the 1936 London Protocol. This entered into force immediately on signature, and was agreed by all the states that were to become major belligerents during the course of the Second World War. Once war broke out in 1939, however, the procès-verbal was side-lined (by both Axis and Allied powers) and unrestricted submarine warfare once again became a contentious feature of war at sea.

Minimal though the conventional law is, it is not as difficult to identify as custom, which has suffered especially from the paucity of naval war since 1945.[40] Although it cannot be regarded as a formal codification of customary law (it is not a treaty), the 1994 *San Remo Manual* was an important and influential attempt at informal codification. Indeed, the ICRC deliberately chose not to cover the customary rules of naval warfare in its major study of customary law published in 2005 because it regarded the *Manual*, published 10 years before, as satisfying that need.[41]

Clearly, the principal sources of the law on the conduct of hostilities at sea are extant treaties, together with custom derived from a combination of practice and *opinio juris* (with official manuals providing evidence of the latter). Treaties are subject to interpretation. The detail of customary law is inevitably subject to some debate provoked by differing interpretations of state practice and the motives behind it. Conveniently, the *San Remo Manual* is a widely accepted and accessible series of rules reliant on both treaty and custom. It also reflects operational realities as they were interpreted by those who compiled it over 20 years ago. In the context of this chapter, therefore, while it is perhaps best regarded as a subsidiary source of law (because it was the considered collective view of an impressive array of specialists, both legal and operational), it is accorded some prominence in the discussions that follow.

IV. Means of Naval Warfare

A. Platforms and Weapon Systems

Strictly speaking, the means of naval warfare are the weapons used in war at sea. Most (though not all) of these are deployed on naval platforms (including aircraft). It is important

[39] For an excellent brief account of these two legally challenging developments, see G Best, *Humanity in Warfare: The Modern History of the International Law of Armed Conflicts* (London, Methuen, 1983) 244–62.

[40] Very clearly, the relative absence of naval war since 1945 is to be welcomed, but it does create a difficulty in relation to the development of the law regulating how navies would operate in any war today or in the future. It is an irony that legal restraints on war actually require wars to occur in order to generate new conventional law and to establish contemporary practice as an influence on customary development.

[41] J-M Henckaerts and L Doswald-Beck, *Customary International Humanitarian Law*, vol I: *Rules* (Cambridge, Cambridge University Press, 2005) (hereinafter 'Study of Customary IHL').

to stress the distinction between weapons and platforms. Modern weapons systems are frequently made up of a system of elements. So, for example, a guided missile will not be able to function without an associated fire-control radar. Given the need to comply with the principle of distinction in targeting, a radar is likely to be a crucial element to be considered during any legal review of the missile system.[42]

Warships can be regarded simply as platforms for carrying weapons and the people who operate them. Alternatively, they can be regarded as complex systems in themselves, with the weapons fitted to them and the crew-members serving in them representing fundamental parts of a whole and single unit capable of use in naval combat.[43] A warship without either its weapons or its crew would be powerless, as, indeed, would a weapons system if a ship's power system were to shut down for some reason. The hull, the people and the weapons operate together as an effective war-fighting unit. With the exception of unmanned maritime systems (see section IV.C), if one of these elements is missing, the unit is powerless.

Nevertheless, for our purposes in this chapter, we maintain a distinction between platforms (eg a guided-missile destroyer or a submarine) and the weapons they carry (eg missiles or torpedoes). Something does need to be said briefly about platforms, however, because particular issues are raised in relation to both submarines and un-manned maritime systems.

B. Submarines

The principal role for submarines during the two World Wars of the twentieth century – and the one that generated substantial legal controversy – was the interdiction and sinking of merchant vessels during offensive economic warfare campaigns. Germany's resort to economic warfare in the earliest days of the Second World War prompted the Allied powers to convoy merchant shipping as a means of defending trade. As soon as they were included in escorted and defended convoys, however, merchant ships became legitimate targets for submarine attack. Ultimately, this meant that a substantial proportion of the civilian manned merchant ships targeted without warning by German submarines during the Second World War were sunk legitimately. Nevertheless, both Axis and Allied submarines did scour the oceans in search of independently steaming enemy merchant ships (or neutral shipping suspected of carrying contraband), and simply sank them without warning. This happened despite the formal confirmation in 1936, by all the major maritime powers, that submarines were to be subject to the same rules as surface warships when conducting economic warfare.

The extant conventional law on the use of submarines remains the 1936 London Protocol. It is as difficult to envisage submarines being used for legitimate *guerre de course* operations against independently steaming merchant ships today, however, as it proved to be in practice during the Second World War. In contrast, when targeting other warships

[42] In common with all other weapons, those to be employed at sea are subject to legal reviews in accordance with Art 36 of the 1977 Additional Protocol.

[43] This is especially the case with submarines (see section IV.B); see, eg, Busuttil's remarks that the 'submarine itself… has long been recognized, and regulated, as a weapon system, *per se*'. JJ Busuttil, *Naval Weapon Systems and the Contemporary Law of War* (Oxford, Clarendon Press, 1998) 101.

or merchant ships in convoy, which are military objectives, they can attack entirely legitimately without giving prior warning. They can most certainly target other warships, be they surface vessels or submarines. The British SSN (nuclear-powered attack submarine) *HMS/M Conqueror*'s sinking without warning of the Argentine cruiser *General Belgrano* during the Falklands/Malvinas War in 1982, for example, was a lawful targeting of a military objective. These SSNs are also excellent anti-submarine warfare platforms.

C. Unmanned Maritime Systems

The use of remotely controlled unmanned maritime systems (UMS), and the possible future emergence of autonomous UMS, is now attracting a significant degree of legal attention.[44] There is, it must be said, nothing new about remotely controlled UMS; they have existed for many years and been used for a variety of activities. Nevertheless, the technology is advancing at a much greater rate than previously, and UMS are becoming a significant factor to be considered in any future conflicts.

All UMS available to date have been remotely controlled to some degree. Strict autonomy is not yet an available and deployable technology, but it is only a matter of time before this changes and some degree of genuine autonomy becomes operationally feasible. Currently, UMS include both unmanned surface and unmanned undersea vehicles (USVs and UUVs, respectively). A very good example of a military application of UMS technology is for mine countermeasures, in which remotely piloted USVs and UUVs have been used to seek out and identify mines and set charges against them to destroy them in situ. Other potential roles include surveillance and intelligence gathering, hydrographic and oceanographic surveying and offensive mining operations. It is by no means difficult to imagine a significant and well-armed USV (or indeed UUV) deploying for sustained periods as part of a naval campaign.

There are a great many legal issues raised by the operation of UMS in both peace and war, not least those to do with how such systems might exercise rights and meet obligations that are ordinarily a function of ship's officers and which demand a degree of human judgement in decision-making. There is some uncertainty as to whether or not they qualify as 'ships' (a term variously and not adequately defined at international law). The range of regulations on such important issues as safety of life at sea, collision avoidance, search and rescue, and marine pollution control all rely on human decision-making and action to ensure compliance. The law would clearly need to change in order for UMS to function as ships within the existing legal framework in peacetime, let alone during war. It seems likely, however, that if the technology produces a solution that is both financially attractive and capable in principle of complying with a general regulatory framework developed for shipping at sea, the regulations will almost inevitably be changed to accommodate new realities.

From the point of view of naval hostilities, two issues need to be addressed. The first is to do with the definition of 'warship' in international law. At present, this includes a manning

[44] As pointed out in an excellent and comprehensive summary of the legal issues raised by UMS: see M Schmitt and D Goddard, 'International Law and the Use of Unmanned Maritime Systems', *International Review of the Red Cross*, vol 98, no 902 (August 2017) 567.

requirement, with warships (those vessels able legitimately to apply force in combat) defined in the 1982 UNCLOS as ships

> belonging to the armed forces of a State bearing the external marks distinguishing such ships of its nationality, under the command of an officer duly commissioned by the government of the State and whose name appears in the appropriate service list or its equivalent, and manned by a crew under regular armed forces discipline.[45]

The second is to do with the need for weaponised UMS to operate in a manner consistent with the law of targeting, including taking precautions in attack. Would a UMS be regarded as a weapon in itself, or merely as a platform used to deploy a weapon? Ultimately what will matter is the degree to which any UMS is capable of compliance with the law regulating the conduct of hostilities. A remotely controlled UMS clearly needs to be under sufficient control that its human operator is able to assume responsibility for tactical decision-making and able to apply judgement to arrive at a lawful targeting solution. The prospect of autonomous UMS adds to the debate about autonomy in general, and whether or not it is even feasible for the necessary precautions in attack to be applied by them in order to meet the requirements of distinction and proportionality. These issues would need to be addressed in any legal review of UMS and the weapons they are used to deploy.

D. Naval Weapons

All weapons deployed on or by naval platforms are subject to the principles and basic rules underpinning the law of weapons. These (dealt with in more detail elsewhere in this book) are summarised as follows:[46]

- The means and methods of warfare are not unlimited.[47]
- The principle of humanity requires that weapons should not inflict either superfluous injury or unnecessary suffering.[48]
- Weapons should not be indiscriminate.[49]
- Neither tactical nor strategic necessity is a justification for non-compliance with the foregoing principles.
- The legality of a weapon is related to its designed purpose.
- Weapon systems must incorporate a means of informing judgement as to possible disproportion in attack.

[45] Art 29, UNCLOS.

[46] S Haines, 'The Developing Law of Weapons: Humanity, Distinction and Precautions in Attack' in A Clapham and P Gaeta (eds), *The Oxford Handbook of International Law in Armed Conflict* (Oxford, Oxford University Press, 2014) 273, 288–89. Not all of these principles are regarded by all as the 'basic' principles of weapons law, with only the first three reflected in the SRM. The present author arrived at this list having been actively involved in the process of legal review of weapons (in accordance with Art 36 of the 1977 Additional Protocol I) within the UK Ministry of Defence.

[47] SRM Rule 38.

[48] SRM Rule 42(a).

[49] SRM Rules 39 and 42(b).

Naval weapons are subject to the considerable body of weapons law that applies to all weapons, regardless of the conflict environment in which they are used, or whether they are used against targets at sea or in power projection operations against targets onshore.[50] The law applying to most weapons deployed at sea is consistent with that applying to other weapons discussed in this volume. The full range of naval weapons includes missiles and projectiles, for example, and their deployment at sea does not alter their legal status or the legitimate use to which they can be put.[51] Three naval weapons deserve additional comment, however. Sea mines and torpedoes remain important additions to the naval armament deployed today. While technology has resulted in a greater measure of sophistication than was evident over a century ago, when these weapons first had a significant impact on naval hostilities, the law regulating them has not changed to the same extent. The third weapon to be discussed below is a more recent phenomenon, and it is one that has so far never been used. Indeed, its use in armed conflict at sea has been avoided by those states that have possessed it. It is the tactical nuclear weapon.

i. Sea Mines

The *San Remo Manual* commentary defines a sea mine as 'an explosive device laid in the water, on the sea-bed or in the subsoil thereof, with the intention of damaging or sinking ships or of deterring ships from entering an area'.[52]

Although sea mines existed before the twentieth century,[53] their general deployment in naval war can be regarded as having commenced with the laying of mines during the Russo-Japanese War in 1904–05. A number of warships on both sides were lost to mining, and their effects raised a general awareness of sea mines' potential as a serious threat to major surface warships.[54] As a consequence, when the powers convened in The Hague in 1907, the regulation of sea mines was included on their agenda. The 1907 Hague Convention VIII was the first conventional law dealing with these weapons. It was also the most recent and remains the basic document on the law relating to sea mines.

It includes rules (in Article 1) addressing the laying of mines and their ability to become harmless if they are either intentionally unanchored/free-floating, or are moored but break free from their moorings. Article 2 forbids the laying of mines with the sole aim of intercepting commercial shipping. Article 3 concerns precautions necessary to reduce the risk

[50] The most comprehensive treatment of weapons law in the round currently available is W Boothby, *Weapons and the Law of Armed Conflict* (Oxford, Oxford University Press, 2009).

[51] There are bans or restrictions on several weapons physically (as distinct from legally) capable of being deployed at sea that have been dealt with in conventional law, including: poison; biological and chemical weapons; expanding and exploding bullets; projectiles containing non-detectable fragments; incendiary weapons; and blinding laser weapons. The Study of Customary IHL (n 41) reflects the relevant conventional bans and/or restrictions in Rules 72–86.

[52] SRM, 169. For recent discussions on the law relating to sea-mines, see S. Haines, '1907 Hague Convention VIII Relative to the Laying of Automatic Submarine Contact Mines', in *International Law Studies* (Stockton Center for the Study of International Law, US Naval War College), Vol. 90 (2014), pp. 412–45; and C O'Flaherty "The Naval Minefield of Customary International Humanitarian Law," *St Antony's International Review*, Vol. 14, No. 1 (2018), pp. 24–52.

[53] H. Levie, *Mine Warfare at Sea* (Dordrecht/Boston/London, Martinus Nijhoff, 1992) 9–19.

[54] The most appropriate starting point for a study of naval operations during the Russo-Japanese War is J Corbett, *Maritime Operations in the Russo-Japanese War 1904–1905* (Annapolis, MD, Naval Institute Press, 2015) (2 vols), with an introduction by J Hattendorf and D Schurman. Corbett wrote this for use within the Royal Navy and it was not originally intended for commercial publication, although limited copies were available from 1915 onwards.

to peaceful shipping, while Article 5 covers the need to clear mines at the end of hostilities. Unfortunately, Article 7 of the Convention restricts its applicability to armed conflicts in which all belligerents are parties and, as a result, the Convention has never formally applied in any conflict since it was negotiated in 1907.

The most important legal question to be raised about sea mines is whether the Hague Convention VIII, originally restricted in its application to automatic submarine contact mines, now applies to other technologies. The basic contact mine remains a formidable weapon in naval armouries, but mine technology has become far more sophisticated. For example, the Italian-manufactured 'Asteria' and Spanish 'Minea' multi-influence sea mines, the most sophisticated mines available today, are capable of being operated in response to a combination of acoustic, magnetic, pressure, seismic and optic influences. They also incorporate technologies designed to counter attempts at mine clearance.[55] For the 1907 Hague Convention VIII to be more broadly applicable than its original wording (and intent) suggests, there would need to have been a development of custom to reflect the provisions of the Convention in relation to contact mines and, then, a further development of custom extending those rules to all other mine technologies.

There is much to be said in favour of customary development along these lines. For example, Article 1 of the Convention requires unanchored contact mines to 'become harmless one hour at most after the person who laid them ceases to control them'. In the case of moored mines, they are required to 'become harmless as soon as they have broken loose from their moorings'. Both conditions are undoubtedly desirable because sea mines in these circumstances are no longer serving the legitimate purpose for which they were laid, and could otherwise become a general and indiscriminate danger to shipping.

While it makes sense for Article 1 to apply to all sea mines, for it to do so in customary law would require sound evidence of a generality of state practice to that effect, as well as an acceptance of a legal obligation (*opinio juris*) for all to comply. Opinion differs on whether the requirements for custom have, strictly speaking, been met. While some believe they have, this might be a case of wishful thinking trumping the facts.[56] No matter. For our purposes it is sufficient to refer to the *San Remo Manual* as an indication of authoritative thinking on the subject (reflected also in contemporary official manuals), with the law from the Hague Convention VIII repeated in *San Remo Manual* Rules 81 and 82.

In all, there are 13 rules in the *San Remo Manual* dealing with sea mines, making them the most regulated of the three weapons dealt with therein.[57] The rules do not merely restate what is contained in the 1907 Hague Convention VIII; they build on the 1907 rules to render them consistent with late-twentieth-century developments in the law of the sea. Mines must only be used for legitimate military purposes, including denial of sea areas to the enemy.[58] The laying of mines must be notified.[59] Those laying mines need to record their location.[60]

[55] For details of these mines see, respectively: https://goo.gl/rBdsnq; and https://goo.gl/FRmojW. The author is most grateful to Captain C O'Flaherty, Royal Navy, for his advice on these, and also for sight of his paper on 'The Naval Minefield of Customary International Humanitarian Law', forthcoming in *St Antony's International Review* (2018).

[56] Dinstein (n 9) 70–71.

[57] Only two other rules deal with weapons: SRM Rule 78 on missiles and other projectiles; and SRM Rule 79 on torpedoes.

[58] SRM Rule 80.

[59] SRM Rule 83.

[60] SRM Rule 84.

Neutral shipping must be allowed free exit from belligerent internal, territorial and archipelagic waters.[61] Mines must not be laid in neutral waters,[62] and must not have the effect of preventing passage between neutral and international waters.[63] Legitimate use of the high seas by neutral states must be ensured.[64] Transit and archipelagic sea-lanes passage must not be impeded unless safe and convenient alternative routes are provided.[65] Lastly, three rules of the *San Remo Manual* deal with aspects of sea-mine clearance.[66]

ii. Torpedoes

While undoubtedly most closely associated with submarines, torpedoes can also be launched from surface warships and from aircraft, and can even be carried to the vicinity of their intended target by ship-launched missiles.[67] They can be used against both surface and submarine targets. At their simplest, they are a very straightforward weapon indeed: an explosive warhead fitted to a powered device fired directly from one ship at another and detonating on impact. Such basic torpedoes, which remain in use today, incorporate no ability to manoeuvre and have to be fired from a submarine or surface vessel whose launching machinery (often incorporating a tube) has to be pointed in the direction of the target to allow the torpedo a free run to it. There is considerable skill required in hitting a target. This involves the operator carrying out the mental calculations necessary to reach a firing solution, the equation combining the distance from launch to target, target course and speed, the time the torpedo will take to reach its target and the direction in which it will need to be fired. Judging correctly the precise moment of launch and the torpedo's required direction of travel to target has always been an essential skill for the successful submarine commander. Later developments in technology have, however, resulted in torpedoes that are wire guided, or which are fitted with a homing mechanism designed to allow the device to seek out its target without input from the launching unit.

The 1907 Hague Convention VIII was not exclusively concerned with sea mines; it also had a provision dealing with torpedoes. Article 1(3) states that it is forbidden 'to use torpedoes which do not become harmless when they have missed their mark'. If they were not to do so they would have potentially indiscriminate effect. Whether one relies on the conventional law of the 1907 Hague Convention or the customary principle of distinction, the need to ensure that torpedoes do not remain live and lethal beyond their immediate purpose is an uncontentious requirement of the law of naval warfare.[68]

[61] SRM Rule 85.
[62] SRM Rule 86.
[63] SRM Rule 87.
[64] SRM Rule 88.
[65] SRM Rule 89.
[66] SRM Rules 90–92.
[67] A substantial proportion of the Italian fleet anchored off Taranto was destroyed or disabled by torpedoes dropped from British aircraft launched from the carrier *HMS Illustrious* in November 1940; the German battleship *Bismarck* was initially disabled by torpedoes dropped from aircraft in May 1941; and the Japanese attack on the US Navy's Pacific fleet in Pearl Harbor in December 1941 included the use of air-dropped torpedoes. An example of torpedoes linked to missile delivery was the *Ikara* anti-submarine system deployed by the Royal Navy and the Royal Australian Navy towards the end of the Cold War.
[68] SRM Rule 79.

iii. Tactical Nuclear Weapons

Although in one sense they are the ultimate weapon of maritime power projection, sea-launched strategic nuclear weapons transcend naval warfare as it is addressed in this chapter. While nuclear strategic systems are not regarded here as a feature of naval warfare, naval operations intended to contain or destroy the platforms from which they are launched would be. Obviously, so too would be the weapons used for that purpose. The principal sea-launched strategic nuclear weapons have been, and continue to be, deployed in ballistic missile-carrying nuclear-powered submarines (commonly referred to as SSBNs). Nuclear weapons used for strategic effect can, however, also include those carried by aircraft launched from aircraft carriers and cruise missiles fitted with nuclear warheads deployed in either surface warships or submarines.

Non-strategic nuclear weapons have been deployed at sea in the past and may continue to be an option for major maritime powers whose navies have roles that include countering a potential enemy's capacity to launch strategic nuclear weapons from naval platforms. Tactical nuclear weapons have certainly been deployed at sea, and have played an important part in the complex pattern of arrangements put in place in relation to nuclear deterrence. The British Royal Navy, for example, deployed nuclear depth-bombs in its anti-submarine surface units (frigates, destroyers and aircraft carriers) as recently as the 1990s. As anti-submarine weapon systems, they had the potential for use in attacks on Soviet SSBNs deployed in the Atlantic and Arctic Oceans during the Cold War.[69] In 1990, the US Navy had almost 6,000 nuclear weapons deployed at sea, which is more than the entire US nuclear stockpile today. Declassified US data reveal these figures and cover nuclear deployments for the 30-year period from 1961. The data release only covers the period up to 1991, after which date non-strategic nuclear weapons were off-loaded from US naval units.[70]

Tactical nuclear weapons for use in naval warfare represent perhaps the most 'useable' nuclear armaments for the simple reason that the issues associated with the principle of distinction (between combatants and civilians or between military objectives and civilian objects) would not be necessarily problematic. A nuclear detonation at sea, far from land and in an ocean region relatively free of civilian-manned shipping, would be most unlikely to harm civilians (notwithstanding the longer-term environmental impact), or not to the point at which civilian casualties would be disproportionate to the military advantage to be gained by their use. There are, of course, other concerns; not least the consequences of a breach of the nuclear threshold that could lead to a wider use of nuclear systems during any war in which sea-based tactical nuclear weapons were used. These concerns are not strictly legal in nature, however, but do have significant political and military-strategic relevance. This was well recognised, for example, by the UK when it deployed units to the South Atlantic in 1982. While tactical nuclear weapons were available in deployed units,

[69] The author of this chapter served in a Royal Navy anti-submarine frigate deployed into the Atlantic during the 1970s, and was one of the four officers on board responsible for the management of nuclear weapon release. If used, the weapons would have been carried in the ship's helicopter to be dropped into the sea above an enemy submarine's datum position. The chances of the ship's helicopter and its crew returning safely on board after deploying the weapon were not generally regarded as high.

[70] See R Farley, 'Declassified: US Nuclear Weapons at Sea During the Cold War', *The Diplomat* (6 February 2016) at https://goo.gl/sm6LQj.

the UK had no intention of using them in the conventional operations that occurred against Argentine naval forces during the armed conflict that ensued.[71]

V. Regions of Operations

Until the developments in the law of the sea negotiated during the series of UN Law of the Sea Conferences,[72] naval hostilities could legitimately take place on both the high seas and in the territorial waters and internal waters of the belligerent states. The only sea areas in which hostilities could not be conducted were the internal and territorial waters of neutral states, but since these extended to only three nautical miles from land, neutral waters represented no great area of restriction for navies involved in hostilities.[73] Since the entry into force of UNCLOS, however, the marked increase in the extent and complexity of coastal state jurisdiction has significantly reduced the extent of the high seas. Jurisdictional zones beyond territorial limits allow coastal states to exercise rights, principally in relation to resource exploitation. These resource rights continue to exist in time of war, with belligerents under an obligation not to jeopardise them. Issues are clearly raised by the activities of naval forces within new jurisdictional zones. Importantly, however, it is still only internal and territorial waters (and, where appropriate, archipelagic waters) that are a part of the territory of states; the zones beyond them do not generate territorial rights, despite representing limited extensions of the coastal state's jurisdiction.

The extent to which navies are now restricted in their actions is best considered under the following headings: (i) on the high seas; (ii) in internal, territorial and archipelagic waters; (iii) in the exclusive economic zone (EEZ) and the waters above the continental shelf; and (iv) in the waters running through international straits.[74]

A. High Seas

The high seas today consist of all sea areas not included in internal waters, territorial waters, archipelagic waters or the EEZ.[75] The high seas extend today from the 200 nautical

[71] The UK Ministry of Defence issued an Unclassified Briefing Paper entitled *Operation CORPORATE 1982: The carriage of nuclear weapons by the Task Group assembled for the Falklands Campaign* (copy in the author's possession).

[72] The two most significant UN Conferences were the First in 1958 and the Third in 1974–82. For the purposes of this chapter, only the outcome of the Third Conference (UNCLOS III) is relied upon.

[73] Norwegian neutral waters (Norway was not yet in the war at that point, although about to become so) were famously entered unlawfully in February 1940 by the German tender *Altmark*, as she attempted to return to Germany from the South Atlantic. She had been supporting the *Graf Spee* and had British Merchant Service prisoners on board, and steamed down the neutral Norwegian coast hoping to avoid British interception. Most of her passage was through Norway's territorial waters and there was some doubt as to whether that act breached Norway's neutrality. Eventually, however, she sought refuge in Jøssingfjord, which was 'internal waters' within which she had no right of innocent passage. Winston Churchill, then First Lord of the Admiralty, ordered the British destroyer *HMS Cossack* to recover the prisoners from the *Altmark*, which she did, herself breaching Norwegian neutrality. See O'Connell (n 23) 41–44.

[74] In the discussions that follow, for the sake of brevity references will in the main be restricted to the rules contained in UNCLOS and the SRM.

[75] Art 86, UNCLOS.

mile outer limit of the EEZ, whereas previously they consisted of all sea areas beyond the 3 nautical mile territorial sea. The high seas have been much reduced in their extent.

All states, including belligerents engaged in armed conflict, are free to exercise the right of free navigation on the high seas,[76] which applies to all ships, including belligerent warships. While free movement is permitted, at first sight the law of the sea appears to rule out the conduct of hostilities by belligerent warships on the high seas, with the provision in Article 88 stating that they 'shall be reserved for peaceful purposes'. Appearances can, however, be deceptive.

The waging of aggressive war is contrary to the UN Charter, and state aggression using naval forces on the high seas for that purpose would most certainly not be a 'peaceful purpose'. Defence against aggression is an inherent right, however, and naval forces resisting aggressive action by opposing belligerent forces on the high seas would not be in breach of Article 88. Unless the UN Security Council determines that one party to a conflict is the aggressor, neither party can be assumed to be so; each will be able lawfully to conduct hostilities, conditional on their compliance with the rules of naval warfare and their respect for the rights of neutral states. If the UN Security Council determines that a state poses a threat to the peace or commits a breach of the peace or an act of aggression, there may be a need lawfully to conduct hostilities on the high seas in the process of imposing military sanctions in accordance with Article 42 of the UN Charter, which expressly mentions operations by sea forces, including the use of blockade.

Where the continental shelf of a coastal state extends beyond its 200 nautical mile EEZ limit, the waters above it constitute a part of the high seas. Hostilities can be conducted in these waters, but belligerents are under an obligation to respect neutral rights relating to the resources of the continental shelf (see the discussion in section V.C).

When conducting naval hostilities on the high seas, belligerents are to pay due regard to neutral states' rights of exploration and exploitation of the resources of the sea-bed, ocean floor and subsoil thereof,[77] and must take care to avoid damage to pipelines and cables laid on the sea-bed which do not exclusively serve other belligerents.[78]

B. Internal, Territorial, and Archipelagic Waters

Internal, territorial and archipelagic waters are a part of the territory of the coastal state. If the coastal state is a belligerent, these sea areas will constitute belligerent waters within which hostilities can be conducted. It follows, of course, that if the coastal state is neutral, these sea areas will be neutral waters, and belligerents are forbidden in law from conducting hostilities within them. That is not to say that belligerent warships and auxiliaries may not enter these waters.

Examples (but not a definitive list) of hostile actions that are forbidden in neutral waters include: attacks on or capture of persons or objects; the use of those waters as a base of

[76] Art 87, UNCLOS.
[77] SRM Rule 36.
[78] SRM Rule 37.

operations; the laying of mines; and the visit, search, diversion or capture of vessels.[79] Belligerent forces may not use neutral waters as a sanctuary[80] but may exercise innocent passage through territorial and archipelagic waters.[81] Of particular note is the requirement for submarines exercising innocent passage to transit through these waters on the surface.[82] If the coastal state has designated sea lanes through its archipelagic waters, belligerent vessels are free to exercise passage through them.[83]

In addition to passage, a neutral state may permit belligerent vessels access to its waters for the purpose of replenishment and repair. The neutral state would not compromise its neutrality by doing so, though there has traditionally been a limit to the access permitted. There is a longstanding rule that denies belligerent warships and auxiliaries the ability to remain in neutral waters for longer than 24 hours, 'unless unavoidable on account of damage or the stress of weather'.[84] This '24-hour rule' was most certainly appropriate in the context of general naval war, when opposing naval forces would confront each other globally. It played an important and notable role in, for example, the confrontation between the *Graf Spee* and British naval forces during the Battle of the River Plate in December 1939.[85] Nevertheless, it is worth questioning the contemporary need for and validity of this rule in the context of geographically limited conflicts. The UK has certainly done this, explaining in its official manual that it no longer reflects state practice or British interests.[86] This position is clearly controversial but may be regarded as a considered reaction to the changing character of naval war. For a customary rule to be overridden or developed, it is obviously necessary to identify evidence of practice inconsistent with the existing rule. The UK's argument is that it would be unnecessary, for example, to apply the 24-hour rule strictly to British warships on visits to states in the Caribbean while other British warships are engaged in a local conflict in a distant region such as the Middle East or South-East Asia.[87]

Given the likely characteristics of the sorts of hybrid conflicts to be discussed in section VI.E of this chapter, in which a fluidity of local circumstances may well result in brief shifts from constabulary applications of force to combat – and back again – strict compliance with such a rule developed in the context of global naval warfare would be unnecessary and inconvenient to the point of appearing bizarre. Nevertheless, the rule remains widely acknowledged and it cannot be assumed that it will no longer apply. Apart from the UK's stated position, there is no evidence of either state practice or opinion sufficient to establish a new customary norm – perhaps because there have been no naval wars in recent years capable of generating the necessary evidence.

[79] SRM Rule 16.
[80] SRM Rule 17.
[81] Arts 19 and 52, UNCLOS.
[82] Arts 20 and 52, UNCLOS.
[83] Art 53, UNCLOS.
[84] SRM Rule 21.
[85] See O'Connell (n 23) 33–36.
[86] UK Ministry of Defence (n 5) para 13.4.
[87] The present author, as the Chairman of the Editorial Board of the *UK Manual* and joint author of its chapter on 'Maritime Warfare', was directly involved in the UK's decision to question the 24-hour rule in this way. He stands by that decision but does not deny its controversial nature. See his discussion of it in Haines (n 12) 103–04.

C. The EEZ and Continental Shelf

The waters within the EEZ and above the continental shelf, all of which were once a part of the high seas, remain a region within which hostilities can be conducted. The continental shelf exists within the limits of the EEZ, but also has the potential to extend beyond those limits into the high seas. Beyond the 12 nautical mile territorial sea limit, the EEZ and continental shelf, while representing jurisdictional zones of the coastal state, are neither neutral nor belligerent waters. Naval hostilities can be conducted within them as long as they are consistent with the laws of naval warfare and belligerent states pay due regard to the rights and duties of the coastal state, amongst other things for the exploration and exploitation of the economic resources of the EEZ and the continental shelf and the preservation and protection of the marine environment.[88] In particular, belligerents should pay due regard to artificial islands, installations and safety zones established by neutral states within their EEZs and on their continental shelves. There is a particular need for care to be exercised by belligerents when laying mines in these waters, which is permitted but which needs to take account of the exploration and exploitation rights of coastal states, with minefields notified to them.[89]

D. International Straits

Strictly speaking, despite being accorded a designated part (Part III) of UNCLOS, international straits are not distinct jurisdictional zones and the navigational rules established for them do not 'in other respects affect the legal status of the waters forming' them.[90] International straits are defined as any straits 'used for international navigation between one part of the high seas or an EEZ and another part of the high seas or EEZ'.[91] Not all such straits require discussion here, however. Those that do are the ones that are less than 24 nautical miles across. If they are more than that distance, they will have stretches of water through them that do not fall within the territorial waters of the opposite littoral states. This means that it is usually possible for all vessels transiting through them to make passage without entering territorial waters, in which case the rules relating to the EEZ outlined in the preceding subsection will apply.

For straits less than 24 nautical miles wide, if opposite littoral states have established 12 nautical mile territorial limits it will be necessary for all vessels to take passage through territorial waters. For these straits, UNCLOS defines a form of passage known as 'straits transit passage'. States' rights and obligations in respect to it are detailed in a series of deliberately negotiated provisions.[92] These were considered an essential element of UNCLOS, by the major maritime powers in particular, ensuring that the pre-existing freedoms of navigation and naval mobility through strategically vital international straits were not undermined by the negotiated agreement extending territorial limits. Indeed, in order to arrive at the

[88] SRM Rule 34.
[89] SRM Rule 35.
[90] Art 34, UNCLOS.
[91] Art 37, UNCLOS.
[92] Arts 37–44, UNCLOS.

negotiated extension of territorial limits from 3 to 12 nautical miles, it was necessary at the same time to agree rules on transit passage.

All vessels (including warships) enjoy the right of unimpeded transit passage for the purpose of continuous and expeditious transit of the strait.[93] Such passage may not be suspended by the littoral states. Belligerent warships and auxiliaries must proceed without delay; refrain from the threat or use of force against the sovereignty, territorial integrity or political independence of the littoral states; and refrain from any activities other than those incidental to their normal modes of continuous and expeditious transit.[94] This last requirement, for normal mode of transit, has resulted in submarines being allowed to transit such straits submerged, contrary to the need for them to transit surfaced when exercising innocent passage through territorial waters.

There are also other differences between the restrictions placed on warships and auxiliaries in straits transit passage and those exercising innocent passage through territorial waters. The transit passage rules are less restrictive. Warships can take defensive measures, including the launching and recovery of aircraft, the formation of defensive screens, and the conduct of acoustic and electronic surveillance,[95] all of which would risk prejudicing the innocence of passage through territorial waters.[96]

VI. Methods of Naval Warfare

A. Sea Control and Sea Denial

All warships – both surface vessels and submarines – engage in sea-control and sea-denial operations as a matter of course. While surface warships are predominantly concerned with achieving and maintaining sea control for themselves, submarines are extremely effective sea-denial platforms.[97] A good way of denying the control of particular sea areas to enemy forces is through the laying of sea mines. All warships, including submarines, need to establish sufficient control of their immediate environment in order to conduct other operations against land targets, against trade or to defend their coastal jurisdictional zones. The conduct of hostilities in all sea-control/sea-denial operations typically involves warships (both surface and sub-surface units) engaging opposing belligerent forces, all of which will be legitimate military objectives.

Warships are the platforms that are entitled to engage in combat operations against other military objectives at sea.[98] In achieving sea control in the regions of naval warfare

[93] Art 38, UNCLOS.

[94] Art 39, UNCLOS; and SRM Rules 27–30.

[95] SRM Rule 30.

[96] Art 19, UNCLOS.

[97] Knowledge of the presence of a single, highly capable enemy submarine in a wide area may cause a naval task force commander considerable anxiety and undermine his ability to achieve his task force's primary mission. The psychological effect of the lawful sinking of the Argentine cruiser *General Belgrano* by the British SSN *Conqueror* in 1982, for example, effectively denied the Argentine Navy the necessary sea control to operate and, in doing so, brought an effective end to the purely naval dimension of the conflict.

[98] This includes merchant vessels converted to warships, allowed for by the 1907 Hague Convention VII Relating to the Conversion of Merchant Ships into Warships. Although this remains extant, the sophistication and

outlined in section V, all warships will be engaged to some degree in threatening or targeting enemy warships. These can be attacked without warning at any time in any of those regions, and, traditionally, such attacks can occur in any legitimate location globally.[99] Geographical restrictions imposed on naval forces that limit their freedom to conduct hostilities to particular areas of the globe will be a political/policy matter and not a matter of law. For example, a conflict in the Indian Ocean involving two Indian Ocean littoral states could lawfully result in the warships of those two states engaging each other in combat in the Mediterranean Sea or the Atlantic or Pacific Oceans. Decisions made by each of the belligerent states to restrict their naval forces to operations within the Indian Ocean may be sensible for a number of reasons, but there would routinely be no international legal obligation placed on those states to impose such limitations.[100]

While the uses of the seas are more varied and intense than in the past, with a great many more civilians present at sea in a wider range of civilian vessels than ever before, the maritime environment is not one in which compliance with the principle of distinction should ordinarily prove especially problematic compared to situations of armed conflict ashore. Clearly, it is necessary to take appropriate precautions in attack, but once a potential target has been identified for what it is (an opposing belligerent warship, for example), the attack may proceed with whatever lawful weapon systems are available. While this is simply stated, it is also necessary to recognise that targeting at distance may result in a naval force (as distinct from single, identifiable warships) becoming the objective. There may be vessels exempt from attack within that naval force or in relatively close proximity (hospital ships and medical transports, for example).[101] While compliance with the principle of distinction may be regarded generally as relatively straightforward in naval warfare, it cannot be assumed to be invariably so.

An important factor to consider when engaging in attacks on enemy naval units is the need to limit the application of force to that which is necessary to render the target incapable of engaging in hostilities. It will frequently not be necessary completely to destroy an enemy warship. Indeed, as the most recent naval combat operations between two naval powers (the Falklands/Malvinas conflict in 1982) demonstrated, modern warships can be taken out of contention by a single hit from a missile. This can result in a catastrophic failure of the warship's power and essential fighting systems, severely disabling the vessel and rendering it incapable of further involvement in combat operations, despite the majority of the crew itself remaining physically capable of doing so. To launch further attacks on an already severely disabled warship would be a disproportionate and unnecessary act. In some circumstances, the capture of a disabled enemy warship may be possible, but if not, and sinking it is considered the most appropriate action to take, all efforts need to be made

complexity of modern warships and the likely characteristics of future naval war are cause for some doubt as to its precise future utility. If it is relied on in the future, it is more than likely to be so in lower-intensity and limited conflicts, rather than as a feature of general naval war between major maritime powers.

[99] Warships are military objectives: by their nature, location, purpose or use they make an effective contribution to military action, and their total or partial destruction capture or neutralisation, in the circumstances ruling at the time, offers a definite military advantage. SRM Rule 40.

[100] It is not inconceivable that such a restriction could be imposed by the UN Security Council in a binding resolution as a measure to limit the effects of an armed conflict.

[101] An extensive list of enemy vessels exempt from attack is contained in SRM Rule 47, with the conditions for and loss of exemption listed in SRM Rules 48–52. (Aircraft exempt from attack are covered in SRM Rules 53–58.)

to place the surviving crew in a position of safety. Indeed, they may be protected persons under the 1949 Geneva Convention II, being effectively shipwrecked (if not also wounded or sick).[102] Attacking an already disabled warship will not only fail to meet the test of military advantage, therefore, it may also constitute a grave breach of Geneva Convention II in relation to its potentially shipwrecked crew.

B. Power Projection

The projection of power ashore from naval platforms at sea is best considered, from a legal point of view, as a matter falling almost entirely within the rules governing the conduct of hostilities in land warfare. It is the location of military objectives being targeted (in compliance with the principle of distinction and the taking of precautions in attack), rather than the position or character of the platforms from which any attacks are to be launched, that is the crucial factor. In conventional law, there are two treaties of relevance: 1907 Hague Convention IX;[103] and the 1977 Additional Protocol I. The latter (the provisions of which are fully discussed elsewhere in this volume) has essentially superseded the former.

If a state is not a party to the 1977 Additional Protocol I, however, it is arguably the case that certain provisions of the Hague Convention IX that have passed into customary law remain binding on it. Those of relevance are Articles 1, 2 and 5. By these, the bombardment of undefended ports, towns, villages, dwellings or buildings is prohibited. Military objectives within these locations can, however, be targeted, although a naval force must first issue a summons of intent to launch an attack in order that civilians can either take shelter or be evacuated. If, for military reasons, an immediate attack is necessary, the naval force must take measures in order that the town suffers as little harm as possible. A bombardment must not take place if it is possible for the military objectives to be destroyed by other means, including by a landing force.

When it comes to amphibious operations, with military forces landing on the coast in order to engage in military operations ashore, as soon as combatants land, they are subject to the rules of land warfare. The important distinction between combatants moving towards a landing and those who have already landed is of relevance in relation to their potential as victims of war (and strictly speaking is not to do with the conduct of hostilities). While still at sea, their protection may well involve the application of Geneva Convention II, under which they may be entitled to shipwrecked status (additional to their potential to be regarded as either sick or wounded). This would be the case, for example, if their landing craft were to be destroyed. Once a landing party has reached the shore, however, Geneva Convention II will no longer have relevance, for the simple reason that combatants on land have no potential to become shipwrecked.

[102] See the discussion in S Haines, 'Who is Shipwrecked?' in A Clapham, P Gaeta, and M Sassòli (eds), *The 1949 Geneva Conventions: A Commentary* (Oxford, Oxford University Press, 2015) 767, 777–78, paras 39 and 40.

[103] Convention (IX) concerning Bombardment by Naval Forces in Time of War; adopted at The Hague, 18 October 1907; entry into force, 26 January 1910.

C. Economic Warfare

Navies can be engaged in either offensive or defensive economic warfare. In terms of the offensive, they have two principal methods at their disposal: the interdiction of shipping (or *guerre de course*), and the mounting of a blockade of the opposing belligerent's coast and ports. The former has been conducted principally on the high seas (and would today take place also in the waters of the EEZ and above the continental shelf), while the latter will certainly be applied within the territorial waters of the opposing belligerent, but would also have the potential to affect significant sea areas beyond territorial limits. Defensive economic warfare operations (the defence of trade) can involve the searching out and destruction of opposing naval forces that pose a threat to trade, or by the direct defence of merchant shipping, the most effective proven method of which has been the formation of protected convoys.

The law regulating economic warfare at sea is the most extensive and complex element of the laws of naval warfare and includes within it the law of prize. Although the first ever instrument of conventional law dealing with naval war (the 1856 Paris Declaration) was about economic warfare, it was brief and there has been little additional conventional law agreed since.[104] The bulk of the law regulating economic warfare is arguably customary. The law of prize, however, which developed over centuries (but especially during the eighteenth and nineteenth centuries[105]), is a complex and extensive body of law that owes its existence to the jurisprudence of various national prize courts. It has been the subject of both national manuals and academic texts, the most recent comprehensive treatment of the subject having been produced immediately following the Second World War.[106] Although the law of prize would be an important source of detailed guidance on the conduct of economic warfare operations, its complexity means that the full body of the law is a matter for legal specialists to understand and to interpret, in order that more accessible rules can be produced as guidance for naval operators to apply at sea during the actual conduct of economic warfare. For convenience here, however, we can rely on the *San Remo Manual* as the principal authoritative reference.

In all, more than 40 *San Remo Manual* rules deal with the conduct of economic warfare operations (including rules dealing with the capture of enemy and neutral civil aircraft, which are not discussed here). They deal with operations against both enemy and neutral

[104] Of the extant 1907 Hague conventions, only the Convention XI Relative to Certain Restrictions with Regard to the Exercise of the Right of Capture in Naval War has any significance here – and that is limited. The 1907 Convention with the greatest potential to codify rules for economic warfare was Convention XII for the establishment of an international prize court. This was not ratified, however, and the subsequent 1909 Declaration of London, intended as a guide to the law of prize to be applied by the Prize Court was, like its 'parent' convention, never ratified.

[105] Essentially, during major naval wars that occurred between the Seven Years War (1756–63) and the end of the Napoleonic Wars in 1815. For an excellent account of the development of the law of prize in the latter stages of this period see R Hill, *The Prizes of War: The Naval Prize System in the Napoleonic Wars 1793–1815* (Stroud, Sutton Publishing, 1998).

[106] For two classic treatments of the law of prize, see: T Holland, *A Manual of Naval Prize Law* (London, Her Majesty's Stationery Office, 1888); and C Colombos, *A Treatise on the Law of Prize*, 3rd edn (London, Sweet & Maxwell, 1949). The former was the UK's official manual at the time of its publication. The latter, the first edition of which appeared in 1926 with an Introduction by A Pearce Higgins, is an academic treatise that takes into account legal developments over prize during the most recent war in which economic warfare was a major feature.

merchant ships, including visit and search, diversion, capture, seizure of cargo, confiscation and destruction, and also with the conduct of blockade operations.[107]

Belligerent warships, in the conduct of economic warfare, can exercise the right of visit and search in relation to any merchant vessels (enemy or neutral) when there are reasonable grounds for suspecting that they are subject to capture.[108] Although belligerents have the right of visit and search in relation to enemy merchant vessels, there is no requirement for this to be exercised prior to their capture.[109] While both enemy and neutral merchant ships may be captured, in relation to the former there are exceptions leading to exemptions, while in relation to the latter there are certain conditions that need to be met if capture is to be legitimate. These enemy exemptions and neutral requirements are dealt with in the paragraphs immediately following. Capture is defined in the *San Remo Manual* as 'taking such a vessel as prize for adjudication' (in a prize court).[110]

i. Enemy Merchant Vessels

All enemy merchant vessels are subject to capture unless they are exempt due to their employment in non-trading activities. The enemy character of a merchant vessel is determined in accordance with Rules 112–117 of the *San Remo Manual.* A vessel flying an enemy flag has enemy character.[111] A vessel flying a neutral flag is assumed to be neutral,[112] but if the commander of a belligerent warship suspects that despite its flag it does have enemy character, the right of visit and search may be exercised.[113] If visit and search raises a reasonable suspicion as to enemy character, the vessel may be captured as prize, subject to adjudication.[114] Enemy character can be determined by reference to registration, ownership, charter or other criteria.[115]

The following enemy merchant vessels are exempt from capture[116] as long as they are innocently employed in their normal role, do not commit acts harmful to the enemy, submit immediately to inspection when required, and do not intentionally hamper the movement of combatants and obey orders to stop or move out of the way when required:[117]

- hospital ships and small craft used for coastal rescue operations
- other medical transports, so long as they are needed for the wounded, sick and shipwrecked on board
- vessels granted safe conduct by agreement between the belligerents, including cartel vessels (for example, those designated for and engaged in the transport of prisoners

[107] For a useful series of discussions on the subject, which provide good background to the rules in the SRM, see R Grunawalt (ed), *The Law of Naval Warfare: Targeting Enemy Merchant Shipping* (Newport, RI, US Naval War College, 1993), including G Walker, 'State Practice Following World War II: 1945–1990', ibid, 121.
[108] SRM Rule 118.
[109] SRM Rule 135.
[110] SRM Rule 138.
[111] SRM Rule 112.
[112] SRM Rule 113.
[113] SRM Rule 114.
[114] SRM Rule 116.
[115] SRM Rule 117.
[116] SRM Rule 136.
[117] SRM Rule 137.

of war) and those engaged in humanitarian missions (including those indispensable to the survival of the civilian population and those engaged in relief actions and rescue operations)
- those carrying cultural property under special protection
- vessels charged with religious, non-military scientific or philanthropic missions
- small coastal fishing vessels and small boats engaged in local coastal trade (although these are subject to the regulation of a belligerent naval commander and to inspection), and
- vessels designed or adapted exclusively for responding to pollution incidents in the marine environment when actually engaged in such activities.

If an enemy merchant vessel subject to capture cannot be taken as prize at sea, it may be diverted to another area or to a port to complete capture, or it may be diverted away from its declared destination.[118] Alternatively, a captured enemy merchant vessel, as an exceptional measure, may be destroyed,[119] subject to certain criteria relating to the safety of crew and passengers and their personal effects, and the safeguarding of documents and papers relating to prize. The destruction of passenger vessels carrying only civilian passengers is prohibited, however; such vessels shall be diverted to an appropriate area or port in order to complete capture.[120]

ii. Neutral Merchant Vessels

Neutral merchant vessels are subject to capture if they are involved in activities that render them liable to attack,[121] or if it is established following visit and search[122] that:

- they are carrying contraband (This is defined in the *San Remo Manual* as goods ultimately destined for the territory under the control of the enemy and which may be susceptible for use in armed conflict.[123] Such goods must appear on a published contraband list produced by the belligerent.[124] Only contraband goods are subject to capture;[125] goods other than contraband are designated as 'free goods'.[126])
- they are on a voyage especially undertaken to transport passengers embodied in the armed forces of the enemy
- they are operating directly under enemy control, orders, charter, employment or direction
- they present irregular or fraudulent documents, lack necessary documents, or destroy, deface or conceal documents

[118] SRM Rule 138.
[119] SRM Rule 139.
[120] SRM Rule 140.
[121] SRM Rule 67.
[122] SRM Rule 146.
[123] SRM Rule 148.
[124] SRM Rule 149.
[125] SRM Rule 147.
[126] SRM Rule 150.

- they are violating regulations established by a belligerent within the immediate area of naval operations, or
- they are breaching or attempting to breach a blockade.

If a neutral merchant vessel subject to capture cannot be taken as prize at sea it may be destroyed, although every effort must be made to avoid doing so. It should not be destroyed without there being entire satisfaction that it can neither be sent into a belligerent port, nor diverted, nor properly released. Destruction can only be ordered if the safety of passengers and crew is assured, if documents relating to the captured vessel are safeguarded and, if feasible, if the personal effects of the passengers and crew are saved. It should not be destroyed simply for carrying contraband, unless by value, weight, volume or freight the contraband forms more than half its cargo. Destruction will be subject to subsequent adjudication.[127] It is prohibited to order the destruction of neutral passenger vessels carrying civilian passengers at sea.[128]

The remaining 12 *San Remo Manual* rules of relevance to economic warfare operations relate to blockade as a method of warfare. The aim of a blockade is to prevent supplies reaching the enemy by sea. Historically, and in the age of sail, it was frequently the case, weather permitting, that the blockading warships sailed close to the coast and to the entrances to belligerent ports. As sail gave way to steam and as weapons technology increased the distances over which warships could threaten each other, the geographical extent of blockade areas increased, and there emerged a debate over the relative value and legality of close and distant blockades.

The defining factor in relation to the legality of a blockade today is the extent of its effectiveness,[129] with the force conducting it to be positioned at a distance which ensures there will be a reasonable risk that access to the blockaded coastline and egress from those waters will be effectively prevented. A blockading force positioned too close to the coast may be at too great a risk from shore-based armaments, or so far from the coast as to be unable effectively to prevent vessels approaching the blockaded ports. The positioning of effective blockading forces will be determined, therefore, by military requirements in the prevailing circumstances; there can be no precise regulation to be applied in all cases determining the sea area to be directly affected by the blockade and from which vessels should be excluded.[130] Nevertheless, when a blockade is to be established, it should be declared to all belligerent and neutral states,[131] and the notification should specify the extent of the blockade, as well as the time of its commencement, the duration and its location. That declaration should also include a period following its commencement during which neutral vessels will be allowed to leave the blockaded coastline.[132]

A blockade does not need to be mounted by surface warships alone. Other warships can be employed, as can a variety of legitimate weapon systems. A blockade cannot, however, be enforced by the use of weapons alone, which means that the laying of a comprehensive

[127] SRM Rule 151.
[128] SRM Rule 152.
[129] SRM Rule 95.
[130] SRM Rule 96.
[131] SRM Rule 93.
[132] SRM Rule 94.

minefield purely for the purpose of enforcing the blockade would be unlawful.[133] Merchant vessels believed to be breaching a blockade may be captured, and if they fail to heed a warning and attempt to resist capture, they may be attacked. Ordinarily the blockade must apply impartially to the vessels of all states,[134] although the blockading power is under an obligation to allow entry to and egress from the blockaded coast and ports in certain circumstances, including vessels in distress and those whose purpose is the delivery of food and essential supplies to the blockaded state's civilian population.[135] A blockade should certainly not have as its objective the starving of the civilian population or damage to it in excess of the concrete and direct military advantage anticipated from it.[136] The passage of medical supplies for both the civilian population and for the wounded and sick members of the armed forces should also be allowed, subject only to regulation and search as necessary.[137]

It remains only to mention the use of convoys for defensive economic warfare. This includes their use by belligerents, but also by neutral powers, as a measure of security for their own and other neutral states' merchant vessels in times and regions of war.

There has been little doubt in the past that the use of convoys by belligerents has been an effective means of protecting their trading activities. Convoys of merchant vessels escorted by warships were a common feature of both World Wars, despite the fact that the merchant ships being convoyed were subject to attack without warning, unlike independently steaming merchant vessels, whose interdiction was subject to the legal conditions for capture already outlined. An operational decision was made by the Allies during the Second World War to convoy merchant ships because they were more effectively defended. Indeed, the convoying of large numbers of merchant vessels served to create 'honey-pots' that came to attract so-called 'wolf-packs' of German U-boats, which then proved vulnerable themselves to the concentrated effort of both Royal Navy anti-submarine escorts and Royal Air Force Coastal Command aircraft. Convoying not only enhanced the survivability of the Allies' merchant shipping, but also rendered Germany's U-boat force more vulnerable to attack from Allied surface and air forces. From a strictly legal perspective, convoyed merchant vessels might appear to be more vulnerable because they are treated as military objectives subject to attack without warning. Overall, however, convoying reduced the vulnerability of merchant ships, despite the fact that some convoys suffered serious losses.

Neutral merchant vessels accompanied by neutral warships benefit from exemption from the belligerent right of visit and search: if they are bound for a neutral port; if they are accompanied by neutral warships of either their own or other neutral states by way of agreement; if their flag state is able to warrant that they are not carrying contraband or otherwise acting contrary to their neutral status; and if the commanders of neutral escorting warships can provide all necessary information to belligerent warships that would otherwise be obtained via visit and search.[138]

[133] SRM Rule 97. And see also the Commentary section of the SRM, 178. The restriction on the use of mines for this purpose derives from Art 2 of the Hague Convention VIII.

[134] SRM Rule 100.

[135] SRM Rule 103.

[136] SRM Rule 102.

[137] SRM Rule 104.

[138] SRM Rule 120.

The foregoing account of those actions that are permitted and those that are not under the extant law governing economic warfare at sea has not attempted to provide detailed comment on the potentially profound practical difficulties that those attempting to apply the law would encounter today given the current characteristics of the international shipping industry. Searching a container ship at sea would be impossible. The characteristics of the majority of merchant vessels today make it extremely difficult to divert them to convenient ports because few ports will be able to take them. This is especially the case with container vessels, which require specialist container terminals. It would also be difficult to put together a prize crew capable of operating a modern merchant vessel. It also seems most unlikely that the lawful destruction of very large container vessels on the high seas would be regarded as appropriate, either politically, or economically or environmentally. The destruction of very large crude carriers would precipitate a major environmental crisis in the immediate vicinity. Since the majority of merchant vessels today are registered in open registry states (most of which would more than likely be neutral), there would be profound consequences to do with neutral rights to the free use of the seas. While the law is as it is, there is considerable doubt as to belligerents' ability – or, indeed, willingness – to apply it as it was applied in the past.

D. Coastal Jurisdiction Integrity

Maintaining the integrity of their areas of jurisdiction is a routine requirement for coastal states, in peacetime as well as in war. In peacetime, naval (and coastguard) operations will be of a constabulary nature, the aim being to enforce the laws of the coastal state as they apply within the various zones of jurisdiction. There may be disputes between opposite or adjacent states over the precise location of maritime boundaries, which could lead to rival naval forces confronting each other. Tensions generated have the potential to result in those confrontations crossing the threshold into armed conflict, at which point the laws of naval warfare would apply.

Regardless of its causes, during an armed conflict between two states it may be tempting for the belligerents to launch attacks on targets within their opponents' coastal jurisdictional zones. There has been one notable naval war so far that has involved attacks on economic activities related to the EEZ or Continental Shelf. During the Iran–Iraq War in the 1980s, offshore platforms within Iranian jurisdiction were attacked initially by Iraqi forces. Installations were damaged, but during the process of repair were again attacked, this time by previously neutral naval forces, when the US attacked Iranian oil platforms as a claimed measure of self-defence following suspected Iranian attacks on US forces in the region. This isolated example provides no evidence sufficient to establish a pattern of relevant practice, and no jurisprudence to suggest adequate answers to questions concerning the potential legality of similar attacks in the future. It does, nevertheless, point to the possibility of exploration and production platforms with resource zones being subjected to attack in the future. The legality of an attack on such a structure would depend, of course, on its status as a military objective. If it had military personnel stationed or weapons systems mounted on it, a platform would become a military objective and might be subject to targeting. Without a military presence, its status as a military objective would clearly be in some doubt. While the issue of the status of Iranian oil platforms during the Iran–Iraq War – and the attacks on them by US forces – provides an interesting vignette, somewhat less ambiguous as a source of potential targeting during operations within disputed areas would be military installations constructed on islands and other features, such as those constructed in recent years in the South China Sea.

Operations either against or in defence of economic activities within zones of coastal state jurisdiction would be subject to the standard rules on targeting. What cannot be in much doubt is that a belligerent state with resource zones of national economic importance would clearly have to consider the need to defend its exploration and exploitation activities in time of war. Indeed, just as in the past economic pressure has been applied on states through attacks on trade, it is possible that attacks on economically important activities within the EEZ or on the Continental Shelf of a belligerent state may come to be seen as an effective way for navies to apply economic pressure.

E. Hybrid Warfare

There is no adequate definition of 'hybrid warfare' – legal or otherwise. In terms of the spectrum of the application of force, it occupies a potentially ambiguous position around the point at which threats to security might be seen to justify a confusing mix of force, sometimes based on law enforcement parameters and at others on the combat paradigm. The identity of those involved is likely to be ambiguous, leading to uncertainty as to the nature of the threat they pose. Forces capable of applying legitimate force at sea include coastguards, but some states may use these deliberately to blur the nature of the threat they pose. Can a coastguard cutter (that looks in most senses identical to a warship, apart from its colour scheme) be responsible for an 'armed attack', or must its use of force be regarded as a form of constabulary action? If a coastguard vessel is applying what is ostensibly constabulary force during an armed conflict, is it to be regarded as directly participating in hostilities and, therefore, subject to attack itself?[139] What is the nature of the cyber-threat within the maritime environment, how will it materialise and what will constitute legitimate responses to it?[140] It is entirely possible, for example, given current and emerging technology, for vessels at sea to be targeted, for their navigation systems to be accessed remotely and for them to be diverted without the knowledge of their crews. Such action might even constitute a new means of engaging in economic warfare at sea. What would be the lawful responses to developments of this sort?

None of these sorts of questions is easy to answer; and there are many more besides that could be posed. The law of naval warfare has not been tested so far against the backdrop of a hybrid and asymmetric conflict involving naval forces, civilians and other paramilitary agencies – both private and public – in low intensity conflicts that appear to remain suspiciously below a conflict threshold. The existing law regulating the conduct of naval hostilities does not deal specifically with the myriad challenges likely to be faced.

[139] Art 51, 1977 Additional Protocol I; and Art 13 of 1977 Additional Protocol II. See also N Melzer, *Interpretive Guidance on the Notion of Direct Participation in Hostilities under International Humanitarian Law* (Geneva, ICRC, 2009).

[140] On cyber-warfare and the application of law to it, see M Schmitt (ed), *Tallinn Manual 2.0: On the International Law Applicable to Cyber Operations* (Cambridge, Cambridge University Press, 2017).

In general terms, however, those laws outlined elsewhere in this chapter relating to means and methods of warfare and to targeting will apply if a situation rises to the level of armed conflict at sea.

For naval forces operating at the nexus between peace and war, their rules of engagement (ROE) will be crucial in relation to the operational options they have for the application of force.[141] Such rules are, importantly, not a fail-safe means of ensuring the lawful application of force; they are, rather, a command and control mechanism for ensuring that tactical action is consistent with strategic objectives – even though they must clearly be promulgated in a manner consistent with the relevant law. While ROE were originally intended for the use of military forces in situations short of armed conflict, they have increasingly been employed during armed conflicts in recent years to influence tactical action in the context of such situations as asymmetric war, NIAC and irregular warfare (including counter-insurgency). As tactical circumstances shift backwards and forwards along the spectrum into and out of armed conflict, they will represent a fundamental reference for commanders at sea. They are not the subject of this chapter, but they will need to be seriously considered as the conduct of hostilities becomes a likely prospect.

F. Deception, Ruses of War, and Perfidy

Naval warfare has traditionally seen the use of camouflage, false flags and other markings by warships as a means of deceiving the enemy. While military aircraft 'are prohibited at all times from feigning exempt, civilian or neutral status',[142] warships are not so constrained. Ruses of war at sea are permitted,[143] false flags may be worn, and simulating other vessels is permitted provided this does not involve the simulation of: hospital ships, small coastal rescue craft or medical transports; vessels on humanitarian missions; passenger vessels carrying civilian passengers; vessels protected by the UN flag; vessels guaranteed safe conduct, including cartel vessels; vessels entitled to be identified by the red cross and associated symbols; and vessels transporting cultural property.[144] While one aim of simulation is to deceive and surprise an enemy, another is undoubtedly to avoid attack. It is perhaps surprising, therefore, that the list of vessels a warship is prohibited from simulating is not identical to the list of enemy vessels exempt from attack in accordance with Rule 47 of the *San Remo Manual*. One official manual (the UK *Manual of the Law of Armed Conflict*) has effectively merged the two lists; it stipulates that no protected or exempt vessels should be simulated. By doing so, it goes further than Rule 110 of the *San Remo Manual*.[145] There is no evidence, however, that this example has been followed by other states.

When simulating other vessels, warships may employ artificial structures and deceptive lighting to alter their appearance, engage in false manoeuvres and deploy misinformation.

[141] For an example of an approach to ROE, see D Mandsager (ed), *Rules of Engagement Handbook* (San Remo, International Institute of Humanitarian Law, 2009).

[142] SRM Rule 109.

[143] SRM Rule 110.

[144] SRM Rule 110.

[145] See the UK Ministry of Defence (n 5) para 13.82. For an explanation, see Haines (n 12) 104–05.

The wearing of a false flag is only a legitimate ruse until such time as the warship engages the enemy. It must, therefore, reveal its true identity before it actually commences an attack. It must be admitted that the wearing of a false flag, while it may have been an effective and frequent ruse in the past, is almost certainly now largely a historical curiosity in the context of naval war between capable naval forces. It is difficult to imagine a modern warship belonging to a naval power relying on such a measure as an attempt to disguise its identity and purpose, given the contemporary sophistication of electronic sensors and other routine modern means of identifying an enemy. Nevertheless, in lower-intensity conflicts involving less sophisticated naval forces belonging to minor powers (including non-state armed groups in NIACs), it might still be possible for such a ruse to have the desired effect. A modern warship operating in asymmetric and hybrid circumstances, while choosing not to employ such ruses itself, will frequently need to be on guard against their being used by potentially hostile forces. If they do so, those hostile forces will not be in breach of the law, as long as they reveal their true identity prior to commencing an attack.

There is a clear need for warships employing ruses not to stray across the line that distinguishes lawful ruses from perfidious attempts to disguise themselves as protected vessels, or, indeed, to attempt to portray their crews as protected persons. Perfidy is explicitly prohibited in the *San Remo Manual*.[146] If, for example, a badly damaged warship's crew acted to create the impression that their ship was incapable of further action, that they were effectively shipwrecked and entitled to protected status under Geneva Convention II, but subsequently attacked an enemy boarding party attempting to either take the ship as booty or provide any injured crew members with medical assistance, this would constitute perfidy, as would a false declaration of surrender. To quote the *San Remo Manual*, perfidy consists of 'acts inviting the confidence of an adversary to lead it to believe that it is entitled to, or is obliged to accord, protection … with intent to betray that confidence'. Perfidious acts include feigning of exempt, civilian, neutral or protected-UN status, or surrender or distress, including by sending distress signals or by the warship's crew taking to life-rafts.

G. Zones

A common feature of recent naval operations is the establishment of zones at sea, variously described as exclusion zones, military areas, war zones or operational zones. These can be defined as geographically fixed zones within a region of conflict, or they can be established around naval forces or task groups, the zones representing a form of mobile protected area around ships as they manoeuvre. Most notably, the British established a series of geographically fixed zones during the armed conflict in the South Atlantic in 1982. The promulgation of these zones resulted in a degree of misunderstanding as to their relationship with the law, not least because of an unfortunate choice of words used by the UK on 28 April 1982 when establishing a 'total exclusion zone'. This served to create the impression that the waters within the zone constituted a form of 'free fire' zone.[147] The subsequent sinking of

[146] SRM Rule 111.

[147] The British statement included the following words: 'Any ship and any aircraft, whether military or civil which is found within this zone without due authority from … London will be regarded as operating in support of the illegal occupation and will therefore be regarded as hostile and will be liable to be attacked by the British forces'.

the Argentine cruiser *General Belgrano* (an entirely lawful act against a legitimate military objective) was assumed by some to have been unlawful because it took place beyond the limits of the declared zone. The issues raised were addressed at some length by those working to draft the *San Remo Manual*.[148] Such zones are now dealt with in Rules 105 to 108. Importantly, while the *Manual* deals with them, there has been no conventional law on the subject of such zones, and evidence of practice is patchy at least. In the absence of any conventional or customary law on the subject, the *San Remo Manual*'s treatment of it may be regarded as provisionally definitive.

The fundamental point made in the *San Remo Manual* is that the establishment or declaration of a zone does not absolve a belligerent 'of its duties under international humanitarian law by establishing zones which might adversely affect the legitimate uses of the defined areas of the sea'.[149] Essentially, the law relating to the conduct of hostilities within the zone is identical to that applying beyond it. An obvious conclusion to be drawn is that the declaration of such zones does not change the applicable law. Indeed, Rule 106 is more emphatic in stating that 'the same body of law applies both inside and outside the zone'.

Such zones are best regarded, therefore, as a matter of policy rather than of the law. In the context of rules of engagement, a naval force might be permitted to take tactical action within a zone that it might, for strategic policy reasons, not be able to take elsewhere – or indeed, it might be more restricted within a zone than it is beyond it. The *San Remo Manual* goes on to posit a series of conditions in Rule 106 that ought to be applied when zones are established. The extent, location and duration of the zone, and any measures imposed, shall not exceed what is necessary and proportionate. Due regard needs to be accorded to the rights of neutral states to use the sea areas within the zone, and necessary safe passage through it must be provided. Lastly, the full details of the zone need to be adequately promulgated.

H. Non-international Armed Conflict

Although naval war is associated principally with conflicts between states (IACs), naval operations are not entirely an irrelevancy when it comes to civil wars (NIACs). During the English Civil War of the seventeenth century, Parliament benefited greatly from its control of naval power, which was able to prevent military forces intervening from the Continent in support of the Royalist campaign.[150] During the American Civil War in the

Quoted in G Politakis, *Modern Aspects of the Laws of Naval Warfare and Maritime Neutrality* (London/New York, Kegan Paul International, 1998) 77. It is easy to see why this statement could be assumed to imply that even a neutral merchant ship found within the zone would be liable to attack. Fortunately, such an attack never occurred and no breach of the law took place.

[148] See the commentary in SRM, 181–83, and also the detailed discussion of the subject (including a lengthy history of zones) in Politakis (n 147) 35–165.

[149] SRM Rule 105.

[150] B Capp, *Cromwell's Navy: The Fleet and the English Revolution 1648–1660* (Oxford, Clarendon Press, 1989). The Parliamentary naval forces were brilliantly led by Robert Blake, who saw off Prince Rupert's Royalist fleet. See M Baumber, *General-at-Sea: Robert Blake and the Seventeenth Century Revolution in Naval Warfare* (London, John Murray, 1989).

nineteenth century, the influence of naval power was strategically significant, not only in the use of blockade at sea but also in operations conducted on the Mississippi-Missouri river system.[151] Naval power was most certainly deployed during the Spanish Civil War in 1936–39.[152] More recently, there have been significant naval dimensions to the NIACs in Algeria, Libya, Sri Lanka and, arguably, Gaza.[153]

During the 'Troubles' in Northern Ireland, which arguably crossed the threshold into NIAC in 1971–74, naval forces were used by the British Government to mount a significant reinforcement of ground forces into Belfast in 1972.[154] The Provisional Irish Republican Army also managed to sink two British-flag merchant vessels in the approaches to the port of Londonderry in 1981 and 1982. While their successes on these occasions were not in the context of an armed conflict, they were certainly indicative of the potential for non-state armed groups to operate in the maritime environment.[155]

The application of the laws of naval warfare to contemporary NIACs is not clear-cut. The core issue is whether or not operations can take place lawfully beyond the territorial limits of the state in which the conflict is taking place. Within those limits, the parties can take advantage of the methods and means of naval warfare, subject to the standard laws relating to distinction and precautions in attack, and provided their conduct of hostilities does not have a substantial negative effect on international navigation. The coastal state does, however, have the right under the law of the sea to take measures within its territorial sea to ensure peace, good order and security through the enforcement of its domestic law. This includes appropriate interference with navigation to stop, board and search merchant vessels in order to establish the innocence of their passage through the coastal state's territorial waters.

Within the territorial waters forming part of an international strait in which unimpeded transit passage rights exist, interference with navigation is more problematic. There is neither treaty law nor established customary law on this matter. Somewhat less certain are the rights of the coastal state to target military objectives beyond its territorial limits, or to mount a blockade of its own coast and ports. It would logically be the case that the targeting of military objectives beyond territorial limits would reflect the state's right to free use of the high seas (subject, of course, to the limitations imposed on it doing so that relate to the rights of other states to legitimate use of those waters). Although blockade is clearly associated with IACs, there would be no legal impediment to a state suspending innocent passage and closing its ports to navigation.[156]

[151] See J McPherson, *Battle Cry of Freedom: The Civil War Era* (Oxford, Oxford University Press, 1988) in particular ch 13 on 'The River War in 1862', 393–427. The key operations were conducted on the Mississippi itself but also on the Cumberland and Tennessee rivers.

[152] H Thomas, *The Spanish Civil War*, 3rd edn (London, Hamish Hamilton, 1986). See also J Cable, *The Royal Navy and the Siege of Bilbao* (Cambridge, Cambridge University Press, 1979).

[153] See the most valuable contribution by W von Heinegg, 'Methods and Means of Naval Warfare in Non-International Armed Conflicts' in K Watkin and AJ Norris (eds), *Non-International Armed Conflict in the Twenty-First Century* (Newport, RI, US Naval War College, 2012) 211.

[154] S Haines, 'Northern Ireland 1968–1998' in E Wilmshurst (ed), *International Law and the Classification of Conflicts*, Oxford, Oxford University Press, 2012) 117, 124–27.

[155] The author was serving as the Royal Navy's head of operations in Northern Ireland at the time of the first PIRA attack on a merchant vessel (the MV *Nellie M*) in February 1981. This was followed by the sinking of the MV *St Bedan* in February 1982.

[156] See the arguments and conclusions drawn by von Heinegg (n 153).

While the laws of naval warfare can at times be less than precise when applied to IACs, the detail of them as applied in NIACs is even less clear. They are not a subject that has been formally considered internationally, and state practice is almost (though not entirely) non-existent.

VII. Concluding Remarks

The laws of naval warfare have developed very little in the years since the last general naval war ended in 1945. While there have been several naval conflicts since then, none has been of sufficient significance to prompt a major reassessment of the law or to establish change through practice. The project that produced the *San Remo Manual* published in 1994 has been the closest to a significant international review of the law, but, as the years pass, aspects of it are appearing increasingly dated. There is, however, a dilemma. Without more naval wars to prompt both conventional and customary developments in the law and to bring it up to date and fit for purpose in the twenty-first century, it is likely to remain as it is. Those faced with the responsibility for conducting naval warfare – as well as their legal advisers – will need to keep this fact very much in mind.

As a final vignette to stress this point, in 1999, during the NATO intervention against Serbia-Montenegro over Kosovo, there was concern that the Montenegrin port of Bar might be used by a third party to provide supplies to Serbia and Montenegro. There was clearly an armed conflict in train between NATO states and Serbia and Montenegro. Under the established laws of naval warfare, it would have been perfectly acceptable for NATO to establish a belligerent blockade of the Montenegrin coast. Significant doubts were expressed in NATO capitals about the legality of such a move, however, and as a result, no blockade was established.[157] The conflict ended before this became critical. One can well imagine similar dilemmas being faced in the future.

[157] The author was serving in the British Ministry of Defence at the time and was asked by the then Director of Naval Operations for his view on the matter – he referred to the existing laws of naval warfare and supported the establishment of a blockade.

12

Armed Conflict in Space

I. Introduction

Based on publicly available information, no armed conflict appears to have yet occurred in space. If the International Committee of the Red Cross (ICRC) is correct, however, that may soon be about to change. In October 2015, in its address to the First Committee of the United Nations (UN) General Assembly, the ICRC raised specific concern over the 'weaponisation' of outer space.[1] Similarly, in recent years, the media has been awash with warnings of the risks of armed conflict in space; *Newsweek* magazine, for example, refers to the belief of many Chinese military analysts that war in space with the United States (US) is inevitable.[2] Meanwhile, in a 2015 novel by political scientists Peter W Singer and August Cole, one of the opening salvoes of the 'Third World War' is a Chinese attack on US communications satellites using high-energy lasers.[3]

In December 2014, the US Air Force Space Command in Colorado Springs, a body set up within the US Air Force in 1982, held a major war game whose scenario was set in outer space in the year 2025. Some 200 US military and civilian experts took part, along with representatives from Australia, Canada, New Zealand and the United Kingdom.[4] The results of the war game were not made public, but as a *Newsweek* journalist warned in May 2016:

> A war in space would have staggering implications. If conflict were to erupt, say, over China's territorial claims to the South China Sea or Russia's aggression in Eastern Europe, America's military satellites wouldn't be the only space assets at risk. Fighting would also likely cripple the civilian satellites that control so much of modern life, from cellphone networks to ATMs and personal GPS units. And although such a conflict might start in space, experts say it could easily turn into full-scale war on Earth. 'If war does extend into space someday – and I hope it never does – the first [nuclear] response is not going to be in space,' warns General John Hyten, head of the US Air Force Space Command.[5]

There is no formally accepted definition under international law of where outer space begins. The threshold between inner and outer space is, though, generally understood to

[1] 'Weapons: ICRC statement to the United Nations, 2015', UN General Assembly, New York, 15 October 2015, at https://goo.gl/3xHoFG (hereinafter '2015 ICRC Weapons Statement to the United Nations').

[2] J Broder, 'Why the Next Pearl Harbor Could Happen in Space', *Newsweek* (4 May 2016) at https://goo.gl/RdrAXx; see also, eg, J Sciutto, 'US military prepares for the next frontier: Space war', *CNN* (29 November 2016) at https://goo.gl/f7nCf2; G Manaugh, 'The Growing Risk of a War in Space', *The Atlantic* (21 June 2016) at https://goo.gl/EgHiZY; and C Bowlby, 'Could a war in space really happen?', *BBC* (19 December 2015) at https://goo.gl/IRwZnq.

[3] PW Singer and A Cole, *Ghost Fleet: A Novel of the Next World War* (Boston, MA, Houghton Mifflin, 2015).

[4] Broder (n 2).

[5] Ibid.

be the Kármán Line, set at 100 kilometres above sea level.[6] This is roughly the height at which a conventional aircraft can no longer fly owing to the lack of air, because at this altitude the craft would have to travel faster than orbital velocity (approximately 8 kilometres per second) to derive the aerodynamic lift necessary to support itself. The Kármán Line is thus the nominal boundary separating aeronautics and astronautics.[7]

Section II of this brief chapter looks at the – limited – treaty law that could govern armed conflict in space, especially the 1967 Outer Space Treaty and the 1979 Moon Treaty. Section III discusses how customary Hague Law rules applied to land and aerial warfare could be transposed to the celestial environment, mentioning briefly the major weapons systems that would likely be used in any armed conflict in space. The concluding section assesses whether new treaty rules are needed to govern the conduct of hostilities.

II. Treaty Law Applicable to Armed Conflict in Space

The most important treaty pertaining to armed conflict in space is the 1967 Outer Space Treaty, although in fact it has more implications for *jus ad bellum* and disarmament law than it does for Hague Law.[8] A creation of the Cold War, the treaty remains in force for its 105 states parties (as at 1 April 2018).[9] The later (1979) Moon Treaty has only 18 states parties and has not attracted adherence from the most important nations engaged in space exploration (and warfare), such as China, Russia and the US. In any event, it adds little of substance to Hague Law rules.

A. The 1967 Outer Space Treaty

According to the UN, the 1967 Outer Space Treaty 'could be viewed as furnishing a general legal basis for the peaceful uses of outer space and providing a framework for the developing law of outer space'.[10] The treaty preamble expressed the desire of the states parties to 'contribute to broad international cooperation in the scientific as well as the legal aspects of the exploration and use of outer space for peaceful purposes'.[11]

Article II of the Treaty prohibits the 'national appropriation by claim of sovereignty, by means of use or occupation, or by any other means' of '[o]uter space, including the Moon and other celestial bodies'. This can be seen as an element of *jus ad bellum*, seeking to prevent

[6] The Line is named after the American-Hungarian physicist, Theodore von Kármán. Though see also S Shostak, 'Where does "outer space" begin?', *NBC News* (25 June 2004) at https://goo.gl/TdmURC.

[7] Dr S Sanz Fernández de Córdoba, '100 km Altitude Boundary for Astronautics', *Fédération Aéronautique Internationale*, at https://goo.gl/MxvgBH.

[8] Treaty on Principles Governing the Activities of States in the Exploration and Use of Outer Space, including the Moon and Other Celestial Bodies, adopted on 19 December 1966; entry into force, 10 October 1967.

[9] This includes all five permanent members of the UN Security Council, as well as India, another state whose interest in space seemingly goes beyond its desire for peaceful planetary exploration. A further 24 states are signatory to the treaty.

[10] *United Nations Treaties and Principles on Outer Space*, UN Publication ST/SPACE/11, vi.

[11] The 1967 Outer Space Treaty, fourth preambular paragraph.

offensive action in space rather than to regulate the terms under which hostilities might be lawful should they nonetheless occur. The provision with potentially the greatest implications for the conduct of hostilities is found in Article IV, according to which:

> States Parties to the Treaty undertake not to place in orbit around the Earth any objects carrying nuclear weapons or any other kinds of weapons of mass destruction, install such weapons on celestial bodies, or station such weapons in outer space in any other manner.
>
> The Moon and other celestial bodies shall be used by all States Parties to the Treaty exclusively for peaceful purposes. The establishment of military bases, installations and fortifications, the testing of any type of weapons and the conduct of military manoeuvres on celestial bodies shall be forbidden …

The first paragraph of the Article is akin to a modified form of disarmament, prohibiting the placement in orbit or on any planet or moon of any weapon of mass destruction (but not conventional weapons).[12] What constitutes a weapon of mass destruction is not defined in the treaty, but it would encompass biological and chemical weapons (although their military utility in outer space is extremely limited) in addition to nuclear weapons, which are explicitly cited. The *use* of these weapons in outer space is, though, not specifically prohibited, nor is the launching of weapons from earth into space. The US Department of Defense notes that the Outer Space Treaty also

> does not ban the use of nuclear or other weapons of mass destruction that go into a fractional orbit or engage in suborbital flight. … For example, intercontinental ballistic missiles (ICBMs) will travel a portion of their trajectory in outer space; but because ICBMs would enter outer space only temporarily, their entry into outer space with nuclear warheads would not violate this prohibition.[13]

The second paragraph of the Article contains both *jus ad bellum* and disarmament provisions. It prohibits recourse to all forms of military action on the Moon (and any planet or associated moon or comet or asteroid). This would outlaw only the offensive use of any weapons, including conventional weapons, as presumably the provision would not extinguish the inherent right of self-defence of any state. Indeed, according to the US Department of Defense, 'lawful military activities in self-defense (eg, missile early warning, use of weapon systems) would be consistent with the use of space for peaceful purposes, but aggressive activities that violate the Charter of the United Nations would not be permissible'.[14] In addition, the testing of any type of weapons is prohibited, which is a disarmament element.

B. The 1979 Moon Treaty

The 1979 Moon Treaty adds little of substance to the minimal Hague Law tenets of the Outer Space Treaty, with states parties expressing their desire in the preamble 'to

[12] See, eg, Y Dinstein, *War, Aggression and Self-Defence*, 6th edn (Cambridge, Cambridge University Press, 2012) 26, para 68; and MN Schmitt, 'International Law and Military Operations in Space' (2006) 10 *Max Planck Yearbook of United Nations Law* 89, 104.

[13] US Department of Defense, *Law of War Manual*, June 2015 (hereinafter 'USDOD 2015 *Law of War Manual*') para 14.10.3.1, at https://goo.gl/uZKhvk.

[14] Ibid, para 14.10.4.

prevent the Moon from becoming an area of international conflict'.[15] It is stipulated in Article 3(2):

> Any threat or use of force or any other hostile act or threat of hostile act on the Moon is prohibited. It is likewise prohibited to use the Moon in order to commit any such act or to engage in any such threat in relation to the Earth, the Moon, spacecraft, the personnel of spacecraft or manmade space objects.

These are again *ad bellum* considerations rather than Hague Law rules. Indeed, they are a general prohibition on the use of force, a modified form of Article 2(4) of the UN Charter for the Moon.[16] Despite being given the moniker of the 'Moon' Treaty, the same rules are explicitly applied to all celestial bodies within the solar system other than the Earth.[17]

Among the major space powers, only India is a signatory (it has never ratified the treaty). The reason for the extremely low level of adherence is unrelated to the rules on the use of force. As one commentator recalls, the most controversial section of the treaty deals with natural resources on the Moon, stipulating that the Moon and its natural resources are the common heritage of mankind and the harvesting of those resources is forbidden except through an international regime established to govern the exploitation of such resources when it becomes feasible to do so.[18] It is, however, unlikely that a state that commits, say, $1 trillion, either to found and maintain a mining operation on the Moon (for example for thorium), or to set up an operation to extract water from the Moon's south pole, is going to share the proceeds among all other states.

III. Customary Law Applicable to Armed Conflict in Space

In its 2015 statement to the UN General Assembly, the ICRC affirmed that it was 'certain' that

> any hostile use of outer space in armed conflict – that is, any use of means and methods of warfare in, from, to or through outer space – must comply with IHL, in particular its rules of distinction, proportionality and precautions in attack.[19]

The organisation went on to stress, though, that, by asserting that the law of armed conflict applies to outer space warfare, the ICRC was 'in no way condoning the weaponisation of outer space, which recurring resolutions of the General Assembly have sought to prevent'.

[15] Agreement Governing the Activities of States on the Moon and Other Celestial Bodies, fourth preambular paragraph.

[16] Upon signature of the Moon Treaty in January 1980, France made an interpretative statement whereby the provisions of Art 3(2) relating to the use or threat of force 'cannot be construed as anything other than a reaffirmation, for the purposes of the field of endeavour covered by the Agreement, of the principle of the prohibition of the threat or use of force, which States are obliged to observe in their international relations, as set forth in the United Nations Charter'. Declaration available at https://goo.gl/1b1n3N.

[17] Art 1(1), 1979 Moon Treaty.

[18] M Listner, 'The Moon Treaty: failed international law or waiting in the shadows?', *The Space Review* (24 October 2011) at https://goo.gl/G7AtX1.

[19] 2015 ICRC Weapons Statement to the United Nations (n 1).

The point, according to the ICRC, is that 'warfare in outer space would not occur in a legal vacuum'.[20]

It would appear both logical and reasonable to apply the rules of distinction, proportionality and precautions in attack to any armed conflict in space. According to the US Department of Defense,

> law of war treaties and the customary law of war are understood to regulate the conduct of hostilities regardless of where they are conducted, which would include the conduct of hostilities in outer space. In this way, the application of the law of war to activities in outer space is the same as its application to activities in other environments, such as the land, sea, air, or cyber domains.[21]

Based on existing knowledge, the most likely targets of any attack would be military communications or intelligence-gathering satellites. These objects would, of course, be lawful military objectives according to the rule of distinction, on the basis that their use makes an undeniable effective contribution to military action and because their total or partial destruction would offer a definite military advantage. Today, the US military and numerous others rely upon satellites for virtually all of their communications and critical surveillance.

As Yoram Dinstein makes clear, however, attacks on such objects 'may raise issues of proportionality in relation to their harmful effects on civilian satellites – through the creation of space debris – and additional questions arise as regards satellites owned by neutral states'.[22] The extent of debris from destroyed space hardware is estimated to number more than 10,000 pieces more than 10 cm in length in orbit around the Earth, many travelling at thousands of miles per hour, such that they can strike an object with potentially devastating kinetic energy. As a consequence of the 'deleterious effects' of space debris, Dinstein suggests that a cyber-attack against military satellites may be preferable.[23]

Although most space weaponry, to the extent it exists, remains classified top secret, it is reasonable to surmise that weapons under particular research and development for use against objects in space include guided missiles, directed energy weapons and cyber weapons.[24] With respect to cyber warfare, it is suggested that hackers might be able to re-programme a US satellite to send false weather reports, coordinates and other disinformation to US forces, affecting planning, navigation and targeting. Singer claims that satellite hackers could even redirect a US missile to strike its own forces.[25]

In 2007, China destroyed one of its own weather satellites using a land-based missile, in an apparent weapons test. Following this test, the then chief of army staff of the Indian Army, General Deepak Kapoor, was quoted as saying that China's space programme was

[20] Ibid.

[21] USDOD 2015 *Law of War Manual*, para 14.10.2.2.

[22] Y Dinstein, *The Conduct of Hostilities under the Law of International Armed Conflict*, 3rd edn (Cambridge, Cambridge University Press, 2016) 124, para 335.

[23] Ibid, 125, para 335.

[24] A US test carried out in 1962, 250 miles above the South Pacific, generated an electromagnetic pulse so powerful that it destroyed the electronics of five US satellites, and caused power, telephone and radio black-outs thousands of miles away. The tests were stopped in 1967 as a result of the Outer Space Treaty. Broder (n 2).

[25] Ibid.

expanding at an 'exponentially rapid' pace in both offensive and defensive capabilities, and that space was becoming the 'ultimate military high ground' to dominate in the wars of the future.[26] China conducted a well-publicised anti-satellite (ASAT) missile test in 2013, when it launched its new Dong Neng-2 from the Earth. The missile climbed to 18,000 miles, high enough to destroy US GPS satellites and almost within reach of the US military's early-warning satellites, which are in geo-stationary orbit 22,000 miles above the Earth.[27]

Concerned about China's intentions, one Indian scholar has argued that India should consider testing ASAT weapons at a low altitude, since the resulting debris would enter the Earth's atmosphere and burn up without causing any damage. He also advocated consideration of 'jamming' satellites using space-based lasers. This method, he claimed, 'falls under the category of "soft-kill" methods and does not create debris'.[28]

Of course, space weaponry could also be used to destroy targets on the Earth. Thus, the so-called 'rod from God' is a non-explosive tungsten cylinder launched downward from orbit and capable of reaching speeds of up to Mach 10 as it descends. The force of the rod's impact alone is said to be equivalent to a small nuclear explosion, causing devastating shockwaves around the target, although as a non-nuclear device its stationing in outer space would not violate the Outer Space Treaty. At such speeds, these 'hypervelocity rod bundles' (as the US Air Force terms them) could penetrate into heavily fortified enemy caves and bunkers deep underground.[29]

IV. A Need for New Law?

In a conference on space security convened by the UN Institute for Disarmament Research (UNIDIR) in 2014, one expert, Professor Li Juqian of the China University of Political Science and Law, suggested that new treaty law would be needed to address the fast-paced evolution of space weaponry and related technologies.[30] In February 2008, China and Russia submitted a draft Treaty on Prevention of the Placement of Weapons in Outer Space and of the Threat or Use of Force against Outer Space Objects to the Conference on Disarmament. In a presentation to the 2014 UNIDIR conference, Vladimir Yermakov, Deputy Director of the Department for Security Affairs and Disarmament of the Russian Ministry of Foreign Affairs, argued that the treaty could become 'a landmark treaty in moving towards universal and complete outer space disarmament'.[31]

In June 2014, China and Russia submitted a new draft of its proposed treaty. Under Article II of the revised draft, states parties would undertake, inter alia:

> Not to place any weapons in outer space;

[26] H Vasani, 'India's Anti-Satellite Weapons', *The Diplomat* (14 June 2016) at https://goo.gl/TNf69p.
[27] Broder (n 2).
[28] Vasani (n 26).
[29] Manaugh (n 2). See also DC Sproull, 'Kinetic Energy Weapons: The Beginning of an Interagency Challenge' (2017) 8:2 *InterAgency Journal* 62, at https://goo.gl/JMjyga.
[30] UN Institute for Disarmament Research (UNIDIR), *UNIDIR Space Security 2014 Conference: The Evolving Space Security Regime: Implementation, Compliance, and New Initiatives*, 2014, 7, at https://goo.gl/NPVRc7.
[31] See ibid, 3.

> Not to resort to the threat or use of force against outer space objects of States Parties to the Treaty.[32]

Responding to the draft in September of that year, the US said that there were a number of issues with the text, including the lack of a verification mechanism and the absence of restrictions on the development and stockpiling of ASAT weapons on the ground. According to Robert Wood, the US Representative to the Conference on Disarmament in Geneva, neither the original treaty nor the revised version addressed 'the most pressing existing threat to outer space systems: terrestrially-based ASAT systems'.[33]

New treaty law would also be an issue of concern to other nations, particularly India, as a scholar at Manipal University points out:

> [A] new treaty banning space weaponisation could inhibit India from demonstrating its ability in the future. After the 2007 test conducted by China, there has been renewed talk of a restrictive treaty banning space weaponisation. Much like the Nuclear Non-Proliferation Treaty (NPT) that forced restrictions on the non-nuclear weapons states of the time (including India), a new restrictive regime on space weaponisation could foreclose India's options, giving the United States, China, and Russia ASAT-weapons-state status à la NPT, while keeping India out of the club.[34]

It remains to be seen whether states will decide to elaborate a treaty to govern armed conflict in outer space. The more likely scenario is that they will not, for fear of being prompted to disclose details of their programmes and capabilities, or being constrained in their ability to target the military satellites of other nations. Perhaps a future UN General Assembly resolution reiterating the common desire for the exclusively peaceful use of outer space could nonetheless include a preambular stipulation that, should any armed conflict break out in space, the customary Hague Law rules of distinction and proportionality in attack would apply? For its part, the US has expressed the view that outer space should be used only for peaceful purposes.[35] Its definition of 'peaceful', however, comprises lawful military activities in self-defence such as missile early warning and even use of weapon systems, because, the Department of Defense argues, citing the words of Carl Christol, 'defensive and deterrent capabilities serve the cause of peace'.[36]

[32] Draft Treaty on the Prevention of the Placement of Weapons in Outer Space, the Threat or Use of Force against Outer Space Objects, Doc CD/1985, 12 June 2014, annexed to Letter dated 10 June 2014 from the Permanent Representative of the Russian Federation and the Permanent Representative of China to the Conference on Disarmament addressed to the Acting Secretary-General of the Conference.

[33] J Foust, 'US Dismisses Space Weapons Treaty Proposal As "Fundamentally Flawed"', *Space Power* (11 September 2014) at https://goo.gl/h1z2MV.

[34] Vasani (n 26). See also, though, an earlier article on 'India's Military Space Program' uploaded to *Global Security*, in which it is asserted that 'India strongly oppose [*sic*] to any attempt to place weapons in space or conducting any unconventional weapons tests in space, as it would pose a perennial threat to all space systems regardless of their use for civilian or military purposes. India is carefully watching the international developments and the attempts of few countries to formulate some legal instruments to prevent any arms race in outer space. Suitable steps would be considered/taken at appropriate time, without causing any prejudice to Indian national interests.' 'India's Military Space Program', *Global Security*, at https://goo.gl/SnRWZ2.

[35] USDOD 2015 *Law of War Manual*, para 14.10.4, citing *National Space Policy of the United States of America*, 28 June 2010, 3.

[36] CQ Christol, 'The International Law of Outer Space', *International Law Studies* (Newport, RI, Naval War College, 1962) 114; see USDOD 2015 *Law of War Manual*, para 14.10.4.

On 5 December 2016, the General Assembly adopted Resolution 71/32 by 130 votes to 4 with 48 abstentions, in which it encouraged all states, 'especially space-faring nations, to consider the possibility of upholding as appropriate a political commitment not to be the first to place weapons in outer space'.[37] A separate resolution, 71/31, adopted the same day by 182 votes to nil with 4 abstentions, invited the Conference on Disarmament to establish a working group under its agenda item entitled 'Prevention of an arms race in outer space' as early as possible during its 2017 session.[38]

[37] UN General Assembly Resolution 71/32, 5 December 2016, para 5.
[38] Ibid, para 6.

13

Cyberwarfare

I. Introduction

In the last 10 years, cyberwarfare[1] has become an issue of great political, economic and military import. As the extent to which Russia influenced the 2016 United States (US) presidential elections continues to be debated – and the effects continue to reverberate – commentators have discussed whether Russia's actions amounted to a violation of the United Nations (UN) Charter, particularly of Article 2(4).[2] In fact, it is hard, in this instance, to see how the release of embarrassing information and the diffusion of propaganda amount to an inter-state use of force, lawful or otherwise. But although, 'so far, instances of cyber warfare have been unusual',[3] it is clear that cyberspace is becoming integral to the conduct of warfare by and between technologically advanced nations.[4]

Although international lawyers were already interested in the implications of the Internet for the law of armed conflict in the 1990s,[5] perhaps the first use of the Internet as a means and method of warfare occurred in the Russia – Georgia conflict in 2008. Russia began Distributed Denial-of-service (DDoS) attacks[6] on Georgian government websites two weeks before its invasion of Georgia.[7] But while communications were interrupted,

[1] There is no accepted definition of what amounts to cyberwarfare. Gary Solis cites a definition by Steven Hildreth of 'warfare waged in space, including *defending* information and computer networks, *deterring* information attacks, as well as denying an adversary's ability to do the same. It can include *offensive* information operations mounted against an adversary.' GD Solis, *The Law of Armed Conflict: International Humanitarian Law in War*, 2nd edn (New York, Cambridge University Press, 2016) 674, citing SA Hildreth, *Cyberwarfare*, Congressional Research Service, Washington, DC (19 June 2001) 16 (original emphasis).

[2] See, eg, N Feldman, 'How US Could Retaliate for Russian Intervention', *Bloomberg View* (12 December 2016) at https://goo.gl/awzrS8; 'Hacking the Election', Blog post by ebm29, *Yale Journal of International Law* (28 October 2016) at https://goo.gl/Ldhjc5. As journalists at *The New York Times* have asserted, 'For Russia, with an enfeebled economy and a nuclear arsenal it cannot use short of all-out war, cyberpower proved the perfect weapon: cheap, hard to see coming, hard to trace.' E Lipton, DE Sanger and S Shane, 'The Perfect Weapon: How Russian Cyberpower Invaded the US', *New York Times* (13 December 2016) at https://goo.gl/1zRfc9.

[3] Solis (n 1) 673.

[4] The US Department of Defense recalls a possible definition of cyberspace as a 'global domain within the information environment consisting of interdependent networks of information technology infrastructures and resident data, including the Internet, telecommunications networks, computer systems, and embedded processors and controllers': US Department of Defense, *Law of War Manual*, June 2015 (hereinafter 'USDOD 2015 *Law of War Manual*') para 16.1.1, at https://goo.gl/uZKhvk.

[5] M Schmitt (ed), *Tallinn Manual on the International Law Applicable to Cyber Warfare* (Cambridge, Cambridge University Press, 2013) (hereinafter 'the *Tallinn Manual*') 1.

[6] DDoS attacks are launched from multiple connected devices that are distributed across the Internet. Such attacks tend to target network infrastructure with a view to saturating it with high volumes of traffic. 'Denial of Service Attacks', *Incapsula* (2017) at https://goo.gl/8MPecm.

[7] DJ Smith, 'Russian Cyber Strategy and the War Against Georgia', *Infocus Quarterly* (17 January 2014) at https://goo.gl/GLgDMS.

the greater impact was in the political sphere rather than on the military. For this reason, some experts have downplayed the significance of the attacks, which might be better characterised as psychological operations rather than cyberwarfare per se.[8] This is not, though, the position taken in the 2013 *Tallinn Manual on the International Law Applicable to Cyber Warfare*, which argues that conducting DDoS operations against enemy military systems is an 'unambiguous' example of direct participation in hostilities.[9]

Perhaps the most potent cyberattack to date, at least in terms of physical damage, was the use of the Stuxnet virus[10] against Iran's Bushehr nuclear power plant at Natanz, which appears to have been initiated in mid-2009.[11] The basic facts of the attack, to the extent they are known, were summarised in chapter 1. The attack, seemingly by the US and probably with Israeli involvement, involved the introduction of the virus, perhaps by means of a USB stick, into the electronic network of the plant, whereupon the virus sought out and infected the Siemens software that operated the 4,600 centrifuges that were enriching uranium. Perhaps as many as 1,000 were damaged as a result of the attack. Gary Solis describes the attack and its effects in valuable case material in *The Law of Armed Conflict: International Humanitarian Law in War*.[12] He cites Michael Hayden, the former head of the Central Intelligence Agency, who stated that this was 'the first attack of a major nature in which a cyberattack was used to effect physical destruction'.[13]

The *Tallinn Manual* asserts that Stuxnet amounted to a use of force.[14] If so, whether or not this use of force was lawful under *jus ad bellum*, this indicates that an armed conflict existed, despite doubt as to whether cyber-attacks or their underlying means of transmission amount to 'arms'.[15,16] In contrast, Fidler argues that since states, including Iran, did not characterise the incident as a use of force, armed attack or act of aggression, the Stuxnet 'episode' was 'a covert cyberoperation that amount[ed], at most, to an illegal intervention in the domestic affairs of Iran'.[17] Indeed, despite the attack's kinetic effects in damaging the

[8] See, eg, 'Iran: West Trying "Psychological Warfare" to Stop Nuclear Activities', *Voice of America* (4 October 2010) at https://goo.gl/xEEQpB.

[9] The *Tallinn Manual*, Commentary on Rule 30, 109, para 10. The *Manual* later describes DDoS as a method of cyber warfare. Ibid, 142, para 4.

[10] Solis states that the virus was named by a Microsoft researcher from an anagram of letters from two sections of its code. Its complexity is such that it has been calculated that 30 experts spent six months preparing the virus. Solis (n 1) 707.

[11] J Markoff, 'Malware Aimed at Iran Hit Five Sites, Report Says', *New York Times* (13 February 2011) at https://goo.gl/o3eMNS.

[12] Solis (n 1) 706–09.

[13] Ibid, 708, citing DE Sanger, *Confront and Conceal* (New York, Crown, 2012) 200.

[14] The *Tallinn Manual*, Commentary on Rule 10, para 9; see also MN Schmitt, 'The Use of Cyber Force and International Law' in M Weller (ed), *The Oxford Handbook of the Use of Force in International Law* (Oxford, Oxford University Press, 2015) 1127.

[15] See, eg, S Watts, 'Who is a Prisoner of War?' in A Clapham, P Gaeta and M Sassòli (eds), *The 1949 Geneva Conventions: A Commentary* (Oxford, Oxford University Press, 2015) 889, 901.

[16] In fact, in early 2016 it was reported that the Stuxnet worm was only one element of a much larger US-prepared cyber-attack plan that would target Iran's air defences, communications systems and key parts of its power grid. The contingency plan, known internally as Nitro Zeus, was to be carried out in the event that diplomatic efforts to curb Iran's nuclear development programme failed and the US was pulled into a war between Iran and Israel. D Goodin, 'Massive US-planned cyberattack against Iran went well beyond Stuxnet', *Ars Technica* (17 February 2016) at https://goo.gl/rtQLbs, citing DE Sanger and M Mazzetti, 'US Had Cyberattack Plan if Iran Nuclear Dispute Led to Conflict', *New York Times* (16 February 2016) at https://goo.gl/JN2ZOD.

[17] DP Fidler, 'Cyberattacks and international human rights law' in S Casey-Maslen (ed), *Weapons under International Human Rights Law* (Cambridge, Cambridge University Press, 2014) 299 at 316–17.

centrifuges, whether it reached the threshold for an international armed conflict (IAC) between Iran and the US is open to serious doubt.[18] In this regard, while the characterisation of the key players is relevant to this determination, it is certainly not conclusive.[19]

The remainder of this chapter summarises the Hague Law rules regulating cyberwarfare and describes how their application might differ in comparison to physical domains. Section II on the applicable law looks at the cyber acts to which Hague Law rules apply and where such acts must occur for the law to apply. It then discusses the application of the rules of distinction and proportionality in attack to cyberattacks. Concluding remarks in section III mention the potential that cyberwarfare may offer in reducing the impact of armed conflict on civilians.

II. The Applicable Law

Although no law of armed conflict treaty specifically governs cyberattacks *in bello*, Solis argues that 'cyber warfare issues may be resolved in terms of traditional law of war concepts'. He cites in evidence the position of the International Court of Justice (ICJ) in the Nuclear Weapons Advisory Opinion, whereby the law of armed conflict applies to 'any use of force, regardless of the weapons employed'.[20] The US Department of Defense has noted that the US

> is actively engaged in the continuing development of norms of responsible state behavior in cyberspace, making clear that as a matter of US policy, long-standing international norms guiding state behavior also apply equally in cyberspace. Among these, applying the tenets of the law of armed conflict are [*sic*] critical to this vision, although cyberspace's unique aspects may require clarifications in certain areas.[21]

A. To which Cyber Acts does Hague Law Apply?

The *Tallinn Manual on the International Law Applicable to Cyber Warfare*, published commercially in 2013, is a soft law expert document that seeks to identify the applicable

[18] The US seemingly sets the bar extremely high for acts that would amount to use of force under Art 2(4) of the UN Charter: 'For example, if cyber operations cause effects that, if caused by traditional physical means, would be regarded as a use of force under *jus ad bellum*, then such cyber operations would likely also be regarded as a use of force. Such operations may include cyber operations that: (1) trigger a nuclear plant meltdown; (2) open a dam above a populated area, causing destruction; or (3) disable air traffic control services, resulting in airplane crashes. … Similarly, cyber operations that cripple a military's logistics systems, and thus its ability to conduct and sustain military operations, might also be considered a use of force under jus ad bellum.' USDOD 2015 *Law of War Manual*, para 16.3.1, citing Harold Hongju Koh, Legal Adviser, Department of State, *International Law in Cyberspace: Remarks as Prepared for Delivery to the USCYBERCOM Inter-Agency Legal Conference* (18 September 2012) reprinted in *Harvard International Law Journal Online*, vol 54 (December 2012), 4.

[19] In 2015, Reuters reported that the US tried to deploy a version of the Stuxnet virus to attack North Korea's nuclear weapons programme in tandem with its attack on Iran's nuclear programme. According to one US intelligence source, Stuxnet's developers produced a related virus that would be activated when it encountered Korean-language settings on an infected machine. But US agents could not access the core machines that ran Pyongyang's nuclear weapons programme. J Menn, 'Exclusive: US tried Stuxnet-style campaign against North Korea but failed – sources', *Reuters* (29 May 2015) at https://goo.gl/gkDd6c.

[20] ICJ, *Legality of the Threat or Use of Nuclear Weapons*, Advisory Opinion, 8 July 1996 (hereinafter 'Nuclear Weapons Advisory Opinion') para 39.

[21] USDOD 2015 *Law of War Manual*, para 16.1.1, fn 1.

lex lata both *ad bellum* and *in bello*.[22] As of the time of writing, it is the most extensive expression of what Hague Law rules governing cyberwarfare might be. (It also addresses *ad bellum* issues.) Rule 20 of the *Manual* states that 'cyber operations executed in the context of an armed conflict are subject to the law of armed conflict'.[23] This seemingly anodyne rule is in fact both extremely broad and contentious, as the associated commentary acknowledges. In particular, the formulation 'in the context of', adopted by the experts as a 'compromise formula', suggests that no direct nexus is required with the armed conflict for law of armed conflict rules to apply. This is legally incorrect.

The example proffered by the commentary in the *Manual* to illustrate the differing views among the experts is further evidence of the misplaced analysis. The example given is of one state's Ministry of Trade taking advantage of the existence of an armed conflict against another state to acquire commercial secrets from a private company located in that enemy state. Some experts suggested that this action was governed by Hague Law rules, while others argued, correctly, that the 'link between the activity and the hostilities' was 'insufficient'. An analogy would be individuals supporting a rebel group that is party to a non-international armed conflict (NIAC) who take advantage of the national police's diversion to the conduct of hostilities to rob a bank. Again, the action takes place in the 'context' of an armed conflict, but certainly does not possess the requisite – direct – nexus to the hostilities.[24]

Existing Hague Law rules govern cyberattacks in the conduct of hostilities. (The notion of cyber 'operations' in general is too broad always to amount to an attack.)[25] Rule 30 of the *Tallinn Manual* defines a cyberattack as a 'cyber operation, whether offensive or defensive, that is reasonably expected to cause injury or death to persons or damage or destruction to objects'. This is a valuable definition. In the commentary on the rule, the *Manual* explains that attacks on data fall within the scope of the definition insofar as the attack results in death, injury or damage.[26] Damage should be deemed to encompass the shutting down of a plan, facility or capacity. The commentary also indicates that the nature of the effects may reasonably be extended to encompass serious illness, severe mental illness and terror.[27] It would probably have been preferable to have included these elements in the rule itself.

[22] The *Tallinn Manual*, 5.

[23] The *Tallinn Manual*, Commentary on Rule 20, 76, para 4. The associated commentary explains that 'cyber operations' is a broader concept than is that of 'cyber-attacks'.

[24] Interestingly, the *Manual* later cites the example of criminals who use cyber means to steal state funds belonging to a party to a conflict, but since they act with a view to private gain, they cannot be regarded as direct participants in hostilities. Some experts suggested that the answer would be different if the funds were to be used to fund particular military operations. The *Tallinn Manual*, Commentary on Rule 35, 120, para 6.

[25] As Dinstein notes, 'cyber attacks cannot be regarded as "attacks" if they *only* break through a "fire wall" or plant malware (such as a virus) in an enemy computer'. Y Dinstein, *The Conduct of Hostilities under the Law of International Armed Conflict*, 3rd edn (Cambridge, Cambridge University Press, 2016) 3, para 9. The US Department of Defense affirms that 'Operations that target an adversary's cyberspace capabilities, but that are not achieved in or through cyberspace, would not be considered cyber operations. For example, the bombardment of a network hub, or the jamming of wireless communications, would not be considered cyber operations, even though they may achieve military objectives in cyberspace.' USDOD 2015 *Law of War Manual*, para 16.1.2.2.

[26] The *Tallinn Manual*, Commentary on Rule 30, 108, para 6.

[27] Ibid, 108, para 8.

At the same time, the US Department of Defense notes, correctly, that the term 'attack' is often used

> in a colloquial sense in discussing cyber operations to refer to many different types of hostile or malicious cyber activities, such as the defacement of websites, network intrusions, the theft of private information, or the disruption of the provision of internet services. Operations described as 'cyber attacks' or 'computer network attacks,' therefore, are not necessarily 'attacks' for the purposes of applying rules on conducting attacks during the conduct of hostilities.[28]

B. Where are Cyber Acts Governed by Hague Law?

Rule 21 of the *Tallinn Manual* stipulates that cyber operations are subject to the relevant provisions of international law applicable during an armed conflict. The commentary on the rule explains:

> As a rule, cyber operations may be conducted from, on, or with effects in the entire territory of the parties to the conflict, international waters or airspace, and, subject to certain limitations, outer space. Cyber operations are generally prohibited elsewhere.[29]

This is a poor expression of extant international law, which appears to mix *ad bellum*, the law of neutrality *in bello*[30] and Hague Law rules. If an act is committed within the geographical scope of hostilities by one party to the armed conflict against another with the requisite direct nexus, it is regulated by Hague Law rules. If, on the other hand, that same act is committed outside the geographical scope of hostilities (a critical issue during a NIAC), it is simply not regulated by Hague Law. *Jus ad bellum* and law of neutrality rules *in bello* will still govern when, where and against which state force may be used. But they operate in parallel with or at least overlap with applicable Hague Law. For if force is used in violation of either of the (or indeed both) other legal regimes, this does not per se preclude the legal application of Hague Law rules.

The difficulty with cyberattacks, of course, is that they may be planned and 'launched' (ie programmed and introduced into the Internet) in a nation that is entirely unconnected with an ongoing armed conflict. The laptop used to launch the attack (the 'means of warfare')[31] can be readily transported anywhere in the world, so the launcher of the attack may then move with his or her weapon to another state, one that again is unconnected with

[28] USDOD 2015 *Law of War Manual*, para 16.1.3.2. Subsequently the *Manual* cites as examples of cyber operations that 'generally would not constitute attacks': defacing a government webpage; a minor, brief disruption of Internet services; briefly disrupting, disabling, or interfering with communications; and disseminating propaganda. Ibid, para 16.5.2.

[29] The *Tallinn Manual*, Commentary on Rule 21, 78, para 1.

[30] The *Manual* describes the law of neutrality as part of the law of armed conflict when in fact it is distinct. Thus, the ICJ in its 1996 Nuclear Weapons Advisory Opinion decides to 'examine the question put to it in the light of the law applicable in armed conflict proper, ie the principles and rules of humanitarian law applicable in armed conflict, and the law of neutrality'. ICJ, Nuclear Weapons Advisory Opinion, para 51. In more than 800 pages of his thoughtful explanation of contemporary law of armed conflict, Gary Solis does not once address the law of neutrality: Solis (n 1). He had no need to do so in order to describe the law of armed conflict.

[31] The *Tallinn Manual* affirms that cyber means of warfare 'include any cyber device, materiel, instrument, mechanism, equipment, or software used, designed, or intended to be used to conduct a cyber attack'. The *Tallinn Manual*, Commentary on Rule 41, 142, para 2.

that armed conflict. In fact, the attacker may never set foot in the area where hostilities are ongoing and where the effects of his or her attack are felt. This effectively renders the attack outside the scope of Hague Law, and seemingly accords the attacker immunity from a war crimes prosecution should his or her actions amount to a serious violation of Hague Law rules. This much is true. However, given that this limited scope of geographical application is only an issue in NIAC, the option to seek the extradition of and then prosecute the individual for terrorist acts would still be open to the victim states.

C. Cyberattacks and the Rules of Distinction and Proportionality in Attack

It is unquestioned that the rules of distinction and proportionality in attack apply to cyberattacks. Thus, as the US Department of Defense affirms, 'If a cyber operation constitutes an attack, then the law of war rules on conducting attacks must be applied to those cyber operations. … For example, such operations must comport with the requirements of distinction and proportionality.'[32]

Consonant with the rule of distinction in attack, cyberattacks must be directed against a military objective. This includes 'dual-use' objects that serve both civilian and military purposes.[33] As an example of a cyberattack prohibited under the rule of distinction, the US Department of Defense cites one that would destroy enemy computer systems belonging to stock exchanges, banking systems and universities, unless those computer systems met the test for being a military objective in the circumstances.[34] Dinstein offers as an example of an indiscriminate attack one that involves the placing of cyber malware on a public website in wartime, which then infects the computer of anyone accessing the site, whether military or civilian.[35] A computer virus that was programmed to spread and destroy uncontrollably within civilian Internet systems would be prohibited as an inherently indiscriminate weapon.[36]

To meet the threshold of harm, a cyber-attack may, for example, be expected to cause a destructive fire in an electricity grid or shut down a life-sustaining software programme.[37] The *Tallinn Manual*'s commentary, however, notes that in case of an cyber operation that shuts down an electricity grid, requiring the control system or critical components thereof to be replaced, experts who agreed that this amounted to an attack were split over the issue of whether the damage requirement would be met where functionality can be restored by reinstalling the operating system.[38] The better view is that this would meet the threshold. Damage is incurred to a system, requiring that resources be devoted to its repair. This would seem to be the very notion of what damage is.

[32] USDOD 2015 *Law of War Manual*, para 16.5.1.
[33] The *Tallinn Manual*, Rule 39.
[34] USDOD 2015 *Law of War Manual*, para 16.5.1.
[35] Dinstein (n 25) 149, para 396(e).
[36] USDOD 2015 *Law of War Manual*, para 16.6.
[37] Dinstein (n 25) 3, para 9.
[38] The *Tallinn Manual*, Commentary on Rule 30, 109, para 10.

In applying the proportionality rule to cyberattacks, the US Department of Defense states that it 'might be important to assess the potential effects of a cyber attack on computers that are not military objectives, such as private, civilian computers that hold no military significance, but that may be networked to computers that are valid military objectives'.[39] At the same time, however, it argues that mere inconveniences or temporary losses, such as a minor, brief disruption of Internet services to civilians that results incidentally from a cyber attack, or the economic harms resulting from civilian businesses being unable to conduct e-commerce, need not be considered.[40] The former seems reasonable; the latter will depend on the extent of the economic harm that is wrought. Indeed, the *Tallinn Manual* affirms that an 'attack on the Internet itself, or large portions thereof', might violate the proportionality rule:

> The Internet is used heavily for civilian emergency response, civil defence, disaster relief, and law enforcement activities. It is also employed for medical diagnosis, access to medical records, ordering medicine, and so forth. Any damage, destruction, injury, or death resulting from disruption of such services would have to be considered in determining whether an attack on the Internet comported with the principle of proportionality.[41]

III. Concluding Remarks

It is clear that cyberwarfare may be a means of warfare that has the potential to reduce significantly the impact of hostilities on the civilian population when compared with kinetic attacks. Indeed, as the US Department of Defense observes, 'cyber capabilities may in some circumstances be preferable, as a matter of policy, to kinetic weapons because their effects may be reversible, and they may hold the potential to accomplish military goals without any destructive kinetic effect at all'.[42] Dinstein suggests the use of a cyber-attack to neutralise enemy air force defence systems in heavily populated areas.[43] Similarly, a cyber-attack that renders an electrical generating station inoperable is likely to result in significantly less civilian harm than a 'comparable kinetic attack from an aerial bomber'.[44] At the same time, as the Department of Defense recalls, 'as with special kinetic weapons, such as precision-guided munitions that have the potential to produce less incidental damage than other kinetic weapons, cyber capabilities usually will not be the only type of weapon that is legally permitted'.[45]

[39] USDOD 2015 *Law of War Manual*, para 16.5.1.1.
[40] Ibid.
[41] The *Tallinn Manual*, Commentary on Rule 39, 136, para 6.
[42] USDOD 2015 *Law of War Manual*, para 16.5.3.1.
[43] Dinstein (n 25) 164, para 441.
[44] Ibid, citing M Gervais, 'Cyber Attacks and the Laws of War' (2012) 30 *Berkeley Journal of International Law* 525 at 570.
[45] USDOD 2015 *Law of War Manual*, para 16.5.3.1.

14

Terrorism and the Law of Armed Conflict

I. Introduction

Certain acts of 'terror' violate Hague Law of armed conflict when they fall within the conduct of hostilities. Often, however, such acts fall outside a situation of armed conflict, or are governed by the domestic counterterrorism laws. When ratifying the 1977 Additional Protocol I, the United Kingdom (UK) entered a declaration whereby 'the term "armed conflict" of itself and in its context denotes a situation of a kind which is not constituted by the commission of ordinary crimes including acts of terrorism whether concerted or in isolation'.[1] According to the International Committee of the Red Cross (ICRC), as international humanitarian law (IHL) 'applies only during armed conflict, it does not regulate terrorist acts committed in peacetime. Such acts are however subject to law, ie domestic and international law, in particular human rights law'.[2]

Under the 1997 Terrorist Bombings Convention,[3] it is stipulated that the 'activities of armed forces during an armed conflict, as those terms are understood under international humanitarian law, which are governed by that law, are not governed by this Convention'.[4] This is generally understood to encompass acts in the conduct of hostilities by both state and non-state armed groups that are party to an armed conflict. A similar provision is included in the 2005 draft of the Comprehensive Convention on International Terrorism.[5]

II. The Primary Rule

Under Hague Law, 'Acts or threats of violence the primary purpose of which is to spread terror among the civilian population are prohibited.' This customary rule, applicable to

[1] Declaration of 28 January 1998, at https://ihl-databases.icrc.org/applic/ihl/ihl.nsf/Notification.xsp?action=openDocument&documentId=0A9E03F0F2EE757CC1256402003FB6D2, see S Sivakumaran, *The Law of Non-International Armed Conflict* (Oxford, Oxford University Press, 2012) 233. See also, eg, International Criminal Tribunal for the former Yugoslavia (ICTY), *Prosecutor v Slobodan Milošević*, Decision on Motion for Judgment of Acquittal (Rule 98bis Decision) (Trial Chamber) (Case No IT-02-54-T), 16 June 2004, para 26; and UK Ministry of Defence, *The Manual of the Law of Armed Conflict* (Oxford, Oxford University Press, 2005) para 5.21.1.

[2] ICRC, 'What does IHL say about terrorism?' (22 January 2015) at https://goo.gl/TWPon2.

[3] 1997 International Convention for the Suppression of Terrorist Bombings, adopted at New York, 15 December 1997; entry into force 23 May 2001. Under Art 2(1) of the Convention, 'Any person commits an offence within the meaning of this Convention if that person unlawfully and intentionally delivers, places, discharges or detonates an explosive or other lethal device in, into or against a place of public use, a State or government facility, a public transportation system or an infrastructure facility: (a) With the intent to cause death or serious bodily injury; or (b) With the intent to cause extensive destruction of such a place, facility or system, where such destruction results in or is likely to result in major economic loss.'

[4] Art 19(2), 1997 Terrorist Bombings Convention.

[5] Comprehensive Convention on International Terrorism, Art 20(2), in App I to UN Doc A/59/894 of 12 August 2005.

the conduct of hostilities in all armed conflict,[6] is reflected in Article 51(2) of the 1977 Additional Protocol I and Article 13(2) of the 1977 Additional Protocol II.[7] According to the ICRC's commentary on the Protocols:

> Air raids have often been used as a means of terrorizing the population, but these are not the only methods. For this reason the text contains a much broader expression, namely 'acts or threats of violence' so as to cover all possible circumstances.[8]

Terror, for the purpose of the war crime, has been defined by the International Criminal Tribunal for the former Yugoslavia (ICTY) as 'extreme fear'.[9] The ICRC commentary notes, though, that while acts of violence during conflict 'almost always give rise to some degree of terror among the population' and 'attacks on armed forces are purposely conducted brutally in order to intimidate the enemy soldiers and persuade them to surrender', the Hague Law prohibition is intended to prohibit acts of violence whose primary purpose is to spread terror among the civilian population 'without offering substantial military advantage'.[10] As Dinstein observes, large-scale aerial bombardments that are 'pounding' military objectives and 'breaking the back of the enemy armed forces' are not unlawful according to this rule, 'even if they lead … to the collapse of civilian morale'.[11] Similarly, according to the ICTY, 'acts of violence' do not include legitimate attacks against combatants but only unlawful attacks against civilians.[12]

The United Nations (UN) Commission of Inquiry on the 2014 Gaza conflict noted that the impossibility for Palestinian armed groups to direct rockets towards military objectives raises the question as to what military advantage the Palestinian armed groups could expect to obtain from launching these rockets.[13] Given the apparent absence of any possible military advantage, and statements by Palestinian armed groups that they intended to hit Israeli cities, the Commission cannot exclude the possibility that the indiscriminate rocket attacks may constitute acts of violence whose primary purpose is to spread terror among the civilian population.[14] In its 2015 *Law of War Manual*, the United States (US) Department of Defense referred to 'indiscriminate terror weapons such as the German V bombs' used in the Second World War.[15]

The UN Commission of Inquiry on Syria has affirmed that Jabhat al-Nusra and affiliated groups used suicide bombings and large-scale vehicle-borne improvised explosive devices

[6] ICRC Study of Customary IHL, Rule 2 ('Violence Aimed at Spreading Terror among the Civilian Population') at https://goo.gl/21Z4mZ.

[7] Acts of terrorism are also prohibited under Geneva Law against protected persons. According to Art 33 of the 1949 Geneva Convention IV, 'all measures of intimidation or of terrorism are prohibited'. See also Art 4(2)(d), 1977 Additional Protocol II.

[8] Y. Sandoz, C Swinarski and B Zimmermann (eds), *Commentary on the Additional Protocols of 8 June 1977 to the Geneva Conventions of 12 August 1949* (Geneva, Martinus Nijhoff, 1987) (hereinafter 'ICRC Commentary on the 1977 Additional Protocols') para 4785.

[9] ICTY, *Prosecutor v Galić*, Judgment (Trial Chamber) (Case No IT-98-29-T), 5 December 2003, para 137.

[10] Ibid, para 1940.

[11] Y Dinstein, *The Conduct of Hostilities under the Law of International Armed Conflict*, 3rd edn (Cambridge, Cambridge University Press, 2016) 146, para 390.

[12] *Galić* (n 9) para 135.

[13] UN Commission of Inquiry on the 2014 Gaza Conflict, para 99.

[14] ICRC Study of Customary IHL, Rule 2 ('Violence Aimed at Spreading Terror among the Civilian Population').

[15] United States (US) Department of Defense, *Law of War Manual*, June 2015, para 1.4.1, fn 54, at https://goo.gl/uZKhvk.

with a view to terrorising the civilian population. Between 6 March and 24 June 2014, Homs governorate, and in particular Homs city, was hit by multiple car bombings in government-controlled areas. On 24 June, a car bomb exploded on in the Wadi al-Dahab neighbourhood of Homs city, killing two civilians and injuring 20 more. 'Such attacks, which have civilians as their primary target, demonstrate a clear intent to spread terror among the civilian population.'[16] The Commission also affirmed that use of barrel bombs in area bombardment is prohibited under the law of armed conflict, 'as a tactic that spreads terror among the civilian population'.[17]

III. The War Crime of Terror

It is generally, though not universally, agreed that acts or threats of violence the primary purpose of which is to spread terror among the civilian population may also amount to a war crime under customary international law. A slight doubt persists, in part because this war crime is not punishable under the 1998 Rome Statute of the International Criminal Court (ICC Statute).[18]

In his Dissenting Opinion in the *Galić* case, Judge Rafael Nieto-Navia argued that the crime of terror did not fall within the jurisdiction of the ICTY.[19] He believed that the Trial Chamber had failed to establish that the offence of inflicting terror on a civilian population attracted individual criminal responsibility under international customary law.[20] General Galić appealed against his conviction on that charge. In its judgment, the Appeals Chamber declared its satisfaction that the prohibition of terror against the civilian population as enshrined in the two 1977 Additional Protocols was a norm of customary international law 'from the time of its inclusion in those treaties'.[21] The Appeals Chamber, by Majority, was also satisfied 'that a breach of the prohibition of terror against the civilian population gave rise to individual criminal responsibility pursuant to customary international law at the time of the commission of the offences for which Galić was convicted'.[22]

In his Dissenting Opinion in the Appeals Chamber, Judge Wolfgang Schomburg believed that there was no basis to find that 'terrorisation against a civilian population' was penalised 'beyond any doubt under customary international criminal law at the time relevant to the Indictment'.[23] He agreed that there could be 'no doubt' that the prohibition per se was part of customary international law.[24] But he questioned the state practice on which the Majority of the Appeals Chamber relied, observing, inter alia, that none of the permanent

[16] Report of the independent international commission of inquiry on the Syrian Arab Republic, UN Doc A/HRC/27/60, 13 August 2014, para 107.

[17] Ibid, para 102.

[18] Statute of the International Criminal Court; adopted at Rome, 17 July 1998; entry into force, 1 July 2002.

[19] *Galić* (n 9) Dissenting Opinion of Judge Nieto-Navia, para 108.

[20] Ibid, paras 113, 114. He did, though, share in the Chamber's conclusion that the crime of attacks on civilians was committed against the civilian population of Sarajevo by Bosnian Serb soldiers.

[21] ICTY, *Prosecutor v Galić*, Judgment (Appeals Chamber) (Case No IT-98-29-A), 30 November 2006, para 86.

[22] Ibid.

[23] *Galić* (n 21) Dissenting Opinion of Judge Wolfgang Schomburg, para 2.

[24] Ibid, para 7.

members of the UN Security Council 'or any other prominent state' had penalised terrorisation against a civilian population (as a war crime).[25] He considered it relevant that the ICC Statute did not have jurisdiction over such a war crime.[26] He could, though, have noted that acts of terror were specified as war crimes under the Statutes of the International Criminal Tribunal for Rwanda (ICTR) and of the Special Court for Sierra Leone (SCSL).[27]

A. The *Galić* Case

The *Galić* case was the first time an ICTY Trial Chamber had considered the charge of terror. Thus, General Galić, as commander of the Bosnian Serbs army around Sarajevo, was accused of having 'conducted a protracted campaign of shelling and sniping upon civilian areas of Sarajevo and upon the civilian population thereby inflicting terror and mental suffering upon its civilian population'.[28] The ICTY Trial Chamber, by Majority, rejected the submissions by both Defence and Prosecution that actual infliction of terror was an element of the crime of terror. It did so on the 'plain wording of Article 51(2), as well as the travaux préparatoires of the Diplomatic Conference'.[29]

General Van Baal, UNPROFOR Chief of Staff in Bosnia and Herzegovina in 1994, testified before the Trial Chamber that sniping in Sarajevo was 'without any discrimination, indiscriminately shooting defenceless citizens, women, children, who were unable to protect and defend themselves, at unexpected places and at unexpected times'.[30] This led him to conclude, the Trial Chamber recalled, 'that its objective was to cause terror; he specified that women and children were the predominant target'.[31]

The Majority of the Trial Chamber 'heard reliable evidence that civilians were targeted during funerals, in ambulances, in hospitals, on trams, on buses, when driving or cycling, at home, while tending gardens or fires or clearing rubbish in the city'.[32] The Majority was convinced by the evidence that civilians in government-held areas of Sarajevo were 'directly or indiscriminately attacked' from Bosnian Serb-controlled territory, and that, as a result and 'as a minimum, hundreds of civilians were killed and thousands others were injured'.[33] The Chamber accepted the Prosecution's assertion that the purpose behind the campaign of sniping and shelling against civilians in Sarajevo was 'a crude application of pressure' on the Bosnian Government. The Prosecution further claimed that the campaign sought to undermine the Government's popular support from within the city to maintain the conflict, and to undermine the morale of Bosniak army combatants, 'by reminding them that so long as they fought, their families behind them were in more danger than themselves'.[34]

[25] Ibid, paras 8–12, 18.
[26] Ibid, para 20.
[27] Art 4(d), ICTR Statute; Art 4(d), Statute of the SCSL.
[28] *Galić* (n 9) paras 65, 66.
[29] Ibid, para 134.
[30] Ibid, para 573.
[31] Ibid.
[32] Ibid, para 584.
[33] Ibid, para 591.
[34] Ibid, para 576.

The Trial Chamber and the Appeals Chamber found, by Majority, that for the crime of terror the following specific elements need to be met:

1. Acts or threats of violence directed against the civilian population or individual civilians not taking direct part in hostilities causing death or serious injury to body or health within the civilian population;
2. The offender wilfully made the civilian population or individual civilians not taking direct part in hostilities the object of those acts of violence; and
3. The above offence was committed with the primary purpose of spreading terror among the civilian population.[35]

B. The *Taylor* Case

In the SCSL's judgment on appeal against conviction by Charles Taylor, the former President of Liberia, for his involvement in the NIAC in Sierra Leone in the late 1980s and the 1990s, the Appeals Chamber declared itself satisfied

> that the Trial Chamber's findings show that the RUF/AFRC [Revolutionary United Front/Armed Forces Revolutionary Council] used acts of terror as its primary modus operandi throughout the Indictment Period. The RUF/AFRC pursued a strategy to achieve its goals through extreme fear by making Sierra Leone 'fearful'. The primary purpose was to spread terror, but it was not aimless terror. Barbaric, brutal violence was purposefully unleashed against civilians because it made them afraid – afraid that there would only be more unspeakable violence if they continued to resist in any way, continued to stay in their communities or dared to return to their homes. It also made governments and the international community afraid – afraid that unless the RUF/AFRC's demands were met, thousands more killings, mutilations, abductions and rapes of innocent civilians would follow. The conflict in Sierra Leone was bloody because the RUF/AFRC leadership deliberately made it bloody.[36]

IV. The Definition of Terrorism under International Law

There is no consensus definition under international law of what amounts to acts of terror outside Hague Law governing the conduct of hostilities. As the ICRC has observed:

> While the legal frameworks governing terrorism and IHL may have some common ground – IHL expressly prohibits most acts that are criminalized as 'terrorist' in domestic legislation and international conventions dealing with terrorism – these two legal regimes remain fundamentally different. They have distinct rationales, objectives and structures.
>
> A crucial difference is that, in legal terms, armed conflict is a situation in which certain acts of violence are considered lawful and others are unlawful, while any act of violence designated as 'terrorist' is always unlawful.[37]

[35] Ibid, para 133; *Galić* (n 21) paras 100, 101.

[36] SCSL, *Prosecutor v Charles Ghankay Taylor*, Judgment (Appeals Chamber) (Case No SCSL-03-01-A), 26 September 2013, para 300.

[37] Extract from ICRC, 'International humanitarian law and the challenges of contemporary armed conflicts', Document prepared for the 32nd International Conference of the Red Cross and Red Crescent, Geneva, 8–10 December 2015, text at https://goo.gl/M12E17.

In 2011, the Appeals Chamber of the Special Tribunal for Lebanon, an ad hoc mechanism set up in relation to the attack that killed former Lebanese Prime Minister Rafik Hariri on 14 February 2005, issued a decision in which it claimed that terrorism during peacetime was defined under customary international law and that it comprised the following three key elements:

(a) the perpetration of a criminal act (such as murder, kidnapping, hostage-taking, arson, and so on), or threatening such an act;
(b) the intent to spread fear among the population (which would generally entail the creation of public danger) or directly or indirectly coerce a national or international authority to take some action, or to refrain from taking it; and
(c) when the act involves a transnational element.[38]

But as Marko Milanovic has observed, this definition is 'controversial to say the least'.[39] Rob Cryer not only disputes that the definition asserted by the Special Tribunal for Lebanon reflects customary international law, but also contests whether any such definition exists. The unwillingness of states to adopt the Comprehensive Convention on International Terrorism, in particular its definition of an act of international terrorism, is therefore regrettable.[40] The draft definition stipulates as follows:

> 1. Any person commits an offence within the meaning of the present Convention if that person, by any means, unlawfully and intentionally, causes:
>   (a) Death or serious bodily injury to any person; or
>   (b) Serious damage to public or private property, including a place of public use, a State or government facility, a public transportation system, an infrastructure facility or to the environment; or
>   (c) Damage to property, places, facilities or systems referred to in paragraph 1 (b) of the present article resulting or likely to result in major economic loss;
>
> when the purpose of the conduct, by its nature or context, is to intimidate a population, or to compel a Government or an international organization to do or to abstain from doing any act.[41]

This definition is opposed by some, notably the Organisation of Islamic Cooperation (OIC) (formerly Organization of the Islamic Conference), which wants to exclude national liberation movements, particularly in the context of the Israel-Palestinian conflict.[42] In contrast,

[38] Special Tribunal for Lebanon (STL), *Interlocutory Decision on the Applicable Law: Terrorism, Conspiracy, Homicide, Perpetration, Cumulative Charging* (Case No STL-11-01/I), 16 February 2011, para 85.

[39] M Milanovic, 'Special Tribunal for Lebanon Delivers Interlocutory Decision on Applicable Law', *EJIL Talk!*, published on 16 February 2011, at https://goo.gl/gVVtxs.

[40] Comprehensive Convention on International Terrorism, Art 20(2).

[41] Comprehensive Convention on International Terrorism, Art 2(1).

[42] 'What is the Comprehensive Convention on International Terrorism?', *Livemint* (28 September 2016,) at https://goo.gl/jbmmwM. As a report published by the European Parliamentary Research Service (EPRS) noted, the oral report on measures to eliminate international terrorism presented by the Chair of the General Assembly Working Group in November 2014 noted a request by the OIC to differentiate between acts of terrorism and 'the legitimate struggle of peoples under foreign occupation and colonial or alien domination in the exercise of their right to self-determination in accordance with the principles of international law'. The report considered that 'particularly problematic, given the ambiguity about what constitutes a "legitimate struggle" and the use of terror tactics by insurgent organisations'. P Pawlak, 'Understanding definitions of terrorism. At a glance', EPRS (November 2015) at https://goo.gl/3Qav6W.

the US insists on excluding acts committed by military forces of states during peacetime.[43] In 2016, India, which had put forward the idea of the Convention in 1996, appealed to the UN General Assembly to act 'with fresh resolve and urgency to adopt this critical Convention'.[44]

In the absence of an international consensus on a definition, states have considerable leeway to define 'terrorism' and 'terrorist' in broad terms. Many have taken full advantage of this opportunity. The US even criminalises the provision of training in the law of armed conflict to groups and individuals it designates as terrorist where it is intended to promote respect for the law. Under US statutes prohibiting material support to terrorism,[45] it is an offence to provide material support or resources to designated terrorist organisations or for the purpose of committing terrorism offences. The term 'material support or resources' is defined to mean any service or tangible or intangible property, which can encompass training, logistical support or expert advice. Violations are punishable by a term of up to 15 years' imprisonment.

A US non-governmental organisation, Humanitarian Law Project, successfully challenged the constitutionality of the provisions before the District and Appellate Courts in California. Humanitarian Law Project wanted to 'train members of [the] Kurdish Workers Party (PKK) on how to use humanitarian and international law to peacefully resolve disputes'. In June 2010, however, in its decision in *Holder v Humanitarian Law Project*,[46] the Supreme Court held that the forms of material support in the challenge before it were not unconstitutionally vague nor was their proscription inconsistent with the freedom of speech and freedom of association requirements of the First Amendment to the US Constitution.[47] In the Majority judgment, Chief Justice Roberts wrote that

> material support 'meant to promot[e] peaceable, lawful conduct' can be diverted to advance terrorism in multiple ways. … A foreign terrorist organization introduced to the structures of the international legal system might use the information to threaten, manipulate, and disrupt. This possibility is real, not remote.

A better view of what the law should be was put forward by the three dissenting judges, in a reasoning drafted by Justice Stephen Breyer, who stated:

> I would read the statute as criminalizing First-Amendment-protected pure speech and association only when the defendant knows or intends that those activities will assist the organization's unlawful terrorist actions. Under this reading, the Government would have to show, at a minimum, that such defendants provided support that they knew was significantly likely to help the organization pursue its unlawful terrorist aims.

Nonetheless, US national criminal law is, today, as set out by Chief Justice Roberts. It applies to acts committed anywhere in the world.

[43] 'What is the Comprehensive Convention on International Terrorism?' (n 42).

[44] Statement of Indian External Affairs Minister Smt. Sushma Swaraj, 71st UN General Assembly, New York (26 September 2016) at https://goo.gl/M7fJ9q.

[45] 18 USC 2339A and 2339B, as amended by the 2001 USA PATRIOT Act and the 2004 Intelligence Reform and Terrorism Prevention Act. The USA PATRIOT Act is an acronym for 'Uniting and Strengthening America by Providing Appropriate Tools Required to Intercept and Obstruct Terrorism'.

[46] US Supreme Court, *Holder, Attorney General, and others v Humanitarian Law Project and others*, 561 US 1 (2010), 130 SC 2705, 21 June 2010, at https://goo.gl/z4P2ST.

[47] See, eg, *Rules of Engagement, Protecting Civilians through Dialogue*, Geneva Academy of International Humanitarian Law and Human Rights (2011) at https://goo.gl/btP1rP.

15

Promoting Respect for Hague Law

I. Introduction

This chapter describes the measures that are in place – both on the battlefield and away from it – to seek to promote respect for Hague Law during the conduct of hostilities. It begins, in section II, by recalling the critical role of the commander in preventing violations of the rules. Section III then considers the extent to which reprisals are a lawful means of bringing a party to conflict back into compliance with the law. Among others, the notion supported in various quarters that reprisals are always unlawful in a non-international armed conflict (NIAC) is contested.

Section IV outlines the responsibility of states to respect and ensure respect for the law of armed conflict: through the duty to investigate and prosecute war crimes, in accordance with the duty to ensure a remedy for violations of internationally wrongful acts under the law of state responsibility, and by virtue of the law restricting the transfer of arms to others who would use them in their own violations of the law. Section V addresses individual criminal responsibility under international criminal law for war crimes. It also summarises the elements of genocide and crimes against humanity as international crimes, which may take place during armed conflict in the conduct of hostilities. The chapter ends with concluding remarks on compliance with Hague Law.

II. The Role of the Commander

It is hard to overstate the importance of commanders in promoting respect for Hague Law rules, both through the discipline and values they instil in their subordinates and by the decisions they make in planning and launching operations. Their potential individual criminal responsibility is addressed in section IV.B, but first it is necessary to stress the preventive nature of their role in the conduct of hostilities.[1] They set the example – good or bad – for others to follow, and have an extraordinary influence on whether Hague Law rules are respected or violated during combat.

[1] According to the United States (US) Department of Defense, military commanders 'have a duty to take appropriate measures as are within their power to control the forces under their command for the prevention of violations of the law of war'. US Department of Defense, *Law of War Manual*, June 2015, Updated December 2016 (hereinafter 'USDOD December 2016 *Law of War Manual*') para 18.4, at https://goo.gl/QMkjqs.

In re Yamashita, a United States (US) Supreme Court decision concerning the trial for war crimes of the Japanese general Tomoyuko Yamashita after the end of the Second World War, included the following affirmation:

> It is evident that the conduct of military operations by troops whose excesses are unrestrained by the orders or efforts of their commander would almost certainly result in violations which it is the purpose of the law of war to prevent. Its purpose to protect civilian populations and prisoners of war from brutality would largely be defeated if the commander of an invading army could, with impunity, neglect to take reasonable measures for their protection. Hence, the law of war presupposes that its violation is to be avoided through the control of the operations of war by commanders who are to some extent responsible for their subordinates.[2]

General Yamashita had been accused of war crimes by virtue of his troops' conduct during the defence of the Philippines in 1944, which saw thousands of civilians summarily executed and many hundreds raped.

The responsibility of the commander is longstanding in Hague Law. Already in the 1907 Hague Regulations, Article 1 laid down, as a condition which an armed force must fulfil in order to be accorded the rights of lawful belligerents, that it be 'commanded by a person responsible for his subordinates'. Decades later, specific obligations were imposed on commanders in the 1977 Additional Protocol I, which obliges parties to an international armed conflict (IAC) to require their military commanders to prevent violations by their subordinates, including by initiating disciplinary or penal action against violators.[3]

That said, the demands placed upon commanders are many and varied, and clearly these demands are especially intense during combat. Moreover, as noted in chapter 9, the complexity and increasing decentralisation of modern battlespace imposes greater responsibility on ever more junior commanders to make tactical decisions that may have strategic repercussions. In the words of Colin Gray, 'The phenomenon of the "strategic corporal" is likely to become highly significant in future land operations.'[4]

Experimental research by the Georgia Tech Research Institute, looking at bias in military decision-making, combined a high volume of data with time pressure to simulate the changing reality of military decision-makers. The project takes account of the fact that in modern warfare senior commanders communicate more directly with field personnel, while the amount and variety of information at their disposal has escalated exponentially, with sources ranging from real-time sensors and voice communications to archived data. 'The result can be ambiguous, disjointed information rather than integrated, organized reports.'[5]

Biases covered by the research include what is termed 'vividness': that when people perceive information directly, it has greater impact than information they receive second hand, even if the second-hand information has more substance. There is also said to be a risk of 'sensationalist appeal', whereby items containing exaggerated claims or threats can influence a decision-maker even when there is no substance to the content.[6] The dangers these provoke for decisions taken during combat are real and substantial.

[2] US Supreme Court, *In re Yamashita*, 327 US 1 (1946), 15.

[3] Art 87, 1977 Additional Protocol I.

[4] CS Gray, 'The Nature of Land Warfare' at https://goo.gl/Z1XiRj, 5.

[5] See Georgia Tech Research Institute, 'Rapid-Fire Reasoning: Research Could Help Military Leaders Make Better Decisions Under Pressure' at https://goo.gl/vMis3W.

[6] Ibid.

III. Reprisals

Belligerent reprisals are one of the few means by which a party to an armed conflict may realistically seek compliance with Hague Law while combat is raging on the battlefield. This is not to deny that reprisals against civilians are, in the words of the International Criminal Tribunal for the former Yugoslavia (ICTY) in the *Kupreškić* case, 'inherently a barbarous means of seeking compliance with international law'.[7] As the ICTY goes on to explain:

> The most blatant reason for the universal revulsion that usually accompanies reprisals is that they may not only be arbitrary but are also not directed specifically at the individual authors of the initial violation. … These retaliatory measures are aimed instead at other more vulnerable individuals or groups. They are individuals or groups who may not even have any degree of solidarity with the presumed authors of the initial violation; they may share with them only the links of nationality and allegiance to the same rulers.[8]

To appreciate why, despite the view of the ICTY Trial Chamber in the *Kupreškić* case, reprisals may still be lawful, it is essential first to appreciate what reprisals are, and especially what they are not. Most importantly, a reprisal is not to be equated with retaliation or revenge for earlier violations by the enemy. These are always unlawful acts.[9] A reprisal seeks to end violations by an adverse party to armed conflict, not to punish it for prior transgressions. It is a form of protection – preventing future violations – albeit wrought in a manner that brings great suffering, and often death, to the innocent.

A. The Meaning of Reprisals

The term 'reprisal' under the law of armed conflict describes an act by one party to an armed conflict that would normally be unlawful, but which is not prohibited on the basis that it seeks, within defined conditions, to bring an adverse party back into compliance with the law. The US Department of Defense describes reprisals in its 2016 *Law of War Manual* as 'extreme measures of coercion used to help enforce the law of war by seeking to persuade an adversary to cease violations'.[10] Although the constituent elements are not found in any law of armed conflict treaty, state practice and jurisprudence have combined to identify the following six conditions for a set of circumstances and acts to amount to a reprisal, *each and every one of which* must be fulfilled:

1. An act of reprisal by one party must be in response to a prior unlawful act by an adverse party.
2. The act of reprisal must be in response to serious violations of the law of armed conflict.

[7] ICTY, *Prosecutor v Zoran Kupreškić and others*, Judgment (Trial Chamber) (Case No IT-95-16-T), 14 January 2000, para 528.

[8] Ibid.

[9] Thus, for instance, when in 1863 the Lieber Code talked of 'retaliation', one must understand instead the modern term of reprisal. USDOD December 2016 *Law of War Manual*, para 18.18.1.1. Indeed, the Code makes it explicit that retaliation will 'never be resorted to as a measure of mere revenge, but only as a means of protective retribution, and moreover, cautiously and unavoidably; that is to say, retaliation shall only be resorted to after careful inquiry into the real occurrence, and the character of the misdeeds that may demand retribution'. 1863 Lieber Code, Art 28.

[10] USDOD December 2016 *Law of War Manual*, para 18.18.

3. Recourse to a reprisal must be necessary in the circumstances.
4. The primary intent of the reprisal must be to end the adverse party's serious violations of the law of armed conflict.
5. The act of reprisal must be proportionate to those serious violations.
6. Reprisals must not be committed against prohibited targets.

These conditions are elaborated in turn.

i. A Response to a Prior Violation of the Law of Armed Conflict

A reprisal may only be conducted in response to a prior act that is or acts that are unlawful under either Geneva Law or Hague Law. Thus, a violation of *jus ad bellum*, even if it is serious, such as in the case of aggression, is not grounds for a reprisal under the law of armed conflict. Moreover, if the prior act is or acts are not clearly unlawful under the law of armed conflict, there is no possibility of lawful recourse to an act of reprisal. As the US Department of Defense cautions, 'a bombardment that results in the death of civilians may be the result of good faith, reasonable mistake, or may have been justified by the importance of destroying the military objective against which the bombardment was directed'.[11] The act(s) potentially justifying recourse to a reprisal must have been conducted by the target armed force, not one of its allies. Furthermore, 'pre-emptive' reprisals are never lawful.

The Nangar Khel massacre was discussed in chapter 6. It concerned the action of Polish soldiers in Afghanistan who, on 16 August 2007, fired mortar shells (and possibly automatic weapons)[12] against the Afghan village of Nangar Khel, killing at least six civilians, including women and children. A central charge was that the defendants had committed the war crime of unlawfully targeting civilians as a reprisal.[13] This was said to be in response to injuries suffered by two other Polish soldiers earlier that day, when their vehicle hit an improvised mine near the village that had been laid by the Taliban. As the Polish soldiers were lawful targets under Hague Law rules in the NIAC with the Taliban, this precluded the possibility of a lawful reprisal.

ii. A Response Only to Serious Violations of the Law of Armed Conflict

A reprisal is only possible in response to serious violations of the law of armed conflict. Such serious violations include, but are not limited to, war crimes.[14] In the words of the United Kingdom (UK) Ministry of Defence, for example, in order to qualify as a legitimate reprisal, an act must be 'in response to serious and manifestly unlawful acts, committed by an adverse government, its military commanders or combatants for whom the adversary

[11] Ibid, para 18.18.2.1.

[12] See, eg, Trial International, 'Lukasz Bywalec', updated 15 June 2016, at https://goo.gl/RgsLk8.

[13] Trial International, 'Tomasz Borysiewicz', 20 July 2016.

[14] The phrase is used in Art 7(1) of the 2013 Arms Trade Treaty, as discussed in section IV. For a discussion of its meaning in that context see, eg, S Casey-Maslen and A Clapham, 'Commentary on Article 7' in S Casey-Maslen et al, *The Arms Trade Treaty: A Commentary* (Oxford, Oxford University Press, 2016) paras 7.39–7.49.

is responsible'.[15] An individual violation will not suffice unless it is exceptionally grave, for instance when many civilians are intentionally killed in a single attack that is not targeted at a lawful military objective.

iii. The Reprisal Must be Necessary

A reprisal is not 'necessary' if other means can achieve the aim of returning an adversary into compliance with the law of armed conflict. Accordingly, other non-violent measures must either be attempted first, or must be doomed to be ineffective.[16] Such measures as are possible should normally include a warning to the offending party to cease its unlawful behaviour, combined with a reasonable time period within which a commitment to renewed compliance must be communicated back, perhaps through a neutral third party. The warning notice should identify clearly the acts that are the basis for a possible future reprisal and make explicit the potential consequences of a failure to respond positively to the notice.

iv. The Reprisal Must Seek to Restore Compliance with the Law of Armed Conflict

Acts ostensibly in reprisal must be conducted with a view to bringing the target state back into compliance with the law of armed conflict, and should be announced as such. Acts carried out purely in revenge or as a form of collective punishment therefore remain wholly unlawful. As Sandesh Sivakumaran observes, though, the relevant test should be whether the *primary* purpose of any reprisal is to seek compliance with the law by the adverse party.[17] Secondary motivations for carrying out a reprisal may be to satisfy public pressure or a particular constituency. In this regard, Sivakumaran is rightly critical of the ICTY Trial Chamber judgment in the *Martić* case, which asserted that the aim of ensuring a return to respect for the law must be the *sole* purpose of the acts taken.[18]

v. Acts of Reprisal Must be a Proportionate Response

Acts of reprisal must be proportionate to the original serious violations of the law of armed conflict while being of a nature and extent such as to effect a return to compliance by the offending party. Excessive or 'unreasonable' use of force is unlawful,[19] and acts of reprisal must cease as soon as their objective, the return to compliance with the law of armed

[15] UK Ministry of Defence, *The Manual of the Law of Armed Conflict* (Oxford, Oxford University Press, 2004) para 16.17.

[16] The US Department of Defense affirms that 'consideration should be given to using protests and demands, retorsion, or reasonable notice of the threat to use reprisals before resorting to reprisals'. USDOD December 2016 *Law of War Manual*, para 18.18.2.2.

[17] S Sivakumaran, *The Law of Non-International Armed Conflict* (Oxford, Oxford University Press, 2012) 455.

[18] ICTY, *Prosecutor v Milan Martić*, Judgment (Trial Chamber) (Case No IT-95-11-T), 12 June 2007, para 465. It is of note, however, that the policy of the UK, as announced in its interpretive declaration upon ratification of the 1977 Additional Protocol I, is that its forces will conduct a reprisal 'to the extent that it considers such measures necessary for the *sole* purpose of compelling the adverse party to cease committing violations' (emphasis added).

[19] 'A reprisal should not be unreasonable or excessive compared to the adversary's violation.' USDOD December 2016 *Law of War Manual*, para 18.18.2.4.

conflict, has been achieved.[20] As Christopher Greenwood has asserted, reprisals 'should exceed neither what is proportionate to the prior violation nor what is necessary if they are to achieve their aim of restoring respect for the law'.[21]

In the *Kappler* case (better known as the *Ardeatine Cave* case), the German Security Service, headed by Lieutenant-Colonel Kappler, executed 10 Italian prisoners for every German policeman killed in a particular bombing. In all, the Security Service retaliated for the bombing by executing 335 prisoners in the Ardeatine caves: 320 for the 32 policemen killed in the bomb attack; 10 for another German killed subsequently; and five others murdered 'due to a culpable mistake'.[22] The Court concluded that the executions were disproportionate 'not only as regards numbers, but also for the reason that those shot in the Ardeatine caves included five generals, eleven senior officers … twenty-one subalterns and six non-commissioned officers'.[23]

The notion of a proportionate response does not require that an act of reprisal employ, for example, the same prohibited weapon, or commit the same violation against a similar group of people. At the same time, as the US Department of Defense has observed, 'Identical reprisals are the easiest to justify as proportionate, because subjective comparisons are not involved.'[24]

vi. Reprisals Must Not be Committed against Prohibited Targets

Certain persons or objects may never be targeted with reprisals. Each of the four 1949 Geneva Conventions includes provisions prohibiting reprisals against protected persons,[25] and these prohibitions today constitute customary law.[26] It is therefore unlawful in any circumstances to conduct reprisals against persons in the power of a party to an IAC, including the wounded, sick and shipwrecked; medical and religious personnel; captured combatants (ie prisoners of war); civilians in occupied territory; and other categories of civilians in the power of an adverse party to the conflict, notably civilian internees.

It is also unlawful to conduct reprisals against medical buildings, vessels and equipment protected by the 1949 Geneva Conventions I and II.[27] It is similarly illegal to conduct reprisals against cultural property protected by the 1954 Hague Convention for the Protection of Cultural Property.[28] These rules are also said by the International Committee of the Red Cross (ICRC) to be customary in nature.[29]

[20] *Kupreškić* (n 7) para 535.

[21] C Greenwood, 'The twilight of the law of belligerent reprisals?' (1989) 20 *Netherlands Yearbook of International Law* 35, 44.

[22] S Darcy, 'The evolution of the law of belligerent reprisals' (2003) 175 *Military Law Review* 184, 195, citing *In re Kappler*, Military Tribunal of Rome, 20 July 1948. See H Lauterpacht (ed), *Annotated Digest and Reports of Public International Law Cases*, vol XV (London, Butterworth & Co, 1948) 471.

[23] See *In re Kappler* (n 22).

[24] USDOD December 2016 *Law of War Manual*, para 18.18.2.4.

[25] Art 46, 1949 Geneva Convention I; Art 47, 1949 Geneva Convention II; Art 13(3), 1949 Geneva Convention III; and Art 33(3), 1949 Geneva Convention IV, respectively.

[26] See ICRC Study of Customary International Humanitarian Law (IHL), Rule 147 ('Reprisals against Protected Objects') at https://goo.gl/YYVrn9.

[27] Art 46, 1949 Geneva Convention I; and Art 47, 1949 Geneva Convention II, respectively.

[28] Art 4(4), 1954 Hague Convention for the Protection of Cultural Property, adopted at The Hague, 14 May 1954; entry into force 7 August 1956.

[29] ICRC Study of Customary IHL, Rule 147.

a. Reprisals against Civilians

The extent to which other law of armed conflict treaty rules prohibiting reprisals reflect customary law is, though, vigorously contested. In particular, this concerns the prohibition on reprisals against civilians and civilian objects in enemy territory during the conduct of hostilities. Thus, for example, Article 51(6) of the 1977 Additional Protocol I stipulates that 'Attacks against the civilian population or civilians by way of reprisals are prohibited.'[30] In its 1987 commentary on this provision, the ICRC asserted:

> The prohibition contained in this article is not subject to any conditions and it therefore has a peremptory character; in particular it leaves out the possibility of derogating from this rule by invoking military necessity. As in the 1949 Conventions, this provision confirms the right of an individual not to be punished for acts which he has not himself committed.[31]

Here the ICRC is overstating the case for the 'peremptory character' of the prohibition on reprisals. The provision was much debated during the negotiations and remains opposed by a number (albeit small) of states. The US, for instance, has expressed the view that the provisions in the 1977 Additional Protocol I on reprisal are 'counterproductive', and that 'they remove a significant deterrent that protects civilians and war victims on all sides of a conflict'.[32] In 1998, the UK attached the following 'understanding' to its ratification of the Protocol, which clarifies its position with regard to reprisals more generally:

> The obligations of Articles 51 and 55 are accepted on the basis that any adverse party against which the United Kingdom might be engaged will itself scrupulously observe those obligations. If an adverse party makes serious and deliberate attacks, in violation of Article 51 or Article 52 against the civilian population or civilians or against civilian objects, or, in violation of Articles 53, 54 and 55, on objects or items protected by those Articles, the United Kingdom will regard itself as entitled to take measures otherwise prohibited by the Articles in question to the extent that it considers such measures necessary for the sole purpose of compelling the adverse party to cease committing violations under those Articles, but only after formal warning to the adverse party requiring cessation of the violations has been disregarded and then only after a decision taken at the highest level of government. Any measures thus taken by the United Kingdom will not be disproportionate to the violations giving rise thereto and will not involve any action prohibited by the Geneva Conventions of 1949 nor will such measures be continued after the violations have ceased. The United Kingdom will notify the Protecting Powers of any such formal warning given to an adverse party, and if that warning has been disregarded, of any measures taken as a result.[33]

In addition, Egypt, Germany and Italy have reserved the right to react to serious violations of the Protocol with any means permitted by international law to prevent further violations, while France has declared that it will apply the provisions of Article 51(8)[34] insofar as their

[30] Attacks in reprisal against civilian objects are prohibited under Art 52(1). Also prohibited are reprisals against objects indispensable to the survival of the civilian population (Art 54(4)), the natural environment (Art 55(2)), and works and installations containing dangerous forces (Art 56(4)).

[31] Y Sandoz, C Swinarski, and B Zimmermann (eds), *Commentary to the Additional Protocols of 8 June 1977 to the Geneva Conventions of 12 August 1949* (Geneva, Martinus Nijhoff, 1987) para 1984.

[32] 'The Position of the United States on Current Law of War Agreements: Remarks of Judge Abraham D Sofaer, Legal Adviser, US Department of State, 22 January 1987' (1987) 2 *American University Journal of International Law and Policy* 460, 469.

[33] Declaration of 28 January 1998, at https://goo.gl/kCB5L9.

[34] 'Any violation of these prohibitions shall not release the Parties to the conflict from their legal obligations with respect to the civilian population and civilians …'

interpretation does not constitute an obstacle to the use, according to international law, of the means which it considers indispensable to protect its civilian population against grave, clear and deliberate violations of the 1949 Geneva Conventions and of the Protocol by the enemy.[35]

In 2005, the ICRC Study of Customary IHL concluded with respect to the legality of reprisals:

> Because of existing contrary practice, albeit limited, it is difficult to conclude that there has yet crystallized a customary rule specifically prohibiting reprisals against civilians during the conduct of hostilities. Nevertheless, it is also difficult to assert that a right to resort to such reprisals continues to exist based on the practice of only a limited number of States, some of which is also ambiguous. Hence, there appears, at a minimum, to exist a trend in favour of prohibiting such reprisals.

In fact, as Louise Doswald-Beck has suggested, in the case of belligerent reprisals against civilian populations in the opposing party's own territory, there may simply be no customary rule at all.[36]

B. Reprisals in the Conduct of Hostilities in International Armed Conflict

It seems generally uncontested that, in an IAC, what would otherwise be prohibited weapons and methods of combat (such as those of a nature to cause superfluous injury or unnecessary suffering) may, in certain circumstances, be used in reprisal against military objectives, including combatants. In case of serious violations of Hague Law rules in which civilians are deliberately targeted in widespread or major attacks by their adversary, states that are not party to the 1977 Additional Protocol I or states parties that have made a relevant interpretive declaration may resort to reprisals, including against the enemy's civilian population.

Of course, that a state engaged in an armed conflict may lawfully avail itself of reprisals in particular circumstances does not mean that it *should* do so. This is emphasised by the US Department of Defense in its 2016 *Law of War Manual*, which affirms that 'potential practical consequences of the use of reprisals … may counsel strongly against taking such measures'. These include the following:

- Taking reprisals may divert valuable and scarce military resources from the military struggle and may not be as effective militarily as steady adherence to the law.
- Reprisals will usually have an adverse impact on the attitudes of governments not participating in the conflict.
- Reprisals may only strengthen enemy morale and will to resist.
- Reprisals frequently lead only to further unwanted escalation of the conflict by an adversary or a vicious cycle of counter-reprisals.
- Reprisals may render resources of an adversary less able to contribute to the rehabilitation of an area after the cessation of hostilities.[37]

[35] Declaration of 11 April 2001 upon ratification in the original French, at https://goo.gl/SkEJWC.
[36] Remarks to experts meeting, Oslo, 17 June 2013; author's notes.
[37] USDOD December 2016 *Law of War Manual*, para 18.18.4.

C. Reprisals in the Conduct of Hostilities in Non-International Armed Conflict

Whether it is possible in certain circumstances to have recourse to reprisals in a NIAC is not settled, despite jurisprudence and the position of a number of international lawyers suggesting that reprisals are always outlawed in such conflicts.

In 2000, an ICTY Trial Chamber concluded, in the *Kupreškić* case, largely on the basis of the 'pervasive influence' of human rights law on the law of armed conflict, that

> belligerent reprisals against civilians and fundamental rights of human beings are absolutely inconsistent legal concepts … Due to the pressure exerted by the requirements of humanity and the dictates of public conscience, a customary rule of international law has emerged on the matter under discussion.[38]

In its subsequent study of customary law, the ICRC, citing the *Kupreškić* case, also asserted that reprisals in a NIAC were unlawful as a matter of custom, averring simply that parties to NIACs 'do not have the right to resort to belligerent reprisals'.[39] Gary Solis, citing the ICRC, appears to concur with this latter conclusion, though he questions the legitimacy of the ICTY's finding more generally.[40] Moir, amongst others, stated simply in 2002 that there is no place for reprisals in a NIAC.[41]

However, no treaty provision expressly prohibits reprisals in such a conflict, despite attempts to read one into Common Article 3 to the 1949 Geneva Conventions and/or the 1977 Additional Protocol II. The reasoning in the *Kupreškić* judgment, such as it exists, is flawed. Custom develops on the basis of *usus* and *opinio juris*, not 'the pressure exerted by the requirements of humanity and the dictates of public conscience'.[42] That is *lex desiderata* – the law as one might wish it to be – not *lex lata*. The ICTY went on to argue that

> while reprisals could have had a modicum of justification in the past, when they constituted practically the only effective means of compelling the enemy to abandon unlawful acts of warfare and to comply in future with international law, at present they can no longer be justified in this manner. A means of inducing compliance with international law is at present more widely available and, more importantly, is beginning to prove fairly efficacious: the prosecution and punishment of war crimes and crimes against humanity by national or international courts.[43]

This is high-minded bunkum. When civilians are being massacred by enemy forces, few will content themselves with the notion that there might, just might, be a prosecution of certain perpetrators or complicit individuals some years down the line. They want the violations to stop, and stop quickly.

Sivakumaran expounded a more reflective position in his 2012 work, *The Law of Non-International Armed Conflict*. Noting that the UK Ministry of Defence contests the

[38] *Kupreškić* (n 7) para 531.

[39] ICRC Study of Customary IHL, Rule 148 ('Reprisals in Non-International Armed Conflict'), at https://goo.gl/SqgYS1.

[40] GD Solis, *The Law of Armed Conflict: International Humanitarian Law in War*, 2nd edn (New York, Cambridge University Press, 2016) 694–95.

[41] L Moir, *The Law of Internal Armed Conflict* (Cambridge, Cambridge University Press, 2002) 240.

[42] See, eg, Lieutenant-Colonel James T Hill, '*Jus in Bello Futura Ignotus*: The United States, The International Criminal Court, and the Uncertain Future of the Law of Armed Conflict' (2015) 223 *Military Law Review* 672.

[43] *Kupreškić* (n 7) para 530.

Trial Chamber's claim in the *Kupreškić* case of the existence of a customary law prohibition on reprisals,[44] he argues, justly, that the view that belligerent reprisals are prohibited in NIACs as a matter of customary IHL 'may be overstating the existing position'.[45] As he notes, the *Martić* case, which concerned what could best be qualified as a NIAC between Croatia and the self-styled Republic of Serbian Krajina, did not, at least at trial or on appeal against conviction,[46] consider reprisals per se unlawful. Instead the relevant chambers adjudged that the claims Martić made for his attacks against Zagreb amounting to a reprisal were not sustained on the facts.[47] And while valid policy reasons may be cited for endorsing a prohibition on any reprisals in NIACs, it is simply premature to assert that a total prohibition exists in customary law.

IV. The Responsibility of States

This section outlines the responsibility of states to respect and ensure respect for the law of armed conflict: through the duty to investigate and prosecute war crimes; in accordance with the duty to ensure a remedy for violations of Hague Law rules under the law of state responsibility for internationally wrongful acts; and by virtue of the law governing the transfer of arms to others who would use them in their own violations of the law. These elements are discussed in turn.

A. The Duty to Investigate and Prosecute War Crimes

There is a duty on each state party to the 1949 Geneva Conventions to search for, and then either prosecute or extradite for prosecution, individuals 'alleged to have committed, or to have ordered to be committed', grave breaches of the Conventions.[48] This duty to prosecute or extradite any such alleged war criminal[49] anywhere in the world is a form of compulsory universal jurisdiction also known under its Latin moniker, *aut dedere aut judicare*. While, of course, the overwhelming majority of these grave breaches involve serious violations of Geneva Law, not Hague Law, in at least one instance this would cover acts of hostilities. If an unlawful attack is intentionally or recklessly launched against a protected medical facility and/or the patients therein, this would potentially fall within the scope of grave breaches as either 'wilful killing' or 'wilfully causing great suffering or serious injury to body or health'.

[44] UK Ministry of Defence (n 15) para 16.19.2, fn 62.

[45] Sivakumaran (n 17) 452.

[46] However, in the pre-trial Rule 61 procedure (a process whereby the indictment against an accused not yet in custody is submitted to the Trial Chamber to determine whether 'there are reasonable grounds for believing that the accused has committed all or any of the crimes charged'), the Trial Chamber ruled that reprisals in an NIAC were outlawed under customary law. ICTY, *Prosecutor v Milan Martić*, Decision (Case No IT-95-11-R61), 8 March 1996, paras 13–17. See, eg, Darcy (n 22) 231–33. Following criticism of this assertion – by Christopher Greenwood and Frits Kalshoven in particular – the Trial Chamber did not refer to its decision a decade earlier when rendering its judgment in the *Martić* case in 2007.

[47] Sivakumaran (n 17) 455.

[48] Art 49, 1949 Geneva Convention I; Art 50, Geneva Convention II; Art 129, Geneva Convention III; and Art 146, Geneva Convention IV.

[49] Art 85(5) of the 1977 Additional Protocol I makes it explicit that grave breaches of the Geneva Conventions or of the Protocol are war crimes.

There is also a duty under customary international law upon each state to investigate and, in all appropriate cases, to prosecute all other war crimes committed by its nationals or members of its armed forces. According to the ICRC, it is a customary rule that states 'must investigate war crimes allegedly committed by their nationals or armed forces, or on their territory'.[50]

Certain war crimes committed in the conduct of hostilities are listed in Article 85 of the 1977 Additional Protocol I:

- attacking the civilian population or individual civilians
- launching an indiscriminate attack affecting the civilian population or civilian objects in the knowledge that the attack will cause excessive civilians harm
- launching an attack against works or installations containing dangerous forces in the knowledge that the attack will cause excessive civilian harm
- attacking non-defended localities and demilitarised zones
- attacking a person in the knowledge that he or she is *hors de combat*,[51] and
- attacking and causing extensive destruction to certain clearly-recognised and specially-protected historic monuments, works of art or places of worship.[52]

While this list is extremely valuable, at least two glaring omissions are remedied by customary law:

- attacking civilian objects, and
- launching an indiscriminate attack, including through the use of indiscriminate weapons.[53]

In all cases, these war crimes apply in NIAC as well as IAC.

Of course, as we have seen in the various chapters, meeting the actus reus and mens rea thresholds for war crimes committed in the conduct of hostilities is exceptionally challenging. Even negligent mistakes do not found criminal responsibility, while the 'fog of war' and a lack of clarity as to the accuracy needed to comply with or violate the rule of distinction combine and contribute to making war crimes charges extraordinarily hard to prosecute successfully. And this is so where a political will exists to punish war crimes; rarely the case in states whose armed forces are engaged in active armed conflict.

B. State Responsibility for Other Serious Violations of Hague Law

There is not only a duty on states to investigate and take remedial action where war crimes are alleged or suspected to have been committed. Each of the 1949 Geneva Conventions

[50] ICRC Study of Customary IHL, Rule 158 ('Prosecution of War Crimes') at https://goo.gl/qyCXGv. See also the Basic Principles and Guidelines on the Right to a Remedy and Reparation for Victims of Gross Violations of International Human Rights Law and Serious Violations of International Humanitarian Law, UN General Assembly Resolution 60/147, 21 March 2006.

[51] Art 85(3)(a)–(e), 1977 Additional Protocol I.

[52] Art 85(4)(d), 1977 Additional Protocol I.

[53] One might also add the war crime of using a weapon or a method of warfare that is of a nature to cause superfluous injury or unnecessary suffering.

requires states parties to 'take measures necessary for the suppression of all acts contrary to the provisions of the … Convention other than the grave breaches'.[54] This applies also to the provisions of the 1977 Additional Protocol I[55] (though not, explicitly, to the 1977 Additional Protocol II). The general duty to suppress violations of Hague Law is complemented by the duty under Article 1 common to the four 1949 Geneva Conventions, whereby each state party undertakes 'to respect and to ensure respect' for all of the provisions of the Conventions 'in all circumstances'.

Consonant with these obligations, the 2016 Minnesota Protocol on the Investigation of Potentially Unlawful Death, which guides the implementation of the 1989 United Nations Principles on the Effective Prevention and Investigation of Extra-legal, Arbitrary and Summary Executions, states:

> Where, during the conduct of hostilities, it appears that casualties have resulted from an attack, a post-operation assessment should be conducted to establish the facts, including the accuracy of the targeting. … Where any death is suspected or alleged to have resulted from a violation of IHL that would not amount to a war crime, and where an investigation ('official inquiry') into the death is not specifically required under IHL, at a minimum further inquiry is necessary. In any event, where evidence of unlawful conduct is identified, a full investigation should be conducted.[56]

Where a violation, especially a serious violation, of Hague Law rules has occurred, such as of the rules of distinction, proportionality or precautions in attack, the state whose forces or agent have perpetrated the violation will bear responsibility under international law. It is a firmly established principle of international law that a state is required to make reparation for any violation of international law that affects another state. In 1928, the Permanent Court of International Justice (PCIJ) was asked to adjudicate the legality of Polish expropriation of a German-owned nitrate factory at Chorzów in Upper Silesia on land that was subsequently ceded to Poland. In its judgment, the PCIJ stated:

> It is a principle of international law that the breach of an engagement involves an obligation to make reparation in an adequate form. Reparation therefore is the indispensable complement of a failure to apply a convention and there is no necessity for this to be stated in the convention itself.[57]

This was endorsed in the 2001 Draft Articles on Responsibility of States for Internationally Wrongful Acts (the '2001 Articles on State Responsibility'), issued by the International Law Commission (ILC):

> Every internationally wrongful act of a State entails the international responsibility of that State.
>
> The responsible State is under an obligation to make full reparation for the injury caused by the internationally wrongful act.[58]

[54] Art 49, 1949 Geneva Convention I; Art 50, Geneva Convention II; Art 129, Geneva Convention III; and Art 146, Geneva Convention IV.

[55] Art 85(1), 1977 Additional Protocol I.

[56] The Minnesota Protocol on the Investigation of Potentially Unlawful Death (2016) at https://goo.gl/Yu17ee, para 21.

[57] PCIJ, *Case Concerning the Factory at Chorzów (Germany v Poland)*, Judgment (Jurisdiction), No 8, 1927, PCIJ Series A, No 9, 21.

[58] Arts 1 and 31(1), ILC Draft Articles on Responsibility of States for Internationally Wrongful Acts, adopted on 10 August 2001, contained in annex to UN General Assembly Resolution 56/83 of 12 December 2001.

An internationally wrongful act is an action or omission attributable to a state under international law that constitutes a breach of an international obligation of that state.[59] In 2005, the International Court of Justice (ICJ) observed 'that it is well established in general international law that a State which bears responsibility for an internationally wrongful act is under an obligation to make full reparation for the injury caused by that act'.[60]

Under the customary law of armed conflict, a state responsible for violations of that law 'is required to make full reparation for the loss or injury caused'.[61] In the view of the ICRC, state practice establishes this rule as a norm of customary international law applicable in both IACs and NIACs.[62] Already in 1907, the Hague Convention IV on the Laws and Customs of War on Land provided that a party that violates the provisions of the annexed Regulations 'shall, if the case demands, be liable to pay compensation'.[63] This provision was repeated, again in the context of IAC, in the 1977 Additional Protocol I.[64] As Emanuela-Chiara Gillard has pointed out, though, 'the obligation to make reparation arises automatically as a consequence of the unlawful act, without the need for the obligation to be spelled out in conventions'.[65]

There is also a duty to provide reparation to individual victims of law of armed conflict violations. In 2005, the UN General Assembly adopted and proclaimed the Basic Principles and Guidelines on the Right to a Remedy and Reparation for Victims of Gross Violations of International Human Rights Law and Serious Violations of International Humanitarian Law.[66] It was stipulated that the obligation to respect, ensure respect for and implement the law of armed conflict includes the duty to:

(a) Take appropriate legislative and administrative and other appropriate measures to prevent violations;
(b) Investigate violations effectively, promptly, thoroughly and impartially and, where appropriate, take action against those allegedly responsible in accordance with domestic and international law;
(c) Provide those who claim to be victims of a human rights or humanitarian law violation with equal and effective access to justice, as described below, irrespective of who may ultimately be the bearer of responsibility for the violation; and
(d) Provide effective remedies to victims, including reparation …[67]

In practice, however, the victims of violations of the law of armed conflict, particularly in the conduct of hostilities, have struggled to secure reparation, and fora under that body of international law that enable the pursuit of justice are lacking. When compensation for harm has been provided by states, it has tended to be on an *ex gratia* basis and without admission of any legal responsibility. For instance, in Afghanistan in addition to the Afghan authorities

[59] Art 2, 2001 Articles on State Responsibility.
[60] ICJ, *Armed Activities on the Territory of the Congo (Congo v Uganda)*, Judgment, 19 December 2005, para 259.
[61] ICRC Study of Customary IHL, Rule 150 ('Reparation') at https://goo.gl/kWeZ6C.
[62] Ibid.
[63] Art 3, 1907 Hague Convention IV Respecting the Laws and Customs of War on Land.
[64] Art 91, 1977 Additional Protocol I.
[65] E-C Gillard, 'Reparation for violations of international humanitarian law', *International Review of the Red Cross*, vol 85, no 851 (September 2003) 529, 532.
[66] UN General Assembly Resolution 60/147, 16 December 2005.
[67] Para 3, pt II: 'Scope of the obligation', 2005 Basic Principles and Guidelines.

themselves, Australia, Canada, Germany, Italy, the Netherlands, Norway, Poland, the UK and the US have each offered *ex gratia* payments for the acts of their armed forces.[68]

The Campaign for Innocent Victims in Conflict (CIVIC) has reported that the UK Ministry of Defence offers compensation when it would be liable under UK law for damage or harm caused to civilians as a result of its negligent actions. The standard of care, or what counts as negligence in the context of UK operations in Afghanistan, is not clear,[69] but would certainly encompass violations of the Hague Law rules of distinction and proportionality in attack. In September 2013, the British newspaper *The Independent* reported that the families of 185 victims of UK military operations in Afghanistan since 2007 had been compensated with barely £3,000 each. The 'fatality claims' included the deaths of Afghan civilians in botched airstrikes, crossfire and road accidents involving British forces.[70] At the end of 2015, it was reported that military officials had paid out £27 million in damages to life, limb and property caused by their actions in Iraq and Afghanistan. Of this, Iraqis received £21.7 million and Afghans £5.3 million for the loss of relatives, wounds and damage to property.[71]

The US Solatia and Condolence Programs offer compensation to Afghan victims to express sympathy towards victims and their relatives for harm suffered as a result of the armed conflict.[72] Maximum payment for death under Solatia was said to be $2,000, while under Condolence it was $2,500.[73] A far greater sum was, though, paid to the victims of the Panjwai massacre on 11 March 2012, when, in what amounted to war crimes, US Army Staff Sergeant Robert Bales murdered in cold blood 16 civilians, including nine children, and wounded six others. By the end of that month, the US had given the equivalent of a total of US$860,000 to the victims' families, allocating $50,000 for each dead relative and $11,000 for each injured survivor.[74]

It is probably the case that states are more disposed to provide compensation when the alleged violation of the law of armed conflict is of Geneva Law rather than Hague Law. One reason may be that evidence of a violation is easier to secure and assess when a person is 'in the power' of a party to the conflict, and when he or she is killed at close range rather than when a death results from the conduct of hostilities. Another may be that there is especial concern about the precedential significance of giving compensation when it is an alleged violation of Hague Law: that it might impact on a state's understanding of the application of the rules of distinction and proportionality and somehow tie its hands in combat.

On 2 September 2012, in the hamlet of Sarar in central Yemen, two armed drones (or possibly manned combat aircraft) bombed a vehicle, killing 12 passengers, including

[68] V Cadelo, 'Redress and reparation for victims of armed conflict: a critical review of practice in 2013' in S Casey-Maslen (ed), *The War Report: Armed Conflict in 2013* (Oxford, Oxford University Press, 2014) 570; see also Campaign for Innocent Victims in Conflict (CIVIC), *Addressing Civilian Harm in Afghanistan: Policies & Practices of International Forces*, Report, June 2010, at https://goo.gl/cy7qPv.

[69] CCC, *Addressing Civilian Harm in Afghanistan: Policies & Practices of International Forces*, 8.

[70] B Brady, 'MoD paid £3,000 compensation for Afghans killed by UK military', *The Independent* (22 September 2013) at https://goo.gl/Aew6gZ.

[71] 'Military pays out £27 mn compensation to Iraqi, Afghan war victims', *RT* (24 December 2015) at https://goo.gl/jgYvXA.

[72] Cadelo (n 68) 570.

[73] See NC Crawford, *Accountability for Killing* (Oxford, Oxford University Press, 2013) 376.

[74] M Rosenberg and S Rahimi, 'US Pays Families of Afghan Victims in Massacre by Soldier', *New York Times* (25 March 2012) at https://goo.gl/Z2bEb5.

three children and a pregnant woman. The driver and a thirteenth passenger survived. According to Human Rights Watch, the strike's apparent target, tribal leader Abd al-Raouf al-Dahab, was not in the vehicle, and it is not clear that he was even a member of al-Qaeda in the Arabian Peninsula (AQAP):

> The Yemeni government admitted the attack was a mistake but for months provided the victims' families only limited compensation: 100 Kalashnikov assault rifles and cash for burial costs. Only in June 2013, after Human Rights Watch and other groups raised the case with the United States, did the Yemeni authorities compensate the families for the deaths.[75]

An exception to the general trend followed the particularly grave incident that occurred early on 3 October 2015, discussed in chapter 4. At around 2am, a US Air Force AC-130 gunship attacked Médecins sans Frontières (MSF)'s Trauma Centre in the city of Kunduz in northern Afghanistan. It is estimated that the airstrikes lasted at least one hour.[76] Doctors and other medical staff were reportedly shot by the aircraft's gunners while running to safety in a different part of the compound.[77] According to MSF's internal report on the air strike, the total number of dead was 'known to be at least 30, including: 10 known patients, 13 known staff, and 7 more bodies that were burnt beyond recognition'.[78] Subsequently, it was reported that 42 people had been killed and 37 wounded.[79]

On 7 October 2015, US President Barack Obama apologised for the airstrike and announced the US would be making condolence payments to the families of those killed. Subsequently, a US Department of Defense report, whose findings were made public on 29 April 2016, stated that condolence payments had been made to more than 170 individuals and families and $5.7 million had been approved to reconstruct the MSF facility. General Joseph Votel, the commander of US Central Command, said in a news briefing to release the report that $3,000 had been paid to the survivors, and $6,000 to the relatives of those killed in the attack.[80]

The investigation found that a combination of factors had caused both the ground force commander and the air crew to believe mistakenly that the air crew was firing on the intended target, an insurgent-controlled site approximately 400 metres away from the MSF Trauma Centre. General Votel said that 'The investigation concluded that certain personnel failed to comply with the rules of engagement and[81] the law of armed conflict. However, the investigation did not conclude that these failures amounted to a war crime.'[82]

[75] Human Rights Watch, 'Between a Drone and Al-Qaeda: The Civilian Cost of US Targeted Killings in Yemen' (22 October 2013) at https://goo.gl/kqzbFv.

[76] MSF, 'Initial MSF internal review: Attack on Kunduz Trauma Centre, Afghanistan', November 2015 (publicly released 5 November 2015) 7.

[77] Ibid, 10.

[78] Ibid, 12.

[79] I Ali, 'US strike on Afghan hospital in 2015 not a war crime: Pentagon', *Reuters Canada* (29 April 2016) at https://goo.gl/sWYZD6.

[80] Ibid.

[81] The CENTCOM press release issued the same day used the word 'and' rather than 'in', which was otherwise reported in the news transcript: April 29: CENTCOM releases investigation into airstrike on Doctors Without Borders trauma center, Press release No 20160429-10, 29 April 2016.

[82] 'News Transcript: Department of Defense Press Briefing by Army General Joseph Votel, commander, US Central Command, Press Operations, Army General Joseph Votel, commander, US Central Command' (29 April 2016) at https://goo.gl/yhVT3z.

C. Arms Transfers and Serious Violations of Hague Law

State responsibility for internationally wrongful acts is also relevant for the transfer of arms to another state or a non-state armed group. For example, a state that is party to the 1992 Chemical Weapons Convention, the 1997 Anti-Personnel Mine Ban Convention or the 2008 Convention on Cluster Munitions, and which transferred one of the weapons falling within the scope of these disarmament treaties and in violation of it, would not only itself be breaching international law, but could also incur international responsibility for the recipient's subsequent unlawful use of the weapon. This latter breach could occur even where it was not unlawful per se to transfer the weapon. Article 16 of the 2001 Articles on State Responsibility ('Aid or assistance in the commission of an internationally wrongful act') stipulates:

> A State which aids or assists another State in the commission of an internationally wrongful act by the latter is internationally responsible for doing so if:
>
> (a) that State does so with knowledge of the circumstances of the internationally wrongful act; and
>
> (b) the act would be internationally wrongful if committed by that State.

In his commentary on the rule, the ILC Special Rapporteur for the 2001 Articles on State Responsibility, James Crawford, introduced an unsupported additional requirement: that a state is not responsible for aid or assistance under Article 16 'unless the relevant State organ intended, by the aid or assistance given, to facilitate the occurrence of the wrongful conduct and the internationally wrongful conduct is actually committed by the aided or assisted State'.[83] This demand for intent is not incorporated in the rule and does not reflect the state of the law. In the *Genocide* case between Bosnia and Herzegovina and Serbia and Montenegro, the ICJ determined that Article 16 represented customary international law, and asserted that the threshold for a finding of complicity in genocide by a state required that

> at the least its organs were aware that genocide was about to be committed or was under way, and … [that] the aid and assistance supplied, from the moment they became so aware onwards, to the perpetrators of the criminal acts or to those who were on the point of committing them, enabled or facilitated the commission of the acts. In other words, an accomplice must have given support in perpetrating the genocide with full knowledge of the facts.[84]

This is the correct test under international law for one state aiding or assisting the unlawful acts of another.

Indirectly, the rules governing state responsibility were given flesh in the 2013 United Nations Arms Trade Treaty (ATT). Under Article 6(3) of the ATT, a state party to the ATT shall not authorise a transfer of a weapon where it has knowledge at the time of authorisation of the proposed transfer that the weapon would be used in the commission of certain war crimes, notably 'attacks directed against civilian objects or civilians protected as such, or

[83] Commentary on Article 16, Report of the International Law Commission on the work of its fifty-third session, *Yearbook of the International Law Commission*, vol II, UN Doc A/CN.4/SER.A/2001/Add.1 (Part 2) (New York, 2007) 66.

[84] ICJ, *Case Concerning the Application of the Convention on the Prevention and Punishment of the Crime of Genocide* (*Bosnia and Herzegovina v Serbia and Montenegro*), Judgment, 26 February 2007, para 432.

other war crimes defined by international agreements to which it is a Party'. It shall also not authorise a proposed export of a weapon where there is an 'overriding' risk of its being used to commit or facilitate a serious violation of international humanitarian law.[85]

The notion of a serious violation of the law of armed conflict is not defined or explained in the treaty, but its scope is certainly broader than a war crime.[86] Any violation of the rules of distinction, proportionality or precautions in attack that results in grave civilian harm (death of or serious injury to a person, or destruction of or severe damage to a civilian object) should be considered a serious violation of Hague Law rules for this purpose. The same applies to a violation of the rule prohibiting the use of a weapon or a method of warfare that is of a nature to cause superfluous injury or unnecessary suffering, the prohibition on starvation of civilians as a method of warfare, and even the wilful denial of humanitarian assistance, at least where quantifiable harm results. This is so irrespective of whether the violation meets the criteria for a war crime, as discussed further in section V.

V. Individual Criminal Responsibility

International criminal law identifies international crimes for which individuals may be held criminally responsible under a range of modes of liability, as discussed in this section. Consonant with the general understanding of a crime under domestic law, to secure any conviction for an international crime it needs to be proven, beyond a reasonable doubt, that an individual suspect had the requisite mens rea (culpable state of mind) at the time he or she committed the relevant actus reus (culpable act).

A. War Crimes

War crimes are thus serious violations of the law of armed conflict that, in addition, entail individual criminal responsibility under international law. These crimes are defined in law of armed conflict treaties, notably the 1899 and 1907 Hague Regulations, the 1949 Geneva Conventions, the 1954 Hague Convention on Cultural Property and the 1977 Additional Protocol I (and, arguably, also Additional Protocol II). The crimes are also set out in the 1998 Rome Statute of the International Criminal Court (ICC Statute) and of course broader customary international law.

i. Perpetrators

The individual perpetrator is the first and most obvious individual who may be held criminally responsible for a war crime. He or she is the person that fired the gun or launched the rocket intentionally to kill civilians or persons *hors de combat*, or tortured to death the detainee, or raped the woman, man or child. Often, however, the identity of the perpetrator

[85] Art 7(1)–(3), ATT.

[86] Casey-Maslen and Clapham (n 14) para 7.45; and see UK High Court, *Campaign Against the Arms Trade (on the application of) v Secretary of State for International Trade* [2017] EWHC 1754 (Admin), paras 16, 18, 24.

is never discovered; this is particularly likely during the conduct of hostilities, as forensic investigations are rare and the potential suspects may be across the front line, long gone or even dead.

It is also important to remember that war crimes are not only committed by members of armed forces. As Gary Solis affirms, 'anyone can commit a war crime. Absent one of the usual exclusions for criminal responsibility, diminished responsibility and insanity, duress, mistake of fact, or mistake of law, both combatants and civilians may be charged.'[87]

Duško Tadić, the first person to be convicted of war crimes (and crimes against humanity) by the ICTY, and indeed the first person to be convicted by an international tribunal since the Nuremberg Trials, was a junior figure in the Bosnian Serb hierarchy. Among a series of brutal and sadistic crimes, Mr Tadić and others forced one prisoner to bite off the testicle of another Muslim, who subsequently died. They forced victims 'to drink water like animals from puddles', and Mr Tadić is said to have let off a fire extinguisher in the mouth of an inmate already battered unconscious.[88]

In January 2000, the ICTY Appeals Chamber reduced the 25-year sentence imposed on Mr Tadić by five years, finding the sentence 'excessive'. Judge Mohammed Shahabuddeen said that, although Tadić was convicted of 'incontestably heinous' crimes, he was at a very low level of command compared with the architects of ethnic cleansing among the Bosnian Serb leadership. During his trial, Mr Tadić was described by one of his defence lawyers as 'a tadpole in a pool of sharks. The sharks have yet to be caught, but one has to ask what sort of sentence they will get and whether there is a proper differentiation.'[89]

ii. Commanders

Commanders will be legally responsible for their own unlawful decisions as well as for the unlawful actions of their subordinates, unless they could not reasonably have foreseen and prevented them.[90] The so-called Yamashita Standard of command responsibility is named after the (contested) case in which the eponymous Japanese general was convicted of war crimes in the aftermath of the Second World War. His conviction was secured even though it was not demonstrated by the Prosecution that he even knew about the crimes, much less ordered them.

Based on treaty law and jurisprudence, dating back in some instances to the First World War, the ICRC identified the following two rules under the customary law of armed conflict:

> Commanders and other superiors are criminally responsible for war crimes committed pursuant to their orders.[91]

[87] Solis (n 40) 339. One may add non-combatants to the list of possible war criminals.

[88] ICTY, *Prosecutor v Tadić*, Judgment (Trial Chamber) (Case No IT-94-1-T), 7 May 1997, paras 198, 206, 305; see also 'World: Europe, Profile of a war criminal', *BBC* (11 November 1999) at https://goo.gl/nGjffq.

[89] 'Sentence cut for Bosnian war criminal', *BBC* (26 January 2000) at https://goo.gl/XyYwju. As a point of reference, General Galić, who was convicted by the ICTY on 5 December 2003 for the shelling and sniping of Sarajevo, was given a 20-year sentence by the Trial Chamber. Galić appealed the judgment, and on 30 November 2006 not only was his appeal rejected, but the Appeals Chamber extended his sentence from 20 years' to life imprisonment.

[90] See, eg, Art 87 ('Duty of commanders'), 1977 Additional Protocol I; Art 49, 1949 Geneva Convention I; Art 50, 1949 Geneva Convention II; Art 129, 1949 Geneva Convention III; Art 146, 1949 Geneva Convention IV; and Art 28, 1954 Hague Convention for the Protection of Cultural Property.

[91] ICRC Study of Customary IHL, Rule 152 ('Command Responsibility for Orders to Commit War Crimes') at https://goo.gl/tseyaU.

> Commanders and other superiors are criminally responsible for war crimes committed by their subordinates if they knew, or had reason to know, that the subordinates were about to commit or were committing such crimes and did not take all necessary and reasonable measures in their power to prevent their commission, or if such crimes had been committed, to punish the persons responsible.[92]

Solis explains clearly the doctrine of command responsibility, also known as *respondeat superior*, as follows:

> The fact that the commander had no hand in the actual crime is immaterial. If she ordered the crime, incited the crime, acquiesced in the crime, ignored her own knowledge of the crime, closed her eyes to an awareness of the crime, passed on a patently unlawful order, or failed to control her troops who were committing war crimes, she may herself be found guilty of those crimes. This is a broad range of situations allowing a finding that a commander is guilty of LOAC/IHL violations committed by subordinates.[93]

iii. Complicity in War Crimes

As is the case under domestic criminal jurisdictions, under international criminal law individual criminal responsibility arises 'not only when a person materially commits a crime but also when he or she engages in other forms or modalities of criminal conduct'.[94] In the words of Telford Taylor, a US prosecutor at the Nuremberg Trials, not under any

> known system of criminal law is guilt for murder confined to the man who pulls the trigger or buries the corpse … [N]ot only are principals guilty but also accessories, those who take a consenting part in the commission of crime or are connected with plans or enterprises involved in its commission, those who order or abet crime, and those who belong to an organization or group engaged in the commission of crime. These provisions embody no harsh or novel principles of criminal responsibility.[95]

a. Joint Criminal Enterprise

Every participant in a common criminal plan is criminally responsible, including under international criminal law, when he or she participates in the criminal acts and intends to engage in the common criminal plan. They are all to be treated as principals in the crime, though varying degrees of culpability can be taken into account in sentencing following conviction.[96] As the ICTY Appeals Chamber stated in its judgment in the *Tadić* case:

> [T]he doctrine of acting in pursuance of a common purpose is rooted in the national law of many States. Some countries act upon the principle that where multiple persons participate in a common purpose or common design, all are responsible for the ensuing criminal conduct, whatever their degree or form of participation, provided all had the intent to perpetrate the crime envisaged in

[92] ICRC Study of Customary IHL, Rule 153 ('Command Responsibility for Failure to Prevent, Repress or Report War Crimes'), at https://goo.gl/Ba6U22.

[93] Solis (n 40) 421. One may assume that his use of the feminine form is not to be taken to imply that there are more female than male commanders, much less more female commanders who are war criminals than their male counterparts.

[94] A Cassese, *International Criminal Law*, 2nd edn (Oxford, Oxford University Press, 2008) 187.

[95] Cited ibid, 190.

[96] ibid.

> the common purpose. If one of the participants commits a crime not envisaged in the common purpose or common design, he alone will incur criminal responsibility for such a crime.[97]

Joint criminal enterprise (JCE) is thus a mode of criminal liability that encompasses all the participants in a common criminal plan. It holds all such individuals criminally responsible for all criminal acts foreseen by the plan (whether or not they materially participated in the commission of these acts), as well as, in certain circumstances, for criminal acts that fall outside the plan but which might foreseeably result.[98]

Three categories of criminal liability exist under JCE, as set out in the *Tadić* Appeals Chamber decision:[99] (i) for a common intentional purpose; (ii) for participation in a common criminal plan within an institutional framework (such as a prison); and (far more controversially) (iii) incidental liability based on foresight and voluntary assumption of risk.[100] All three types share a common actus reus, namely that there is a plurality of persons; a common plan, design or purpose exists that involves the commission of a war crime; and the accused's participation in the common plan involving the perpetration of a war crime.[101]

A decision to deliberately kill civilians would clearly amount to a criminal plan that would entail responsibility under JCE. The level of proof required for any prosecution, though, is high even for the customary law war crime of 'launching an indiscriminate attack resulting in loss of life or injury to civilians or damage to civilian objects', let alone the war crime of deliberately attacking civilians.[102]

b. Joint Criminal Responsibility

The ICC has, to date at least, preferred Claus Roxin's Control Theory of Perpetration to JCE as a mode of liability for war crimes. The theory, which dates back to the 1960s, requires a finding that the defendant performed an essential contribution to a crime. This joint criminal responsibility as a mode of liability is set out in Article 25(3) of the ICC Statute:

> In accordance with this Statute, a person shall be criminally responsible and liable for punishment for a crime within the jurisdiction of the Court if that person:
>
> (a) Commits such a crime, whether as an individual, jointly with another or through another person, regardless of whether that other person is criminally responsible.

[97] ICTY, *Prosecutor v Tadić*, Judgment (Appeals Chamber) (Case No IT-94-1-A), 15 July 1999, para 224.

[98] Cassese (n 94) 191.

[99] *Tadić* (n 97) para 220. See Cassese (n 94) 191; R Cryer, H Friman, D Robinson and E Wilmshurst, *An Introduction to International Criminal Law and Procedure*, 2nd edn (Cambridge, Cambridge University Press, 2010) 369.

[100] Of note, in February 2016 the UK Supreme Court overturned a longstanding decision (dating from 1984) on the common law of joint enterprise in England and Wales, according to which foresight that an accomplice to one crime might go on intentionally to commit another, means the accomplice could be found guilty of the second offence without having taken part in it. F FitzGibbon, 'Joint Enterprise' (2016) 38(5) *London Review of Books* 26, at https://goo.gl/vVDxzj. For the decision, see *R v Jogee* [2016] UKSC 8.

[101] *Tadić* (n 97) para 227.

[102] ICRC Study of Customary IHL, Rule 156 ('Definition of War Crimes'), ii(vii). According to the ICRC: 'It is clear that launching an attack knowing that civilian casualties are likely to occur does not in itself necessarily amount to an indiscriminate attack, because incidental injury or damage is not as such prohibited. However, launching an attack without attempting to aim properly at a military target or in such a manner as to hit civilians without any thought or care as to the likely extent of death or injury amounts to an indiscriminate attack. Launching such an attack knowing that the degree of incidental civilian deaths, injuries or damage will be excessive is categorized as a grave breach in Additional Protocol I.'

In its March 2012 judgment in the *Lubanga* case, the ICC Trial Chamber held that to be liable as a co-perpetrator the accused must, at a minimum, associate with a group whose purpose entails 'a sufficient risk that, if events follow the ordinary course, a crime will be committed'. This appears, however, to be close to the – much criticised[103] – third form of liability for JCE (incidental liability based on foresight and voluntary assumption of risk) and is potentially very wide in scope.

In terms of the actus reus under Article 25(3)(a) of the ICC Statute, the majority of the Chamber concluded that

> the commission of a crime jointly with another person involves two objective requirements: (i) the existence of an agreement or common plan between two or more persons that, if implemented, will result in the commission of a crime; and (ii) that the accused provided an essential contribution to the common plan that resulted in the commission of the relevant crime.

It asserted that these two requirements 'must be assessed on the basis of all the evidence related to the alleged crime'.[104] With respect to the requisite mens rea, the Majority decided that the standard was 'awareness that a consequence will occur in the ordinary course of events', meaning that 'the participants anticipate, based on their knowledge of how events ordinarily develop, that the consequence will occur in the future. … A low risk will not be sufficient.'[105]

In its 2014 judgment in the *Katanga* case, the ICC Trial Chamber declared that 'it need not discard the interpretation of the law on individual responsibility founded on the theory of control over the crime'.[106] Indeed, the Chamber decided to rely on the criterion of control, considering that under Article 25(3)(a) of the ICC Statute,

> the perpetrators of a crime are those who control its commission and who are aware of the factual circumstances allowing them to exert such control. Thus, the indirect perpetrator has the power to decide whether and how the crime will be committed[107] insofar as that person determines its perpetration.[108]

c. Aiding and Abetting

Under the ICC Statute, the ICC has potential jurisdiction over anyone who, with respect to a crime within the jurisdiction of the Court, 'for the purpose of facilitating the commission of such a crime, aids, abets or otherwise assists in its commission or its attempted commission, including providing the means for its commission'.[109] Thus, under international criminal

[103] See, eg, Cryer et al (n 99) 373.

[104] ICC, *Prosecutor v Thomas Lubanga Dyilo,* Judgment (Trial Chamber) (Case No ICC-01/04-01/06), 14 March 2012, para 1006.

[105] Ibid, para 1012.

[106] ICC, *Prosecutor v Germain Katanga*, Judgment (Trial Chamber) (Case No ICC-01/04-01/07), 7 March 2014, para 1382.

[107] ICC, *Prosecutor v Germain Katanga*, Decision on the confirmation of charges (Case No ICC-01/04-01/07), 30 September 2008, para 518. See also GP Fletcher, *Rethinking Criminal Law* (Oxford, Oxford University Press, 2000) 672–73; C Roxin, 'Crimes as Part of Organized Power Structures' (2011) 9 *Journal of International Criminal Justice* 193 at 198–99.

[108] *Katanga* (n 106) para 1396.

[109] Art 25(3)(c), ICC Statute.

law, as under domestic criminal law, a person may be convicted (as an accessory) of aiding or abetting a crime where he or she assists a principal in the commission of a crime, but without sharing his or her criminal intent to commit that crime. Indeed, as the Appeal Chamber's decision in the *Krstić* case implied, the critical difference between JCE and aiding and abetting an international crime resides in the mens rea.[110] In the *Lašva Valley* case, the ICTY Trial Chamber stated:

> With regard to mens rea, the Trial Chamber must determine whether it is necessary for the accomplice to share the mens rea of the principal or whether mere knowledge that his actions assist the perpetrator in the commission of the crime is sufficient to constitute mens rea in aiding and abetting the crime. The case law indicates that the latter will suffice.[111]

In general, the acts of a participant in a JCE are 'more serious than those of an aider and abettor to the principal offender since a participant in a joint criminal enterprise shares the intent of the principal offender whereas an aider and abettor need only be aware of that intent'.[112] In the *Ngirabatware* case, the International Criminal Tribunal for Rwanda (ICTR) Trial Chamber observed that the actus reus of aiding and abetting is constituted by

> acts or omissions specifically aimed at assisting, encouraging or lending moral support to the perpetration of a certain specific crime, and which have a substantial effect on the perpetration of the crime. Whether a particular contribution qualifies as substantial is a fact-based inquiry, and need not serve as condition precedent for the commission of the crime. The contribution may occur before, during or after the principal crime has been perpetrated, and the location where the actus reus takes place may be removed from the location of the principal crime.[113]

In its judgment in the *Katanga* case, the Trial Chamber found that Article 25(3) of the ICC Statute differentiates between persons whose conduct constitutes commission of the crime per se and 'those whose conduct is solely connected to the commission of a crime by another person'. This latter scenario 'specifically corresponds to various forms of accessoryship'.[114] It held that an accessory 'can be held criminally liable as such, only where a person commits or attempts to commit a crime within the jurisdiction of the Court. Principal liability, however, imports in essence autonomy as it does not hinge on the liability of a third person.'[115] An accessory, it stated, exerts no control over the decision whether and how the crime will be committed.[116]

B. Crimes against Humanity

The concept of 'crimes against humanity' was first raised in 1915 in a protest from the British, French and Russian Governments following mass killings of Armenians in the

[110] ICTY, *Prosecutor v Krstić*, Judgment (Appeals Chamber) (Case No IT-98-33-A), 19 April 2004. See Cassese (n 94) 211.
[111] ICTY, *Prosecutor v Furundžija ('Lašva Valley')*, Judgment Trial Chamber (Case No. IT-95-17/1-T), 10 December 1998, para 236.
[112] ICTY, *Prosecutor v Krnojelac*, Judgment (Appeals Chamber) (Case No IT-97-25-A), 17 September 2003, para 75.
[113] ICTR, *Prosecutor v Ngirabatware*, Judgment (Trial Chamber) (Case No ICTR-99-54-T), 20 December 2012, para 1294.
[114] *Katanga* (n 106) para 1384.
[115] Ibid, para 1385.
[116] Ibid, para 1396.

Ottoman Empire by Turkish forces.[117] Following a suggestion by the international lawyer Hersch Lauterpacht, the Charter of the International Military Tribunal that judged Nazi war crimes at Nuremberg included a provision authorising the Tribunal to prosecute persons guilty of crimes against humanity.[118]

Antonio Cassese affirmed that under international law, 'the category of crimes against humanity is sweeping but sufficiently well defined'.[119] He described four elements that characterise a crime against humanity under contemporary international law, three of which are not contentious and a fourth that is disputable. First, they are particularly odious offences in that they constitute a serious attack on human dignity, or a grave humiliation or degradation of one or more persons. Second, and critically, they are not isolated or sporadic events but are part of a widespread or systematic practice of atrocities. Third, they are prohibited and may be punished regardless of whether they are perpetrated during armed conflict or in peacetime. Fourth, while the victims are generally civilians, controversially Cassese argued that under customary law the victims might also be enemy combatants.[120] His argument was that since crimes against humanity may be committed in times of peace, 'it no longer makes sense to require that such crimes be perpetrated against civilians alone'. This is not, though, persuasive.[121] The argument, based on ICTY jurisprudence,[122] that former combatants who are *hors de combat* should be protected is stronger.[123]

In August 2012, the third report by the UN Commission of Inquiry on Syria concluded that the Syrian regime and the *Shabbiha* government militia had committed the crimes against humanity of murder and of torture.[124] It set out the Commission's view of the applicable law as follows:

> Crimes against humanity are those crimes which 'shock the conscience of humanity'. Under the Rome Statute, crimes against humanity occur where certain acts are undertaken as part of a widespread or systematic attack against a civilian population where the perpetrator has knowledge of the attack. The elements of crimes against humanity are well established in international criminal law:
>
> 1. There must be one or more attacks;
> 2. The acts of the perpetrator must be part of the attack(s);
> 3. The attack(s) must be directed against any civilian population;

[117] See, eg, Cassese (n 94) 101–02.

[118] Ibid, 102–04.

[119] Ibid 98.

[120] Ibid, 99 and 112–13.

[121] Nonetheless, in the revision of his 2008 work, which was completed after his death by a number of leading international criminal lawyers, the thrust of Cassese's argument was not only maintained, it was actively promoted. See A Cassese, *International Criminal Law*, 3rd edn (Oxford, Oxford University Press, 2013) 101–05.

[122] See, e.g., ICTY, *Prosecutor v Blaškić*, Judgment (Trial Chamber) (Case No IT-95-14-T), 3 March 2000, paras 208–14.

[123] As Cryer et al observe, however, the Appeals Chamber judgment in the *Martić* case affirmed that 'civilian' does not include persons *hors de combat*, and that therefore such persons would not be the victims of crimes against humanity unless the broader attack was directed at civilians defined narrowly. 'The unfortunate effect of this interpretation is that large-scale extermination or torture directed against prisoners of war would not constitute crimes against humanity.' Cryer et al (n 99) 242, citing ICTY, *Prosecutor v Martić*, Judgment (Appeals Chamber) (Case No IT-95-11-A), 8 October 2008, paras 295–314.

[124] *Third report of the independent international commission of inquiry on the Syrian Arab Republic*, UN Doc A/HRC/21/50, 16 August 2012, 1–2.

4. The attack(s) must be widespread or systematic;
5. The perpetrator must know that his or her acts constitute part of a pattern of widespread or systematic crimes directed against a civilian population and know that his or her acts fit into such a pattern.

Surprisingly, in its February 2017 report on the siege of Aleppo, the Commission did not find that any crimes against humanity had been committed by any of the various parties. Acts that may constitute crimes against humanity include the following: murder, extermination, enslavement, forcible transfer of population, imprisonment, torture, rape, sexual slavery, enforced prostitution, forced pregnancy, enforced sterilisation, sexual violence, persecution, enforced disappearance and *apartheid*.[125]

C. Genocide

Genocide, the so-called 'crime of crimes',[126] was first coined as a term by Raphael Lemkin in his 1944 book *Axis Rule in Occupied Europe*. Lemkin wrote:

> Generally speaking, genocide does not necessarily mean the immediate destruction of a nation, except when accomplished by mass killings of all members of a nation. It is intended rather to signify a coordinated plan of different actions aiming at the destruction of essential foundations of the life of national groups, with the aim of annihilating the groups themselves. Genocide is directed against the national group as an entity, and the actions involved are directed against individuals, not in their individual capacity, but as members of the national group.[127]

In 1946, UN General Assembly Resolution 96(I) proclaimed that genocide was a crime under international law, although it was not formally prohibited by treaty until the adoption in December 1948 of the Convention on the Prevention and Punishment of the Crime of Genocide. Its prohibition, which was recognised by the ICJ as a general principle of law in 1951,[128] is also a norm of *jus cogens*.[129] Acts of genocide may be committed in peacetime as well as during armed conflict.[130]

The definition of the crime, as set out in Article 2 of the 1948 Genocide Convention, is also considered to have attained customary law status. Thereunder, genocide comprises:[131]

> any of the following acts committed with intent to destroy, in whole or in part, a national, ethnical, racial or religious group, as such:
>
> (a) Killing members of the group;
> (b) Causing serious bodily or mental harm to members of the group;

[125] Art 7(1)(a–k), ICC Statute.

[126] See, eg, WA Schabas, 'National courts finally begin to prosecute genocide, the "crime of crimes"' (2003) 1(1) *Journal of International Criminal Justice* 39.

[127] US Holocaust Memorial Museum, 'Coining a word and championing a cause: the story of Raphael Lemkin', *Holocaust Encyclopedia*, at https://goo.gl/HkKAmt.

[128] ICJ, *Reservations to the Convention on the Prevention and Punishment of the Crime of Genocide*, Advisory Opinion, 28 May 1951, 12.

[129] ICJ, *Case Concerning Armed Activities on the Territory of the Congo* (New Application: 2002) (*Democratic Republic of the Congo v Rwanda*), Judgment (Jurisdiction of the Court and Admissibility of the Application), 3 February 2006, para 64.

[130] Cryer et al (n 99) 204.

[131] See, eg, Cassese (n 94) 57.

(c) Deliberately inflicting on the group conditions of life calculated to bring about its physical destruction in whole or in part;
(d) Imposing measures intended to prevent births within the group;
(e) Forcibly transferring children of the group to another group.

Thus, *dolus specialis* (special intent) is explicitly required for the crime of genocide under international law: 'intent to destroy, in whole or in part, a national, ethnical, racial or religious group, as such'. Moreover, case law within the ICTR as well as the ICJ evidences that the intent must be to target a 'substantial' part of the particular group. In the words of the ICJ:

> That is demanded by the very nature of the crime of genocide: since the object and purpose of the Convention as a whole is to prevent the intentional destruction of groups, the part targeted must be significant enough to have an impact on the group as a whole. That requirement of substantiality is supported by consistent rulings of the ICTY and the ... ICTR ... and by the Commentary of the ILC to its Articles in the draft Code of Crimes against the Peace and Security of Mankind.[132]

On 2 August 2001, in the *Krstić* case, the ICTY Trial Chamber I stated that it was 'convinced beyond any reasonable doubt that a crime of genocide was committed in Srebrenica' and that General Radislav Krstić was guilty of genocide. His crime involved the summary execution of many thousands of Muslim men and boys *hors de combat* after the city had fallen in July 1995. The Trial Chamber pointed out that the decision to kill all the Bosnian Muslim men of fighting age was taken after the decision to transfer the women, children and old people. For this reason, the Serbian forces had to realise the impact such a decision would have on the group's survival. By deciding to kill all the men of Srebrenica of fighting age, a decision was taken to make it impossible for the Bosnian Muslim people of Srebrenica to survive. Stated otherwise, what was ethnic cleansing became genocide.[133]

In April 2004, the Appeals Chamber unanimously found that genocide had indeed been committed in Srebrenica in 1995. It overturned Krstić's conviction as a participant in a JCE to commit genocide, deciding instead that he had aided and abetted[134] the so-called 'crime of crimes':

> Krstić knew that buses he had assisted in procuring for the transfer of the women, children and elderly were being used to transfer the males to various detention sites. He also knew that Drina Corps vehicles and personnel were being used to scout for detention sites and to escort and guard the Bosnian Muslim prisoners at various detention sites. He also knew that heavy vehicles and equipment belonging to the Drina Corps under his command were being used to further the execution of the Bosnian Muslim civilians. This knowledge and these modes of assistance constitute a substantial contribution to the commission of the crimes as required for a conviction for aiding and abetting the genocide of the Bosnian Muslims of Srebrenica.[135]

As an aider and abettor of genocide rather than a participant in the JCE, Mr Krstić's sentence was reduced to 35 years' imprisonment.

[132] ICJ, *Case Concerning Application of the Convention on the Prevention and Punishment of the Crime of Genocide* (*Bosnia and Herzegovina v Serbia and Montenegro*), Judgment, 26 February 2007, para 198.

[133] ICTY, 'Radislav Krstić becomes the First Person to be Convicted of Genocide at the ICTY and is Sentenced to 46 Years Imprisonment', Press Release OF/P.I.S./609e, The Hague (2 August 2001) at https://goo.gl/Cp3qUE.

[134] ICTY, *Prosecutor v Krstić* (n 110), para 237.

[135] Ibid, para 238.

VI. Concluding Remarks

Rules are one thing, their respect on the battlefield quite another. Given that it is likely that fewer than one in 100,000 perpetrators are brought to trial each year for even a limited number of the war crimes they have committed, it is hard to gainsay the argument that compliance with the duty to 'respect and ensure respect' for Hague Law rules is anything other than an abject failure.

Indeed, when reflecting on the level of respect for Hague Law rules in most situations of armed conflict one is tempted to recall the old joke about the difference between an optimist and a pessimist. A pessimist says 'things are so bad; they just can't get any worse', but an optimist says, 'Oh yes they can.' While one may, justly, lament the lack of 'implementation' of the law of armed conflict – diplomatic parlance for the barbarity wrought during widespread and flagrant violations of Hague Law rules – one must resist the temptation to believe that warfare cannot be other than an unrelenting series of crimes.

To those who argue that there has been too much focus on prosecuting war crimes in recent decades, the counter-argument is that there has been far too little. And to those who argue it is pointless to elaborate rules for warfare – to seek to civilise the barbaric – the obvious riposte is that they are more needed than ever. While appalling loss of life continues to occur during the conduct of hostilities, things could – and may yet – get worse. One day, Syria could be the new normal.

INDEX